OXFORD WORLD'S CLASSICS

THE INTERPRETATION OF DREAMS

SIGMUND FREUD was born in 1856 in Moravia, but was brought to Vienna by his parents at the age of 4 and lived there until his flight to England after the German annexation of Austria in 1938. Having received a broad classical education, he trained as a doctor at the Vienna Medical School. He worked initially on the nervous system, then became interested in the therapeutic uses of cocaine, in speech disorders, and in using hypnosis in treating psychological afflictions. His *Studies in Hysteria* (1895), written jointly with his older colleague Josef Breuer, maintained that 'hysterics suffer mainly from reminiscences' which could be recalled and discharged by the 'talking cure'. In 1897, however, Freud concluded that hysterical and neurotic patients most often suffered from fantasies stemming from their relations with their parents in childhood. He embarked on the investigation of unconscious fantasy-life which produced *The Interpretation of Dreams* (1899), *The Psychopathology of Everyday Life* (1901), and *Jokes and their Relation to the Unconscious* (1905). His *Three Essays on the Theory of Sexuality* (1905) argued that patterns of sexual development, involving such mechanisms as identification and repression, were central to the unconscious forces shaping the personality. From there he developed psychoanalysis as a therapeutic technique and a theory of the unconscious which underwent many mutations, both in Freud's work and in that of followers, from Jung onwards, who successively established independent schools of psychoanalytic thought and treatment. Freud died in exile in Hampstead in 1939.

JOYCE CRICK was, until her retirement, Senior Lecturer in the Department of German at University College London. Previous translations include texts by Hamann, Herder, Friedrich Schlegel, Novalis, and Solger selected for Cambridge University Press's volumes of *German Aesthetic and Literary Criticism*. She has edited the German material for the Princeton edition of Coleridge's *Notebooks* and (forthcoming) his translation of Schiller's *Wallenstein*. Interest in translation theory took her to the problems raised by Freud's texts. She has also written on Thomas and Heinrich Mann, Christa Wolf, Bertolt Brecht, and Günter Grass.

RITCHIE ROBERTSON is Taylor Professor of German at Oxford University and a Fellow of the Queen's College. His books include *Kafka: Judaism, Politics, and Literature* (OUP, 1985), *Kafka: A Very Short Introduction* (OUP, 2004), and *Mock Epic Poetry from Pope to Heine* (OUP, 2009). His translations include Kafka's *The Man who Disappeared (America)* for Oxford World's Classics.

OXFORD WORLD'S CLASSICS

SIGMUND FREUD

The Interpretation of Dreams

Translated by
JOYCE CRICK

with an Introduction and Notes by
RITCHIE ROBERTSON

OXFORD
UNIVERSITY PRESS

OXFORD

UNIVERSITY PRESS

Great Clarendon Street, Oxford OX2 6DP

Oxford University Press is a department of the University of Oxford.
It furthers the University's objective of excellence in research, scholarship,
and education by publishing worldwide in

Oxford New York

Athens Auckland Bangkok Bogotá Buenos Aires Calcutta
Cape Town Chennai Dar es Salaam Delhi Florence Hong Kong Istanbul
Karachi Kuala Lumpur Madrid Melbourne Mexico City Mumbai
Nairobi Paris São Paulo Shanghai Singapore Taipei Tokyo Toronto Warsaw

with associated companies in Berlin Ibadan

Oxford is a registered trade mark of Oxford University Press
in the UK and in certain other countries

Published in the United States
by Oxford University Press Inc., New York

Translation © Joyce Crick 1999
Editorial material © Ritchie Robertson 1999

British Library Cataloguing in Publication Data

Data available

Library of Congress Cataloging in Publication Data

Data available

ISBN 978-0-19-953758-7

15

Typeset by RefineCatch Limited, Bungay, Suffolk
Printed in Great Britain by
Clays Ltd, Elcograf S.p.A.

CONTENTS

CONTENTS

THE INTERPRETATION OF DREAMS

INTRODUCTION

Freud's Work Before The Interpretation

The Interpretation of Dreams (*Die Traumdeutung*), a slimmer volume than the much-expanded version that has hitherto been available, was published in November 1899, though postdated by the publisher to 1900. Its muted but respectful reception by reviewers disappointed Freud's hopes and led him to complain unjustly that it had been ignored.[1] For Freud, it was and remained the central book of his prolific career. In 1932 he wrote, in the preface to the third English edition: 'It contains, even according to my present-day judgement, the most valuable of all the discoveries it has been my good fortune to make. Insight such as this falls to one's lot but once in a lifetime' (SE iv. p. xxiii).[2]

When the book came out, however, Freud was more sombre. Writing to his medical colleague, confidant, and fellow-Jew Wilhelm Fliess (1858–1928), he compared the effort of writing it to the struggle with the angel which left the biblical Jacob permanently lame: 'When it appeared that my breath would fail in the wrestling match, I asked the angel to desist; and that is what he has done since then. But I did not turn out to be the stronger, although since then I have been limping noticeably. Yes, I really am forty-four now, an old, somewhat shabby Jew . . .'[3] Behind the wry self-disparagement lies a desperate need for professional success, understandable in a member of the upwardly mobile Jewish middle class of the Habsburg Empire. Freud's parents, Jacob Freud, a wool-merchant, and Amalia Nathansohn, twenty years his junior, both came from Galicia (now the Western Ukraine, then the north-easternmost Habsburg province). They settled first in Freiburg (now Příbor) in Moravia, where their eldest child, Sigmund, was born in 1856, then moved in 1859 to

[1] On the book's reception, see Frank J. Sulloway, *Freud, Biologist of the Mind: Beyond the Psychoanalytic Legend*, 2nd edn. (Cambridge, Mass., and London, 1992), 448–53.

[2] References in this form are to *The Standard Edition of the Complete Psychological Works of Sigmund Freud*, ed. James Strachey, 24 vols. (London, 1953–74).

[3] Letter of 7 May 1900, in *The Complete Letters of Sigmund Freud to Wilhelm Fliess, 1887–1904*, tr. and ed. J. M. Masson (Cambridge, Mass., and London, 1985). Future quotations from this book are identified in the text by the date of the letter.

Leipzig and in 1860 to Vienna, where Sigmund was to live until his escape from National Socialism in 1938.

Freud's medical training at Vienna University was stamped by the scientific, positivistic spirit of the later nineteenth century. The Romantic approach to natural science, which sought to disclose a harmonious universal order and saw in it the expression of an indwelling world-soul, was now outdated. Freud's own belief in the unity of nature was based on Darwin, whose *Origin of Species* (1859) explained how one living species changes into another and thus made human beings continuous with all other organisms. Freud tells us in his *Autobiography* (1925) that 'the theories of Darwin, which were then of topical interest, strangely attracted me, for they held out hopes of an extraordinary advance in our understanding of the world' (SE xx. 8). In his first year at university he chose to attend Carl Claus's lectures on 'General Biology and Darwinism'. However, his principal mentor was Ernst von Brücke, who was in turn a follower of the great physiologist and physicist Hermann von Helmholtz, and, like him, was intent on explaining organisms entirely by physical and chemical forces. Occult forces like vital energy were to be excluded. Darwinian evolution, operating through conflict without any animating purpose, suited this hard-nosed approach. Freud adhered to the Helmholtz school's tenets in his early neurological work. Beginning with publications on the nervous systems of fish, he moved on to the human nervous system, exploring the anaesthetic properties of cocaine, speech disorders, and cerebral paralyses in children. He was thus a reputable neurologist before psychoanalysis was ever thought of. It is not surprising, therefore, that his first attempt at devising a psychological theory was thoroughly materialist.

This was the 'Project for a Scientific Psychology', which Freud wrote at great speed in September and October 1895 and never published.[4] Its assumptions and method, however, are still visible in *The Interpretation of Dreams* and indeed underlie much of his later psychoanalytic thought. Briefly, Freud, like the Hehmholtz school, supposes that nervous or mental energy is analogous to physical energy. It works on particles, called neurones (posited by

---

[4] For an introduction, see Ernest Jones, *Sigmund Freud: Life and Work*, 3 vols. (London, 1953–7), i. 422–31; a fuller analysis in Richard Wollheim, *Freud* (London, 1971), ch. 2.

H. W. G. Waldeyer in 1891), which it fills like an electrical charge. This energy circulates within a closed system, occasionally inhibited by contact barriers. Within this system, wishes arise which seek satisfaction. Satisfaction takes the form of discharging energy. At the same time, the system is governed by a principle of constancy which seeks to keep the amount of energy constant. The system is in contact with the external world through the self or ego (*Ich*), imagined as an organization of neurones constantly charged with energy, and able to receive or inhibit stimuli from the outside world. When energy remains unconnected with the outside world, as in dreaming, it flows freely; when connected with the outside world via the ego, its flow is weakened and inhibited. This distinction between the free-flowing energy of the primary process, where desire takes no account of reality, and the hesitant flow of the secondary process, where desire has to compromise with reality, will meet us again at the end of *The Interpretation of Dreams*, and will reappear in Freud's later writings as the contrast between the id and the ego; while the circulation of energy will also appear later as the movement of libido among objects of desire. And it is in the 'Project' that Freud first states that dreams 'are *wish-fulfilments*—that is, primary processes following upon experiences of satisfaction' (SE i. 340).[5]

Also in 1895, Freud and his fellow-physician Josef Breuer published a book, *Studies in Hysteria*, which inaugurates the interactive therapy soon to be known as psychoanalysis. Breuer had in 1880 met a young Viennese woman with a bizarre and varying range of symptoms: she could not drink water, she could speak only English, she had a squint, visual disturbances, partial paralyses. Under hypnosis she related the events that had initiated these afflictions: for example, she had been unable to drink water since seeing a dog drinking out of a glass. Freud applied Breuer's 'talking cure' to other unfortunate women. A British governess, Miss Lucy R., suffered from a depression made worse by a continual smell of burnt pudding.[6] Freud traced this olfactory illusion back to an occasion when, as she was cooking pudding with her charges, a letter arrived from her mother and was seized by the children; during this tussle the pudding got burnt. Not satisfied with this explanation, Freud probed further and elicited from Miss R. the admission that she was in love with her employer and distressed by a scene in which he reprimanded her. Having got this off her chest, she regained her good cheer and her sense of smell. Their case studies led Breuer and Freud to maintain, in their preface to *Studies in Hysteria*, that '*Hysterics suffer mainly from reminiscences*' (SE ii. 7). Hysterical symptoms, apparently bizarre, did have a meaning: they were displaced recollections of experiences too painful to remember consciously. Freud makes the further, tacit, assumption that those experiences are always sexual; and he did not scruple to confirm his assumption by asking Miss R. leading questions.

On this basis, Freud theorized that the buried memory tormenting hysterics was of sexual abuse in childhood. He attached huge importance to this theory, equating it with discovering the source of the Nile. Slowly, however, it crumbled, till on 21 September 1897 he confided to his friend Wilhelm Fliess that he no longer believed his own theory. It did not help him cure his patients; it implied that child abuse must be implausibly widespread; and it ignored his patients' tendency to confuse reality with fantasy (especially, perhaps, when Freud was prompting them). Freud was not denying that child abuse often really occurred, though he may have underestimated its frequency.[7] He was accepting—with a cheerfulness that puzzled him—a major defeat to his ambitions.

While gradually abandoning this theory, Freud was also reacting to his father's death on 23 October 1896. Grief, overwork, and worry brought on what has plausibly been called a creative illness.[8] It was a painful spell of inner isolation, following his intense preoccupation with his ideas, and resulting in the exhilarating conviction that he had discovered a great new truth. Freud worked through his illness by probing his own past. He recollected his sexual arousal in infancy by his nurse; he remembered seeing his mother naked during a train journey when he was two and a half; and he acknowledged hostility towards his father. 'Being totally honest with oneself is a good exercise,' he told Fliess on 15 October 1897. 'A single idea of general value dawned on me. I have found, in my own case too,

[7] See J. M. Masson, *The Assault on Truth: Freud's Suppression of the Seduction Theory* (London, 1984), which overstates the case against Freud.

[8] Henri F. Ellenberger, *The Discovery of the Unconscious: The History and Evolution of Dynamic Psychiatry* (London, 1970), 447.

[the phenomenon of] being in love with my mother and jealous of my father, and I now consider it a universal event in early childhood.' The expression of these primordial emotions, he continued, might explain the power of Sophocles' *Oedipus Rex* and Shakespeare's *Hamlet*.

This is the germ of the famous 'Oedipus complex', an idea whose power consists in representing ordinary life as tragic. To become a man—that is, to become like one's father—every man must oppose and overcome his father, paying in guilt the price of maturity. The objections are obvious. *Is* this universal? What about women? What about non-European cultures? Is the 'Oedipus complex' perhaps a self-aggrandizing masculine myth, a generalization from Freud's personal myth of the hero?[9] Whatever the answers, this notion at any rate helped Freud through his personal crisis, in which the main therapeutic activity was writing *The Interpretation of Dreams*. After the book's completion, Freud even overcame what he considered the neurotic travel phobia that had prevented him, despite many Italian trips, from visiting Rome, and spent twelve days in the Holy City in September 1901. *The Interpretation of Dreams* is, among other things, a disguised autobiography, drawing on the dreams that provided Freud with material for self-analysis. But before exploring that dimension, let us examine the argument and structure of the book itself.

Freud's Argument

In summarizing Freud's argument, it will be convenient to stay reasonably close to the structure of *The Interpretation of Dreams*. For although the book is composed with the rhetorical skill, the attention to the reader, characteristic of Freud, its structure is not wholly clear. As the book's guiding metaphor, that of a journey, indicates, it follows in some measure the process by which Freud devised and developed his theories. Thus the key concepts on which the theory is based, the primary and secondary processes, are explained only near the end; and certain nagging problems, like the place of anxiety-dreams in his theory, are not dealt with once and for all, but are treated at different points with solutions that are not always consistent.

[9] See Sulloway, *Freud*, 476–80.

Freud knew that he had to convince his readers of his scholarly respectability by reviewing previous studies of dreams, and he accomplishes this laborious task in a lengthy survey which shows his skill in abstracting the essential points from voluminous and only intermittently rewarding authors. In keeping with his own classical education and the cultural standards of his milieu, he also quotes what classical authors said about dreams. Aristotle is quoted as differing from his predecessors by assigning dreams a physiological rather than a divine origin; Lucretius and Cicero testify to the view that people dream about the things that concern them in waking life. These references, along with the book's epigraph from Virgil, signal that Freud is not writing a narrowly medical treatise but placing the problem of dreams in the mainstream of cultural tradition.

After these preliminaries, which need not detain readers for long, the real substance of the book begins in Chapter 2. Here, preparing to illustrate his own method of dream-interpretation by means of a specimen dream, Freud gives his work yet another genealogy by referring to the symbolic dream-interpretations carried out by Joseph in Genesis 41, to the ancient dream-book of Artemidorus of Daldis (second century AD), and to the popular dream-manuals which circulate at the present day. The folk-belief that dreams have a meaning is nearer the truth than the scepticism of scientists; Freud proposes to place this belief on a scientific footing. To do so, he employs the method of free association, already practised with hysterical patients, in which one relaxes one's concentration and waits for ideas to enter one's mind spontaneously. He first recounts a dream relating to his professional life, that of 'Irma's injection', then reports the associations that occur to him, and finally extracts the desire that gave rise to the dream—the desire that a mistaken diagnosis should be a colleague's fault instead of Freud's. The dream shows how recollections of one's everyday life can be worked into a structure where one person can be substituted for another, where unacknowledged feelings like envy and guilt can find expression, where ideas can be linked by verbal similarities, and where the laws of logic can be suspended. We may wonder that the concealed wish should be a petty piece of professional rivalry, and suspect that the interpretation of the dream could be extended much further even than Freud hints. For the moment, however, the dream has neatly served its purpose of showing that dreams are the fulfilments of wishes.

Having made this point, Freud invites us to pause on our journey and consider the next step. For even if all dreams are wish-fulfilments, very few are obviously so. When thirsty, one may dream of drinking. Children may dream of forbidden food or desirable outings. But in most dreams the manifest content differs from the latent content, and the latter can only be discovered by undoing the mechanisms of censorship and dream-distortion that have hidden it. Often the latent content is unflattering to our vanity. Freud disarms us by recounting a dream in which his ostensible affection for a friend disguised latent malice. Thus we are prepared to accept malevolent motives as the explanation in cases where a wish is apparently *not* fulfilled. A lady's ostensible disappointment at being unable to give a supper-party conceals her wish to prevent a rival from becoming plump and attractive. Another lady's dream, apparently contradicting Freud's theory, is said to stem from a desire to contradict Freud's theory. Another lady, who is distressed by a dream that her daughter is dead, has her dream attributed to long-past wishes, during her unwanted pregnancy, that the embryo might die. A young man's unpleasant dream of being arrested for infanticide turns out to mask the yet more unpleasant fear that his mistress might get pregnant. And in anxiety-dreams—a tough challenge for the theory of dreams as wish-fulfilments—the anxiety is explained as a transformation of unused libido and hence as revealing the presence of inadmissible sexual desires.

As these examples show, Freud's theory is resourceful, perhaps dangerously so, in incorporating apparently recalcitrant counter-examples. His argument proceeds by confronting difficult cases, including many remarkable dreams of his own, absorbing them into the theory, and expanding the theory more and more in the process. Faced with the objection that dreams are mostly trivial, Freud replies that trivial recollections from the previous day (*Tagesreste*, 'day's remainders' or 'residues') are used by the dream to encode its latent content. Hence, although they use trivial material, no dreams are themselves trivial. Somatic stimuli, like physical discomfort while in bed, are similarly employed by the dream as part of its material. Dreams are not bound by our conceptions of time. They have access to material from our childhood, so that embarrassing dreams of being naked in public can be explained as harking back to children's pleasure in nakedness, with the embarrassment introduced by the censorship. And dreams about the deaths of our loved ones point to the emotional ambivalence felt most intensely in childhood, when children may feel intense antagonism towards their siblings and their parents. Here Freud inserts the argument that love for one parent and hostility to the other form a universal pattern illustrated in Sophocles' *Oedipus* and, in more veiled form, in Shakespeare's *Hamlet*. The reader may feel that by introducing this portentous theory of emotional conflict and illustrating it by the masterpieces of Western literature Freud risks bursting the bounds of his dream-book. But for readers sceptical of Freud's theory, there could hardly be more powerful witnesses than Shakespeare and Sophocles. And by citing the classics Freud again conveys his ambition. He wants to show that dreams are central to psychic life, and therefore central to the themes of human culture.

Having led the reader thus far through a large number of dreams and suggested a link between dreams and literature, Freud adopts a more systematic approach. Labelling the activity of the dream 'the dream-work', he discusses the four ways in which a latent dream-thought is reshaped into a dream. One is condensation, in which different dream-elements are fused. Different people may be identified; different ideas may be linked by a pun, as when Freud found at least four ideas combined in the dream-word 'Autodidasker'. At the same time, the dream-work practises displacement, transferring emotional intensity from the centre of the dream-thought to its marginal components. Meanwhile, the dream-thought must be adapted to fit the representational resources of the dream. For example, the dream cannot express logical relations like 'because' or 'either/or'. Hence the illogicality which Freud noted in his dream of Irma's injection. The dream excels, however, in turning thoughts into pictures. It uses visual images that are also found in relatively primitive forms of expression like proverbs, jokes, and songs. However, the absurdity of dreams is limited by a fourth activity which Freud is uncertain whether or not to assign to the dream-work. This is 'secondary revision', which censors the exuberance of the dream, reassures the dreamer by introducing thoughts like 'It's only a dream', and fills in gaps in the dream's structure so as to make it more logical and coherent. Hence the final form of the dream is fully determined, with nothing owed to chance, but at first glance indecipherable. It is like a hieroglyphic inscription, consisting partly of pictures and partly of verbal symbols, which has been distorted, blurred, and defaced.

The last chapter, grandiosely entitled 'The Psychology of the Dream-Processes', does not offer the final clarification we might expect. Instead, Freud warns us that our journey will descend once more into darkness, uncertainty, and speculation. Dealing apparently with several separate topics, he restates some of the assumptions underlying his dream-theory and opens up more mysterious per-spectives, indicating the place of his dream-theory within a wider, still half-obscure theory of the mind.

One of these assumptions, operative throughout *The Interpret-ation* but now reaffirmed, is that all psychical activity is determined by the pursuit of an unconscious purpose. None of it is arbitrary or haphazard. Even the manner in which one recounts one's dreams is shaped by an extension of the dream-work: so there is no need to fear that dreamers give mistaken accounts of their dreams. For the pur-poses of interpretation, the account of the dream *is* the dream. Hence, though some dreams will in practice elude us, all dreams can in principle be interpreted by Freud's method.

Another assumption is labelled 'regression', and here the reader encounters strange diagrams purporting to represent the direction of psychical energy within the mind. Freud gave these conceptions spatial form because he still thought, as in his 'Project', that it would eventually be possible to locate them within the brain as described by neurology. The normal sequence is that energy is prompted at the perceptual system, passes into consciousness, and thence to the motor system, where it is discharged by action. (I feel an unpleasant sensation, realize that I have been bitten by a mosquito, raise my hand, and swat the insect.) But in dreaming energy flows the other way. Barred by the censor from consciousness, and hence from dis-charge through action, wishes flow back, collecting unconscious memories on their way, and present themselves once again, now transformed by the dream-work, to the sleeper's lowered conscious-ness. In this scheme, the 'unconscious' and the 'preconscious' are agencies or authorities (*Instanzen*) which the wish has to satisfy; the unconscious is more tolerant, and helps the wish to smuggle itself past the censorship of the preconscious. As a result, psychical energy is discharged without disturbing sleep.

Even if we prefer to set aside these schemes as residues of Freud's misplaced neurological ambitions, we need to realize how lasting such ambitions were, for the concept of regression leads on to Freud's account of the primitive character of dream-thought. He prepares for this description by likening the unsatisfied wish underlying the dream to the Greek Titans, the giants overthrown by the Olympian gods and buried under mountains which still quake when the prisoners move their huge limbs. Then he formulates the distinction between two kinds of thinking: the rational, realistic kind that is supposedly normal in waking life, and the irrational kind, found in hysterical patients, which denies unacceptable facts and takes refuge in fantasies. Freud calls the latter kind the primary process. Infants, with their imperious desires, think only in this manner. As one matures, one learns to adjust one's wishes to reality, to repress many infantile desires into the unconscious recesses of the mind, and to replace irrational, associative thinking with logical reasoning. But since Freud still conceives the mind as a closed system, desires are not expelled but only hidden away. They reassert themselves most riotously in dreams, where the primary process engages in conflict with the censor; but they also manifest themselves in neurotic symptoms, and, as Freud would argue in his next books, in jokes, slips of the tongue, and seemingly casual but in fact deeply significant mistakes. And in later works, Freud would relate the childhood of the individual to the early stages of humanity, and seek the origins of art and religion in the supposedly irrational thought-processes of primeval man.

Arguing with Freud

What Freud offers as a scientific theory looks more like an imaginative vision. With its scale and sweep, and its revelation of profound and unwelcome truths about human life, the theory invites an awed suspension of disbelief. We are, it seems, embedded in the organic world and in thrall to the past more deeply even than Darwin had envisaged. The violently ambivalent emotions of our childhood still shape our adult experiences and are themselves shaped in a structure inherited, as Freud would later contend, from the primitive past of humanity.

> Archaic fevers shake
> Our healthy flesh and blood
> Plumped in the passing day
> And fed with pleasant food.
> The fathers' anger and ache
> Will not, will not away
> And leave the living alone . . .[10]

And this archaic heritage makes itself known both in the master-pieces of our literature and in the seemingly nonsensical productions of our dreaming minds. Freud has delivered a rebuke to our vanity.

Still, we should respect Freud's intellectual ambitions by arguing with his theory. We should also remember that the passage of a century will inevitably have revealed the flaws in this, as in any thesis, and will also have disclosed its underlying presuppositions. What Freud took for granted may now strike us as dated, implausible, or absurd, insofar as we inhabit a different cultural world and follow a different intellectual paradigm. But that difference itself is partly of Freud's making.

We may wonder, first, whether the theory is too powerful for its own good. As Freud's theoretical apparatus rolls onward, it chews up all the counter-evidence in its path, at the risk of rendering the theory unfalsifiable and vacuous. For if no counter-evidence were conceivable, the theory could not be tested and could not be developed. As we have seen, the theory that all dreams are wish-fulfilments finds it hardest to cope with dreams of fear and punishment. Having claimed that anxiety in dreams comes from transformed libido, Freud finally adopts another, evasive strategy by saying that anxiety-dreams concern him only insofar as they illustrate the dream-work and really belong to the psychology of the neuroses. As for punishment-dreams, they express the desire to be punished for indulging a forbidden wish. In any case, every successful dream is a wish-fulfilment because it fulfils the wish to sleep. To Freud's credit, he resorts to this desperate argument—for the wish to sleep can hardly be the latent dream-thought—only once and in passing, while his explanation of punishment-dreams is clearly an interim solution which he will worry away at until, in *The Ego and the Id* (1923), he proposes the concept of the superego.

---

[10] Edwin Muir, 'The Fathers', in his *Collected Poems* (London, 1984), 139.

Turning to particular instances, Freud's interpretations reveal a gender-bias that is both comical and discreditable. As with his hysterics, he assumes that his female patients are unconsciously obsessed with sex and reveal their obsession through involuntary puns. A 'reserved' young woman dreams that she goes to market, cannot buy butcher's meat, but is offered strange-looking vegetables (p. 140). The 'butcher' makes Freud think of a vulgar expression, 'to shut the butcher's shop' (= to button one's fly), while the vegetables are identified as black radish (*schwarzer Rettich*) and decoded as 'Schwarzer, rett' Dich!' (Black, save yourself!). Apparently Freud is imputing both sexual and racial fantasies to his patient.[11] A footnote mentions that she accused him of sexually provocative behaviour: whatever happened in the consulting-room, the atmosphere must have been highly charged, and Freud's interpretations might well have been felt as sexual aggression. Another woman patient dreams about Italy (p. 179); since she has never been there, Freud interprets as 'Genitalien' (genitals) the phrase 'gen Italien' (Italy-wards) which, be it noted, is so obsolete that the woman is highly unlikely to have actually used it. Freud's double standard becomes obvious when he fails to see any sexual meaning in his own dream about riding a horse through a narrow passage between two carts (p. 177).

Freud's weakness for doubles entendres illustrates a striking feature of his dream-interpretations: their heavy reliance on word-play. He draws freely on colloquial expressions, as when a basket in a dream evokes the standard expression 'einen Korb geben' (to give someone a basket, i.e. to reject a suitor). A dream about a box evokes the English word 'box' and hence the sexual connotations of *other* German words for box. Freud's own dream about Count Thun brings in English, Latin, and Spanish. His dreams often turn on invented portmanteau words like 'norekdal' and 'Autodidasker'. This reliance on puns gives Freud an interpretative freedom which might often be considered licence. It anticipates the verbal bias of *Jokes and their Relation to the Unconscious* (1905), which deals with witticisms rather than humour in general, and of *The Psychopathology of Everyday Life* (1901), which deals with many

[11] The 'black' may have been suggested by the Ashanti village from West Africa, complete with inhabitants, which was displayed in the Prater in Vienna in 1896 and attracted innumerable visitors. See Andrew Barker, *Telegrams from the Soul: Peter Altenberg and the Culture of fin-de-siècle Vienna* (Columbia, SC, 1996), 63–74.

kinds of mistake but especially with the verbal parapraxes now famous as 'Freudian slips'.

Evidently Freud, like many writers, was under the spell of words. This is not surprising if we consider his multilingual education. Although his family, as Jews intent on assimilation, had provided him only with perfunctory Hebrew teaching, his education had given him a solid grounding in the Greek and Latin classics. As a school-boy he corresponded with a friend in Spanish; he translated several books by John Stuart Mill from English; his French was good enough for him to study in Paris. The effect of his classical education should be underlined. He wrote that his classical learning had brought him 'as much consolation as anything else in the struggle of life' (SE xiii. 241). Throughout his life he astonished people by his familiarity with classical philology.[12] His theory of parapraxes has been most searchingly criticized by a classical scholar, who compares them to textual errors.[13] Indeed Freud's preferred analogy for dream-interpretation is decipherment, suggesting how a philologist tries to restore the original sense of an inscription blurred by time or a text corrupted by a succession of inaccurate copyists. In philology, as in dream-analysis, the original may be remote from the text, as in the example quoted by A. E. Housman from a German critic: 'If the sense requires it, I am prepared to write *Constantinopolitanus* where the MSS. have the monosyllabic interjection *o.*'[14]

The extremely verbal character of Freud's mind leads him to underestimate visual imagery in dreams. Freud admits that his own dreams are not very visual: 'my own dreams have in general fewer sensory elements than I have to reckon with in the dreams of others' (p. 358). Punning dreams are apparently not uncommon, though seldom as lapidary as the dream-declaration 'Iona Cathedral'.[15] But most people report dreaming principally in visual images. Freud, however, assumes that dreams start from a dream-thought that is best expressed in words and translate it into a picture-language

---

[12] See Ernest Jones, *Free Associations: Memories of a Psycho-Analyst* (London, 1959), 35.

[13] See Sebastiano Timpanaro, *The Freudian Slip*, tr. Kate Soper (London, 1974).

[14] Housman, 'The Application of Thought to Textual Criticism', in his *Selected Prose*, ed. John Carter (Cambridge, 1962), 142.

[15] See Charles Rycroft, *The Innocence of Dreams*, 2nd edn. (London, 1991), 124–5.

which is intellectually inferior because it cannot convey logical connections; the analyst restores to the dream its verbal character. However, the first edition of *The Interpretation of Dreams* at least stops short of the crude doctrine of sexual symbolization with which Freud's dream-theory is popularly but misleadingly associated. It was only in later editions that Freud, influenced by his colleague Wilhelm Stekel, added all the mechanical equivalences—staircases signify the sexual act, tables represent women, losing one's hair or teeth symbolizes castration, etc.—which have given so much satisfaction to the simple-minded and done so much to bring Freudian analysis into disrepute. Freud revelled in linguistic play, but, despite his appreciation of painting and especially sculpture, he did not know what to make of visual imagery in dreams. Freud's own dream-theory is, in this respect, seriously skewed and unfaithful to most people's experience.

As a scientific rationalist, Freud distrusts the manifest content of dreams. But his distinction between the meaningless manifest content and the all-important latent content has been questioned by Jung and others. Why should not the manifest content be meaningfully related to problems and tensions that preoccupy the dreamer? If, as surveys suggest, American blacks dream more often than whites about loss, injury, and violence, this is presumably not because they suffer more from castration-anxiety but because they are more exposed to violence. The astonishing dreams collected by Charlotte Beradt during the Third Reich show how the atmosphere of terror penetrated into people's unconscious minds.[16] Many dreams can make sense without Freud's tortuous decipherments.

In assigning dreams to the primary process, the mode of thought that refuses to acknowledge reality as an obstacle to its desires and regresses from logic to images, Freud seems to distrust the imaginative activity by which dreams are shaped. The shortcomings in his theory of dreams are linked to his inability to account for artistic creation. He thought that both activities were forms of daydreaming, fantasies in which the censorship is relaxed, desire is allowed to roam, the constraints of reality are temporarily ignored, and infantile experience again comes to the fore. In his essay 'Creative Writers and Day-Dreaming' (1908) he maintained that the

---

[16] Beradt, *The Third Reich of Dreams*, tr. Adriane Gottwald (Chicago, 1968).

creative artist indulged such fantasies by softening their egoistic character so that the reader could share the vicarious pleasure of overcoming obstacles and gaining love and fortune. But this notoriously inadequate essay does nothing to explain the power of great art, although or because it deals with painful material, to give us a feeling of satisfaction, harmony, and uplift; nor the power of even simple stories and pictures to give shape to our experience and make us feel more at home in the world. The idea that some dreams at least may be like imaginative creations, restoring our psychic balance and helping us towards wholeness, was again left to Jung.[17]

Another deficiency in Freud's account of dreams is his downplaying of their emotional power. For him, emotion in dreams shows that the censorship has failed in its normal task of reducing the affective strength of dream-material. Unlike Jung, he shows no interest in those 'big dreams' which tend to come at important thresholds in one's life—puberty, early middle age, the approach of death—and can give one's life a new direction. A famous example is the symbolic dream which the philosopher Descartes dreamt on the night of 10–11 November 1619 and associated with an intellectual breakthrough.[18] In other cultures such dreams can be accommodated within a meaningful pattern. They may be understood as revelations by the gods or as initiating the dreamer into a preordained role as seer or shaman. Thus young Ojibwa boys in North America used to undergo a 'dream fast' to induce dreams of the animals or birds that would become their guardian spirits. When the culture disintegrates under colonial pressure, however, such 'culture pattern' dreams vanish and only 'individual' dreams remain.[19] One of Freud's later patients, the young Russian who has gone down in psychoanalytic history as the Wolf Man, brought him an extraordinary childhood dream about seven white wolves sitting in a tree outside the dreamer's bedroom window (SE xvii. 29). By dubious reasoning, Freud traced the dream back to a speculative episode in which the dreamer saw his parents

---

[17] See C. G. Jung, 'On the Nature of Dreams', *The Collected Works*, ed. Herbert Read, Michael Fordham, and Gerhard Adler, tr. R. F. C. Hull, 2nd edn. (London and Princeton, 1970), viii. 281–97.

[18] See Stephen Gaukroger, *Descartes: An Intellectual Biography* (Oxford, 1995), 106–11; Marie-Louise von Franz, 'The Dream of Descartes', in her *Dreams* (London and Boston, 1998), 107–91.

[19] See Jackson Steward Lincoln, *The Dream in Primitive Cultures* (London, 1935).

copulating.[20] But its analogues in Russian folklore, and some unusual features of the patient, suggest that it was an initiatory dream; the Russian was Westernized enough to have lost the key to its meaning, and Freud's analysis ensured that he never found it.[21]

The Interpretation *as Autobiography*

Although the applicability of Freud's theory may be limited, it enabled him to make sense of his own dreams, many of which are recounted and analysed in great detail. Freud tempered his indiscretion by prudently withholding much further material, some of which researchers have since brought to light. With their help, we can see how far *The Interpretation of Dreams* is a semi-disguised autobiography. Carl Schorske, who explores this dimension in his inspiring study of fin-de-siècle Vienna, remarks: 'Imagine St Augustine weaving his *Confessions* into *The City of God*, or Rousseau integrating his *Confessions* as a subliminal plot into *The Origins of Inequality*: such is the procedure of Freud in *The Interpretation of Dreams*.'[22]

Many autobiographical elements are of course present on the surface. We learn much about Freud's dealings with his father, other relatives, and colleagues, about his medical training, his daily life, his health, his holidays with his family. The book also incorporates much of 1890s Vienna, from its politics to its sexuality and its slang; as a contemporary document, it should be read alongside the early chapters of Stefan Zweig's *The World of Yesterday* and Arthur Schnitzler's recently published diaries for the 1890s. Our present concern, however, is with what remains half-concealed in Freud's major dreams.

Professional ambition and anxiety play an important role. We should remember that in 1899, when Freud published *The Interpretation of Dreams*, he was more than halfway through a long life which had hitherto brought many disappointments. His appointment as

[20] For a tart summary of Freud's argument see Roy Porter, *A Social History of Madness: Stories of the Insane* (London, 1987), 223–8 (with further references, p. 251); on Freud's rhetoric, Stanley Fish, 'Withholding the Missing Portion: Psychoanalysis and Rhetoric', in his *Doing What Comes Naturally* (Oxford, 1989), 525–54.

[21] See Carlo Ginzburg, 'Freud, the Wolf-Man, and the Werewolves', in his *Myths, Emblems, Clues*, tr. John and Anne C. Tedeschi (London, 1990), 146–55.

[22] Schorske, *Fin-de-siècle Vienna: Politics and Culture* (Cambridge, 1981), 183.

lecturer in neuropathology at Vienna University enabled him in 1886 to marry Martha Bernays, to whom he had been engaged for four years, but in order to support a family he had also to open a private medical practice. Despite his prolific research, his promotion to professor was delayed till 1902, partly by anti-Semitism. In 1897, when his name was unavailingly put forward, he had a dream identifying another Jewish colleague, R., with his Uncle Josef. Since this uncle had been sentenced to ten years' imprisonment for handling forged banknotes, Freud's dream equates Jewishness with criminality as professional handicaps and displaces them onto a colleague.

Despite his frequent disclaimers, Freud was intensely ambitious. He hoped to make his name by an epoch-making scientific discovery. In 1884 he narrowly failed to win credit for discovering the anaesthetic properties of cocaine. Although Freud published an article on this topic, the crucial research was done just afterwards by his friend Carl Koller. Freud's resentment finds expression in the dream of the botanical monograph, dating from early March 1898. The dried plant specimen in the monograph is associated, via the leaves of an artichoke, with the pages that Freud and his sister were encouraged by their father to tear out of an illustrated book. Thus books here are consigned to desiccation and destruction, implying Freud's own failure as a writer. His father, who had died some sixteen months earlier, is cast here as an enemy of books and thus covertly blamed for Freud's failure. To atone for this hostile thought, however, Freud recalls how in 1885 his father's glaucoma was operated on, with Koller administering the cocaine anaesthesia, and he puts himself in his father's place by imagining how he too might undergo such an operation.

The friend who restores Freud's sight by supervising his glaucoma operation is the Berlin ear, nose, and throat specialist Wilhelm Fliess, who makes many covert appearances in *The Interpretation of Dreams*. After their first meeting in autumn 1887, when Fliess, visiting Vienna, attended Freud's lectures, they soon became close friends. Freud's letters to Fliess, an invaluable source for his personal and intellectual biography, have embarrassed Freudians by showing how their hero temporarily accepted Fliess's eccentric-sounding theories. Fliess maintained, for example, that the female menstrual cycle of twenty-eight days corresponded to a male cycle of twenty-three days and that these two periodicities governed much of life; that all human beings were essentially bisexual; and that many nasal disorders could be explained by positing a physiological link between the nose and the genitals. As Frank Sulloway has shown, these theories were neither unique to Fliess nor lacking in physiological evidence.[23] The theory of universal bisexuality powerfully influenced Freud's later theory of sexual development and is highly relevant to present-day debates in gender theory.[24]

Freud's acceptance of Fliess's naso-genital theory led to the events that underlie his specimen dream of Irma's injection. In March 1895 Freud treated a young woman called Emma Eckstein for hysteria.[25] Assuming that her hysteria was sexual in origin, he thought Fliess might cure it by operating on her nose. After the operation Emma kept having nosebleeds, till a fortnight later a massive and near-fatal haemorrhage obliged Freud to call in another doctor, who removed from her nasal cavity half a metre of gauze left there by Fliess. Deeply distressed by Fliess's incompetence, Freud assured him that he was not to blame for this 'minimal oversight' (13 March 1895) and that Emma's nosebleeds were really motivated by her desire for the doctor's love (4 May 1896). In the dream, Freud defends himself against similar charges of professional incompetence by illogically blaming his colleagues. But his self-defence is made harder by other guilty associations. He recalls how a dear friend hastened his own death by cocaine abuse. This friend was Ernst Fleischl von Marxow (1846–91), a physiologist in Brücke's laboratory, whom Freud greatly admired. Fleischl had a painful infection in his right hand which required repeated surgery. To dull the pain, he took morphine, and became addicted to it. Freud, who had helped pioneer cocaine as an anaesthetic, encouraged him to overcome his morphine addiction by switching to cocaine, which was then thought to be normally non-addictive. Thus a dream which, according to the discreet interpretation Freud gave his readers, deals only with professional rivalry, turns out to encode some of Freud's most searing experiences of guilt. It also reveals the intense, almost homosocial bonds linking male colleagues. Emma Eckstein is blamed for her own

---

[23] Sulloway, _Freud_, ch. 5.

[24] See Marjorie Garber, _Vice Versa: Bisexuality and the Eroticism of Everyday Life_ (London, 1995).

[25] For a detailed narrative of the Eckstein affair, see Masson, _The Assault on Truth_, 55–72.

haemorrhages and serves as a channel for affection between Freud and Fliess, while Irma in the dream, surrounded by doctors who examine, percuss, and inject her, seems almost to be the passive victim of male group sexuality.

Freud's dreams not only express his own frustration at finding his career apparently blocked by scientific failure and anti-Semitic prejudice; they reveal much about his feeling of isolation in an Austro-Hungarian Empire that was falling under the sway of demagogic nationalism. As Austrian Jews, Freud and his family identified strongly with the central Imperial government which had gradually extended civil liberties to the Jews, beginning in 1781 with the Toleration Patents of the enlightened despot Joseph II and ending in 1867 with complete emancipation as part of the constitutional compromise (*Ausgleich*) between the Austrian and Hungarian halves of the Empire. They were loyal to the German language and culture and often cast longing eyes northwards to Germany, where political Liberalism seemed to have more effective spokesmen. Freud himself, as a student at Vienna University, belonged to the radical and German-nationalist Leseverein der deutschen Studenten Wiens (Reading Club for German Students at Vienna). This placed him at one extreme of the Liberal camp. The heyday of Liberalism in Austria began in 1868, when the Emperor Franz Joseph appointed a cabinet led by the liberally inclined aristocrat Prince 'Carlos' Auersperg and consisting mainly of middle-class ministers. Freud refers to this 'Bourgeois Ministry' in connection with his dream about his uncle, saying that it seemed to assure Jews that they could scale the heights of political power, and thus explaining the ambition in his dream as the residue of youthful hopes. From this, Schorske and others have concluded that the young Freud held political ambitions which were displaced into science; but the evidence is slight.[26]

By the 1890s, when Freud dreamt the dreams analysed in *The Interpretation*, the political outlook was much bleaker. The Liberals had fallen from power in 1879: their free-market economics led to financial scandals and failed to help the growing number of industrial workers, who turned instead to the Socialists and to the welfare

[26] Schorske, *Fin-de-siècle Vienna*, 189. Seminal though his book has been, Schorske, who is also the historian of German Social Democracy, tends to assume that political activity forms the whole duty of man and that cultural activity is only a substitute or sublimation.

policies of the Christian Social Party, founded by Dr Karl Lueger and others. Lueger, who presented himself as defender of the common man against Jewish capitalism, alarmed Freud and many others by his distasteful anti-Semitism. He was elected Mayor of Vienna five times before the Emperor consented to let him assume office in April 1897. Meanwhile, conservative governments were anxious to conciliate the increasingly powerful nationalist movements elsewhere in the Empire. In April 1897 the Prime Minister, Count Badeni, issued two language decrees requiring all public employees in Bohemia and Moravia to know both German and Czech. The Germans replied by rioting throughout the summer in Prague, other Bohemian towns, and Vienna. They also borrowed the Czechs' tactics of parliamentary obstruction: it was on this occasion that the Liberal deputy, Dr Lecher, spoke for thirteen hours, and, more amazingly still, always stuck to the point. On 28 November Franz Joseph accepted Badeni's resignation. These turbulent events interested Freud all the more since his family were German-speaking Jews who had come to Vienna via Moravia, one of the areas where German culture was retreating before militant Czech nationalism.

This is the background to Freud's 'revolutionary dream' of early August 1898, inspired by seeing the Prime Minister, Count Thun—successor to the unfortunate Badeni, and himself obliged to resign the following year—setting off to consult with the Emperor in the summer resort of Bad Ischl (p. 160) Freud's conscious rebelliousness, shown by whistling the aria in which Mozart's Figaro challenges Count Almaviva, is strengthened in the dream by recalling his early German nationalism and the revolution of 1848, eight years before his own birth. He brings in his reading of Zola's revolutionary novel *Germinal* and the defeat of the Spanish Armada by England, a nation to which Freud was so attached that he named one of his sons Oliver after Oliver Cromwell. His dream-rebellion, however, extends to the lower bodily stratum. Zola's description of a farting competition provides a link with the wind that dispersed the Armada, while the French word *pissenlit* (dandelion, literally 'piss-in-bed') is connected with holding the glass for an old, half-blind man to urinate into, with Freud's early bed-wetting, and with his desire to prove to his father (the blind man) that he has achieved something in life. Associating urine with childhood megalomania, Freud thinks also of Rabelais's giant Gargantua, who floods the city of Paris with his urine. In his unconscious, then, Freud imagines himself as a giant who can mobilize his prodigious powers of pissing and farting against the over-polite aristocracy. Although historians have made much of this dream's revolutionary content, it might more aptly be called Freud's Rabelaisian dream.

A different kind of rebellion is suggested in Freud's many dreams concerned with Rome. Despite his fondness for Italy, some inhibition prevented him from visiting Rome until September 1901. In the dreams Rome appears as an object of both enmity and desire. Freud associates it with the Roman Catholic Church, which represented for him the stronghold of religious obscurantism in contrast to his own scientific enlightenment. To a German nationalist, who undoubtedly sympathized with Bismarck's campaign against the political power of the Church in the 1870s, Rome would also represent a deadly political enemy. And when Freud recalls how his father, as a young man, meekly submitted to the insults of a 'Christian' (i.e. a Gentile), Rome comes also to typify the anti-Semitism which was indeed rife, often with clerical support, in Freud's Vienna. Against this Rome, Freud casts himself as a military assailant. He identifies himself with Hannibal, the Carthaginian and hence Semitic general who defeated the Romans but failed to take Rome, and with Napoleon's marshal Masséna, who was popularly but wrongly supposed to be Jewish, and who fought, unsuccessfully, against British forces in the Peninsular War.

Why, however, does Freud identify only with unsuccessful assailants? Why does he not think of Alaric the Goth, who conquered Rome in AD 410, or the Imperial forces that sacked Rome in 1527? To Freud, Rome is also an object of desire. He wants to get there one day; he does not want it to be destroyed. More than that: it is precisely Catholic Rome that Freud desires. For he associated the Catholic Church with the Czech nanny who, as he told Fliess, took him to church as a child, aroused his sexual desires, and was then dismissed for stealing (letters of 3, 4, 15 October 1897). The anxiety caused by her loss may, as Paul Vitz has argued, underlie the taboo on visiting Rome which he only overcame after working through his fears by writing *The Interpretation of Dreams*.[27] And on his many visits to Rome from 1901 onwards, it was not classical but Christian

---

[27] Vitz, *Sigmund Freud's Christian Unconscious* (New York, 1988), 22.

Rome that fascinated him, particularly of course Michelangelo's statue of Moses in the church of San Pietro in Vincoli, about which he wrote an essay in art history (SE xiii. 209–36).

If we accept the terms of Freud's theory, the historical and cultural material that Freud's unconscious shapes into dreams is always based on the template of early family relations. His professional friendships and rivalries correspond to the model he describes late in *The Interpretation of Dreams*: 'An intimate friend and a hated foe have always been necessary to my emotional life' (p. 314). Thus his friend Fliess and his rival Koller fit into the model of his ambivalent childhood relationship with his nephew John, who was one year older. His rebellion against Count Thun is ultimately directed against his father. And his ambivalence towards Rome is based on his early attitude to those two contrasting mother-figures, his taboo-breaking nurse and his dominating mother. If we were to adopt Jung's theory of dreams, however, we would want to turn things round and say that individual relationships fit the mythical templates of the collective unconscious. We need to bear both these interpretive possibilities in mind as we approach the dream which, of all those in this long book, has the best claim to rank as a 'big dream', that of the Three Fates (p. 157).

In itself, this dream may not seem impressive, but Freud's associations to it introduce, via far-fetched puns, a dense thematic network. He identifies the three women in the kitchen as the three Fates. The first, who seems to be making dumplings, is a mother providing nourishment. Freud then recalls how his mother proved that we are made of earth by rubbing her hands together, as though making dumplings, and producing black scales (a result not easy to reproduce experimentally, by the way). Thus the dumplings suggest also our eventual return to the earth in death. In his strange mythographic essay of 1913, 'The Theme of the Three Caskets', Freud connects the three caskets in *The Merchant of Venice* and the three daughters in *King Lear* with 'the three forms taken by the figure of the mother in the course of a man's life—the mother herself, the beloved one who is chosen after her pattern, and lastly the Mother Earth who receives him once more' (SE xii. 301). Returning to the dream, we note how Freud's puns and quotations introduce repeated motifs of food (fish, flesh, milk) and of earth ('dirt' and 'dust' in the quotations from Herder and Goethe). Shakespeare is significantly misquoted: Prince Hal's words in 2 *Henry IV*, 'Thou owest God a death', turn into 'You owe Nature a death', supporting Freud's naturalistic myth of man's passage from birth to burial. The third Fate, the beloved, is vestigially present in the name 'Pélagie'. Alexander Grinstein has traced it back to Charles Kingsley's novel *Hypatia* (1853), where Pelagia is a seductive dancer and sister to the ascetic monk Philammon.[28] In this haunting dream, therefore, the father, otherwise ubiquitous in Freud's theories, has yielded to the ambivalent, archetypal figure of the mother who dispenses nourishment, love, and finally death.

Freud's Disputed Legacy

In its reception, *The Interpretation of Dreams* shares the curious fate that Freud's work as a whole has encountered. Nowadays, anyone who studies psychology at university may never be required to read anything by Freud or his followers. But anyone who studies literature will almost certainly find that the course has a theoretical component in which knowledge of Freud and recent Freudian thinkers is mandatory. The scientific study of the mind can proceed with little reference to Freud, but for the study of literature, and more generally for the study of culture, the approaches first developed in *The Interpretation of Dreams* are indispensable.

The failure of psychoanalysis to demonstrate its scientific status has been the starting-point for some wide-ranging critiques of Freud and his thought. We may distinguish two versions of such critiques. The scientific version, represented especially by Adolf Grünbaum, judges Freud's work by the standards of scientific method and finds it wanting.[29] It especially points out that the analytic session cannot provide objective and testable clinical data, because the psychoanalytic method depends on emotional interaction between analyst and analysand, and because it is thus all too easy for the analyst to suggest to the analysand the emotional connections which the latter is supposed to discover. Such critics also doubt the effectiveness of

[28] Grinstein, *On Sigmund Freud's Dreams* (Detroit, 1968), 179–86.
[29] See Adolf Grünbaum, *The Foundations of Psychoanalysis: A Philosophical Critique* (Berkeley, Los Angeles, and London, 1984); for a reply, David Sachs, 'In Fairness To Freud', in Jerome Neu (ed.), *The Cambridge Companion to Freud* (Cambridge, 1991), 309–38.

psychoanalysis as a therapy, on the grounds that there are no clear criteria by which its success can be measured. The more polemical version of anti-Freudian criticism is represented especially by Frederick Crews, who was once a distinguished Freudian literary critic but who now calls himself a 'Freud-basher'. In this account, Freud was not only unscientific in his methods: he was a charlatan who browbeat his patients, falsified his findings, tyrannized his followers, and (for good measure) cheated on his wife.[30] And despite his constant hostility to all religion, expressed most uncompromisingly in *The Future of an Illusion* (1927), he has even been pilloried as an impostor who sought to found a false religion.[31]

What are we to make of these critiques, and what is really at stake? Often, Freud's critics are stating the obvious. Psychoanalysis does not and cannot conform to the objective and experimental model of science. Although Freud drew up guidelines to minimize the analyst's influence on the analysand, the analytic session is very different from a laboratory experiment. Psychoanalysts and psychotherapists constantly try to revise the clinical models which help them to understand their patients, and they have produced a rich and varied body of reflection. But such revision should be seen as the refinement of analytic and therapeutic techniques rather than the construction of hypotheses to be tested experimentally. Many psychoanalysts accept that their work is 'a craft rather than a science'.[32]

In other respects, Freud's detractors show a strange tunnel vision. They make many valid points about Freud's therapeutic blunders and his undoubted tendency to steer patients in the direction he wanted. They show an irreproachable concern for reason and evidence, but they seldom present any positive purpose to which these intellectual tools should be applied. In their obsession with Freud himself, they forget that psychoanalysis has developed into a variety

[30] See especially Frederick Crews *et al.*, *The Memory Wars: Freud's Legacy in Dispute* (New York, 1995), and, in reply, Jonathan Lear, 'On Killing Freud (Again)', in his *Open Minded: Working out the Logic of the Soul* (Cambridge, Mass., 1998), 16–32. On Freud's relations with his sister-in-law, see Lisa Appignanesi and John Forrester, *Freud's Women* (London, 1992), 50–3.

[31] See Richard Webster, *Why Freud Was Wrong: Sin, Science and Psychoanalysis* (London, 1995), which incorporates numerous earlier critiques.

[32] Anthony Bateman and Jeremy Holmes, *Introducing Psychoanalysis: Contemporary Theory and Practice* (London, 1995), 243.

of schools of thought engaged in healthy competition. Beyond that, psychoanalytic theories have been absorbed into the common-sense understanding with which we approach other people and ourselves. Psychoanalysis has helped us to understand the psyche as deep, complex, and mysterious. Hence psychoanalysis is not, as its detractors often imply, an alternative to treatment by mind-altering drugs like Prozac, nor to self-help manuals that offer us useful knowledge—but, too often, only knowledge—about one another. It approaches people, not as essentially transparent beings who can be studied, adjusted, and manipulated, but as creatures who have—to use a word Freud would not have liked—souls, and who are characteristically enigmatic to themselves and to others.

Like any healthy intellectual and spiritual movement, psycho-analysis, despite the constant dangers of orthodoxy and funda-mentalism, has been rich in creative heresy. One development, associated with Jung, places more trust than Freud did in the mani-fest content of dreams and visions, taking them as guides to the individual's spiritual development, and thus reasserting the Roman-tic heritage of psychoanalysis.[33] Another, associated with the maverick Jacques Lacan, builds on Freud's conception of the verbal character of unconscious processes, combines it with structural linguistics, and proclaims that 'the unconscious is structured like a language'.[34] Yet a third development in psychoanalytic reflection places the emphasis on the act of interpretation and argues that psychoanalysis is less a scientific theory of the mind than a hermeneutic, a technique of understanding, and hence a branch of the humanities like biography and philology.[35] Like any classic, *The Interpretation of Dreams* has retreated into the past while fructifying the present.

Within dream research, *The Interpretation of Dreams* anticipates both the major directions of subsequent study: the inquiries into the *function* and into the *meaning* of dreams. Neurophysiologists have found that our sleep alternates between deep sleep, with slow breath-ing and heartbeat, and light sleep in which rapid eye movements

---

[33] See Polly Young-Eisendrath and Terence Dawson (eds.), *The Cambridge Companion to Jung* (Cambridge, 1997), esp. Douglas A. Davis, 'Freud, Jung, and Psychoanalysis', 35–51.

[34] See David Macey, *Lacan in Contexts* (London and New York, 1988), ch. 5.

[35] See Jürgen Habermas, *Knowledge and Human Interests*, tr. J. J. Shapiro (Boston, 1971).

(hence REM-sleep) suggest that we are following interior events in our mind's eye. Dreams occur in the latter state, which occupies about a quarter of our sleeping time. If repeatedly woken during REM-sleep, we become anxious, irritable, sometimes distressed. It is likely, therefore, that in addition to the physiological function of maintaining our sleep, dreams often have the psychological function of helping our minds to process and eliminate trivial or threatening material. The dreamer by definition does not know about this function, just as, in Freud's view, the latent dream-thoughts could be disclosed by the analyst but not by the dreamer. At least some dreams, however, may have not only a function but also a meaning, which may be apparent in the manifest content. There need be no universal key, no system of symbols, to explain this meaning; a dream has been successfully interpreted when its meaning suddenly clicks for the dreamer. The dream may be a message from one part of the self to another, seeking, as in Jung's theory, to restore psychic balance. The message may be shaped by the individual's creative and artistic capacities. Some imaginative people may have a special talent for dreaming, as for singing, drawing, or storytelling.

Despite Freud's commitment to scientific rationalism, he created a psychology which, in Lionel Trilling's words, 'makes poetry indigenous to the very constitution of the mind'.[36] Freud himself made an over-sharp distinction between the irrationality of the primary process, which produces the absurd manifest content of the dream, and the rational reflection which restores the latent content. But what if we see 'irrational', or (more politely) symbolic thinking, not as the antithesis to rational reflection but as the basis from which conceptual thinking develops?[37] A dream-interpretation would then take dream-symbolism seriously and educe from it a conceptual meaning, just as the interpretation of a poem accepts symbolism as a valid mode of expression and gingerly educes conceptual implications from it, while taking care not to substitute the interpretation for the poem. Hence the importance of *The Interpretation of Dreams* for the study of culture. Freud and the other early psychoanalysts were highly cultured people who wanted to apply their theories to literature, art, and history: Ernest Jones wrote about *Hamlet*,

[36] Trilling, 'Freud and Literature', in *The Liberal Imagination* (London, 1951), 52.

[37] See Jonathan Lear, *Love and its Place in Nature: A Philosophical Interpretation of Freudian Psychoanalysis* (London, 1990), 8.

Theodor Reik about Schnitzler, Marie Bonaparte about Edgar Allan Poe, Otto Rank about the representation of incest in world literature and mythology, while Lou Andreas-Salomé was herself a writer of fiction. Psychoanalysis seemed potentially able to bridge the division between the 'two cultures'.

The impact on creative literature of *The Interpretation of Dreams*, and of Freudianism in general, is less than is sometimes assumed. As Freud was the first to admit, creative writers anticipated his findings by their own psychological intuition. Writers do not create by anxiously following the instructions of a psychological theorist; and insofar as writers do absorb the psychological theories of their time, the early twentieth century offered many others besides Freudianism. The greatest psychological novelists—Marcel Proust, Robert Musil, Virginia Woolf—took little interest in Freud.[38] The dreamlike fluidity of stream-of-consciousness narrative antedates Freud: its earliest practitioner, Édouard Dujardin (*Les Lauriers sont coupés*, 1888), was inspired by Wagner's 'continuous melody'. On the other hand, Franz Kafka, recording what had passed through his mind while writing his 'breakthrough' story 'The Judgement' in 1912, wrote: 'Thoughts about Freud, naturally', and it is possible that first- or even second-hand acquaintance with Freud's early works helped him to make a confident and concentrated use of images, especially in his haunting story 'A Country Doctor'.[39] A more deliberate use of Freud's dream-theory was made by the Surrealists, who in poetry and painting tried to abandon rational control and juxtapose images from the unconscious. Above all, the verbal character that Freud imputed to the unconscious formed the foundation for Joyce's epic in dream-language, *Finnegans Wake*, where an archetypal narrative emerges through a multilingual swirl.

It is not in literature, but in literary criticism, that Freudianism has had a lasting impact. The great critics of the mid-twentieth century, like William Empson, W. H. Auden, Edmund Wilson, and Lionel Trilling, absorbed psychoanalysis as part of the intellectual equipment that enabled them to relate literature to the emotional,

[38] See 'Freudian Fictions' (1920), in *The Essays of Virginia Woolf*, ed. Andrew McNeillie, vol. 3 (London, 1988), 195–8.
[39] See Edward Timms, 'Kafka's Expanded Metaphors: A Freudian Approach to *Ein Landarzt*', in J. P. Stern and J. J. White (eds.), *Paths and Labyrinths: Nine Papers from a Kafka Symposium* (London, 1985), 66–79.

social, and philosophical fabric of human existence. Criticism that ignored psychoanalysis would nowadays look naive; but criticism that relies exclusively on psychoanalysis can easily be tiresome and sectarian. Freud's conception of interpretation as the disclosure of a hidden dream-thought is a doubtful precedent. Most critics would rather agree with Conrad's Marlow, for whom 'the meaning of an episode was not inside like a kernel but outside, enveloping the tale which brought it out only as a glow brings out a haze'.[40] Even in his pro-Freudian period, Frederick Crews conceded: 'It must be admitted that Freudian criticism too easily degenerates into a grotesque Easter-egg hunt: find the devouring mother, detect the inevitable castration anxiety, listen, between the syllables of verse, for the squeaking bedsprings of the primal scene.'[41] Crews's own study of Nathaniel Hawthorne's fiction inquires subtly and astutely into the buried fantasies of guilt, incest, parricide, and sadism which he presents as the real meanings concealed beneath Hawthorne's moral and theological surface meanings. In dealing with Hawthorne's inquiry into New England's Puritan heritage, however, Crews himself risks narrowness by insisting that Hawthorne was not really interested in the Puritans, who simply represent the repressive side of the author, and that Hawthorne's sense of the past refers only to symbolic family conflict.[42] Here, and still more in some post-Freudian criticism, we see the danger that a single-minded use of psychoanalytic theory to illuminate literature ends up presenting literature as an expression of psychoanalytic theory.

The Interpretation of Dreams has been fruitful for literary study by developing the hermeneutic principle illustrated in Freud's explorations of dreams: that interpretation and analysis are interminable. Freud says repeatedly that the latent content of a dream always exceeds its interpretation. Later he was to declare that psychoanalytic treatment could never really reach a final conclusion. Similarly, the implications of an imaginative work reach

[40] Joseph Conrad, *Heart of Darkness*, in *Youth, Heart of Darkness, The End of the Tether*, Collected Edition (London, 1947), 48.

[41] Crews, *Out of My System: Psychoanalysis, Ideology, and Critical Method* (New York, 1975), 166.

[42] Crews, *The Sins of the Fathers: Hawthorne's Psychological Themes* (New York, 1966), 31, 60.

down into the buried regions of our imagination, so that the meaning of a literary masterpiece is inexhaustible. There cannot in practice be a single, conclusive interpretation, though such a concept may be necessary as a regulative idea to direct our interpretative efforts and save them from mere vacuous subjectivity. The exploration of a work of literature must be undertaken afresh by each reader and involves an element of (perhaps unwitting) self-exploration.

Psychoanalytic criticism most successfully avoids becoming an Easter-egg hunt when it transfers its attention from the supposed latent content to the mechanisms of condensation and displacement through which a text can communicate, and when psychoanalysis is integrated with formalist and social approaches. The literary genre where psychoanalysis has proved most rewarding is Gothic fiction, in which surface realism is fractured by half-hidden terrors and obsessions.[43] Unacknowledged impulses may be displaced onto a Doppelgänger, as in Robert Louis Stevenson's *Dr Jekyll and Mr Hyde*; meanings may be forcefully condensed into a single figure, as when the monster in Mary Shelley's *Frankenstein* embodies the guilty, self-punishing fears of its creator, the nemesis of overweening science, and the reckless resentment of victims of injustice. A critical eye thus sharpened can find mechanisms of doubling, displacement, and mirroring even in the most ostensibly solid works of realism.[44] One can also understand fictional characters, like those in dreams, as being formed on the templates of parents and siblings, and hence as revenants. Thus, in *David Copperfield* the father whom the orphan David never knew has a sinister revenant in Mr Murdstone and a benign, ineffectual counterpart in Mr Micawber, while sibling conflict emerges with the admired Steerforth and the hated Uriah Heep, both of whom appear as sexual rivals.

The wider legacy of Freud's early work is too all-enveloping to be readily visible. It is the interpretive approach to culture, and the understanding of much social life *as* culture, that currently domin-

[43] For an exemplary study, see David Punter, *The Literature of Terror: A History of Gothic Fictions from 1765 to the Present Day*, 2nd edn., 2 vols. (London and New York, 1996).
[44] For a critically agile and eclectic example, see Andrew J. Webber, *The Doppelgänger: Double Visions in German Literature* (Oxford, 1996).

ates the humanities. It has been influentially formulated by Clifford Geertz: 'Believing . . . that man is an animal suspended in webs of significance he himself has spun, I take culture to be those webs, and the analysis of it to be therefore not an experimental science in search of law but an interpretive one in search of meaning.'[45] If we want to historicize this search for meaning, a good starting-point would be Darwin's study, *The Expression of the Emotions in Man and Animals* (1872), which shows how bodily actions that originally served some practical purpose survive by finding a new use as means of expression. Freud extended this approach to the hysterical symptoms which had previously been thought meaningless. 'All these sensations and innervations', he wrote, 'belong to the field of "The Expression of the Emotions" which, as Darwin has taught us, consists of actions which originally had a meaning and served a purpose' (SE ii. 181). Freud went on to disclose meaning in other unconsidered trifles of everyday life: in dreams, jokes, slips of the tongue, and seemingly casual lapses of memory. Thanks to Freud, vast areas of social life became intelligible: they formed a text which could be read. But while Freud provided a vocabulary for the social text, it also needed a syntax, and that was supplied by his contemporary, the Swiss linguist Ferdinand de Saussure, who showed how far language depends not on reference to non-linguistic realities but on its internal systematic character. Understood as a system of signs, language could provide the model for 'a science that studies the life of signs within society', to which Saussure gave the name 'semiotics'.[46] When Saussure's conception of a semiotic system is combined with Freud's extension of its potential scope, the way lies open for the transformation of the humanities into a study of meanings, their construction, perception, and interpretation. We now have semiotic and cultural studies not only of the arts, but of gesture, clothes, food, manners, ritual, and all forms of social classification.[47] We have learnt to apply to ourselves the distant, half-perplexed gaze which an anthropologist turns on another culture, and it is no accident that

---

[45] Geertz, *The Interpretation of Cultures* (New York, 1973), 5.

[46] Saussure, *Course in General Linguistics*, tr. Wade Baskin (London, 1974), 16.

[47] For a concise example, dealing with American classifications of domestic animals, clothes, and colours, see Marshall Sahlins, 'La Pensée Bourgeoise: Western Society as Culture', in his *Culture and Practical Reason* (Chicago, 1976), 166–204.

the 'cultural turn' in the humanities was pioneered by anthropologists like Geertz.[48]

What, finally, enabled Freud to see his society with the detached gaze of the anthropologist? Like many middle-class German and Austrian Jews of his time, he was deeply and intimately imbued with Western culture, from the Greeks to Mark Twain. But this profound acculturation was not accompanied by full social integration. Much as Freud admired many Gentiles among his teachers and colleagues, including especially Brücke and Fleischl von Marxow, he felt most at ease among fellow-Jews with whom he shared, as he told the B'nai B'rith Society in Vienna, 'a clear consciousness of an inner identity, the safe privacy of a common mental construction' (SE xx. 274). Freud's sense of marginality has been claimed as an important spur to his creativity.[49] Not only did he feel obliged to prove himself, but he sought to construct a universal science which would submerge Jewish difference within an all-embracing account of the irrational, hidden, often shameful forces that governed the mind.[50] Thus he looked at his society from a position partly within, partly outside it, the classic position of the participant observer, and from his standpoint on its margins he revolutionized its self-understanding.

[48] As one particularly influential example, see the early work of Mary Douglas, especially *Purity and Danger: An Analysis of the Concepts of Pollution and Taboo* (London, 1966) and *Natural Symbols: Explorations in Cosmology* (London, 1970).

[49] In the English-speaking world, many anthropologists have been either Jewish émigrés or Roman Catholics (e.g. E. E. Evans-Pritchard and Mary Douglas); in a Protestant-dominated society the latter can easily occupy a marginal position analogous to Freud's.

[50] See Stanley Rothman and Phillip Isenberg, 'Sigmund Freud and the Politics of Marginality', *Central European History*, 7 (1974), 58–78; Sander L. Gilman, *Freud, Race, and Gender* (Princeton, 1993); id., *The Case of Sigmund Freud: Medicine and Identity at the Fin de Siècle* (Baltimore and London, 1993).

NOTE ON THE TEXT

The text presented here is translated from the first edition of *Die Traumdeutung*, published in November 1899 with the date '1900'. It was hardly an instant bestseller: the initial print run of 600 copies took eight years to sell out. A sign of the importance Freud nevertheless attached to this book is that he kept it up to date by adding new material in each subsequent edition. Since the additions themselves were not always dated, the contours of Freud's original dream theory became increasingly blurred. The first collected edition of Freud's works, the *Gesammelte Schriften* (published at Vienna from 1924 to 1934), reprinted in 1925 the first edition of *Die Traumdeutung* as volume 2 and the additions separately in volume 3. Later, however, the *Gesammelte Werke,* published in London by the Imago Publishing Company from 1940 to 1952, reverted to a single text, that of the eighth (1930) edition, and reprinted it with all its additions. The English translation by James Strachey which forms part of the Standard Edition of Freud's works was based on this eighth edition, but Strachey, by indicating when each of the additions had been made, provided a variorum text which could enable a diligent reader to reconstruct how Freud elaborated his dream theory from the original edition onwards.

The main difference between the original edition, translated here, and the eighth edition which Strachey worked from, consists in the inclusion of a long section on symbolism as part of Chapter VI. Under the influence especially of Wilhelm Stekel, Freud came to think that dreams relied heavily on a repertoire of symbols whose meanings were partially at least independent of their context, and some such notion has passed into popular currency. One effect of making the first edition available in English should be to dispel this misconception by showing that the original dream theory is based on a much more flexible and sensitive interpretation of dream imagery.

Freud scholars have often wished for a critical edition which would retrace how Freud composed his work. In the case of *The Interpretation of Dreams,* and of most of the texts Freud wrote before the First World War, such an edition is impossible, because the manuscripts do not survive. In 1936, when Abraham Schwadron of the Hebrew University of Jerusalem asked Freud to donate his papers to the University Library, Freud replied: 'I have a probably unjustifiable antipathy to personal relics, autographs, collections of handwriting specimens, and everything that springs from these. This goes so far that I have, for example, handed all my manuscripts before 1905 into the wastebasket, among them that of the *Interpretation of Dreams*.'[1] Not till about 1913 did Freud realize that his manuscripts could have monetary value. He bequeathed a large number of them to his daughter Anna, and they are now stored in the Library of Congress in Washington. The scholar most familiar with Freud's manuscripts, Ilse Grubrich-Simitis, makes no great claims for the surprises that a critical edition might bring.[2]

However, an annotated edition which went beyond Strachey's useful notes in elucidating the cultural references and the conceptual changes in Freud's work would be an extremely valuable project. The present edition provides more annotations than Strachey's, thanks in part to the endeavours of subsequent scholars, though a few of Freud's references remain obscure; but we can at least see how steeped Freud was in literature, including the classics, and how much *The Interpretation of Dreams* reflects the professional and domestic life of a highly cultured medical academic in turn-of-the-century Vienna, not least his trips with his family to the environs of Vienna, to holiday resorts in southern Austria, and to Italy and the Adriatic.

R.R.

[1] Letter of 12 July 1936, quoted in Peter Gay, *Freud: A Life for our Time* (London, 1988), 612.

[2] Ilse Grubrich-Simitis, *Zurück zu Freuds Texten* (Frankfurt, 1993), 315.

NOTE ON THE TRANSLATION

Although the basis of this text is the first edition of Freud's *Die Traumdeutung*, as a translation it is a latecomer, and enters a much-ploughed field that has been the scene of some controversy. The first version was done in 1913, after Freud's third edition, by A. A. Brill, the Austro-Hungarian follower of Freud who settled in New York. This was replaced in 1953 by James Strachey's monumental variorum edition, which became volumes IV and part of V of the *Standard Edition of the Complete Psychological Works of Sigmund Freud*.[1] As such, it has become part of the memorializing and institutionalizing of Freud's life's work that was Ernest Jones's grand project.[2] It has become a classic and a touchstone. But, also as such, it has of recent years come under fire both ideologically and linguistically. Notoriously—by now—many of its linguistic solutions (and hence its conceptualization) to the problems posed by Freud's professional terminology fall in with Jones's avowed intentions of reinforcing the claims of psychoanalysis to scientific status and of making the controversial new science acceptable to the medical establishment. By now, Strachey's Greek- and Latin-based neologisms are deeply embedded in the language of English psychoanalysis. So are his much-debated rendering of 'Seele' by 'mind', and his general tendency to use terms implying structure rather than process for the workings of the—mind? soul? psyche? Moreover, his great editorial achievement in the Standard Edition as a whole in doing just that—*standardizing*, making an evolving and often contradictory oeuvre coherent over many years and topics and writings—has not entirely escaped the danger of a retrospectively induced uniformity. His own language, though perhaps rather dated now, is graceful and idiomatic; he is often interventionist, but his interventions are mainly in the interests of greater clarity and consistency (often greater, that is, than Freud's). But *Die Traumdeutung*,

---

[1] This translation is made from Freud's first edition: *Die Traumdeutung* (Leipzig und Wien: Franz Deuticke 1900).

[2] See Riccardo Steiner, '"To explain our point of view to English readers in English words"', in *Translation in Transition: The Question of the Standard Edition, The International Review of Psycho-Analysis*, 18 (1991), 351–92.

especially in its first form, is an early work—a founding work, it is true, but one in which terms and ideas are still provisional aids—'scaffolding' was Freud's metaphor—not yet set in stone, not yet subject to Jones's glossaries.[3]

Nothing can replace Strachey's *The Interpretation of Dreams*, just as nothing will replace the Authorized Version. It is, quite simply, THERE. It has for half a century belonged to that rare category of translations which Goethe described as read not instead of the original, but in their place. Many of its inventions are ingenious and necessary and have entered the language ('unpleasure' for 'Unlust', for example). Where they are successful and uncontroversial, it would seem perverse not to adopt them. There is no starting all over from scratch, no going back to 1899. The present translator has had admiring recourse to Strachey again and again. Nevertheless, in the light of so many objections, and with the imminent prospect of a Revised Standard Edition,[4] it may be timely to risk another version, a variant made on rather different principles (though, in the agony of the workshop, principles have a way of yielding to expediency). It is not done from inside the psychoanalytic profession, but by a Germanist with, it is hoped, an ear for the literary and cultural resonances of Freud's German, and an eye on the lay reader prepared to tackle a work which is in any case demanding enough without having to enter the arcanum of a specialized terminology. The advantage, and the opportunity, of being 'Not the SE' is that the criticisms can be listened to, tested in the active workshop of practical translation, and followed up—or not. It may be possible to go behind the interventionist nature of the SE and approach Freud's text more closely. This is not so much a matter of being more literal (though the present version probably is that—but these are matters of degree), as of attempting to render Freud's varying registers, listening for latent metaphors as well as his grand elucidatory analogies, and for not freezing uniform renderings when he is still thinking his way into new areas of thought.

[3] As early as 1918, Jones drew up a *Glossary for the Use of Translators of Psycho-Analytical Works* (Supplement 1 to *The International Journal of Psycho-Analysis*). He notes (p. 2) by way of introduction that it is 'to be regarded purely as a useful aid to translators, in no sense a lexicon of psycho-analytic terms, though conceivably it may later form the basis of one'. It did.

[4] Announced by the Institute of Psycho-Analysis in London in conjunction with the Hogarth Press for publication from 2000.

It is not only a matter of terminology, but of register, syntax, and the dynamics of German grammar that enable Freud to think in the way he does.[5] In the workshop, one wrestles with more than the concept-carrying noun, but also with sentence-structure and emphasis, with verbs and their modes. How to render these in the inevitable mismatch, which one can only hope to mitigate, of another language, and another mindset? What follows is a catalogue of some of the difficulties encountered on this secondary journey, and of the decisions they called forth. They may, negatively, as it were, serve to characterize some selective aspects of Freud's style in this treatise-cum-autobiography for the English speaker, at least those that emerged in the workshop. What strikes one in retrospect is how many of them are problems not only of Freud's language but of the German language *überhaupt*, as they say in German.

Broadly, this text is written in at least three main modes: theoretical, narrative, and analytic-exploratory, with fine-tuned registers within them. There is first the discursive, formal language of the argued treatise, presenting evidence, argument, rebuttal, qualification, inference. (The pace is stately, but will quicken as a point is clinched or an authority—'Autor'—refuted.) Now in German, the logical connectives necessary for such discourse—'daher', 'dennoch', 'also', 'doch', 'allerdings', 'zwar . . . aber', and so on—are comfortably current in everyday speech. Their unobtrusiveness helps to give formal argument a certain ease, apparent in much of Freud's prose. Not so their English equivalents, the hences and thuses, the nonethelesses and notwithstandings, which are the first steps into the arcanum. I have not been able to avoid them entirely, but I have reduced, simplified where possible ('all the same' instead of 'nevertheless', for example).

One of the main criticisms levelled at the SE is that this same everydayness characterizes many of Freud's apparently technical terms. Here too, Freud is following the habit of his own language: medical and scientific German has no alternative learned Latinate idiolect, as English has—or at least to a lesser extent. German patients are in a position to understand the language of their

[5.] See Ilse Grubrich-Simitis, 'Reflections on Sigmund Freud's Relationship to the German Language and to Some German-Speaking Authors of the Enlightenment', *The International Journal of Psycho-Analysis*, 67 (1986), 287–94, quoted by Patrick Mahoney in *Translating Freud*, edited by Darius Ornston (New Haven and London, 1992), 24–5.

diagnosis. To convey this accessibility, the challenge for the late translator is how to surmount Strachey's technical renderings. It may be easy enough to replace 'coenaesthesia' (Gemeingefühl) by the more immediate 'general vital feeling', but other terms are more problematic. In *Die Traumdeutung* Freud had not yet fully developed the language of psychoanalysis; it was still in the making. All the same, the famously ordinary 'Besetzung' ('occupation', 'investment', 'charge', with their latent military or electrical metaphors) expresses a concept essential to its arguments, as its notoriously medical rendering by 'cathexis' also does, that contentious coinage which by now has become deeply established in English analytic discourse.[6] I have dispensed with it and opted for 'charge' and its cognates (though this sometimes requires silent extension into 'charge [of energy/intensity]'). That is something a variant translation can allow itself. On the other hand, other neurological terms—'stimulus', 'excitation'—appear incorrigible.

So, on the whole, does another characteristic of German which is also an essential characteristic of Freud's German—in this work in particular. That is its ease in making word-combinations, specifically combinations with 'Traum': 'Traumarbeit', 'Trauminhalt', 'Traum-gedanke', 'Traumvorstellung', 'Traummaterial', and many, many more besides. On the whole such combinations sit uneasily in English, and there are small strategies for getting round them. But these five indicate fundamental theoretical concepts. Indeed, the distinction between 'Trauminhalt' and 'Traumgedanke' is essential to the analysis of dreams (or to 'dream-analysis'?). Freud explicates the terms with the adjectives 'manifest' and 'latent' quite early, but develops his argument using the less lucid noun-combinations, making his way towards clarification as he rediscovers 'manifest' and 'latent'. So in these instances in particular, and in a number of others, I have gone against the grain of English idiom, and rendered the combinations literally. They are in fact all-pervasive, and contribute to the general character of Freud's text. But they do signal that this English text is translated.

---

[6] See Darius Ornston, 'The Invention of "Cathexis" and Strachey's Strategy', *International Review of Psycho-Analysis*, 12 (1985), 391–9. Ornston (see note 5) has been a leading advocate of rethinking the SE. As far as this particular word is concerned, however, John Forrester bows to the reality-principle: 'It is much too late to suggest an alternative translation [for 'Besetzung'], even if one were to find one that was satisfactory.' *Language and the Origins of Psychoanalysis* (London, 1980), 224.

The debate reached a wider public with criticism of a range of words designating aspects of the inner life where Freud simply employed terms long familiar and in popular use, having rich, older, theological or philosophical resonances: first of all with 'Seele', and its cognates 'seelisch' and 'Seelenleben'.[7] I have rendered these by 'psyche' and 'psychical', moving into more literary language by rendering the third as 'inner life'. I have used 'soul' on occasion when Freud quotes one of his older authorities. 'Das Ich', too, for the figure seen in one's dreams, or even for the dreamer herself, I have rendered in more literary fashion as 'the self', for when he wrote *Die Traumdeutung* Freud had not yet undertaken a sharper conceptualization of what became 'the ego' in English. However, that term was current in philosophical and psychological discourse, and I have sometimes used it, once again, when Freud quotes from others—from Meynert, for example.

In the course of translating Freud's theoretical language, I let myself be guided but not constricted by the rule-of-thumb of using the same rendering for the same term; but I also let myself be deflected by the occasional intractability of English idiom, by context, and by the growing sense that Freud himself was exploring possible ways of saying what was on the brink of the unsayable: hence those frequent verbal forms of 'stirring', 'emerging', 'arising'—'regen', 'entstehen', 'hervorgehen', 'auftauchen'—to express the dynamics of the strictly *Un*conscious; hence the obscurity of some of his formulations—which I have often left obscure,[8] so that there might perhaps be some virtue, not in *in*consistency, but in not forcing consistency. For example, Freud uses 'Bildung' both statically, as 'a formation', and dynamically as a transitive process of 'forming', related to 'shaping', 'producing', 'creating'; and he uses 'Gebilde' mainly as 'structure'. But the distinction is not clear-cut, and on occasion (p. 80) the two words are even interchangeable. Such fluidity raises even greater problems in the workshop in rendering the philosophical/psychological term 'Vorstellung' and its cognate 'vorstellen', both of which are terms in common usage

---

[7] See Bruno Bettelheim, *Freud and Man's Soul* (New York, 1983).

[8] An example, which will also illustrate SE's elucidatory approach: 'Das seelisch Unterdrückte, welches im Wachleben durch die *gegensätzliche Aufhebung der Widersprüche* . . .' (1st edn., Chapter VII (e), p. 262, Freud's italics). JC: 'by the removal of contradictions by their opposite'; SE: 'the fact that the contradictions present in it are eliminated—one being disposed of in favour of the other.'

too (as 'idea' and 'to imagine', i.e. 'to generate ideas'). Initially, the translator has a choice between the traditional philosophical terms of 'idea' and 'representation', with a possible preference for the second.[9] But as Freud goes on to argue that the dream-content consists of disguises, substitutions, and stand-ins for the dream-thoughts, in terms of 'vertreten' and 'darstellen'—that is, of 'representing' in a quite different sense—that word-of-all-work had to be co-opted for a different office, and I had on the whole to return to 'idea'. It is not entirely satisfactory; not because the word is normally also used to render 'Einfall', for there are ways of getting round that little hurdle; but because of the occasional overlap in Freud's usage of 'Vorstellung' with 'Bild', rendered by 'image'. The two words are further apart in English than 'image' and 'representation'. (Confusion is greatest where Freud quotes his authorities, who have their own uses for the term.) So, in cases where greater clarity is required, I have found two ad hoc strategies useful: in contexts where there is no danger of confusing 'Vorstellung' with 'Darstellung' I have sometimes recalled 'representation' into service; and to guard against 'ideas' by itself being misunderstood as formulated conceptions, I have more often used 'imagined ideas'. This may rouse objections as not being a standard philosophical formulation, or perhaps even as being tautological, but I would defend it as being relatively close to what I think is Freud's meaning and register—and it rescues 'imagine' for the simple 'vorstellen', which I will not translate as 'generate representations'. Once again we are moving in a field where German terms of art are closer to everyday usage than English ones.

As a last item in discussing Freud's theoretical language, there is one specific psychoanalytic concept—'Nachträglichkeit'—where Strachey's rendering (as 'deferred action') has been disputed. I would not dream of entering this difficult debate, but I find that rendering the cognate adjective as 'retrospective', varied in context on occasion as 'retroactive', seems to serve Freud's argument, at least in this early text.

[9] 'Classical term in philosophy and psychology for that which one represents to oneself, that which forms the concrete content of an act of thought' and 'in particular the reproduction of an earlier perception'. Quoted in the entry on 'Idea (or Representation or Presentation)', in J. Laplanche and J.-B. Pontalis, *The Language of Psycho-Analysis*, tr. Donald Nicholson-Smith (London, 1973), 200–1. They go on to point out that to Freud, the 'act of thinking' can be unconscious.

But his theoretical mode is not his only mode. Another major register is to be found in the accounts of dreams, his own and others. His own are told in more lively fashion, and though he responds to a colourful dream from a patient (his words of praise are 'witty', 'ingenious', 'beautiful'), the narrative language is plain, even bald, and the storyline appropriately full of gaps. Importantly, Freud conveys the immediacy of the dream's experience by using the present tense. The present indicative is also the appropriate verb-form for the dream's sense of time and actuality: the past is present and the wish is realized. So I have followed him in this.

The narrative present also characterizes the third major mode of *Die Traumdeutung*, which I have called the exploratory-analytical. This is to be found mainly in the dream-analyses. Here the tense conveys the immediacy of process, the excitement of making discoveries on the hoof, sometimes the sudden 'Aha!' To use the past tense in translating would close the whole adventure. The analyses are by far the most varied writing in the text, in pace, material, and colour. The importance Freud ascribes to 'ordinary linguistic usage' as the 'Urtext' of dream-images, the reliance of many of his analyses on the picturesque suggestiveness of poetry—or Viennese slang—and his fondness for verbal play and punning, which is put to full use here, are the despair of the translator, who can only refer the reader to the explanations in the notes,[10] for to fabricate equivalents would be to negate the authenticity of the dreams. However, in their inventiveness and variety, their finely modulated ironies (so difficult to capture without exaggeration), their conversations and their ventriloquism, these analyses have given one translator a great deal of pleasure.

From declaring that dreams have a meaning which can be interpreted, Freud went on to compare the operation of the dream-work in transposing the text of the dream-thoughts into the new language of the dream-content to an act of translation. But that kind of transposition takes place unconsciously. Not this.

My warm thanks are due to Dr Ritchie Robertson for reading this text so closely and carefully; his comments and suggestions were

---

[10] I owe a debt of gratitude to Strachey's elucidation of a number of the grosser plays on words.

always constructive, and saved me from a number of errors, while his historical knowledge of Freud's social world—which enters Freud's dreams so palpably—made a context for a work which has itself become historical. My thanks too to Judith Luna for spur and encouragement, and to Jeff New for his patience and editorial labours. And not least to the strong predecessor. As one of Freud's favourite poets wrote: 'Mach's einer nach, und breche nicht den Hals.'

J. C.

SELECT BIBLIOGRAPHY

Biography

Anzieu, Didier, *Freud's Self-Analysis*, tr. Peter Graham (London, 1986).

Appignanesi, Lisa, and John Forrester, *Freud's Women* (London, 1992).

Clark, Ronald W., *Freud: The Man and the Cause* (London, 1980).

Gay, Peter, *Freud: A Life for our Time* (London, 1988), with an invaluable bibliographical essay.

Jones, Ernest, *Sigmund Freud: Life and Work*, 3 vols. (London, 1953–7).

Krüll, Marianne, *Freud and his Father*, tr. Arnold J. Pomerans (London, 1987).

Margolis, Deborah P., *Freud and his Mother: Preoedipal Aspects of Freud's Personality* (Northvale, NJ, 1996).

Roazen, Paul, *Freud and his Followers* (New York, 1975).

Vitz, Paul C., *Sigmund Freud's Christian Unconscious* (New York, 1988).

General Studies

Fisher, Seymour, and Roger P. Greenberg, *The Scientific Credibility of Freud's Theories and Therapy* (New York, 1977).

Grubrich-Simitis, Ilse, *Back to Freud's Texts: Making Silent Documents Speak*, tr. Philip Slotkin (New Haven and London, 1996), on Freud's manuscripts.

Grünbaum, Adolf, *The Foundations of Psychoanalysis: A Philosophical Critique* (Berkeley, Los Angeles, and London, 1984).

Laplanche, J., and J.-B Pontalis, *The Language of Psycho-Analysis*, tr. Donald Nicholson-Smith (London, 1973).

Lear, Jonathan, *Love and its Place in Nature: A Philosophical Interpretation of Freudian Psychoanalysis* (London, 1990).

Mitchell, Juliet, *Psychoanalysis and Feminism* (London, 1974).

Rieff, Philip, *Freud: The Mind of the Moralist* (Chicago, 1959).

Stevens, Richard, *Freud and Psychoanalysis* (Milton Keynes, 1983), a good introduction.

Webster, Richard, *Why Freud Was Wrong: Sin, Science and Psychoanalysis* (London, 1995), the most comprehensive negative critique.

Wollheim, Richard, *Freud* (London, 1971).

On The Interpretation of Dreams

Forrester, John, 'Dream Readers', in his *Dispatches from the Freud Wars* (Cambridge, Mass., and London, 1997), 138–83.

Grinstein, Alexander, *On Sigmund Freud's Dreams* (Detroit, 1968).

Hopkins, James, 'The Interpretation of Dreams', in Jerome Neu (ed.), *The Cambridge Companion to Freud* (Cambridge, 1991), 86–135, a sympathetic philosophical critique.

Schorske, Carl E., 'Politics and Patricide in Freud's *Interpretation of Dreams*', in his *Fin-de-siècle Vienna: Politics and Culture* (Cambridge, 1981), 181–207.

Steiner, George, 'The Historicity of Dreams', in his *No Passion Spent: Essays 1978–1996* (London, 1996), 207–23, an imaginative and stimulating critique.

Intellectual and Historical Contexts

Beller, Steven, *Vienna and the Jews, 1867–1938: A Cultural History* (Cambridge, 1989).

Buhle, Mari Jo, *Feminism and its Discontents: A Century of Struggle with Psychoanalysis* (Cambridge, Mass., and London, 1998).

Ellenberger, Henri F., *The Discovery of the Unconscious: The History and Evolution of Dynamic Psychiatry* (London, 1970).

Forrester, John, *Language and the Origins of Psychoanalysis* (London, 1980).

Gay, Peter, *Freud, Jews and Other Germans* (New York, 1978).

Geehr, Richard S., *Karl Lueger, Mayor of Fin de Siècle Vienna* (Detroit, 1990).

Gilman, Sander L., *et al.* (eds.), *Reading Freud's Reading* (New York and London, 1994).

Gresser, Moshe, *Dual Allegiance: Freud as a Modern Jew* (Albany, NY, 1994).

McGrath, William J., *Freud's Discovery of Psychoanalysis: The Politics of Hysteria* (Ithaca and London, 1986).

Micale, Mark S., *Approaching Hysteria: Disease and its Interpretations* (Princeton, 1995), with extensive recent bibliography.

Price, S. R. F., 'The Future of Dreams: From Freud to Artemidorus', *Past and Present*, 113 (Nov. 1986), 3–37.

Ritvo, Lucille, *Darwin's Influence on Freud* (New Haven and London, 1990).

Ryan, Judith, *The Vanishing Subject: Early Psychology and Literary Modernism* (Chicago, 1991).

Sulloway, Frank J., *Freud, Biologist of the Mind: Beyond the Psychoanalytic Legend*, 2nd edn. (Cambridge, Mass., and London, 1992).

Wistrich, Robert S., *The Jews of Vienna in the Age of Franz Joesph* (Oxford, 1989), including a thorough study of Freud's Jewish identity.

Select Bibliography

Freud's Legacy

Beharriell, Frederick J., 'Psychoanalysis and Literature: The Freud-Denial Syndrome', in Karl Konrad Polheim (ed.), *Sinn und Symbol: Festschrift für Joseph P. Strelka zum 60. Geburtstag* (Berne, 1987) 593–610.

Collier, Peter, and Judy Davies (eds.), *Modernism and the European Unconscious* (Cambridge, 1990).

Crews, Frederick, *Out of My System: Psychoanalysis, Ideology, and Critical Method* (New York, 1975).

Hoffman, Frederick J., *Freudianism and the Literary Mind* (Baton Rouge, La., 1945).

Metz, Christian, *Psychoanalysis and Cinema: The Imaginary Signifier*, tr. Celia Britton *et al.* (London, 1982).

Trilling, Lionel, 'Freud and Literature', in his *The Liberal Imagination* (London, 1951).

Wright, Elizabeth, *Psychoanalytic Criticism*, 2nd edn. (Cambridge, 1998).

Dreams

Béguin, Albert, *L'Âme romantique et le rêve* (Marseilles, 1937).

Burke, Peter, 'The Cultural History of Dreams', in his *Varieties of Cultural History* (Cambridge, 1997), 23–42, with many further references.

Engel, Manfred, '"Träumen und Nichtträumen zugleich": Novalis' Theorie und Poetik des Traumes zwischen Aufklärung und Hochromantik', in Herbert Uerlings (ed.), *Novalis und die Wissenschaften* (Tübingen, 1997), 143–67.

Franz, Marie-Louise von, *Dreams: A Study of the Dreams of Jung, Descartes, Socrates, and other Historical Figures* (Boston and London, 1998).

Hobson, J. Allan, *The Dreaming Brain* (London, 1990), combining neurological with interpretive approaches.

Jung, C. G., *Dreams*, tr. R. F. C. Hull (London, 1985), a handy collection of Jung's essays on dreams.

Rycroft, Charles, *The Innocence of Dreams*, 2nd edn. (London, 1991), on dreaming as imaginative activity.

Stevens, Anthony, *Private Myths: Dreams and Dreaming* (London, 1995), broadly Jungian.

Freud as a Writer

Frankland, Graham, *Freud's Literary Culture* (Cambridge, 1999).

Hyman, Stanley Edgar, *The Tangled Bank: Darwin, Marx, Frazer and Freud as Imaginative Writers* (New York, 1959).

Mahony, Patrick, *Freud as a Writer* (New Haven and London, 1987).

Schönau, Walter, *Sigmund Freuds Prosa: Literarische Elemente seines Stils* (Stuttgart, 1968).

Translating Freud

Bettelheim, Bruno, *Freud and Man's Soul* (London, 1983).

Gilman, Sander L., 'Reading Freud in English: Problems, Paradoxes, and a Solution', in his *Inscribing the Other* (Lincoln, Nebr., and London, 1991), 191–210.

Ornston, Darius Gray (ed.), *Translating Freud* (New Haven and London, 1992).

Timms, Edward, and Naomi Segal (eds.), *Freud in Exile: Psychoanalysis and its Vicissitudes* (New Haven and London, 1988).

A CHRONOLOGY OF SIGMUND FREUD

This chronology focuses mainly on the period up to and soon after the publication of *The Interpretation of Dreams*.

1856   6 May: Sigismund (later Sigmund) Freud born at Freiberg (now Příbor) in Moravia.

1860   The Freud family settles in Vienna, after a stay in Leipzig.

1873   Freud enters Vienna University as medical student.

1876–82 Works under Ernst Brücke at the Institute of Physiology in Vienna.

1881   Graduates as Doctor of Medicine.

1882   Becomes engaged to Martha Bernays.

1882–5 Works in Vienna General Hospital, concentrating on cerebral anatomy.

1884   Begins research on the clinical uses of cocaine. July: publishes his paper 'On Cocaine'.

1885   Appointed *Privatdozent* (university lecturer) in neuropathology.

1885   October: begins studies under J. M. Charcot at the Salpêtrière (hospital for nervous diseases) in Paris (until February 1886); becomes interested in hypnosis.

1886   Marries Martha Bernays.

1886–93 Continues work on neurology at the Kassowitz Institute in Vienna.

1887   Birth of eldest child, Mathilde.

        Gets to know the Berlin physician Wilhelm Fliess; their intellectual relationship, intense throughout the 1890s, cools by 1902.

1888   Begins to follow Josef Breuer in using hypnosis for cathartic treatment of hysteria.

1889   Birth of eldest son, Martin.

        Foundation of Austrian Social Democratic Party.

1891   Birth of second son, Oliver.

1892   Birth of youngest son, Ernst.

1893   Birth of second daughter, Sophie.

1895   Birth of youngest child, Anna (later a distinguished psycho-analyst in her own right).

Publication with Breuer of *Studies on Hysteria*.

1896   Death of Freud's father Jakob, aged 80.

1897   Freud's self-analysis and 'creative illness', leading to the theory of the Oedipus complex.

Appointment of Gustav Mahler as director of Imperial Opera in Vienna; his informal analysis with Freud took place in 1910.

April: appointment of the anti-Semite Karl Lueger as Mayor of Vienna; only after his fifth electoral victory would the Emperor confirm him in office.

August: First Zionist Congress organized in Basle by Theodor Herzl.

November: 'Badeni language riots' in response to proposals by the Prime Minister, Count Badeni, for appeasing nationalists by giving Czech and other languages equal status with German in Austrian provinces.

1899   Founding of Karl Kraus's satirical periodical *Die Fackel* (*The Torch*).

1899   November: publication of *The Interpretation of Dreams*.

1901   Publication of *The Psychopathology of Everyday Life*.

Freud's first visit to Rome.

1902   Appointed Professor Extraordinarius.

1903   Publication of Otto Weininger's notorious *Sex and Character*, which shares with Freud and Fliess a theory of bisexuality.

1905   *Three Essays on the History of Sexuality*.

1906   Contact with C. G. Jung, whose adherence to psychoanalysis Freud particularly values; close relationship till their final breach in 1914.

1913   *Totem and Taboo*, in which Freud applies psychoanalysis to explain the origins of culture.

1914   Assassination of heir to the Austrian throne, Archduke Franz Ferdinand, at Sarajevo and outbreak of First World War, in which Austrian troops suffered heavy losses especially on the Russian and Italian fronts.

1915   Freud responds to the War with 'Thoughts for the Times on War and Death'.

1916   21 November: death of Emperor Franz Joseph I of Austria.

1918   Dissolution of Austro-Hungarian Empire; November: proclam-
        ation of Austrian Republic.

1920   Death of Freud's daughter Sophie.

1923   *The Ego and the Id*: the conscious/unconscious/preconscious
        triad of *The Interpretation* is finally replaced with the division of
        the mind into ego, id, and superego.

1930   *Civilization and its Discontents*, perhaps the greatest of Freud's
        sociological works.

        Awarded the Goethe Prize for his literary and scientific
        achievement by the City of Frankfurt.

        Death of Freud's mother Amalie, aged 95.

1933   After Hitler's seizure of power in Germany, books by Freud are
        burnt in Berlin.

1938   Hitler's annexation of Austria; Freud leaves Vienna for London.

1939   23 September: death in London.

THE INTERPRETATION
OF DREAMS

*Flectere si nequeo superos, Acheronta movebo**

THE INTERPRETATION
OF DREAMS

CONTENTS

FOREWORD

In making this attempt at presenting an interpretation of dreams I do not think I have gone beyond the bounds of neuro-pathological interests. For under psychological scrutiny the dream turns out to be the first item in the series of abnormal psychical formations, whose further members—hysterical phobia, obsession, and delusion—are bound to occupy the physician in his practice. Although, as we shall see, the dream cannot claim a comparable significance for practice, its theoretical value as a paradigm is all the greater for that, and if we are not able to explain how dream-images originate, we will also labour in vain to understand and possibly treat the phobias, obsessions, and delusions.

However, the same connection that makes our subject so important can also be held responsible for the shortcomings of the present work. The disjunctions to be found so frequently in this account correspond to those points of contact where the problem of dream-formation intervenes in wider problems of psychopathology. These could not be dealt with here, but if time and strength allow and further material presents itself, later revisions will be devoted to them.

The peculiarities of the material I use to elucidate the interpretation of dreams have also made this publication difficult for me. It will become apparent from the work itself why for my purposes I could make no use of any of the dreams related in the literature or of any I might have collected from strangers. The only choice I had was between my own dreams and those of my patients under psychoanalytic treatment. I could not use the latter material, as the processes of the dream were undesirably complicated here by interference from neurotic characteristics. Reporting my own dreams, however, turned out to be inextricably tied to revealing more of the intimacies of my psychical life than I could wish or than usually falls to the task of an author who is not a poet, but a scientist. This was painful and embarrassing, but unavoidable; I have bowed to it then, so that I should not entirely do without presenting the evidence for my psychological conclusions. But of course I have been unable to resist the temptation to take the sting out of many an indiscretion by omitting or substituting certain material; though whenever I did this, it was definitely detrimental to the value of my examples. I can only express the hope that readers of this work will put themselves in my difficult position and be forbearing with me; and further, that all those who find that the dreams related here allude to them personally in any way, will not wish to deny freedom of thought—at least to the life of dreams.

                                                                    Freud

THE SCIENTIFIC LITERATURE ON
THE PROBLEMS OF DREAMS

In the following pages I shall provide proof that there is a psychological technique which allows us to interpret dreams, and that when this procedure is applied, every dream turns out to be a meaningful psychical formation which can be given an identifiable place in what goes on within us in our waking life. I shall further try to explain the processes that make the dream so strange and incomprehensible, and infer from them the nature of the psychical forces in their combinations and conflicts, out of which the dream emerges. Having got so far, my account will break off, for it will have reached the point at which the problem of dreaming opens out into more comprehensive problems which will have to be resolved on the basis of different material.

I shall begin with a survey both of what earlier authorities have written on the subject and of the present state of scientific inquiry into the problems of dreams, as I shall not often have occasion to return to it in the course of this treatise. In spite of being concerned with the subject over many thousands of years, scientific understanding of the dream has not got very far. This is admitted by the writers so generally that it seems superfluous to quote individual authors. In the writings I list at the end of my work many stimulating observations and a great deal of interesting material can be found relating to our subject, but little or nothing touching the essential nature of the dream or offering a definitive solution to any of its riddles. And of course, even less has passed into the knowledge of the educated layman.

The first work to treat the dream as an object of psychology seems to be Aristotle's* *On Dreams and Dream Interpretation* [1]. Aristotle concedes that the nature of the dream is indeed daemonic, but not divine—which might well reveal a profound meaning, if one could hit on the right translation. He recognizes some of the characteristics of the dream-life, for example, that the dream reinterprets slight stimuli intruding upon sleep as strong ones ('we believe we are passing through a fire and growing hot when this or that limb is only being slightly warmed'), and he concludes from this that dreams could very well reveal to the physician the first signs of impending changes in the body not perceptible by day. Lacking the requisite knowledge and teaching and without informed assistance, I have not been in a position to arrive at a deeper understanding of Aristotle's treatise.

As we know, the ancients prior to Aristotle regarded the dream not as a product of the dreaming psyche, but as an inspiration from the realm of the divine, and they already recognized the two contrary trends which we shall find are always present in evaluations of the dream-life. They distinguished valuable, truth-telling dreams, sent to the sleeper to warn him or announce the future to him, from vain, deceptive, and idle dreams intended to lead him astray or plunge him into ruin. This pre-scientific conception of the dream held by the ancients was certainly in full accord with their world-view as a whole, which habitually projected as reality into the outside world what had reality only within the life of the psyche. Their conception also took account of the main impression made on the waking life by the memory of the dream remaining in the morning, for in this memory the dream is opposed to the other contents of the psyche as something alien, coming as it were from another world. It would be wrong, by the way, to think that the theory of the supernatural origin of dreams has no followers in our own day. Quite apart from all the pietistic and mystical writers—who do right to occupy the remains of the once extensive realm of the supernatural, as long as it has not been conquered by scientific explanation—we also encounter clear-sighted men averse to the fantastic who use this very inexplicability of the phenomena of dreams in their endeavours to support their religious belief in the existence and intervention of superhuman powers. The high value accorded to the dream-life by many schools of philosophy, for example, by Schelling's* followers, is a distinct echo of the undisputed divinity accorded to dreams in antiquity; and the divinatory, future-predicting power of dreams remains under discussion because the attempts at a psychological explanation are not adequate to cope with all the material gathered, however firmly the feelings of anyone devoted to the scientific mode of thought might be inclined to reject such a notion.

The reason why it is so difficult to write a history of our scientific knowledge of the problems of dreams is that, however valuable our knowledge may have become under single aspects, no progress along a particular line of thought is to be discerned. No foundation of confirmed results has been constructed on which the next researcher might have built further, but every new author tackles the self-same problems afresh as though from the very beginning. If I were to discuss the writers in chronological sequence and summarize what each of them had to say on the problems of dreams, I would have to abandon any clear overall survey of the current state of our knowledge of dreams. That is why I have chosen to construct my account according to topics rather than authors, and in dealing with each dream problem I shall cite whatever material for its solution exists in the literature.

However, this literature is very scattered and encroaches upon many other subjects, and I have not been able to cope with it all: so I must ask my readers to rest content as long as no fundamental fact or significant point of view has escaped my attention.

Until recently, most writers have felt obliged to deal with sleep and dreams within the same context, as a rule also linking to this their evaluations of analogous states extending into psychopathology, and their assessments of occurrences similar to dreams (such as hallucinations, visions, etc.). The most recent work, on the other hand, endeavours to restrict the subject and take some single question from the field of the dream-life as its object of inquiry. This change of emphasis is, I believe, an expression of the conviction that in such obscure matters enlightenment and agreement may only be reached by a set of detailed investigations. It is a detailed investigation of this kind, specifically of a psychological nature, that I am able to offer here. I have had little occasion to occupy myself with the problem of sleep, for this is essentially a problem of physiology, though a characterization of the sleeping state has to include changes in the conditions under which the psychical apparatus functions. So in my account I have disregarded the literature on sleep.

Scientific interest in the phenomena of dreams as such leads to the following, partly overlapping, questions:

(a) *The Relationship of Dreams to Waking Life*

The naive judgement of someone who has just woken up assumes that the dream—even if it does not come from another world—has still transported the sleeper to one. The old physiologist Burdach [8], to whom we owe a scrupulous and sensitive description of the phenomena of dreams, has expressed this conviction in a celebrated passage (p. 474): '... the life of the day, with its exertions and pleasures, its joys and sorrows, is never repeated: the dream is rather bent on freeing us from it. Even when our entire soul has been engrossed with one object, when our heart has been riven with a deep sorrow or some task has exercised all our mental powers, the dream either gives us something completely alien, or takes for its combinations only individual elements from reality, or only enters into the key of the mood we are in and symbolises reality.'

In his justly acclaimed study of the nature and origin of dreams, L. Strümpell [66] expresses a similar view (p. 16): 'The dreamer has turned away from the world of waking consciousness ...' (p. 17): 'In dreams our memory of the ordered content of waking consciousness and its normal behaviour is as good as completely lost ...' (p. 19): 'The almost memory-less isolation of the soul in dreams from the routine content and course of waking life ...'

But the great majority of writers have taken the opposite view-point. Haffner [32] writes as follows (p. 19): 'At first the dream continues the waking life. Our dreams always follow the ideas present in our consciousness not long before. Meticulous observation will almost always discover a thread in which the dream links up with the experiences of the previous day.' Weygandt [75] (p. 6) directly contradicts Burdach's assertion quoted above, 'for apparently it can often be observed in the great majority of dreams that, rather than freeing us from ordinary life, they lead us right back into it'. Maury [48] (p. 56) says in a succinct formula: 'Nous rêvons de ce que nous avons vu, dit, désiré ou fait.'* In his *Psychologie* of 1855 (p. 530), Jessen [36] puts it at rather greater length: 'The content of dreams is always more or less determined by the individual personality, by age, sex, class, level of education, mode of life and by all the events and experiences of our lives hitherto.'

The ancients shared this idea of the dependence of the content of dreams on life. To cite Radestock [54] (p. 134): about to begin his campaign against Greece, Xerxes* was dissuaded from this decision by sound advice, but was spurred on to it again and again by his dreams; at this, the rational old dream-interpreter of the Persians, Artabanos, told him quite rightly that dream-images usually contain what the dreamer already thinks when awake.

In Lucretius'* didactic poem, *De rerum natura*, we find the passage (IV. v. 959):

> Et quo quisque fere studio devinctus adhaeret,
> aut quibus in rebus multum sumus ante morati
> atque in ea ratione fuit contenta magis mens.
> in somnis eadem plerumque videmur obire;
> causidici causas agere et componere leges,
> induperatores pugnare ac proelia obire, etc. etc.

Cicero* (*De Divinatione*, ii) says exactly what Maury said so much later: 'Maximeque reliquiae earum rerum moventur in animis et agitantur, de quibus vigilantes aut cogitavimus aut egimus.'

The contradiction between these two views of the relationship between dream-life and waking life seems to be indeed irresolvable. So this is a good place to recall F. W. Hildebrandt's [35] discussion. He takes the view that the peculiarities of the dream cannot be described at all except as a 'series of opposites which seem to intensify to the point of becoming contradictions' (p. 8). 'The *first* of these opposites is the *strict seclusion or isolation* of the dream from real, true life on the one hand, and on the other the continual *encroachment* of the one on the other, the constant dependence of the one on the other.—The dream is something altogether separate from the reality we experience when awake; one might call it an existence hermetically closed within itself, cut off from real life by an unbridgeable chasm. It frees us from reality, extinguishes our normal recollection of it, and places us in another world and in a quite different life-story, which has fundamentally nothing to do with our real one . . .' Hildebrandt then explains how, when we fall asleep, our whole being, with the forms of its existence, disappears 'as though beneath an invisible trap-door'. Then perhaps we dream we are making a sea-voyage to St Helena in order to offer the imprisoned Napoleon something special by way of Moselle. We are received by the ex-Emperor in the friendliest fashion and are almost sorry to see the interesting illusion disrupted by our awakening. But then we compare the situation in the dream with reality. We have never been a wine-merchant, and have never wanted to be one. We have never been on a sea-voyage, and St Helena is the last place we would choose to take one to. For Napoleon we feel no kind of sympathy, but on the contrary harbour a fierce patriotic hatred towards him. And on top of all that, the dreamer was not yet even among the living when Napoleon died on his island; to enjoy any personal relationship with him was beyond the bounds of possibility. Thus the dream-experience appears as something alien interpolated between two divisions of our life which otherwise fit into each other perfectly and continuously.

'And yet,' Hildebrandt goes on, 'the apparent *opposite* is just as true and correct. In my view, the most intimate relationship and connection nevertheless goes hand in hand with this isolation and seclusion. We may even say: whatever the dream may present, it acquires its material from reality and from the intellectual life which goes along with this reality . . . However strangely the dream may employ it, it can never actually get free from the real world: its most sublime and its most farcical phenomena alike must always borrow their raw material either from what has appeared before us in the world of the senses or from what has somehow already found a place in our waking thoughts—in other words, from what we have already experienced, outwardly or inwardly.'

(b) *The Dream-Material—Memory in Dreams*

That all the material composing the content of the dream derives in some way from our experience, and so is reproduced, *remembered*, in the dream—this at least we may count as undisputed knowledge. But it would be an error to assume that such a connection between the dream-content and waking life is bound to emerge effortlessly as the obvious result of comparing the two. It has rather to be attentively sought, for in a large number of cases it is capable of concealing itself for a long time. The reason for this lies in a number of peculiarities shown by our powers of memory in dreams, and which, although they have been generally remarked, have so far resisted every attempt at an explanation. It will be worth our while to examine these characteristics in detail.

The first thing to emerge is that material appears in the dream-content which, when subsequently awake, we do not recognize as part of our knowledge or experience. We may well remember that we dreamed this or that, but not that we ever experienced it. We are then in a quandary as to what source the dream has drawn on, and may well be tempted to believe that the dream possesses the power of independent production, until, often after a long interval, a new experience restores the memory of the earlier experience and so reveals the source of the dream. We then have to admit that we had known and remembered something in our dream which had escaped our powers of recollection when awake.

A particularly impressive example of this kind is told by Delboeuf [16] from his own dream-experience. In his dream he saw the yard of his house covered in snow and found two little lizards half-frozen and buried under the snow. Being an animal-lover he took them up, warmed them, and restored them to the little hole in the wall intended for them. In addition he gave them a few leaves from a little fern-plant growing on the wall which he knew they were very fond of. In his dream he knew the name of the plant: *Asplenium ruta muralis.*—The dream then continued, after an interval returned to the lizards, and to Delboeuf's astonishment showed him two new little lizards which had set upon the remains of the ferns. Then he turned and looked into the distance, saw a fifth and a sixth lizard making their way to the hole in the wall, until finally the whole road was covered with a procession of lizards all moving in the same direction, etc.

In his waking life, Delboeuf was familiar with the Latin names of only a few plants, and the *Asplenium* was not among them. So he was greatly astonished to discover that a fern of this name actually existed: its correct designation was *Asplenium ruta muraria*, which the dream had slightly distorted. It seemed hardly credible that the name had occurred by coincidence; but where his knowledge of it in his dream had come from, remained a mystery to him.

The dream took place in 1862. Sixteen years later the philosopher was visiting a friend when he noticed a little album containing dried flowers of the sort that are sold as souvenirs to visitors in many parts of Switzerland. A memory arose within him, he opened the herbarium, found in it the *Asplenium* from his dream, and recognized his own handwriting in the Latin name added to it. Now the connection could be made: in 1860—two years before the dream of the lizards— a sister of this friend had visited Delboeuf while on her honeymoon. She had had this album with her, intending it for her brother; and

Delboeuf had taken the trouble to write its Latin name, at a botanist's dictation, beside each of the little dried plants.

A happy accident, of the sort that make this example so very much worth relating, allowed Delboeuf to trace yet another part of the content of this dream back to its forgotten source. One day in 1877 an old volume of an illustrated magazine came into his hands, and there he saw a picture of the entire procession of lizards as he had dreamed it in 1862. The volume bore the date 1861, and Delboeuf was able to recall that he had been a subscriber to the magazine from the time of its appearance.

The fact that the dream has at its disposal recollections which are inaccessible to the waking person is so remarkable and theoretically significant that I should like to reinforce it by recounting some more 'hypermnestic' dreams. Maury [48] relates that for some time the word *Mussidan* kept coming into his mind during the day: he knew it was the name of a French town, but nothing more. One night he dreamed of a conversation with a certain person, who told him she came from *Mussidan*, and when he asked where the town was she replied that *Mussidan* was the main town in the *Département de la Dordogne*. When he awoke, Maury gave no credence to the information in the dream. But from the gazetteer he learned that it was perfectly correct. In this case the dream's superior knowledge is confirmed, but the forgotten source of this knowledge has not been traced.

Jessen [36] relates (p. 551) a very similar event in a dream from older times: 'Among these is the dream of the elder Scaliger* (Hennings p. 300), who wrote a poem in praise of the famous men of Verona. A man calling himself Brugnolus appeared to him in a dream, complaining that he had been forgotten. Although Scaliger could not recall ever having heard anything of him, he composed lines about him all the same, and his son afterwards learned in Verona that a Brugnolus had indeed once been famous there as a critic.'

In a publication unfortunately not available to me (*Proceedings of the Society for Psychical Research*), Myers is said to have produced a collection of such hypermnestic dreams. In my view, anyone engaged in the study of dreams is bound to recognize that it is a very common phenomenon for a dream to bear witness to knowledge and recollections which the waking person does not believe he possesses. In my psychoanalytic work with nervous patients, which I shall refer to later, I find myself several times every week in the position of proving to my patients from their dreams that they really do know certain quotations, obscene words, and the like very well, and that they use them in dreams even though they have forgotten them in waking life. I should like to add here a further innocuous case of dream-hypermnesia, for in this instance the source that gave rise to the knowledge accessible only to the dream is very easy to detect.

As part of a lengthy dream a patient dreamed that in a coffee-house he had ordered a 'Kontuszowka'. But after relating the dream he asked what it could be: he had never heard the name. I was able to reply that 'Kontuszowka' was a Polish schnapps which he could not have invented in his dream, as the name had long been familiar to me from posters. At first the man would not believe me. A few days later, after he had made his dream come true in a real coffee-house, he noticed the name on a poster, and what is more, on one at a street corner which he must have passed at least twice a day for several months.

One of the sources that dreams draw upon for material for reproduction, some of it not remembered or employed in the mental activity of waking life, is the life of childhood. I shall cite only a few of the writers who have noticed this and emphasized it:

Hildebrandt [35] (p. 23): 'It has already been expressly conceded that dreams faithfully bring quite remote and even forgotten events from the distant past back to our minds, sometimes with a marvellous power of reproduction.'

Strümpell [66] (p. 40): 'The issue becomes even more complex when we remark how sometimes dreams draw forth images of individual places, things, and persons quite unscathed and in all their original freshness, as it were out from under the deepest and most massive accumulations deposited by later years on the earliest experiences of our youth. This is not confined merely to those impressions which we were vividly conscious of when they first arose, or were associated with strong psychical values and now recur later in a dream as actual recollections in which the wakened consciousness takes pleasure. Rather, the depths of the dream memory also include those images of people, things, places, and experiences from our earliest years which either impressed themselves only slightly on our consciousness, or possessed no psychical value, or have long since lost both, and so, both in the dream and after we have woken up, they appear quite alien and unfamiliar to us until their early origin is discovered.'

Volkelt [72] (p. 119): 'It is particularly remarkable how easily recollections of childhood and youth enter dreams. The dream never tires of reminding us of things we have long since ceased to think about, things which have long since lost all importance to us.'

The dream's command of childhood material, most of which, as we know, falls through the gaps in our conscious power of recollection, occasions interesting hypermnestic dreams, a few of which I would again like to relate.

Maury [48] tells us (p. 92) that as a child he often travelled from his home town of Meaux to the nearby town of Trilport, where his father was directing the construction of a bridge. One night a dream transported him to Trilport and set him playing again in the streets of the town. A man approached him wearing a kind of uniform. Maury asked him what his name was; the man introduced himself as C., and said he was a watchman at the bridge. After he woke, Maury still doubted the truth of this recollection, so he asked an old servant who had been with him since childhood whether she could remember a man of this name. Certainly, came her reply, he was the watchman at the bridge your father was constructing at that time.

Maury reports another example, just as satisfyingly confirmed, of the reliability of childhood recollection as it appears in dreams. It came from a Montsieur F., who had grown up as a child in the town of Montbrison. Twenty-five years after he had left it, this man decided to revisit his home town as well as old friends of the family whom he had not seen since. In the night before his departure he dreamed that he had arrived, and in the vicinity of Montbrison encountered a man unknown to him by sight, who told him he was Monsieur T., a friend of his father's. The dreamer knew that as a child he had known a man of this name, though when awake he could no longer remember what he looked like. A few days later, now actually arrived in Montbrison, he found the locality of his dream again, which he had thought was unfamiliar to him, and encountered a man whom he promptly recognized as the T. of his dream. Only that the real person was much older than the dream had represented him.

At this stage I can relate a dream of my own, in which the impression to be recalled is replaced by an association. In a dream I saw a person who I knew in the dream was the doctor of my home town. His face was not clear, but was blended with the impression of one of my teachers at the *Gymnasium*, whom I occasionally still meet today. After I woke, I could not make out what association linked these two people. But when I asked my mother about this doctor from my earliest years, I learned that he had had only one eye—and the schoolteacher whose figure in the dream had covered that of the doctor also has only one eye. I had not seen the doctor for thirty-eight years, and to my knowledge I have never thought about him in my waking life.

It sounds as if there was an intention to set up a counterweight to the overly great role played by childhood impressions in dreams, when several authorities maintain that most dreams can be shown to contain elements from the days most recently preceding the dream. Robert [55] (p. 46) even asserts that in general the normal dream is concerned only with the days just past. We shall in any event discover that the theory of dreams Robert has constructed makes it imperative for him to push back the oldest impressions and bring forward the most recent. I can, however, confirm from my own investigations that what Robert says in this respect is a fact. An American writer, Nelson [50], takes the view that what most often happens is that the dream makes use of impressions from the day before the day of the dream or from the third day before, as though the impressions from the day immediately preceding the dream were toned down, not remote enough.

Several writers who would not doubt the intimate connection between the content of dreams and waking life have observed that impressions that occupy the waking thoughts intensely appear in dreams only when they have to some extent been pushed to one side by the thinking activity of the day. Thus we do not as a rule dream of a dead person dear to us in the time right after their death, while the survivor is still filled with grief (Delage) [15]. Meantime, however, one of the most recent observers, Miss Hallam [33], has collected examples of the opposite behaviour, and in this regard claims for each of us the right to our psychological individuality.

The third, most remarkable and incomprehensible characteristic of memory in dreams is to be seen in the choice of material reproduced. For what is considered worth remembering is not, as in waking life, only the things that are of most significance, but also on the contrary the most trivial and nondescript things. At this point I shall cite those authors who have expressed their amazement most forcefully.

Hildebrandt [35] (p. 11): 'For the remarkable thing is that as a rule the dream takes its elements not from the important and far-reaching events, not from the great and motivating interests of the previous day, but from the trivial extras, from the worthless scraps, as it were, of the recent or more remote past. A distressing death in the family, whose impressions send us late to sleep, is blotted from our memory until our first waking moment brings it back to us vividly in all its sadness. On the other hand, a wart on the forehead of a stranger we encountered and did not give a moment's thought to after we had passed him by—this plays a part in our dream . . .'

Strümpell [66] (p. 39): '. . . cases where the analysis of a dream discovers elements which, though it is true they derive from the experiences of the previous day or the day before that, were so worthless and insignificant to the waking consciousness, that they sank into oblivion soon after they were experienced. Experiences of this kind are for instance words heard by accident, someone else's actions scarcely noticed, fleeting perceptions of things or persons, brief passages from our reading, and the like.'

Havelock Ellis [23] (p. 727): 'The profound emotions of waking life, the questions and problems on which we spread our chief voluntary mental energy, are not those which usually present themselves to dream consciousness. It is so far as the immediate past is concerned mostly the trifling, the incidental, the "forgotten" impressions of daily life which reappear in our dreams. The psychic activities that are awake most intensely are those that sleep most profoundly.'

Binz [4] (p. 45) takes these very peculiarities of memory in the dream as the occasion for expressing his dissatisfaction with the explanations of the dream he himself supports: 'And the natural dream raises similar questions. Why is it that we do not always dream the memory-impressions of the most recent day we have spent, but often plunge without any recognizable motive into a past that lies far behind us, almost obliterated? In dreams why does the consciousness so often receive the impression of *trivial* recollections, while the brain-cells, the very place where the most sensitive register of our experience is lodged, mostly lie still and silent, unless they have been freshly aroused in waking hours shortly before?'

It is easy to see how the strange preference of the dream-memory for trifling and hence unnoticed things among the experiences of the day was largely bound to lead to a general failure to understand the dream's dependence on the life of the day, or at least to making this very difficult to demonstrate in individual cases. Consequently, in Miss Whiton Calkins's [12] statistical analysis of her (and her companion's) dreams, it was possible for her to be left with 11 per cent of the total in which no relation to the life of the day was perceptible. Hildebrandt is certainly right in maintaining that all dream-images could be explained genetically, if we spent sufficient time and concentration on tracing their origin. True, he calls this 'an extremely laborious and thankless task. For it would mostly amount to tracking down all sorts of things with no psychical value in the remotest corners of the chamber of memory, and bringing to light all sorts of utterly trivial impulses from times long past from depths where they had been buried perhaps the very hour after they had occurred.' But I must express my regret that this penetrating writer failed to pursue this path from this modest beginning; it would have led him straight to the centre of the explanation of dreams.

The way the memory behaves in dreams is certainly most important for any theory of memory in general. It teaches us that 'nothing that is once mentally our own can ever be entirely lost' (Scholz [59] p. 34). Or, as Delboeuf [16] puts it, 'que tout impression même la plus insignifiante, laisse une trace inaltérable, indéfiniment susceptible de reparaître au jour',* a conclusion which so many other—pathological—phenomena of the psychical life likewise force us to make. Now if we keep this extraordinary capability of the dream-memory in mind, we will be keenly aware of the contradiction which certain dream-theories, referred to later, are bound to set up, as they try to explain the absurdity and incoherence of dreams by the partial forgetting of what is known to us by day.

It might perhaps occur to us to reduce the phenomenon of dreaming entirely to that of remembering and regard the dream as the expression of a reproductive activity, unresting even at night, which is an end in itself. Accounts such as that given by Pilcz [51] would accord with this, for he claims that firm connections can be demonstrated between the time of dreaming and the content of the dream, such that in deep sleep the dream reproduces impressions from the earliest times, but reproduces recent ones towards morning.

But such a conception is made improbable from the outset by the way the dream deals with the material to be remembered. Strümpell [66] rightly points out that in the dream repetitions of experiences do not occur. True, the dream makes a start at it, but the next link is missing; it appears in altered form, or something entirely strange appears in its place. The dream presents only fragmentary reproductions. Certainly, this is so often the rule that we can make theoretical use of it. However, exceptions do occur in which a dream will repeat an experience just as completely as our waking recollection can. Delboeuf tells of how in a dream one of his university colleagues (who teaches at present in Vienna) repeated a dangerous coach journey in all its detail, where he escaped an accident only as if by a miracle. Miss Calkins [12] mentions two dreams whose content consisted of the exact reproduction of an experience from the previous day, and I myself will later take the opportunity of relating an instance known to me of the return in a dream, unaltered, of a childhood experience.

(c) *Dream-Stimuli and Dream-Sources*

What we are to understand by dream-stimuli and dream-sources can be clarified by referring to the popular saying, 'dreams come from the stomach'. Behind these concepts there is concealed a theory which regards the dream as the consequence of a disturbance of sleep; we would not have dreamed if something to disturb us had not stirred in our sleep—and the dream is the reaction to this disturbance.

Discussion of the causes that generate dreams occupies more space than any other topic in the writings about them. It goes without saying that the problem could only arise after the dream had become an object of biological inquiry. The ancients, who regarded the dream as divine inspiration, had no need to seek for its source; the dream proceeded from the will of the divine or daemonic power, its content from their knowledge or intention. For science, the question arose straight away whether the incentive to dreaming was always the same, or whether there might be several incentives— which brought with it the need to consider whether the explanation for the causes of dreams fell to psychology or to physiology. Most authorities seem to assume that there can be many kinds of cause for disturbances of sleep, that is, for the sources of dreaming, and that both somatic stimuli and psychical excitations can act as causative agents of dreams. But there is wide disagreement in privileging the one or the other among the sources of dreams, and in establishing a hierarchy among them according to their importance for the genesis of the dream.

With a complete enumeration of the sources of dreams it emerges that there are ultimately four kinds, which have also been used for the classification of dreams:

1. External (objective) sensory excitation;
2. Internal (organic) sensory excitation;
3. Internal (organic) somatic stimulus;
4. Purely psychical sources of stimulus.

1. External sensory stimuli

Strümpell the younger, son of the philosopher whose work on dreams has already served us several times as a guide to the problems of dreams, has, as we know, reported on his observation of an invalid afflicted with general anaesthesia of the skin and paralysis of several of the higher sensory organs. When this man's few remaining sensory gateways were cut off from the outside world, he fell asleep. When we want to go to sleep, we all try to attain a situation similar to the one in Strümpell's experiment. We close the most important sensory gateways, our eyes, and try to protect our other senses from any stimulus or change in the stimuli acting on them. We then go to sleep, though we are never completely successful in carrying out our aim. We can neither isolate our sensory organs entirely from the stimuli, nor wholly neutralize their excitability. The fact that we can always be woken by stronger stimuli may be taken as proof 'that even in sleep the psyche has remained in constant contact with the world external to the body'. The sensory stimuli that reach us in sleep could well become sources for dreams.

Now among such stimuli there are a great number, ranging from the unavoidable ones entailed in the sleeping state itself or occasionally admitted to it, to the chance stimulus to waking which is likely or intended to put an end to sleep. A rather strong light can penetrate the eyes, a sound become audible, or an odour agitate the nasal membrane. While we are asleep, involuntary movements may uncover parts of our body and in this way expose them to the sensation of getting colder, or by changing our position we may produce sensations of pressure or contact. A fly may sting us, or a slight nocturnal accident assail several of our senses at once. Attentive observers have collected a large number of dreams in which the stimulus established on waking and a part of the dream-content coincide so closely that the stimulus could be recognized as the source of the dream.

I shall cite here from Jessen [36] (p. 527) a collection of dreams of this kind which derive from objective—more or less accidental—sensory stimulation. Each indistinctly heard sound arouses corresponding dream-images: the rumble of thunder transports us to the midst of a battle; the crowing of a cock can be transformed into a human cry of fear; the creaking of a door call forth dreams of burglars breaking in. If we lose our bedclothes at night, we might dream that we are walking about naked or that we have fallen into the water. If we are lying at an angle in bed and our feet project over the edge, we might dream that we are standing at the edge of a terrible abyss, or that we are falling from a steep cliff. If by accident our head gets under the pillow, there is a great rock hanging over us about to bury us beneath its weight. Accumulations of semen produce lascivious dreams, localized pains the idea of abuses we have suffered, hostile attacks or the infliction of bodily injuries . . .

'Meier (*Versuch einer Erklärung des Nachtwandelns*, Halle: 1758, p. 33) once dreamed that he was set upon by a number of people who stretched him out on the ground on his back and drove a stake into the ground between his big toe and the one next to it. As he was imagining this in his dream, he woke and felt a straw sticking between his toes. On another occasion, according to Hennings (*Von den Träumen und Nachtwandlern*, Weimar: 1784, p. 258), Meier had fastened his shirt rather tightly around his neck, and dreamed he was being hanged. Hoffbauer dreamed as a young man that he was falling from a high wall, and discovered when he woke that the bedstead had come apart and that he really had fallen . . . Gregory reports that he once laid a hot-water bottle at his feet when he went to bed and then dreamed he had made a journey to the top of Mount Etna, where he found the heat of the ground almost unbearable. Another dreamed after he had had a poultice applied to his head that he was being scalped by Red Indians. A third, who went to sleep in a damp shirt, dreamed he was being dragged through a river. An attack of gout while he was asleep led an invalid to believe he was in the hands of the Inquisition and was being tortured (Macnish).'

The argument from the similarity between stimulus and dream-content is strengthened if by this systematic application of sensory stimuli it is possible to produce in the sleeper dreams corresponding to the stimulus. According to Macnish, Giron de Buzareingues had already tried such experiments. 'He left his knee uncovered, and dreamed that he was travelling by post-chaise at night. He observes in his account that travellers would certainly know how cold the knees would become in a coach at night. At another time he left the back of his head uncovered and dreamed that he was attending a religious ceremony in the open air. For in the country where he lived, it was the custom to keep the head covered, except on such occasions as the one just mentioned.'

Maury [48] reports a number of new observations of dreams he himself had produced. (A further series of experiments proved unsuccessful.)

1. He is tickled on the lips and tip of the nose with a feather.— Dreams of a terrible torture; a mask of pitch is placed on his face, then torn away, taking the skin with it.

2. A pair of scissors is sharpened against a pair of tweezers.—He hears bells pealing, then warning-bells, and is transported to the June days of 1848.*

3. He smells eau de Cologne.—He is in Cairo in the shop of Johann Maria Farina. There follow wild adventures which he is unable to reproduce.

4. He is squeezed gently in the neck.—He dreams that he is having a poultice applied, and thinks of a doctor who treated him in childhood.

5. A hot iron is held to his face.—He dreams of the 'stokers'[1] who have crept into the house and are forcing the inhabitants to hand over their money by thrusting their feet into a brazier. Then the Duchess of Abrantés, whose secretary he is in the dream, appears on the scene.

8. A drop of water is poured on to his forehead.—He is in Italy, perspiring heavily and drinking the white wine of Orvieto.

---

[1] 'Chauffeurs' was the name given to bands of robbers in the Vendée using this form of torture.

9. The light from a candle, filtered through a red paper, is made to fall on him repeatedly.—He dreams of storms, of heat, and finds himself once again in a storm at sea which he once experienced in the English Channel.

Other attempts at producing dreams experimentally have been made by d'Hervey [34], Weygandt [75], and others.

Many have noticed the 'striking skill of the dream in weaving sudden impressions from the sensory world into its creations in such a way that they come to form a catastrophe whose onset has already been gradually prepared and ushered in' (Hildebrandt [35]). 'When I was younger,' this author relates, 'in order to get up regularly at a certain hour in the morning, I sometimes used the familiar alarm usually attached to clocks. It must have happened a hundred times that the sound of this alarm fitted into an apparently very long and coherent dream, as if the whole dream were directed towards it as its logically indispensable point and natural goal.'

I shall refer to three more of these alarm-clock dreams in another connection.

Volkelt (p. 68) relates: 'A composer once dreamed that he was giving a class and wanted to make something clear to his pupils. He had just done so and turned to one of the boys with the question: "Did you understand me?" The boy shouted like a madman "O ja" ["Oh yes"]. Annoyed at the shouting, he reprimanded the boy. But the whole class was already shouting "Orja". Then: "Eurjo". And finally "Feuerjo!" ["Fire! Fire!"]. And then he was awakened by real cries of "Fire! Fire!" in the street.'

Garnier (*Traité des Facultés de l'âme*, 1865), quoted by Radestock [54], reports that Napoleon I was awakened from a dream while he was sleeping in his carriage by the explosion of an infernal machine,* and that in the dream he once again experienced the crossing of the Tagliamento* and the Austrian bombardment, until he woke with a start, crying: 'We have been undermined.'

A dream Maury [48] once had has become famous (p. 161). He was unwell and lay in bed in his room. His mother was sitting beside him. He dreamed of the Reign of Terror at the time of the Revolution, took part in dreadful scenes of murder, and was finally brought before the court himself. There he saw Robespierre, Marat, Fouquier-Tinville,* and all the sombre heroes of that terrible epoch, addressed them, after all kinds of incidents which escaped his recollection was condemned, and then, accompanied by an enormous crowd, led to the place of execution. He mounts the scaffold, the executioner fastens him to the plank; it tips up; the guillotine blade falls; he feels his head being severed from his body, wakes in a torment of fear—and discovers that the headboard of the bed has collapsed and, just like the blade of a guillotine, struck the back of his neck.

This dream gave rise to an interesting discussion, set off in the *Revue philosophique* by Le Lorrain [45] and Egger [20], as to whether and how it was possible for the dreamer to concentrate such an apparently full and abundant dream-content in the brief interval between waking-stimulus and waking.

Examples of this kind make objective sensory stimuli appear to be the most firmly established among the sources of dreams. Such stimuli are also the only ones that play any part in the knowledge of the layman. If you ask an educated man otherwise unfamiliar with the literature of dreams how dreams come about, he will no doubt reply by referring to a case he has heard of, in which a dream was explained by an objective sensory stimulus recognized after waking. Scientific inquiry cannot stop there; it becomes the occasion for it to question further why the stimulus acting upon our senses while we are asleep should appear in the dream in nothing like its true form, but be represented by some other imagined idea, which stands in some kind of relationship to it. But the relationship linking the dream-stimulus and the dream it produces is, in Maury's [47] words, 'une affinité quelconque, mais qui n'est pas unique et exclusive'* (p. 72). Take, for example, Hildebrandt's three alarm-clock dreams. We shall have to raise the question why the same stimulus produced such differing dreams, and why exactly these dreams, as its consequence.

(p. 37) 'So I am taking a walk one spring morning and strolling through the early green of the fields as far as a neighbouring village. There I see a crowd of villagers in their best clothes, their hymn-books under their arms, making their way in droves towards the church. Of course! It is Sunday, and morning service is due to begin soon. I decide to take part, but first, because I am rather hot and out of breath, I decide to cool off in the churchyard that surrounds the church. While I am reading some of the inscriptions on the grave-stones there, I hear the bell-ringer climb the tower, and then see the little village bell at the top which will give the signal for the service to begin. For a while it still hangs there motionless, then it begins to swing—and suddenly its strokes ring out loud and clear—so loud and clear that it puts an end to my sleep. But the sound of the bell comes from the alarm-clock.

'A second connection. It is a bright winter's day. The streets are deep with snow. I have agreed to take part in a sleigh-ride, but I have to wait a long time before the message comes that the sleigh is standing at the door. There follow the preparations for getting in—the fur rug is spread out, the foot-muff brought out—and at last I am sitting in my seat. But the departure is still delayed until the reins let the waiting horses feel the signal to start. Then the horses move off. The sleigh-bells, vigorously shaken, strike up their familiar janissary music with such force that in a moment the cobweb of the dream is torn apart. Again it is nothing but the shrill tone of the alarm-clock.

'Now a third example! I see a kitchen-maid walking along the corridor to the dining-room carrying several dozen plates piled up. The column of china in her arms seems to me to be in danger of toppling over. "Take care", I warn her, "the whole load is going to fall." The usual contradiction is, of course, forthcoming: she is used to carrying such things, etc., while I still follow her progress with concern. Sure enough, at the threshold she stumbles—the fragile crockery falls and clatters and shatters in a hundred pieces over the floor. But—the endlessly unceasing sound is, as I soon notice, not really a clattering, but a proper ringing;—and, as I now recognize as I wake, the ringing is only the alarm-clock doing its duty.'

The question why in the dream the psyche fails to recognize the nature of the objective sensory stimulus has been answered by Strümpell [66]—and almost to the same effect by Wundt [76]—by supposing that the stimuli encroaching upon the psyche in sleep place it under conditions which enable an illusion to be created. We *recognize and correctly interpret* a sensory impression, that is, we place it in the class of memories where, according to all our previous experience, it belongs, if the impression is strong, clear, and long-lasting enough, and if we have sufficient time to reflect on it. If these conditions are not met, we fail to recognize the object that gives rise to the impression; instead we use it as the basis of an illusion. 'If someone goes for a walk in the open country and perceives a distant object indistinctly, it can happen that at first he takes it to be a horse.'

Observing it more closely, he may be urged to interpret it as a cow lying down, until finally the sight resolves itself with certainty into a group of seated people. Now, the impressions which the psyche receives in sleep from external stimuli are of a similar indefinite nature. These stimuli are the basis on which the psyche creates illusions, for the impression summons up a greater or smaller number of remembered images, through which it acquires its psychical value. Which of the many relevant spheres of memory the appropriate images are summoned up from, and which of the possible associative connections thereby come into play, even Strümpell regards as indeterminable and left as it were up to the arbitrary will of the psyche.

We have a choice here. We can admit that the laws governing the formation of dreams cannot really be pursued any further, and so refrain from asking whether our interpretation of the illusion produced by the sensory impression may not be determined by other factors. Or we can speculate that the objective sensory stimulus encroaching upon sleep plays only a modest part as a source for dreams, and that other factors determine which images from our store of memories we chose to be aroused. In fact, if we examine Maury's experimentally produced dreams—which I have related in such detail for just this purpose—we are tempted to say that the experiment set up really covers the origin of only one of the elements of the dream, and that the rest of the dream-content seems rather too independent, too definite in its details, to be explained by the one requirement that it has to be consistent with the element introduced experimentally. Indeed, one even begins to have doubts about the illusion-theory and the power of the objective impression to shape the dream when one learns that on occasion in the dream it undergoes the strangest, most far-fetched interpretation. For example, M. Simon [63] recounts a dream in which he saw gigantic figures seated at table and distinctly heard the fearful gnashing of their jaws as they chewed. When he woke, he heard the hoofbeats of a horse galloping past his window. If in this case the sound of horses' hooves roused ideas from a cluster of recollections from *Gulliver's Travels,** of sojourns with the giants of Brobdingnag and the virtuous Houyhnhnms—as, without any support from the author, I would be inclined to interpret it—would not the choice of this sphere of memories so remote from the stimulus have been more easily motivated by different factors?

2. *Internal (subjective) sensory excitation*

Despite all the objections, we have to concede that the part played by objective sensory excitations during sleep in initiating dreams is indisputable, and if the nature and frequency of these stimuli seem perhaps inadequate to explain every dream-image, this indicates that we should be looking for other sources of dreams which are different from these but analogous in their effect. I do not know where the idea first arose of enlisting internal (subjective) excitations of the sensory organs as well as external sensory stimuli; but it is in fact done in all the more recent accounts of the aetiology of dreams. 'In the production of dream-illusions,' says Wundt [76], 'I believe an essential role is played by those subjective visual and aural perceptions familiar to us when we are awake, such as dazzling light on a dark field of vision, ringing or buzzing in the ears, etc., among them especially subjective excitations of the retina. This would explain the remarkable tendency of the dream to conjure up large numbers of similar or wholly identical objects before our eyes. We see countless birds, butterflies, fishes, many-coloured beads, flowers, and the like spread out before us: here the scattered light of the dark field of vision has assumed fantastic shapes, and the numerous particles of light which go to make it up are embodied by the dream in as many individual images. Because the shimmering light is so mobile, these are perceived as *moving* objects. Probably this is also at the root of the great inclination of the dream to form such a variety of animal figures, whose inventiveness of form adapts easily to the particular form of the subjective light-images.'

As a source of dream-images, subjective sensory excitations have the obvious advantage that, unlike objective ones, they are not dependent on external chance. They are as it were available for service whenever an explanation requires them. But they take second place to objective sensory stimuli as explanations, for it is either difficult or impossible to confirm their role as instigators of dreams in the way observation and experiment can do for objective stimuli. The main proof of the dream-arousing power of subjective sensory excitations is provided by what are called hypnagogic hallucinations, described by Johann Müller as 'fantastic visual phenomena'. These are images, often very vivid and fluctuating, which habitually appear—with many people quite regularly—while we are falling asleep, and which can also persist for a time after we have opened our eyes. Maury [48], who was very prone to them, has examined them in detail and maintains they are related, indeed identical, to dream-images (a view also held by Müller). For them to emerge, Maury says, a certain psychical passivity, a relaxation of attention, is required (p. 59 f.). But if we are in the right mood, a second of such lethargy is enough to make a hypnagogic hallucination appear, after which perhaps we reawaken, until the often-repeated performance is brought to an end by sleep. If we then wake up again after not too long an interval, we are, according to Maury, often able to establish that we have experienced the same image in our dream as hovered before us as a hypnagogic hallucination before we fell asleep (p. 134). It once happened in this way to Maury with a hallucination of a number of grotesque figures with distorted features and strange hair-styles who were harassing him with incredible persistence while he was falling asleep. After he woke, he remembered that he had also dreamed of them. Another time, when he had put himself on a diet and so was feeling hungry, he had a hypnagogic vision of a dish, and of a hand armed with a fork which took some of the food in the dish. In his dream he found himself at a well-laden table and heard the sounds the diners were making with their forks. Another time, when he had fallen asleep with sore and painful eyes, he had the hypnagogic hallucination of microscopically small signs which he had to strain to decipher one by one: an hour after he had woken he recalled a dream in which there was an open book, printed in very small letters, which he had to read through laboriously.

In just the same way as these images, auditory hallucinations of words, names, etc., can also appear hypnagogically and then be repeated in dreams, forming the overture, as it were, announcing the leitmotifs of the opera to follow.

The same path as the one followed by Johann Müller and Maury has been taken by a more recent observer of hypnagogic hallucinations, G. Trumbull Ladd [40]. By practising he was able to wrench himself suddenly awake two to five minutes after gradually falling asleep, but without opening his eyes: he then had the opportunity of comparing the sensations on his retina as they were just fading with the dream-images as they survived in his memory. He affirmed that a close relationship was recognizable between the two each time, for the luminous particles and lines of the retina's own light made as it were the outline sketch, the diagram, of the figures perceived in the dream. For example, a dream in which he saw before him clearly printed lines, which he read and studied, matched an arrangement of parallel lines of luminous particles in the retina. As he put it himself: the clearly printed page he read in his dream resolved itself into an object which appeared to his waking perception like part of a real printed page seen through a small hole in a piece of paper from too far away to make out anything distinctly. Ladd, who does not underestimate the central part played by the phenomenon in other respects also, takes the view that hardly a single dream unfolds within us which does not depend on the material of the inner excitations of the retina. This applies especially to dreams shortly after falling asleep in a darkened room, whereas in morning dreams when we are close to waking, he suggests, the objective light penetrating to the eyes in the brightened room supplies the source of the stimulus. The fluctuating character of the excitations of light in the retina, with their endless changeability, corresponds exactly to the restless flow of images which our dreams present to us. If we regard Ladd's observations as significant, we cannot doubt that this subjective source of stimulus is most productive in the creation of dreams, for as we know, visual images constitute the main component of our dreams. The contribution of the other senses, apart from that of hearing, is slighter and irregular.

3. *Internal, organic somatic stimulus*

As we are still looking for sources of dreams not outside but within the organism, we must remind ourselves that when they are in a state of health almost all our internal organs give us hardly a sign of their existence, but that when they are irritated—as we put it—or when we are ill, they become a source of mainly painful sensations for us, which must be put on the same footing as those external agencies which arouse excitations of pain or feeling. These are very ancient experiences, prompting Strümpell [66], for example, to say (p. 107): 'The psyche attains in sleep to a much more profound and wide-ranging sensory consciousness of its bodily nature than it does when awake, and cannot but receive and be affected by impressions of certain stimuli that originates in parts of the body and in changes there, which it was unaware of when awake.' Even as early a writer as Aristotle [1] declared it might very well be possible that in dreams our attention might be drawn to incipient illnesses whose traces we have not noticed when awake (by virtue of the magnification the dream gives to the impressions, see p. 1); and medical writers who were certainly very far from believing in the prophetic powers of dreams have granted them this importance at least as heralds of illness. (See M. Simon [63] (p. 31) and many earlier authors.)

There appear to be plenty of authenticated instances of success in diagnosis by dreams from more recent times too. For example, Tissié [68], following Artigues (*Essai sur la valeur séméiologique des rêves*), reports the story of a woman of forty-three who was afflicted by anxiety-dreams over several years of apparently perfect health, and who then, under medical examination, displayed an incipient heart condition to which she soon succumbed.

Advanced disorders of the internal organs clearly act in quite a large number of people as initiators of dreams. The frequency of anxiety-dreams among those suffering from diseases of the heart or lungs has been generally remarked: indeed, many authors have brought this association of the dream-life so much to the fore that I can content myself here with merely referring to the literature (Radestock [54], Spitta [64], Maury, M. Simon, Tissié). Tissié even considers that diseased organs impose a particular character on the dream-content. The dreams of someone with a heart condition are usually very brief and end with his awakening in terror; the situation of death under frightful circumstances almost always plays a part in their content. Sufferers from lung disease dream of suffocation, crowding, and fleeing, and a striking number are prey to the familiar nightmare—which Börner [5] has also been able to produce experimentally by lying on his face and covering the respiratory organs. Indigestion evokes in the dream ideas from the field of enjoyment and disgust. The influence, finally, of sexual arousal on the content of dreams will be comprehensible to every one of us from our own experience and provides the whole theory that dreams are initiated by organic stimulus with its strongest support.

As we work our way through the literature on dreams, it also becomes unmistakable that some of the authors concerned (Maury [48], Weygandt [75]) were led to their interest in the problems of dreams by the influence of their own illnesses on the content of their dreams.

However, although these undoubtedly established facts increase the sources of dreams, this is not as significant as one might like to think: for after all the dream is a phenomenon occurring in those in good health—perhaps to everyone, perhaps every night—and organic disease is obviously not one of its indispensable conditions. But for us, the issue is not where exceptional dreams come from, but what the source of stimulation for the ordinary dreams of normal people might be.

Meanwhile it requires only one step further for us to come upon a source of dreams that flows more abundantly than any of the previous ones and really shows no prospect at all of drying up. If it has been established that the interior of the body in a state of sickness becomes a source of dream-stimuli, and if we concede that, in a sleeping state, diverted from the external world, the psyche is able to devote greater attention to the body's interior, then we are tempted to assume that the organs do not first have to become sick for excitations—which somehow turn into dream-images—to reach the sleeping psyche. What we dimly apprehend when we are awake only in its quality as a general vital sense, to which in medical opinion all the organ-systems contribute, would, when working powerfully at night and with its individual components active, supply the strongest and at the same time the most common source for the arousal of representations.

We have touched here on that theory of the genesis of dreams which has become the favoured one among all medical authors. The darkness in which the core of our being, the 'moi splanchnique', as Tissié [68] calls it, is shrouded from our knowledge, and the darkness in which dreams originate correspond too well not to be brought into association with one another. The train of ideas which makes the vegetative sensations of our organs into makers of dreams has this further appeal to the physician that it also enables us to make the dream and mental disturbance, which have so much in common in their manifestations, compatible in their aetiologies as well; for changes in the general vital sense and in the stimuli which proceed from the internal organs are also accorded far-reaching importance in the genesis of psychoses. So it is not surprising if the theory of physical stimulation can be traced back to more than one first thinker who proposed it independently.

The line of thought developed by the philosopher Schopenhauer*

[60] in 1851 has become definitive for a number of authors. Our conception of the world arises in us as our intellect recasts the impressions it receives from without into the forms of time, space, and causality. The stimuli from the interior of our organism, communicated by the sympathetic nervous system, manifest by day at most an unconscious influence on our mood. At night, however, when the deafening effect of the impressions of the day has ceased, those impressions surging from within are able to call attention to themselves—just as at night we can hear the murmuring of the stream which the noise of the day made inaudible. But how else is the intellect to react to these stimuli but by fulfilling its distinctive function? It will transform the stimuli accordingly into figures occupying space and time and moving on the connecting thread of causality, and that is how the dream comes into being. On this assumption, Scherner [58], and after him Volkelt [72], attempted to go deeper into the relationship between physical stimuli and dream-images. However, we shall reserve consideration of their work until the section on theories of dreams.

In a particularly rigorous inquiry the psychiatrist Krauss [39] derived the origin of dreams as well as of hallucinations and delusions from the same element, *sensations caused organically*. In his view, there is scarcely a place in the organism conceivable which cannot become the starting-point for a dream or a delusion. The organically caused sensation 'can, however, be divided into two groups: 1. those of the overall temper of feeling (general vital feelings), 2. the specific sensations immanent in the main systems of the vegetative organism, in which we have distinguished five groups, (*a*) muscular sensations, (*b*) respiratory, (*c*) gastric, (*d*) sexual, and (*e*) peripheral' (p. 33 of the second article).

Krauss assumes that the emergence of dream-images on the basis of physical stimuli takes the following course: in accordance with some associative law the awakened sensation arouses an imagined idea related to it and combines with it into an organic formation. However, the way the consciousness acts towards this is different from its normal behaviour. It does not heed the sensation itself, but turns its attention entirely to the accompanying imagined ideas—which is also the reason why this fact could remain unrecognized for so long (pp. 11 ff.). Krauss also coins the special term *transubstantiation* of the sensations into dream-images for this process.

The influence of organic physical stimuli on the formation of dreams is almost universally accepted today, but the question as to what law governs the relationship between the two gets very different and often obscure answers. Accordingly, when dream-interpretation is based on the theory of physical stimulus, it has the particular task of tracing the content of a dream back to the organic stimulus which caused it; and if we do not accept the rules for interpretation devised by Scherner [58], we are often faced with the awkward fact that the only way the organic source of stimulation reveals itself is precisely by means of the very content of the dream.

However, a degree of agreement has been reached in the interpretation of various forms of dreams which have been designated 'typical' because they recur with very similar content in so many people. These are the familiar dreams of falling from a height, of the teeth falling out, of flying, and of the embarrassment of finding oneself naked or ill-clad. This last dream is supposed to derive simply from our awareness while asleep that we have thrown off the bedclothes and are now lying uncovered. The dream that our teeth are falling out is attributed to a 'sensitivity of the teeth'—which does not, however, need to imply that the excitation is due to bad teeth. The dream of flying, according to Strümpell [66], is the appropriate image used by the psyche to interpret the quantum of stimulus proceeding from the rise and fall of the lungs when the cutaneous sensation of the thorax has simultaneously sunk into unconsciousness. The latter condition is responsible for the sensation associated with the idea of floating. The cause of falling from a height is supposed to be that as we lose consciousness of the feeling of pressure on the skin, we either let an arm sink from the body or suddenly straighten a bent knee; as we do so we become conscious once more of the feeling of pressure on the skin, but this transition to consciousness is psychically embodied in the dream of falling (Strümpell, p. 118). The weakness of these plausible attempts at explanation clearly lies in the fact that without offering any further grounds for doing so, they allow this or that group of organic sensations to disappear from psychical perception or to force themselves upon it, until the constellation favourable to the explanation is produced. I shall, by the way, have occasion later to return to typical dreams and their genesis.

By comparing a number of similar dreams, M. Simon [63] has

attempted to deduce some rules for the influence of organic stimuli in determining their ensuing dreams. According to him (p. 34), if in sleep any organic apparatus normally involved in the expression of an affect is put by some other cause into the state of arousal into which it is usually placed by that affect, the dream arising will contain imagined ideas which are appropriate to that emotion.

According to another rule (p. 35), if in sleep an organic apparatus is in a state of activity, arousal, or disturbance, the dream will introduce imagined ideas related to the exercise of the organic function which that apparatus performs.

Mourly Vold [73] has undertaken to demonstrate the influence on the production of dreams assumed by the theory of physical stimulus by experiment in one particular field. He has done so by changing the position of the sleeper's limbs, and then comparing the consequent dreams with the changes he had made. He reports his findings in the following propositions:

1. The position of a limb in a dream corresponds roughly to its position in reality, i.e. we dream of a static condition of the limb corresponding to the real one.

2. If we dream of a limb moving, it is always the case that one of the positions taken in the course of the movement corresponds to the real position.

3. In the dream, we can also ascribe the position of our own limb to another person.

4. We can also dream that the movement in question is impeded.

5. In the dream, the position in question can also appear as an animal or a monster, setting up a certain analogy between the two.

6. In the dream, the position of a limb can call up thoughts which have some sort of connection with the limb. Thus, for example, if the fingers are involved, we dream of numbers.

I would conclude from such results that even the theory of physical stimulus cannot entirely extinguish our apparent freedom in determining the dream-images to be awakened.

4. Sources of stimulation in the psyche

In discussing the connections between dreams and waking life, and the origin of dream-material, we found that both the most ancient and the most recent inquirers into dreams held the view that people dream of what they do by day, and of what interests them when they are awake. This interest continuing from waking life into sleep is, they claim, not only a psychical bond linking the dream to life, but it also provides us with a source of dreams not to be underestimated. This, in addition to the interests developing during sleep—the stimuli affecting us while asleep—should be sufficient to explain the origin of all dream-images. However, we have also heard the objection to this claim: that the dream withdraws the sleeper from the interests of the day, and that we—mostly—dream of the things that have moved us most intensely by day only when they have lost their immediate relevance to our waking life. Thus at every step in the analysis of the dream-life, we get the impression that it is inadmissible to set up general rules unless we anticipate reservations with an 'often', an 'as a rule', or a 'usually', and provide for the validity of exceptions.

If the interests of our waking lives together with the internal and external stimuli acting upon sleep were sufficient factors in the aetiology of dreams as a whole, we ought to be in a position to give a satisfactory account of the origin of all the elements in a dream. The riddle of where dreams have their sources would be solved, and all that would be left would be the task of distinguishing the respective shares of the psychical and the somatic dream-stimuli in any particular dream. In reality, there has been no case as yet in which this complete resolution of a dream has been successful, and anyone who has attempted it has been left with—usually very many—components whose origin could not be accounted for. The interests of the day are clearly not such influential psychical sources of dreams as confident assertions that in dreams we all continue the business of the day would lead us to expect.

No other sources in the psyche for dreams are known. All the explanations of dreams represented in the literature—with the possible exception of Scherner's [58], which we will discuss later—thus leave a great gap when it comes to tracing back to source the material for the images most characteristic of dreams. In this embarrassing situation, most of the authors tend as far as possible to minimize the share of psychical factors, so difficult of approach, in the arousal of dreams. It is true, they distinguish major categories of *dreams aroused by nervous stimuli* and *dreams aroused by association*, the latter having its source exclusively in reproduction (Wundt [76]), but they cannot rid themselves of the doubt 'whether they ever appear without the impetus from a physical stimulus' (Volkelt [72] p. 365). Even the description of the pure association-dream does not work: 'In true association-dreams, there can no longer be a question of such a firm core. Here, the looseness of the grouping enters even the centre of the dream. In this kind of dream, the life of the imagined ideas, in any case released from sense and reason, is no longer held together even by the more substantial excitations of body and psyche, and so is left to its own variegated devices and desires, its own confusions and contortions' (Volkelt, p. 118). Wundt too attempts to reduce the share of the psyche in initiating dreams by arguing that it is probably wrong to regard the phantasmagoria of dreams as pure hallucinations. Probably most dream-images are in reality illusions, arising from faint sense-impressions which are never extinguished in sleep (pp. 359 f.). Weygandt [75] has adopted this view and applied it generally. He maintains that all dream-representations 'have their immediate cause in sensory stimuli, to which reproductive associations only then attach themselves' (p. 17). Tissié [68] (p. 183) goes even further in repressing the sources in psychical stimuli: 'Les rêves d'origine absolument psychique n'existent pas', and elsewhere (p. 6): 'les pensées de nos rêves nous viennent de dehors . . .'*

Those authors who take a middle position, like the influential philosopher Wundt, make a point of remarking that in most dreams somatic stimuli work together with psychical initiators of dreams, whether unknown or recognized as coming from the interests of the day.

We shall find out later that the riddle of how dreams are formed can be solved by the discovery of an unsuspected source of stimulus in the psyche. For the moment, let us not be surprised at the overestimation of those stimuli to dream-formation which do not derive from the life of the psyche. It is not just that these are the only ones easy to detect, and even to confirm by experiment; the somatic conception of the origin of dreams is also in complete accord with the prevailing line of thought in psychiatry today. True, the dominance of the brain over the organism is given great emphasis, but anything possibly showing that the life of the psyche might be independent of demonstrable organic changes, or could act spontaneously, fills the psychiatrist of today with alarm, as if to acknowledge this would inevitably mean a return to the days of Natural Philosophy and the metaphysics of the soul. This mistrust on the part of the psychiatrist has placed the psyche as it were under the supervision of a guardian, and demands that it should make no movement that might reveal that it possesses a competence of its own. Yet what this attitude in fact implies is a lack of trust in the causal chain extending between the body and the psyche. Even where investigation shows the primary cause of the phenomenon to be psychical, if we go deeper, we shall one day discover that the way continues until it reaches the organic basis for the psychical. But where in the present state of our knowledge, we cannot but regard the psychical as the end of the road, that is no reason for denying it.

(d) *Why Do We Forget Our Dreams After We Wake?*

It is proverbial that a dream 'fades' in the morning. Of course, it can be remembered. For after all we only know of its existence from our recollection of it after waking; but we very often believe that we are remembering it only imperfectly, that there was more of it present in the night; we can observe how a recollected dream, still vivid in the morning, will vanish in the course of the day, leaving only fragments behind; we often know that we have dreamed, but not *what* we have dreamed, and we are so accustomed to knowing that dreams can be forgotten that we do not even reject as absurd the possibility that we could have been dreaming in the night, but know nothing in the morning of either the content of the dream or the fact that we have been dreaming. On the other hand, it does happen that dreams can retain an extraordinary hold on the memory. I have analysed dreams of my patients which occurred twenty-five or more years previously, and I can remember a dream of my own which happened at least thirty-seven years ago, but which is still as fresh as ever in my memory. All this is very remarkable, and at first impossible to understand.

The most detailed treatment of forgetting dreams has been provided by Strümpell [66]. This forgetting is clearly a complex phenomenon, for Strümpell traces it back not to a single cause but to a whole set of them.

In the first place, all the reasons for forgetting in our waking life are also operative in forgetting dreams. When we are awake we habitually forget a vast number of sensations and perceptions straight away, because they were too weak, because the degree of psychical arousal connected with them was too slight. The same applies to many of our dreams. They are forgotten because they were too weak, while stronger images close to them are remembered. However, the element of intensity is not in itself decisive for the retention of dream-images; Strümpell as well as other authors (Calkins [12]) concedes that we often forget very quickly dreams that we know were very vivid, while very many shadowy, faintly perceived images are to be found among those retained in our memory. Moreover, when we are awake it is usually easy for us to forget what has only happened once, and easier for us to remember what we have been able to perceive repeatedly. Most dreams, however, are once-and-for-all experiences.[2] This will contribute to some extent to all dreams and their forgetting. There is a third reason for forgetting which is far more important. For sensations, images, thoughts, etc. to attain a certain degree of memorability, it is necessary that they should not remain isolated, but enter into connections and associations of an appropriate kind. If we break up a little line of poetry into its single words and shake them up together, it will become very hard to remember. 'Neatly ordered and in proper sequence, one word aids another, and the whole makes sense and remains firmly in our memory. In general it is as difficult and as rare for us to remember the absurd as it is to retain the confused and disordered.' Now in most cases dreams have no intelligibility or order. Dream-compositions are essentially devoid of any possible memory themselves, and are forgotten because they usually merge into one another from one moment to the next. However, these observations are not entirely in accord with what Radestock [54] claims to have observed: that the strangest dreams are the very ones we retain best.

It seems to Strümpell that other elements deriving from the relationship between dreams and waking life are still more effective as factors in forgetting dreams. The ease with which the waking consciousness can forget dreams is plainly just the counterpart to the fact we discussed earlier that the dream (almost) never borrows ordered recollections from waking life, but only details, which it tears out of their accustomed psychical connections where they are remembered when we are awake. This means that the dream-composition has no

[2] Dreams recurring periodically have often been noted. See those collected by Chabaneix [11].

place in the community of the ordered series with which the psyche is filled. It has nothing that would help us to remember it. 'In this way the dream rises up from the ground of our inner life, as it were, and floats in our psychical space like a cloud in the sky, which any fresh breeze will quickly blow away' (p. 87). The same tendency is furthered by the fact that when we wake the onrush of the sensory world occupies our attention so fully that only very few dreams can withstand its force. They retreat before the impressions of the new day, as the brightness of the stars gives way to the light of the sun.

Finally, it has to be considered that forgetting dreams is aided by the fact that most people show little interest in their dreams anyway. Anyone who is interested in dreams for a certain time, for example, for scientific inquiry, will also dream more during that period than usual, which probably means that he remembers his dreams more easily and more often.

Two other reasons for forgetting dreams which Bonatelli (cited by Benini [3]) adds to Strümpell's are probably already covered by the latter: (1) that the change in general vital feeling which takes place between sleeping and waking makes it unfavourable for one to reproduce the other, and (2) that the different arrangement of the material of the imagined ideas in the dream makes it impossible for the waking consciousness to translate, as it were.

After all these reasons for forgetting, it really is strange, as Strümpell himself emphasizes, that we still retain so much of our dreams in our memory. The continual efforts of our authors to formulate rules for remembering dreams amount to an admission that here too there is something enigmatic and unsolved. Some particular aspects of the remembrance of dreams have rightly been noted of late, for example, that a dream which in the morning we thought we had forgotten can return to our memory in the course of the day, triggered by some perception which chances to touch on the—forgotten—content of the dream (Radestock [54], Tissié [68]). However, the entire issue of dream recollection is open to an objection calculated to reduce its value substantially in critical eyes. We may very well doubt whether our memory, which retains so little of the dream, might not falsify what it does retain.

Strümpell too expresses doubts of this kind as to whether we can reproduce our dreams exactly: 'It happens so easily that the waking consciousness involuntarily introduces many things into its recollection of the dream: we imagine we have dreamed all kinds of things which the actual dream did not contain.'

Jessen [36] is particularly emphatic on this point (p. 547): 'But in investigating and interpreting coherent and consistent dreams, we should also consider very carefully a circumstance which has, it seems, so far received little attention: there is always the tricky problem of truth. For when we call to memory a dream we have had, without noticing or intending it we fill out the gaps in our dream and add to it. Rarely and perhaps never has a coherent dream been as coherent as it appears to us in recollection. However much a man may love truth it is scarcely possible for him to relate a remarkable dream he has had without adding to it or embellishing it: the human mind's endeavour to see everything in coherent connection is so great that when it remembers a relatively incoherent dream it involuntarily makes good the flaws in the coherence.'

Egger's [20] remarks on the subject sound like a translation of these words of Jessen's, though he will certainly have arrived at them independently: '. . . l'observation des rêves a ses difficultés spéciales et le seul moyen d'éviter toute erreur en pareille matière est de confier au papier sans le moindre retard ce que l'on vient d'éprouver et de remarquer; sinon, l'oubli vient vite ou total ou partiel; l'oubli total est sans gravité; mais l'oubli partiel est perfide; car si l'on se met ensuite à raconter ce que l'on n'a pas oublié, on est exposé à compléter par imagination les fragments incohérents et disjoints fournis par la mémoire . . .; on devient artiste à son insu, et le récit périodiquement répété s'impose à la créance de son auteur, qui, de bonne foi, le présente comme un fait authentique, dûment établi selon les bonnes méthodes . . .'*

A very similar observation is made by Spitta [64] (p. 338), who seems to assume that we only introduce order at all into the loosely associated elements of the dream simply when we try to reproduce the dream, attempting—'out of mere juxtaposition to create succession and development, that is, to introduce the process of logical connection which the dream lacks'.

Now, as we do not have another control to act as an objective check on the fidelity of our recollection—which in any case is impossible in the case of a dream, as it is our own personal experience and we have only our memory as its known source—what value is left in our recollection of it?

(e) *The Distinctive Psychological Features of Dreams*

In the scientific consideration of dreams, we start from the assumption that they are the products of our own psychical activity; yet the finished dream seems to us something alien, and we feel so little disposed to admit to its authorship that we are just as happy to say 'a dream came to me' as 'I dreamed'.* Where does this 'psychical strangeness' come from? After our discussion of the sources of dreams, we ought not to think that it is determined by the material that enters the content of the dream, for this is for the most part common to both the dream life and the waking life. We can ask ourselves whether this impression is not produced by modifications brought about by the psychical processes in the dream, and in this way attempt a characterization of the dream in psychological terms.

No one has emphasized the essential difference between dream and waking, or used it to draw such far-reaching conclusions, as G. T. Fechner [25] has (in some observations in his *Elemente der Psychophysik*, part II, p. 520). In his view, 'neither simply the reduction of the conscious life of the psyche below the main threshold' nor the withdrawal of attention from the influences of the external world is sufficient to explain the particular characteristics of the dream-life in contrast to waking life. He suspects rather that the *location of the dream is different from that of waking mental life*. 'If the location of psycho-physical activity during sleep were the same as during waking life, the dream could in my opinion merely be a continuation of waking mental life at a lower degree of intensity, and would, moreover, have to share the same material and the same form. But that is not how things are.'

What Fechner means by such a relocation of psychical activity is by no means clear; nor, as far as I know, has anyone else gone further along the path he indicated in these remarks. We will no doubt have to reject an anatomical interpretation in the sense of localization in different parts of the brain, or even with reference to the histological stratification of the cerebral cortex. But the idea may perhaps one day prove useful and fruitful if it is applied to a psychical apparatus made up of several agencies set up one behind the other.

Other writers have contented themselves with emphasizing one or other of the more tangible psychological features that distinguish the dream-life and making it the starting-point, say, for further attempts at explanation.

It has rightly been observed that one of the chief peculiarities of the dream-life already enters the scene while we are in the state of falling asleep, and can be described as the phenomenon introducing sleep. According to Schleiermacher [61] (p. 351), what characterizes the waking state is that thinking takes place in *concepts* and not in *images*. Now the dream thinks mainly in images, and it can be observed that as sleep approaches, to the degree that voluntary activity becomes more sluggish, so *involuntary ideas emerge*, which all belong to the class of images. This incapacity for the kind of thinking that we feel is intentional, and the emergence of images that is regularly associated with this absent state of mind are two features which persist in the dream, and which psychological analysis compels us to recognize as essential characteristics of the dream-life. These images—the hypnagogic hallucinations—are, as we have learned, even as regards content identical with the images in dreams.

Dreams, then, think mainly in visual images, but not exclusively. They also work with auditory images, and to a lesser extent with impressions from the other senses. A great deal is also simply thought or imagined in dreams (probably represented by the residual representations left from words) just as it is in waking life. But what are really characteristic of dreams are only those elements in the content that behave like images, that is, they are more like perceptions than remembered representations. Disregarding all those discussions familiar to the psychiatrist on the nature of hallucinations, we can state that the dream *hallucinates*, that it replaces thoughts with hallucinations. In this respect there is no difference between visual and acoustic representations. It has been observed that the recollection of a sequence of musical notes heard as we fall asleep is transformed into a hallucination of the same melody as we sink further into sleep, but that whenever we wake in the course of nodding off, alternating as these frequently do as we drowse, the hallucination gives way to the softer and qualitatively different remembered (acoustic) representation.

The dream's transformation of representations into hallucinations is not the only way it differs from the waking thought that might correspond to it. The dream creates a situation out of these images, it enacts something as immediately present, it *dramatizes* an idea, as Spitta [64] (p. 145) puts it. However, the description of this aspect of the dream-life will not be complete until we add that when we dream—as a rule, that is, for exceptions require a separate explanation—we believe not that we are thinking, but that we are experiencing, that is, we accept the hallucinations in good faith. Criticism of this belief—that we have not been experiencing anything, but have only been thinking in a peculiar form, dreaming—arises only when we wake up. This characteristic distinguishes the true dream in sleep from day-dreaming, which is never confused with reality.

Burdach [8] has summarized the characteristics of the dream-life so far observed as follows (p. 476): 'The essential features of the dream include (a) that the subjective activity of our psyche appears as objective, for the faculty of perception regards the products of the imagination as though they were apprehended by our senses; . . . (b) in sleep our autonomy is suspended. Hence falling asleep requires a certain passivity . . . Images called up in slumber are determined by a reduction in our autonomy.'

The point now is to try to explain why the psyche places such faith in these dream-hallucinations, which can appear only after a certain independent activity on our own part has been put on hold. Strümpell [66] argues that in doing this the psyche is behaving correctly and according to its own mechanism. According to him, the elements of the dream are not at all mere presentations, but *real and genuine experiences of the psyche*, such as occur when we are awake through the mediation of our senses (p. 34). Whereas the psyche thinks and imagines in verbal images and language when awake, in dreams it imagines and thinks in real sensory images (p. 35). In addition, there is a consciousness of space present in the dream, for sensations and images are transported into an external space, as they are when we are awake (p. 36). So we have to concede that with regard to its images and perceptions, the psyche is in the same position in dreams as it is in waking life (p. 43). If nevertheless it goes astray in dealing with them, this is because in sleep it lacks the criterion able to distinguish between sense-perceptions coming from without and those coming from within. It cannot subject its images to the only tests that can demonstrate their objective reality. It *also* disregards the distinction between images which are *arbitrarily* interchangeable and others where this arbitrariness does not exist.

It goes astray because it is unable to apply the law of causality to the content of its dreams (p. 58). In short, the psyche's act of turning away from the external world also holds the grounds for its belief in the subjective world of the dream.

The same conclusion is reached, after a partly different psychological argument, by Delboeuf [16]. According to him, we believe in the reality of the images in our dreams because in sleep we are removed from the external world and so have no other impressions to compare them with. But surely this is not why we believe in the truth of our hallucinations, for in sleep we have lost the possibility of applying tests. The dream can create the illusion of all these tests: it can, for instance, show us that we are touching a rose we see, and yet we are still dreaming. According to Delboeuf there is no valid criterion whether something is a dream or waking reality except—and this only in practice and in general—the sheer fact of awakening. I declare everything I have experienced between going to sleep and waking up to be an illusion when I notice on awakening that I am lying on my bed undressed (p. 84). While asleep I took my dream to be true on account of the *habit of thought*, which is itself not to be lulled asleep, and assumes an external world with which I contrast my self.[3] If

[3] Like Delboeuf, but describing the condition in rather different words, Haffner [32] has attempted to explain the activity of dreaming by the modification which is bound to result from introducing an abnormal condition to the otherwise correct functioning of the psychical apparatus. According to him, the dream is primarily characterized by the absence of any location in place or time, i.e. by the emancipation of the dream-idea from the dreamer's position in time and place. This is connected with the second fundamental feature of the dream: its confusion of hallucinations, products of the imagination and combinations of the fantasy with external perceptions. 'As all the higher powers of the psyche, in particular the powers of conceptualization, judgement, and inference on the one hand and free self-determination on the other, are attached to imaginary sensory images and always have these as their foundation, it follows that these activities also have their part in the uncontrolled irregularities of the dream-images. They have their part, we say, for in itself our power of judgement, like our will, is by no means altered. These activities are just as keen and just as free as when we are awake. In our dreams too we cannot contravene the laws of thought, i.e. we cannot propose that the image represented is identical with its opposite etc. In our dreams too we can only desire what we imagine to be a good (*sub ratione boni*). But in thus applying the laws of thinking and willing, the human mind is led astray in the dream by confusing one idea with another. Thus it happens that in dreams we propose and perform the wildest contradictions, while on the other hand we can reach the most clear-sighted judgements, draw the most logical conclusions, and make the most virtuous and saintly decisions. *Lack of orientation* is the entire secret of the flight of our imagination in dreams, and *lack of critical reflection*, as well as of communication with others, is the chief source of the boundless extravagances in our dreams of our judgements, our hopes, and our desires' (p. 18).

the psyche's act of turning away from the external world is given prominence in this way as one of the determining factors in shaping the most striking features of the dream-life, it is worth citing some subtle observations made by Burdach [8] long ago, which throw light on the relationship between the sleeping psyche and the external world and are calculated to restrain us from overestimating the conclusions we have just been discussing. 'Sleep occurs', says Burdach, 'only under the condition that the psyche is not roused by sensory stimuli ... but the condition for sleep is not so much a lack of sensory stimuli as a lack of interest in them; some sensory impressions are even necessary in so far as they serve to soothe the psyche, for instance, when a miller can go to sleep only when he hears the sound of his mill, or when someone who needs a night-light as a precaution cannot get to sleep in the dark' (p. 457).

'In sleep the psyche isolates itself from the external world and draws back from its periphery ... At the same time, connection is not entirely broken off: for if we did not hear and feel while we were asleep, we could not be woken up at all. The continuation of sensation is demonstrated even more strongly by the fact that we are not always woken by the mere sensory strength of an impression, but by its psychical associations; an insignificant word will not wake the sleeper, but if you call him by name he will wake up ... which means that in sleep the psyche distinguishes between sensations ... So it appears that we can also be woken by the lack of a sensory stimulus if this relates to something we regard as important; in this way we wake when the night-light is put out, as the miller does when his mill ceases grinding, that is to say, when the sensory activity comes to a stop. That assumes that this activity has been perceived, but as something indifferent, or rather as satisfying, without disturbing the psyche' (pp. 460 ff.).

Even if we disregard these not inconsiderable objections, we still have to concede that the strangeness of the dream cannot fully be accounted for by those characteristics of the dream-life we have discussed so far, which derived from a turning away from the external world. For otherwise it ought to be possible to transform the hallucinations of the dream back into ideas and the situations of the dream back into thoughts, and in that way resolve the task of the interpretation of dreams. This, in fact, is what we do when we reproduce a dream from memory after we awake, and whether this back-translation is wholly or only partly successful, the dream retains its enigmatic quality undiminished.

All our authors also assume without a second thought that in dreams other and profounder changes have occurred to the ideational material of waking life. Strümpell [66] attempts to unearth one of them in the following discussion (p. 17): 'With the cessation of active sensory perception and normal awareness of life, the psyche also relinquishes the ground in which its feelings, desires, interests and actions are rooted. Even those mental states, those feelings, interests, value-judgements which still cling to the remembered images when we are awake, are subject to . . . an obscuring pressure, with the result that their link with the images is dissolved. The perceptual images of the things, people, places, events, and actions of waking life are reproduced in great numbers individually, but none of them carries with it its *psychological* value. This has been removed from them, and so they hover around in the psyche on their own resources . . .'

According to Strümpell, stripping the images of their psychical value in this way—a process which again is itself traced back to the subject's turning from the external world—accounts to a large extent for the impression of strangeness that the dream leaves in our memory by contrast with waking life.

We have heard that even in the act of falling asleep we relinquish one of our psychical activities, the direction by our will of the course of our ideas. In this way we are forced to the suspicion, obvious in any case, that the sleeping state may also extend to the operations of the psyche. One or other of these operations is perhaps entirely suspended; the question then is whether the remainder work on undisturbed, whether they are able to perform their normal work under such circumstances. The thought arises that it might be possible to explain the peculiarities of the dream by the reduced performance of the psyche in the sleeping state—and the impression which the dream makes on our waking judgement does support such an idea. The dream is incoherent, without compunction it unites the grossest contradictions, permits impossibilities, sets aside the knowledge that influences us by day, and exposes us as ethically and morally obtuse. Anyone who behaved while awake in the way the situations in the dream present him would be regarded as insane; anyone who while awake uttered or sought to communicate the kind of things that occur in the content of dreams would gives us the impression of being confused or weak-minded. Accordingly we believe we are only stating a fact when we express a very low opinion of psychical activity in dreams, and in particular declare the higher intellectual capacities to be in suspension, or at least seriously impaired, in them.

With rare unanimity—the exceptions will be discussed elsewhere—our authors have passed judgements on the dream that also lead directly to a particular theory or explanation of the dream-life. It is time for the summary I have just made to give way to a collection of statements made by various writers—philosophers and physicians—on the psychological characteristics of the dream.

According to Lemoine [42] the incoherence of the dream-images is the one essential characteristic of the dream.

Maury [48] agrees with him: he says (p. 163): 'il n'y a pas des rêves absolument raisonnables et qui ne contiennent quelque incohérence, quelque anachronisme, quelque absurdité.'*

According to Hegel (cited by Spitta [64]) the dream lacks all intelligent objective coherence.

Dugas [19] says: 'Le rêve, c'est l'anarchie psychique, affective et mentale, c'est le jeu des fonctions livrées à elles-mêmes et s'exerçant sans contrôle et sans but; dans le rêve l'esprit est un automat spirituel.'*

Even Volkelt [72], whose theory regards psychical activity during sleep as not in the least purposeless, admits to the 'loosening, dissolution, and confounding with one another of ideas held coherently together in waking life by the central ego's force of logic' (p. 14).

The *absurdity* of the connections between ideas occurring in dreams could hardly be more severely condemned than it was long ago by Cicero (*De divinatione*, ii): 'Nihil tam praepostere, tam incondite, tam monstruose cogitari potest, quod non possimus somniare.'*

Fechner [25] says (p. 522) it is as if psychological activity had been transferred from the brain of a rational man to that of a fool.

Radestock [54] (p. 145): 'It does in fact seem impossible to recognize any firm laws in these crazy antics. Evading the attention of that stern policing power, the rational will, which directs the course of our waking ideas, the dream whirls everything madly together like a kaleidoscope.'

Hildebrandt [35] (p. 45): 'What strange escapades the dreamer permits himself, for example, in the rational conclusions he draws! With what unconcern he sees the most familiar empirical laws stood on their heads! What ludicrous contradictions to the rules of nature and society he can endure before, as we say, it all gets too much for him and the extremity of the nonsense wakes him up! Occasionally we will multiply three by three and in all innocence make twenty; we are not in the least surprised if a dog recites poetry, a corpse walks to its own grave, a rock floats on water; in all seriousness we go on a mission to the Duchy of Bernburg or the Principality of Liechtenstein to inspect their navies, or let Charles XII enlist us as a volunteer just before the battle of Pultava.'*

Binz [4] (p. 33), referring to the theory of dreams founded on these impressions: 'Out of every ten dreams, the content of at least nine is absurd. We couple together in them people and things which have absolutely nothing to do with one another. As in a kaleidoscope, one grouping is the next moment changed into another, if possible into one crazier and more senseless than its predecessor; and so the interplay within the imperfectly sleeping brain goes on until we wake up, clutch our brow, and ask ourselves whether we are still in possession of the faculty of rational thought.'

Maury [48] discovers a comparison for the relationship between dreams and waking thoughts which a physician will find very impressive: 'La production de ces images que chez l'homme éveillé fait le plus souvent naître la volonté, correspond, pour l'intelligence, à ce que sont par la motilité certains mouvements que nous offrent la chorée et les affections paralytiques . . .' For the rest, the dream is to him 'toute une série de dégradations de la faculté pensante et raisonnante' (p. 27).*

It is hardly necessary to cite those writers who repeat Maury's proposition with respect to the various higher functions of the psyche.

According to Strümpell [66], in the dream all the logical operations of the psyche based on relations and connections withdraw—also, of course, where the irrationality is not immediately obvious (p. 26). According to Spitta [64] (p. 148), in the dream the ideas seem to be completely detached from the law of causality. Radestock [54] and others emphasize the weakness of the powers of judgement and deduction characteristic of the dream. According to Jodl [37]

(p. 123), in the dream there is no criticism or correction of a set of perceptions by reference to the content of the total consciousness. The same writer maintains: 'All kinds of conscious activity occur in dreams, but incompletely, impeded, isolated from one another.' Stricker [77, 78] (together with many others) explains the ways in which the dream contradicts our waking knowledge as deriving from the fact that in dreams events get forgotten, or the logical relations between ideas get lost (p. 98), etc. etc.

Those authors who pass such a generally unfavourable judgement on the performance of the psyche in dreams still concede that a certain amount of psychical activity remains in the dream. Wundt [76], who has become an authority in the theory of dream-problems for so many others who have dealt with them, expressly admits as much. We could ask what the nature of this remnant of normal psychical life in dreams might be. It is fairly generally agreed that the faculty of reproduction, the memory, seems to have suffered least, indeed, it is even able to show a certain superiority over the same function in waking life (see p. 12 above), even though part of the absurdity of dreams is supposed to be explained by the very forgetfulness of the dream-life. According to Spitta [64], it is the *emotional life* of the psyche which is not affected by sleep and which directs the dream. He defines 'emotion' as 'the unfluctuating concentration of feelings that make up the innermost subjective nature of man' (p. 84).

Scholz [59] sees the 'allegorizing reinterpretation' which the dream-material undergoes as one of the activities of the psyche expressing itself in dreams. Siebeck [62] also detects in the dream 'that activity of supplementary interpretation' (p. 11) of the psyche which it practises on everything it perceives and experiences. A special difficulty in assessing dreams is presented by the role of our supposedly highest psychical function, consciousness. Since consciousness is our only means of knowing, there can be no doubt that consciousness is maintained; however, Spitta takes the view that only consciousness is maintained in dreams, but not *self*-consciousness. Delboeuf [16] confesses he is unable to grasp this distinction.

The laws of association according to which ideas combine also apply to dream-images; indeed, their rule is expressed more clearly and strongly there. Strümpell [66] (p. 70): 'The dream runs its course, it seems, either governed exclusively by the laws of bare ideas, or by those of organic stimuli together with such ideas, that is to say, neither reflection nor reason, aesthetic taste nor moral judgement is able to affect the process.' The authorities whose views I am reproducing here imagine dreams to be formed rather as follows: the sum of sensory stimuli arising from the various sources already discussed operates during sleep first of all to arouse a number of ideas in the psyche which present themselves as hallucinations (according to Wundt as genuine hallucinations, because they derive from internal and external stimuli). These combine with one another according to the known laws of association, and, in accordance with the same rules, call up a fresh set of ideas (images). The entire material is then processed by the active remnant of the organizing and thinking powers of the psyche as best it can (see for instance Wundt [76] and Weygandt [73]). All they have not yet succeeded in discovering are what motives decide whether the images that do not come from outside are aroused according to one law of association or another.

However, it has often been observed that the associations linking the dream-ideas with one another are of a quite distinctive sort, and quite different from those active in waking thoughts. As Volkelt [72] says (p. 15): 'In dreams, ideas chase and catch one another on the basis of chance similarities and barely perceptible connections. Every dream is permeated by such casual, haphazard associations.' Maury [48] sets great store by this way of connecting ideas, for it allows him to draw a close analogy between the dream-life and certain forms of mental disturbance. He recognizes two main features in 'délire': '(1) une action spontanée et comme automatique de l'esprit; (2) une association vicieuse et irrégulière des idées' (p. 126).* Maury himself supplies two excellent examples of dreams in which mere similarity in the sound of words is sufficient to link the dream-ideas together. He once dreamed he undertook a pilgrimage (*pélerinage*) to Jerusalem or Mecca. Then, after many adventures he found himself with the chemist *Pelletier*, who, following a conversation, gave him a shovel (*pelle*) made of zinc, which at a later stage in the dream became his great sword of battle (p. 127). In another dream, he went out on to a country road and read the *kilo*metres on the milestones, after which he found himself in the shop of a grocer who had a huge pair of scales, and a man placed *kilo*-weights on the scales in order to weigh Maury; then the grocer said to him: 'You aren't in Paris, you are on the island of *Gilolo*.' There followed several episodes in which he saw the *lobelia* flower, then General *Lopez*, whose death he had read of shortly before; finally he woke, playing a game of *lotto*.

But we are not surprised to find that this low opinion of the psychical powers of the dream has not gone uncontradicted by others—though contradiction on this point seems difficult. It also does not mean very much when one of the detractors of the dream-life (Spitta [64], p. 118) assures us that the same psychological laws that govern us when we are awake also rule over the dream, or when another (Dugas [19]) says: 'Le rêve n'est pas déraison ni même irraison pur',* if neither of them takes the trouble to reconcile this judgement with the anarchy and dissolution of all functions they have described in the dreaming psyche. But the possibility does seem to have dawned on others that the madness of the dream may not be without method, may perhaps be only pretence, like that of the Prince of Denmark, referred to in this perceptive judgement. Either these authors must have refrained from judging by appearances, or the appearance presented by the dream looked different to their eyes.

Accordingly, without wishing to dwell on its apparent absurdity, Havelock Ellis [23] recognizes the dream as being 'an anarchic world of vast emotions and imperfect thoughts', whose study might teach us something of the primitive stages in the development of the psychical life. A thinker like Delboeuf [16] maintains—though without producing the evidence to counter the material that contradicts him, and so really without good reason: 'Dans le sommeil, hormis la perception, toutes les facultés de l'esprit, intelligence, imagination, mémoire, volonté, moralité, restent intactes dans leur essence; seulement, elles s'appliquent à des objets imaginaires et mobiles. Le songeur est un acteur qui joue à volonté les fous et les sages, les bourreaux et les victimes, les nains et les géants, les démons et les anges' (p. 222).* The most energetic opponent of the detractors of the psyche's performance in dreams appears to have been the Marquis d'Hervey; Maury [41] argues vigorously against him, but despite every effort, I have been unable to get hold of his work. Maury says of him (p. 19): 'M. le Marquis d'Hervey prête à l'intelligence, durant le sommeil, toute sa liberté d'action et d'attention et il ne semble faire consister le sommeil que dans l'occlusion des sens, dans leur fermeture au monde extérieur; en sorte que l'homme qui dort ne se distingue guère, selon sa manière de voir, de l'homme qui laisse vaguer sa pensée en se bouchant les sens; toute la différence qui sépare alors la pensée ordinaire de celle du dormeur c'est que, chez celui-ci, l'idée prend une forme visible, objective, et ressemble, à s'y méprendre, à la sensation déterminée par les objets extérieurs; le souvenir revêt l'apparence du fait présent.'*

Maury adds, however: 'qu'il y a une différence de plus et capitale à savoir que les facultés intellectuelles de l'homme endormi n'offrent pas l'équilibre qu'elles gardent chez l'homme l'éveillé.'*

Estimations of the dream as the product of the psyche cover a wide gamut in the literature: they extend from the deepest disdain of the kind we have become familiar with, through the presentiment of a value not yet revealed, to an overestimation which places the dream far above the achievements of waking life. Hildebrandt [35], as we know, represents the psychological characteristics of the dream-life in three antinomies, and the third of his antitheses finally sums up this set of judgements (p. 19): 'They lie between *an intensification*, an *enhancement* which not rarely rises to the point of *virtuosity*, and on the other hand a decided *reduction* and *enfeeblement* of the life of the psyche, often to a level below the human.

'As to the first, which of us could not confirm from his own experience that in the working and weaving of the spirit of the dream there is sometimes a profundity and warmth of feeling, a clarity of vision, a subtlety of observation, a quickness of wit, which we would modestly disclaim as our own in waking life? The dream possesses a marvellous poetry, a capacity for allegory, an incomparable sense of humour, a delicious irony. It beholds the world in an idealizing light unique to it, and intensifies the effect of its manifestations often by the aptest understanding of their fundamental nature. It presents earthly beauty to us in truly heavenly splendour, the sublime in the height of majesty, our ordinary fears in the most frightful form, the ridiculous with ineffably graphic comedy. Sometimes we are so full of one of these random impressions when we wake that it seems to us that the real world has never offered us anything to compare with it.'

We may well ask ourselves whether the contemptuous remarks and the enthusiastic praise are really referring to the same thing. Has the one overlooked the idiotic dreams and the other the profound and subtle ones? And if both kinds occur—dreams deserving the one judgement and dreams deserving the other—does it not seem idle to look for a psychological description of the dream? Is it not enough to say that in dreams everything is possible, from the lowest degradation of our psychical life to an intensification of it rare when we are awake? Attractive though this solution would be, it has this one thing against it: the efforts of all those investigating the dream seem to be based on the assumption that a characterization of the dream does exist, universally valid in its essential features, which would reconcile these contradictions.

It is indisputable that the psychical achievements of the dream were given readier and more positive recognition in the intellectual period, now behind us, in which philosophy and not the exact sciences, dominated the mind. Views such as Schubert's,* that the dream is a liberation of the mind from the power of external nature, a release of the soul from the fetters of sensuality, and similar judgements by the younger Fichte[4]* and others, which all represent the dream as an ascent of the inner life to a higher level, seem hardly comprehensible to us today; nowadays they are repeated only by mystics and religious fanatics. The rise of the scientific mode of thinking is accompanied by a reaction in the appreciation of the dream. Medical writers in particular are most inclined to brand psychical activity in dreams as insignificant and valueless, while philosophers and observers outside the profession have mostly clung to the psychical value of dreams—amateur psychologists whose contribution is not to be neglected in this of all fields. Anyone inclined to disdain the performance of the psyche in dreams understandably favours somatic sources of stimuli as their aetiology; naturally, those who consider that the dreaming psyche has left most of its abilities behind in the waking world also have no motive for granting the inner life any stimulus of its own to dreaming.

Among the great achievements which we are tempted to ascribe to the dream-life even in sober comparisons, that of memory is the most striking; we have dealt in detail with the—quite frequent—experiences demonstrating it. Another distinction enjoyed by the dream-life often commended by older writers, its sovereign ability to transcend space and time, is easily recognized as an illusion. This distinction, as Hildebrandt [35] remarked, is just that: illusory. Dreaming transcends space and time in just the same way that waking thought does, simply because it is no more than a form of thought. Dreams are also supposed to enjoy a further distinction

_____
[4] Cf. Haffner [32] and Spitta [64].

with regard to temporality, that of being independent of the passage of time in another sense. Dreams like the one related above by Maury [48] (pp. 24–5) of his execution by the guillotine seem to demonstrate that dreams are capable of compressing far more perceptions into a very short space of time than our psychical activity can cope with in our thoughts while we are awake. However, various arguments have disputed this inference: since the essays of Le Lorrain [45] and Egger [20] 'on the apparent duration of dreams', an interesting discussion has developed which has probably not yet reached a clarification of this profound and difficult question.

That the dream is capable of continuing the intellectual work of the day and bringing it to a conclusion which had not then been reached; that it can resolve doubts and problems and be the source of fresh inspiration for poets and composers—in the light of many different accounts, and after the collection made by Chabaneix [11], this seems to be incontestable. But though the fact may admit of no doubt, we must have many reservations touching matters of principle about the way it is understood.

Finally, the alleged divinatory powers of the dream form an object of contention where a scepticism very hard to overcome encounters assurances obstinately repeated. There is a reluctance—no doubt justified—to reject the notion outright, because in many cases we may be on the threshold of a natural psychological explanation.

(f) *Ethical Feelings in Dreams*

For reasons which will become apparent only after I have presented my own investigations into dreams, I have separated the specific problem of whether or how far the moral dispositions and feelings of waking life extend into our dream-life from the general topic of the psychology of dreams. Here too we are dismayed to see the same contradictions we have observed with surprise and exasperation in the accounts we have already noted of all the other achievements of the psyche. The certainty with which one writer asserts that the dream knows nothing of moral demands is matched by the assurance with which another affirms that mankind's moral nature also holds good in our dream-life.

Appeal to our dream-experience every night seems to put the first assertion beyond all doubt. Jessen [36] says (p. 553): 'We do not grow better or more virtuous in sleep; rather, the conscience seems to be silent in dreams, for we feel no pity, and we are able to commit the gravest crimes, stealing, murdering, and killing with perfect indifference, and without any subsequent remorse.'

Radestock [54] (p. 146): 'It has to be considered that in dreams associations run on and ideas are linked together without any part being played by reason or reflection, aesthetic taste or moral sense; the judgement is extremely weak and what predominates is *ethical indifference*.'

Volkelt [72] (p. 23): 'In dreams, as everyone knows, sexual behaviour is especially unrestrained. Just as the dreamer himself is shameless to the last degree and devoid of all moral feeling or judgement, so he also beholds everyone else, including even the most respected, caught up in the performance of acts he would shrink from associating them with in waking life, even in his thoughts.'

The sharpest contrast to these views is provided by assertions such as Schopenhauer's that in dreams everyone acts and speaks wholly in accordance with his character. R. P. Fischer[5] maintains that subjective feelings and efforts, or affects and passions, are revealed in the arbitrary acts of the dream-life and that people's individual moral peculiarities are reflected in their dreams.

Haffner [32] (p. 25): 'Apart from rare exceptions . . . a virtuous man will also be virtuous in dreams; he will resist temptation and be invulnerable to hatred, envy, wrath, and every vice; the man of sin, however, will as a rule also find in his dreams the images he has before him when awake.'

Scholz [59] (p. 36): 'In the dream there is truth, in spite of all the disguising; in dignity or degradation we recognize our own self . . . The honest man could not commit a crime that would dishonour him, even in a dream, or if he does he is horrified at it as something alien to his nature. So the Roman Emperor who had one of his subjects executed because the latter had dreamed he had had the emperor's head cut off was not altogether wrong when he justified this by saying that whoever dreamed of such a thing was bound to have similar thoughts in mind when awake. It is telling that we say of something that is totally foreign to our nature: "I wouldn't even dream of it."'

---

[5] *Grundzüge des Systems der Anthropologie* (Erlangen: 1850), cited after Spitta.

Pfaff[6] says outright, varying a familiar proverb: 'Tell me your dreams for a while and I will tell you what you are really like.'

Hildebrandt's [35] little book, which I have already quoted so many times—formally the most perfect contribution to the inquiry into the problems of dreams, and the most fertile in ideas I have found in the literature—places this very problem of morality in dreams at the centre of its interests. For Hildebrandt too it is a firm rule that the purer the life the purer the dream, the more impure the one, the more impure the other.

The moral nature of man persists even in dreams: 'But whereas no error in arithmetic however obvious, no reversal of science however romantic, no anachronism however comic ever offends us or even arouses our suspicions, we never lose our sense of the difference between good and evil, right and wrong, virtue and vice. However much of what accompanies us by day may fade during the hours of slumber, Kant's categorical imperative* has clung to our heels so firmly as our inseparable companion that we cannot get rid of him, even in sleep . . . However, this fact can only be explained by supposing that the fundamental basis of human nature, the moral being, is too firmly constructed to have any part in the effects of the kaleidoscopic shake-up which imagination, reason, memory, and other faculties of the same order undergo in dreams' (pp. 45 ff.).

In the wider discussion of the subject some remarkable inconsistencies and evasions can be observed in both groups of writers. Strictly speaking, for all those who believe that the moral personality of man disintegrates in dreams, any interest in immoral dreams would come to an end with this statement. They could reject the attempt to make the dreamer responsible for his dreams, and from the wickedness of his dreams conclude the existence of an evil tendency in his nature with as much composure as they would the apparently equivalent attempt to demonstrate from the absurdity of his dreams the worthlessness of his intellectual attainments when awake. The others, for whom the 'categorical imperative' extends even into dreams, would have to assume responsibility for immoral dreams without reservation: it is only to be hoped that if they themselves have dreams of a reprehensible kind this does not oblige them to lose faith in the soundness of their own morals.

[6] *Das Traumleben und seine Deutung* (1868), in Spitta, p. 192.

However, it seems that no one can really know how far he is good or wicked, and that no one can deny the memory of his own immoral dreams. For beyond these opposing judgements on the morality of dreams, the writers of both groups endeavour to explain the origin of immoral dreams, and a new opposition develops according to whether the origin is sought in the functioning of the psychical life or in impairments to it from some somatic cause. The compelling power of the facts then enables the advocates of both responsibility and irresponsibility in the dream-life to meet in acknowledging that the immorality of dreams has a distinctive psychical source.

All the same, all those who would have morality persist in dreams still guard against assuming full responsibility for their dreams. Haffner [32] says (p. 24): 'We are not responsible for dreams, because our thinking and willing have been deprived of the sole basis on which our life has truth and reality . . . That is why no willing or acting in dreams can be virtue or sin.' Yet man is responsible for sinful dreams insofar as he is their indirect cause. As in waking, so quite particularly before going to sleep he has the duty of morally purifying his soul.

Hildebrandt's analysis of this mixture of rejection and recognition of responsibility for the moral content of dreams goes much deeper. After explaining that the dream's dramatic mode of presentation, its compression of the most complicated thought-processes into the briefest periods of time, and what he too concedes is a devaluation and confusion of the ideational elements in the dream all have to be allowed for and discounted when it comes to the dream's appearance of immorality, he admits that all the same we should have the gravest reservations about denying altogether our responsibility for sins and crimes committed in dreams.

'When we want to deny an unjust accusation emphatically, especially one that touches on our fundamental views and beliefs, we will probably use the expression: I wouldn't think of it even in my dreams. However, when we say that, we are stating that we regard the domain of the dream as the furthest and remotest domain in which we would have to vouch for our own thoughts, for there our thoughts are connected with our real being so loosely that they can hardly be considered still our own; on the other hand, by feeling obliged to deny the presence of such thoughts even here, we indirectly concede that our justification would not be complete if it did not reach as far as this. And I believe that here, even if unconsciously, we are speaking the language of truth' (p. 49).

(p. 52) 'For there is not a deed can be imagined in our dreams whose primary motive has not in some way previously passed through our soul when awake, as wish, desire, or impulse.' We would have to say of this primary impulse that the dream did not invent it—the dream only imitated it and expanded it, only adapted in dramatic form a scrap of historical material it had discovered in us; it enacts the saying of the Apostle that whosoever hateth his brother is a murderer.* Aware of our moral probity, we can smile at the extended recollection of a sinful dream, but we do not find anything to laugh at in the original material from which the dream was formed. We feel ourselves responsible for the aberrations of the dreamer: not for their sum, but for a certain percentage. 'In short, if we understand Christ's saying: "Out of the heart proceed evil thoughts"* in this indisputable sense, then we shall hardly be able to resist the conviction that every sin committed in dreams brings with it at least an obscure minimum of guilt.'

Hildebrandt, then, discovers the source of the immorality of dreams in the germs and hints of evil impulses passing through our soul during the day as thoughts of temptation, and he does not hesitate to include these immoral elements in the moral evaluation of the personality. It is these same thoughts, and the same judgement of them, which have, as we know, led the pious and saintly of every age to lament that they are miserable sinners.

There can surely be no doubt that these *utterly contrasting* ideas occur universally, in most people and in other fields besides the ethical. Judging them has on occasion been treated less seriously. Spitta [64] quotes a relevant passage from A. Zeller's article 'Irre' ['Lunatics'] in Ersch and Gruber's *Encyklopädie der Wissenschaften* (p. 144): 'A mind is rarely so fortunately organized that it possesses full authority over itself at all times, and is not interrupted again and again in the clear and steady course of its thoughts by ideas which are not only uncharacteristic but altogether grotesque and nonsensical; indeed, the greatest thinkers have had cause to complain of this dreamlike, teasing, and embarrassing rabble of ideas, as it disturbs their profoundest meditations and most solemn and serious intellectual work.'

More light is cast on the psychological position of these contrasting ideas by a further remark of Hildebrandt's that the dream sometimes allows us to see into the depths and crevices of our nature which are mostly still barred to us when we are awake (p. 55). Kant* reveals the same insight in a passage in his *Anthropologie* when he says that the dream no doubt exists to disclose to us our hidden dispositions and reveal, not what we are, but what we could have become if we had had a different upbringing; Radestock [54] (p. 84) does the same when he says that often the dream reveals to us what we do not want to admit to ourselves, and that we are wrong to call it a liar and a deceiver. Our attention is drawn to the fact that the emergence of these impulses alien to our moral consciousness is only analogous to what the dream does with other ideational material lacking or playing only a minor role in waking life, processes already familiar to us from observations such as those made by Bernini [3]: 'Certe nostre inclinazioni che si credevano soffocate e spente da un pezzo, si ridestano; passioni vecchie e sepolte rivivono; cose e persone a cui non pensiamo mai, ci vengono dinanzi'* (p. 149), and by Volkelt [73]: 'Even ideas which have entered the waking consciousness almost unnoticed and which perhaps have never again been recalled to memory often have the habit of making their presence in the psyche known to the dream' (p. 105). Finally, this would be the place to remind ourselves that according to Schleiermacher [61] even the act of falling asleep is attended by the emergence of *involuntary* ideas (images).

We may, then, sum up all this ideational material whose occurrence in immoral as well as in absurd dreams arouses our surprise and displeasure as '*involuntary ideas*'. The only important difference is that in the moral domain the involuntary ideas can be recognized as the opposite of our normal feelings, while the others seem to us merely alien. So far no advance has been made in dealing with the problem which might enable us to resolve this distinction by deeper understanding.

What significance, then, has the emergence of involuntary ideas in dreams? What conclusions can be drawn for the psychology of the waking and dreaming soul from this nightly appearance of contrasting ethical impulses? Here we have to note a fresh difference of opinion and yet another regrouping among the writers on the subject. The line of thought taken by Hildebrandt and others sharing his views can surely continue only in the direction of recognizing that the immoral impulses have a certain power in waking life too, though this power is inhibited from going as far as action; also of supposing that something is suspended in the state of sleep which, likewise operating as an inhibition does, has prevented us from noticing the existence of this impulse. The dream would thus exhibit the real, if not the whole, nature of man, and is one of the means of making the hidden interior of the psyche accessible to us. It is only on the basis of such assumptions that Hildebrandt can assign to the dream the role of *warning voice* drawing our attention to hidden moral defects in our soul, just as according to physicians it can alert our consciousness to previously unnoticed physical illness. And Spitta [64] too must be adopting the same view when he points to the sources of arousal which enter the psyche at the period of puberty, for example, and when he reassures the dreamer that he has done everything in his power if he leads a strictly virtuous life when awake and tries to suppress sinful thoughts whenever they appear, preventing them from maturing into action. According to this view, we could call the *involuntary* ideas the ideas *suppressed* by day, and would have to regard their emergence as a genuine psychological phenomenon.

Other writers would deny us the right to this last conclusion. For Jessen [36] the involuntary ideas—in dreams as in waking, in the delirium of fever as well as in other kinds—have 'the quality of a volitional activity laid to rest and of *a more or less mechanical* procession of images and ideas caused by motions within' (p. 360). An immoral dream would demonstrate nothing further of the dreamer's inner life than that he had at some time acquired knowledge of its ideational content, but certainly not that it revealed an impulse of his own psyche. Another writer, Maury [48], leaves us in doubt as to whether he too does not ascribe to the dream-state the ability to dismantle psychic activity into its component parts rather than unsystematically to destroy it. He says of those dreams where we put ourselves outside the bounds of morality: 'Ce sont nos penchants qui parlent et qui nous font agir, sans que la conscience nous retienne, bien que parfois elle nous avertisse. J'ai mes défauts et mes penchants vicieux; à l'état de veille, je tâche de lutter contre eux, et il m'arrive assez souvent de n'y pas succomber. Mais dans mes songes j'y succombe toujours ou pour mieux dire j'agis par leur impulsion, sans crainte et sans remords . . . Évidemment les visions qui se déroulent devant ma pensée et qui constituent le rêve, me sont suggérées par les incitations que je ressens et que ma volonté absente ne cherche pas à refouler' (p. 113).*

If we believed in the capacity of the dream to disclose a real but suppressed or hidden moral disposition on the part of the dreamer we could not express this opinion more plainly than in these words of Maury's (p. 115): 'En rêve l'homme se révèle donc tout entier à soi-même dans sa nudité et sa misère natives. Dès qu'il suspend l'exercice de sa volonté, il devient le jouet de toutes les passions contre lesquelles, à l'état de veille, la conscience, le sentiment de l'honneur, la crainte nous défendent.' In another passage he observes acutely (p. 462): 'Dans le rêve, c'est surtout l'homme instinctif qui se révèle . . . L'homme revient pour ainsi dire à l'état de nature quand il rêve; mais moins les idées acquises ont pénétré dans son esprit, plus les *penchants en désaccord* avec elles conservent encore sur lui l'influence dans le rêve.'* Then as an example he cites the fact that his dreams often show him to be a victim of that very superstition which in his writings he has combated most vigorously.

But the value of all these insights of Maury's for our knowledge of the psychology of the dream-life is diminished when he insists on regarding the phenomena he has so correctly observed only as proofs of the 'automatisme psychologique' which in his view dominates the dream-life. This automatism he conceives as being the absolute antithesis to psychical activity.

A passage in Stricker's [77] studies of consciousness states that dreams do not consist solely and wholly of delusions. For example, if we are afraid of robbers in a dream, the robbers are certainly imaginary, but the fear is real. This draws our attention to the fact that the development of affects in dreams is not amenable to the judgement we make of the rest of the dream-content, and we are faced with the problem of what part or aspect of the psychical processes of the dream may be real, that is, what can lay claim to being included among the psychical processes of waking life.

(g) *Theories of Dreams and the Function of Dreams*

A proposition about the dream which attempts to explain as many of its observed features as possible from a single standpoint, at the same time determining the position of the dream in relation to a more comprehensive field of phenomena, may be called a theory of the dream. Particular theories of the dream are distinguished from one another according to which of its features they elevate into its essential characteristic and treat as the point of reference for the explanations and connections they set up. That dreams have a function, that is a use or other capacity, does not necessarily have to be inferred from the theory, but, as we are accustomed to thinking teleologically, we are still likely to be attracted to those theories which include an insight into a function for dreams.

We have already met several views of the dream which more or less deserved the name of dream-theories in this sense. The belief of the ancients that the dream was a gift of the gods for the purpose of directing the actions of men was a complete theory of the dream which provided information about everything worth knowing about it. Since then the dream has become an object of biological research, and a large number of dream-theories have appeared, though many of them are far from complete.

Without making any claim to comprehensiveness, we can perhaps attempt the following loose grouping of dream-theories according to their fundamental assumptions about the degree and kind of psychical activity present in the dream.

1. Theories such as Delboeuf's, which propose that the full psychical activity of waking life continues in dreams. According to these, the psyche does not sleep; its apparatus remains intact; but under the conditions of sleep, which differ from those of the waking state, in normal functioning it is bound to produce different results from those of the waking state. With these theories the question is whether they are in a position to derive all the differences between dreams and waking thought from the conditions of the sleeping state. Moreover, they have no means of explaining the function of the dream: we cannot understand to what end we dream, or why the complex mechanism of the psychical apparatus carries on working even when it is placed in a situation which it does not seem to be intended for. To sleep without dreaming, or, on the intervention of disturbing stimuli, to wake up, remain the only appropriate reactions, rather than the third, of dreaming.

2. Theories which on the contrary assume a lowering of psychical activity in the dream, a loosening of connections, an impoverishment

of usable material. These theories would entail an entirely different psychological description of sleep from Delboeuf's, for instance. Sleep would extend over the entire psyche; it would not merely shut off the psyche from the external world, but rather would penetrate into its mechanism and render this temporarily unusable. If I may draw a comparison with material from psychiatry, I would say that the former theories construe the dream as a form of paranoia, the latter make of it a model of mental deficiency, or amentia.

The theory that in the dream-life only a fragment of our psychical activity finds expression, as it has been largely paralysed by sleep, is by far the most favoured among medical authors and by the scientific world at large. As far as we may assume a more general interest in the explanation of dreams, this must certainly be called the *dominant* theory of the dream. It has to be emphasized how easily this theory above all is able to get over the worst hurdle in the way of any explanation of dreams—that is, coming to grief over one of the contradictions embodied by the dream. As it regards the dream as the product of a partially waking state ('a gradual, partial and at the same time very anomalous waking state', Herbart's *Psychologie* says of the dream), it is able to explain the entire gamut—from the dream's defective performance as displayed in absurdities up to fully concentrated thinking—by a series of states from ever-increasing wakefulness up to full waking alertness.

Those who cannot dispense with physiological terms of description, or who think them more scientific, will find this theory of dreams outlined by Binz [4] (p. 43): 'This condition [of numbness], however, draws an end only gradually in the early morning hours. The fatigue-producing agent accumulated in the brain-protein grows sparser and sparser and more of it is dissipated or carried away by the restlessly active bloodstream. Here and there particular clusters of awakened cells are already brightening, while all around everything is still in repose. The *isolated action of the individual clusters* now appears before our clouded consciousness, and they lack control by the other parts of the brain that direct association. That is why the images created, most of which correspond to material impressions of the recent past, come about in a wild and unruly manner. The number of liberated brain-cells continually increases, the irrationality of the dream continually diminishes.'

We shall certainly find this conception of dreaming as an

imperfect, partial waking among all modern physiologists and philosophers—or at least traces of its influence. Maury [48] presents it in its fullest form, and here it often seems as if the author imagined that being awake or being asleep could be shifted to different regions of the anatomy—though this entails his thinking that a particular anatomical province and a particular psychical function are apparently connected to each other. However, I would merely suggest here that if the theory of partial waking were confirmed, a great deal of discussion would have to be spent on differentiating it more finely.

This conception of the dream-life naturally fails to show what function the dream might have. Rather, its judgement on the status and significance of the dream is put quite consistently by Binz (p. 357): 'As we see, all the facts urge us to characterize the dream as a *physical* process, one which is in every instance useless and in many instances downright pathological . . .'

The expression 'physical' in connection with the dream, emphasized by the author himself, surely has a very wide range of reference. It refers first of all to the aetiology of dreams, which, of course, was particularly important for Binz when he was studying the experimental production of dreams by the administration of poisons. For this kind of dream-theory is related to the argument which would have the stimulus to dreaming proceed if possible solely from the somatic side. To put it in its most extreme form: after we have lapsed into sleep through the removal of stimuli there would be no need or occasion for dreaming until morning, when our gradual awakening through newly arriving stimuli could be reflected in the phenomenon of dreaming. But we cannot succeed in keeping sleep free from stimuli; just as Mephisto* complains of the germs of life constantly stirring, stimuli which the sleeper has paid no heed to when awake now approach him from all directions, from without, from within, from every region of the body. Thus sleep is disturbed, the psyche is shaken awake, tweaked at the corners now here now there, then functions with its wakened part for a little while, glad if it can go back to sleep again. The dream is the reaction to this disturbance of sleep caused by the stimuli, though it is of course a perfectly superfluous reaction.

However, there is a further significance to calling the dream, which after all is still an activity of the psyche, a physical process. The dream is denied the *dignity* of being a process of the psyche.

Perhaps the best illustration of what valuation the exact sciences mostly place on the activity of dreams is that metaphor, already applied long ago to the dream, of the 'ten fingers of someone wholly ignorant of music strumming on the keys'. Viewed in this way, the dream becomes something altogether uninterpretable: for how should the ten fingers of an unmusical player produce a piece of music?

From very early on there have been plenty of objections to the theory of partial waking. In 1830 Burdach [8] wrote: 'When we say that the dream is a partial waking, in the first place this explains neither waking nor sleeping, and in the second all it does say is that some forces of the psyche are active in the dream, while others are at rest. But such an imbalance occurs throughout our entire life . . .' (p. 483).

There is a further, very interesting conception of the dream dependent on the prevailing dream-theory which regards the dream as a 'physical' process. It was first put forward by Robert [55], and is especially attractive because it is able to propose a function, a beneficial outcome, for dreaming. As the basis for his theory, Robert takes two observed facts which we have already dwelt on in our assessment of the dream material (see p. 17): that we so often dream of the most trivial impressions of the day, and so rarely carry over its major interests into our dreams. Robert insists that things we have fully thought through never become the impulses of our dreams, but always and only those which lie in our mind unfinished or have only fleetingly touched our thoughts (p. 10). The reason why we usually find a dream inexplicable is that its causes are *'those sensory impressions of the previous day which the dreamer has not been sufficiently aware of'*. Thus the condition for an impression to become part of a dream is either that its processing was disturbed or that it was too insignificant to be worth processing.

So Robert represents the dream 'as a physical process of elimination and excretion which we become aware of in our mental reaction to it'. *Dreams are the excretion of undeveloped thoughts, thoughts nipped in the bud.* 'A man deprived of the ability to dream would in time go insane, because a mass of unfinished, incomplete thoughts and superficial impressions would accumulate in his brain, and what should have been incorporated in his memory as a finished whole would be stifled under their weight.' The dream serves the over-burdened brain as a safety-valve. *Dreams possess the power to heal and to relieve* (p. 32).

It would be a misunderstanding to ask Robert how generating ideas in a dream can bring relief to the psyche. The author clearly concludes from those two peculiarities of the dream-material that during sleep this evacuation of worthless impressions is carried out *somehow* as a somatic course of events, and that dreaming is not a distinct psychical process but only the information reaching us that this elimination is occurring. Moreover, excretion is not the only thing going on in the psyche at night. Robert himself adds that in addition the stimulations of the day are being processed, and that 'anything from the thought-material lying undigested in the mind which cannot be excreted is bound into a rounded whole with *threads of thought borrowed from the imagination* and so becomes part of the memory as a harmless imaginary picture' (p. 23).

However, in its evaluation of the sources of the dream, Robert's theory stands in the starkest opposition to the one now prevailing. Whereas in the latter dreaming would not occur at all if the psyche were not repeatedly awakened by external and internal sensory stimuli, in Robert's theory the impulse to dreaming lies within the psyche itself, in the overloading which it desires to have relieved, and he judges, quite consistently, that the causes of the dream lying in our physical condition have a subordinate place and could in no way give rise to dreaming in a mind which held no raw material from the waking consciousness to form its dreams upon. All he concedes is that the fantasy-images developing in the dream out of the depths of the psyche may be influenced by nervous stimuli (p. 48). So, according to Robert, the dream is not so very dependent on somatic factors after all; true, it is not a psychical process, has no place among the psychical processes of waking life: it is a nightly somatic process operating on the apparatus of psychical activity, and it has a function to fulfil, to protect this apparatus from overload or, to vary the metaphor, to clear out the stables for the psyche.

The same characteristics of the dream apparent in its selection of material provide support for the theory of another writer, Yves Delage [15], and it is instructive to observe how only a slight change in the way the same things are conceived produces a result with quite different implications.

On the death of someone dear to him, Delage observed from his own experience that one does *not* dream of what has filled one's thoughts during the day, or does so only when it begins to give way during the day to other interests. His researches with other people confirmed to him how universal this was. He makes a nice observation of this kind, should it turn out to be universally true, on the dreaming of young married couples: 'S'ils ont été fortement épris, presque jamais ils ont rêvé l'un de l'autre avant le mariage ou pendant la lune de miel; et s'ils ont rêvé d'amour c'est pour être infidèles avec quelque personne indifférente ou odieuse.'* But what *do* people dream of, then? Delage recognizes that the material occurring in our dreams consists of the fragments and remains of impressions from recent days and earlier times. Everything appearing in our dreams which we may at first be inclined to regard as created by our dream-life turns out on closer inspection to be unrecognized reproduction, 'souvenir inconscient'. But all this ideational material has one feature in common: it originates in impressions which have probably affected our senses more powerfully than our mind, or in impressions from which our attention was diverted very soon after they arose. The less conscious and at the same time the more powerful an impression, the greater its prospect of playing a role in our next dream.

These are essentially the same two categories of impression—the trivial and the unprocessed—which Robert [55] emphasizes, but Delage gives a different turn to the connection in his opinion that these impressions are capable of generating dreams not because they are trivial, but because they are unprocessed. The trivial impressions, too, have to a certain extent not been fully processed, they too are by their nature new impressions, 'autant de ressorts tendus',* which will be relaxed during sleep. A powerful impression whose processing has been accidentally halted or deliberately suppressed will be even more entitled to a role in the dream than one that is weak or almost unnoticed. The psychical energy accumulated through the day by inhibition and suppression becomes the mainspring of the dream at night. What appears in the dream is what has been psychically suppressed.

Unfortunately Delage breaks off his train of thought at this point: he can concede only the most minor role to the independent activity of the psyche in the dream, and so with his theory of the dream he promptly returns to the prevailing doctrine that the brain is only partly sleeping: 'En somme le rêve est le produit de la pensée errante, sans but et sans direction, se fixant successivement sur les souvenirs, qui ont gardé assez d'intensité pour se placer sur sa route et l'arrêter au passage, établissant entre eux un lien tantôt faible et indécis, tantôt plus fort et plus serré, selon que l'activité actuelle du cerveau est plus ou moins abolie par le sommeil.'*

One can create a third group of dream-theories out of those which ascribe to the dreaming psyche the capacity and inclination for exceptional psychical achievements that are either beyond its powers or that it can only carry out imperfectly when awake. On the whole the exercise of these capacities produces a beneficial function for the dream. The evaluations of the dream made by earlier writers on psychology mostly belong in this group. However, instead of quoting them, I shall content myself with referring to an observation of Burdach's [8], to whom dreaming 'is the natural activity of the soul, which the power of the individual does not restrict, self-consciousness does not disturb, self-determination does not direct, but is the vitality of our centres of sensibility revelling in free and uninhibited play' (p. 486).

Burdach and others clearly envisage this indulgence in the free use of its own powers as a state in which the psyche refreshes itself and gathers new energy for the day's work, rather like taking a holiday. That is why Burdach also quotes in acknowledgement the winning words in which the poet Novalis praises the free run of the dream: 'The dream is a defence against the ordinary regularity of life, a recreation for the fettered fantasy, a place where it can throw all the images of life into confusion and interrupt the earnestness of grown men with joyful children's play; without dreams we would certainly grow old sooner, and so we can regard the dream, if not as a direct gift from above, still as a delightful task, a friendly companion on our pilgrimage to the grave.'*

The refreshing and healing action of the dream is described even more forcefully by Purkinje [53] (p. 456): 'Productive dreams especially would convey these functions. They are effortless products of the imagination in free play, unconnected with the events of the day. The psyche does not wish to continue the tensions of waking life, but to resolve them, recover from them. First and foremost it produces states that are the very opposite of those in our waking state. It cures sadness with joy, care with hope and cheerful diverting images, hatred with love and kindness, fear with courage and confidence; doubt it soothes with conviction and firm faith, vain expectations with fulfilment. Many sore places in the heart, which the day would keep ever open, are healed by sleep, which covers them over and keeps them from fresh irritation. This is what the healing effect of time in part depends upon.' We all feel that sleep is a benefaction to our psychical life, and the obscure awareness of the popular mind is clearly unwilling to be robbed of its prejudice that the dream is one of the ways in which sleep confers its benefactions.

The most original and far-reaching attempt to explain the dream as an activity peculiar to the psyche which can develop freely only in sleep is the one undertaken in 1861 by Scherner [56]. Scherner's book, written in a heady, florid style, exhibits an almost intoxicated enthusiasm for its subject and, if it does not sweep us along with it, is bound to put us off. It resists analysis to such an extent that we turn readily to the clearer and briefer account of Scherner's theories as the philosopher Volkelt [72] presents them. 'A mysterious appearance of sense does flash and gleam out of the mystical conglomerations, out of all the surging splendour, only it fails to illuminate the philosopher's path.' Such is the judgement passed on Scherner's mode of presentation even by a follower.

Scherner is not one of those writers who permit the psyche to take its capacities with it into the dream-life undiminished. He even explains how the centrality, the spontaneous energy, of the ego becomes enervated in dreams, how as a result of this decentralization cognition, feeling, willing, and the generation of ideas are altered, and how the remnants of these psychical forces no longer possess the true character of mind but only the nature of a mechanism. But instead, the activity of the psyche which we may call the *imagination*, free of all control by reason and so, too, free of all restraint, soars to absolute domination in the dream. True, it does take its ultimate building-blocks from waking memory, but it uses them to construct buildings vastly different from the structures of waking life; in dreams it is not only reproductive, it is *productive* as well. These peculiarities are what lend the dream-life its particular character. It has a preference for what is *unrestrained, exaggerated, monstrous.* At the same time, however, its liberation from the inhibiting categories of thought gives it a greater suppleness, agility, flexibility of shifting shape; it is highly sensitive to the delicate stimuli that arouse moods of tender warmth or emotions that disturb; straight away it gives the inner life the vividness of outwardly perceived forms. The dream-imagination *lacks a conceptual language*: what it has to say it has to paint visibly, and since it is not weakened by the presence of concepts, it paints it with all the richness and power of the thing seen. But clear though this language is, its visual nature also makes it rambling, awkward, clumsy. Its clarity is especially impeded because it is reluctant to express an object by its own image and prefers a *different image* as long as this is capable of expressing the aspect of the object the imagination wants to present. This is the *symbolizing activity* of the imagination ... It is also very important that the dream-imagination does not reproduce objects exhaustively but only in outline, and very freely at that. Its paintings thus seem like brilliant improvisations. However, the dream-imagination does not stop at merely representing an object; it is under an inner compulsion to involve the dreaming self with it more or less deeply and so produce a dramatic action. A dream roused by a visual impression, for example, paints pieces of gold in the street: the dreamer gathers them up, rejoices, and carries them off.

The material which the dream-imagination takes for its artistic powers to work upon is, according to Scherner, mainly that offered by the stimuli of the bodily organs so dimly perceived by day. So, though otherwise poles apart, in this respect—in their assumptions about what the sources and instigators of dreams may be—Scherner's all-too-fantastical theorizing and the perhaps overly sober theses put forward by Wundt and other physiologists are in entire agreement. Now according to the physiological theory, the psyche's reaction to the inner bodily stimuli is over and done once the ideas somehow appropriate to them are aroused; by way of association these ideas then call others to their aid, and at this stage the course of the psychical processes in dreams seems to be concluded. According to Scherner, on the other hand, the bodily stimuli only offer the psyche material it can make use of for its imaginative purposes. For Scherner the formation of dreams is only beginning at the stage where in the eyes of others it has come to an end.

Of course, we cannot regard what the dream-imagination does with the bodily stimuli as exactly purposeful. It plays a teasing game with them and imagines the organic sources from which the stimuli in a particular dream originate in some kind of palpable form. Indeed, Scherner believes—though Volkelt and others do not follow him here—that the dream-imagination has a certain favourite way of representing the whole organism, and that is as a *house*. Fortunately, though, it does not seem to confine itself to this subject-matter for its representations: contrariwise, it can use large numbers of houses to designate one particular organ, for instance, a very long street of houses for the stimulus from the intestines. At other times particular parts of the house represent in reality particular parts of the body; for example, in a headache dream the ceiling of a room (which the dreamer sees covered with disgusting, toad-like spiders) represents the head.

Quite apart from the house symbolism, all kinds of other objects are employed to represent the parts of the body sending out a stimulus to dreaming. 'Thus the respiring lung finds its symbol in the fiery oven with its breathlike roar, the heart in empty baskets and chests, the bladder in pouch-shaped objects or hollowed-out objects generally. The male sexual dream has the dreamer find the upper part of a clarinet in the street, beside it the same part of a tobacco pipe, and beside that again a fur coat. The clarinet and the pipe represent the approximate form of the male member, the fur coat the pubic hair. In the female sexual dream the crotch of the thighs can be symbolized by a narrow courtyard enclosed by houses, the vagina by a very narrow, slippery soft footpath leading across the middle of the yard which the dreamer has to cross, perhaps to deliver a letter to a gentleman' (Volkelt, p. 39). It is especially important that at the end of a physically stimulated dream of this kind the dream-imagination as it were throws off its mask and presents the arousing organ or its function unconcealed. Thus a 'toothache dream' usually concludes with the dreamer taking a tooth out of his mouth.

But the dream-imagination can do more than turn its attention only to the form of the arousing organ; it can just as well take the substance contained in it as the object of symbolization. Thus, for example, a dream stimulated by the intestines leads the dreamer through muddy streets, a dream stimulated by urine leads him beside foaming water. Or the stimulus itself, the nature of its excitation, the object it desires, are represented symbolically; or the dream-self enters into a concrete connection with the symbolizations of its own condition; for example, when aroused by pain we struggle in desperation with snapping dogs or raging bulls, or when in a sexual dream a woman sees herself pursued by a naked man. Quite apart from the abundance of its possible forms of representation, the central force in every dream is still a symbolizing activity of the imagination. Volkelt [72] then attempted to penetrate more closely into the nature of this imagination and assign a place in a system of philosophical thought to the psychical activity. His book is written beautifully and with ardour, but it is too difficult to understand for anyone whose early training has not prepared him for an intuitive grasp of the conceptual schemes of philosophy.

There is no useful function attached to the activation of Scherner's symbolizing imaginaton in dreams. As it dreams, the psyche plays with the stimuli it is offered. We might even surmise that it plays with them mischievously. But we could also be asked whether our own detailed consideration of Scherner's theory of dreams could possibly lead to anything useful, for its arbitrariness and disconnection from all the rules of scientific research seem only too obvious. If so, it would be proper to register a veto against the arrogance of rejecting Scherner's theories before scrutinizing them. This theory is built on the impression made on someone by his dreams; he has paid great attention to them and he seems to have a strong personal aptitude for pursuing the dark aspects of the psyche. Moreover, this theory deals with a subject which for thousands of years mankind has certainly found mysterious, but rich in content and associations, and which rigorous science has on its own admission done little to elucidate beyond attempting, wholly counter to popular feeling, to deny it any meaning or importance. Finally, let us frankly admit that it does seem that our attempts to explain the dream cannot easily avoid the fantastic. Even the ganglion-cells are subject to it: the passage quoted on p. 64 from so sober and exact a scientist as Binz [4], which describes how the aurora of awakening passes across the sleeping cell-clusters of the cerebral cortex, is no whit less fantastic—and improbable—than Scherner's attempts at interpretation. I hope to be able to show that behind the latter something real does exist, though it has been recognized only vaguely and is not characterized by the universality which a theory of dreams may claim. For the present, Scherner's theory of dreams, by its contrast to the medical theory, for instance, shows us clearly the extremes between which explanations of the dream still fluctuate today.

(h) *The Relations Between Dreams and Mental Illnesses*

In speaking of the relation of dreams to mental disturbances we can mean three different things: (1) aetiological and clinical relationships, as when a dream takes the place of a psychotic condition, inaugurates it, or is left over after it; (2) changes the dream-life undergoes in the case of mental illness; and (3) inner relationships between dreams and psychoses, analogies indicating essential similarities. These various relationships between the two sets of phenomena were a favourite theme of medical writers in earlier ages of medicine—and have been again more recently, as we learn from the literature on the subject collected by Spitta [64], Radestock [54], Maury [48], and Tissié [68]. Not long ago Sante de Sanctis [56, 57] turned his attention to them. It will be sufficient for the interests of our own account if we merely touch on the subject.

As to the clinical and aetiological relations between dreams and psychoses, I propose to refer to the following observations as model examples. Hohnbaum (cited in Krauss [39]) reports that the first outbreak of madness was often ascribed to origins in a terrible anxiety-dream, and that the predominant idea was connected with this dream. Sante de Sanctis presents similar observations of paranoiacs, and says that in individual cases the dream was the 'vraie cause déterminante de la folie'.* Psychosis can spring to life at a stroke with the operative dream containing the explanation, or it can develop slowly through further dreams which still have to struggle with doubts. In one case of de Sanctis's, the disturbing dream was followed by mild attacks of hysteria, and then further by a melancholy-anxious condition. Féré (cited by Tissié) reports a dream which resulted in a hysterical paralysis. In these instances the dream is presented to us in terms of the aetiology of mental disturbance, although we can account for the facts of the case just as well if we say that the mental disturbance first manifested itself in the dream-life, or broke out first of all in the dream. In other examples the dream-life contains the pathological symptoms, or the psychosis remains restricted to the dream-life. Thus Thomayer [70] draws attention to *anxiety-dreams* which must be regarded as equivalent to epileptic attacks. According to Radestock, Allison has described cases of 'nocturnal insanity' in which individuals are apparently quite healthy throughout the day, while hallucinations, fits of rage, and the like regularly appear at night. Similar observations can be found in de Sanctis (a dream equivalent to paranoia in the case of an alcoholic—voices accusing his wife of infidelity), and in Tissié. Tissié presents a wealth of recent observations in which actions of a pathological nature (based on delusory assumptions, obsessive compulsions) derive from dreams. Guislain describes a case in which sleep was intermittently replaced by insanity.

There can be no doubt that one day physicians will also concern themselves with a psychopathology of dreams as well as their psychology.

In cases of recuperation after mental illness it often becomes particularly clear that, although the patient may be functioning soundly by day, his dream-life can still be in the grip of the psychosis. According to Krauss [39], Gregory is said to be the first to have drawn attention to this phenomenon. Macario (cited by Tissié) tells of how a manic patient, a week after his full recovery, experienced over again in his dreams the flight of ideas and the passionate impulses belonging to his illness.

Up to now only very few studies have been made into what changes the dream-life undergoes in permanent psychotics. On the other hand, the deep affinity between dreams and mental disturbance, revealed in the general correspondence between the phenomena of both, was noticed from the first. According to Maury [47], Cabanis was the first to draw attention to it in his *Rapports du physique et du moral*; after him came Lélut, J. Moreau, and especially the philosopher Maine de Biran. Comparison between the two certainly dates from before this, however. Radestock [54] introduces the chapter in which he deals with it with a collection of quotations drawing an analogy between dreams and madness. Kant says in one place: 'The lunatic is one who dreams while awake.' Krauss: 'Madness is a dream with waking senses.' Schopenhauer calls the dream a brief madness and madness a long dream. Hagen describes delirium as dream-life brought about not by sleep but by illness. Wundt says, in his *Physiologische Psychologie*: 'Indeed, in our dreams we are able to experience ourselves almost all the phenomena we encounter in lunatic asylums.'

The individual correspondences which provide the basis for accepting this kind of equivalence are listed by Spitta [64] (very much as Maury did) in the following series: (1) Abolition or at least retardation of self-consciousness, consequently ignorance of the condition as such, hence impossibility of surprise at it, lack of moral consciousness. (2) Modified perception by the sense-organs, in dreams reduced, in madness generally very much intensified. (3) Connection of ideas with one another merely in accordance with the laws of association and reproduction, thus the automatic construction of sequences, hence disproportionate relationships between the ideas (exaggerations, fantasies) and everything resulting from them. (4) Changes or reversal of the personality, and occasionally character-changes (perversions).

Radestock adds a few other features, analogies in the material: 'most hallucinations and illusions are to be found in the domain of the senses of sight and hearing and in the general vital feeling. As in dreams, the fewest elements are provided by the senses of smell and taste. The deliriums of fever and the recollections of dreams both rise out of the remote past: what the waking and the healthy seem to have forgotten, the sleeping and the sick remember.' The analogy between dream and psychosis achieves its full force, however, only when it extends like a family resemblance to the subtler gestures and to the distinctive individual features of facial expression.

'To the man who is tormented by physical or mental suffering the dream grants what reality has denied: well-being and happiness; so too there arise for the mentally ill bright images of happiness, greatness, grandeur, and wealth. The supposed possession of goods and the imaginary fulfilment of desires whose refusal or loss was in fact a cause of the madness usually make up the main content of the delirium. A woman who has lost a dear child experiences the joys of motherhood in her delirium, someone who has suffered a loss of property considers himself extraordinarily rich, the deserted girl sees herself tenderly loved.'

(This passage from Radestock is an abridgement of a sensitive account by Griesinger [31] (p. 111), which reveals, with all possible clarity, that *wish-fulfilment* is one of the forms of imagining common to the dream and the psychoses. My own investigations have taught me that this is where the key to a psychological theory of the dream and of the psychoses is to be found.)

'Bizarre combinations of ideas and weakness of judgement are what chiefly characterize dreams and madness.' The *overestimation* of one's own intellect, which to the sober judgement seems only to produce absurdities, occurs in both; the *rapid succession of images* in the dream corresponds to the *rapid flight of ideas* in the psychoses. Both lack any *measure of time*. The *splitting of the personality* in dreams, where for instance our own knowledge is divided between two people, with the alien figure correcting our own ego, is exactly equivalent to the division of the personality in hallucinatory paranoia: the dreamer, too, hears his own thoughts uttered by alien voices. Even persistent delusory ideas find their analogy in stereotypically recurring pathological dreams (le rêve obsédant).—After recovering from a delirium sufferers quite often say that the entire period of their sickness seems like a dream to them, and often a not unpleasant one; they tell us, indeed, that during their illness they have occasionally felt that they were only trapped in a dream, just as often happens in dreams occurring in sleep.

After all this, it is not surprising when Radestock sums up his own views and those of many others by saying that 'madness, an abnormal, pathological phenomenon, is to be regarded as an intensification of the normal, periodically recurring, state of dreaming' (p. 228).

Krauss [39] has sought to establish a relationship between dream and madness, more intimate perhaps than the analogy between the two overt phenomena will really admit, by grounding it in their aetiology (or rather in their sources of excitation). In his view the basic element common to both is, as we have heard, the organically caused sensation, the somatic sensation, the general vital feeling to which all the organs together contribute (see Peisse, in Maury [48], p. 52).

The undeniable correspondence between dreams and mental disturbance, which extends even to characteristic individual details, offers one of the strongest supports to the medical theory of the dream-life, according to which the dream presents itself as a useless and disturbing process and as the expression of a reduced psychical activity. We cannot, however, expect to arrive at a definitive explanation of dreams by reference to psychical disturbance so long as our insight into the course of these latter disorders is still, as we well know, in such an unsatisfactory state. On the other hand, it seems probable that a revised conception of the dream is bound to influence our view of the inner mechanism of mental disturbance; and so we may say that we are also working towards an explanation of the psychoses when we seek to cast light on the mystery of the dream.

THE METHOD OF INTERPRETING DREAMS

Analysis of a Specimen Dream

The title I have given my treatise makes it clear which tradition I would like to take up in the way dreams are understood. I propose to show that dreams are capable of yielding an interpretation; and any contribution this may make towards elucidating those problems of dreams we have just been discussing, will in my eyes turn out to be merely a by-product gained in the course of carrying out my own task. This assumption that dreams are interpretable brings me at once into opposition to the prevailing theory of dreams, indeed to every dream-theory except Scherner's, for 'to interpret a dream' means to determine its 'meaning', to substitute for it something that fits into the chain of our psychical acts as a full and equally valid member. However, as we have learned, the scientific theories of the dream have no room for a problem of dream-interpretation, for to them the dream is not a psychical act at all but a somatic process which makes its occurrence known by indications in the psychical apparatus. Popular opinion has at all times thought differently. It exercises its right to inconsistency, on the one hand admitting that dreams are incomprehensible and absurd, but on the other unable to bring itself to deny them all significance. A dim presentiment seems to lead it to assume that the dream does possess a meaning, though a hidden one, that it stands as a substitute for another mode of thinking, and that it is only a matter of finding the right way to reveal this substitute for the hidden significance of the dream to be disclosed.

So it is that popular opinion has always endeavoured to 'interpret' dreams, and in doing so has tried two essentially different methods. The first procedure takes the dream-content as a whole and seeks to replace it with a different, intelligible, and in certain respects analogous content. This is *symbolic* dream-interpretation: it comes to grief from the start, of course, with those dreams which appear not only incomprehensible but also confused. An example of this procedure might be the interpretation Joseph provides for Pharaoh's dream in the Bible. Seven fat kine followed by seven lean kine which consume them—that is a symbolic substitute for the prophecy of seven years of famine in the land of Egypt which will consume all the surplus created by seven years of plenty. Most of the artificial dreams invented by the poets are intended for this kind of symbolic interpretation, for they render the author's thoughts in a disguise found to match those characteristics of our dreaming familiar to us from experience. The view that dreams are mainly concerned with the future, having a premonition of what form it will take—a remnant of the prophetic significance once accorded to dreams—then becomes the motive for transposing the meaning of the dream discovered by symbolic interpretation into the future tense by means of an 'it will'.

There are of course no instructions for discovering the route to such symbolic interpretation. Success remains a matter of inspiration, of sudden intuition, and that is how the interpretation of dreams by means of symbolism was able to raise itself to the practice of an art which seemed to be bound up with an especial gift.[1] The other popular method of dream-interpretation is very far from making any such claim. It might be called the 'decoding method', as it treats the dream as a kind of secret writing in which every sign is translated by means of a fixed key into another sign whose significance is known. I have had a dream of a letter, for example, but also of a funeral or the like; I now consult a 'dream-book' and discover that 'letter' is to be translated as 'ill humour', 'funeral' as 'betrothal'. It is then up to me to make some connection between the catchwords I have deciphered, which I then accept as lying in the future. An interesting variant of this decoding procedure, which to some extent corrects its character as a purely mechanical transposition, appears in the treatise on dream-interpretation by Artemidorus* of Daldis [2]. Here not only the content of the dream but also the personality and the circumstances of the dreamer are taken into account so that the same element in the dream has a different meaning for the rich man, the married man, or the orator from the meaning it has for the poor man, the unmarried man, or, say, a merchant. The essential thing about this procedure is that the work of interpretation is not

---

[1] After I had completed my manuscript, I had access to a work by Stumpf [65], which is in agreement with my own in its aim to prove that dreams have a meaning and can be interpreted. But he interprets according to an allegorizing symbolism without any guarantee that the procedure is universally valid.

directed towards the dream as a whole, but at each piece of the dream-content by itself, as if the dream were a conglomerate in which each little fragment of rock required a separate definition. It is certainly the incoherent and confused dreams that provided the first impetus to the creation of the decoding method.

There is not a moment's doubt that neither of the popular methods of dream-interpretation is of any use in the scientific treatment of the subject. The symbolic method is limited in its application and incapable of being stated in general terms. As for the decoding method, everything would depend on whether the 'key', the dream-book, is reliable. And of that there is no guarantee whatever. We might be tempted to agree with the philosopher and the psychiatrist, and join them in dismissing the problem of the interpretation of dreams as a chimaera.

But I have come to learn better. I have had to realize that here is another of those not infrequent cases where an ancient, stubbornly held popular belief seems to have come closer to the truth of things than the judgement of contemporary science. I have to maintain that dreams really do possess a meaning, and that a scientific method of dream-interpretation is possible. I came to my knowledge of this method in the following way.

For many years I have been occupied with unravelling certain psychopathological structures, hysterical phobias, obsessional ideas, and the like, for therapeutic purposes—in fact ever since I learned from an important contribution by Josef Breuer that for these formations, experienced as symptoms of illness, the unravelling and the cure, solution, and resolution, amount to the same thing.[2] If one has been able to trace a pathological idea of this sort back to the elements in the patient's inner life which produced it, then it will disintegrate and the patient will be freed from it. Given the inadequacy of our other attempts at therapy, and considering the puzzling nature of these conditions, I was tempted, despite all the difficulties, to go further along the path pioneered by Breuer all the way to a complete solution. How this technique has ultimately developed, and what the results of this endeavour have been, are things I shall have to report on in detail another time. In the course of these psychoanalytical studies I came upon the interpretation of dreams. Patients who had

[2] Breuer and Freud, *Studien über Hysterie* [*Studies on Hysteria*], Vienna, 1895.

undertaken to inform me of all the thoughts and ideas that beset them on a certain subject told me their dreams, and in this way taught me that a dream can be interpolated into the psychical chain which, starting from a pathological idea, can be traced backwards in the memory. This suggested that the dream itself might be treated as a symptom, and that the method of interpretation developed for symptoms might be applied to dreams.

Now, for this the patient's psyche requires a certain preparation. I want him to do two things: to pay attention to his psychical perceptions more intently, and to switch off the critical faculty he normally uses to sift the thoughts arising in him. In order to give all his attention to self-observation, it is helpful for him to lie down and close his eyes; he must be expressly bidden to abstain from any critical judgement of the thoughts he forms and becomes aware of. He is told, that is, that the success of the psychoanalysis depends on his paying attention to everything that passes through his mind, reporting it, and on not allowing himself to be tempted, for instance, to suppress one idea occurring to him because it appears to him unimportant or irrelevant to the subject, another because it appears nonsensical. He has to be wholly impartial towards the ideas that come to him; for it was just this critical judgement that was to blame for any earlier failures to find the solution to the dream, the obsessional idea, or whatever.

In the course of my psychoanalytical work I have noticed that the psyche of a man engaged in reflection is in a very different frame of mind from that of someone who is observing his own psychical processes. In reflection, one psychical activity comes into play more than in even the most attentive self-observation, as the tense expression and creased brow of a man occupied in reflection shows, by contrast to the expression of repose in someone engaged in self-observation. In both cases a concentration of attention must be taking place. But the man who is reflecting is exercising a critical activity as well. Consequently, once he has become aware of the ideas arising within him, he rejects some and cuts others off short so that he does not pursue the paths of thought they might open up for him. Towards still other thoughts he acts in such a way that they never become conscious at all, that is, they are suppressed before they are perceived. On the other hand, the only trouble the self-observer has to take is to suppress this critical activity. If he is successful, a tremendous number of thoughts which he would otherwise have been unable to grasp enter his consciousness. It is with the aid of this new-found material for his self-awareness, that the interpretation of both pathological ideas and dream-formations can be carried out. As we see, it is a matter of producing in the psyche a condition sharing a certain similarity in distribution of psychical energy (mobile attention) with the condition present just before falling asleep (and certainly with the hypnotic state too). As we fall asleep, the 'involuntary ideas' emerge on account of the reduction of a certain willed (and certainly also critical) operation which we allow to affect the course of our ideas; the cause of this reduction we usually call 'tiredness'; the involuntary ideas emerging are transformed into visual and acoustic images. (Compare the remarks of Schleiermacher [61] and others, p. 60.) In the condition we employ for the analysis of dreams and pathological ideas we deliberately and voluntarily abstain from that critical activity and use the psychical energy saved (or part of it) for the attentive pursuit of the involuntary thoughts now emerging, which retain their character as ideas (this being the distinction between this condition and the one that attends falling asleep). *We thus turn the 'involuntary' ideas into 'voluntary' ones.*

In general it is not difficult to transport oneself or someone else into the required state of uncritical self-observation. Most of my patients manage it after their first instruction. I myself can achieve it very completely by the help of writing down the thoughts that occur to me. This reduces the critical activity by a certain amount of psychical energy, which can then be used to heighten the intensity of the self-observation. It varies considerably, however, according to the subject which is to be the focus of attention.

Now, the first step in employing this procedure teaches us that the object of attention has to be not the dream as a whole, but only the separate parts of its content. If I ask an unpractised patient: 'What does this dream make you think of?', as a rule there is nothing within his mental horizon he can call to mind. I have to present him with his dream bit by bit, and then for each bit he will provide me with a series of ideas occurring to him which can be called the 'ulterior motives' of this part of the dream. With this first important condition, then, the method of dream-interpretation I practise already departs from the popular method of interpretation by symbols, famous in history and legend, and it approaches the other method, the 'decoding method'. Like this, it is an interpretation *en detail*, not *en masse*; like this, it conceives the dream from the first as something put together, as a conglomorate of psychical formations.

In the course of my psychoanalyses of neurotics I have probably interpreted more than a thousand dreams at least, but I would rather not use this material here as an introduction to the technique and theory of dream-interpretation. Quite apart from the fact that I would expose myself to the objection that these are, after all, the dreams of neuropaths which do not allow any conclusions to be drawn about the dreams of those of sound mind, there is another reason why I am compelled to reject them. The subject-matter these dreams are aiming for, of course, is always the clinical history lying at the root of the neurosis. This would require an over-lengthy pre-amble for each dream, going deep into the nature and aetiological conditions of the psychoneuroses. These are things which are in themselves novel and highly disturbing, and so they would distract attention from the problem of dreams. My intention is rather to make the unravelling of the dream a preliminary to elucidating the more difficult problems of the psychology of neuroses. But if I dis-pense with the dreams of neurotics, my main material, I cannot be too nice in my dealings with the remainder. All that is left are the dreams which have occasionally been told me by persons of sound mind from among my acquaintance, or which I have found described as examples in the literature on the dream-life. Unfortunately I have no analysis for any of these dreams, and lacking this, I am unable to discover their meaning. For my procedure is not so easy to practise as the popular decoding method, which translates the given dream-content according to a fixed key; rather, I expect to find that with different people and in different contexts the identical dream-content might well conceal a quite different meaning. So I have to rely on my own dreams, resorting to them as an abundant and con-venient fund of material coming from a more-or-less normal person and relating to a variety of occasions in daily life. The reliability of such 'self-analyses' will certainly be called into question. There is a risk of arbitrary conclusions, it will be said. Rather, in my judge-ment, the conditions for self-observation are more favourable than the conditions for the observation of others. At any rate, we can try to see how far self-analysis will take us in the interpretation of dreams. There are other difficulties which I will have to overcome within myself. There is an understandable diffidence about exposing so many intimate things in one's psychic life, knowing too that others might well misinterpret them. But this is something one has to be able to go beyond. 'Tout psychologiste', says Delboeuf [16], 'est obligé de faire l'aveu même de ses faiblesses s'il croît par là jeter du jour sur quelque problème obscure.'* And I trust I may assume that in the reader, too, an initial interest in the indiscretions I shall have to commit will very soon give way to an absorption solely in the psychological problems they serve to illuminate.

I shall therefore take one of my own dreams and use it to explain my method of interpretation. Every dream of this sort requires a preliminary statement. But now I must ask the reader to make my interests his own for some little time, and immerse himself with me in the minutest details of my life, for our interest in the hidden significance of dreams absolutely demands a transference of this kind.

Preamble: In the summer of 1895 I had been giving psychoanalytic treatment to a young lady who was a very close friend of my family and myself. It will be understood that mixed relationships of this kind can become the source of various perturbations for the physician, especially for the psychotherapist. The physician's personal interest is greater, his authority less. A failure is a threat to his friendship with his patient's relatives. The course terminated in partial success: the patient lost her hysterical anxiety but not all her somatic symptoms. At the time I was not yet quite certain of the criteria which would indicate that a hysterical illness had been definitively cured, and I suggested to my patient a solution which seemed to be unacceptable to her. It was in this state of disagreement that, on account of the summer holidays, we broke off the treatment.—One day I was visited by a younger colleague, one of my closest friends, who had also visited my patient—Irma*—and her family where they were staying in the country. I asked him how he had found her, and received the answer: She is better, but not entirely recovered. I know I was annoyed by these words of my friend Otto,* or by the tone in which they were spoken. I thought I heard a criticism in them, perhaps that I had promised my patient too much, and—rightly or wrongly—I attributed Otto's apparent opposition to me to the influence of her relatives, who, so I assumed, had never really approved of my treating her. In any case, the unpleasant feeling I had was unclear to me, nor did I give expression to it. That same evening I wrote out Irma's clinical history, in order to give it to Dr M.,* a friend we had in common and the dominant personality in our circle at that time, as though to justify myself. During the night after this evening (or more probably in the early morning) I had the following dream, which I set down immediately after waking.

Dream of 23–24 July 1895

A large hall—many guests, whom we are receiving.—Among them Irma, whom I take aside at once, as it were to answer her letter and reproach her for not having yet accepted the 'solution'. I say to her: If you are still having pain it is really only your own fault.—She replies: If only you knew what pain my throat and stomach and abdomen are giving me. I feel I am choking.—I am startled and look at her. She looks pale and puffy; I think perhaps I have overlooked something organic after all. I take her to the window and examine her throat. At this she shows some reluctance, like women who wear dentures. I think to myself: but she has no need to. Her mouth then opens wide and I discover to the right a big white patch, and elsewhere I see large, greyish-white scabs set on remarkable curled structures clearly modelled on the nostrils.—I quickly call Dr M.* over, who repeats the examination and confirms it . . . Dr M. looks quite different from usual; he is very pale, walks with a limp, and his chin has no beard . . . My friend Otto is now also standing beside her, and my friend Leopold* is percussing her through her bodice, saying: She has an attenuation low to the left, also pointing out an infiltrated part of the skin on the left shoulder (which like him I felt, in spite of her dress) . . . M. says: No doubt about it, it is an infection, but it doesn't matter; dysentery will set in and the poison will be eliminated . . . We also know directly where the infection originated. Not long before, when she felt unwell, my friend Otto gave her an injection of a propyl preparation, propylene . . . propionic acid . . . trimethylamine (I see its formula before me printed in bold type) . . . Such injections are not to be given so lightly . . . Probably the syringe was not clean, either.

This dream has one advantage over many others. It is immediately clear which events of the previous day it is connected to and what subject it deals with. The preamble supplies the details. The news from Otto about Irma's condition and the clinical history I had written far into the night were still engaging the activity of my psyche, even in sleep. All the same, no one knowing the preamble and the content of the dream could have any idea of what the dream means. I myself do not know. I am surprised at the symptoms Irma complains of to me in the dream, for they are not the same as those I have been treating her for. I smile at the nonsensical idea of giving an injection of propionic acid, and at the consolation Dr M. offers. Towards its conclusion the dream seems to me more obscure and condensed than it is at the start. To discover the meaning of all this I have to resolve on a detailed analysis.

Analysis

The hall—many guests, whom we are receiving. That summer we were living at Bellevue, a house standing by itself on one of the hills adjoining the Kahlenberg. The house was once intended to be a dance-hall, hence the unusually lofty, hall-like rooms. I had the dream at Bellevue a few days before the celebration of my wife's birthday. During the day my wife had said that she expected that several friends, including Irma, would becoming to us as guests on her birthday. So my dream anticipates this occasion: it is my wife's birthday and many people, Irma among them, are being received by us in the large hall at Bellevue.

I reproach Irma for not having accepted the solution I had suggested; I say: If you are still having pain, it is really only your own fault. I could also have said this to her in waking life, or I did in fact say it to her. I was then of the opinion (which I later recognized to be incorrect) that my task did not go beyond informing my patients of the hidden meaning of their symptoms; whether or not they accepted this solution, on which the success of the treatment depended, was no longer my responsibility. I am grateful to this error, now happily overcome, for having lightened my existence at a time when, with all my unavoidable ignorance, I was supposed to be producing successful cures.—But I note from the sentence I speak to Irma in my dream that above all I am refusing to be blamed for all the pain she still has. If it is Irma's own fault it cannot be mine. Is the intention of the dream to be sought for in this direction?

Irma's complaining; pains in her throat, abdomen, and stomach, a feeling of choking. Stomach pains were among my patient's symptoms, although they were not very prominent: she complained rather of sickness and nausea. Pains in the throat and abdomen, choking sensations, scarcely featured. I wonder why I decided on this choice of symptoms in my dream, but for the moment cannot find an answer.

She looks pale and puffy. My patient was always rosy-cheeked. I suspect that here another person is being foisted on her.

I am startled to think I have overlooked an organic illness after all. This is, as one may well believe, a perpetual anxiety on the part of a specialist who sees almost no one but neurotics and is used to ascribing to hysteria so many phenomena other physicians treat as organic. On the other hand, a faint doubt steals over me—I do not know where it comes from—as to whether my alarm is entirely genuine. If Irma's pains are organic in origin, again I am not responsible for curing them, for after all, my course of treatment removes only hysterical pains. So it actually seems to me as if I wanted my diagnosis to be faulty: for then the reproach of failure would also be removed.

I take her to the window to examine her throat. She shows some reluctance, like women who wear false teeth. I think to myself: but she has no need to. I never had occasion to inspect Irma's mouth. The event in my dream reminds me of an examination some time previously of a governess who had at first given the impression of youthful beauty, but on opening her mouth took some measures to hide her denture. This instance recalls other medical examinations and the other little secrets they reveal—to the pleasure of neither party.—'But she has no need to' is in the first place, no doubt, a compliment to Irma: but I also suspect a another meaning as well. In carrying out an analysis attentively one gets a feeling whether the ulterior motives expected are exhausted or not. The way Irma is standing at the window suddenly reminds me of another experience. Irma has a close woman friend I regard very highly. When I visited her one evening I discovered her at the window in the situation reproduced in the dream, and her physician, the same Dr M., was explaining that she had a diphtheritic membrane. In fact, the person of Dr M. and the membrane recur in the continuation of the dream. It occurs to me now that in recent months I have had every reason to suppose that this other lady was also a hysteric. Indeed, Irma herself betrayed this to me. But what did I know about her condition? Only this very thing, that like my Irma in the dream she suffers from hysterical choking. So in the dream I have replaced my patient by her friend. Now I recall I have often played with the thought that, like Irma, this lady too might make a claim on me to free her from her symptoms. But I thought it was very unlikely myself, for she has a very reserved nature. She *shows reluctance*, as the dream indicates. Another explanation might be *that she has no need to*: in fact she has so far shown herself strong enough to control her condition without the help of others. Then there are a number of other traits which I could attach to neither Irma nor her friend: pale, puffy, false teeth. The false teeth led me to that governess; I feel inclined to settle for bad teeth. Then another person occurs to me to whom these traits could allude. She too is not my patient, and I would not like to have her as one, as I have observed that she is shy in my presence, and I do not think she would make a compliant invalid. She is usually pale, and on one occasion when she had had a good time she was puffy.[3] So I have been comparing my patient Irma with two other people who would be equally reluctant to submit to treatment. What can be the sense in my having exchanged her in my dream for her friend? Perhaps it is that I would like to exchange her: either the other woman rouses stronger feelings of sympathy in me or I have a higher opinion of her intelligence. For I regard Irma as foolish because she does not accept my solution. The other would be wiser and so would give way the sooner. *Her mouth then opens wide*: she would tell me more than Irma.[4]

What I see in the throat: a white patch and nostrils with scabs. The white patch reminds me of diphtheritis and thus of Irma's friend, but it also reminds me of the serious illness my eldest daughter suffered from nearly two years before and of all the fear we went through in that terrible time. The scabs on the nostrils bring to mind a problem I once had with my own health. At that time I frequently used cocaine to suppress bothersome swellings in my nose and a few days ago I had heard that a woman patient who did the same had contracted an extensive necrosis of the nasal mucous membrane. My recommendation of cocaine, which I made in 1885,* also brought

---

[3] Irma's unexplained complaints in the dream of abdominal pains can also be traced back to this third person. I am referring, of course, to my wife; the abdominal pains remind me of one of the occasions when I noticed her shyness. I have to confess that in my dream I do not treat Irma or my wife very kindly. But in excuse be it noted that I am measuring them both against the ideal of the good, compliant patient.

[4] I have the feeling that the interpretation of this part is not taken far enough to follow all its hidden meaning. If I were to pursue the comparison of the three women, I would digress too far. Every dream has at least one place where it is unfathomable, the navel, as it were, by which it is connected to the unknown.

severe criticism upon me. A dear friend, who was already dead in 1895, had hastened his death by misuse of this remedy.

I quickly call Dr M. over, who repeats the examination. This would simply correspond to the position M. held among us. But the 'quickly' is sufficiently striking to require a special explanation. It reminds me of an unhappy experience I had as a doctor. I had once produced a severe toxic state in a woman patient by the repeated prescription of a remedy which was then still considered harmless (sulphonal), and rushed to my experienced elder colleague for assistance. That this really is the case I have in mind is substantiated by another detail: the patient who succumbed to the poisoning had the same name as my eldest daughter. Until now I had never thought of the fact: now it seems to me almost like the retribution of fate. As though the substitution of persons were continued here in a different sense; this Mathilde for that Mathilde; an eye for an eye and a tooth for a tooth. It is as though I were seeking out every occasion which could be turned into grounds for accusing myself of a lack of medical conscientiousness.

Dr M. is pale, with a clean-shaven chin, and a limp. Of this so much is true, that his friends are often concerned at how unwell he looks. The other two characteristics must belong to another person. My elder brother occurs to me; he lives abroad, is clean-shaven, and, if I recall correctly, on the whole bore a resemblance to the M. of the dream. A few days previously news came of him that on account of an arthritic affliction in his hip he has a limp. There must be a reason for me to merge the two into one in my dream. I actually remember that I was out of humour with both of them, and for a similar reason. Both had rejected a certain suggestion I had recently made to them.

My friend Otto is now standing beside the patient and my friend Leopold is examining her and indicating an attenuation low to the left. My friend Leopold is also a physician, a relative of Otto's. As they both practise the same specialization fate has made of them rivals who are constantly being compared with one another. They both assisted me for years when I ran a surgery for children with nervous disorders. Scenes such as the one reproduced in the dream often took place there. While I was debating the diagnosis of a case with Otto, Leopold had made a fresh examination of the child and produced an unexpected contribution to our decision. There existed between them a difference of character similar to that between

Inspector Bräsig and his friend Karl.* The one was distinguished by his 'quick thinking', the other was slow, deliberate, but thorough. When I contrast Otto with the cautious Leopold in my dream, I am clearly doing so in order to praise Leopold. It is an act of comparison similar to the one between Irma the disobedient patient and her—in my view—wiser friend. I notice now another track on which the thought-connections of the dream are moving: from the sick child to the children's clinic. From the attenuation low to the left I get the impression that it corresponds to the details of a particular case where Leopold struck me by his thoroughness. In addition, I have vaguely in mind something like a metastatic affection, but it might also relate to the patient I would like to have in place of Irma. For, as far as I can judge, this lady imitates a tubercular condition.

An infiltrated part of the skin on the left shoulder. I know straight away that this is my own rheumatic shoulder, which I regularly feel if I have stayed awake deep into the night. The wording of the dream, too, sounds ambiguous: 'which like him I *feel* . . .' 'To feel in oneself' is a common expression. It occurs to me, incidentally, how curious the description 'an infiltrated part of the skin' sounds. 'Infiltration in the upper left back' is a more familiar phrase: it would refer to the lung, and so again to tuberculosis.

In spite of her dress. This is certainly no more than a parenthesis. When we examined children at the children's clinic they were naturally undressed; it is one of the contrasts to the way we have to examine adult female patients. It used to be said of an excellent clinician that he only ever conducted a physical examination of his patients through their clothes. The rest is in the dark to me, and, to speak frankly, I have no inclination to probe any deeper.

Dr M. says: It is an infection, but it doesn't matter. Dysentery will set in and the poison be eliminated. At first this seems ludicrous to me, but like everything else it still has to be carefully taken apart. Considered more closely, a kind of meaning does appear. What I discovered in the patient was a localized diphtheritis. From the time my daughter was ill I recall a discussion of diphtheritis and diphtheria: the latter is the general infection which starts with the localized diphtheritis. Leopold has indicated from the attenuation a general infection of this kind, which leads one to think of metastatic foci. I believe, it is true, that metastases of this kind do not occur in diphtheria. They remind me, rather, of pyaemia.

It doesn't matter is a consolation. I believe it fits in as follows. The last part of the dream has for its content the idea that the patient's pains derive from a serious organic infection. I sense that all I want with this too is to shift the blame from myself. The psychological treatment cannot be held responsible for the persistence of a diphtheritic condition. But I still feel troubled at having invented for Irma a serious illness wholly and solely to exonerate myself. It seems so cruel. So I need some assurance that all will be well, and it does not seem to me to be a bad choice to put this consolation into the mouth of Dr M. himself. But in this I am putting myself in a superior position to the dream, which itself requires explaining.

But why is this consolation so nonsensical?

Dysentery: some remote theoretical idea that diseased matter can be removed through the bowels. Am I trying to make fun of Dr M.'s wealth of far-fetched explanations and unusual pathological linkages? With regard to dysentery something else comes to mind. A few months before I had taken on a young man who had very remarkable difficulties with defecating, and whom other colleagues of mine had treated as a case of 'anaemia with under-nourishment'. I recognized that it was a case of hysteria, wanted to try my psychotherapy out on him, and sent him on a sea voyage. Now, a few days previously I received a desperate letter from him in Egypt telling me he had had a new attack there, which the doctor declared was dysentery. True, I suspect that the diagnosis is only an error on the part of an ignorant colleague who is letting himself be deceived by the hysteria, yet I could not spare myself the reproach of putting my patient into a situation in which to his hysterical bowel affection he may have added one that was organic. Furthermore, dysentery was reminiscent in sound to diphtheria,* a name under taboo which was not mentioned in the dream.

Yes, it must be that with the consoling prognosis 'Dysentery will set in, etc.' I am making fun of Dr M., for I remember that he once told me, laughing, something quite similar of another colleague years before. He had been called by this colleague to a consultation over a seriously sick patient, and felt induced to reproach his colleague, who had seemed very hopeful, with the fact that he had found albumen in the patient's urine. But the colleague refused to be disconcerted, and calmly replied: '*It doesn't matter*, my dear colleague, the albumen will be eliminated, you'll see!'—So I am no longer in any doubt that this part of the dream contains mockery at the expense of those of my colleagues ignorant of hysteria. As though to confirm this, the thought now passes through my mind: Does Dr M. know that the symptoms shown by his patient, Irma's friend, which are giving rise to fears of tuberculosis, also derive from hysteria? Has he recognized this hysteria, or has he been 'taken in' by it?

But what motive can I have for treating my friend so badly? It is very simple: Dr M. disagrees with my 'solution' for Irma every bit as much as Irma herself does. So in this way I have already taken revenge on two people in this dream: on Irma with the words: 'If you are still having pain it is really only your own fault', and on Dr M. with the wording of the nonsensical consolation I have put in his mouth.

We know immediately where the infection originated. This immediate knowledge in the dream is very curious. Just previously we did not know, as the infection was only pointed out by Leopold.

When she felt unwell, my friend Otto gave her an injection. Otto had actually told me that during the short time he had stayed with Irma's family he was called to a nearby hotel to give an injection to someone who suddenly felt unwell. The injections again remind me of my unhappy friend who poisoned himself with cocaine. I had advised him to take the drug only orally during withdrawal of morphia, but he started injecting it immediately.

Of a propyl preparation . . . propylene . . . proprionic acid. How on earth do I get on to these? On the evening when I had later worked on the clinical history, and then had the dream, my wife opened a bottle of liqueur on which the word 'Ananas' [pineapple][5] could be read. It was a gift from our friend Otto. For he has the habit of giving presents on every possible occasion. I hope one day he will have a wife who will cure him of this. This liqueur gave out such an odour of cheap alcohol, of fusel oil in fact, that I refused to taste it. My wife said: 'We'll give this bottle to the servants', but even more prudently I forbade it with the philanthropic remark that the servants ought not to be poisoned either. The odour of alcohol (Amyl . . .) clearly stirred in me the recollection of the entire series: propylene, methyl, etc. . . . which supplied the dream with the propyl preparation. True, I made a substitution. I dreamed 'propyl' after having smelled

---

[5] 'Ananas', by the way, contains a curious echo of my patient Irma's family name.

'amyl': but such substitutions are perhaps permissible in organic chemistry more than anywhere else.

Trimethylamine. In my dream I see the chemical formula for this substance, which at any rate witnesses to a considerable effort of memory; actually, I see it printed in bold type, as though I wanted something of quite special importance to stand out strongly from its context. But with my attention thus drawn to it, what is trimethyl-amine leading me to? To a conversation with another friend* who has followed the development of my work for years, as I have his. On that occasion he had told me about certain ideas of his concerning a chemistry of sexuality, and mentioned among other things that he believed he recognized trimethylamine to be one of the products of sexual metabolism. So this substance leads me to sexuality, that fac-tor to which I attribute the greatest significance in the origin of the nervous afflictions I want to cure. My patient Irma is a young widow; if my concern is to find an excuse for the failure of the treatment I gave her, my best course will surely be to appeal to this state of affairs, which her friends would be very glad to alter. How strangely, by the way, a dream like this is put together! The other woman, who is my patient in the dream instead of Irma, is also a young widow.

I sense why the formula for trimethylamine has taken up so much of the dream. So many important things come together in this one word: trimethylamine is an allusion not only to the overwhelming factor of sexuality but also to a person whose approval, at a time when I felt myself alone and deserted, I remember with gratification. Was it likely that this friend, who played so great a role in my life, might not make any further appearance in this dream's chain of ideas? He does so, of course: he is an expert in the effects that proceed from the affections of the nose and the cavities adjacent to it, and has revealed to science some very remarkable connections between the nostrils and the female sexual organs. (The three curled structures in Irma's throat.) I had Irma examined by him to see whether her stomach pains might have a nasal origin. He himself, however, suffers from nasal abscesses which cause me concern, and the pyaema called to mind by the metastases in the dream probably alludes to these.

Such injections are not to be given so lightly. Here the charge of rashness is flung directly at my friend Otto. I believe I thought something of the kind on the afternoon when, by word and glance, he seemed to be opposing me. It was something like: how easily he can be influenced; how quickly he comes to a decision.—Also, the sentence quoted above again points to my dead friend, who had so rashly decided to inject himself with cocaine. As I said, I had in no way intended the drug to be injected. With my criticism of Otto for treating those chemical substances lightly, I note that again I am touching on the story of that unfortunate Mathilde which provoked the same accusation against me. It is clear that I am collecting examples of my conscientiousness here, but also of its opposite.

Probably the syringe was not clean, either. Another criticism of Otto, but one with its origin elsewhere. Yesterday I happened to meet the son of a lady of eighty-two to whom I have to administer two injections of morphia daily. She is at present staying in the country, and I learned that she is suffering from phlebitis. I thought at once that there must have been an infiltration caused by a contaminated syringe. It is my pride that over a period of two years I have not introduced a single infiltration; I take constant care, to be sure, to see that the syringe is clean. I am, simply, conscientious. From phlebitis I come back to my wife, who suffered from a blockage of the veins during a pregnancy. And now three similar situations surface in my memory—involving my wife, Irma, and the dead Mathilde—the identity of these situations has clearly given me the right to substitute these three people for one another in my dream.

I have now completed the interpretation of the dream. During this work I had trouble in keeping at bay all the many ideas which were bound to be set going by the comparison between the dream-content and the dream-thoughts concealed behind it. In the course of the work, the 'meaning' of the dream also became clear to me. I noticed an intention which was realized by the dream and which must have been the motive for dreaming. The dream fulfilled a number of wishes which had been aroused in me by the events of the previous evening (Otto's news, writing down the clinical history). For the outcome of the dream is that I am not to blame for the pain Irma continues to suffer, and that Otto is to blame for it. Otto annoyed me by his comments on Irma's incomplete recovery, and the dream takes revenge on him for me as it turns the criticism back onto him. The dream exonerates me of responsibility for Irma's condition in tracing it back to other factors (a whole series of reasons). The dream represents a certain state of affairs as being as I would wish it to be: *its content is thus a wish-fulfilment, its motive a wish*.

So much leaps to the eye. But many of the details of the dream, too, become comprehensible to me when seen in terms of wish-fulfilment. I take my revenge on Otto not only for his having rashly opposed me by ascribing to him an equally rash medical treatment (the injection), but also for having given me a bad liqueur which smelled of fusel oil. And I find an expression in my dream which unites both charges: the injection with a propyl preparation. Even then I am not satisfied, but carry on my revenge by contrasting him with his more reliable rival. In doing so I seem to be saying: I prefer him to you. But Otto is not the only one who has to feel the weight of my wrath. I also revenge myself on my disobedient patient by exchanging her for a wiser, more compliant one. Nor do I quietly accept Dr M.'s disagreement with me, but clearly insinuate to him that in my view he is incompetent to judge the matter in hand ('Dysentery will set in, etc.'). Indeed, it seems to me that I am appealing over his head to someone else of greater competence (the friend who told me of the trimethylamine), just as I turned away from Irma to her friend, and from Otto to Leopold. Get rid of these people, replace them with three others of my own choice, then I shall be free of the accusations which I don't believe I have deserved! How baseless these accusations are is demonstrated to me in the dream in the most detailed fashion. Irma's painful condition cannot be charged to me, for she herself is to blame for it in rejecting the solution I had offered. Irma's illness has nothing to do with me, for it is organic in nature and in no way curable by a course of psychical treatment. Irma's illness can be satisfactorily explained by her widowhood (trimethylamine!), which of course I can do nothing to alter. Irma's illness has been caused by an incautious injection on Otto's part with an inappropriate substance, a thing I would never have done. Irma's illness comes from an injection with a dirty syringe, like the phlebitis contracted by my elderly patient, whereas nothing of the kind occurs when I give injections. I note, to be sure, that these explanations of Irma's illness, which unite to relieve me of blame, are not consistent with one another, but on the contrary are mutually exclusive. The entire plea—for the dream is nothing but just that—vividly recalls the defence offered by the man accused by his neighbour of returning a kettle to him in a damaged condition: in the first place the kettle wasn't damaged at all, in the second it already had a hole in it when he borrowed it, and in the third he had never borrowed a kettle from his neighbour. But so much the better: if only one of these three defences is acknowledged to hold good, the man has to be acquitted.

Other subjects are woven into the dream whose relevance to exonerating me from responsibility for Irma's illness is not so transparent. My daughter's illness and that of my patient with the same name, the harmful effect of cocaine, the illness that affected my patient on his travels in Egypt, concern for the health of my wife, my brother, Dr M., my own bodily ailments, concern for my absent friend who suffered from nasal abscesses. Yet when I take a good look at it, all these things are linked together to form a single sphere of ideas, perhaps with the label: concern for health, my own and others', the physician's conscientiousness. I recall having a vaguely disagreeable feeling when Otto brought me the news of Irma's condition. From the sphere of ideas which played a part in my dream I think I can find words retrospectively to describe this momentary feeling. It is as if he had told me: 'You don't take your duties as a physician seriously enough, you aren't conscientious, you don't perform what you promise.' As a consequence, that sphere of ideas would have placed itself at my disposal so that I could demonstrate how very conscientious I am, how much I have at heart the health of my relations, friends, and patients. Remarkably enough, this ideational material also includes painful recollections calculated rather to support the accusation ascribed to my friend Otto than to vindicate me. The material does not take sides, as it were, but there is still an unmistakable connection between the broader raw material on which the dream was based and the narrower subject of the dream, out of which my wish to be innocent of blame for Irma's illness emerged.

I do not claim that I have uncovered all the meaning of this dream or that its interpretation is without any gaps.

I could linger much longer over this dream, extract from it further elucidations and discuss fresh puzzles which it has thrown up. I myself know the passages from which fresh connections among the thoughts can be pursued; but considerations of the sort that apply to all dreams of one's own deter me from this work of interpretation. Anyone who is prepared to censure me for this reserve is welcome to try being franker than I have been. For the moment I shall content myself with this one newly gained insight: if we follow the method of dream-interpretation indicated here, we discover that dreams really do have a meaning and are in no sense an expression of brain-activity in a state of fragmentation, as the authorities on the subject would have it. *After the work of interpretation has been completed the dream reveals itself as a wish-fulfilment.*

III

THE DREAM IS A WISH-FULFILMENT

After passing through a narrow defile and suddenly arriving at the top of a rise where the paths divide and the most fertile prospect opens out in all directions, one may pause for a moment and consider where to make for next. A similar situation confronts us now that we have got through this first dream-interpretation. We are standing in the clear light of a sudden insight. The dream cannot be compared to the random resonation of a musical instrument struck not by the hand of a player but by the impact of an external force; it is not meaningless, not absurd, it does not assume that one part of our store of ideas slumbers while another begins to wake. It is a fully valid psychical phenomenon, in fact a wish-fulfilment; it is to be included in the series of intelligible psychical acts of our waking life; it has been constructed by a highly elaborate intellectual activity. But just as we are about to rejoice in this knowledge, we are assailed by a host of questions. If, as the dream-interpretation would have it, the dream represents a fulfilled wish, what is the source of the striking and disconcerting form in which this wish-fulfilment is expressed? What change has taken place in the dream-thoughts for them to assume the shape of the manifest dream as we recall it on waking? In what way has this change come about? Where does the material come from that has been fashioned into the dream? What is the origin of the peculiarities we noticed in the dream-thoughts, for example, that they might quite acceptably contradict one another? (The comparison with the kettle, p. 95.) Can the dream teach us anything new about our inner psychical processes, can its content rectify opinions we have held during the day? I propose to leave all these questions aside for the present and to pursue one particular path. We have learned that the dream represents a wish as fulfilled. Our next concern must be to find out whether this is a general characteristic of dreams or only the chance content of the dream our analysis began with ('the dream of Irma's injection'): for even if we prepare ourselves to expect that every dream has a meaning and psychical value, we still have to leave the possibility open that this meaning may not be the same in every dream. Our first dream was a wish-fulfilment; another may perhaps turn out to be the fulfilment of a fear; a third may have a reflection for its content, a fourth simply reproduce a recollection. Are there any other wishful dreams, or are wishful dreams perhaps the only dreams there are?

It is easy to show that dreams frequently display the features of wish-fulfilment without disguise, so that one may wonder why their language has not been understood long ago. There is, for example, a dream I can produce for myself by way of experiment, as it were, whenever I wish to. If I eat anchovies, olives, or some other strongly salted dish in the evening, I develop a thirst at night which wakes me up. But the awakening is preceded by a dream which always has the same content, which is that I am drinking. I gulp down water in deep draughts, and it tastes as delicious as only a cool drink can be when one is parched, and then I wake up and have to drink in reality. The occasion for this simple dream is the thirst, which of course I become aware of when I wake up. It is this sensation that produces the wish to drink, and the dream shows me this wish as fulfilled. In doing so it serves a function which I can quickly guess. I am a good sleeper, not used to being awakened by some need. If I manage to quench my thirst by dreaming that I am drinking, I shall not need to wake up to satisfy it. So the dream is a dream of convenience: dreaming replaces action, as it also does in other areas of life. Unfortunately, the need for water to quench my thirst is not to be satisfied by a dream, as my thirst for revenge on my friend Otto and Dr M. was, but the will and wish to do so are the same. Not long ago the same dream appeared in modified form. I was thirsty even before I went to sleep, and drank up the glass of water standing on the table beside my bed. A few hours later I was again assailed by thirst and by the inconveniences that attend it. To get water for myself I would have to get up and fetch the glass that stood on my wife's bedside table. So I dreamed, appropriately, that my wife was offering me a drink out of a vessel; this vessel was an Etruscan urn which I had brought home from a trip to Italy and had since given away. But the water it contained tasted so salty (obviously from the ashes), that I had to wake up. One sees how conveniently the dream can arrange things: since its only objective is wish-fulfilment it can be completely egotistical. Love of comfort is really not compatible with consideration for others. The involvement of the urn is probably another wish-fulfilment: I am sorry I no longer own this vessel, just as the glass on my wife's side, for that matter, is also inaccessible to me. The cinerary urn is also appropriate to the increasing sensation of a salty taste which I knew would compel me to wake up.[1]

When I was young, I had dreams of convenience like this very frequently. Accustomed to working late into the night, I always found it difficult to wake betimes; then I used to dream that I was out of bed and standing at the washstand. After a while I was unable to ignore the fact that I had not got up yet, but in the meantime I had slept a while longer. A young colleague* who seems to share my fondness for sleep told me of a similar sloth-dream which took a particularly clever form. The landlady he lodged with close to the hospital had strict orders to wake him punctually every morning, but she always had a hard time doing so. One morning his sleep was especially sweet. The woman called into his room: 'Get up, Herr Pepi, you've got to get to the hospital.' Straight away the sleeper dreamed of a room in the hospital, a bed where he was lying, and a headboard on which was written: 'Pepi H . . . . medical student, age 22.' He said to himself in his dream: 'If I am already in hospital, I don't have to go there,' turned over, and carried on sleeping. In doing so he had openly admitted to himself what was motivating his dreaming.

Here is another dream where the stimulus again produces its effect during sleep itself: one of my female patients had been obliged to undergo an operation on her jaw which turned out to be unsuccessful. Her physicians required her to wear a cooling appliance on her ailing cheek day and night, but she was in the habit of flinging it off as soon as she fell asleep. One day I was asked to reprove her for this; she had flung the appliance to the floor again. The invalid made her excuses: 'This time I really can't help it; it was the result of a dream I had in the night. In my dream I was in a box at the opera, taking a lively interest in the performance. But Herr Karl Meyer was

---

[1] The existence of thirst dreams was also familiar to Weygandt [75], who wrote (p. 41): 'The sensation of thirst is perceived most precisely of all: it always produces the idea of quenching it. The dream represents quenching thirst in various ways, which take their special form from some close memory. Here too it is a general phenomenon that after imagining that his thirst is quenched, the dreamer is promptly disappointed by the very slight effect of the supposed refreshment.' But Weygandt fails to see the universal validity in the reaction of the dream to the stimulus. —If others are overcome by thirst at night and wake up without having dreamed beforehand, this is not an objection to my experiment, it only indicates that they are not such good sleepers.

lying in the sanatorium and complaining fearfully of pains in his jaw. I said to myself: since I don't have the pains, I don't need the appliance; that is why I threw it off.' This dream of the poor sufferer's sounds like the representation of a phrase one might find oneself uttering in an unpleasant situation: 'I could think of more agreeable ways to pass the time.' The dream shows this more agreeable way. Herr Karl Meyer, on whom the dreamer had foisted her pain, was the least attractive young man of her acquaintance she could think of.

It is no less easy to detect the wish-fulfilment in several other dreams I have collected from people in good health. A friend who is familiar with my dream-theory and told his wife about it says to me one day: 'My wife has asked me to tell you that yesterday she dreamed she had started her period. You will know what that means.' Indeed I do; if the young woman has dreamed she is having her period, then she is missing it. I can imagine she would have liked to enjoy her freedom a little longer before the difficulties of motherhood begin. It was a clever way of announcing her first pregnancy. Another friend writes that his wife dreamed recently that she saw spots of milk on the front of her blouse. This too is the announcement of a pregnancy, but not of a first one; the young mother is wishing she might have more nourishment for her second child than she had for her first.

A young woman whose child had an infectious illness and who was cut off from social life for several weeks while she was caring for it dreams after the child's recovery that she is attending a party at which Alphonse Daudet, Bourget, Marcel Prévost,* and others are present, and that they are all very charming to her and entertain her most delightfully. In her dream these authors have the same features as their portraits; Marcel Prévost, whose portrait she has never seen, looks like—the disinfection man who had come to fumigate the sick-room the previous day and had been the first visitor to enter it for a long time. I think I can translate the dream perfectly: now at last, she thinks, it is time for something more entertaining than this everlasting nursing.

This selection will perhaps be enough to demonstrate that dreams of the most various kinds are very frequently found which can only be understood as wish-fulfilments, and which display their content undisguised. Most of these are short and simple dreams—which makes a pleasant contrast to the confused and extravagant dream-compositions which have attracted the attention of the authors on the subject. But it would be worth our while to linger for a time with these simple dreams. We may well expect the simplest forms of dreaming of all to be children's dreams, for their psychical attainments are certainly less complex than those of adults. Child psychology is in my opinion destined to perform a service for the psychology of adults similar to what has been done for the study of the structure of the highest classes of animals by the investigation into the anatomy or development of the lower animals. Until now not many purposeful steps have been taken to make use of the psychology of children to this end.

The dreams of small children are simple wish-fulfilments and so of no interest at all compared with the dreams of adults. They present no puzzles to solve, though they are of course invaluable as proof that in its innermost nature the dream signifies a wish-fulfilment. I have been able to collect a number of such dreams from what my own children have told me.

It is to an excursion from Aussee to the beautiful village of Hallstatt* in the summer of 1896 that I owe two dreams, one from my daughter, who was then eight and a half years old, the other from a boy of five and a quarter. By way of preamble I must explain that this summer we were staying on a hill near Aussee from which we could enjoy a glorious view of the Dachstein* when the weather was fine. With a telescope it was easy to pick out the Simony mountain lodge. The children repeatedly tried to view it through the telescope, though with what success I do not know. Before the outing I had told the children that Hallstatt lay at the foot of the Dachstein. They were greatly looking forward to the day. From Hallstatt we walked along the vale of E[s]cher,* and its changing prospects delighted the children. Only one of them, the five-year-old boy, gradually grew fractious. Whenever a new mountain came into sight he asked: 'Is that the Dachstein?' to which I had to reply: 'No, only a foothill.' After the question had been repeated several times he fell completely silent; and he frankly refused to climb the path up to the waterfall. I thought he had become tired. But next morning he came up to me radiantly happy, and said: 'Last night I dreamed we were at the Simony lodge.'* Now I understood him: when I talked about the Dachstein he had expected that on the excursion to Hallstatt we were going to climb the mountain and get to see the lodge the children had talked about so much when they were looking through the telescope. Then, when he noticed he was being fobbed off with foothills and a water-fall, he felt cheated and became cross. The dream compensated him for this. I tried to find out the details of his dream, but they were meagre. 'You walk up steps for six hours,' as he had been told.

Wishes also stirred in the eight-and-a-half-year-old girl which had to be satisfied by a dream. We had taken the twelve-year-old son of our neighbours with us to Hallstatt, a perfect little gentleman whom, it seemed to me, the little lady already found very attractive. The next morning she related the following dream: 'Just think, I dreamed that Emil is one of us, calls you Papa and Mama, and sleeps with us in the big room the same as our boys. Then Mama comes into the room and throws a handful of big chocolate bars wrapped in blue and green paper under our beds.' Her brothers, who have not, it would seem, inherited any skill in interpreting dreams, declared, just like our authorities on the subject, 'This dream is nonsense'. The girl defended part of the dream at any rate, and it is useful for the theory of neuroses to learn which part: that Emil was one of us, that was nonsense, but not the bit about the chocolate bars. Now, I was in the dark about this very part. Their mother gave me the explanation. On the way home from the railway station the children had stopped at the vending-machine and had wanted chocolate bars of just this sort, wrapped in shiny metallic foil, which they knew the machine had for sale. Their mother had rightly decided that they had had enough wishes fulfilled for one day, and left this wish to their dreams. I had missed the little scene. The part of the dream my daughter had dismissed I understood without further ado. On the road I had myself heard our well-mannered guest asking the children to wait for Papa or Mama to catch up. The child's dream had turned this temporary kinship into permanent adoption. Other forms of companionship than those mentioned in her dream, which she had drawn from her relation to her brothers, were as yet unknown to her affections. Why the bars of chocolate were thrown under the beds could not be explained, of course, without questioning the child.

A dream very similar to my boy's was told me by a friend of mine. It concerned a girl of eight. Her father had taken several children on a walk to Dornbach* with the intention of visiting the Rohrer moun-tain lodge, but because it had grown too late he had turned back, promising the children to make up for it some other time. On the way back they passed a sign pointing the way to the Hameau. The children now wanted to be taken to the Hameau, but again for the same reason had to be put off with the promise of the trip for another day. The next morning the eight-year-old girl told her father contentedly: 'Papa, today I dreamed you were with us at the Rohrer lodge and on the Hameau.' So it was that her impatience had anticipated the fulfilment of her papa's promise in her dream.

Just as straightforward is another dream which the beauty of the Aussee scenery roused in my daughter, then aged three and a quarter. The little girl had crossed the lake for the first time and the voyage had been all too brief for her. When we reached the landing-stage she did not want to leave the boat and wept bitterly. The next morning she said: 'Last night I went on the lake.' Let us hope the length of time this dream-voyage lasted gave her greater satisfaction.

My eldest son, then eight years old, is already dreaming the realization of his fantasies. He has been riding in a chariot with Achilles, and Diomedes was the charioteer. The previous day, of course, he was fired with enthusiasm for the legends of Greece, which his elder sister had been given as a present.

If I am right that when children talk in their sleep this also belongs to the sphere of dreaming, in what follows I can relate one of the youngest dreams in my collection. My youngest daughter, nineteen months old at the time, vomited one morning and for that reason was given nothing to eat for the rest of the day. During the night that followed this day of fasting, we heard her cry excitedly in her sleep: '*Anna F.eud, Er(d)beer, Hochbeer, Eier(s)peis, Papp* [strawberry, wild strawberry, scrambled eggs, mash]'. At that time she used her name to express taking possession of something; the menu no doubt included everything that would have seemed to her a desirable meal; the strawberries' appearance in two variations was a demonstration against the domestic policing of her diet and originated in the fact—which she had very likely noticed—that the children's nurse had ascribed her indisposition to eating too many strawberries; so that is how she took her revenge in her dream for this annoying report.[2]

---

[2] Shortly afterwards her grandmother, whose age added to the little girl's would come close to seventy, had a dream which achieved the same feat as her youngest grandchild's. After the disturbance of a floating kidney had compelled her to go without food for a day, she dreamed—evidently carried back to her happy prime as a young woman—that she was 'invited out' to both the main meals of the day, and both times was offered the most delicious morsels.

If we consider childhood a happy time because it does not yet know sexual desire, we should not forget what a rich source of disappointment, renunciation, and so of dream-arousal the other great vital drives can be for it. Here is a second example. On my birthday my twenty-two-month-old nephew was given the task of congratulating me and presenting me with a little basket of cherries, which at that time of year are still counted among the earliest fruits. He seems to find it difficult to do, for he says repeatedly: 'There's cherries in it,' and cannot be persuaded to let go of the basket. But he is able to compensate for this. Every morning until then he was in the habit of telling his mother that he had dreamed of the 'white soldier', a guards officer in a cloak whom he once admired in the street. On the day after the birthday sacrifice he wakes with the joyful announcement, which can only have derived from a dream: '*Hermann ate all the cherries!*'

What animals dream of I do not know. There is a proverb, mentioned to me by one of my students, which claims to know, for it asks the question: *What does a goose dream of?* and answers: *Corn*. The entire theory that the dream is a wish-fulfilment is contained in these two sentences.

We observe now that we would have found the shortest route to our theory of the hidden meaning of dreams if we had only looked to linguistic usage. Proverbial wisdom often speaks scornfully enough of dreams, it is true—it seems to want to admit that science is right when it judges: *Träume sind Schäume* [dreams are froth]—but in linguistic usage the dream is nevertheless the sweet fulfiller of wishes. 'I wouldn't have imagined it in my wildest dreams,' we cry in delight when we find our expectations surpassed in reality.

IV
DREAM-DISTORTION

Now if I make the assertion that wish-fulfilment is the meaning of *each and every* dream, and hence that there can be no other dreams besides wishful dreams, I am sure in advance that I shall encounter the strongest opposition. It will be objected: 'That there are dreams which can be understood as wish-fulfilments is nothing new: authorities on the subject have long recognized the fact.' (See Radestock [54] (pp. 137–8), Volkelt [72] (pp. 110–11), Purkinje [53] (p. 456), Tissié [68] (p. 70), M. Simon [63] (p. 42 on Baron Trenck's hunger-dreams in prison), and the passage in Griesinger [31] (p. 111).) But that there are no other kinds of dream besides wish-fulfilling dreams is just another of those unjustified generalizations with which you have been pleased to draw attention to yourself of late.* There are in fact plenty of dreams which have the most painful and embarrassing content but no trace of wish-fulfilment. The pessimist philosopher Eduard von Hartmann is perhaps most firmly opposed to the theory of wish-fulfilment. In his *Philosophie des Unbewussten*, Part II (stereotype edition p. 344), he says:

'As for dreams, all the little miseries of our waking life also pass over with them into the state of sleep, but not the one thing that can at least partly reconcile the cultivated person to life: the enjoyment of science and art . . .' But less discontented observers too have emphasized that in dreams pain and unpleasure occur more frequently than pleasure. Scholz [59] (p. 33), Volkelt [72] (p. 80), and others do so. Indeed, the ladies Sarah Weed and Florence Hallam have given a numerical term, based on a study of their own dreams, to the preponderance of unpleasure in dreams: they identify 58 per cent of dreams as being distressed and only 28.6 per cent as positively pleasant. Apart from these dreams, which extend the various disagreeable feelings of our life into sleep, there are also anxiety-dreams, when this most terrible of all unpleasurable feelings holds us in its grip until we wake. And it is anxiety-dreams like this that afflict children above all, whose dreams we have found to be wishful dreams undisguised (see Debacker [17] on the *pavor nocturnus*).

Anxiety-dreams really do seem to make it impossible to make a generalization of the principle we have drawn from the examples in the previous section, that the dream is a wish-fulfilment. Indeed they seem to brand it as an absurdity.

All the same, it is not very difficult to get round these apparently compelling objections. One should merely bear in mind that our theory does not rest on a consideration of the manifest content of the dream, but refers to the thought-content which the work of interpretation enables us to recognize behind the dream. Let us compare the *manifest dream-content* and the *latent content* with each other. It is true that there are dreams whose manifest content is of the most distressing kind. But has anyone tried to interpret these dreams, to reveal their latent thought-content? If not, these two objections no longer apply to us: it is still possible all the same that once interpreted, even distressing dreams and anxiety-dreams will be revealed as wish-fulfilments.

In scientific work, when there are difficulties in solving one problem it is often helpful to add another, in much the same way as it is easier to crack two nuts against one another than to crack each separately. In this way we not only confront the question: how can distressing dreams and anxiety-dreams be wish-fulfilments? but from our previous discussions of the dream we can also raise a second question: why is it that dreams with a neutral or trivial content which turn out to be wish-fulfilments do not reveal this meaning of theirs undisguised? Take the dream of Irma's injection which we treated in such detail: its nature is not in the least distressing, and through the interpretation it can be recognized as a flagrant wish-fulfilment. But why does it require an interpretation at all? Why does it not say straight out what it signifies? In fact, even the dream of Irma's injection does not at first give the impression of representing a wish of the dreamer as fulfilled. The reader will not have received this impression, but I too failed to grasp it before I undertook the analysis. If we call this tendency of the dream to require explanation the *fact of dream-distortion*, then the further question arises: Where does this dream-distortion come from?

First thoughts on the subject may suggest a variety of possible answers, for example, that during sleep there is an inability to create an appropriate expression for our dreaming thoughts. But the analysis of certain dreams compels us to admit a different explanation of dream-distortion. I would like to demonstrate this with a second dream of my own: again, it will require a number of indiscretions, but a thorough clarification of the problem will compensate for this personal sacrifice.

Preamble: In the spring of 1897 I learned that two professors of our university had proposed me for appointment as *professor extraordinarius*.* This news came as a surprise to me, and gave me great pleasure as an expression of recognition from two outstanding men which was not to be accounted for by any personal connections. However, I told myself at once that I should not expect anything to come of this occurrence. The ministry had in recent years ignored proposals of this kind, and several colleagues who were older than I and at least my equal in merit were still waiting in vain for their appointments. I had no reason to suppose I should fare any better. So I decided privately to reconcile myself to this. I am not, as far as I know, ambitious; I pursue my medical practice with gratifying success, even without the recommendation of a title. Besides, it was not a question of my calling the grapes sweet or sour, for undoubtedly they hung too high for me.

One evening a colleague paid me a visit, a friend who was one of those whose fate I had allowed to serve as a warning to me. For some time a candidate for promotion to professor—a title which in our society raises a physician to a demigod in the eyes of a patient—and less resigned than I was, he was in the habit of appearing at the offices of the ministry from time to time in order to advance his case. He came to me straight from one of these visits. He told me that this time he had driven the high official into a corner and asked him straight out whether the delay in his appointment was not really due to—considerations of religion.* The reply had been that, to be sure—given the present tendency—His Excellency was for the moment not in a position to, etc. 'Now at least I know where I stand,' my friend concluded. His tale told me nothing new, though it was bound to strengthen me in my attitude of resignation. For the same religious considerations also apply to my own case.

On the morning after this visit I had the following dream, which was also remarkable in respect of its form. It consisted of two thoughts and two images, in such a way that one thought and one image gave way to the other. However, I shall put down only the first half of the dream, as the other has nothing to do with my purpose in reporting it.

I. *My friend R. is my uncle. — I feel great affection for him.*

II. *I see his face before me, rather altered. It is as though elongated; a yellow beard framing it is emphasized with particular clarity.*

Then there follow the two other parts, again a thought and an image, which I shall ignore.

The interpretation of this dream proceeded as follows:

When the dream occurred to me in the course of the morning, I laughed aloud and said: 'The dream is nonsense.' I could not get rid of it, however; it pursued me all day, until in the evening I finally reproached myself with the words: 'If one of your patients had nothing to contribute to the interpretation of a dream but "It is nonsense", you would reprimand him and assume that the dream conceals an unpleasant history which he wants to spare himself the pain of acknowledging. Deal with yourself in the same way: your view that the dream is nonsense signifies only an inner resistance to interpreting it. Don't be deterred.' So I set about the interpretation.

'R. is my uncle.' What could that mean? For I have only one uncle, my Uncle Josef.[1] His story was a sad one.* More than thirty years earlier his desire for gain had misled him into an act severely punishable by the law, and he was punished accordingly. My father, whose hair turned grey with grief in a few days, always used to say that Uncle Josef had never been a bad man, he had been a numbskull: that was the expression he used. So if my friend R. is my Uncle Josef, what I want to say is: R. is a numbskull. Hardly credible and very unpleasant! But there it is, that face I see in my dream, with the elongated features and the yellow beard. My uncle really had a face like that, longish, framed by a fine, fair beard. My friend R. was extremely dark, but when the dark-haired start to go grey they have to pay for the splendour of their youth. Their dark beards pass, hair by hair, through a disagreeable succession of colours: first reddish-brown, then yellowish-brown, and only then definitely grey. My friend R.'s beard has now reached this stage, and so, by the way, has my

[1] It is remarkable how my — waking — recollection is reduced here for the purposes of the analysis. I have known five of my uncles, and one of them I have loved and honoured. But the moment I overcame my resistance to interpreting my dream, I said to myself: I have really only had one uncle, the one who is meant in the dream.

own, as I note with chagrin. The face I see in my dream is at the same time both my friend R.'s and my uncle's. It is like a composite photograph by Galton,* who had several faces photographed on the same plate in order to trace family likenesses. So there is no possible doubt: I really think my friend R. is a numbskull—like my Uncle Josef.

At first I have no idea what purpose I have in producing this identification, which I feel I have to resist constantly. But it does not go very deep, for my uncle was a criminal and my friend R. has not a stain on his character, if we except the penalty imposed on him for knocking down an apprentice with his bicycle: but could this misdeed be what I meant? That would reduce the comparison to the ludicrous. But then I call to mind another conversation I had a few days earlier with another colleague, N., about the same subject, in fact. I met N. in the street. He too was proposed for a professorship, knew of my own honour, and congratulated me on it. I rejected his congratulations firmly. 'You of all people should not make that kind of joke, for you have learned yourself what such proposals are worth.' He replied, probably not seriously: 'You never know. And there is a black mark against me. Don't you know that a woman once made a legal complaint against me? I don't need to tell you that the investigation was called off: it was a low attempt at blackmail, and I had my work cut out to save the blackmailer from being prosecuted herself. But perhaps the ministry is holding this affair against me so as not to approve my appointment. But you haven't a stain on your character.' There, indeed, I have the criminal, and at the same time the interpretation and tendency of my dream as well. My Uncle Josef represents to me both my colleagues who have not been appointed to professorships, the one because he is an idiot, the other because he is a criminal. I also know now why I need this representation. If 'religious' considerations are decisive in the delay experienced by my friends R. and N. in securing appointments, then my own appointment is also called into question; but if I can ascribe their rejection to other grounds which do not apply to me, my hopes will remain undisturbed. This is what my dream is doing: it makes a numbskull of one, R., and a criminal of the other, N. But I am neither the one nor the other; the common ground between us is cut away; I can look forward to my appointment as professor, and I have avoided the distress of having to apply to myself R.'s news of what the high official told him.

I have to continue further with the interpretation of my dream. I do not feel that I have dealt with it satisfactorily as yet. I am still perturbed by the ease with which I degrade two respected colleagues in order to keep my way open to a professorship. True, I am less dissatisfied with my behaviour now that I know how to assess the value of the statements made in the dream. I would dispute with anyone that I really regard R. a numbskull or that I do not believe N.'s account of the blackmailing affair. Nor, of course, do I believe that Irma was dangerously infected* by Otto with a propyl preparation: here as there, what my dream is expressing is only my *wish that that is how it might be*. The assertion in which my wish is realized sounds less absurd in the second dream than in the first: in the second it is formed by an adroit use of a basis in fact, rather like a well-made slander where 'there is something in it', for my friend R. had the vote of a specialist professor against him at the time, and my friend N. unsuspectingly handed me the material for blackening his character himself. Nevertheless, I repeat, the dream still seems to me to need further elucidation.

Now I recall that the dream contains a further element which the interpretation has not heeded so far. Once it occurred to me that R. was my uncle, I feel a warm affection for him in my dream. Where am I to place this feeling? For my Uncle Josef, I have naturally never had any affectionate feelings. My friend R. has for years been very dear to me, but if I were to go up to him with words expressing an affection close to the degree of fondness I felt in the dream, he would certainly be astonished. My fondness for him appears false and exaggerated to me, much like my judgement of his intellectual qualities as I expressed it when I merged his personality with my uncle's, though exaggerated in the opposite sense. But then a new fact dawns upon me. The affection in the dream does not belong to the latent content, to the thoughts behind the dream, it stands in opposition to this content; it is calculated to hide the true interpretation of the dream from me. Probably this is its very purpose. I recall how reluctantly I approached interpreting it, how long I wanted to put it off, declaring the dream to be sheer nonsense. From my psycho-analytic practice I know how such a dismissive judgement is to be interpreted: it has no value as knowledge but merely as the expression of an affect. When my little daughter does not want an apple she has been offered, she maintains that the apple tastes sour, without having even tried it. If my patients behave like the little girl, then I know they have been confronted with an idea they want to *repress*. The same applies to my dream: I do not want to interpret it because the interpretation will contain something I am baulking at. The interpretation once completed, I learned what it is I baulked at: it is the assertion that R. is a numbskull. I cannot trace the affection I felt for R. back to the latent thought of the dream, but I can trace it back to this resistance of mine. If my dream is distorted on this point when compared with its latent content, into its opposite in fact, then the affection manifest in the dream serves this distortion, or in other words, the distortion and deformation here turn out to be intentional, a means of *pretence*. The thoughts in my dream contain a defamation of R.: so that I might not notice this, the opposite, a feeling of tenderness towards him, makes its way into my dream.

This insight could be a generally valid one. As the examples given in Chapter III have shown, there are indeed dreams which are undisguised wish-fulfilments. Where the wish-fulfilment is unrecognizable, disguised, there must have been a tendency to defensiveness against this wish, and as a consequence of this defensiveness the wish was only able to express itself in distortion. I propose to seek a parallel in social life to this event in the inner life of the psyche. Where in social life do we find a similar distortion of a psychical act? Only in the case of two people where the one possesses a certain power and the other has to take this power into account. This second person then distorts his psychical acts or, as we can also put it, he *pretends*. The politeness I practise every day is to a large extent a pretence of this kind; when I interpret my dreams for the reader I am compelled to resort to such distortions. The poet too laments the need for such distortion:

Das Beste, was du wissen kannst, darfst du den Buben doch nicht sagen.*
['The best that you can know, you cannot tell to boys.']

The political writer who has unpleasant truths to tell to those in power finds himself in a similar position. If he utters them openly the ruler will suppress his words—retrospectively if it is a question of words spoken, preventatively if they are to be made known in print. The writer has the *censorship* to fear: and so he moderates and distorts the expression of his opinion. According to the degree of severity and sensitivity of this censorship, he will find himself forced either just to hold back on certain forms of attack or to speak allusively instead of in plain statement, or he will have to conceal his objectionable views behind a harmless-seeming disguise—he may, for example, tell of incidents involving two mandarins of the Middle Kingdom, whereas he has the bureaucrats of the Fatherland in mind. The stricter the censorship, the more far-reaching the disguise and often the cleverer the devices which nevertheless put the reader on the track of what is really meant.

The correspondence, traceable down to the last detail, between the phenomena of censorship and dream-distortion justifies us in assuming similar preconditions for both. Accordingly we would assume two psychical forces (currents, systems) to be the originators of dream-formation in the individual; one of these forms the wish uttered by the dream, while the other imposes a censorship on the dream-wish and by this censorship distorts its expression. Only the question arises: 'What is the nature of the authority empowering this second agency to impose its censorship?' If we bear in mind that prior to analysis the latent thoughts of the dream are not conscious, but that the manifest dream-content they generate is recalled as being conscious, then it is a short step to assuming that the prerogative of this second agency consists simply in permitting access to consciousness. We might say: nothing from the first system can become conscious which has not previously been passed by the second agency, and the second agency lets nothing pass without exercising its rights and making whatever changes it thinks fit to the applicant for consciousness. Saying this reveals a quite distinct conception of the 'nature' of consciousness: in our view, the entry of something into consciousness constitutes a specific psychical act, different from the process by which ideas are generated or imagined and independent of it; and we regard consciousness as a sensory organ perceiving a content given from elsewhere. It can be shown that psychopathology simply cannot do without this basic assumption. We may reserve a more detailed discussion of this for later.

If I hold on to the idea of two psychical agencies and their relationship to consciousness, then the striking affection I felt in my dream for my friend R., who was so much disparaged in the interpretation, turns out to have a wholly congruent analogy in the political life of mankind. According to this, I imagine myself in a society where a ruler jealous of his power and a lively public opinion are in conflict with each other. The people rise up against an unpopular official and want him removed; to show that he does not have to take account of the popular will, the tyrant chooses just this moment to bestow a high distinction on the official, though there is no other reason for doing so. In this way my second agency, which rules over access to consciousness, bestows a distinction on my friend R. by an outpouring of excessive affection, because the wishful endeavours of the first system, in their own particular all-absorbing interest, would slander him as numbskull.

Perhaps at this point we have a presentiment that the interpretation of dreams is capable of providing us with information about the structure of our psychical apparatus which till now we have sought in vain from philosophy. However, this is a track we shall not follow: now that we have explained distortion in dreams we shall return to the problem from which we started. The question was how dreams with a distressing content can be resolved as wish-fulfilments. We see now that this is possible if a distortion of the dream has taken place, if the distressing content serves only to disguise a desired content. Taking into account our assumptions about the two psychical agencies, we can now also add that distressing dreams in fact do contain something which is distressing to the second agency but at the same time fulfils a wish of the first agency. They are wishful dreams insofar as every dream does indeed come from the first agency, while the second only acts defensively, not creatively, towards the dream. If we confine ourselves to assessing what the second agency contributes to the dream we shall never be able to understand the dream. All the puzzles of the dream noticed by the authorities will still remain.

That the dream really does have a secret meaning which turns out to be a wish-fulfilment still has to be demonstrated by analysis for each case in turn. So I shall select a number of dreams with a distressing content and attempt to analyse them. Some of them are the dreams of hysterics, requiring a lengthy preamble and in places an intrusion into the psychical events that attend hysteria. But this is a difficulty in reporting I cannot avoid.

As I have already mentioned, when I undertake the analysis of a psychoneurotic his dreams are regularly the subject of our discussions. In the course of these I have to inform him of all the psychological explanations which helped me to reach an understanding of his symptoms, and as I do so I get criticism as unsparing as any I might expect from my professional colleagues. What my patients object to with great regularity is the proposition that all their dreams are wish-fulfilments. Here are a few examples of evidence to the contrary which have been held up to me.

'You always say the dream is a fulfilled wish,' a bright woman patient begins. 'Well, I will tell you a dream which was just the opposite, in which a wish I had was *not* fulfilled. How will that fit your theory?' This is the dream:

'*I am going to give a dinner-party but I have nothing in the house except some smoked salmon. I think of going shopping, but I remember it is Sunday afternoon and all the shops are shut. Then I want to 'phone the delivery people but the 'phone is out of order. So I have to give up my wish to give a dinner party.*'

Of course I reply that only an analysis can decide the meaning of this dream, though I do concede that at first glance it does appear rational and coherent and looks like the opposite of a wish-fulfilment. 'But what is the material this dream proceeded from? You know the stimulus to a dream is always to be found in the experiences of the previous day.'

Analysis: The patient's husband, a worthy and capable wholesale butcher, told her the previous day that he was getting too fat and intended to start losing weight. He would get up early, do exercises, keep to a strict diet, and above all accept no more invitations to dinner parties.—Of her husband she said further, laughing, that on his regular evening out with his friends he had made the acquaintance of a painter who had insisted he wanted to paint him because he had never seen such an expressive head. However, her husband replied in his coarse way that he thanked him very much but he felt sure that the painter would prefer a piece of a pretty young girl's backside to the whole of his face.[2] She tells me she is now very much in love with her husband and teases him a lot. She has also asked him not to give her any caviare.—What can that mean?

For a long time, she says, she has wanted a bread-roll with caviare every morning, but has grudged the expense. She would, of course, have got the caviare from her husband at once if she had asked for it,

---

[2] To sit for a portrait. Goethe:* 'Und wenn er keinen Hintern hat, | Wie kann der Edle sitzen?' ['And if he hasn't a backside, | How can the lord be seated?']

but on the contrary she asked him not to give her any caviare, so that she could go on teasing him about it.

(This explanation strikes me as flimsy. Such unsatisfying information usually conceals unacknowledged motives. Consider Bernheim's* experiments in hypnotism in which the subjects hypnotized carry out post-hypnotic instructions, and when asked about their motives do not reply: 'I don't know why I did that' or some such answer, but have to invent a palpably inadequate reason. It is likely to be something of the sort with my patient's caviare. I note that she needs to create an unfulfilled wish for herself in waking life. Her dream also shows a wish failing or refusing to come true. But why does she want an unfulfilled wish?)

The ideas coming to her mind so far are inadequate for interpreting the dream. I press her for more. After a short pause, congruent with overcoming a resistance, she goes on to say that the previous day she paid a call on a friend she is actually jealous of because her husband always speaks so well of her. Fortunately this woman is very thin and skinny and her husband is fond of the buxom type. What was it this skinny friend had talked about? Naturally, about her wish to put on some weight. She also asked her: 'When are you going to invite us over again? One eats so well at your table.'

Now the meaning of the dream is clear. I can tell my patient: 'It is exactly as if you had said to youself when you heard this suggestion: "Of course I'll invite you so that you can eat plenty at my house, get fat, and be even more attractive to my husband. I'd rather never give a dinner party again." The dream then tells you that you cannot give a dinner party, and in this way it fulfils your wish to contribute nothing to filling out your friend's figure. Indeed, your husband's intention to accept no more invitations to dinner parties in the interest of slimming already informs you that we get fat from the food set before us on social occasions.' All that is still lacking is some kind of connection that will confirm this solution. And the smoked salmon is still unaccounted for. 'What made you think of the salmon referred to in the dream?' 'Smoked salmon is this friend's favourite dish,' she replies. I happen to know the lady as well, and can confirm that she is as fond of salmon as my patient is of caviare.

The same dream also admits of a different, and subtler, interpretation, which a minor circumstance even makes necessary. The two interpretations do not contradict each other; they coincide and present a splendid example of how dreams, like all other psychopathological formations, carry more than one meaning. We have heard how at the same time as dreaming of a wish refused my patient took the trouble to provide herself in real life with a wish denied (the bread-roll with caviare). Her friend too had expressed a wish—to get plumper, that is—and it would not surprise us if our lady had dreamed that a wish of her friend's would not be fulfilled. It is in fact her own wish that her friend's wish—to put on more weight—should not be fulfilled. Instead of this, however, she dreams that she herself has not had a wish fulfilled. The dream is given a new interpretation if in her dream she means not herself but her friend, if she has put herself in the place of her friend, or, as we may say, she has *identified* herself with her.

In my view this is what she really did, and as an index of this identification, in real life she created for herself the wish refused. But what is the sense of this hysterical identification? To explain this we need a fuller exposition. Identification is an extremely important factor in the mechanism of hysterical symptoms: it is the means which enables patients to express in their symptoms the experiences of a large number of people, not just their own, to suffer as it were for a whole host of others, and to play all the roles in a drama solely out of their own personal resources. It will be objected that this is the hysterical imitation we are already familiar with, the ability of hysterics to imitate all the symptoms belonging to other sufferers which have made an impression on them, an empathy, as it were, intensified to the point of reproduction. But this only indicates the path run by the psychical process in the case of hysterical imitation; the path is one thing, the psychical act that takes it is another. The latter is a little more complicated than the imitation of hysterics is usually imagined to be: it corresponds to an unconscious inferential process, as an example will make clear. A physician who has a patient with a certain kind of convulsion in the same hospital room with other patients will not be surprised if he discovers one morning that this particular hysterical attack has found imitators. He will simply say to himself: 'the others have seen it and imitated it; this is what we call psychical infection.' That is so: but psychical infection proceeds more or less in the following way. As a rule the patients know more about one another than the physician does about any one of them, and they are concerned for one another after the physician has paid his visit. Today one of them has had an attack: the others soon learn that a letter she has received from home, revival of lovesickness, or the like, is the cause of it. Their empathy is aroused, and the following inference is made within them, without its reaching consciousness: if one can get attacks like this from causes like this, then I too can get them, for I have the same occasions for them. If this inference had the potential to become conscious, it would perhaps result in the *anxiety* that one might get a similar attack; however, it takes place on different psychical terrain, and therefore ends in a realization of the dreaded symptom. The identification is thus not simple imitation but *appropriation* on the basis of a claim to the same aetiology: it expresses a 'just like' and refers to some factor held in common which remains in the unconscious.

In hysteria the common factor most frequently expressed is sexual. The hysterical woman identifies herself in her symptoms most readily—though not exclusively—with those people with whom she has had sexual intercourse, or who have sexual intercourse with the same partners as she herself has. Language also acknowledges a view of this kind: two lovers are 'one'. In hysterical fantasies, as in dreams, it is sufficient for the identification that sexual relations are thought of: it is not necessary to assume they are real. So my patient is merely following the rules of hysterical thought-processes when she expresses her jealousy of her friend (which, by the way, she herself recognizes to be unjustified) by putting herself in her friend's place in the dream, and when she identifies with her by creating a symptom (the wish refused). One might clarify the process with a play on words: she is putting herself in the friend's place in the dream because the friend is putting herself in her place in the eyes of her husband, because she—the friend—would like to occupy her place in her husband's affections.[3]

The objection to my dream-theory was resolved in the case of another of my patients, the cleverest of all my female dreamers— more simply, but still in conformity with the pattern that the non-fulfilment of one wish signifies the fulfilment of another. I had been arguing with her one day that the dream was a wish-fulfilment; the

---

[3] I myself regret the inclusion of such examples from the psychopathology of hysteria; represented in such a fragmentary way and torn out of all context, they cannot after all be very illuminating. If they are able to indicate the close connections between my subject of the dream and the psychoneuroses, then they will have fulfilled my intention in using them.

following day she brought me a dream in which she was travelling with her mother-in-law to the house they were to share in the country. Now, I knew that she had vehemently resisted spending the summer in the company of her mother-in-law, and also knew that in recent days she had happily succeeded in avoiding this dreaded companionship by renting a house in the country a long way from her mother-in-law's residence. Now the dream cancelled this desired solution: was this not the very opposite of my theory of wish-fulfilment through dreams? Certainly, I only had to pursue the logic of the dream to reach its interpretation. According to this dream I was wrong: *so it was her wish that I should be wrong, and the dream showed her that her wish was fulfilled*. However, the wish that I should be wrong, which was fulfilled by using the theme of the house in the country, referred in reality to a different and more serious object. At this time I had concluded from the material provided by her analysis that something important for her illness must have taken place at a certain period in her life. She had denied it because there was nothing she could recollect. We soon discovered that I was right. Her wish that I might be wrong, transformed into the dream that she was travelling to the country with her mother-in-law, thus corresponded to the justified wish that those things, which I was only then beginning to suspect, might never have happened.

Without analysis, but only by supposition, I allowed myself to interpret a little incident that occurred to a friend who had been a fellow-pupil of mine through the eight classes of the Gymnasium. He once attended a lecture I gave to a small circle on the novel thesis that the dream was a wish-fulfilment, went home, dreamed *he had lost all his cases*—he was a lawyer—and complained to me about it. I availed myself of the excuse 'You can't win every case,' but privately I thought: since I was top of the class for eight years, while he moved about somewhere in the middle, might the wish from those school years that I would for once make a thorough fool of myself be still not so far from his mind?

Another dream of a darker nature was told to me by a patient—again as an objection to the theory of wishful dreams. My patient, a young girl, began: 'You will recall that my sister now has only one boy, her Karl; she lost her elder son, Otto, while I was still living with her. Otto was my favourite, and I was the one who really brought him up. I am fond of the little one, but naturally not nearly as much as I was of the one who died. Well last night I dreamed *that I saw Karl lying dead before me. He is lying in his little coffin, his hands folded, candles all around—in short, just like little Otto, whose death was such a blow to me.* Now tell me, what does that mean? You know me well enough: am I so wicked as to wish that my sister should lose the only child she still has? Or does the dream mean that I wish Karl were dead instead of Otto, whom I so much preferred?'

I assured her that she could discount this latter interpretation. After brief reflection I was able to tell her the correct interpretation of the dream, which I then got her to confirm. I was able to do this because I was familiar with her entire previous history.

Orphaned young, the girl had been brought up by her much older sister, and among the friends and visitors who came to the house she met a man who made an enduring impression on her heart. For a while it seemed that this relationship, though not openly declared, would end in marriage, but this happy outcome was thwarted by her sister from motives that never became entirely clear. After they had broken with each other, the man our patient loved avoided the house; some time after the death of little Otto, on whom she had meanwhile turned her affection, she herself left to make an independent life. However, she failed to free herself from the dependency she had fallen into in her love for her sister's friend. Her pride bade her avoid him; but she found it impossible to transfer her love to other suitors who subsequently appeared on the scene. Whenever the man she loved, a man of letters, announced a lecture anywhere, she was unfailingly to be found among the audience, and she would also seize any opportunity that arose of seeing him elsewhere from a distance. I recalled that the previous day she had told me that the professor was going to a certain concert and she wanted to go too, so as to enjoy the sight of him once again. This was the day before the dream: the concert was to take place on the day on which she told me the dream. Knowing this, I found it easy to construct the correct interpretation, and I asked her if she could remember an event of any kind that had happened after the death of little Otto. She replied at once: 'Certainly, the professor came back after he had stayed away a long time, and I saw him again standing beside little Otto's coffin.' It was just as I expected. So I interpreted the dream in the following way: 'If the other boy were to die, the same thing would be repeated. You would spend the day with your sister, the professor would certainly come along to offer his condolences, and under the same circumstances as before you would see him again. The dream signifies nothing but this wish of yours to see him again, which inwardly you are fighting against. I know you have a ticket for today's concert in your purse. Your dream was a dream of impatience: it put seeing him again, which is to take place today, forward by a few hours.'

To conceal her wish, she had obviously chosen a situation in which such wishes are usually suppressed, a situation in which one is so full of sadness that one gives no thought to love. And yet it is quite possible that even in the real situation, which the dream so faithfully copied, beside the coffin of the first boy whom she had loved more, she had been unable to suppress her tender feelings for the visitor she had missed for so long.

A different explanation was given to a similar dream by another patient, one who had shone in her earlier years with her quick wit and a cheerful disposition, and who still showed these qualities at least as far as the ideas occurring to her during her treatment were concerned. In the context of a lengthy dream it seemed to this lady that she saw her only daughter, a girl of fifteen, lying dead in a box. She was minded to use this dream as an objection to the theory of wish-fulfilment, but suspected herself that the detail of the box must point the way to a different understanding of the dream.[4] In the course of the analysis it occurred to her that the previous evening the company had fallen to discussing the English word 'box' and the many ways it could be translated into German: as *Schachtel* [case], *Loge* [box in a theatre], *Kasten* [chest], *Ohrfeige* [box on the ear], etc. From other components of the same dream it emerged that she guessed the connection between the English 'box' and the German '*Büchse*' [tin can] and was then plagued by the recollection that '*Büchse*' is also used as a vulgar term for the female genitals. So making allowances for her knowledge of anatomical topography I could assume that the child in the 'box' signified a child in the womb. Enlightened to this extent, she now no longer denied that the dream really did represent a wish of hers. Like so many young women she was by no means happy when she found herself pregnant, and had more than once admitted to herself that she wished the child might die in her womb; indeed, in an outburst of anger after a violent scene

---

[4] As the smoked salmon did in the dream of the thwarted dinner-party.

with her husband she had beat her body with her fists so as to strike
the child within it. The dead child was thus truly a wish-fulfilment,
but the fulfilment of a wish abandoned fifteen years previously, and it
is not to be wondered at that when it arrives so late a wish-fulfilment
is no longer recognized. Too much has changed in the meantime,
after all.

The group to which the last two dreams belong, having the death
of a dear relative as their content, will be considered again among the
typical dreams. I shall be able to show there by means of fresh
examples how all these have to be interpreted as wish-fulfilments,
despite their unwished-for content. I am indebted not to a patient
but to an intelligent jurist of my acquaintance for the following
dream, which again was told me with the intention of restraining me
from rashly generalizing my theory of wishful dreams. '*My dream*',
says my informant, '*is that I am arriving at my house with a lady on my
arm. A closed carriage is waiting there, a man comes up to me, identifies
himself as a police agent, and invites me to follow him. I ask only for time
to put my affairs in order.*—Do you believe that it is perhaps a wish of
mine to be arrested?' Certainly not, I have to admit. Do you know
what you were being arrested for?—'Yes, I believe it was for
infanticide.'—Infanticide? But you know that this is a crime that
only a mother can commit against her newborn child?—'That
is so.[5]—And what were the circumstances of your dream: what
happened the evening before?—'I would rather not tell you, it is a
delicate matter.'—I need it, however, or we must forgo the interpretation of the dream.—'Well then, listen. I spent the night not at
home but with a lady who means a lot to me. When we woke in the
morning we again did something together. Then I went back to sleep
and dreamed what I told you.'—Is the lady married?—'Yes.'—And
you don't want to have a child by her?—'No, no, that could give us
away.'—So you don't practise normal coitus?—'I take care to withdraw before ejaculating.'—May I assume you had performed this
feat several times that night, and after repeating it in the morning
you were a little uncertain whether or not you had succeeded?—
'That may well be so.'—Then your dream is a wish-fulfilment. You

---

[5] It often happens that a dream gets related incompletely and the recollection of the
parts omitted only surfaces in the course of analysis. As a rule it is these elements
inserted retrospectively that yield the key to the interpretation of the dream.

received from it a reassurance that you have not begotten a child, or, what is almost the same thing, that you had killed a child. I can easily demonstrate the connecting links to you. You will recall that a few days ago we were talking about the distress of marriage, and of the inconsistency which permits coitus in ways which avoid pregnancy, although once ovum and semen have met and formed a foetus, any kind of interference is punished as a crime. In connection with this we also considered the medieval dispute over the point in time when the soul enters into the foetus, since it is only from that moment that the concept of murder becomes admissible. You are also sure to know Lenau's* ghastly poem in which infanticide and contraception are equated.—'Remarkably enough, I happened to think of Lenau only this morning.'—That too is an echo of your dream. And now I shall demonstrate to you a little subsidiary wish-fulfilment in your dream. You are arriving at your house with the lady on your arm: you are therefore *taking her home*, instead of spending the night at her house, as you did in reality. That the wish-fulfilment forming the core of the dream should conceal itself in such an unpleasant form has perhaps more than one cause. From my essay on the aetiology of anxiety neurosis you could learn that I claim that coitus interruptus is one of the causal factors in the creation of neurotic anxiety. It would accord with this if, after several acts of coitus of this kind, you were left with a feeling of unease which then became an element in the composition of your dream. You also use this ill-humour to conceal the wish-fulfilment from yourself. By the way, doesn't this also explain your reference to infanticide? How is it you hit upon what is specifically a woman's crime?—'I will confess that some years ago I was once involved in an affair like this. It was my fault that a girl tried to save herself from the consequences of a relationship with me by having an abortion. I had nothing at all to do with carrying out the intention, but for a long time, as you will understand, I was anxious lest the matter might be discovered.'—I understand; this recollection provided a second reason for being troubled by your suspicion that you might have failed in your usual practice.

A young physician who heard this dream related in my course of lectures must have felt personally affected by it, for he hastened to dream a similar dream, applying the form of its thinking to a different subject. The previous day he had submitted his income-tax return: it was an entirely honest return, for he had little income to declare. He then dreamed that an acquaintance came from a meeting of the tax commissioners and told him that all the other tax returns had been approved, but his had aroused general mistrust and he would incur a severe penalty. The dream is the barely concealed fulfilment of a wish to be accounted a physician with a large income. By the way, it recalls the familiar tale of the young girl who is advised to reject her suitor because he has a violent temper and would certainly beat her when they were married. The girl replies: 'If only he would beat me!' Her wish to be married is so intense that she is prepared to accept the trouble it was suggested would go with the marriage, and even comes to wish for it.

I hope that these examples will—pending any further objections—be enough to make it seem plausible that even dreams with a painful content can be resolved as wish-fulfilments. Nor is anyone likely to think it a matter of chance that, when these dreams are interpreted, we should always light upon subjects one would prefer not to speak of or think about. No doubt the disagreeable feeling aroused by these dreams is simply identical with the aversion which would keep us, mostly with success, from dealing with such subjects or from discussing them, and which each of us has to overcome if we find ourselves nevertheless obliged to tackle them. However, this feeling of unpleasure which recurs thus in dreams does not exclude the existence of a wish: everyone has wishes he would not like to communicate to others, and wishes he prefers not to admit to himself. On the other hand, we consider we are justified in connecting the unpleasure that characterizes all these dreams with the fact of dream distortion; and we are also justified in concluding that these dreams are distorted in the way they are, and the wish-fulfilment in them disguised to the point of unrecognizability, because an aversion exists towards the subject of the dream or towards the wish derived from it, together with an intention to repress it. Dream-distortion thus proves to be in fact an act of censorship. But we will have taken into account everything our analysis of unpleasurable dreams has brought to light if we alter our formula for the nature of the dream to read: *The dream is the (disguised) fulfilment of a (suppressed, repressed) wish.*

There now remain anxiety-dreams as a special sub-species of dreams with a distressing content, which the unenlightened will be least willing to accept as being wishful dreams. All the same, I can deal with anxiety-dreams very briefly here, for what is involved is not some new aspect of the problem of dreams but an understanding of neurotic anxiety in general. The anxiety we feel in dreams is only apparently explained by the content of the dream. If we subject the dream-content to interpretation we notice that the anxiety in the dream is not justified by the content of the dream any more than, say, the anxiety of a phobia is by the idea to which the phobia clings. It is perfectly true, for example, that one can fall out of a window and so have reason to exercise a certain caution when standing next to one: but that does not explain why in the corresponding phobia the anxiety is so great and pursues its victim far beyond its occasions. The same explanation then proves to be valid both for the phobia and for the anxiety-dream. In both instances the anxiety is only *soldered on* to the idea that attends it, and originates from a different source.

On account of this intimate connection between dream anxiety and neurotic anxiety, in discussing the former I must at this point refer to the latter. In a little essay on 'Anxiety Neurosis' (*Neurolog. Centralblatt*, 1895 [SE iii. 87]) I maintained a while ago that neurotic anxiety originates in the sexual life and corresponds to a libido deflected from its purpose and unable to find employment. Since then this formula has proved increasingly sound, and from it one can derive the proposition that anxiety-dreams are dreams with a sexual content whose accompanying libido has undergone a transformation into anxiety. We shall have an opportunity later to support this assertion with the analysis of some of the dreams of neurotics. In the course of my further attempts to approach a theory of dreams, I shall also return to the causes of anxiety-dreams and their compatibility with the theory of wish-fulfilment.

V

THE MATERIAL AND SOURCES OF DREAMS

When we gathered from our analysis of the dream of Irma's injection that the dream is a wish-fulfilment, our interest was first captured by whether this discovery had led us to identify a universal characteristic of dreams, and for the time being we silenced any other kind of scientific curiosity which might have arisen in our mind in the course of that interpretive work. Now that we have reached our goal by the one route, we may go back and choose a new starting-point for our expeditions through the problems of dreams, even though for a while we may lose sight of the subject of wish-fulfilment, which we have certainly not finished with for good.

Now that applying our method of dream interpretation has enabled us to uncover the existence of a *latent* dream-content which is far more significant than the *manifest* dream-content, it becomes pressing for us to take up the separate problems of the dream afresh in order to see whether puzzles and contradictions which appeared insuperable as long as we only knew the manifest content of the dream may not now resolve themselves to our satisfaction.

What the authorities have said about the connection between dreams and waking life, and about the provenance of the dream-material, has been reported fully in the introductory section. We may also remind ourselves of those three distinctive features of the dream-memory which have been remarked on so often but never explained:

1. that the dream clearly prefers the impressions of the days immediately past (Robert [55], Strümpell [66], Hildebrandt [35], and Weed-Hallam [33]);

2. that it selects according to different principles from those applied by our waking memory, remembering not what is vital and important, but what is trivial and unnoticed (see p. 18);

3. that it has at its disposal our earliest childhood impressions, and even fetches forth details from this period of our life which again

seem to us trifling and in our waking life were thought to have been forgotten long ago.[1]

These peculiarities in the selection of dream-material were of course observed by the authorities in the manifest dream-content.

(a) *Recent and Insignificant Material in Dreams*

If at this point I consult my own experience with regard to the provenance of the elements appearing in the dream content, I must first of all affirm the proposition that a reference to the events of the *day just past* is to be discovered in every dream. Whatever dream I choose, one of my own or someone else's, will confirm this experience every time. Knowing this fact, I can begin the dream-interpretation perhaps by first looking for the daytime experience which has set the dream off; in many cases, indeed, this is the shortest route. In the two dreams I subjected to close analysis in the previous section (the dream of Irma's injection and the dream of my uncle with the yellow beard) the connection with the day is so obvious that it requires no further elucidation. But to show how regularly this connection can be demonstrated, I should like to examine some items from my chronicles of my own dreams with this in view. I shall report the dreams only to the extent needed to uncover the dream-source we are looking for.

1. I am visiting a house where I am admitted only with difficulty, etc.; in the meantime I keep a woman *waiting* for me.

Source: Conversation with a relative in the evening, who said she would have to *wait* for a purchase she wished to make until, etc.

2. I have written a *monograph* on a certain (unclear here) species of plant.

Source: In the morning I saw a *monograph* on the genus cyclamen in the window of a bookshop.

3. I see two women in the street, *mother and daughter*, the latter a patient of mine.

Source: A patient I was treating told me in the evening what

---

[1] Clearly Robert's view that the dream is intended to relieve our memory of the trivial impressions of the day is no longer tenable if often quite trivial images recalled from childhood appear in the dream. We would have to conclude that the dream habitually fulfils its appointed task in a most inadequate way.

difficulties her *mother* was placing in the way of continuing the treatment.

4. At the bookshop of S. and R. I take out a subscription for a periodical costing 20 florins a year.

Source: My wife reminded me during the day that I still owed her 20 florins in housekeeping money.

5. I receive a *letter* from the Social Democrats' *committee* treating me as though I were a member.

Source: I received *letters* at the same time both from the Liberal electoral committee and from the board of the Humanitarian Society, of which I really am a member.

6. A man standing on a *steep rock in the middle of the sea*, in the style of Böcklin.*

Source: *Dreyfus** on *Devil's Island*, at the same time news of my relatives in *England*, etc.

One might ask whether the dream invariably relates to the events of the preceding day, or whether the connection can extend to impressions from a longer period of the immediate past. The issue is probably not a matter of principle, but for my part I would plump for the exclusive privilege of the last day before the dream (the dream-day). Whenever I thought that an impression from two or three days previously was the source of a dream, closer examination was able to convince me that I had recalled this impression on the previous day, that a demonstrable reproduction of it had thus been interpolated between the day on which the event occurred and the time I had the dream; and what is more, I was able to establish the recent occasion which could have prompted my recollection of the earlier impression.

So it is my view that for every dream there is a stimulus drawn from those experiences 'we have not yet slept on'.

Thus the relationship to the dream-content of impressions from the immediate past (except the day before the night of the dream) is no different from that of other impressions from any time more remote. The dream can choose its material from any period of our life, provided only that a train of thought extends from the experiences of the day of the dream (the 'recent' impressions) back to these earlier experiences.

But why do we prefer recent impressions? This point will be

clarified to some extent if we submit one of the dreams referred to above to a more detailed analysis. I shall choose the dream about the monograph.

Dream-content: *I have written a monograph on a certain plant. The book is lying in front of me, I am just turning to a coloured plate inserted into it. Each illustration has a dried specimen of the plant affixed to it, in the manner of a herbarium.*

Analysis: During the morning I saw a new book in the window of a bookshop entitled *The Genus Cyclamen*, obviously a monograph on this plant.

Cyclamen is my wife's *favourite flower*. I am reproaching myself for so rarely thinking of *bringing her flowers*, which would please her. On the subject of *bringing flowers*, I recall a story I told to some of my friends not long before and have used to support my assertion that forgetting is very often the execution of an intention of the Unconscious, and at all events allows us to make an inference about the secret sentiments of the one who forgets. A young woman who was accustomed to finding a bouquet from her husband on her birthday misses this expression of his affection one birthday and bursts into tears. The husband arrives and cannot understand why she is crying until she tells him: 'Today is my birthday.' Then he strikes his forehead, exclaiming: 'I'm sorry, I completely forgot,' and makes to go off and get *flowers* for her. But she is inconsolable, for she sees in her husband's forgetfulness a proof that she no longer plays the same part in his thoughts she once had.—Two days ago, my wife met this Frau L., who told her she was in the best of health, and asked after me. Some years earlier I had been her physician.

A fresh approach: I once really did write something rather like a *monograph* on a plant, an essay on the *coca plant*, which drew the attention of K. Koller to the anaesthetizing property of cocaine. I had referred to this use of the alkaloid myself in my publication, but was not thorough enough to take the matter further. In this connection it occurs to me that on the morning of the day following the dream (I only found time for its interpretation in the evening) I was thinking about cocaine in a kind of daytime fantasy. If I were ever to get glaucoma I would go to Berlin and be operated on there incognito in my Berlin friend's* surgery by a physician he has recommended. The surgeon, not knowing who his patient is, would speak highly of how easy these operations had become since the introduction of cocaine; I would not betray by the slightest word or gesture that I myself had a part in this discovery. This fantasy was followed by thoughts of how awkward it is for a physician to claim medical treatment for himself from his colleagues. I would be able to pay the Berlin eye specialist, who does not know me, like anyone else. It is only after recalling this daydream that it strikes me that the memory of a particular experience is hidden behind it. Shortly after Koller's discovery, my father contracted glaucoma. He was operated on by my friend the eye specialist Dr Königstein; Dr Koller attended to the cocaine anaesthesia and remarked that on this occasion all three people who had a part in the introduction of cocaine found themselves together.

My thoughts now move on to when I was last reminded of this story of the cocaine. It was a few days previously, when I received the *Festschrift* with which grateful students had celebrated the fiftieth birthday of their teacher and head of their laboratory. Listed among the laboratory's claims to fame I also found it mentioned that K. Koller discovered the anaesthetizing property of cocaine there. Suddenly I notice that my dream is connected with an event on the previous evening. I had accompanied home none other than Dr *Königstein* himself and had been discussing a matter with him which always rouses intense interest in me whenever it is broached. As I was lingering in the hallway with him, Professor *Gärtner* and his young wife came up, and I could not resist congratulating them on how *blooming* they looked. Now Professor *Gärtner* is, as it happens, one of the authors in the *Festschrift* I have just spoken of, and probably caused me to recall it. Frau L., whose birthday disappointment I have just related, had also been mentioned in my conversation with Dr *Königstein*, though in another connection.

I shall try to interpret the other determinants of the dream-content as well. A *dried specimen* was included in the monograph, as though it were a *herbarium*. I have a recollection from my schooldays connected with a herbarium. Our headmaster once called the pupils in the top classes together and gave them the task of checking and cleaning the institution's herbarium. Little *worms* had been found in it—*bookworm*. He does not seem to have placed much trust in the assistance I could give, for he gave me only a few leaves out of it to deal with. I can remember even now that they contained *cruciferae*. I was never much interested in botany. At my botany examination I was again given a *crucifera* to identify and failed to recognize it. I would have done badly if my theoretical knowledge had not helped me out. From the *cruciferae* I move on to the *compositae*. Actually, the artichoke is a *composita* too, and in fact the one I might call my *favourite flower*. More thoughtful than I, my wife often brings me these favourite flowers home from the market.

I *see* the monograph I have written *lying before me*. This too is not without relevance. My friend in Berlin, a strong visualizer, wrote to me yesterday: 'I am very much engaged with your dream-book. *I can see it lying finished before me and I am leafing through the pages.*' How I have envied him this prophetic gift! If only I could see it lying finished before me!

The folded-in coloured plate: When I was a medical student I suffered a great deal from the impulse to learn only from *monographs*. Despite my limited means I possessed runs of several medical journals whose *coloured plates* were my delight. I was proud of this inclination to thoroughness. When I myself began to publish I had to draw the plates for my treatises myself, and I know that one of them came out so poorly that a well-disposed colleague laughed at me on account of it. On top of that, I do not know why, a memory comes to me from my very early years. My father once amused himself by handing over a book with *coloured plates* (an account of travels in Persia) to me and my eldest sister for us to destroy. Hardly justifiable as a way of educating the young. I was then five years old, and my sister not yet three, and the picture of us children blissfully pulling this book to pieces (*like an artichoke*, leaf by leaf, I must add) is almost the only clear memory of this period of my life I still retain. Then, when I became a student I developed a decided preference for collecting and owning books (analogous to my inclination to study from monographs, a hobbyist's enjoyment of the kind that is already apparent in my dream-thought about cyclamen and artichokes). I became a *bookworm* (cf. *herbarium*). Ever since I began to reflect on myself, I have always traced this first passion of my life back to this childhood impression, or rather, I recognized that this childhood scene was a 'screen memory' for my later bibliophilia.[2] Naturally I learned very early that passions today can mean sorrow tomorrow.

---

[2] See my essay 'Über Deckerinnerungen' ['On Screen Memories'] in the *Monatschrift für Psychiatrie und Neurologie*, 1899 [SE iii. 301].

When I was seventeen I had a considerable account with a bookseller and no means of meeting it, and my father was unwilling to accept it as an excuse that my inclinations had not been for anything worse. However, mentioning this experience from my later youth brings me back at once to the conversation with my friend Dr Königstein. For the same reproach as before—that I devoted myself too much to the *enjoyment of my hobbies*—was also the subject of our conversation on the evening of the dream-day.

For reasons that have no place here I shall not pursue the interpretation of this dream, but merely indicate the path leading towards it. During the work of interpretation I am reminded of my conversation with Dr Königstein, of more than one part of it, in fact. If I keep in mind the things that were touched on in this conversation, the meaning of the dream will become intelligible to me. All the trains of thought it set going—my wife's particular enjoyments and my own, cocaine, the difficulties of medical treatment by one's colleagues, my preference for monographs, and my neglect of such subjects as botany—all these continue and converge into one of the many ramifications of our wide-ranging conversation. The dream again acquires the character of a justification, a plea on my own behalf, like the dream just analysed of Irma's injection; indeed, it was a continuation of the theme begun in that dream, airing it in terms of new material which had ensued in the interval between the two dreams. Even the seemingly neutral form of expression of the dream acquires a certain tonality. Now the implication is: 'But I am the man who wrote the valuable and successful treatise (on cocaine)', just as in the earlier dream I protested: 'But I am an excellent and industrious student'; in both cases, then: 'I am justified in claiming this.' However, I can dispense with completing my interpretation of the dream at this point, for my only intention in relating it was to use it as an example with which to investigate the relationship between the dream-content and the experience of the previous day which prompted it. As long as I know only the manifest content of this dream, all I am able to notice is a relationship between the dream and one daytime impression; after I have done the analysis, it turns out that the dream has a second source in another experience from the same day. The first of the impressions to which the dream relates was an indifferent matter, a triviality: I see a book in the bookshop window whose title I notice only fleetingly and whose contents could hardly interest me. The second experience was of great psychical value: I engaged my friend, the eye specialist, in eager conversation for what must have been an hour, made suggestions to him that were bound to affect us both, and roused memories in myself which led me to notice a great range of disturbances within me. What is more, this conversation was broken off when acquaintances approached. Now, how are these two daytime impressions related to each other and to the dream that occurred that night?

In the dream-content I can find only one allusion to the trivial impression, and this enables me to confirm that dreams have a preference for taking unimportant elements from our lives into their content. In the dream-interpretation, on the contrary, everything leads to the significant experience which had rightly stirred me. If I assess the meaning of the dream according to the latent content brought to light by the analysis—the only correct way of doing so— all of a sudden I come upon a new and important insight. The puzzle of the dream's preoccupation with worthless fragments of daily life dissolves before my eyes; I must also contradict the assertion that the waking life of the psyche does not not continue into the dream, and that the dream squanders its psychical activity on foolish material instead. The opposite is true: what has claimed our attention by day also governs the thoughts of our dream, and we put ourselves to the trouble of dreaming only on the basis of material such as would have given us occasion for thought in the daytime.

There is an obvious explanation of why I persist in dreaming of trivial and unimportant impressions from the day, even though the one that truly stirred me is what actually set me dreaming: it is likely that here again we are looking at a manifestation of dream-distortion, which we have already traced back to a psychical force exercising its power as a censorship. My recollection of the monograph on the genus cyclamen is put to use as though it were an *allusion* to the conversation with my friend, very much as, in the dream of the thwarted dinner-party, a reference to the friend is represented by the allusion to 'smoked salmon'. But the question is: what are the intermediary links by which the impression of the monograph could come to constitute an allusion to the conversation with the eye specialist, for such a relationship is not immediately apparent. In the example of the thwarted dinner-party the relationship is given from the outset: it goes without saying that, as her friend's favourite dish, 'smoked salmon' belongs to the sphere of ideas which the person of her friend is able to suggest to the dreamer. In our new example we have a case of two separate impressions which at first have nothing in common except that they happen on the same day. The monograph catches my attention in the morning; then I have the conversation in the evening. The answer offered by the analysis goes like this: connections between the two impressions of this kind, which were not present at first, are passed on retro-actively from the ideas contained in the one impression to the ideas contained in the other. I have already identified the links in question in my account of the analysis. Without some influence from else-where it is likely that the idea of the monograph on cyclamen would only have attached itself to the thought that this was my wife's favourite flower, and also perhaps to a recollection of the bouquet Frau L. had not received. I do not believe that these ulterior thoughts would have been sufficient to produce a dream.

> There needs no ghost, my lord, come from the grave
> To tell us this,

as it says in *Hamlet*.* But behold, in the analysis I am reminded that the man who interrupted our conversation was called *Gärtner* [gardener] and that I thought his wife 'blooming'; indeed, I only now remember in retrospect that one of my patients with the lovely name of *Flora* was for a while the main subject of our conversation. What must have happened is that these intermediaries from the botanical sphere of ideas effected a linkage between the two experiences of the day, the unimportant one and the one that initiated the dream. Then further relationships emerged, involving cocaine, which can quite appropriately mediate between the person of Dr Königstein and a botanical monograph I wrote, and they consolidate this merging of the two spheres of ideas into one, so that one element from the first impression could be used as an allusion to the second.

I am prepared for this explanation to be challenged as being arbi-trary or forced. What would have happened if Professor Gärtner and his 'blooming' wife had not appeared, if the patient we discussed had not been called Flora, but Anna? And yet the answer is easy. If these thought-connections had not presented themselves, others would probably have been chosen. It is so easy to create connections of this kind, as indeed the riddles and conundrums we amuse ourselves with during the day amply demonstrate. The scope of wit and humour has no bounds. To go a step further: if intermediate connections of sufficient range and variety could not be created between these two impressions of the day, then the dream would have just turned out differently: some other trivial daytime impression—of the sort that impinge on us in droves and are forgotten by us—would have taken the place of the 'monograph' in the dream, contrived some connection with the content of the conversation, and would have stood in for it in the dream-content. Since the impression of the monograph alone met this fate, this must have been the one most suited to establishing the linkage. We have no need to be amazed, like Lessing's Hänschen Schlau,* 'that it is only the wealthy of this world who possess the most money'.

The psychological process by which, as we explain it, the trivial experience comes to stand for the psychically valuable one must still strike us as surprising and disconcerting. In a later section we shall be faced with the task of reaching a closer understanding of the peculiarities of this apparently irrational operation. But at this point we are concerned only with the outcome of the process, which we are urged towards treating as our basic assumption by countless experiences recurring regularly in the course of dream-analysis. But as for the process itself, it is as if a *displacement*—of psychical emphasis, shall we say—were taking place by way of intermediaries, until ideas initially weak in intensity, by borrowing from those initially more intensely charged, attain a degree of power which enables them to force an entry into consciousness. We are not at all surprised by displacements of this kind when it is a matter of finding an attachment for quantities of affect, or a question of motor actions in general. The lonely spinster who transfers her affections to animals, the bachelor who becomes a passionate collector, the soldier who defends a strip of coloured cloth, the flag, with his life's blood, the feelings of ecstasy roused in a love affair by a handclasp lingering for a second, the outburst of rage engendered in Othello by a lost handkerchief—these are all examples of psychical displacements which seem to us incontestable. But that the same means and the same principles should decide what enters our consciousness and what is withheld from it—in other words, what we think—that strikes us as pathological; and when it occurs in waking life, we call it a flaw in reasoning. Let us reveal the outcome of later discussions at this point and say that the psychical process we have recognized in dream-displacement will prove to be, not a pathologically disturbed process, but rather one differing from the normal, a process of a more *primary* nature.

Accordingly, we interpret the fact that the dream-content admits remnants of trivial experiences as a manifestation of *dream-distortion* (through displacement), and we recall that we recognized dream-distortion to be the result of a censorship controlling the transit between two psychical agencies. In doing so we expect that the analysis of the dream will invariably uncover for us the real, psychically significant source of the dream in the life of the day, though our recollection of the real source has displaced its emphasis onto the unimportant one. This conception has brought us into complete conflict with Robert's [55] theory, which for us has become quite unusable. For the fact Robert wanted to explain simply does not exist; the assumption that it does rests on a misunderstanding, on a failure to put the real meaning of the dream in the place of the apparent dream-content. There is a further objection to Robert's theory: if the dream really had the task of removing the 'dross' of our recollections of the day by means of a particular psychical activity, our sleep would have to be more disturbed and put to more strenuous work than we could claim for it in our waking mental life. For it is obvious that the number of indifferent daytime impressions which we would have to shield our memory from is immeasurably large; the night would be too short for us to cope with such a sum. It is far more likely that we forget trivial impressions without any active engagement of our psychical powers.

All the same something warns us not to dismiss Robert's ideas without further consideration. We have left unexplained the fact that one of the trivial impressions of the day—of the most recent day, that is—invariably makes a contribution to the dream-content. The relationships between this impression and the actual dream-source in the Unconscious do not always exist from the outset; as we have seen, they are produced only retroactively, during the dream-work, in the service of the intended displacement as it were. So there must be present some pressure to develop connections in the particular direction of the recent, though trivial, impression; this impression must have some quality that makes it especially suitable for this, for otherwise it would be just as easy for the dream-thoughts to displace their emphasis onto an insignificant component from their own sphere of ideas.

At this point the following experiences may help us on our way to clarification. If a single day has brought us two or more experiences suitable to initiate a dream, the dream will unite reference to them both into a single whole; it obeys a *compulsion to form a unity out of them*. For example, one summer afternoon I got into a train compartment where I encountered two acquaintances who were, however, strangers to one another. One was an influential colleague, the other a member of an aristocratic family which I attended as a physician. I introduced the two gentlemen to each other; but throughout the long journey they conducted their conversation through me, so that I had to converse now with the one, now with the other. I asked my colleague to recommend to others an acquaintance we had in common who had just started up in medical practice. My colleague replied that he was convinced that the young man was a good doctor, but his unprepossessing appearance would make it difficult for him to gain an entry into better-class houses. I replied: 'That is exactly why he needs recommendation.' I inquired of my other travelling companion soon after how his aunt was doing—she was the mother of one of my patients and was at that time seriously ill. During the night following this journey I had a dream: the young friend on whose behalf I had asked for patronage is in an elegant salon in a select company I had assembled of all the distinguished and wealthy people I knew, and with all the poise of a man of the world he delivers a funeral oration in their presence on the old lady who was the aunt of my travelling companion—and who for the sake of the dream had already died. (I confess frankly that I was not on good terms with her.) So again my dream had made out connections between two daytime impressions and with them had composed a unified situation.

On the basis of many similar experiences I am led to put forward the proposition that some kind of compulsion exists for the dream-work to put together all the sources of dream-stimuli present into a unity in the dream itself.[3]

---

[3] The inclination of the dream-work to merge all items of interest occurring at the same time into one operation has already been observed by several writers on the subject, e.g. Delage [15] (p. 41), Delboeuf [16]: *rapprochement forcé* (p. 236).

I would now like to discuss the question whether the dream-initiating source to which the analysis leads us must always be a recent (and significant) event, or whether some inner experience, that is to say, the memory of a psychically valuable event, can assume the role of initiator of the dream. The very definite answer provided by numerous analyses is the latter: the initiator of the dream can be an inner process which has, as it were, become recent if the dreamer has been actively thinking about it during the day. This is probably the right moment to set out a table of the various conditions which can be recognized as the sources of dreams.

The source of a dream can be:

(a) A recent and psychically significant experience which is represented directly in the dream.[4]

(b) Several recent, significant experiences which are combined into a unity by the dream.[5]

(c) One or more recent and significant experiences which are represented in the dream-content by reference to an—unimportant—experience occurring at the same time.[6]

(d) A significant inner experience (a memory, train of thought) which is then represented in the dream by reference to a recent but trivial impression.[7]

As we see, for the interpretation of dreams one condition always holds good: one constituent of the dream-content is a repetition of a recent impression from the previous day. This part, meant to act as the proxy in the dream, can either belong to the sphere of ideas of the actual initiator of the dream itself—either as an essential or as an unimportant component of it—or it will derive from the field of some trivial impression which has been drawn into into relationship with the sphere of the dream-initiator by a more or less dense web of connections. The apparent number and variety of conditions only arises as a consequence of whether *a displacement has or has not occurred*, and we may note here that these alternatives offer us the same easy explanation of the array of contrasts possible between dreams as the range from partial to fully awakened

---

[4] Dream of Irma's injection; dream of the friend who is my uncle.

[5] Dream of the young doctor's funeral oration.

[6] Dream of the botanical monograph.

[7] Most of my patients' dreams during analysis are of this kind.

states of the brain cells does for the physical theory of dreams (see p. 64).

What is also to be noted about this list is that for the purposes of dream-formation the element that is psychically valuable but not recent (the train of thought, the memory) can be replaced by a recent but psychically trivial element, as long as the two conditions obtain: (1) that the dream-content retains a reference to the recent experience, and (2) that what initiates the dream is still a psychically valuable occurrence. In only one case, (a), are both conditions fulfilled by the same impression. And if we consider further that the same trivial impressions which the dream employs for as long as they are recent will forfeit their suitability as soon as they have grown a day (or at most several days) older, we must be prepared to assume that the very freshness of an impression in itself lends it a certain psychical value for dream-formation which is somehow on a par with the value of memory or trains of thought imbued with affects. Only in the course of certain later psychological reflections shall we be able to discern what the basis for this value of *recent* impressions for dream-formation can be.[8]

In addition, our attention is drawn here to important changes which the material of our memories and ideas can undergo at night and without our being conscious of them. The demand that we should sleep on a thing before coming to a final decision about it is plainly quite justified. But we note that at this point we have left the psychology of dreaming and are encroaching upon the psychology of sleep—a step which we shall have occasion to take later from time to time.

Now there is an objection which threatens to upset the conclusions we have just drawn. If trivial impressions can enter the dream-content only as long as they are recent, how is it that in the dream-content we also find elements from early periods of our life which, when they *were* recent, as Strümpell put it, possessed no psychical value, and so ought to have been forgotten long ago—elements, that is, which are neither fresh nor psychically significant?

This objection can be dealt with fully if one refers to the results of the psychoanalysis of neurotics. The solution runs as follows: the displacement which substitutes unimportant matter for psychically

---

[8] Cf. the passage in Chapter VII on 'transference'.

valuable material (in dreaming just as in thinking) has in their case already taken place in those early periods of life and has been fixed in their memory ever since. For those originally trivial elements are no longer trivial once they have assumed by means of displacement the value of psychically significant material. What has remained really trivial can no longer be reproduced in a dream.

It will rightly be concluded from this discussion that I maintain there are no trivial initiators of dreams, and thus no innocuous dreams. This is my strict and single-minded opinion, excepting the dreams of children and perhaps brief dream-reactions to nocturnal sensations. Apart from these, either what we dream is manifestly recognizable as having psychical significance, or it is distorted and can only be assessed after a dream-interpretation has been carried out, when it too will reveal its significance. The dream never wastes its time on trifles; we do not allow a mere nothing to disturb our sleep. The apparently innocuous dreams turn out to be pretty bad when we take the trouble to interpret them: if I may be permitted the expression, the dream 'wasn't born yesterday'. As this is another point where I may anticipate contradiction, and as I am glad to seize the opportunity to demonstrate dream-distortion at work, I shall now subject a number of 'innocuous' dreams from my collection to analysis.

I

A clever and refined young lady who is, however, even in her daily dealings, one of the reserved, one of the 'still waters', relates her dream: '*I arrive at the market too late and can get nothing either from the butcher or the vegetable woman.*' An innocuous dream, to be sure, but dreams do not look like this: I get her to tell it to me in detail. Then her account runs as follows: *She goes to the market with her cook, who is carrying the basket. The butcher tells her, after she has asked for something: 'That is no longer available', and makes to give her something else, with the remark: 'This is good too'. She refuses it and goes to the vegetable woman, who wants to sell her a peculiar vegetable tied up in bundles but black in colour. She says: 'I don't recognize that. I won't have it.'*

The daytime connection of this dream is simple enough: she really had gone to the market too late and had got nothing. *The butcher's shop was already shut* strikes one as a description of the experience. But wait: is that not a rather vulgar phrase which refers—or rather its opposite does—to a certain kind of carelessness* in a man's dress? The dreamer, by the way, did not use these words; perhaps she avoided them; let us look for an interpretation of the individual details contained in the dream.

When something in a dream has the character of speech, that is, when it is said or heard and not merely thought—a distinction which is usually perfectly clear—it derives from something that has been said in waking life, though this has been treated as raw material, broken up, slightly altered, but above all wrenched from its context.[9] We can take such spoken words as our starting-point in the work of interpretation. So where do the butcher's words '*That is no longer available*' come from? In fact, from myself: a few days previously I had explained to her 'that the earliest experiences of childhood as such *are no longer available*, but are replaced in the analysis by "transferences" and dreams'. So I am the butcher, and she is reject- ing these transferences of earlier modes of thought and feeling to the present day.—Where do her dream-words come from: '*I don't recog- nize that. I won't have it*'? For the purpose of analysis this has to be divided up. '*I don't recognize that*' she said herself to her cook the previous day when she had a quarrel with her; but then she added: '*Behave properly*'. A palpable displacement is emerging here: of the two sentences she used towards her cook, she took the insignificant one into her dream; the one she suppressed, however—'Behave properly!'—is the only one appropriate to the remainder of the dream-content.* It is what one might exclaim to someone who had made an improper demand and omitted to 'shut the meat shop'. That we were really on the track of the interpretation is then demon- strated by the similarity between this and the allusions present in the scene with the vegetable woman. A vegetable sold tied together in bundles (and long and narrow, as she adds in retrospect), and at the same time black, what can that be but a dream-merging of asparagus and black radishes? Asparagus I have no need to interpret to any knowledgeable person; but the other vegetable too—as a warning shout: 'Black, look out!' [*Schwarzer, rett' dich!*, cf. *schwarzer Rettich*, black radish]—seems to me to point to the same sexual theme as

---

[9] Cf. the passage on speech in dreams in the section on the dream-work. Only one of the authorities on the subject seems to have recognized the origin of utterances in dreams, Delboeuf [16] (p.226), who compares them with 'clichés'.

we divined at the beginning when we wanted to substitute 'the meat-shop was shut' for the dream-narrative. There is no need to understand the meaning of this dream in its entirety: what has been established is that it is meaningful and in no sense innocuous.[10]

II

Another innocuous dream by the same patient, in some respects a counterpart to the preceding one: *Her husband asks: Shouldn't we have the piano tuned? She: It's not worth while, and besides the hammers need re-leathering.* Again a repetition of a real event from the previous day: her husband asked this question and she replied along these lines. But what does it mean, that she should dream this? True, she says of the piano that it is a *disgusting* chest with a *dreadful tone*, something her husband owned before they were married,[11] etc., but the key to the solution is only provided by her words: '*It's not worth while*'. This has its origin in a visit she paid to a friend the day before. She was invited to take off her jacket and declined with the words: 'No thanks, *it's not worth while*, I have to go soon.' As she tells me this, it occurs to me that while we were engaged in the work of analysis the previous day, she suddenly grasped at her jacket, where a button had come undone. It is as though she wanted to say: 'Please, don't look, it's not worth while.' Thus the *chest* [*Kasten*] is amplified to *her chest* [*Brustkasten*], and the interpretation of the dream leads directly to the time when she was developing physically, when she began to be dissatisfied with her figure. It is likely it could lead to even earlier times if we take account of the '*disgusting*' and the '*dreadful tone*', and recall how frequently the smaller hemispheres of the female body stand in—as opposite and as substitute—for the large ones in allusions and dreams.

III

I shall interrupt this series to interpolate the brief innocuous dream

---

[10] For the curious I would note that the patient's dream conceals a fantasy of indecent, sexually provocative behaviour on my part, which she repulses. This may seem incredible to some, but I would remind them of the numerous cases where physicians have been accused in this way by hysterical women, in whom the same fantasy does not appear in distorted form and in their dreams, but has become undisguisedly conscious in the form of a delusion.

[11] A substitution by its opposite, which will become clear after the interpretation.

of a young man. He dreamed *that he was putting on his winter coat again, which was terrible*. According to him, the occasion for this dream is the cold snap that has suddenly set in. However, a subtler judgement will notice that the two brief parts of the dream do not suit each other very well, for what could be 'terrible' about wearing a thick or heavy coat in the cold? It also does no good for the innocuousness of this dream that the first idea occurring to the young man during analysis is the recollection that on the previous day a lady confessed to him in confidence that her latest child owed its existence to a burst condom. He now reconstructs what he thought on this occasion: a thin condom is risky, a thick one is no good. The condom was the 'overcoat' [*Überzieher*]—rightly, for one puts it on [*zieht ihn über*]; a lightweight coat also has the same name. An event such as the one the lady related would certainly have been 'terrible' for this unmarried man.—And now back to our female dreamer of innocuous dreams.

IV

She is putting a candle into the candlestick; but the candle is broken, so that it does not stand very well. The girls at school say she is clumsy; but the mistress says it is not her fault.

Here too there is a real occasion: she really did put a candle into the candlestick the previous day; but it was not broken. A transparent symbolism is being employed here. A candle is an object that rouses the female genitalia; if it is broken, so that it does not stand very well, this signifies the impotence of the man ('*it is not her fault*'). But, carefully raised as she is, and a stranger to everything ugly, does this young woman know of this use of the candle? As it happens she is able to quote the experience through which in fact she acquired this knowledge. During a trip on the Rhine in a rowing-boat, a boat passes them by in which a group of students are sitting and singing, or rather bellowing with great gusto, a song that goes: 'When the Queen of Sweden, with the window-shutters shut, takes Apollo candles . . .'*

She fails to hear or understand the last words, and her husband has to enlighten her. In the dream-content these lines are replaced by the innocuous recollection of a task she once performed *clumsily* at her boarding-school, doing so, indeed, under the same circumstances: *with the window-shutters shut*. The connection between the theme of masturbation and impotence is clear enough. 'Apollo' in the latent dream-content links this dream to an earlier one in which the virginal Pallas was referred to. Indeed, not at all innocuous.

V

In case it may be imagined that drawing inferences from the dream about the life the dreamer really leads is all too easy, I shall add another dream which seems equally innocuous and comes from the same person. *I have dreamed of something*, she said, *which I really did during the day, that is, I was filling a little trunk so full of books that I had trouble in closing it, and I dreamed it just as it really happened.* Here the narrator herself places the emphasis on the correspondence between dream and reality. Now, although they have created a place for themselves in waking thought, all such judgements of the dream or comments on it nevertheless invariably belong in the latent dream-content, as later examples will confirm. So, then, we are told that what the dream relates really happened on the previous day. It would take us too far afield to describe the route by which in the course of the interpretation we hit upon the idea of calling on English to assist us. It is enough to say that again we are dealing with a little *box* (compare the dream of the dead child in the box, pp. 119–20) which was filled so full that nothing more would go in. This time at least nothing bad.

In all of these 'innocuous' dreams, it is the sexual element which thrusts itself forward so conspicuously as the motive for censorship. But this is a topic of fundamental importance which we shall have to set aside.

(b) *Material from Infancy as a Source of Dreams*

As the third distinctive characteristic of the content of dreams, like all the writers on the subject (except Robert), we have indicated that impressions from the earliest years of our life can appear in our dreams, which do not seem to be at the disposal of our memory when we are awake. How rarely or how often this occurs is understandably hard to judge, because the origins of these elements in the dream cannot be recognized after we wake. So proof that we are dealing with impressions from childhood has to be produced by means of objective evidence, and the conditions for this come together only rarely. A. Maury [48] tells a story for its particular value as evidence of a man who decided to visit his home town after having been away for twenty years. The night before he left, he dreamed he was in a village quite unfamiliar to him and in the street he met a man he did not know, with whom he had a conversation. When he did return to his home, he was able to assure himself that this unfamiliar village really existed in the vicinity of his hometown, and the unknown man of his dream turned out to be a friend of his late father's who lived there. A compelling proof, certainly, that he had seen both, man and village, in his childhood. In addition, the dream can be interpreted as an impatience-dream, like that of the girl who had a ticket for the concert in her purse (pp. 120–1), or of the child whose father had promised him an excursion to the Hameau, and others of the kind. The motives for reproducing just this impression from the dreamer's childhood rather than any other, of course, cannot be uncovered without analysis.

Someone attending my lectures, who boasted that his dreams were only very rarely subject to dream-distortion, told me that a while ago he dreamed he saw *his former tutor in the bed of the maid* who had been employed in the house up to his eleventh year. The locality of this scene occurred to him while he was dreaming. His interest aroused, he told the dream to his older brother, who laughed and confirmed the reality of what he had dreamed. He remembered it very well, he said, for he was six years old at the time. The loving couple used to get him, the elder boy, drunk on beer when circumstances were favourable to nocturnal dalliance; the younger child, then three years old—our dreamer—who slept in the maid's room, was not regarded as an inconvenience.

There is a further instance where it can be determined with certainty and without the aid of dream-interpretation that a dream contains elements deriving from childhood and that is when the dream is what we call a *recurrent* one, that is, one first dreamed in childhood, which repeatedly reappears from time to time in the sleep of the adult. To the familiar examples of this kind of dream I can add some I have been told, though I have never had a recurrent dream of this sort myself. A physician in his thirties told me that from the earliest years of his childhood up to the present day, a yellow lion which he is able to describe exactly has made frequent appearances in his dream-life. Now this lion, familiar to him only in his dreams, turned up one day *in natura* as a long-lost porcelain object, and the young man then heard from his mother that this object had been his best-loved toy during his early childhood, though he himself could no longer remember it. One of my women patients had dreamed four or five times in the course of her thirty-eight years the same frightening scene: she is being pursued, flees into a room, shuts the door, then opens it again in order to take out the key, which is in the outside lock; then, with the feeling that something dreadful will happen if she does not succeed, seizes the key to lock the door from the inside; after which she breathes a sigh of relief. I am unable to say at what early age this little scene could have taken place, which of course she only witnessed.

If we now turn from the manifest dream-content to the dream-thoughts disclosed only after analysis, we are astonished to find the active involvement of childhood experiences in dreams whose content would in no way lead us to suspect it. I owe an especially charming and instructive example of a dream of this kind to my honoured colleague of the 'yellow lion'. After reading Nansen's* account of his polar expedition, he dreamed that on an icefield he was giving galvanic treatment to the intrepid explorer on account of a sciatica which the latter was complaining of! In the analysis of this dream he recalled an incident from his childhood without which the dream would certainly have remained incomprehensible. One day when he was three or four years old he was listening intently to the grown-ups talking about journeys of discovery, and then asked his father if that was a serious illness. He had clearly confused 'journeys' [*Reisen*] with 'aches' [*Reissen*], and the laughter of his brothers and sisters made sure he did not forget the embarrassing experience.

Something rather similar is involved in the analysis of the dream about the monograph on the genus cyclamen when I come upon the memory of my father giving the five-year-old boy a book with coloured plates to destroy. It may perhaps be doubted whether this memory really did play a part in forming the dream-content, or whether the work of analysis is not rather creating a connection only in retrospect. But the wealth of associations, and the way they were intertwined together vouch for the former idea. (Cyclamen—favourite flower—favourite food—artichoke; pull to pieces like an artichoke, leaf by leaf (an expression one hears every day in connection with the division of the Chinese Empire*);—herbarium—

bookworm, whose favourite food is books.) Moreover, I can testify that the ultimate meaning of the dream, which I have not given in full here, is very intimately connected with the content of that childhood scene.

In the case of another set of dreams, we learn from analysis that the very wish that initiated the dream, and whose fulfilment the dream represents, has its origin in childhood, so that to our surprise we *find the child, with its impulses, living on in the dream.*

At this point I shall continue the interpretation of a dream from which we have already learned much that is new; I mean the dream in which my friend R. is my uncle (p. 109). We have pursued its interpretation to the point when the wishful motive to be appointed professor came palpably to meet us; and we explained the affection I felt for my friend R. in the dream as a defiant creation made in opposition to the slander of my two colleagues in my dream-thoughts. The dream was my own, so I may continue its analysis by saying that the solution I had reached still failed to satisfy my feelings. I knew that my judgement of the colleagues who were so ill-used in my dream-thoughts was quite different in waking life, and the strength of my wish not to share their fate with regard to the academic appointment seemed to me inadequate to explain fully the contrast between my opinion of them when awake and that of the dream. If my need to be addressed by a different title was so strong, it pointed to a pathological ambition which I do not recognize in myself and which I believe is quite foreign to me. I do not know how others who think they know me would judge me in this matter: perhaps I really have been ambitious; but if so, my ambition has long since been aimed at other goals than the rank and title of a professor extraordinarius.

So where, did the ambition that inspired my dream come from? Suddenly there comes to my mind mind a tale I was told so often in my childhood, how at my birth an old peasant woman made a prophecy to my mother as she rejoiced in her first-born child, that she had given the world a great man. Such prophecies must be very frequent: there are so many mothers full of expectations for their children, and so many old peasants or other old women who have lost what power they had on earth and so have turned their attention to the future. Nor will such a prophecy have been to the disadvantage of the prophetess. Could this be the source of my desire for greatness?

But just at this point I recall another impression from the later years of my childhood which might offer an even better explanation: one evening, in one of the hostelries on the Prater* where my parents would often take me to when I was eleven or twelve, we noticed a man going from table to table and for a small sum improvising verses on any subject he was given. I was sent to invite the poet to our table, and he showed his gratitude to the messenger. Before he asked what his subject was to be, he devoted a few rhymes to me and declared in his inspiration that one day I would probably become a 'minister'. I can still remember very clearly the impression this second prophecy made on me. It was during the period of the Bourgeois Ministry;* shortly before, my father had brought home portraits of those middle-class academics Herbst, Giskra, Unger, Berger, and others, and we had illuminated the house in honour of these gentlemen. There were even Jews among them: which meant that every industrious Jewish boy carried a ministerial portfolio in his satchel.* It must even have something to do with the effect of those times that until shortly before I enrolled at the university I intended to read law, and changed course only at the last moment. For a ministerial career is certainly not open to a medical man! So then, what of my dream? I notice only now that it is transporting me back from the troubled present to the hopeful period of the Bourgeois Ministry and is doing its best to fulfil the wish I nurtured *then*. In treating my two learned and worthy colleagues so badly because they are Jews—one as if he were a numbskull, the other as if he were a criminal—in acting in this way, I am behaving as though I were the minister, I am putting myself in the minister's place. What a thorough revenge on His Excellency! He declines to appoint me professor extraordinarius, and in return, in my dream I put myself in his place.

In another instance I was able to note that the wish that initiated the dream, though belonging to the present, was all the same powerfully reinforced by memories reaching deep into childhood. It concerns a set of dreams which have their basis in my longing to go to *Rome*.* I anticipate that for some time yet I shall have to satisfy this desire only in my dreams, for at the time of year when I am free to take a holiday, a stay in Rome is inadvisable for reasons of health. So I dream on one occasion that I am seeing the Tiber and the Ponte Sant'Angelo through a train window; then the train starts moving, and it occurs to me that I have not even set foot in the city. The view

I saw in the dream was copied from a familiar engraving which I had noticed briefly the previous day in the drawing-room of one of my patients. Another time someone is leading me to a hill and showing me Rome, half-veiled in mist and still so far away that I wonder at the clarity of the view. The content of this dream is richer than I would wish to go into here. The motif 'to see the Promised Land from afar' is easy to recognize. The city I first saw thus hidden in mist is *Lübeck*;* the model for the hill is—*Gleichenberg*.* In a third dream I am in Rome at last, or so the dream tells me. But to my disappointment what I see is not city scenery at all: *a little river with dark waters, one side of it black rocks, on the other meadows with large white flowers. I notice a Herr Zucker* (whom I know slightly) *and decide to ask him the way to the city.* It is obvious that I am labouring in vain to see in my dream a city I have not seen in waking life. When I break up the dream's landscape into its elements, the white flowers indicate *Ravenna*, a town I know, which had for a time at least taken precedence over Rome as Italy's capital. In the marshes around *Ravenna* we found the most beautiful water-lilies in the midst of dark waters; the dream has them growing in meadows, like the narcissi in our own Aussee, because in *Ravenna* it was so difficult to gather them from the water. The dark rocks, so close to the water, remind me vividly of the vale of *Tepl*, near *Karlsbad*.* 'Karlsbad' now puts me in a position to explain the strange feature of asking Herr Zucker the way. In the material from which the dream was spun I was able to recognize two of those comic Jewish anecdotes which conceal so much profound and often bitter wisdom, and which we always enjoy quoting in conversation and letters. One is the story of the 'constitution', which tells of how a poor Jew steals onto the express train to Karlsbad without a ticket, is then caught out, at every ticket-inspection told to get off and treated worse and worse, until, when asked by an acquaintance who encountered him at one of the stations of his suffering, where he is travelling to, he replies: 'If my *constitution* holds out—to *Karlsbad*.' Close to this my memory holds another story of a Jew who does not know any French and who has it drummed into him that in *Paris* he must ask the way to the Rue Richelieu. *Paris* too was for many years a goal of my desire, and the joy I felt when I first set foot there I took as a guarantee that I should also see the fulfilment of my other wishes. Moreover, asking the way is a direct allusion to Rome, for it is well known that all roads lead to

Rome. The name *Zucker* [sugar] also points to *Karlsbad*, for that is where we send all those suffering from the *constitutional* complaint of diabetes [*Zuckerkrankheit*]. What occasioned this dream was a suggestion of my Berlin friend that we should meet in Prague at Easter. The things I intended to discuss with him there would give rise to a further connection with *sugar* and diabetes.

A fourth dream, shortly after the last one, again takes me to *Rome*. I see a street-corner before me and am surprised that so many German posters have been put up there. On the previous day I had written prophetically to my friend that probably *Prague* would not be a very comfortable place for Germans* to take a walk in. The dream thus expressed at the same time both the wish to meet him in *Rome* rather than in a Bohemian city, and the desire, probably originating in my student days, that the German language might be treated with greater toleration in Prague. In any case, in the earliest years of my childhood I must have understood the Czech language, for I was born in a little town in Moravia with a Slav population. A Czech children's poem which I heard in my seventeenth year* imprinted itself so effortlessly on my memory that I can repeat it even today, though I have no idea what it means. So these dreams too are not without multiple connections to the impressions of my earliest years.

On my last visit to Italy, which among other things took me along *Lake Trasimene*, I saw the *Tiber*, but with sadness in my heart I was obliged to turn back 80 kilometres from Rome: it was then at last that I discovered that my longing for the Eternal City was reinforced by impressions from my youth. I was just working out a plan to travel to *Naples* via *Rome* one year quite soon when I recalled something I must have read in one of our classic writers:* 'It is a nice question who paced his room more restlessly after he had conceived the plan to go to *Rome*—*Winckelmann*,* the headmaster's deputy, or *Hannibal*,* the general.' And there I was, following in *Hannibal's* footsteps; like him, I had not been granted a sight of *Rome*; he too had moved to *Campania* when all the world had expected him in *Rome*. But *Hannibal*, whom I had managed to resemble so much, had been my favourite hero when I was at the Gymnasium: like so many of that age, my sympathies in the Punic Wars did not lie with the Romans but with the Carthaginians. Then, in the upper school, when I first became aware of the consequences of being descended from an alien race, and the stirrings of anti-Semitism among my schoolfellows urged me to take up a position, the figure of the Semitic general rose even higher in my eyes. *Hannibal* and *Rome* symbolized to me the opposition between the tenacity of Jewry and the organization of the Catholic Church. The significance which the anti-Semitic movement has since acquired for our emotional life later helped to fix the thoughts and feelings of that early period. Thus the wish to go to *Rome* became for my dream-life a cloak and symbol for several other fervent wishes; and I would work with all the endurance and single-mindedness of the Carthaginian for their realization, even though their fulfilment seems for the time being to be as little favoured by fate as *Hannibal's* lifelong wish to enter *Rome*.

And this is the moment when I hit on the experience from my youth which is still exerting its power in all these dreams and feelings even today. I must have been ten or twelve years old when my father began to take me with him on his walks and in conversation tell me his views on the things of this world. In this vein, to show me how I had been born into better times than he had, he once told me: 'When I was a young man I went for a walk on a Saturday in the town you were born in, wearing my best clothes and with a new fur cap on my head. Then a Christian comes along, knocks my cap in the mud with a single blow, and shouts: "Jew, get off the pavement!"' — 'And what did you do?' — 'I stepped into the road and picked up my cap,' came the impassive reply. That did not seem to me very heroic of the big, strong man who was leading me by the hand. I compared this situation, which I was not happy about, with another more suited to my feelings: the scene where *Hannibal's* father, *Hasdrubal*,* makes his son swear before the domestic altar to take revenge on the Romans. From that time on, Hannibal had a place in my fantasies.

I believe I can trace this enthusiasm for the Carthaginian general even further back into my childhood, so that here too all that may be involved is the transference to a new bearer of an affective relationship that had already been formed. One of the first books that came into my hands once I could read was Thiers's* *History of the Consulate and the Empire*; I recall that I had stuck little labels onto the flat backs of my wooden soldiers, bearing the names of the Napoleonic marshals, and that *Masséna** (as a Jew: *Menassa*) was my declared favourite even then. *Napoleon* himself was connected with *Hannibal* by his crossing of the Alps. And perhaps the evolution of this warrior ideal can be pursued even further back into childhood—back to the wishes which the company, during my first three years, of a boy a year older, friendly one moment, belligerent the next, must have aroused in the weaker of the two playmates.

The deeper we descend into the analysis of dreams, the more frequently we are put on the track of childhood experiences which act as dream-sources in the latent dream-content.

We have heard (p. 20) that the dream very rarely reproduces recollections in such a way that they form the only manifest dream-content, unabbreviated and unchanged. All the same, some examples of this occurrence have been confirmed, and to these I can add some new ones which again relate to scenes of infancy. In the case of one of my patients, a dream once presented a barely distorted reproduction of a sexual incident which he immediately recognized as a faithful recollection. Its memory had never been completely lost in waking life, it is true, though it had become much obscured, and its revival was the result of the preceding work of analysis. At twelve years old the dreamer had visited a schoolfriend confined to his bed, and by making some movement, probably quite accidentally, his friend exposed himself. Seized by a kind of compulsion at the sight of his friend's genitals, he exposed himself also, and took hold of the other's member; but his friend looked at him with surprise and indignation, and he grew embarrassed and desisted. A dream repeated this scene twenty-three years later, together with all the feelings that had attended it, except that now the dreamer assumed the passive instead of the active role, and the person of the schoolfriend was replaced by someone from the present.

As a rule, it is true, the scene from infancy is represented in the manifest dream-content only by an allusion, and has to be developed out of the dream by means of interpretation. The report of such examples cannot be very conclusive as evidence, because of course there is usually no other guarantee that these are in fact childhood experiences: if they occur at an early age they will no longer be acknowledged by the memory. The justification for inferring them at all from the evidence of dreams is provided by a large number of factors arising during the work of psychoanalysis which, operating in combination, seem sufficiently dependable. Torn out of context for the purpose of dream-interpretation, these derivations of dreams from childhood experiences will not perhaps seem very impressive, especially as I am not even reporting all the material on which the interpretation is based. But this will not deter me from reporting them.

I

All the dreams of one of my women patients have the character of 'being rushed' [*gehetzt*]: she rushes to be on time so as not to miss the train, and so forth. In one of her dreams she is to visit a friend of hers; her mother has told her to go by transport, not to walk; *but she runs, — and as she does so she keeps falling down.* — The material emerging in the analysis allows me to recognize a recollection of romping and rushing about in childhood [*Kinderhetzereien*] — of the sort the Viennese call '*eine Hetz*' [a bit of fun] — and in the specific case of this dream I can trace it back to the joke children are fond of, the sentence 'Die Kuh rannte bis sie fiel' [the cow ran until she fell] said as quickly as if it were a single word, which again is a 'rush' [*Hetzen*]. All these innocuous rushings with her little friends are recalled because they take the place of other, less innocuous ones.

II

Another patient has the following dream: *She is in a big room in which all kinds of machines are standing, as she imagines an orthopaedic institution to be. She hears that I have no time and that she will have to receive treatment at the same time as five others. But she baulks at this, and refuses to lie in the bed — or whatever it was — intended for her. She stands in a corner and waits until I say it isn't true. In the meantime the others are laughing at her and saying she is fooling around.* — Besides this, *as though she were going to make a lot of little squares.*

The first part of this dream's content is a connecting link to her treatment and a transference to me. The second contains the allusion to the childhood scene; with the reference to the bed the two parts are soldered together. The orthopaedic institution could be traced back to a remark of mine in which I had compared her treatment, as regards both its nature and its duration, to an *orthopaedic* treatment. When I began it, I had to tell her *that for the moment I had little time for her*, but that later I would devote a whole hour to her every day. This aroused in her the old sensitivity which is one of the main character traits of children heading for hysteria. They are insatiable for love. My patient was the youngest of six siblings (hence *five*

others) and as such her father's favourite, though even so she seems
to have found that her beloved father devoted too little time and
attention to her.—Her waiting until I say it isn't true has the following derivation: a little tailor's boy had brought her a dress, and
she had given him the money for it. Then she asked her husband if
she would have to pay again if the boy lost the money. To *tease* her,
her husband assured her 'yes' (the *teasing* in the dream-content), and
she asked him again and again *and waited for him finally to say it
wasn't true*. So for the latent dream-content, this thought can be
construed as wondering whether she may have to pay me double if
I devote double the time to her, a thought that is mean or *dirty*.
(Dreams very often replace the uncleanliness of childhood with
meanness over money: the word 'dirty' forms the bridge.) If all the
business of waiting until I say, etc., is intended in the dream to be a
circumlocution for 'dirty', then *standing in a corner* and *not lying in
bed* correspond to it as constituents of a childhood scene in which
she has dirtied the bed, and is *sent to stand in the corner* as a punishment, with the threat that her father won't love her any more, her
brothers and sisters will laugh at her, etc. The little squares pointed
toward her little niece, who showed her the arithmetical trick of
writing numbers in, I think, nine squares in such a way that in
whatever direction you add them up, they come to 15.

III

The dream of a man: *He sees two boys who are scrapping; they are
cooper's boys, as he concludes from the tools lying around; one of the boys
has knocked the other down, the boy on the ground has earrings with blue
stones. He runs after the miscreant, his stick raised with the intention of
beating him. The boy flees to a woman standing beside a wooden fence, as
though she were his mother. She is a labouring woman, with her back to
the dreamer. At last she turns round and looks at him with a horrible
gaze, so that he runs away in fear. The red flesh of her lower eyelids can be
seen protruding.*

The dream made full use of trivial events from the previous day.
He really did see two boys in the street that day, one of whom
knocked the other down. When he ran up to settle the quarrel they
both took flight.—'Cooper's boys' is explained only by a subsequent
dream; in the course of its analysis he used the phrase *dem Faß den
Boden ausschlagen* [to knock the bottom out of the barrel—to be the

absolute limit].—He has observed that earrings with blue stones are mostly used by *prostitutes*. In this way the familiar line of doggerel about *two boys* was added: 'The other boy, he was called Marie' (i.e. he was a girl).—The standing woman: after the scene with the two boys he went for a walk along the Danube and took advantage of the solitude there to urinate *against a wooden fence*. As he walked on, a decently dressed older woman smiled at him in a very friendly way and tried to hand him her visiting card.

As the woman in the dream is standing as he had done when urinating, what is involved is a urinating woman, and the horrible '*sight*' also belongs to this, the protrusion of red flesh, which can only relate to the genitals gaping when a woman crouches down and which, seen in childhood, reappeared in the later recollection as '*proud flesh*', as a 'wound'. The dream unites two occasions on which the little boy was able to see the genitals of little girls, that is, when they were *knocked down* and when they *urinated*, and, as the other context indicates, it preserves the memory of a beating or a threat from his father on account of the sexual curiosity shown by the boy on these occasions.

IV

A large number of childhood recollections, combined in a rough and ready fashion, lies behind the following dream of an elderly lady.

She is rushing out to do some shopping. Then on the Graben* she sinks to her knees as if she has collapsed. Lots of people gather around her, especially the cab-drivers; but no one helps her up. She makes many vain attempts; finally she must have succeeded, for she is put into a cab which is supposed to take her home; through a window a large, heavily laden basket (similar to a shopping-basket) is thrown in after her.

This is the same patient who is being rushed in her dreams, just as she rushed about in play as a child. The first situation in the dream is clearly derived from the sight of a fallen horse, just as the 'collapse' indicates a horse-race. In her early years she was a *horsewoman*, and earlier still probably a *horse*. Falling down belongs to her earliest childhood memory of the seventeen-year-old son of the caretaker, who was seized in the street with epileptic convulsions and taken home in a carriage. Of course, she only heard of this, but the idea of epileptic convulsions, of 'someone falling', gained great power over her imagination and later influenced the form assumed by her own hysterical attacks.—When a woman dreams of falling, it almost always has a sexual significance, she becomes a '*fallen woman*'; in the case of the present dream this interpretation will hardly admit of any doubt at all, for her fall is on the *Graben*, the place in Vienna well known as a parade for prostitutes. The *shopping-basket* allows of more than one interpretation: as a basket it recalls the many *baskets* [colloquial: 'refusals'] she once handed to her suitors, and later, as she thought, she received herself. That *no one will help her up* also belongs here: she herself interprets it as being spurned and rejected. The *shopping-basket* further recalls fantasies, already familiar from the analysis, in which she married far below her station and now has to go and do the shopping herself. Finally, however, the shopping-basket can be interpreted as a symbol for a *servant*. Then further childhood recollections appear of a *cook* who was dismissed because she stole: she too *sank to her knees* and pleaded. The dreamer was twelve years old at the time. Then the memory of a housemaid who was dismissed because she consorted with the *coachman* [*Kutscher*] of the house, who, by the way, later married the girl. This recollection thus supplies us with the source for the *cab-drivers* [*Kutscher*] in the dream (who, unlike the real one, refused to look after the fallen woman). But what still remains to be explained is throwing the basket in after her, specifically *through the window*. This reminds her of dispatching luggage on the railway, of the country practice of '*Fensterln*' [visiting a girl by climbing in through her window], of little impressions from a stay in the country, when a man threw *blue plums* into a lady's room through her window, and how her little sister was afraid because a passing idiot looked into the room through the window. And then behind these there surfaces an obscure recollection from her tenth year of a maid in the country who was engaged in love-scenes with a servant of the house, which the child could have noticed something of, and who was '*dispatched*', '*thrown out*' (in the dream the opposite: '*thrown in*') together with her lover. Now in Vienna, the luggage, the suitcase of a servant is described as her '*sieben Zwetschken*' [seven little plums—bits and pieces]: 'Pack' deine sieben Zwetschken zusammen und geh' [Pack your bits and pieces together and go].

Of course my collection of dreams has plenty of dreams supplied by my patients, which, when analysed, lead back to dim or altogether forgotten childhood impressions, often from the first three years of life. But it is difficult to draw conclusions from these which are to hold good for dreams in general, for as a rule the dreamers are neurotics, hysterics especially, and the role ascribed in these dreams to childhood scenes could well be determined by the nature of the neurosis and not by the character of the dream. All the same, it happens just as often when I interpret my own dreams—which I do not undertake on account of any gross pathological symptoms—that in the latent dream-content I come unexpectedly upon a scene from infancy, and that all at once a whole series of dreams leads on to paths which have their beginnings in a childhood experience. I have already given examples of this, and shall give more when occasion arises. Perhaps I cannot conclude this section better than by relating some of my own dreams in which recent occasions and long-forgotten childhood experiences appear together as dream-sources.

I

After I sought my bed, tired, hungry, and weary from travel, I am visited in sleep by the great vital needs, and I dream: *I am going into a kitchen for a pudding. Three women are standing there, one of whom is the landlady, and she is turning something in her hand as though making dumplings* [Knödel]. *She answers that I must wait until she is finished (not clearly as speech). I grow impatient and go away offended. I put on an overcoat: but the first one I try is too long for me. I take it off again, rather surprised that it is trimmed with fur. A second that I put on has a long stripe with Turkish markings on it. A stranger with a long face and a short pointed beard comes up and prevents me from putting it on, declaring it is his. Then I show him that it is covered all over with Turkish embroidery. He asks: 'What are the Turkish (markings, stripes . . .) to you?' But then we are quite friendly with one another.*

In analysing this dream there comes quite unexpectedly to my mind the first novel I ever read, when I was perhaps thirteen years old, beginning it, that is, at the end of the first volume. I never knew the name of the novel, nor that of its author, but I can remember its conclusion very vividly: the hero declines into madness, and continually calls out the names of the three women who brought him the greatest happiness and the greatest misfortune in his life. One of these names is Pélagie.* I still don't know what I can do with this recollection in the analysis. Then the three women are joined in my thoughts by the three Fates who spin man's destiny, and I know that one of the three women, the landlady in the dream, is the mother who gives life, and sometimes, as in my case, the earliest nourishment. At the woman's breast love and hunger meet. An anecdote tells how a young man, who became a great admirer of female beauty, once said, when the conversation turned to the pretty nurse who had suckled him as an infant, that he regretted that he had not used the opportunity to greater advantage. It is my habit to use this anecdote to elucidate the element of retrospective action in the mechanism of the psychoneuroses.—One of the Fates is rubbing the palms of her hands together as though making *dumplings*: a strange occupation for a Fate and in urgent need of explanation! This comes now from another, and earlier, childhood memory. When I was six years old and enjoying my earliest instruction from my mother, I was supposed to believe that we are made of earth and must therefore return to earth. I did not like this idea, however, and expressed my doubts of it. At this my mother rubbed the palms of her hands together— just as though making dumplings, except that they held no dough— and showed me the blackish *epidermis* scales she had rubbed off as a sample of the earth of which we are made. My astonishment at this demonstration *ad oculos* was boundless, and I resigned myself to what I was later to hear expressed in the words: you owe Nature a death.*[12] So it really is the Fates I am visiting in the kitchen, then, as I did so often as a child when I was hungry, and from the stove my mother would tell me to wait until lunch was ready. And now for the dumplings! At least one of my university teachers, in fact the very one to whom I owe my *histological* knowledge (*epidermis*), will be reminded by the name Knödl of a person he was forced to sue because he had *plagiarized* his writings. To plagiarize, to appropriate what one can get even if it belongs to someone else, plainly leads to the second part of the dream, in which I am treated like the *overcoat thief* who was up to his thieving tricks for a time in the lecture halls. I have written the word *plagiarism* down without any particular purpose, just because it occurred to me, and now I see that it must belong to the latent dream-content because it is able to serve as a bridge between the various parts of the manifest dream-content.

[12] Both affects belonging to these childhood scenes, the astonishment and the acceptance of the inevitable, were to be found in a dream I had shortly beforehand, which first restored the memory of this childhood experience to me.

The chain of associations—*Pélagie*—*plagiarism*—*plagiastomes* [large fish, sharks][13]—*fish's bladder*—link the old novel with the Knödl affair and with the overcoats [*Überzieher*], which obviously signify a piece of sexual equipment (cf. *Maury's* dream of *Kilo*—*Lotto*, p. 51). An utterly forced and nonsensical connection, it is true, but all the same one that I could not have created when awake if it had not already been created by the dream-work. Indeed, as if nothing were sacred to my urge to create connections by force, the well-loved name of Brücke* [bridge] (word-bridges, see above) now serves to remind me of the institution where I passed my happiest hours as a schoolboy without any further needs ('So wird's Euch an der Weisheit *Brüsten* mit jedem Tage mehr gelüsten'* ['Suck on at Wisdom's *breasts*, you'll find | She daily grows more sweet and kind.']), in total contrast to the desires which *plague* me while I am dreaming. And finally, there arose the recollection of another dear teacher whose name, *Fleischl** [from *Fleisch*—flesh, meat], like Knödl, again sounded like something to eat, and of a sad scene in which *epidermis scales* played a role (the mother—landlady), and disturbance of mind (the novel), and a substance for reducing *hunger*, from the pharmacy, or 'Latin Kitchen' [Küche], cocaine.

I could pursue the intertwined trains of thought further in this way and explain fully the part of the dream which I have neglected in this analysis, but I must refrain from doing so, as the personal sacrifices it would demand are too great. I shall take up only one of the threads, which is able to lead directly to one of the dream-thoughts lying behind the tangle. The stranger with the long face and pointed beard who tries to prevent me from putting on the overcoat has the features of a merchant in Spalato* from whom my wife purchased a great quantity of *Turkish* cloth. He was called *Popović*, a suspicious name [Popo = bottom] which has also given the humorist *Stettenheim** the occasion for a suggestive remark. ('He told me his name and blushed as he shook my hand.') The same misuse of names, by the way, as with *Pélagie, Knödl, Brücke, Fleischl*. Of course, playing games with names in this way is a bad habit of children—so much I can say without contradiction; but if I am indulging in it myself, it is an act of retribution, for my own name has fallen victim countless

---

[13] The plagiastomes are not an arbitrary addition; they recall a vexatious occasion when I disgraced myself before the same teacher.

times to such idiotic joking [Freud(e) = joy]. *Goethe* once remarked
about how sensitive we are about our names, which we feel as closely
attached to as we do to our *skin*: the occasion for his remark was
Herder's play upon his name in the lines:

'Der Du von *Göttern* abstammst, von *Gothen* oder vom *Kothe*'—*
['Thou who art descended from Gods, from Goths or from dung'—]
'So seid ihr *Götterbilder* auch zu *Staub*.'*
['You godlike figures too have turned to dust.']

I note that this digression on the misuse of names was intended
only to prepare the way for my own complaint. But let us break off
here.—The purchase in Spalato reminds me of another one, in Cattaro,* when I was much too cautious and missed the opportunity of a
bargain. (See above: the missed opportunity with the nurse.) For one
of the dream-thoughts which hunger inspires in the dreamer is:
*Don't miss a thing, take what you can, even if it involves doing a little
wrong; don't let any opportunity slip by, life is so short, death inevitable.*
Since it is also meant sexually, and since desire will not stop at doing
wrong, this '*carpe diem*' has the censorship to fear, and has to hide
behind a dream. And then all the thoughts countering the desire
make their presence felt as well: recollection of the time when *spiritual nourishment* alone satisfied the dreamer, all the restraints and even
the threats of repellent sexual punishments.

II

A second dream requires a lengthier preamble:

I have arrived at the Westbahnhof to set off for my holiday at
Aussee, but I reach the platform while the train for Ischl,* due to
leave earlier, is still there. There I see Count *Thun*★ on the platform,
who for his part is bound for Ischl to see the Emperor. In spite of the
rain he arrived in an open carriage, getting out and going straight
through the entrance for local trains; when the ticket-collector, who
did not know him, made to take his ticket, he waved him away
without explanation with an abrupt gesture. After he has departed
on the train for Ischl, I am supposed to leave the platform again and
go back to the stifling waiting-room, but with some difficulty I succeed in being allowed to stay. I pass the time watching out for anyone
coming along and claiming the patronage of the great to get a compartment allocated to them: if that happens, I intend to kick up a

fuss, that is, demand equality of treatment. Meantime I am singing to myself something which I then recognize as an aria from *The Marriage of Figaro*:*

> Will der Herr Graf ein Tänzelein wagen, Tänzelein wagen,
> Soll er's nur sagen,
> Ich spiel ihm eins auf.
> [If milord Count should want to go dancing
> He'll pay the piper,
> I'll call the tune.]

(I doubt if anyone else would have recognized the melody.)

I had been in an exuberant, aggressive mood the whole evening, and had needled waiters and cab-drivers—without offending them, I hope; now all kinds of impudent and revolutionary thoughts are going through my mind, appropriate to Figaro's words and reminiscent of Beaumarchais's comedy, which I had seen at the Comédie Française. His remark about the great lords who took the trouble to be born; the *droit du seigneur* the Count tries to exercise on Susanna; the jokes which our wicked journalists from the opposition make on the name of Count Thun by calling him Count Nichtsthun [*Thun* = do, *Nichtsthun* = do-nothing]. Truly, I don't envy him; he is now on his way to a difficult visit to the Emperor, and *I* am really Count *Nichtsthun*: I am going on holiday. With all sorts of enjoyable plans for my holiday into the bargain. Along comes a gentleman who is familiar to me as the government representative at examinations for medical students, and whose performance in this role has earned him the flattering epithet of the 'Government Sleeping-partner'. On the strength of his official status he demands half a first-class compartment, and I hear one official say to another: 'Where shall we put the gentleman with the half first-class ticket?' A nice piece of preferential treatment: I pay my first-class fare in full. But then I do get a compartment to myself, though it is in a coach without a corridor, so that I will have no use of a lavatory the whole night long. I complain to the official, but to no avail, and I revenge myself by suggesting that he should have a hole made in the floor of the compartment in case travellers might have need of it. And at 2.45 in the morning I really do wake up from the following dream with the desire to urinate:

A crowd of people, a students' assembly.—*A count (Thun or*

Taaffe) is speaking. Called upon to say something about the Germans,
he declares derisively that their favourite flower is the coltsfoot [Huflat-
tich], and then sticks something resembling a torn leaf in his buttonhole,
actually the crumpled skeleton of a leaf. I flare up in indignation,*[14] *so I
flare up in indignation, but all the same I wonder at being in this state of
mind.* Then, less clearly: *it was as though it were the main hall [Aula]
of the university, the entrances crowded, and I would have to escape. I
force my way through a series of handsomely furnished rooms, obviously
rooms belonging to the administration, with furniture of a colour between
brown and mauve, and at length I arrive in a corridor where a housekeeper, a fat, elderly woman, is sitting. I avoid speaking to her; but she
clearly considers I have a right to get past, for she asks whether she should
accompany me with a lamp. I indicate, or tell her, that she should remain
on the stairs, and as I do so feel how cunning I am in finally eluding
inspection as I leave. In this way I get below and find a narrow, steeply
rising path, which I follow.*

Again unclear . . . *As if I now have the second task of getting out of
the city, just as earlier I got out of the house. I am riding in a hansom-cab
and tell him to drive to a railway station. 'I can't drive with you on the
railway line itself,' I say, after he raised an objection, as though I had
tired him out. At the same time it is as though I had already driven with
him on a stretch one usually travels by train. The stations are crowded; I
reflect whether I should go to Krems or Znaim,* but think that the Court
might be there and decide for Graz* or somewhere like that. Now I am
sitting in the carriage, which resembles a city tram, and I have in my
buttonhole a strangely entwined, long thing, with mauve-brown violets on
it made of a stiff material, which attracts a lot of attention.* Here the
scene breaks off.

*I am again in front of the railway station, but in the company of an
older man; I devise a plan for remaining unrecognized, but also see that
this plan has already been carried out. Thinking and experiencing are
here, as it were, one. He is pretending to be blind, at least in one eye, and I
am holding out a male urine-bottle to him (which we had to buy, or have
bought, in the city). I am his male nurse, then, and have to give him the
bottle because he is blind. If the ticket-collector sees us like this he is bound
to let us pass, as we are quite inconspicuous. At the same time the posture*

---

[14] This repetition slipped into my written account of the dream, presumably from
absent-mindedness. I retain it, as the analysis shows that it has its significance.

of the man in question and his urinating member can be seen very vividly. This is when I wake up with a desire to urinate.

The entire dream makes something of the impression of a fantasy transporting the dreamer to the revolutionary year of 1848. My memories of this had in fact been renewed by the anniversary celebration of 1898, as they had been by a little excursion to the *Wachau*.* Here I had got to know Emmersdorf,* the place where Fischhof,* the student leader, had retired, who might be indicated by certain features of the manifest dream-content. My train of thought then leads me to England, to the home of my brother, who had the habit of teasing his wife with 'Fifty years ago',* after the title of a poem by Lord *Tennyson*, which the children would always correct to '*fifteen* years ago'. But this fantasy, which is linked to the thoughts that had been called up by the sight of Count *Thun*, is only like the façade on Italian churches, placed in front of a building with no organic connection to it, being full of gaps, confused, and with components from the interior protruding in many places. The first situation in the dream is concocted from several scenes which I can separate out. The Count's arrogant posture in the dream is copied from a scene at the Gymnasium which occurred during my *fifteenth year*. We had formed a conspiracy against an unpopular and ignorant teacher. Its moving spirit was a fellow-student* who seems since then to have taken *Henry VIII of England* as his model. It fell to me to direct the principal assault, and a discussion of the importance to Austria of the Danube (*the Wachau!*) was the occasion when it came to open rebellion. One of our fellow-conspirators was the only aristocrat* in our year, called 'the *giraffe*' on account of his strikingly tall stature: summoned to explain himself by the school tyrant, the professor of *German*, he stood there before him like the Count in my dream. The declaration of the favourite flower and sticking in the buttonhole something that again must be a flower (which recall the orchids I had given a woman friend on the same day, and also a rose of *Jericho*), is strikingly reminiscent of the scene in *Shakespeare* which inaugurates the civil wars of the *white* and *red* roses;* the reference to Henry VIII paved the way to this recollection. Then, it was not far from the roses to the red and white carnations. (Between these the analysis interpolates two little verses, one *German*, the other *Spanish*: *Rosen, Tulpen, Nelken, alle Blumen welken*. [Roses, tulips, carnations, all flowers wither].—*Isabelita*, no llores que se marchitan las flores

[Little Isabel, do not weep because the flowers wither]. The Spanish comes from *Figaro*.) Here in Vienna the white carnation has become the emblem of the *anti-Semites*, the red that of the *Social Democrats*. Behind it a recollection of an anti-Semitic challenge during a railway journey through the beautiful land of Saxony (*Anglo-Saxon*s). The third scene contributing elements to the first dream situation comes from my earliest student days. In a *German* students' union there was a discussion of the relationship between philosophy and the natural sciences. Green youth that I was, full of materialist theories, I pushed myself forward to advocate an extremely one-sided point of view. A colleague,* my senior and my better, who has subsequently proved his ability to lead men and organize the masses, and, by the way, also has a name from the animal kingdom, then rose and gave us a sound drubbing; he too, he said, had in his youth tended swine and then returned repentant to his father's house. I *flared up in indignation* (as in the dream), became *swinishly* offensive [*saugrob*], and replied that now that I knew he had tended *swine, I was no longer surprised* at his manner of speech. (In the dream I am *surprised* at my nationalistic German state of mind.) Uproar followed; I was urged from many directions to retract my words, but I remained steadfast. The offended party was too sensible to accept the suggestion that he should offer a *challenge*, and let the matter rest.

The remaining elements of the dream-scene have their origin in deeper strata. What could the Count's proclamation of the 'colts-foot' mean? Here I must ask my chain of associations: *Huflattich* [coltsfoot]—*lattice* [lettuce]—*Salat* [salad]—*Salathund* [the dog-in-a-manger who grudges others what he nevertheless does not eat himself]. Here one can see a stock of insults showing through these expressions: *Gir-affe* [ape], *Schwein, Sau, Hund*; by the roundabout way of a name I can also arrive at an *ass*, and thereby again at mockery of an academic teacher. In addition I translate—I do not know whether correctly or not—*Huflattich* as *pisse-en-lit*. I learned this from *Zola*'s *Germinal*,* in which the children are invited to bring salad leaves of this sort with them. Dog—*chien* contains in its name an echo of the greater bodily function (*chier*, as *pisser* was used for the lesser). Before long we will have all three kinds of indecency together, for in this same *Germinal*, which has plenty to do with the coming revolution, a singular contest is described relating to the production of gaseous excretions called *flatus*.[15] And now I am bound to see that the path to this 'flatus' has been laid down for a long time, from the '*flowers*' via the *Spanish* verse, *Isabelita* to *Isabella* and *Ferdinand*, via *Henry VIII*, the sailing of the Armada against England, after whose defeat the English had a commemorative medallion struck bearing the inscription '*Flavit* et dissipati sunt',* for the tempest had scattered the Spanish fleet. But I intended, only half in jest, to use this inscription as the title of the chapter 'Therapy', if ever I were to get round to writing a detailed account of my conception and treatment of hysteria.

As for the second scene, I am not able to analyse it in such detail—for reasons of censorship. For in this scene I am putting myself in the position of one of the great of that revolutionary period who also had an adventure with an *eagle* and is said to have suffered from *incontinentia alvi** and the like, and *I believe I would not be justified in getting past* the censorship here, even though a *Hofrat* [lit: Court Councillor, senior civil servant] (*Aula*, consilarius *aulicus*) told me the greater part of that story. The series of rooms [*Zimmer*] in the dream owe their inspiration to His Excellency's Pullman car, into which I was able to glance for a moment; as so often in dreams, however, they signified *women* [*Frauenzimmer*] (public women). In the figure of the housekeeper I am repaying a clever elderly lady most ungratefully for her hospitality and for the many enjoyable stories I have been told at her house.—The feature of the lamp goes back to *Grillparzer*,* who noted a charming experience of similar tenor and then used it in his play about *Hero* and *Leander* (Des *Meeres* und der Liebe *Wellen* [The *Waves* of the *Sea* and of Love]—the Armada and the *storm*).

I must also withhold a detailed analysis of the two remaining parts of the dream; I shall pick out only those elements leading to the two childhood scenes which are my reason for considering the dream at all. It will rightly be supposed that it is sexual material that obliges me to make this suppression: but one does not need to be entirely satisfied by this explanation. For there are many things which are no secret to ourselves but which we are nevertheless obliged to keep secret from others, and what is at issue here is not the reasons for concealing the solution to the dream, but the motives of inner

---

[15] Not in *Germinal* but in *La Terre*, an error I only noticed after the analysis. In addition, I would draw attention to the identical letters in *Huflattich* and Flatus.

censorship which hide the actual content of my own dream from myself. I have to say, therefore, that the analysis reveals these three parts of the dream to be impertinent boasting, the issue of a ludicrous megalomania long since suppressed in my waking life, which even ventures at particular points into the manifest dream-content (*I feel how cunning I am*), and in any event offers an excellent explanation of my exuberant mood on the evening before the dream. Boasting in every field: thus the reference to *Graz* alludes to the saying: '*What does Graz cost?*' which we are fond of repeating when we feel we have more than enough money. Anyone who recalls Master *Rabelais's** unsurpassed account of the life and deeds of *Gargantua* and his son *Pantagruel* will be able to include the implied content of the first part of the dream among the instances of boasting. What follows belongs to the two scenes of childhood I promised to relate: I had bought a *new* suitcase for this journey, whose colour, a *brownish-mauve*, appears several times in the dream (*mauve-brown* violets made of a stiff material beside a thing they call a 'girl-catcher'—the furniture in the administration's rooms). It is a well-known childhood belief that something *new* will *attract attention*. The following scene from my childhood was told me, and my memory of it has been replaced by the recollection of that account. Before the age of two I am supposed to have occasionally still *wet the bed*, and when I was rebuked for this, so I am told, I *consoled* my father with the promise that in N. (the nearest town of any size) I would buy him a lovely *new, red* bed. (Hence the parenthesis in the dream that *we bought* the bottle *in the city, or had to buy it*: what we have promised we *have* to perform.) (Notice, too, the combination of the male bottle and the female case, *box*.) The child's entire megalomania is contained in this promise. We have already been struck, in the course of an earlier dream-interpretation, by the significance for the dream of the problems children experience over urination (compare the dream on p. 154).

Then there was another domestic incident when I was seven or eight which I remember very well. One evening before going to bed I broke the rule that one must not relieve oneself in one's parents' bedroom in their presence, and in the course of rebuking me for this, my father let fall the remark: 'Nothing will come of the boy.' It must have been a terrible blow to my ambition, for allusions to this scene recur in my dreams again and again and are invariably connected with enumerations of my successes and achievements, as though I wanted to say: 'You see, something did come of me.' This childhood scene also provided the material for the last image in the dream, in which, of course, the roles were reversed in revenge. The older man, plainly my father, since the blindness in one eye signifies the glaucoma he suffered in one eye,[16] is now urinating in front of me as I once did in front of him. With the glaucoma I am reminding him of the cocaine which had been of help to him during his operation, as if thereby I had fulfilled my promise. Besides this, I am making fun of him: because he is blind, I have to hold the bottle out to him, and I am revelling in allusions to my knowledge of the theory of hysteria, which I am proud of.[17]

---

[16] Another interpretation: he has one eye, like *Odin*, father of the gods. *Odhin's Consolation**—The *consolation* I offer my father that I will buy him a new bed.

[17] Some of the material on which the interpretation is based: holding out the bottle [*Glas*] recalls the story of the peasant at the optician's who tries glass after glass but still cannot see.—Bauern*fänger* [peasant-catcher = con-man]—Mädchen*fänger* [girl-catcher] in the previous part of the dream.—The treatment of the weak-minded father by the peasants in Zola's *La Terre*.*—The unhappy satisfaction of seeing how in the last days of his life my father dirtied his bed like a child; hence in the dream I am his male nurse.— 'Thinking and experiencing are here, as it were, one' recalls a violently revolutionary literary drama by Oscar Panizza* in which God the Father is treated pretty shamefully as a paralysed old man; it says there: 'Will and deed with him are one,' and his archangel, a kind of Ganymede, has to restrain him from scolding and cursing, as these imprecations would instantly be fulfilled.—The *devising of plans* is a criticism of my father, originating from a later period, just as the entire rebellious content of the dream, full of *lèse-majesté* and mockery of the authorities as it is, goes back to rebellion against the father. The prince is called *Landesvater* [father of his country], and the father is the oldest, first, and sole authority for the child, from whose absolute power the other social authorities have proceeded in the course of the history of human culture (insofar as 'Matriarchy' does not impose limits on this proposition).—The version in the dream, 'Thinking and experiencing are one', points to the explanation of hysterical symptoms, to which the *male bottle* also related. A Viennese would not need me to explain the meaning of the principle of 'Gschnas': it consists in producing objects of a rare and valuable appearance out of trivial, preferably ludicrous and worthless material, e.g. arms and weapons out of cooking-pots, straw, and salt-sticks, as our artists do on their social evenings. Now, I had noticed that hysterics do the same; beside what has actually happened to them, they unconsciously create for themselves horrible or extravagant fantasy events which they construct from the most innocuous and banal material of their experience. It is on these fantasies, and not on the recollection of actual events, that their symptoms depend, and this is so, whether the symptoms are serious or equally innocuous. This explanation had helped me over many difficulties and given me much pleasure. I was able to use it to explain the dream-element of the '*male bottle*' because I had been told at the last 'Gschnas' evening that a poison chalice of Lucretia Borgia's had been put on display, which had as its centre-piece and main component a *urine bottle* for men of the sort customarily used in hospitals.

If the two urinating scenes from childhood are in any case closely linked in my history to the theme of megalomania, their arousal on the journey to Aussee is helped by the circumstance that my compartment had no WC, and I had to be prepared for an embarrassing situation in the course of the journey, which is just what did happen in the morning. I then woke with the sensations of a call of nature. One might be inclined to attribute the role of actual initiator of the dream to these sensations, but I would rather give precedence to a different idea: that it was the dream-thoughts which first called forth the desire to urinate. It is very unusual for me to be aroused from sleep by a need of any kind, least of all at the time I woke on this occasion, quarter to four in the morning. I would counter a further objection by saying that on other journeys under more comfortable conditions, I hardly ever felt a desire to urinate after waking too early. In any case, it will not matter if I leave this point undecided.

My experience in the analysis of dreams has, further, made me aware that even dreams whose interpretation at first seems complete because both the source of the dream and the initiator of the wish are easily demonstrable—even these dreams set vital trains of thought reaching out which go back to earliest childhood: and so I have had to ask myself whether this feature too does not constitute an essential condition of dreaming. If I might generalize this idea: in its manifest content, every dream would be characterized by a connection with what has been experienced recently; in its latent content, however, by a connection with the experiences from our earliest years—which, as I really can demonstrate from my analyses of hysteria, have remained in a strict sense still recent, right up to the present. However, this supposition still seems very difficult to prove; I shall have to return in another context to the probable part played by our earliest childhood experiences in the formation of dreams (Chapter VII).

Of the three peculiarities of the dream-memory we considered at the start, we have explained one satisfactorily—its preference for the trivial in the dream-content—by tracing it back to dream-distortion. We have been able to confirm the existence of the other two—the special choice made of recent and of infantile material—but we have not been able to account for them by the motives for dreaming. Let us keep these two characteristics in mind, for their explanation and utility remain to be dealt with: they are bound to find their place

elsewhere, either in the psychology of sleep, or in those considerations of how the psychical apparatus is constructed, which we shall
have to undertake later once we have noted that the interpretation of
dreams enables us, like a window, to cast a glance into its interior.

However, I should like to emphasize one other result of these last
dream-analyses before going on. The dream frequently appears *to
have several meanings*; not only can several wish-fulfilments be united
in it alongside one another, as we have seen; but one meaning, one
wish-fulfilment can overlay another, until right at the bottom we
come upon the fulfilment of a wish from earliest childhood; and here
again we are bound to wonder whether in this sentence 'frequently'
should not be replaced by 'invariably'.

(c) *The Somatic Sources of Dreams*

If we try to interest an educated layman in the problems of dreaming, and with this in mind ask him what sources he thinks dreams
might flow from, we usually find that he believes he is quite sure of
this part of their solution. He recalls at once the influence on the
formation of dreams exercised by a disturbed or overburdened
digestion ('dreams come from the stomach'), or by the position the
body happens to take, or by little eventualities while we are asleep,
and he seems quite unaware that after all these motives have been
taken into consideration there still might be something left that
needs explaining.

What part the scientific literature has assigned to somatic sources
of stimulus in the formation of dreams has already been discussed in
detail in the opening chapter (pp. 30–5), so all we need do here is
recall the results of this review. We heard that three kinds of somatic
stimulus-source are to be distinguished: objective sensory stimuli
proceeding from external objects; purely subjective excitations of
the sensory organs; and physical stimuli originating from within
the body. And we noted that, in contrast to somatic sources, the
authorities tended to push any possible psychical sources of dreams
into the background, or even exclude them entirely (p. 36). In testing
the claims made in favour of these groups as somatic sources of
stimulus we learned that the significance of objective excitations of
the sense-organs—partly chance stimuli during sleep, partly those
which the psyche is unable to ward off even in sleep—is confirmed

by numerous observations and corroborated by experiment
(pp. 23-4). We found that the role of subjective sensory excitations
appears to have been proved by the recurrence of hypnagogic
sensory images in dreams (p. 28). And we learned that—although it
cannot be demonstrated that the entire range of images and ideas
occurring in our dreams is traceable to internal physical stimuli—
this widely assumed derivation can be supported by the influence
patently exerted on the content of our dreams by the excitations of
the digestive, urinary, and sexual organs.

'*Nervous stimulus*' and '*physical stimulus*' then, it is claimed, are the
somatic sources of dreams, that is, according to several authorities,
the only sources there are.

On the other hand, we have also paid heed to a number of doubts
which seem to attack not so much the correctness as the adequacy of
the somatic stimulus theory.

However certain all its advocates must have felt about its factual
basis—especially with regard to accidental and external nervous
stimuli, which can be recognized in the dream-content with no
trouble whatever—still, not one of them was unaware of the likeli-
hood that the sheer abundance of ideas contained in dreams might
not be derived from external nervous stimuli alone. Miss Mary
Whiton Calkins [12] examined her own dreams and those of a
second person from this point of view over six weeks, and found
only 13.2 per cent and 6.7 per cent respectively in which the element of external sense-perception could be demonstrated; only two
instances in her collection could be traced back to organic sensations.
On this point, statistics confirm what a superficial survey of our own
experiences had led us to expect.

Many have settled for giving prominence to the 'nervous-stimulus
dream' over other forms of dream, as being a well-researched sub-
species. Spitta [64] divided dreams into those aroused by *nervous-
stimulus* and those by *association*. However, it was clear that this
solution could not be considered satisfactory as long as it failed to
demonstrate the bond linking the somatic dream-sources to the ideas
contained in the dream.

Accordingly, as well as the first objection—the insufficient frequency of external stimuli—there is now a second, the inadequate
elucidation of the dream that is reached by introducing this kind of
dream-source to explain it. The advocates of this theory owe us two

explanations in this respect: first, why we do not recognize the external stimulus as we dream for what it is, but invariably misunderstand it (compare the alarm-clock dreams, p. 25); and second, why the reaction of the perceiving psyche to this misunderstood stimulus can vary so unpredictably in its outcome. By way of answer to this question we have heard from Strümpell [66] that, as a consequence of its withdrawal from the external world in sleep, the psyche is not in a position to offer the correct interpretation of the objective sensory stimulus, but is obliged to create illusions on the basis of this stimulus with its range of indeterminate potentialities. As he puts it himself (p. 108):

'As soon as an external or internal nervous stimulus produces in the psyche a sensation or a complex of sensations, a feeling, a psychical event of any kind, and as soon as this is perceived by the psyche, this event summons up sensory images left there from the sphere of its waking experience, from earlier perceptions, that is, either naked or clad in the appropriate psychical values. It gathers around itself, as it were, a larger or smaller number of such images, which are the means by which the impression deriving from the nervous stimulus acquires its psychical value. Here too we usually say, as we do of waking behaviour, that when asleep the psyche *interprets* the impressions produced by the nervous stimuli. The outcome of this interpretation is what we call the *nervous-stimulus dream*, that is, a dream whose constituents are determined by a nervous stimulus producing its effects in the life of the psyche in accordance with the laws of reproduction.'

Wundt's [76] view is identical in all essentials to this theory; he maintains that the ideas appearing in dreams proceed in the main at least from sensory stimuli, including especially stimuli of our general vital feeling. So they are mainly illusions of the fantasy, and probably only to a minor extent pure remembered ideas intensified into hallucinations. To express the relation between the dream–content and the dream–stimuli according to this theory, Strümpell hits on the excellent comparison (p. 14): it is 'as though the ten fingers of a player wholly ignorant of music are running up and down the keyboard'. In this view the dream would appear to be not a psychical phenomenon arising from psychical motivations but the consequence of a physiological stimulus expressing itself in psychical symptoms, because the apparatus affected by the stimulus is incapable of any other form of expression. A similar assumption lies, for example, behind the explanation of obsessional ideas which Meynert put forward in his famous comparison with a dial on which certain numbers stand out more strongly than others.

However popular this theory of somatic dream-stimuli has become, and however attractive it may appear, it is nevertheless easy to point out its weak point. Every somatic dream-stimulus that requires the sleeping psychical apparatus to interpret it by constructing an illusion can arouse countless such attempts at interpretation, that is, can get itself represented in the dream-content in a tremendous variety of different ideas. However, the theory put forward by Strümpell and Wundt is unable to suggest any motive which would govern the relation between the external stimulus and the dream-idea selected for its interpretation, that is, which would explain the 'strange selection' that the stimuli 'make often enough in their reproductive activity' (Lipps, *Grundthatsachen des Seelenlebens*, p. 170). Other objections can be raised against the assumption at the basis of the entire theory of illusion, which holds that the sleeping psyche is not capable of recognizing the real nature of objective sensory stimuli. The physiologist Burdach [8] showed us long ago that even in sleep the psyche is perfectly capable of interpreting correctly the sense-impressions reaching it, capable too of reacting in accordance with the correct interpretation, for he argues that we are able to exclude sense-impressions that seem important to us (nurse and child) from the oblivion into which we fall when asleep, and that we are much more certain to be wakened by our own name than by some indifferent impression on the ear—which of course presupposes that even in sleep the psyche distinguishes between sensations (Section I, p. 36). Burdach concludes from these observations that what should be assumed is not our inability to interpret sensory stimuli while asleep, but *our lack of interest in them*. The same arguments as Burdach was using in 1830 recur unaltered in 1883 in Lipps's criticism of the theory of somatic stimulus. According to this, the psyche appears to be like the sleeper in the anecdote: when asked 'Are you asleep?', he replies 'No', but in response to the request that follows, 'Then lend me ten guilders', takes refuge behind the excuse 'I'm asleep'.

The inadequacy of the theory of somatic dream-stimuli can also be demonstrated in other ways. Observation shows that I am not compelled by the external stimuli to dream, even though these promptly appear in the dream-content in the event of my dreaming. I can react in a number of ways to a stimulus that comes over me in sleep, to the skin, say, or to one caused by pressure. I can simply not notice it, and then discover on waking up that, for instance, a leg has been uncovered or an arm squashed; indeed, pathology shows me countless examples of the most various and violent stimuli from sensations or movements during sleep which have failed to produce any effect at all. I may feel a sensation during sleep—penetrating my sleep, as it were—which is usually the case with painful stimuli, but without weaving the pain into a dream; and I may, thirdly, wake in response to the stimulus in order to remove it. It is only as a fourth possible reaction that the nervous stimulus might cause me to dream; but the other possibilities will be realized at least as often as that of forming a dream. This could not happen if the *motivation for dreaming did not lie outside the somatic sources of stimulus.*

A fair assessment of these gaps in the explanation that dreams are due to somatic stimuli has been made by other writers—Scherner [58], joined by the philosopher Volkelt [72]; they have attempted to determine more precisely the psychical activities which create such varied and colourful dream-images out of the somatic stimuli, that is, they have moved dreaming essentially back into the inner realm again, and into an activity of the psyche. Scherner not only gave a vivid and imaginative poetic description of the psychical character-istics revealed in the formation of dreams, he also believed he had divined the principle governing the psyche's treatment of the stimuli presented to it. According to Scherner, as the dream-work bestirs the imagination, soaring freely and unburdened by the fetters of the day, it strives to represent *in symbolic form* the nature of the organ that gives rise to the stimulus and the kind of stimulus it may be. In this way a sort of dream-book develops containing instructions for the interpretation of dreams and enabling us to make inferences from the dream-images about our bodily feelings, the condition of our organs, and the nature of the stimuli. 'Thus the image of a cat will express a mood of ill-humour, the image of a smooth, shining loaf of bread, bodily nudity. The human body as a whole is repre-sented by the dream-imagination as a house, the separate bodily organs as parts of the house. In "toothache dreams" a high-vaulted entrance-hallway corresponds to the mouth, and a flight of stairs to the descent from the throat to the gullet; in "headache dreams" the ceiling of a room covered with disgusting toad-like spiders is chosen to designate the top of the head' (Volkelt, p. 39). 'A wide selection of these symbols is used by the dream to represent the same organ; thus the breathing lung finds its symbol in a blazing, roaring stove, the heart in empty chests and baskets, the bladder in round, bag-shaped, or generally hollowed-out objects. It is especially important that at the conclusion of the dream the organ producing the stimulus, or its function, is often presented undisguised, in fact, mainly as it affects the dreamer's own body. Thus the "toothache dream" usually ends with the dreamer's drawing a tooth out of his mouth' (p. 35). This theory of dream-interpretation cannot be said to have found much favour with the authorities on the subject. More than anything, it seemed so far-fetched; and there has even been some reluctance to recognize the morsel of justification which in my judgement it can claim. As we see, it leads to a revival of dream-interpretation by means of *symbolism* such as the ancients employed, except that the sphere from which the interpretation is drawn is limited to the extent of the human body. The applicability of Scherner's theory is bound to be seriously restricted by the absence of a scientifically comprehensible technique of interpretation. Arbitrariness in the dream-interpretation is certainly not to be discounted, especially as here too a stimulus can express itself in the dream-content in several forms of representation; thus, even Scherner's follower Volkelt was unable to confirm the representation of the body as a house. It is bound to cause offence, too, that here again the psyche has the dream-work foisted on it as a useless and purposeless activity, for according to this theory the psyche is content to generate fantasies about the stimulus engaging it without even the remotest prospect of removing it.

But there is one objection which deals a heavy blow to Scherner's theory of the dream's symbolization of physical stimuli. These physical stimuli are present at all times, and it is generally assumed that the psyche is more accessible to them during sleep than when we are awake. So it is difficult to understand why the psyche does not dream continually the whole night through, indeed, why it does not dream every night about all the organs. If this objection is met by stipulating that to arouse dream-activity special excitations would have to proceed from the eye, ear, teeth, gut, etc., then there is still the difficulty of demonstrating that these intensifications in the stimuli are objective—which is possible only in a small number of cases. If the dream of flying symbolizes the rise and fall of the lungs while breathing, then, as Strümpell already observed, either this dream would have to be dreamed much more frequently, or one ought to be able to demonstrate an increase in breathing activity during the dream. Yet a third case is possible, the most probable of all, that is, that special motives may be intermittently operative to draw attention to visceral sensations uniformly present—but this case already takes us beyond Scherner's theory.

The value of Scherner's and Volkelt's views lies in the fact that they draw our attention to a number of characteristics of the dream-content which need explanation and seem to obscure further insight. It is quite correct that dreams contain symbolizations of bodily organs and functions, that in dreams water often indicates a stimulus from the bladder, that the male member can be represented by an upright staff or a column, and so forth. One can hardly reject the interpretation of dreams displaying a very mobile field of vision and brilliant colours as 'visual-stimulus dreams', in contrast to the pallid colouring of others, nor dispute the contribution of illusion-formation in dreams containing noise and a babble of voices. A dream such as Scherner's, in which two rows of fine fair-haired boys stand facing one another on a bridge, attack one another, and then take up their former positions again, until finally the dreamer sits down on a bridge and draws a long tooth from his jaw; or a similar dream of Volkelt's, which involves two rows of cupboard-drawers and which again ends with pulling out a tooth: dream-images of this kind, described in great detail by both writers, will not allow us to cast Scherner's theory aside as idle invention without first investigating the core of truth it contains. Our task will then be to produce an alternative explanation for the supposed symbolization of the alleged toothache.

All the time we have been engaged with the theory of somatic dream-sources I have refrained from advancing any argument based on our dream-analyses. If we have been able to show, by a procedure which other authorities have not applied to their material on dreams, that the dream possesses a value of its own as a psychical act, that a wish is the motive for its formation, and that the experiences of the previous day provide the immediate material for its content, then every other dream-theory that neglects such an important investigative procedure, and consequently makes the dream seem a useless and puzzling psychical reaction to somatic stimuli, stands condemned even without any specific criticism. Otherwise—most improbably—there would have to be two quite different kinds of dream, of which we have encountered only one, and the earlier judges of the dream only the other. All that remains for us to do now is to find a place within our own theory of dreams for the facts on which the current theory of somatic dream-stimuli is based.

We have already taken the first step in this direction by putting forward the proposition that the dream-work is under the compulsion to process into a unity all the initiators to dreaming that are present at the same time (p. 137). We saw that when two or more experiences capable of producing an impression are left from the previous day, the wishes arising from them are united in a dream; we also saw that the psychically valuable impression and the trivial experience come together to form the material of the dream, provided that ideas mediating between the two can be generated. Hence the dream appears as a reaction to everything that is simultaneously present and currently active in the sleeping psyche. As far as we have analysed the dream-material up to now, we have recognized it as being a collection of psychical remnants, memory-traces, to which (on account of the preference for recent and childhood material) we had to ascribe a psychologically—as yet—indeterminable characteristic of current activity. It will not be very difficult for us now to predict what will happen if these active memories are joined during sleep by new material from the senses. These excitations in turn become important for the dream because they are current and active; they are combined with the other factors currently active in the psyche to provide material for forming the dream. In other words, the stimuli occurring during sleep are processed into a wish-fulfilment whose other constituents are the familiar psychical remains of the day. This combination does not *have* to take place; indeed, we have heard that more than one kind of response is possible towards bodily stimuli in our behaviour when asleep. Where it does take place is in those dreams where it has been possible to find representational material for the dream-content able to express both kinds of dream-source, the somatic and the psychical.

The essential nature of the dream is not changed if the psychical sources of the dream are supplemented by somatic material: it remains a wish-fulfilment, no matter how its expression is determined by the current material.

At this point I should like to make room for a number of distinctive factors which can shape the importance of external stimuli for the dream in variously shifting ways. I imagine that a combination of individual, psychological, and fortuitous elements working together in any given circumstances will decide how we behave in particular instances of more intense objective stimulation during sleep; the habitual or accidental depth of our sleep, combined with the intensity of the stimulus, will in one instance make it possible to suppress the stimulus in such a way that it does not disturb our sleep, in another force us to wake up, or support our efforts to overcome the stimulus by weaving it into a dream. In accordance with the diversity of these constellations, external objective stimuli will find expression more frequently or more rarely in one person's dreams than in another's. In my own case, as I am an excellent sleeper and stubbornly resist any attempt to disturb me while I am asleep, external causes of excitation very rarely intrude into my dreams, whereas psychical motives evidently cause me to dream very easily. In fact I have recorded only one single dream in which an objective, painful source of stimulus can be recognized, and this dream in particular will be most instructive for us to see what effect the external stimulus had in shaping it.

I am riding a grey horse, at first timidly and clumsily, as though I were only holding on. Then I encounter a colleague, P., who is sitting high in the saddle, dressed in a suit of loden cloth, and warning me of something (probably that I have a bad seat). Now I gradually find that I am sitting more and more easily and comfortably on my highly intelligent horse, and I note that I feel quite at home up here. For a saddle I have a kind of cushion which completely fills the space between the horse's neck and crupper. Thus saddled, I ride through the narrow space between two heavy waggons. After I have ridden some distance down the road, I turn round and make to dismount, at first before a little chapel with open door, built as part of the street frontage; but then I really dismount in front of one very near it; my hotel is in the same street; I could let the horse go on there alone, but I prefer to lead it there myself. It is as if I were ashamed to arrive at the hotel on horseback. A hotel-boy is standing in front of it. He shows me a note of mine which has been found, and laughs at me over it. On the note, underlined twice, is written: 'Nothing to eat', and then a second instruction (unclear) *something like: 'No work'; in addition a vague idea that I am in a strange town, where I am not doing any work.*

At first one cannot tell from the dream that it arose under the influence, or rather under the compulsion, of a painful stimulus. But the day before I had been suffering from boils that made every movement a torment, and finally a boil at the base of the scrotum had grown as big as an apple, causing me the most unbearable pain with every step. Feverish fatigue, lack of appetite, carrying on in spite of it all with the day's hard work, all combined with the pain to distress me. I was not really capable of pursuing my duties as a physician, but the nature and location of the trouble raised the thought of a different activity—the one for which I would certainly have been more unfit than for any other, and that is *riding*. Now this is the very activity my dream sets me doing; it is the most energetic denial of my complaint that can be imagined. I cannot ride in any case; apart from this once, it never enters my dreams; I have only ever sat on a horse once, and then it was without a saddle, and I did not enjoy it. But in this dream I am riding as if I had no boil on the perineum, *no, I am riding for the very reason that I do not want to have one.* To judge from its description, my saddle is the poultice which made it possible for me to sleep. Protected by it, I probably felt nothing of my pain in the early hours of sleep. Then the painful sensations made themselves felt and tried to wake me up, whereupon the dream came and said soothingly: 'Sleep on still, you won't wake up anyway! You haven't got a boil, look, you're riding a horse after all, and you can't ride if you've got a boil.' And the dream succeeded. The pain was numbed and I slept on.

But the dream was not content with 'suggesting away' the boil by obstinately clinging to an idea incompatible with my complaint—in this respect behaving like the hallucinatory delusions of the mother who has lost her child[18] or the merchant whose losses have destroyed his fortune. In addition, the details of the sensation denied in the dream and the image used to repress it also serve the dream as material to link other material currently active in the psyche to the dream-situation, and to find a way of representing it. I am riding a *grey* horse; the colour of the horse matches exactly the *pepper-and-*

---

[18] Compare the passage in *Griesinger* [31] and the observation in my second paper on the psychoneuroses of defence, *Neurologisches Zentralblatt*, 1896 [in fact in his first paper, SE iii. 43].

salt-coloured suit my colleague P. was wearing when last I encountered him in the country. *Highly spiced food* has been suggested to me as the cause of my boils, in any case preferable as an aetiology to *sugar*, which one might think of in connection with boils. My friend P. is fond of *getting on his high horse* with me ever since he took over a woman patient of mine with whom I had performed great *feats* [*Kunststücke*] (in my dream I am sitting on the horse crosswise at first, like a *circus-rider* [*Kunstreiter*]), but who really led me, like the horse in the anecdote leading the Sunday rider,* whither she would. So symbolically the horse comes to signify a patient (in my dream it is *highly intelligent*); '*I feel quite at home up there*' goes back to the position I occupied in her house before I was replaced by P. '*I thought you were firmly in the saddle there*' was a remark made to me recently about my connections with the same house by one of my few well-wishers among the great physicians of this city. It was also a great *feat* to practise psychotherapy for eight to ten hours a day in such pain, but I know that unless I am physically well, I cannot carry on my particularly difficult work for long, and the dream is full of dark allusions to the situation that is bound to arise (the note, of the sort neurotics keep and show their physician): '*Nothing to eat and no work*'. Interpreting further, I see that the dream-work has contrived to find the route from the wish-fulfilling situation of riding to very early scenes of childhood quarrels which must have taken place between myself and a nephew, only a year older than I by the way, who now lives in England. In addition, it has taken up elements from my travels in Italy; the street in my dream is made up of impressions from Verona and Siena. Interpretation going still deeper leads to sexual dream-thoughts, and I recall what dream-allusions to this beautiful country were thought to mean in a woman patient of mine who had never been in Italy (*gen Italien—Genitalien* [to Italy—genitals]); at the same time this has some connection with the house where I preceded my friend P. as physician, and with the place where my boil was located.

Among the dreams mentioned in earlier sections there were already several which could serve as examples of processing nervous stimuli, as they are called. The dream of drinking water in great draughts is one of these; in this case the somatic stimulus is apparently the sole source of the dream, and the wish deriving from the sensation—thirst—its only motive. It is similar in other simple dreams, if the somatic stimulus by itself is capable of creating a wish. The dream of the invalid who cast the cooling appliance off her cheek at night shows an unusual way of reacting to painful stimuli with a wish-fulfilment. It seems that the invalid had temporarily contrived to numb her own sensations, and in doing so she foisted her pain onto someone else.

My dream of the three Fates is obviously a hunger-dream, but it contrives to push the need for nourishment back to the infant's longing for the mother's breast, and to use this harmless desire as a screen for a more serious one which may not express itself so openly. The dream about Count *Thun* showed us the paths by which a fortuitous physical need can be linked with the most powerful—but also with the most powerfully suppressed—emotions of the inner life. And when, as in the case reported by Garnier, the First Consul weaves the noise of an exploding infernal machine into a dream of battle before it wakes him, this reveals very clearly the nature of the only aim served at all by the psyche's activity as it engages with sensations during sleep.

Let us compare this dream by Napoleon I, who was, by the way, an excellent sleeper, with the dream of the lie-abed student woken by his landlady to get to the hospital, who dreamed he was in a hospital bed and then slept on with the motivation: 'If I am already at the hospital, I don't need to get up in order to go there.' The latter is an obvious dream of convenience. The speaker frankly admits his motive for dreaming, but in doing so, he reveals one of the secret motivations for dreaming at all. In a certain sense all dreams are *dreams of convenience*: they serve the purpose of continuing sleep instead of waking up. *The dream is the guardian of sleep, not its disturber.* We shall produce the arguments to justify this view at a later point, contrasting it with those psychical factors which wake us from sleep; at this stage we are already able to establish that it is applicable to the part played by objective external stimuli. Either the psyche does not concern itself at all with the causes of sensations during sleep, if it is able to do this despite the intensity of the stimuli and despite under-standing very well what they signal; or it uses the dream to deny these stimuli; or, thirdly, if it *has* to acknowledge them, it seeks out that interpretation which presents the currently active sensation as a constituent of a situation which is both wished-for and compatible with sleeping. The actual sensation is woven into a dream *in order to* *rob it of reality.* Napoleon may go on sleeping: for all that is trying to disturb him is a dream-recollection of the rumble of cannon at Arcole.*[19]

Thus the wish to sleep must always be included among the motives for the formation of dreams, and every successful dream is a fulfilment of this wish. How this universal, invariably present, and constant wish to sleep relates to the other wishes fulfilled in their turn by the dream-content, will be the subject of another discussion. However, in the wish to sleep we have uncovered the factor that is able to fill the gap in the Strümpell–Wundt theory and explain the oddity and capriciousness of the way the dream interprets the external stimulus. The correct interpretation—which the sleeping psyche is perfectly capable of making—would make claims on our active interest and demand an end to sleep; so out of all the interpretations possible only those are admitted which are compatible with the absolute censorship exercised by the wish to sleep. As who should say: it is the nightingale* and not the lark. For if it is the lark, our night of love is at an end. From among the interpretations now admissible, the one then selected will be the interpretation that is able to make the best link with the wishful impulses lurking in the psyche. Thus everything is unambiguously determined, and nothing left to arbitrary choice. The misinterpretation is not illusion but—if you like—evasion. But again, as in the case of substitution by displacement at the behest of the dream-censorship, we have to concede that here too is an act which puts the normal psychical process out of joint.

If the external nervous and internal somatic stimuli are sufficiently intense to compel the attention of the psyche, then—always provided that they result in dreaming and not in waking up—they represent a firm point for the formation of the dream, a nucleus in the dream-material, for which a corresponding wish-fulfilment can be sought much as mediating ideas (see above) are sought between two psychical dream-stimuli. It is in so far true of a number of dreams that in them the somatic element is in command of the dream-content. In this extreme case, in order to create the dream even a wish that is not actively present will be roused. However, all the dream can do is represent a situation in which a wish appears as fulfilled; it is, as it were, faced with the task of seeking out the wish

---

[19] The two sources from which I learned of this dream do not agree in their accounts.

that can be represented as fulfilled by the sensation actively present. Even if this active material is painful or distressing in character, that does not make it useless for forming a dream. The life of the psyche also has at its disposal wishes whose fulfilment arouses unpleasure—which seems a contradiction, but can be explained if we take into account the presence of the two psychical agencies and the censorship prevailing between them.

As we have heard, there are in the life of the psyche *repressed* wishes belonging to the first system whose fulfilment the second system resists. When I say 'there are', I do not mean it historically, as if to say that these wishes once existed and have been abolished; on the contrary, the theory of repression, which the study of the psychoneuroses requires, maintains that such repressed wishes still continue in existence, but at the same time so does the burden of an inhibition. Language has hit upon the right term when it speaks of the 'suppression' of such impulses. The psychical organization enabling these wishes to break through to their realization remains intact and in working order. But if it happens that such a suppressed wish is in fact realized, then the inhibition set up by the second system (which is capable of consciousness) and now overcome, expresses itself as unpleasure. To conclude this discussion: when unpleasurable sensations from somatic sources are present in sleep, this constellation is utilized by the dream-work, maintaining the censorship to a greater or lesser degree, to represent the fulfilment of an otherwise repressed wish.

One set of anxiety-dreams is made possible by this state of affairs, while another set of these dream-formations unfavourable to the wish-theory displays a different mechanism. For anxiety in dreams can be psychoneurotic, originating in psychosexual excitations, and in their case the anxiety corresponds to repressed libido. In such instances, this anxiety has the significance of a neurotic symptom, as the entire anxiety-dream does, and we are standing on the border where the dream's wish-fulfilling intention breaks down. But there are other anxiety-dreams where the feeling of anxiety has a somatic origin (for instance, with breathing difficulties experienced by invalids with lung or heart trouble), and then it is exploited to assist energetically suppressed wishes towards their fulfilment in a dream, though their dream, had it arisen from psychical motivations, would have resulted in the same release of anxiety. It is not difficult to reconcile the two apparently disparate cases. If either of two factors belonging intimately together in the psyche—an inclination towards an affect together with a representational content—is currently active and given, it will evoke the other, even in a dream; in the one instance the somatically given anxiety will call up the suppressed ideas contained in the psyche; in the other, these ideas, freed from repression and accompanied by sexual excitation, will call up the release of anxiety. We can say of the one case that a somatically given affect receives a psychical interpretation; in the other, though everything is psychically given, the content, which had been suppressed, is easily replaced by a somatic interpretation appropriate to the anxiety. The difficulties our understanding has with this have little to do with dreams: they arise because with this discussion we are touching on the problems of how anxiety develops, and of repression.

The stimuli from within our body which command our dreams undoubtedly include our general physical feeling. Not that it is able to provide the content of the dream, but it does compel the dream-thoughts to select from the material which is to act as representation in the dream-content, as it brings one part of this material close to mind as appropriate and keeps another distant. Moreover, it is very likely that this general feeling from the life of the day is linked to the psychical residue important for the dream.

When the somatic sources of stimulus during sleep—that is to say, the sensations felt in sleep—are not unusually intense, their part in the formation of dreams is similar, in my view, to that played by the recent but trivial impressions of the day. I think that they are brought into play in the formation of a dream only when they are suitable for combination with the ideas contained in the psychical source of the dream, but otherwise not. They are treated like a cheap material always available and put to use whenever needed, rather than a precious material itself prescribing how it should be used. The case is rather as if a patron brought an artist a rare stone, an onyx, for him to make into a work of art. The size of the stone, its colouring and flaws, will help to decide what head or scene is to be represented in it, whereas in the case of uniform and abundant material such as marble or sandstone the artist only follows the idea which has formed in his mind. It is only in this way, it seems to me, that we can understand why the content of our dreams provided by bodily stimuli of ordinary intensity nevertheless does not appear in every dream, nor every night.

Perhaps I can best explain my view by an example which will also take us back to dream-interpretation. One day I was struggling to understand the significance of the sensation we sometimes have of inhibited movement, of being unable to stir, unable to have done with something, and the like, which appears so often in dreams, and which is so similar to the feeling of anxiety. That night I had the following dream: *I am going, very incompletely dressed, from an apartment on the ground floor up a flight of stairs to a floor higher up. As I go I jump three steps at a time, pleased that I can climb stairs so nimbly. Suddenly I see a maidservant coming down the steps, that is, towards me. I feel embarrassed, try to hurry, and then that sensation of inhibition appears. I am stuck to the steps and cannot move.*

Analysis: The situation in the dream is taken from everyday reality. I have two flats in an apartment-building in Vienna which are connected only by the main flight of stairs outside them. My consulting-room and study are on the upper ground floor, the living rooms on the floor above. When I have finished my work in the lower apartment late in the evening, I go up the flight of stairs to my bedroom. On the evening before the dream I had in fact gone this short distance in rather dishevelled dress, that is, I had taken off my collar, tie and cuffs; in the dream this had become a greater degree, as usual vague, of undress. Jumping the steps is my customary way of going upstairs, though here it was a wish-fulfilment as well, already recognized as such in the dream, for my ease in performing this feat reassured me as to the condition of my heart. Moreover, this way of going upstairs is the effective opposite to the inhibition in the second half of the dream. It shows me what needs no proof: that the dream has no difficulty in imagining motor actions being performed to perfection: think, for instance, of flying in dreams!

However, the flight of stairs I am going up is not that of my own house; at first I do not recognize it and only the person coming towards me enlightens me as to the place intended. This person is the maidservant of the old lady I visit twice a day to give her injections; the flight of stairs is also quite similar to those I have to climb there twice a day.

How have these stairs and this woman got into my dream? The embarrassment at not being fully dressed is undoubtedly sexual in character; the maidservant I dreamed about is older than I, surly and not at all attractive. The only answer I can think of to these questions is the following: whenever I make my morning visit to this house, I usually have to clear my throat; the product of my expectoration lands on one of the steps. For there is no spittoon on either of these two floors, and I take the view that keeping the stairs clean ought not to be at my expense, but aided by the provision of a spittoon. The housekeeper, likewise an elderly and surly person, but, I willingly grant, with an instinct for cleanliness, takes a different point of view from mine over this matter. She lies in wait for me to see if I will again permit myself this liberty, and when she has established that I have, I hear her grumbling audibly. Then for days she will deny me the usual marks of respect when we encounter each other. On the day before my dream, the housekeeper acquired an ally in the maid. I had completed my visit to the invalid, hurriedly, as always, when the maidservant stopped me in the hallway and uttered the pronouncement: 'Doctor, you might have wiped your boots today before you came into the room. Your feet have made the red carpet all dirty again.' This is the entire claim the flight of stairs and the maidservant can make for appearing in my dream.

Between my flying over the stairs and spitting on the steps there is a close connection. Throat catarrh and heart trouble are both supposed to represent a punishment for the vice of smoking, which of course has given me as low a reputation for cleanliness with the lady in charge of domestic affairs in my own house as in the other; the dream had fused both into a single structure.

I must postpone further interpretation of this dream until I can explain the origin of the typical dream of being incompletely clothed. As a provisional conclusion to be drawn from the dream, I shall say only that the dream-sensation of inhibited movement is always called up wherever a certain context requires it. The cause of this dream-content cannot have been any particularly immobile condition of mine while asleep, for not a moment before I had seen myself leaping light of foot up steps as though to reassure myself on this question.

(d) *Typical Dreams*

In general we are unable to interpret someone else's dream if the person concerned is unwilling to yield us the unconscious thoughts behind its content—which is a serious restriction on the practical utility of our method of interpreting dreams. But, quite in contrast to the individual's usual freedom to trick out his dream-world in his own peculiar way and so make it inaccessible to others, there are a certain number of dreams which almost everyone has dreamed in the same way, and which we usually assume have the same meaning for everyone too. These typical dreams are also particularly interesting because they presumably derive from the same sources in all dreamers and so they seem particularly well suited to provide us with information about the sources of dreams.

In dealing with these typical dreams, I find I am hampered by the chance circumstance that I have not had access to enough of them in my own experience. So I shall do no more than give a fuller assessment of some model examples in this category, and to do this I shall select what we call the embarrassment-dream of being naked, and the dream of the death of relatives dear to us.

Dreams of being naked or ill-clad in the presence of strangers also occur with the added feature of not being ashamed of this, and the like. But we are interested in dreams of nakedness only when the dreamer feels shame or embarrassment in this kind of dream, wants to run away or hide, and then is subject to the peculiar inhibition of being unable to move from the spot and feeling incapable of doing anything to alter the embarrassing situation. It is only in this combination that the dream is typical; in other respects its content may be involved at its core in all sorts of other connections and shot through with additional elements personal to the individual. What is essential is the embarrassing sensation of shame, of wanting to hide one's nakedness, usually by mobility, and of being unable to do so. I believe that most of my readers at some time will have found themselves in this situation in their dreams.

Usually the nature and kind of undress is not very distinct. We hear it said, for instance, 'I was in my shirt', but this is rarely a clear image. Mostly the unclad state is so indefinite that when it is related an alternative is given: 'I was in my shirt or underwear.' As a rule the deficiency in dress is not so bad that the shame associated with it would seem justified. For someone who has worn the Emperor's uniform, nakedness is often replaced by incorrect dress: 'I am in the street without my sabre and I can see a group of officers coming towards me', or 'without my necktie', or 'I am wearing checked civilian trousers', and the like.

The people in whose presence one feels ashamed are almost always strangers, their faces left indefinite. It never happens in a typical dream that they raise objections or draw attention to the form of dress which is so embarrassing to oneself. On the contrary, these people are indifferent or, as I could see from one particularly clear dream, stiff and solemn in demeanour. This is worth reflecting on.

Between them the shame and embarrassment of the dreamer and the indifference of the other people produce a contradiction of the kind that often occurs in dreams. After all, the only thing appropriate to the dreamer's feeling would be for the strangers to gaze at him with astonishment and laugh at him, or be indignant at the sight. But as I see it, this offensive feature is removed from the dream by wish-fulfilment, while the other, sustained by some power or other, remains in place, and in this way the two parts are out of harmony with each other. We have interesting testimony that this dream, partly distorted as it is by wish-fulfilment, has not been rightly understood. It has, of course, become the basis of a fairy-tale familiar to us all in the version by Hans Andersen,[20]* and has recently been put to poetic use by L. Fulda* in his *Talisman*. Andersen's tale tells of two deceivers who weave a precious garment for the Emperor which is supposed to be visible only to the virtuous and loyal among his subjects. The Emperor goes forth clad in this invisible garment, and, for fear of the power of the raiment as a touchstone of their loyalty, everyone pretends not to notice that the Emperor is naked.

But this is the very situation in our dream. We do not have to be very bold to assume that as the dream-content was not understood, this provided a spur to inventing a guise in which the situation on the brink of memory makes some sense. The situation is thereby robbed of its original meaning and put at the service of other purposes. But we shall hear that a misunderstanding of this kind—of the dream-content by the conscious thinking of a second psychical system—occurs frequently and is to be acknowledged as a factor in the final form of the dream; and further, that similar misunderstandings—also within the same psychical personality—play a major part in the creation of obsessions and phobias. As for our dream, it is also possible to say where the material for this reinterpretation is taken from. The deceiver is the dream, the

---

[20] 'The Emperor's New Clothes'.

Emperor the dreamer himself, and the moralizing tendency betrays an obscure awareness that what is involved in the latent dream-content are forbidden wishes which have been sacrificed to the power of repression. In fact, the context in which dreams of this kind appear in the course of my analyses of neurotic cases leaves no room for doubt that what lies at the bottom of the dream is a memory from our earliest childhood. It is only in our childhood that we are seen in inadequate clothing by our relatives, as well as by strange nurse-maids, servant-girls, and visitors, and in those days we were not ashamed of our nakedness.[21] With many children we can observe that even in later years being undressed has an exhilarating effect on them rather than inducing shame. They laugh, leap around, and slap themselves, and their mother or whoever else is by reprimands them and says: 'Stop it! That's naughty! You mustn't do that.' Children often display exhibitionist pleasure in the wish to show themselves off: you can hardly walk through a village in the countryside around here without encountering a two- or three-year-old who lifts his little shirt to the traveller, perhaps in his honour. One of my patients has preserved a conscious memory of a scene from his eighth year in which, after undressing before going to bed, he tried to dance out in his shirt to his little sister in the next room, and the maidservant who was looking after him prevented it. Exposure before children of the opposite sex plays a large part in the early lives of neurotics; in paranoia the illusion of being observed while dressing and undressing is to be traced back to this experience; among adults remaining in the perverse stage there is a class in whom this infantile impulse has been raised to the point of becoming a symptom: the class of *exhibitionists*.

When we look back, this childhood where shame is absent appears to us as a paradise, and Paradise itself is nothing but the mass fantasy of the childhood of the individual. This is why in Paradise too human beings are naked and feel no shame in each other's presence, until a moment comes when shame and anxiety awaken and sexual life and the work of culture begins.* Now, dreams can take us back to this Paradise every night. We have already raised the supposition that impressions from our earliest childhood (the prehistorical

---

[21] The child also makes an appearance in the fairy-tale, for in it a small child suddenly calls out: 'But he has nothing on.'

period up to about the end of our third year) demand reproduction for their own sake, perhaps regardless of their content, and that their repetition is a wish-fulfilment. Thus nakedness-dreams are *exhibition-dreams.*

The heart of the exhibition-dream is formed by one's own figure, seen not as a child's, but as it is in the present, and by the inadequate clothing, which looks indistinct, overlaid as it is by so many later recollections of undress or to please the censorship; then there are also the persons in whose presence one feels ashamed. I know of no instance in which the actual spectators of these infantile exhibitions reappear in the dream: for the dream is hardly ever a simple recollection. Curiously enough, the people in whom we did have a sexual interest when we were children are left out of all the reproductions found in dreams, hysteria, and obsessive neurosis: it is only paranoia which restores the spectators, deducing with fanatical conviction that although they have remained invisible, they are really present. What the dream puts in their place, 'a lot of strangers' who take no notice of the spectacle offered them, is virtually the *wishful opposite* to the one familiar person in front of whom one exposed oneself. Incidentally, 'a lot of strangers' frequently appear in dreams in any number of other contexts: as wishful opposites, they always signify 'secrets'. It is noticeable that the restoration of the earlier state of affairs occurring in paranoia also takes this opposite into account. One is no longer alone, one is certainly being observed, but the observers are 'a lot of strangers, left curiously indefinite'.

Moreover, in the exhibition-dream repression finds a voice. The embarrassing feeling in the dream is, after all, the reaction of the second psychical system to the fact that the content of the exhibition scene which it repudiated has nevertheless contrived to reach representation. To spare it this, the scene should not have been brought to life again.

We will deal with the feeling of inhibition again later. In dreams it is an excellent means of representing the *conflict of will*, the *No*. The unconscious intention is to continue the exhibition, the demand of the censorship is to break it off.

The relationships of our typical dreams to fairy-tales and other poetic materials are certainly neither isolated nor accidental. The poet is normally the instrument of the transformation process, but on occasion the keen poet's eye has understood it analytically and

pursued it backwards, tracing the poem back to the dream. A friend
has drawn my attention to the following passage from G. Keller's
Green Henry: 'It is not my wish, my dear Lee, that you should ever
learn from experience the exquisitely piquant truth in Odysseus'
situation when he appears naked and covered with mud before
Nausicaa and her companions! Do you want to know what is going
on in it? Some time, when you are separated from your homeland
and all you hold dear, roaming in foreign lands, and when you have
seen much and experienced much, when you are acquainted with
grief and sorrow, are wretched and deserted, then at night you are
sure to dream that you are drawing near your homeland. You will
see it shining, radiant in the loveliest colours. Fair and gracious figures
come to meet you. Then you suddenly discover that you are walking
in rags, naked and covered in dust. A nameless shame and fear take
hold of you. You try to cover yourself, to hide, and you wake bathed
in sweat. As long as mankind has existed, this has been the dream of
the sorrowful, storm-tossed man, and thus it is that Homer has taken
that situation from the depths of man's eternal nature.'*

The depths of mankind's eternal nature, which the poet invariably
counts on arousing in his listeners, are made of those motions of our
inner life rooted in that time of our childhood which later becomes
prehistoric. From behind the irreproachable wishes of the homeless
man which are suitable for consciousness, infantile wishes break
out which have become impermissible, and that is why the dream
externalized in the legend of Nausicaa invariably turns into an
anxiety-dream.

My own dream, referred to on p. 184, of running up the stairs,
which turned soon afterwards into being rooted to the spot, is also an
exhibition-dream, as it shows the essential elements of its kind. So it
should be traceable back to childhood experiences, and knowledge of
these should enlighten us as to how far the maidservant's behaviour
towards me, her objection that I dirtied the carpet, helps her to the
position she has in the dream. In fact I can supply the desired
explanation. In a psychoanalysis one learns to reinterpret closeness
in time as closeness in subject-matter. Two ideas, apparently unconnected, following immediately upon each other, belong to a unity
which is to be inferred, just as an 'a' and a 'b' which I write down one
after the other have to be spoken as a syllable, 'ab'. Likewise in
relating elements to one another in dreams. The dream of the stairs

referred to is taken from a series of dreams, and I am familiar with the interpretation of the other items in it. This dream, surrounded by the others, must belong in the same context. Now at the basis of the other dreams around it there was the memory of a nursemaid who looked after me from some date when I was still being breast-fed until I was two-and-a-half years old. According to information I recently gathered from from my mother, she was old and ugly, but very intelligent and competent. From what I may conclude from my dreams, she did not always treat me with the most loving care, and had harsh words for me if I failed to respond satisfactorily to her upbringing in cleanliness. So, in taking it on herself to continue this work of education, the maidservant earns the right to be treated as an incarnation of the prehistoric old nurse in my dream. We may assume that, despite her ill-treatment, the child was fond of this tutelary figure.[22]

Another group of dreams which may be called typical are those in which a dear relative, a parent, or brother or sister, a child, and so on, has died. We must immediately distinguish two classes of these dreams: those where the dreamer remains untouched by sorrow, so that on waking he wonders at his lack of feeling; and the others, in which the dreamer feels profound grief at the death, indeed, express-ing it even by weeping passionately in his sleep.

The dreams of the first group we may put aside. They have no claim to be regarded as typical. On analysis we find that they mean something different from what they contain, that they are intended to conceal some other wish. Take the dream of the aunt who sees her sister's only son before her in his coffin (p. 120). That does not mean that she wishes her little nephew were dead but, as we learned, it means the wish to see a certain much-loved person again after a long parting, the same person she had once seen again after a similar long interval at the dead body of another nephew. This wish, which is the true content of the dream, offers no occasion for grief, and that is why no grief is felt in the dream either. We note here that the affect contained in the dream does not belong to the manifest but to the

---

[22] An over-interpretation of this dream would run: spitting [*Spucken*] on the steps would lead—since *Spuken* [haunting] is an activity of spirits—by way of rough transla-tion to '*esprit d'escalier*'. *L'esprit d'escalier* means much the same as lack of ready wit [*Schlagfertigkeit* = (lit.) readiness with a blow]. That is a fault I really must admit to. Or was the nursemaid not ready enough with her blows, perhaps?

latent dream-content, and that the emotional content of the dream has remained free of the distortion that affected its representational content.

The case of dreams where the death of a dear relative is represented is different when emotions of sorrow are also felt. These mean what their content says: the wish that the person concerned might die. And as I may expect that all my readers' feelings and those of everyone who has had a dream of this kind will baulk at my interpretation, I must attempt to prove it on the broadest of foundations.

We have already explained one dream which taught us that the wishes that are represented as fulfilled in our dreams are not always current wishes. They can also be wishes that are past, over and done, overlaid or repressed, but which we are still obliged to credit with a kind of continued existence only because they surface again in our dreams. They are not dead as we conceive the dead, but are like the shades in the *Odyssey*** who wake to a kind of life once they have drunk blood. That dream (p. 121) of the dead child in the box is concerned with a wish that was active fifteen years before and frankly admitted to be from that time. It is perhaps not unimportant for the theory of dreams if I add that at the basis even of this dream there lies a memory from earliest childhood. As a little girl—it cannot be said for certain when—the dreamer had heard that during the pregnancy of which she was the product her mother had fallen into a deep depression and with all her heart had wished the child in her womb dead. Now an adult and pregnant herself, she was only following her mother's example.

If anyone has a dream filled with grief that their mother or father, brother or sister has died, I never take this dream for evidence that the dreamer wishes them dead *now*. The theory of dreams does not make so great a demand; it is content to conclude that—some time in childhood—he *has* wished them dead. But I am afraid this qualification will still do little to pacify my critics; they may dispute just as energetically the possibility that they ever had such a thought, just as they feel sure that they do not nurse such wishes at the present time. That is why I have to restore a part of the lost inner life of childhood, according to the evidence that the present still has to show.

Let us first look at the relationship children have to their brothers and sisters. I do not know why we assume that it must be a loving one, for there are insistent examples of hostility between adult siblings in everyone's experience, and we are so often able to establish that these quarrels began in childhood or have always existed. But very many adults too, who are very close to their siblings today and support them, lived in a state of scarcely interrupted enmity with them during childhood. The older child has mistreated the younger, told tales about him, stolen his toys; the younger, in helpless rage at the older, admires him, envies him, and fears him, or turns his first conscious stirrings for freedom and justice against the oppressor. The parents say the children don't get on well, and cannot find the reason for it. It is not difficult to see that even the character of a good child is different from what would be desirable in an adult. Children are absolutely self-centred, they feel their needs intensely and aim quite ruthlessly at their satisfaction, particularly at the expense of their rivals, other children, and above all their brothers and sisters. But that does not make us call the child 'wicked'; we call him 'naughty'; he is not responsible for his bad deeds, neither in our judgement nor before the law. And rightly so. For we may expect that within the lifespan we ascribe to children, stirrings of altruism and a sense of morality will awaken, and that, as Meynert puts it, a secondary ego will overlay the primary and inhibit it. Morality probably will not develop at the same time in every child; also, the length of the amoral childhood period is different in different individuals. If this morality fails to develop, it pleases us to speak of 'degeneration', though obviously it is a matter of hampered development. Where the primary character has already been overlaid by later development, it can still come to the surface again at least partially, if the subject falls ill with hysteria. The similarity of what we call the hysterical character with that of a naughty child is really quite striking. Obsessional neurosis, by contrast, corresponds to an excessive morality, reinforcing the burden on the primary character as this begins to stir again.

Thus many people who love their brothers and sisters today, and would feel bereft at their death, carry ill wishes towards them in their unconscious from long ago, which can be realized in dreams. But it is particularly interesting to observe small children of up to three years old or a little more in their behaviour towards their younger siblings. Until now, the child was the one and only. Now he is told that the stork has brought a new baby. The child inspects the new arrival and declares firmly: 'The stork can take it away again.' It is my entirely serious opinion that the child has the measure of the disadvantage it has to expect from the stranger. I was told by a lady close to me, who gets on very well today with her sister, four years her junior, that when she heard the news of the new arrival, she answered with the reservation: 'But I won't give her my red cap.' Even if the child did not reach this insight until later, the arousal of her hostility would still date from that moment. I know of a case in which a little girl not yet three years old attempted to strangle the baby in its cradle, sensing that no good would come of its further presence. Children of about this age are capable of jealousy, intensely and unmistakably. Or it can happen that the baby really does disappear quite soon, and once again the child is the centre of all the tenderness in the house. But then a new one arrives, sent by the stork. Is it not quite reasonable that our darling should generate within him the wish that his new competitor might meet with the same fate as the earlier one, so that things go as well again for him as they did before and in the interim? Of course, in normal circumstances this behaviour of the child to the later infant is a simple function of the difference in their ages. If the interval in age is greater, motherly instincts towards the helpless newborn baby will already begin to stir in the older girl.

Feelings of hostility towards siblings must be far more frequent in childhood than the imperceptive adult may observe.

In the case of my own children, who followed quickly on one another, I missed the opportunity to make observations of this kind. I am catching up on them now with my little nephew, whose sole reign was disturbed after fifteen months by the appearance of a rival. True, I am told that the young man behaves very chivalrously towards his little sister, kisses her hand, and strokes her. But I am becoming convinced that even before he is two years old he is using his ability to talk to criticize a creature who does, after all, appear superfluous in his eyes. Whenever the talk turns to her, he joins in the conversation and exclaims with displeasure: 'Too little, too little.' In recent months, weaned away from this contemptuous attitude by his excellent development, he has found different grounds for his admonition that she does not deserve so much attention. He reminds us on every occasion that offers: 'She hasn't got any teeth.' We all recall the story of the eldest daughter of another sister: six years old at the time, for half an hour she kept asking all her aunts to reassure her: 'Lucie can't understand that yet, can she?' Lucie was her rival, two-and-a-half years her junior.

I have come upon the dream of a sibling's death appropriate to this intensified hostility in every one of my women patients, for example. I found only one exception, which could easily be interpreted as proving the rule. Once during a consultation I was explaining this state of affairs to a lady whose symptoms seemed worth considering under this aspect. To my astonishment she responded that she never had dreams of this kind. Another dream occurred to her which ostensibly had nothing to do with it. It was a dream she first had when she was four years old, as the youngest child at the time, and had then dreamed many times. *A flock of children, all her brothers, sisters, and cousins, were romping in a meadow. Suddenly they grew wings, flew up in the air, and were gone.* She had no idea what the dream meant. It will not be hard for us to recognize it as a dream of the death of all her brothers and sisters in its original form, very little affected by the censorship. I will venture to replace it with the following analysis. At the death of one of the flock—in this case the children of two brothers were brought up together as brothers and sisters—our little mourner, not yet four years old, will have asked a wise grown-up: 'What happens to children when they are dead?' The answer will have been: 'Then they grow wings and become little angels.' In the dream, in accordance with this explanation, all the brothers and sisters have wings like angels and—and this is the main thing—they fly away. Our little angel-maker* is left alone—think of it!—the only one left after such a great flock! The children romping in a meadow and then flying away from it is surely an unmistakable reference to butterflies, as if the child were drawn by the same combination of ideas as moved the ancients to picture the psyche with butterflies' wings.

Now perhaps someone will interject: 'Granted the hostile impulse of children towards their siblings, but how could a tender infant disposition reach such heights of wickedness as to wish its rivals or sturdier playfellows dead, as if every offence were only to be expiated by the death penalty?' Anyone who says this is not taking into account the child's idea of 'being dead', which has only the word and very little else in common with ours. The child knows nothing of the horrors of decomposition, of freezing in the cold grave, of the terror of endless Nothingness which the adult's imagination cannot bear to contemplate, as all the myths of the world to come bear witness. The fear of death is unknown to the child; that is why he will play with the terrible word and threaten another: 'If you do that again, you'll die, like Franz!'—which makes his poor mother shudder, for she may be unable to forget that the greater part of mankind born on this earth will not outlive the years of childhood. Even at the age of eight, back from a visit to the Science Museum, a child can say to his mother: 'Mama, I love you so much; when you die I'll have you stuffed and set you up here in this room so that I can see you for ever and ever!' That is how little the child's idea of being dead resembles ours.

To the child, who is, after all, spared the scenes of suffering before death, being dead is much the same as 'being away', no longer disturbing the survivors. The child does not distinguish how this absence comes about, whether on account of a journey, an estrangement, or death. If in the prehistoric years his nurse is sent away and his mother dies a while later, the two events as they are uncovered in the course of analysis overlay each other in his memory. That the child does not miss them very intensely in their absence is something many a mother has learned to her sorrow on returning home after a summer trip of several weeks, when, in response to her enquiries she has to hear: 'The children haven't asked after their mama, not once.' But if she really has made the journey to 'That undiscovered country from whose bourne | No traveller returns',* the children will seem to have forgotten her at first and they will begin to remember her only *in retrospect*.

So if the child has motives for wishing another child away, there is nothing to stop him giving this wish the form of wanting him dead, and the psychical reaction to the wishful dream of death is evidence that, despite all the differences in content, the child's wish is nevertheless somehow the same as the consonant wish in the adult.

But if this wish for his brothers or sisters to die is explained by the child's self-centredness, which makes him see them as rivals, how are we to explain his death-wish towards his parents, who are for the child the givers of love and fulfillers of his needs, and whose preservation he should wish for simply from selfish motives?

We are led to a solution of this difficulty by our experience that dreams of a parent's death most frequently concern the parent who shares the same sex as the dreamer, so that a man mostly dreams of his father's death, a woman of her mother's. I cannot set this up as the rule, but the predominance of the pattern I have indicated is so distinct that it requires to be explained by a factor of general significance. Put crudely, it is as though a sexual preference were established very early, as though the boy saw a rival for love in his father, and the girl in her mother, and removing them could only be of benefit to the child.

Before this idea is rejected as monstrous, let us take a good look at the real relationships between parents and children. We have to distinguish what the cultural demand to honour our parents requires of this relationship from what daily observation tells us is the case. There is more than one occasion for hostility hidden in the relationship between parents and children; the conditions for creating wishes which will not pass the censorship are present in abundance. Let us dwell first on the relation of father and son. It is my opinion that the sanctity we have accorded the Ten Commandments blunts our perception of reality. Perhaps we do not dare to notice that the greater part of mankind put themselves above obeying the Fourth Commandment.* At the lowest levels of human society as much as at the highest, parental respect habitually yields to other interests. The dark tidings that reach us in myth and legend from the primeval days of human society give us some idea of the power of the father and the ruthlessness with which he wielded it that is most disagreeable. Cronos devours his children, rather as the boar devours the mother-sow's farrow, and Zeus castrates his father and takes his place as ruler. The more absolute the father's rule in the ancient family, the more the son as rightful successor is forced into the position of enemy, and the greater his impatience to come to power himself through the death of the father. Even in our middle-class families, by refusing his son his independence and the wherewithal to support it, the father is helping to develop the natural seeds of enmity in him. The physician is often enough in a position to notice that in his grief at the loss of his father, the son cannot suppress his satisfaction at gaining his freedom at last. The father habitually keeps a rigid grip on the remnants of the dreadfully antiquated *potestas patris familias* in our society today, and every writer is sure of making an impact if, like Ibsen, he pushes the ancient battle between father and son to the foreground in his plot. The occasions for conflict between daughter and mother arise when the daughter grows up and sees her mother as her wardress while she herself desires her sexual freedom; on the other hand, as her daughter blossoms the mother is reminded that the time has come for her to give up her own claims to sexuality.

All these relationships are plain for everyone to see. But they do not take us any further in our aim to explain the dreams of a parent's death in persons whose honour for their father and mother has long been something sacrosanct. Moreover, our previous discussions have prepared us to expect that the death-wish towards the parents will derive from earliest childhood.

This assumption is confirmed by our analyses in the case of psychoneurotics with a certainty that excludes any doubt. We learn from them that sexual wishes in the child—insofar as they can be called that at such an early stage—develop very early, and that the girl's first affection is for her father, and the boy's first infant desire is for his mother. Thus the father becomes an intrusive rival for the boy, as the mother does for the girl, and we have already explained in the case of siblings how little the child needs for this feeling to lead to a death-wish. As a rule their sexual choice is already determined by the parents' preferences. A natural inclination sees to it that the husband will spoil his little daughter, the wife take her son's part, while both of them—as long as the magic of sex does not upset their judgement—will be strict in their influence on the little ones' upbringing. The child is quite aware of the preference and rebels against the parent who opposes it. To be loved by the grown-ups means for him not only the satisfaction of a particular need, but also that he will get his way in all other respects too. Thus the child follows his or her own sexual impulses and at the same time perpetuates what the parents initiated by choosing between them along the same lines as they did.

The signs of these infantile affections in children are, most of them, usually overlooked; a few can be noticed even after the first childhood years. An eight-year-old girl of my acquaintance took advantage of the opportunity offered when her mother was called away from table to proclaim herself her successor: '*I'*ll be mama now. Karl, do you want more vegetables? Do help yourself, please,' and so on. A particularly gifted and lively girl, not yet four years old and particularly transparent with regard to this aspect of child psychology, declared point-blank: 'Mummy can go away now. Then daddy will have to marry me and I'll be his wife.' In the life of children this wish does not in the least exclude the child's tender love for her mother. If the little boy is allowed to sleep close to his mother when his father is away, and when his father returns he has to go back to the nursery to someone far less to his liking, then a wish could easily form that his father should always be absent so that he can keep his place near his dear, sweet mama, and one means of achieving this wish is obviously if his father were dead. For one thing his experience has taught him: 'dead' people, like grandpapa, for example, are always absent, and never come back.

Although such observations of small children neatly fit the interpretation I have suggested, still they do not have the same persuasive power that the psychoanalyses of adult neurotics have to convince the physician entirely. When neurotics tell me their dreams in this respect, they do so with introductory material of a kind that makes interpreting them as wishful dreams inescapable. I discover a lady one day in low spirits with eyes red from weeping. She says: 'I don't want to see my relatives again; the sight of me must fill them with horror.' Then, almost without transition, she tells me that she remembers a dream but of course she doesn't know what it means. She dreamed it when she was four, and it goes as follows: *A lynx or a fox is going for a walk on the roof, then something falls down, or she falls down, and then her mother is carried out of the house dead*, at which she weeps bitterly. I have scarcely informed her that this dream must mean a wish from her childhood to see her mother dead, and that this dream must be why she thinks her relations are filled with horror at her, when she promptly offers some material to explain the dream. 'Lynx-eyes' is a rude name she was once called by a street urchin when she was a very small child; when she was three years old, a tile fell from the roof onto her mother's head, so that she bled heavily.

I once had the opportunity to make a close study of a young girl who was going through a variety of psychical conditions. In the state of raving confusion with which her illness began, the patient showed a particular revulsion from her mother, struck her and swore at her whenever she came near her bed, while at the same time she remained loving and obedient towards a much older sister. There followed a lucid but apathetic condition, with very disturbed sleep;

in this phase I began her treatment and analysed her dreams. A vast number of them dealt, in more or less disguised form, with the death of her mother; in one dream she was attending the funeral of an old woman; in another she saw herself and her sister sitting at table in mourning. There was no doubt as to the meaning of these dreams. As she improved further, hysterical phobias made an appearance; the most tormenting was that something had happened to her mother. Then, wherever she might be, she had to hurry home to convince herself that her mother was still alive. This case, in combination with what I had learned elsewhere, was very instructive. It showed the variety of ways the psychical apparatus has of reacting to the same initiating idea, translated, as it were, into many languages. In her confused condition, when, as I see it, the second psychical agency was overwhelmed by the normally suppressed first, her unconscious hostility towards her mother powerfully affected her motor activity; then, as she first grew calmer, and her turmoil was suppressed and the power of the censorship restored, this hostility had only the field of dreaming left open to it to realize the wish for her mother's death; as this state of normality grew still stronger, it created the excessive concern for her mother as a hysterical counter-reaction and defensive phenomenon. In this connection, it is no longer inexplicable why hysterical girls so often cling to their mothers with such extravagant tenderness.

Another time I had the opportunity to see deep into the unconscious inner life of a young man whose obsessional neurosis had made him almost incapable of living; he could not go out into the street because he was tormented by the fear that he might kill every passer-by. He spent his days sorting out the evidence for his alibi in case he should be accused of any murder that occurred in town. It goes without saying that he was as moral a person as he was highly cultured. The analysis—which, by the way, led to his recovery—revealed the basis of this painful obsession to be murderous impulses towards his rather too severe father, which to his astonishment had expressed themselves consciously when he was seven years old, though of course they derived from much earlier childhood years. After his father's painful illness and death, when he was thirty years old the obsessional accusation appeared, transferred to strangers in the form of this phobia. Anyone capable of wanting to hurl his own father from a mountain-peak into the abyss below cannot, to his way of thinking, be trusted to spare the lives of those less close to him; so he is quite right to lock himself up in his room.

In my experience, which is already very extensive, parents play the main parts in the inner life of all children who later become psychoneurotics. Being in love with the one parent and hating the other belong to the indispensable stock of psychical impulses being formed at that time which are so important for the later neurosis. But I do not believe that in this respect psychoneurotics are to be sharply distinguished from other children of Adam with a normal development in their capacity to create something absolutely new and theirs alone. It is far more likely—and this is supported by occasional observations of normal children—that with these loving and hostile wishes towards their parents too, psychoneurotics are only revealing to us, by magnifying it, what goes on less clearly and less intensely in the inner life of most children. In support of this insight the ancient world has provided us with a legend whose far-reaching and universal power can only be understood if we grant a similar universality to the assumption from child-psychology we have just been discussing.

I refer to the legend of King Oedipus* and the drama of that name by Sophocles. Oedipus, son of Laius, King of Thebes, and Jocasta, is abandoned as an infant because an oracle had proclaimed to his father that his son yet unborn would be his murderer. He is rescued and grows up as a king's son at a foreign court, until he himself consults the oracle about his origins, and receives the counsel that he should flee his home city, because he would perforce become his father's murderer and his mother's spouse. On the road from his supposed home city he encounters King Laius and kills him in a sudden quarrel. Then he arrives before Thebes, where he solves the riddle of the Sphinx as she bars his way, and in gratitude he is chosen by the Thebans to be their king and presented with Jocasta's hand in marriage. He reigns long in peace and dignity, and begets two sons and two daughters with his—unbeknown—mother, until a plague breaks out, occasioning fresh questioning of the oracle by the Thebans. At this point Sophocles' tragedy begins. The messengers bring word that the plague will end when the murderer of Laius is driven from the land. But where is he?

> . . . Where shall we hope to uncover
> The faded traces of that far-distant crime?*

The action of the play consists now in the gradually intensified and skilfully delayed revelation—comparable to the work of a psychoanalysis—that Oedipus himself is Laius' murderer, but also that he is the son of the murdered king and Jocasta. Shattered by the abomination he has in his ignorance committed, Oedipus blinds himself and leaves his homeland. The oracle is fulfilled.

Oedipus the King is what we call a tragedy of fate; its tragic effect is supposed to depend on the contrast between the all-powerful will of the gods and the vain struggles of men threatened by disaster. What the deeply moved spectator is meant to learn from the tragedy is submission to the will of the divinity and insight into his own powerlessness. Consequently, modern dramatists have tried to achieve a similar tragic effect by weaving the same contrast into a plot of their own invention. But the spectators have looked on unmoved as, despite all the efforts of innocent humans, some curse or oracle is fulfilled. The later tragedies of fate* have failed in their effect.

If *Oedipus the King* is able to move modern man no less deeply than the Greeks who were Sophocles' contemporaries, the solution can only be that the effect of Greek tragedy does not depend on the contrast between fate and human will, but is to be sought in the distinctive nature of the subject-matter exemplifying this contrast. There must be a voice within us that is ready to acknowledge the compelling force of fate in *Oedipus*, while we are able to reject as arbitrary such disposals as are to be found in *Die Ahnfrau* or other tragedies of fate. And a factor of this kind is indeed contained in the story of King Oedipus. His fate moves us only because it could have been our own as well, because at our birth the oracle pronounced the same curse upon us as it did on him. It was perhaps ordained that we should all of us turn our first sexual impulses towards our mother, our first hatred and violent wishes against our father. Our dreams convince us of it. King Oedipus, who killed his father Laius and married his mother Jocasta, is only the fulfilment of our childhood wish. But, more fortunate than he, we have since succeeded, at least insofar as we have not become psychoneurotics, in detaching our sexual impulses from our mothers and forgetting our jealousy of our fathers. We recoil from the figure who has fulfilled that ancient childhood wish with the entire sum of repression which these wishes have since undergone within us. As the poet brings Oedipus' guilt to light in the course of his investigation, he compels us to recognize our own inner life, where those impulses, though suppressed, are still present. The contrast with which the chorus takes its leave:

> . . . behold: this was Oedipus,
> Greatest of men; he held the key to the deepest mysteries;
> Was envied by all his fellow-men for his great prosperity;
> Behold, what a full tide of misfortune swept over his head. (p. 68)

this admonition refers to us too and our pride, who have grown so wise and powerful in our own estimation since our childish years. Like Oedipus we live in ignorance of those wishes, offensive to morality and forced upon us by Nature, and once they have been revealed, there is little doubt we would all rather turn our gaze away from the scenes of our childhood.

There is an unmistakable indication in the text of Sophocles' tragedy itself that the legend of Oedipus sprang from that ancient dream material which contains the painful disturbance of our relations with our parents by the first stirrings of our sexuality. Jocasta consoles Oedipus at a stage where he has not yet learned the truth, but is troubled by the memory of what the oracle proclaimed. She refers to a dream which many indeed do dream, but without—or so she thinks—its having any significance:

> Nor need this mother-marrying frighten you;
> Many a man has dreamt as much. Such things
> Must be forgotten, if life is to be endured. (p. 53)

The dream of having sexual intercourse with the mother is dreamed by many today as it was then, and they recount it with indignation and amazement. It is clearly the key to the tragedy and the complement to the dream of the father's death. The Oedipus story is the imagination's reaction to these two typical dreams, and just as the dreams of the adult are filled with feelings of revulsion, the legend too is bound to include the horror and self-punishment in its content. Its further revision derives from a misleading secondary revision of the subject-matter, which seeks to make use of it for theological ends. (Compare the subject-matter of the exhibition-dream, p. 186.) (The attempt to reconcile divine omnipotence with human responsibility, of course, is bound to be defeated by this material, as by any other.)[23]

I cannot leave the typical dreams of the death of dear relatives without adding some words to elucidate their general significance for the theory of dreams. These dreams present the very unusual

[23] Another great creation of tragic poetry is rooted in the same soil as *Oedipus the King*: Shakespeare's *Hamlet*. But the change in treatment of the same material reveals the difference in the inner life of these two cultural periods so remote from each other: the advance of repression over the centuries in mankind's emotional life. In *Oedipus* the child's wishful fantasy on which it is based is out in the open and realized—as it is in dreams; in *Hamlet* it remains repressed, and we learn of its existence—as we learn of a neurosis—only through the inhibiting effects it produces. Curiously, *Hamlet* has shown that the overwhelming power of modern drama is compatible with the fact that we can remain quite unclear about the hero's character. The play is based on Hamlet's hesitation in fulfilling the task of revenge laid upon him; what the reasons or motives are for this hesitation the text does not say; the most various attempts at interpretation have not been able to identify them. According to the view argued by Goethe and still dominant today, Hamlet represents the type of human being whose power of action is paralysed by the over-development of the activity of thought ('sicklied o'er with the pale cast of thought').* According to others, the poet has attempted to portray a pathological, irresolute character close to neurasthenia. However, the drama's plot tells us that Hamlet should certainly not appear to be entirely incapable of action. We see him in action twice, once in sudden passion, when he stabs the eavesdropper behind the arras, the second time purposefully, indeed cunningly, when with all the insouciance of a Renaissance prince he dispatches the two courtiers to the death intended for himself. So what inhibits him from fulfilling the task laid upon him by his father's ghost? Here again we have at our disposal the knowledge that it is the particular nature of this task. Hamlet can do anything—except take revenge on the man who removed his father and took the latter's place beside his mother, the man who shows him his own repressed infant wishes realized. The revulsion that should urge him to revenge is thus replaced by self-recrimination, by the scruples of conscience which accuse him of being, quite literally, no better than the sinner he has to punish. I have translated into conscious terms what is bound to remain unconscious in the hero's psyche; if anyone wants to call Hamlet a hysteric, I can only acknowledge that it is an inference my interpretation admits. The sexual revulsion which Hamlet expresses in the dialogue with Ophelia is congruent with it—the same sexual revulsion which was to take increasing hold of the poet's psyche in the following years, reaching its extreme in *Timon of Athens*. Of course it can only have been the poet's own inner life that confronts us in *Hamlet*; I note from the work on Shakespeare by Georg Brandes* (1896) that the drama was written immediately after his father's death (1601), that is, when Shakespeare's mourning for his father was still fresh, and when presumably his childhood feelings towards him were revived. It is also known that Shakespeare had a son called Hamnet* (identical with Hamlet) who died young. Just as *Hamlet* deals with the relationship of the son to his parents, so *Macbeth*, written in much the same period, deals with the theme of childlessness.* Incidentally, just as every neurotic symptom, even the dream, is capable of over-interpretation, indeed demands it, if we are to understand it fully, so every truly poetic creation will have arisen from more than one motive and more than one impulse in the poet's psyche, and will admit of more than one interpretation. What I have attempted here is only an interpretation of the deepest layer of the impulses in the psyche of the creative poet.

instance of a dream-thought formed by a repressed wish escaping any censorship and entering the dream unaltered. There must be quite special conditions to make this fate possible. I think these dreams are encouraged by the following two factors. First, we cannot think of a wish more remote from us than this one; we believe that to wish *that* 'would not occur to us in our wildest dreams', and that is why the dream-censorship has no weapons against this monstrous thing, rather as Solon's laws were unable to decree any punishment for parricide. Secondly, however, it is just here that a remnant of the day very frequently comes halfway to meet the suppressed and unsuspected wish in the shape of a *care and concern* for the life of the dear person. The only way this concern can enter the dream and leave its mark is by making use of the congruent wish; but the wish is able to mask itself with the care and concern which has come to life during the day. If we take the view that all this happens more simply, that we are only continuing at night and in our dreams what we are concerned about by day, then we are just cutting off these dreams of the death of someone dear from their explanation, and holding on unnecessarily to an easily soluble puzzle.

It is also instructive to pursue the relation of these dreams to anxiety-dreams. In the dreams of the death of someone dear the repressed wish has found a way of escaping the censorship—and the distortion it imposes. Then it is unfailingly accompanied by feelings of pain or grief in the dream. Similarly, an anxiety-dream only comes about if the censorship has been entirely or partially overcome, while on the other hand the censorship is overcome the more easily if anxiety is already present as a current sensation deriving from somatic sources. In this way it becomes obvious what tendency the censorship pursues in exercising its office and practising dream-distortion: it is *in order to prevent the development of anxiety or other forms of distressing affect.*

In the previous discussion I spoke of the self-centredness of the child's psyche. I shall pick up on this with the aim of suggesting a connection: that dreams have preserved this characteristic too. They are all of them absolutely self-centred; in all of them the self, our own dear self, makes an appearance, even though disguised. The wishes fulfilled in them are invariably this self's wishes. Any dream said to have been called forth by interest in another is only a deception and a show. I shall submit to analysis a few examples contradicting this assertion.

I

A boy not yet four years old relates: *he saw a big dish, with veget-ables and a big joint of roast meat on it, and all of a sudden the meat was eaten up whole, all in one piece—not cut up. He did not see the person who ate it.*[24]

Who can the stranger be, whose sumptuous repast of roast meat fills our little one's dream? What the boy experienced on the day of the dream is bound to enlighten us on this score. For some days he has been on a milk diet prescribed by the physician; but on the evening of the day of the dream he was naughty and as a punishment he was not given any supper. He had endured a fast of this kind once before and behaved very bravely throughout. He knew that he would get nothing to eat, but he also did not dare to give the slightest indication that he was hungry. Upbringing is beginning to have its effect on him. It is already expressed in his dream, which shows the beginnings of dream-distortion. There is no doubt that he himself is the person whose wishes were directed at such a lavish meal, of roast meat in fact. But since he knows that this has been forbidden him, he does not dare, as hungry children do in their dreams (compare my little daughter Anna's dream of the strawberries, p. 104), to sit down to the meal himself. The person remains anonymous.

II

I dream on one occasion that I see displayed in a bookshop a new volume of a particular series in binding for connoisseurs, which I usually buy (monographs on art, world history, places famous for their art, etc.). *The new collection is called: 'Famous Speakers' (or 'Speeches') and the first volume bears the name 'Dr Lecher'.**

In the analysis, it seems improbable to me that the fame of Dr Lecher, the never-ending speechmaker of the German Obstruction in Parliament, should concern me in my dreams. It is in fact the case that a few days ago I took on new patients for psychological treat-

---

[24] The sheer size too, the excessive abundance, scale, and exaggeration of dreams, could be an infantile characteristic. The most ardent wish of children is to grow up and get as big a share of everything as the grown-ups; they are hard to satisfy; do not know the meaning of 'enough'; insatiably demand the repetition of anything that has given them pleasure or tasted nice. They only learn to moderate their demands, restrain themselves, and give in to others though the cultural process of their education. It is well known that the neurotic is also inclined to immoderation and excess.

ment, and am now compelled to speak for ten or eleven hours a day. So I am that kind of never-ending speechmaker myself.

III

Another time I dream that a teacher of my acquaintance at the University says: *My son, the myope.** Then there follows a dialogue consisting of brief remarks and replies. But then there follows a third part of the dream in which I and my sons are present, and as for the latent dream-content, father and son and Professor M. are only straw men corresponding to myself and my eldest son. On account of another peculiarity, I shall deal further with this dream later on.

IV

The following dream gives an example of really base egoistic feelings hiding themselves behind tender care.

My friend Otto is looking ill; he is brown in the face and has protruding eyes.

Otto is my family doctor, and I am still hopelessly in his debt because for years he has watched over the health of my children, treated them successfully when they were ill, and on top of that given them presents on every occasion that offered a pretext. He paid a visit on the day of the dream, and my wife remarked that he looked tired and under stress. At night my dream comes and lends him some of the symptoms of Basedow's disease.* Anyone who discards my rules in analysing dreams will understand this dream to mean that I am worried about my friend's health, and that this worry is realized in the dream. This would contradict not only the proposition that the dream is a wish-fulfilment, but also the other proposition that it is only accessible to egoistic impulses. But I would ask anyone who takes this line to explain my fears that Otto might be suffering from Basedow's disease, when his appearance does not give the slightest occasion for such a diagnosis. My analysis, on the other hand, provides the following material drawn from an event that took place six years ago. We were travelling, a small group of us, which also included Professor R., in deep darkness through the forest of N., a few hours from the place where we were spending the summer. Our driver, not entirely sober, tumbled us together with the carriage down a hillside, and it was fortunate that we all escaped unhurt. But we were forced to spend the night at the nearest inn, where the news of our accident aroused great sympathy for us. One gentleman, showing the unmistakable symptoms of *Morbus Basedowii*—but only browning of the facial skin and protruding eyes, by the way, just as in the dream, no sign of struma—placed himself entirely at our disposal and asked what he could do for us. Professor R., in his forthright way, replied: 'Just lend me a nightshirt.' 'So sorry, I can't,' rejoined the noble fellow, and went his way.

In continuing the analysis, it occurs to me that Basedow* is not only the name of a physician but also of a famous educator. (Now that I am awake I do not feel entirely sure of this knowledge.) But my friend Otto is the person I have asked to take care of my children's physical welfare, particularly during puberty (hence the nightshirt), if anything were to happen to me. In seeing my friend Otto in my dream with the symptoms of our noble helper, I obviously mean to say: 'If anything happens to me, I can expect just as little from him for the children as from Baron L. on that occasion, despite his obliging offers.' The egoistic thread in this dream now seems to be revealed.

But where is the wish-fulfilment here? Not in my revenge on my friend Otto, who is fated to be badly treated in my dreams, but in the following association. In representing Otto as Baron L. in my dream, I have at the same time identified my own person with someone else, that is, with Professor R., for of course I am demanding something of Otto, just as on that occasion R. demanded something of Baron L. And there we have it. Professor R., with whom I would not otherwise dare to compare myself, is like me in one respect: he made his way independently outside the university and only late in life attained the title he had long merited. So once again, I want to become a professor! Even that 'late in life' is a wish-fulfilment, of course, for it means that I shall live long enough to see my boys through puberty myself.

I have no knowledge from my own experience of other typical dreams in which the dreamer is flying at his ease, or falling filled with feelings of anxiety, and everything I have to say about them I owe to my psychoanalyses of patients. From the information gathered from them, one is bound to conclude that these dreams too repeat impressions from childhood, and relate to the motion-games children find so enjoyable. What uncle is there who has not made a child fly by rushing through the room with him, arms outstretched, or played 'falling' by bouncing the child on his knees and then suddenly stretching out his legs, or by lifting the child up high and then suddenly pretending to take away his support? The children shout with pleasure and never tire of wanting it repeated, particularly when some fear and giddiness are involved. Then, years afterwards, they create the repetition in their dreams, but in their dreams they leave out the hands that held them, so that now they hover and fall freely. The pleasure all small children take in games such as swinging and bouncing is well known; when they see acrobatic tricks in the circus their memory is renewed. In many young boys a hysterical attack is made up of reproducing tricks of this kind, which they perform with great skill. Not infrequently in these motion-games, innocuous in themselves, sexual feelings will be aroused.[25] To use a common word covering all these games, it is the 'romping' [*Hetzen*] of childhood that is repeated in these dreams of flying, falling, growing giddy, and the like, but its feeling of pleasure is now turned into its opposite, changed into anxiety. But as every mother knows, the romping of childhood too ends often enough in quarrels and tears.

Thus I have good reason for rejecting the explanation that dreams of flying and falling are called up by the state of our tactile feelings during sleep or sensations of the movement of our lungs. As I see it, these sensations are themselves reproduced from the memory to which the dream relates, that is, they are the content of the dream and not its source.

Everyone who has finished his senior years at school with the final matriculation examination complains how persistently he is pursued by the dream that he has failed, has to repeat a year, and the like. For someone who possesses an academic degree, this typical dream is replaced by another, which offers the prospect of not holding his own at the viva for his doctorate, though he may object in vain in his sleep that he has been practising medicine for years, is a university

[25] Apropos, a young colleague, entirely free of nervous troubles, told me: 'I know from my own experience that when swinging as a child, and at the very moment when the downward movement had the greatest impact, I had a peculiar feeling in the genitals which, though it was not really very agreeable, I have to describe as a feeling of pleasure.'—I have often heard from patients that the first pleasurable erections they remember appeared in boyhood when they were climbing.—It emerges from psycho-analyses with great certainty that the first stirrings of sexuality frequently have their roots in childhood scuffling and wrestling.

lecturer, or head of a government department. These are the ineradicable memories of punishments we suffered in childhood for our misdeeds stirring within us again, attaching themselves to the two decisive stages of our studies, the 'dies irae, dies illa'* of these strict examinations. The 'examination-fear' of neurotics, too, is reinforced by this infantile anxiety. Once we have ceased to be schoolchildren, it is no longer our parents and nurses, or later our teachers, who see to our punishment, as once they did; the implacable causal chain of life has taken over our further education and now we dream of the matriculation or the viva—and which of us has not trembled at undergoing them, even the righteous?—whenever we expect that the outcome will punish us because there is something we have not done right, or have not finished properly, or whenever we feel the pressure of some responsibility.

But I certainly do not deceive myself that I can produce a full explanation for this set of typical dreams. In my attempts to do so, my material really has left me in the lurch. I must hold on to the general viewpoint that all the sensations of movement and tactile feeling in these typical dreams are roused as soon as some psychical motive requires them, and they can be ignored if a need of this kind does not come halfway to meet them. The relation to infantile experiences also seems to me to emerge with certainty from the indications I have received in the analysis of psychoneurotics. But what other meanings may have attached themselves in the course of life to the memory of those sensations—different in each individual perhaps, despite the typical appearance of these dreams—I cannot say, and I would very much like to be in a position to fill this gap by careful analysis of good examples. To anyone who is surprised that I should complain of the lack of good material, despite the frequency of dreams of flying, falling, drawing teeth, and the like, I owe the explanation that I have not had such dreams in my own experience since I have been giving my attention to the topic of dream-interpretation. Moreover, the dreams of neurotics which are otherwise at my disposal are not all of them interpretable, and often not into the last nook and cranny of their hidden intentions; a certain psychical force that had a share in constructing the neurosis and is reactivated in resolving it resists being interpreted down to the last riddle.

THE DREAM-WORK

Until now every other effort to solve the problems presented by dreams has latched directly on to the dream's manifest content as it is present in the memory, and has attempted to use this as the basis of an interpretation; or, if it dispensed with an interpretation, it sought to substantiate its judgement of the dream by reference to its content. We are alone in confronting a different state of affairs; as we see it, there is a new kind of psychical material intervening between the content of the dream and the results of our reflections: the *latent* dream-content reached by our procedure, or the dream-thoughts. It is from this latent content, not the manifest, that we worked out the solution to the dream. This is why a new task faces us which did not exist before, the task of investigating the relationship of the manifest dream-content to the latent dream-thoughts, and of tracing the processes by which the latter turned into the former.

The dream-thoughts and the dream-content lie before us like two versions of the same content in two different languages, or rather, the dream-content looks to us like a translation of the dream-thoughts into another mode of expression, and we are supposed to get to know its signs and laws of grammatical construction by comparing the original and the translation. Once we have learnt what these are, the dream-thoughts will be easy for us to understand without any further ado. The content of the dream is given as it were in the form of hieroglyphs whose signs are to be translated one by one into the language of the dream-thoughts. We would obviously be misled if we were to read these signs according to their pictorial value and not according to their referentiality as signs. Suppose I have a picture-puzzle, a rebus, before me: a house with a boat on its roof, then a single letter of the alphabet, then a running figure with his head conjured away, and the like. Now I could fall into the trap of objecting that this combination and its constituent parts are non-sense. A boat does not belong on the roof of a house and a person without a head cannot run; besides, the person is bigger than the house, and if the whole is supposed to represent a landscape, then single letters of the alphabet do not fit in there, as they certainly do not occur in Nature. Obviously the correct solution to the rebus can only be reached if I raise no such objections to the whole or to the details, but take the trouble to replace each picture by a syllable or a word which, through some association, can be represented by the picture. The words connected in this way are no longer non-sense, but can yield the most beautiful and meaningful poetic saying. The dream is a picture-puzzle of this kind, and our predecessors in the field of dream-interpretation made the mistake of judging the rebus as if it were a pictorial composition. As such, it seemed to them to have no meaning or value.

(a) *The Work of Condensation*

The first thing the investigator comes to understand in comparing the dream-content with the dream-thoughts is that *work of condensation* has been carried out here on a grand scale. The dream is scant, paltry, laconic in comparison to the range and abundance of the dream-thoughts. Written down, the dream will fill half a page; the analysis containing the dream-thoughts will require six, eight, twelve times as much space. The ratio varies for different dreams; as far as I can check, it never changes its intent. As a rule, in taking the dream-thoughts brought to light to be all the dream-material there is, one is underestimating the degree of compression that takes place, whereas further work of interpretation is able to reveal fresh thoughts hidden behind the dream. We have already had to note that actually one is never certain of having interpreted a dream in its entirety; even when the solution seems satisfying and complete, it is always possible for a further meaning to announce its presence through the same dream. *The quota of condensation* is thus, strictly speaking, indeterminable. One conclusion to be drawn from this disproportion between dream-content and dream-thoughts might be that a wholesale con-densation of the psychical material takes place during the dream's formation. However, one could raise an objection to this which at first sight seems very tempting. After all, we so often have the feeling that we have dreamed a great deal all through the night and then forgotten most of it. Accordingly, the dream we remember when we wake would be just a remnant of the total dream-work, which would probably equal the dream-thoughts in extent, if only we were able to remember the dream in its entirety. This is certainly correct in part; it is evident that a dream is reproduced most faithfully when we try to recollect it soon after waking, and that its memory becomes more and more sketchy towards evening. On the other hand, however, it emerges that the feeling that we have dreamed a great deal more than we can reproduce very often rests on an illusion, whose origins will be explained later. Moreover, the assumption that condensation is operative in the dream-work is not affected by the possibility of forgetting our dreams, for its activity is proven by the masses of ideas belonging to the separate bits of the dream that *are* retained. If a great deal of the dream is in fact lost to memory, this more or less cuts off our approach to a fresh set of dream-thoughts. There is nothing to justify any expectation that the lost parts of the dream would only have related to the thoughts already known to us from our analysis of the parts that *have* been retained.

In face of the vast number of ideas analysis can offer for every element in the dream-content, many readers will feel the stirrings of doubt as to whether all the things coming into someone's mind retrospectively in the course of analysis may in principle be counted as the dream-thoughts, that is, whether it may be assumed that all these thoughts were already active during sleep and played their part at the time in forming the dream. Or rather, whether fresh thought-associations might not arise in the course of analysing which had no part in forming the dream. I can only give qualified assent to this doubt. It is certainly correct that particular thought-associations do arise only during the analysis; but on each occasion one can satisfy oneself that fresh associations of this kind only come about between thoughts which are already associated in some other way in the dream-thoughts; the new associations are, as it were, parallel connections, short-circuits made possible by the existence of other and deeper connecting paths. As for the greater mass of the thoughts revealed in the analysis, it has to be recognized that they were already active in forming the dream, for after working through a chain of these thoughts, which seem to be quite unconnected to the formation of the dream, one suddenly comes upon one which is represented in the dream-content and which is essential to its interpretation, but which was only accessible by way of that chain. In this respect, see the dream of the botanical monograph, for example, which appears to be the result of an astonishing feat of condensation, even though I have not reported its analysis in full.

But how, then, are we to imagine the conditions prevailing in the psyche during the sleep which precedes dreaming? Are all the dream-thoughts present side by side, or will they follow one after the other, or are there several simultaneous trains of thought formed from different centres, which then converge? I do not think it is necessary to make an imaginary picture of the psychical conditions prevailing in the process of dream-formation. However, we should not forget that this is a matter of unconscious thinking, and that the process could easily be very different from the one we are aware of in ourselves in the course of purposeful reflection accompanied by consciousness.

However, the fact that the formation of dreams is based on condensation is established beyond question. Now, how does this condensation come about?

When one considers that only very few indeed of the dream-thoughts discovered by the analysis are represented in the dream by one of their ideational elements, one might suppose that condensation proceeds by way of *exclusion*, for the dream is not a faithful translation or point-by-point projection of the dream-thoughts, but an exceedingly incomplete and fragmentary reproduction. But, as we shall soon discover, this is a most inadequate view. All the same, let us use it as a basis to start from and go on to ask ourselves: if only a few elements of the dream-thoughts reach the dream-content, what are the conditions that determine their selection?

For light on this question we shall turn our attention to those elements in the dream-content which must in fact have fulfilled the conditions we are seeking. The most suitable material for this inquiry will be a dream which has been formed by a particularly strong process of condensation. I shall choose the dream of the botanical monograph reported on p. 129.

I

Dream content: *I have written a monograph on a species (which kind is left open) of plant. The book is lying in front of me. I am just turning over a folded colour plate. Bound into the copy is a dried specimen of the plant.*

The most immediately striking element in this dream is the *botanical monograph*. This derives from the impressions of the dream-day.

I had in fact seen a *monograph on the species 'cyclamen'* displayed in the window of a bookshop. The dream does not mention species, retaining only the monograph and its reference to botany. The 'botanical monograph' promptly shows its connection to the *work on cocaine* which I once wrote. From cocaine the train of thought moves on the one hand to the *Festschrift* and to certain events in a university laboratory, on the other hand to my friend, the eye specialist *Dr Königstein*, who had a share in the medical application of cocaine. The figure of Dr K. links up with my recollection of the interrupted conversation I had with him the previous evening, and to my various thoughts on payment for medical services among colleagues. Now, it is this conversation which is actually the active initiator of the dream. The monograph on cyclamen is also an agent, but an unimportant one. As I see it, the *botanical monograph* in the dream turns out to be a *mediating common factor* between the two experiences of the day, taken over unchanged from the unimportant impression, but linked by a wealth of associative connections with the psychically significant experience.

But not only the composite idea *botanical monograph*, but also each of its elements separately, *botanical* and *monograph*, enters by way of multiple connections deeper and deeper into the maze of the dream thoughts. *Botanical* is the link to my recollections of the figure of Dr *Gärtner*, of his '*blooming*' wife, of a patient of mine who was called *Flora*, and of the lady with the forgotten flowers whose story I recounted. *Gärtner* leads again to the laboratory and to my conversation with *Königstein*; the reference to both patients belongs in the same conversation. The dream-thoughts branch along one path from the woman with the flowers to my wife's *favourite flowers*, and their other route ends in the title of the monograph seen fleetingly during the day. In addition, *botanical* recalls an episode at school and an examination from my university days, and a fresh theme broached in that conversation, that of my favourite hobbies, is linked via what I call in jest my *favourite flower*, the artichoke, to the train of thoughts that started out from the forgotten flowers. Behind 'artichoke' there is hidden the recollection of Italy on the one hand and a scene from childhood on the other, where I inaugurated my relationship to books which has since become so intimate. So *botanical* is a real point of intersection, where very many trains of thought contributing to the dream converge; and I can vouch for it that these were all brought quite fittingly into connection with one another in that conversation. This is where we find ourselves in the middle of a thought-factory where, as in the weaver's masterpiece,

> Ein Tritt tausend Fäden regt,
> Die Schifflein herüber, hinüber schiessen,
> Die Fäden ungesehen fliessen,
> Ein Schlag tausend Verbindungen schlägt.*

> ['One thrust of his foot, and a thousand threads
> Invisibly shift, and hither and thither
> The shuttles dart—just once he treads
> And a thousand strands all twine together.']

Monograph in the dream touches again on two themes: how specialized my studies were and how expensive my hobbies.

This first examination suggests that the elements 'botanical' and 'monograph' have been admitted into the dream because they are able to show the widest range of contacts with the most dream-thoughts, that is, they represent *points of intersection* where a great number of the dream-thoughts converge; and because they have *many meanings* with respect to the interpretation of the dream. The fact at the basis of this explanation can also be put differently: each element of the dream-content turns out to be *over-determined*, to be represented many times and in many ways in the dream-thoughts.

We shall learn more if we scrutinize the remaining components of the dream for their appearance in the dream-thoughts. The *coloured plate* I unfold refers to a fresh theme (see p. 131), my colleagues' criticism of my work; and to one already represented in the dream, my hobbies; besides these, to the childhood memory in which I pull apart the leaves of a book with coloured plates; the dried specimen of the plant touches on my experience at school with the herbarium and gives particular emphasis to this recollection. So I perceive what kind of relationship this is between the content and the thoughts of the dream: it is not only that the elements of the dream are determined *many times over*, but also that the individual dream-thoughts are represented in the dream by several elements. The path of associations leads from one element of the dream to several dream-thoughts; and from one dream-thought to several dream-elements. Thus, the formation of a dream does not come about by a process of one dream-thought or a group of them supplying a shorthand term for the dream-content, and then by the next dream-thought providing a further shorthand term as its deputy, much as representatives are elected from the population for Parliament. Rather, the entire mass of the dream-thoughts undergoes a certain procedure whereby those elements with the most and best support are best qualified for admission to the dream-content, rather like election by means of the list system. Whatever dream I submit to this kind of analysis, I always find the same principles confirmed: the elements formed into the dream are drawn from the entire mass of the dream-thoughts, and in its relation to the dream-thoughts each one of the elements seems to be determined many times over.

It is certainly not idle to demonstrate this relationship of dream-content and dream-thoughts with a fresh example, one which is remarkable for the particularly intricate way it intertwines its interacting associations. The dream comes from a patient I am treating for claustrophobia. It will soon become apparent why I feel occasioned to give this exceptionally clever feat of dreaming the heading of:

II. 'A Pleasant Dream'

He is travelling in a large private party to X Street, where a modest hostelry is located (which is not the case). *A play is being performed in its rooms; one moment he is a spectator, the next an actor. Finally someone says they will have to change their clothes to return to town. Some of the party are directed to the rooms on the ground floor, others to those on the first floor. Then a quarrel ensues. The ones up above are annoyed that those down below are not yet ready, so that they cannot come down. His brother is up above, he himself down below, and he is annoyed at his brother that he is being hurried so.* (This part is unclear.) *In any case, it was already decided and disposed on their arrival who should be up above and who should be down below. Then he is walking by himself up the rise made by X Street towards the town, and his steps are so heavy, so laborious, that he cannot stir from the spot. An elderly gentleman joins him and rails against the King of Italy. Then at the end of the rise he walks with much greater ease.*

The difficulties he had in climbing the rise were so distinct that when he woke he wondered for a while whether it was dream or reality.

The manifest content scarcely moves one to praise this dream. Against the rules, I shall begin with that part described by the dreamer as the most distinct.

The difficulty dreamed of and probably felt as it was dreamed, the laborious climb accompanied by dyspnoea,* is one of the actual symptoms my patient had displayed years ago, which was then attributed, together with other symptoms, to tuberculosis (probably in hysterical imitation). We are already familiar with this peculiar sensation of inhibited movement from exhibition-dreams, and here again we find it as material present and always available to be used for any other representational purpose. The part of the dream-content describing how difficult climbing was at the beginning and how easy the rise became at the end, reminded me as he recounted it of the well-known, masterly opening of Alphonse Daudet's *Sappho*.* There, a young man is carrying his beloved up the staircase; at first she is light as a feather; but the further he climbs, the more heavily she weighs in his arms, and this scene is a model for the course of their relationship; in describing it thus, Daudet intends to warn young men not to squander their more serious affections on girls of low origin and doubtful past. Although I knew that my patient had recently had a love affair with a lady from the theatre and had broken it off, I really did not expect to find my idea for the interpretation confirmed. In any case, the situation in *Sappho* was the reverse of the one in the dream; in the dream, the climb was difficult at the start and became easier later; in the novel, the symbolism was only served if what was taken easily at first turned out to be a heavy burden at the end. To my astonishment my patient remarked that the interpretation chimed very well with the content of the play he had seen the previous evening in the theatre. The play was called *Rund um Wien* [*Round about Vienna*], and dealt with the life of a young woman who begins as a good girl, but then enters the *demi-monde*, has affairs with highly placed personages, and so '*rises high up*', but finally sinks '*down lower and lower*'. The play had reminded him of another one performed years before, entitled *Von Stufe zu Stufe** [*From Step to Step*], with advertisements showing a flight of stairs made up of several steps.

Now for further interpretation. The actress with whom he had had this latest affair, so full of associations, lived in X Street. There is no inn in the street. However, he spent part of the summer in Vienna on account of the lady, and *put up* [*abgestiegen*; lit: got *down*] at a small hotel nearby. As he left the hotel, he said to the cabby: 'At least I haven't caught any vermin, I'm glad to say'—another of his phobias, by the way. The cabby replied: 'But how can anyone stay there! That's not a proper hotel, it's only a *hostelry*.'

The inn links up at once in his memory with a quotation:

> Bei einem Wirthe wundermild
> Da war ich jüngst zu Gaste,
> ['Not long ago I was a guest,
> My host was wond'rous kind.']

But the host in Uhland's* poem is an *apple-tree*.

Now a second quotation continues the train of thought:

> *Faust* (mit der Jungen tanzend).
>
> Einst hatt ich einen *schönen Traum*;
> Da sah ich einen *Apfelbaum*,
> Zwei schöne Aepfel glänzten dran,
> Sie reizten mich, ich *stieg hinan*.

> *Die Schöne*
>
> Der Aepfelchen begehrt ihr sehr
> Und schon vom Paradiese her,
> Von Freuden fühl' ich mich bewegt,
> Daß auch mein Garten solche trägt.*

> [*Faust* (dancing with the young witch).
>
> A *pleasant dream* once came to me:
> I saw a lovely *apple-tree*,
> And two fine apples hanging there;
> I *climbed to pick* that golden pair.

> *The Fair One*
>
> You men were always apple-mad;
> Adam in Eden was just as bad.
> I've apples in my garden too—
> How pleased I am to pleasure you!]

There is not the slightest possible doubt about what is meant by the apple-tree and the apples. A beautiful bosom was high among the charms binding my dreamer to his actress.

The interrelations revealed by the analysis gave us every reason to assume that the dream goes back to an impression from childhood. If this was correct, it was bound to relate to the wet-nurse of this nearly thirty-year-old man. For a child the nurse's breast is indeed the hostelry. The nurse, as well as Daudet's Sappho, appears to be an allusion to the lover he had recently broken with.

My patient's (elder) brother also appears in the dream-content, the brother being *up above* and he himself *down below*. This is again a *reversal* of their real relationship, for the brother, to my knowledge, has lost his social position, and my patient has maintained his. In recounting the dream-content, the dreamer avoided saying his brother was 'up above' and he himself 'on the ground floor'. That would have been much too explicit a declaration, for here in Vienna we say of persons who have lost wealth and position that they are '*on the ground floor*', that is, we are using a similar metaphor to saying 'they have *come down in the world*'. There must be some meaning to the representation of something *in reverse* at this point in the dream. The reversal must also apply to another connection between dream-thoughts and dream-content. There is an indication as to where this reversal is to be found. Clearly it is at the end of the dream, where a similar *reversal* applies to climbing as to *Sappho*. Then it easily emerges what reversal is meant: in *Sappho* the man is carrying the woman who has a sexual relationship with him; in the dream the situation is *reversed* and it is the woman who is carrying the man; as this can only happen in childhood, the reference is again to the nurse, who finds it hard to carry the baby she is breast-feeding. The end of the dream sums it up in representing *Sappho* and the nurse by the same allusion.

Just as the name of *Sappho* as chosen by the poet is not without reference to a lesbian disposition, so those parts of the dream in which figures are involved *above* and *below* point to the dreamer's being preoccupied by fantasies with a sexual content which, being suppressed desires, are not unconnected with his neurosis. The interpretation of the dream does not itself indicate that these are fantasies and not recollections of actual events; it only provides us with the content of the thought and leaves it to us to decide what it is worth as reality. Actual and imaginary events appear at first to be of equal value here—and not only here, but also in the creation of more important psychical formations than dreams. A large social gathering, as we already know, signifies a secret. The brother is nothing but the representative, introduced into the childhood scene by 'imagining back', of all his later rivals for women. The episode of the gentleman who railed against the King of Italy relates again, mediated by a recent experience of slight importance, to the intrusion by persons of the lower orders into higher society. It is as if, alongside Daudet's warning to the young man, a similar one was meant for the suckling child.[1]

As a third example to hand for studying condensation in the formation of dreams, I shall report the partial analysis of another dream which I owe to an elderly lady under psychoanalysis. In accordance with the grave anxiety-state from which this patient suffered, her dream thoughts contained a wealth of sexual material which disconcerted as much as alarmed her when she came to learn of it. As I am not able to pursue the interpretation of her dream to the end, the dream material appears to break up into a number of groupings without visible connection.

III

Dream content: *She recalls that she has two may-beetles* in a box which she must set free or else they will suffocate. She opens the box; the beetles are exhausted; one of them flies up out of the opened window, but the other is squashed by the casement as she is closing the window, which someone wants her to do (expression of disgust).*

Analysis: Her husband is away on a journey. Her fourteen-year-old daughter sleeps in the bed next to her. In the evening the girl draws her attention to a moth which has fallen into her water-glass; but she neglects to rescue it and next morning she feels very sorry for the poor little beast. The book she had been reading that evening told how some boys threw a cat into boiling water, and described the animal's convulsions. These are the two intrinsically unimportant occasions for the dream. The theme of *cruelty to animals* continues to engage her. Years before, when they were staying in a certain district for the summer, her daughter had been very cruel to all kinds of

---

[1] The imaginary nature of the situation relating to the dreamer's nurse is demonstrated by the objective circumstance that the wet-nurse in this case was his mother. I recall, moreover, the regret referred to on p. 158 of the young man in the anecdote that he had not made better use of the situation with his wet-nurse—which is probably the origin of this dream.

creatures. She made a collection of butterflies and asked her mother for *arsenic* in order to kill them. On one occasion a moth flew around the room for a long time with a pin through its body. Another time some caterpillars which were being kept till they developed to the chrysalis stage were left to starve. While still very young the same child was in the habit of pulling off the wings of *beetles* and butterflies. Today she would recoil in horror at all these acts of cruelty; she has grown so tender-hearted.

My patient's thoughts are occupied by this contradiction. It reminds her of another one, between *appearance* and attitude, as it is presented by [George] Elliot [*sic*] in *Adam Bede*.* A girl who is beautiful but vain and very stupid, beside her one who is plain but high-minded. The *aristocrat* who seduces the silly little thing; the working-man of noble feeling who behaves accordingly. You can't tell that from *looking at* people's appearance, she thinks. Who could tell from looking at *her* that she was tormented by desires of the senses?

The same year as the little girl made her butterfly collection, the region suffered badly from a plague of *may-beetles*. The children waged war on the beetles, *squashed* them mercilessly. She saw a man tear off their wings and then eat the bodies. She herself was born in *May* and had been married in *May*. Three days after the wedding she wrote a letter home to her parents saying how happy she was. But she was not in the least happy.

On the evening before the dream she had been looking through old letters and had read out various serious and amusing letters to her family, including one most ridiculous letter from a piano-teacher who had paid court to her as a girl, and also one from an *aristocratic* admirer.[2]

She reproaches herself that one of her daughters had got hold of a bad book by Maupassant.[3]* The *arsenic* demanded by her small daughter reminds her of the *arsenic pills* that restored his youthful powers to the Duc de Mora in *Le Nabab*.*

Regarding 'setting free', the passage from *The Magic Flute** occurs to her:

---

[2] This is the actual initiator of the dream.

[3] To develop the point: in her view, reading-matter of this kind is *poison* for a young girl. She herself had learned a great deal as a girl from forbidden books.

Zur Liebe kann ich Dich nicht zwingen,
Doch geb ich Dir die *Freiheit* nicht.
[I cannot force you to love,
But I will not give you your *freedom*.]

Regarding the may-beetles, there is also the line from Kleist's *Das Käthchen von Heilbronn:**

Verliebt ja wie ein *Käfer* bist Du mir.[4]
[You are as much in love with me as a may-*beetle*.]

And between them Tannhäuser:* 'Weil Du von *böser Lust* beseelt—' ['Because your soul is filled with *evil desire*—'].

She lives in a state of worry and anxiety about her absent husband. The fear that something should *happen* to him on the journey is expressed in numerous daytime fantasies. Shortly before, in the course of the analysis, she had discovered a complaint in her unconscious thoughts about his 'senility'. The wishful thought disguised by this dream can perhaps best be guessed at if I relate that several days before the dream, going about her daily business, she was suddenly alarmed at the imperative she had aimed at her husband: '*Go hang yourself*.' It emerged that a few hours previously she had read somewhere that a powerful erection sets in when a man is hanged. It was the wish for this erection returning from its repressed state in this alarming disguise. 'Go hang yourself' says as much as 'Get an erection at all costs'. Dr Jenkins's arsenic pills in *Le Nabab* belong here; but my patient also knew that the strongest aphrodisiac, *cantharides* ('Spanish flies', as it is called), is prepared by crushing beetles. This is the meaning that the main component of the dream-content is getting at.

Opening and closing the *window* is an issue of constant dispute with her husband. She herself needs fresh air to sleep, her husband dislikes it. The main symptom she was complaining of in these days is *exhaustion*.

In reporting all three of these dreams I have used italics to highlight the points where one of the dream-elements recurs in the dream-thoughts. But since none of these dreams is analysed through to the end, it will probably be more rewarding to look at a dream

---

[4] A further train of thought leads to the same poet's *Penthesilea:** *cruelty* to the beloved.

where the analysis is reported more fully, and use that to demonstrate the over-determination of the dream-content. To do so I shall select the dream of Irma's injection. It will not be difficult for us to see from this example that the work of condensation employs more than just one device in the formation of dreams.

The main figure in the dream-content is my patient Irma, who is seen with the features belonging to her in real life, and so in the first place represents herself. However, her posture as I examine her at the window is taken from my recollection of someone else, the lady for whom I would like to exchange my patient, as the dream-thoughts indicate. Insofar as Irma displays a diphtheritic attenuation recalling my concern for my eldest daughter, she comes to stand for this child of mine, behind whom there is hidden the figure of the patient I lost from the severe toxic condition, linked to her by having the same name. As the dream proceeds, the meaning of Irma's person changes (without any alteration in her visible image); she turns into one of the children we are examining in the public surgery at the children's clinic, when my friends demonstrate the difference in their intellectual gifts. The transition was obviously made by way of my little daughter. By her reluctance to open her mouth this same figure of Irma turns into an allusion to another lady whom I once examined, and, in the same context, to my own wife. In the pathological changes I discover in her throat, moreover, I gathered together allusions to further persons still.

All these persons whom I came upon in my pursuit of 'Irma' do not appear in the dream in their own form; they are hidden behind the dream-figure of 'Irma', which in this way becomes a collective image, though endowed, it is true, with contradictory features. Irma becomes the proxy for these other persons sacrificed in the process of condensation, in which I have her go through everything, item for item, that reminds me of them.

I can also create a *collective figure* for the dream-condensation in a different way by combining the actual features of two or more persons into a dream-image. This is how the figure of Dr M. in my dream came about; he bears the name of Dr M.; he speaks and acts like him; his physical build and his illness belong to someone else, to my eldest brother; one single characteristic, his pallor, is doubly determined, being shared by both persons in real life. In the dream of my uncle, Dr R. is a similar composite figure. But here the dream-image was created in another way again. I did not combine features belonging to the one with features of the other, thereby reducing the remembered image of each by certain features; rather, I adopted the procedure Galton used in making his family portraits, that is, I projected both images onto each other; in this way the features they have in common emerge more prominently, and those that do not match obliterate each other, and become blurred in the image. In the dream of my uncle the reinforced characteristic that stands out among blurred facial features—blurred because they belong to two people—is the *yellow beard*, which also contains an allusion to my father and to myself, by way of the association with growing grey.

The production of collective and composite figures is one of the main methods of condensation in dreams. We shall soon have occasion to deal with them in a different context.

Similarly, the idea of 'dysentery' in the dream of the injection is determined several times over, on the one hand by the resemblance of its sound to 'diphtheria', on the other by its association with the patient I sent to the Near East whose hysteria goes unrecognized.

The reference to '*propyls*' in the dream turns out to be an interesting case of condensation. The dream-thoughts did not have '*propyls*' in them, but '*amyls*'. One might think that a simple displacement had been effected in the formation of the dream. That is so; however, this displacement also serves the purposes of condensation, as the following addition to my analysis will show. If my attention pauses for a moment at the word '*propyls*', what occurs to me is the similarity of its sound to the word '*Propylea*'.* But there are *Propylea* not only in Athens but also in Munich. This was the town where a year before my dream I visited the friend—who was very ill at the time—unmistakably referred to by the *trimethylamine* following hard upon *propyls*.

I shall pass over the striking circumstance that, here and elsewhere in the analysis of dreams, associations of the most varying quality are used in connecting thoughts as if they were of equal value, and I shall yield to the temptation to imagine, as it were visually, the process by which *amyls* was replaced by *propyls* in the dream-thoughts.

Suppose, on the one hand, there is the group of ideas around my friend Otto, who does not understand me, puts me in the wrong, and gives me a liqueur smelling of amyl; on the other, connected by contrast, there are the ideas relating to my Berlin friend, who does understand me, would say that I am in the right, and to whom I owe so much valuable information, including his thoughts on the chemistry of sexuality.

From Otto's group, what ought especially to arouse my attention is determined by the recent events occasioning the dream; *amyls* belongs to these distinctive elements, predestined to enter the dream-content. The wealth of ideas in the 'Wilhelm' group virtually draws its life from its contrast with 'Otto', and it is the elements in it alluding to those already aroused in 'Otto' that are given prominence. Indeed, in this entire dream I move to and fro from one person who annoys me to another whom I can contrast with him at will; point for point, I can call up my friend against my adversary. Thus, 'amyls' from the Otto group wakes memories from the sphere of chemistry in the other group too; trimethylamin, supported from many sides, enters the dream-content. '*Amyls*' too might be able to enter the dream-content unchanged; however, it is subject to the influence of the 'Wilhelm' group, as out of the entire range of memories covered by this name, one element is picked out that is capable of yielding a double determination for amyls. '*Propyls*' is close to '*amyls*' for this association; it is met half-way by Munich and the *Propylea* from the 'Wilhelm' sphere. In *propyls-Propylea* both fields of ideas come together. As though by compromise, this middle element then enters the dream-content. A *mediating common factor* is created here admitting of multiple determination. This makes it utterly clear that if an element is determined many times over, its entry into the dream-content is bound to be made much easier. For this mediating factor to be formed, our attention is displaced from what is actually meant to something closely associated with it.

Studying the injection-dream has already given us an insight into the processes of condensation in dream-formation. We have been able to identify as particular functions of the work of condensation: its selection of elements occurring many times in the dream-thoughts; its formation of new unities (collective figures, composite structures), and its production of mediating common factors. What the larger purpose of condensation may be, and what helps to bring it about, are questions we shall not raise until we come to deal with the psychical processes of dream-formation in relation to one another. For the moment, let us be content with affirming that *condensation* in dreams constitutes a remarkable relationship between dream-thoughts and dream-content.

The work of condensation in a dream can most easily be grasped if it has selected words and names for its objects. Words are often treated as things in dreams, and then they go through the same combinations, displacements, substitutions and also condensations as the representations of things.

I

A colleague once sent me an article he had written in which, in my judgement, a physiological discovery of modern times had been overestimated, and above all dealt with in extravagant language. The next night I dreamed a sentence which clearly referred to this article: '*That is a really norekdal style.*' At first I had difficulty in analysing this word-formation; there was little doubt that it was created in parodic imitation of the superlatives 'coloss*al*' and 'pyramid*al*'; but it was not easy to say where it came from. Finally I broke down the monster into the two names '*Nora*' and '*Ekdal*' from two well-known dramas by Ibsen.* I had previously read a newspaper article about Ibsen by the same author whose latest opus I had criticized in this way in my dream.

II

One of my patients recounted a short dream to me which ended in a nonsensical word-combination. She is with her husband at some peasant celebration and then says: '*That will end in a general Mais-tollmütz.*' It is accompanied in her dream by the obscure thought that it is a pudding made of maize, a kind of polenta. The analysis broke the word down into *Mais* [maize]—*toll* [crazy]—*mannstoll* [man-crazy]—*Olmütz*,* all of them recognizable as remnants from a conversation at table. Hidden behind *Mais*, as well as an allusion to the recently opened Jubilee Exhibition,* were the words: *Meissen* (a figurine of *Meissen* porcelain representing a bird); *Miss* (her relative's English governess had travelled to *Olmütz*); *mies*=nasty, miserable, used in Jewish slang in jest; and a long chain of ideas and connections started off from each separate syllable of this lump of a word.

III

A young man had his door-bell set ringing late in the evening by an acquaintance handing in a visiting-card. That night he has this dream: *a workman is waiting late at night to put the room-telephone*

[*Zimmertelegraph*] *to rights. After he has gone, it still goes on ringing, not with one continuous ring but only intermittently. The servant fetches the man back, and he says: 'It's odd how even people who are tutelrein don't know how to deal with this kind of thing.'*

As we see, the unimportant occasion for the dream refers only to one element in it. It only becomes significant once it has attached itself to an earlier experience of the dreamer's, just as slight in itself, which he has endowed with the significance of a proxy. As a boy living with his father, when drowsy with sleep he once spilt a glass of water on the floor so that the cable of the room-telephone was soaked and the *continuous ringing* disturbed his father's sleep. As the continuous ringing correlates to getting wet, the *intermittent ringing* is then used to stand for *drops falling*. But the word '*tutelrein*' can be analysed along three lines, aiming at three kinds of dream-material: '*Tutel*' = *Curatel*, which means guardianship; *Tutel* (perhaps '*Tuttel*') is a vulgar term for a woman's breast, and the component '*rein*' [clean] takes over the first syllables of '*Zimmertelegraph*' to form '*zimmerrein*' ['house-trained'], which has a great deal to do with wetting the floor, and in addition echoes a name present in the dreamer's family.[5]

IV

In a fairly long, chaotic dream of my own, which is apparently centred on a journey by ship, it happens that the next landing-station is called *Hearsing* and the one after that *Fliess*. This latter is the name of my friend in B.,* which has often been the goal of my journeys. But *Hearsing* is made up of the place-names of our local railway line in Vienna, which end so frequently in-*ing*: *Hietzing*,

---

[5] We employ the same analysis and synthesis of syllables—truly a syllabic chemistry—in inventing all kinds of witticisms when we are awake. 'What is the cheapest way of acquiring silver [*Silber*]? You go to an avenue of silver poplars [*Silberpappeln*], order them to be silent, then the '*Pappeln*' [gossiping] will stop and the silver is free.' The first reader* and critic of this book made the objection—which will probably be repeated by those who follow him—that 'the dreamer often appears too witty'. That is correct, as long as it refers only to the dreamer; it only involves disapproval if it is meant to apply to the interpreter too. In real, waking life I can make little claim to the description 'witty'; if my dreams appear witty, that is not because of my disposition, but on account of the peculiar psychological conditions under which the dream is worked out, and it is closely connected with the theory of Wit and the Comic. The dream is made witty because the straight and nearest way to express its thoughts is barred to it; it is made witty of necessity. My readers can be assured that my patients' dreams produce an impression just as witty (at least forced-witty)—or even more so—than mine.

Liesing, Mödling (Medelitz, 'meae deliciae' in its old name, that is, 'my delight' [*meine Freud'*]), combined with the English *hearsay*, which indicates slander, and sets up the connection with the unimportant daytime initiation of the dream, a poem in the *Fliegende Blätter** about a slanderous dwarf 'Sagter Hatergesagt' [Sez-he He-sed]. By connecting the final syllable '-ing' to the name *Fliess* one gets '*Vlissingen*', in reality the port in the sea-journey where my brother puts in when he comes to visit us from England. But the English name of *Vlissingen* is *Flushing*, which is the same as blushing, and recalls the woman patient I am treating who suffers from a 'blushing-anxiety'; it also reminds me of a recent publication on this neurosis by Bechterew which caused me feelings of annoyance.

V

Another time I had a dream made up of two separate parts. The first is the word '*Autodidasker*', which I recall vividly; the other is identical with a brief and innocuous fantasy I entertained some days before, to the effect that when next I see Professor N., I have to say: 'The patient I last consulted you about really does suffer only from a neurosis, just as you surmised.' Now not only does the new coinage '*Autodidasker*' have to satisfy the requirement that it should contain or represent a compromise-meaning, this meaning should also relate coherently to my intention, repeated from waking life, to give Professor N. that satisfaction.

Now *Autodidasker* breaks down easily into *Autor* [author], *Autodidakt* [self-taught] and *Lasker*,* which is also associated with the name *Lassalle*.* The first of these words leads to the—this time significant—occasion for the dream. I had brought my wife several volumes by a well-known author who is a friend of my brother's and who comes, so I have heard, from the same village as I do (J. J. David).* One evening she talked to me about the profound impression made on her by the sad and moving story of a wasted talent in one of David's novellas, and our conversation then turned to the signs of talent we perceived in our own children. Influenced by what she had just been reading, she expressed her concern about the children, and I consoled her with the remark that dangers of this sort are just the kind that can be averted by education and upbringing. That night my train of thought continued, took up my wife's worries, and wove all kinds of things into them. An observation the writer had made to my brother with regard to getting married showed my thoughts a side-path which made it possible to represent them in my dream. This path led to Breslau,* where a lady who was a very close friend of ours had got married. In Breslau I found examples in *Lasker* and *Lassalle* for my concern about wasting one's life for a woman, which formed the heart of my dream-thoughts. The two enabled me to represent both kinds of this disastrous influence at the same time.[6] 'Cherchez la femme', the phrase summing up these thoughts, leads me, though in a different sense, to my brother, who is still unmarried, and who is called *Alexander*. Now I note that *Alex*, our shortened form of his name, sounds almost like *Lasker* back-to-front, and that an impulse from this must have shared in effectively directing my thoughts to the roundabout route via Breslau.

However, my games with names and syllables in this dream contain a further meaning. They stand for the wish that my brother should enjoy a happy family life, and they do in the following way. In the novel of an artist's life, *L'Œuvre*,* whose subject-matter must have suggested itself to my dream-thoughts, it is well known that the writer has portrayed himself and his own family happiness in certain episodes, appearing in this role under the name of *Sandoz*. He probably reached this change of name along the following route. If we reverse *Zola* (as children like to do), we get *Aloz*. That was probably not sufficiently disguised for him; so he replaced the syllable *Al*, which also introduces the name *A*lexander, by the third syllable of that name, *sand*, and that is how *Sandoz* came about. And it is in much the same way that my *Autodidasker* was made.

My fantasy of telling Professor N. that the patient we had both seen only suffered from a neurosis entered my dream in the following way. Shortly before the end of my working year I acquired a patient who utterly baffled my diagnostic skills. A severe organic complaint, perhaps some change to the spinal cord, suggested itself, but was not to be demonstrated. It would have been tempting to diagnose a neurosis, which would have brought an end to all my difficulties, were it not that the sexual case-history, without which I refuse to diagnose a neurosis, was so energetically rejected by my

---

[6] *Lasker* died of progressive paralysis, that is, as the consequence of an infection (lues) caught from a woman; *Lassalle*, it is well known, died in a duel fought on account of a lady.

patient. Not knowing what to do, I turned to the physician whom I revere most deeply for his humanity (as do others) and to whose authority I most readily defer. He listened to my doubts, said they were justified, and then said: 'Keep the man under further observation; it will be a neurosis.' As I know that he does not share my views on the aetiology of neuroses, I did not contradict him, but neither did I hide my scepticism. A few days later I told my patient that I did not know how to treat him, and advised him to turn to someone else. Then to my great surprise he began to ask me to forgive him for lying to me; he was so ashamed, and then he revealed to me that very item of sexual aetiology which I had expected, and which I needed if I was to assume a neurosis. It was a great relief to me, but at the same time a source of embarrassment; I had to admit that my adviser, not thrown off course by requiring a case-history, had seen more correctly. I intended to tell him, when I saw him again—to tell him that he was right and I was wrong.

Now this is just what I am doing in my dream. But what sort of a wish-fulfilment is it supposed to be if I admit I am wrong? That is just what I do wish. I would like to be wrong in my worries and fears, or rather, I would like my wife, whose fears I have taken over into my dream, to be wrong. The theme associated with being right or wrong in the dream is not too far away from the one which is really interesting for the dream-thoughts. The same alternatives—organic or psychological damage caused by a woman—or rather, by sexuality: tabetic paralysis or neurosis. The way *Lassalle* met his end is connected more loosely to the latter.

Professor N. plays a part in this tightly knit (and, when carefully interpreted, quite transparent) dream, not only on account of this analogy, nor of my wish to be wrong, nor yet on account of his further connections with Breslau and with the family of our friend who married there—but also because of the following little occurrence which followed our consultation. After he had finished his professional task with that speculation, he turned his interest to personal matters. 'How many children do you have now?' 'Six.'—A dubious, respectful gesture.—'Girls? Boys?' 'Three of each. They are my pride and my wealth.' 'Now take care, the girls are no problem, but bringing up boys can have its difficulties later.' I rejoined that they had been quite well-behaved so far. Clearly this second diagnosis pleased me just as little as his earlier judgement that my patient only had a neurosis. These two impressions, then, are connected by proximity, being experienced all at once. In taking the story of the neurosis into my dream, I am substituting it for our conversation about bringing up children, which reveals still further connections with the dream-thoughts, as it touches so closely on my wife's worries as she later expressed them. Thus, even my anxiety that N. might be right in his remarks about the difficulties in bringing up boys makes its way into the dream-content by hiding behind the representation of my wish that I was wrong to nurse such fears. The same fantasy functions unaltered to represent the two opposite sides of the alternative.

These verbal distortions in our dreams are very like those familiar to us from paranoia, but which are also present in hysteria and obsessive ideas. The linguistic tricks of children, who at certain times really do treat words as if they were objects, inventing new languages and artificial word-combinations, are in this respect the common source for dreams and for the psychoneuroses.

Where the dream contains speech expressly distinct from thoughts, the rule applies without exception that the words spoken in the dream derive from words remembered in the dream-material. The words spoken are either retained intact or are slightly altered in expression; frequently they are a patchwork of various utterances remembered from the day. In this process the actual words remain the same, but their sense is altered to yield a different meaning, or multiple meanings. Speech in dreams often functions merely as an allusion to an event which was accompanied by the words remembered.

(b) *The Work of Displacement*

While we were collecting examples of dream-condensation, another relationship, probably no less significant, must already have caught our attention. We could not fail to observe that the elements pushing to the fore in the dream-content as essential components certainly did not play the same part in the dream-thoughts. As a corollary, this statement can also be reversed. What is clearly essential in the content of the dream-thoughts does not need to be represented in the dream itself at all. The dream, one might say, is *centred differently*; its content is ordered around a centre made up of elements other than the dream-thoughts. Thus, for example, the centre of the dream-content in the dream of the botanical monograph is clearly the element 'botanical'; the dream-thoughts, on the other hand, are concerned with complications and conflicts arising from obligations incurred by services between colleagues; thereafter they focus on the charge that I am giving up too much for the sake of my hobbies—and the element 'botanical' has no place at all here in the heart of the dream-thoughts, unless it is loosely related to it by contrast, for botany had never been one of my favourite subjects. In my patient's Sappho dream, *climbing up and down, being up above and down below* are made to be its centre; but in fact the dream deals with sexual relations with persons of the *lower* orders, so that only one of the elements in the dream-thoughts seems to have entered the dream-content, but then to an undue extent. Similarly, though it is true that cruelty reappears as a factor in the content of the may-beetles dream, which is about the relations of sexuality to cruelty, it does so in a connection of a different kind and without any reference to sexuality, that is, it is torn from its context and recast in a different, unfamiliar form. Again, in the dream of my uncle the meaning of the yellow beard that forms its centre seems to bear no relation to the ambitious wishes we have acknowledged to be the heart of the dream-thoughts. Dreams of this kind give the impression of *displacement* with good reason. In complete contrast to these examples, the dream of Irma's injection shows that in the formation of a dream individual elements are also able to retain the place they occupy in the dream-thoughts. When we first recognize this new relation, which is entirely variable in meaning, between dream-thoughts and dream-content, it is likely to fill us with astonishment. If in the course of some normal psychical process we find one idea being singled out from many others and becoming particularly vivid in our consciousness, we usually regard this success as proof that it has been accorded the especially high psychical value (a certain degree of interest) which is its due. But now we discover that this value accorded to particular elements in the dream-thoughts is not retained or not taken into account in forming a dream. After all, there is no doubt as to which are the most valuable elements in the dream-thoughts; our judgement needs no help to tell us. But in dream-formation these essential elements, charged though they are with intense interest, are dealt with as if they were of little value, and instead their place is taken in the dream by other elements which certainly had little value in the dream-thoughts. At first this gives the impression that the psychical intensity[7] of the particular ideas was not taken into consideration at all in their selection for the dream, but only the varying nature and degree of their determination. What enters the dream, one might think, is not what is important in the dream-thoughts, but what appears frequently and variously in them. However, this assumption will not take our understanding of dream-formation much further, as from the outset it leaves no room for thinking that these two factors in selecting elements for the dream—multiple determination and inherent value—must necessarily work along the same lines to produce the same meaning. It supposes that the ideas which are the most important in the dream-thoughts are likely to be the ones that recur in them most often, for the particular dream-thoughts radiate from them as it were from a centre. And yet the dream can reject these elements, even though they are emphasized so intensely and reinforced so variously, and it can take up into its content other elements which are characterized by the second quality, inherent value, alone.

To solve this problem we shall make use of another impression we had when we were examining the over-determination of the dream-content. Perhaps a number of my readers have already made their own judgement that this over-determination of the dream-elements is not a remarkable discovery at all, as it is quite self-evident. After all, the analysis starts out from the dream-elements and registers all the ideas that are associated with them; no wonder, then, that in the thought-material acquired in this way these are the very elements to emerge with particular frequency. I doubt if I could accept this objection, but I shall put into words something that sounds rather like it: among the thoughts brought to light in the analysis there are many which are more remote from the heart of the dream, standing out like artificial elements interpolated for some purpose. Their purpose is easy to discover; these are the very ones that set up the connection, often forced and far-fetched, between the dream-content and the dream-thoughts, and if these elements were eliminated from the analysis, the components of the dream would lose not

---

[7] The psychical intensity, value, weight of interest, of an idea is of course to be kept separate from the sensory intensity of its representation.

only their over-determination by the dream-thoughts, but any adequate determination by them at all. This leads us to the conclusion that very probably the multiple determination which decides the selection of elements for the dream is not always a primary factor in forming it, but often a secondary result of some power at work in the psyche as yet unknown to us. All the same, over-determination must be an important factor for the entry of particular elements into the dream, for we can observe that it is produced in some profusion in cases where it arises with some assistance from the dream-material.

The thought suggests itself that a psychical power is operative in the dream-work which on the one hand strips the psychically valuable elements of their intensity, and on the other creates new values *by way of over-determination* out of elements of low value; it is the new values that then reach the dream-content. If this is what happens, then *a transference and displacement of the psychical intensity* of the individual elements has taken place; as a consequence, the difference between the texts of the dream-content and the dream-thoughts makes its appearance. The process we are assuming here is *the* essential part of the dream-work; it has earned the name of *dream-displacement*. *Dream-displacement* and *dream-condensation* are the two foremen in charge of the dream-work, and we may put the shaping of our dreams down mainly to their activity.

It is also easy for us, I think, to recognize the psychical power which manifests itself in the facts of dream-displacement. The result of this displacement is that the dream-content no longer looks the same as the heart of the dream-thoughts, that the dream reproduces only a distortion of the dream-wish present in the unconscious. But dream-distortion is already familiar to us; we traced it back to the censorship exercised by one psychical agency in our mental life against another. Dream-displacement is one of the main means of bringing this distortion about. *Is fecit cui profuit.** We may assume that dream-displacement comes about through the influence of that censorship, the censorship of endopsychic defence.

The way in which these factors—displacement, condensation, and over-determination—interact in the process of dream-formation, and the question of which becomes dominant and which secondary, are things we shall set aside for later inquiries. For the moment we can state a second condition which the elements reaching the dream have to fulfil: *they should have evaded the censorship set up by resistance.* But from now on in interpreting dreams we propose to take account of dream-distortion as an indubitable fact.

(c) *The Means of Representation in Dreams*

Besides the two factors of dream-*condensation* and dream-*displacement* which we discovered were at work in the transformation of latent thought-material into the manifest dream-content, in pursuing our inquiry we shall encounter two further conditions which undoubtedly have an influence on the selection of material reaching the dream. But before continuing, even at the risk of appearing to pause on our way, I would like to look for the first time at what goes on in the course of interpreting a dream. If I am not deceived, the best way of explaining this clearly and ensuring it is proof against any objections would be for me to take one particular dream as a model, work out its interpretation, as I did in Chapter II with the dream of Irma's injection, but then to put together the dream-thoughts I have uncovered and from them reconstruct the process by which the dream was formed, that is, to complete the analysis of the dream by its synthesis. I have carried out this work on many examples for my own instruction; but I am unable to use them here because I am prevented by a number of considerations regarding the psychical material which most fair-minded people would approve of. These considerations were less troublesome when analysing dreams, for the analysis did not need to be complete, and retained its value even if it took us only a little way into the fabric of the dreams. But for their synthesis, the only way I knew for it to be convincing was for it to be complete. I could only give a complete synthesis of the dreams belonging to people unknown to the reading public. And as the means of doing so is only available to me from my patients, that is, from neurotics, this part of my account of dreams will have to be postponed until—in some other place—I am in a position to take the psychological explanation of neuroses to the point where it is possible to make the connection to our topic.

I know from my attempts at synthesizing dreams out of the dream-thoughts that the material emerging in the course of interpretation varies in value. One part of it is made up of the essential dream-thoughts, that is, those which completely replace the dream and would be sufficient by themselves to take its place, if the dream were not subject to censorship. The other part can be summed up under the name of '*collaterals*'; taken all together, they represent the paths along which the real wish rising up from the dream-thoughts is translated into the wish expressed in the dream. One group of these collaterals consists of associations to the real dream-thoughts, corresponding in my scheme to displacements from the essential onto the trivial. A second group comprises those thoughts which make combinations from among these materials, once trivial but now turned into important items by the displacement, and which lead from these to the dream-content. A third group, finally, contains the thought-combinations and ideas occurring to us which enable us to come upon the intermediate collaterals in the course of interpreting the dream-content; but it is not the case that *all of these ideas and combinations together should necessarily* have been involved in the formation of the dream.

At this point we are interested solely in the essential dream-thoughts. These mostly reveal themselves to be a complex of thoughts and memories with the most complicated structure, having all the features of the trains of thought familiar to us from waking life. Quite often they are lines of thought starting out from more than one centre, but not without their points of contact; almost invariably one train of thought is accompanied by its contradictory opposite, associatively linked to it by contrast.

Of course, the individual parts of this complicated structure stand in the most various logical relations to one another. They form foreground and background, digressions and explanations, they set terms and conduct proofs and raise objections. Then, when the entire mass of these dream-thoughts is subject to the pressure of the dream-work, and the pieces are whirled about, broken up, and pushed up against one another, rather like ice-floes surging down a river, the question arises: what has become of the bonds of logic which had previously given the structure its form? What kind of representation does the dream give to 'when', 'because', 'just as', 'although', 'either–or', and all the other relational terms without which we can understand neither sentences nor speech?

Our first answer must be that the dream has no means at its disposal among the dream-thoughts of representing these logical relations. Mostly it disregards all these terms and takes over only the factual substance of the dream-thoughts to work upon. It is left to the interpretation of the dream to re-establish the connections which the dream-work has destroyed.

This inability to express such relations must be due to the nature of the psychical material which goes to make the dream. After all, the fine arts, painting and sculpture, are subject to a similar limitation in comparison with literature, which can make use of speech. Here too the cause of the incapacity lies in the material which both arts use as their medium of expression. Before painting came to recognize the laws of expression applying to it, it used to go to some lengths to make up for this disadvantage. In ancient pictures we read scrolls issuing from the mouths of painted figures, reproducing in writing the spoken words the painter despaired of representing pictorially.

It may be that an objection will be raised at this point, disputing the dream's inability to represent logical relations. True, there are dreams where the most complicated intellectual operations go on, reasoning and counter-reasoning, chopping logic and drawing analogies. But here too appearances are deceptive. If we go further into the interpretation of dreams of this kind, we will learn that this is all *dream-material, not the representation of intellectual activity in the dream*. The ostensible thinking in the dream reproduces the *subject-matter* of the dream-thoughts, not the *relations of the dream-thoughts to one another*; and establishing such relations is what constitutes thinking. I shall offer some examples of this. However, the easiest thing is to make the point that everything spoken in dreams and expressly identified as such is always an—unaltered or only slightly modified—reproduction of words which are also present in the recollected material of the dream-thoughts. Words spoken are often only an allusion to an event retained in the dream-thoughts; the meaning of the dream is something quite different.

However, I do not dispute that work of critical thinking, which does not simply repeat material from the dream-thoughts, also has a share in forming the dream. I shall have to elucidate the influence exercised by this factor at the end of the present discussion. It will then emerge that this work of thinking is not produced by the dream-thoughts, but by the dream, which in some sense has already been completed.

For the moment, then, let us continue to accept that dreams do not have a particular way of representing logical relations between dream-thoughts. Where, for example, a contradiction is present in a dream, it is either a contradiction to the dream or a contradiction from the content of one of the dream-thoughts; the contradiction in the dream corresponds to a contradiction *between* the dream-thoughts only in a very indirectly mediated way.

But just as painting finally succeeded in finding a way of expressing at least the intention of the words spoken by the figures represented—tenderness, menace, warning, and the like—by a different means from fluttering scrolls, so it has emerged that it is possible for the dream to take into account particular logical relations between its dream-thoughts by suitably modifying its distinctive mode of representation. We may learn that different dreams take them into consideration to a different extent. One dream will disregard the logical coherence of its material entirely, while another will try to suggest it as fully as possible. In this respect dreams depart to a varying extent from the text they have before them to work upon. By the way, dreams show a similar variability in the way they behave towards the temporal sequence of the dream-thoughts, if the sequence is set up in the unconscious (as it is, for example, in the dream of Irma's injection).

What means, then, is the dream-work able to use to indicate these relations, which are so difficult to represent, in the dream-thoughts? I shall attempt to list them one by one.

First of all, the dream does justice to the connection undeniably existing between all the pieces of the dream-thoughts by concentrating them into the unified representation of a situation or an event. It renders logical connections in terms of simultaneity; in doing so, it proceeds like the painter who assembles all the philosophers or poets to present a picture of the School of Athens* or of Parnassus, for though they never gathered in one hall or on one mountain-top, they surely form a community in our thoughts.

The dream continues this method of representation in its details. Whenever it shows two elements close together, this is a guarantee that there is a particularly intimate relation between their equivalents in the dream-thoughts. It is not unlike what happens in our system of writing: *ab* means that both letters should be spoken as one syllable; *a* and *b* with a space between is a sign that *a* is to be read as the last letter of one word and *b* as the first of another. Accordingly, the combinations in the dream are not formed of random, completely disparate elements from the dream-material, but from ones which are also intimately related in the dream-thoughts.

To represent *causal relations* the dream has two procedures which, in essentials, amount to the same thing. When the dream-thoughts run something like: 'because this was so and so, then such and such was bound to happen', the dream's main way of representing this is to present the subordinate clause as an introductory dream and then add the main clause as the main dream. If I have interpreted aright this sequence can also be reversed, but the main clause will always correspond to the main part of the dream.

A patient of mine once gave me a beautiful example of this way of representing causality. I shall give a full account of her dream later. It consisted of a short prologue and a very elaborate part, with a very strong thematic centre, which might be entitled: 'Told by the Flowers'. The preliminary dream went like this: *She is going into the kitchen to the two maidservants and scolding them for not having finished preparing 'the bite to eat'. As she does so she sees a lot of crude kitchen-ware turned on end to dry off and piled in a heap on top of one another. The two maids go to fetch water, and to do so it is as if they have to wade into a river coming up as far as the house or into the yard.*

Then the main dream followed, introduced like this: *she is climbing down from high up over curiously shaped railings, glad that her dress does not catch on anything, etc*. The dream-prologue refers to the lady's parental house. It is likely that she has often heard the words in the kitchen from her mother. The piles of coarse crockery derive from the modest hardware shop in the same building. The second part of the dream contains an allusion to her father, who used to chase after servant-girls and caught a fatal illness during a flood—the house stood very near the riverbank. The thought hiding behind this preliminary dream, then, is: because I come from this house, from such modest and disagreeable circumstances. The main dream takes up the same thought, presenting it transformed by wish-fulfilment: I am of high degree; that is, rather: because I am of such low degree, my life has been such and such.

As far as I can see, a division of the dream into two unequal parts does not always signify a causal relation between the thoughts in both parts. It often seems as if the same material were being presented in the two dreams from different points of view; or the two dreams have arisen from separate centres in the dream-material, overlapping in content in such a way that what is the centre of one dream may play a part in the other as an allusion, and the other way round. In a certain number of dreams, however, the division into a shorter introductory dream and a longer dream following it does in fact signify a causal relation between the two parts. The second method of representing causal relations is employed where the material is meagre; it operates by transforming one image in the dream, whether a person or a thing, into another. We can seriously maintain that this connection is a causal one only in cases where we actually see this transformation happening; not where we merely observe that the one person or thing has now taken the place of the other. I said that the two methods of representing causal relations amounted to the same thing: in both cases *causation* is represented by *succession*, in the first case by one dream following another; in the second by the immediate transformation of one image into another. Admittedly, in most cases the causal relation is not represented at all, but submits to the inevitable one-after-the-other of the elements, inevitable even in the working of our dreams.

The dream has no way at all of expressing the alternative 'either ... or'. It usually takes up the two options into one context as if they had equal rights. The dream of Irma's injection contains a classic example. Its latent thoughts clearly state: it is not my fault that Irma continues to suffer pain; the blame is to be ascribed *either* to her resistance to accepting my solution *or* to the unfavourable sexual conditions under which she lives, which I cannot change, *or* the nature of her pain is not hysterical at all, but organic. However, the dream presents all three of these all-but mutually exclusive possibilities and has no difficulty in adding the dream-wish as a fourth explanation. The 'either ... or' was then introduced into the interconnections of the dream-thoughts by me after I had interpreted the dream.

However, where a dreamer wants to use an 'either ... or' in recounting a dream: 'it was either a garden or a living-room, etc.', what is present in the dream-thoughts is not an alternative but an 'and', a simple addition tacked on. With this 'either ... or' we are mostly describing a still insoluble characteristic in a dream-element: its haziness. The rule for interpretation in this case is: the separate options of the apparent alternative are to be treated as equal and linked by 'and'. For example, I dream that after waiting for a long time in vain for the address of my friend, who is staying in Italy, I receive a telegram giving me this address. I see it printed in blue on the paper slip of the telegram; the first word is blurred, something like:

> *via,*
> or   *villa,* the second clearly: *Sezerno.*
> or even (*casa*).

The second word, which sounds like an Italian name and reminds me of our etymological discussions, also expresses my annoyance that he should have kept the place where he is staying *secret* for so long; but in the analysis it can be seen that each one of the three items suggested as alternative possibilities for the first word offers an independent and equally valid starting-point for the chain of thoughts.

The night before my father was buried* I had a dream of a printed panel, a placard or notice nailed up, rather like the notices forbidding smoking in railway waiting-rooms. Written on it is either:

> *You are requested to close your eyes.*

or

> *You are requested to keep an eye closed.*

which I am used to representing in the following form:

>   *your*
> *You are requested to keep   eye(s) closed*
>   *an*

Each of the two versions has its particular meaning and leads the dream-interpretation along particular paths. I had arranged for the ceremony to be as simple as possible, because I knew what the departed thought about such events. However, other members of the family did not approve of such puritan simplicity; they considered it would let us down in front of the funeral guests. That is why one phrase in the dream makes the request to 'close an eye', that is, to be forbearing, or 'turn a blind eye'. In this case it is particularly easy to grasp the meaning of the haziness we have described as expressing an 'either . . . or'. The dream-work has not been successful in producing for the dream-thoughts a unified form of words which will also carry two meanings. The two main lines of thought have already separated in the dream-content.

Alternatives are difficult to represent, and in some cases they are expressed by the division of the dream into two halves of equal length.

The dream has a very striking way of dealing with the category of *opposites* and *contradictions*. This is simply disregarded. To the dream 'No' does not seem to exist. In particular, it prefers to draw opposites together into a unity or to represent them as one. Indeed, it also takes the liberty of representing some random element by its wished-for opposite, so that at first one cannot tell which of the possible poles is meant positively or negatively in the dream-thoughts. In one of the dreams just referred to, whose preliminary we have already interpreted ('because I am of such low degree'), the dreamer is climbing over a railing. As she does so, she is holding a branch of blossom in her hands. What this image brings to her mind is how the angel in pictures of the Annunciation (she herself is called Maria) carries a tall lily, and how the girls dressed in white walk in the Corpus Christi procession when the streets are decked with green branches. From these ideas it is quite certain that the blossoming branch in her dream alludes to sexual innocence. But the branch is covered with red blossoms, each one resembling a camellia. By the end of the way she has taken, her dream continues, the blossoms are rather faded; this is followed by unmistakable allusions to her period. Thus the same branch, which is carried as if it were a lily and borne by an innocent maiden, is at the same time an allusion to the *dame aux camélias*,* who always wore a white camellia, as we know, but wore a red one at the time of her period. The same blossoming branch ('des Mädchens Blüthen' ['the maiden's blossoms'] in Goethe's poem*) represents both sexual innocence and its opposite. The same dream, too, which expresses her joy at going through life immaculate, in some places allows the opposite train of thought—that she has been guilty of various sins against sexual purity (in childhood, that is)—to shimmer through. In analysing the dream we found it easy to distinguish the two trains of thought from each other; of these, the consolatory one seems to lie in a surface stratum, the reproachful one much deeper; both directly contradict each other, while their equal but opposite elements have come to be represented by the self-same dream-elements.

There is only one of the logical relations to benefit—to a very great extent—from the mechanism of dream-formation. It is the relation of similarity, congruence, or convergence, the *just like*, which dreams have the most various means of expressing better than anything else. Indeed, the mergers, or cases of 'just like' present in the dream-material constitute the basis for the formation of the dream, and a considerable part of the dream-work consists of creating new mergers of this kind, if those already present are prevented from entering the dream by the censorship of resistance. Finding representations for the relation of similarity is aided by the dream-work's activity of condensation.

In general, dreams represent *similarity, congruence, having features in common* by concentration into a *unity*, which is either already present in the dream-material or newly formed. The first case can be called an *identification*, the second a *composite formation*. Identification is applied when personages are involved; *composite formation* in cases where objects are the material to be unified, though composites can also be generated by personages. Places are often treated like persons.

In identification, only one of the figures linked by some common factor gets to be represented in the dream-content, while the other figure or figures seem to be suppressed. However, this one figure goes through all the relationships and situations which are generated both by the cover-figure itself and by the figure it covers. In composite formations that include persons, the dream-image will already contain features belonging to the figures individually but not shared by them, so that when these features are combined, a new unity, a composite figure, is certain to appear. The composite itself can be brought about in various ways. Either the figure in the dream takes its name from one of the persons it refers to—we know then that such and such a person is intended, rather as we know such things when awake—while its visual appearance belongs to the other person; or the dream-image is composed of visual features which in real life are distributed between both. Instead of being represented by visual features, the second person's share can also be rendered by the gestures we ascribe to him, the words we have him speak, or the situation we place him in. In this last instance the sharp distinction between identification and the formation of composite figures begins to get blurred.

The common quality or thing that justifies—that is, occasions—the merging of the two persons can be represented in the dream, or it can be absent. As a rule it is this very identification or formation of a composite figure that serves to make such representation of this common factor superfluous. Instead of repeating: *A* is hostile towards me, but so is *B*, I form a composite figure of *A* and *B* in my dream, or I imagine *A* performing the kind of action which does not belong to him, but which we know to be characteristic of *B*. The dream-figure obtained in this way encounters me in my dream in some new connection, and the circumstance that it signifies both *A* and *B* justifies me in entering what the two have in common, that is, their hostility towards me, into the appropriate place in the dream-interpretation. In this way I can often achieve an extraordinary degree of condensation in the dream-content; I do not need to make a direct representation of a complicated set of circumstances relating to a person, if I have found someone else to associate with him who has the same claim on some of those circumstances. It is easy to see the extent to which using identification as a means of representation can also serve to circumvent the censorship set up by resistance, which creates such harsh conditions for the dream-work. It may be that the impulse towards censorship is to be found in the very ideas associated in the dream-material with the one person; so then I find a second person who also has connections with the offensive material, but only with a part of it. This contact at a point where censorship is operative now entitles me to form a composite figure characterized by unimportant features from both persons. Being free of censorship, this composite figure is now fit to be taken up into the dream-content, and by making use of condensation in my dream I have satisfied the requirements of the dream-censorship.

Where a feature common to the two figures is also represented in the dream, this is usually a hint to look for some other, hidden common feature which the censorship has made impossible to represent. A displacement with regard to the shared feature has taken place here, to some extent in order to facilitate its representation. The presence in my dream of a composite figure having unimportant shared features allows me to infer that a different common feature, one by no means unimportant, is present in the dream-thoughts.

Accordingly, identification, or the formation of composite figures, serves different purposes: first, to represent a feature both persons have in common; secondly, to represent a *displaced* common feature; but thirdly, to find expression for a common feature that is merely *wished for*. Since wishing it to be the case that two people have something in common is often the same as *exchanging* them, this relation too is expressed in the dream by identification. In the dream of Irma's injection, I wish to exchange this patient for another, that is, I wish that the other were my patient, as Irma is; the dream takes account of this wish in showing me a figure who is called Irma, but who is examined in a posture in which I have only had occasion to see the other. In the dream of my uncle, this exchange is made into the centre of the dream; I identify myself with the minister by treating and judging my colleagues no better than he does.

It has been my experience that every dream without exception deals with oneself. Dreams are absolutely self-centred. Where a strange figure, not my self, appears in the dream-content, I can assume without hesitation that my self is concealed behind that figure. I can add to my self. At other times when my self appears in the dream, its situation tells me that another person is concealed behind it by a process of identification. The dream should then remind me to transfer something attached to this figure to myself, that is, the hidden thing we have in common. There are also dreams in which my self appears together with other figures, which again, once the identification is resolved into its components, reveal themselves to be my self. These identifications then allow me to associate my self with certain ideas, whose entry the censorship has stepped in to prevent. Thus I can represent my self in a dream in many ways, directly, or by means of identification with other figures. Several identifications of this kind make it possible for a tremendous wealth of dream-thoughts to be condensed.[8]

Identifications of localities bearing their own names can be resolved into their constituents even more transparently than those of persons, because in these cases there is no disturbance from the overweening self. In one of my Rome-dreams (p. 150), the place I am visiting is called *Rome*; I am astonished at the number of German placards on a streetcorner. This is a wish-fulfilment which makes me

---

[8] If I am in doubt as to which of the figures in my dream is concealing my self, I keep to the following rule: the figure in the dream which is subject to some affect, which I sense in my sleep, is the one that conceals my self.

promptly think of *Prague*; the wish may derive from a nationalistic German period of my youth. At the time I had the dream, a meeting in *Prague* with my friend was in prospect. So the identification of Rome and Prague can be explained by a wished-for common factor: I would prefer to join my friend in *Rome* than in *Prague*, and for this meeting I would rather exchange *Prague* for *Rome*.

The possibility of creating composite formations is high among the features which often give dreams their fantastic character, as they import into the dream-content elements which could never have been the objects of our perception. The psychical process of forming composites in a dream is clearly the same as when we imagine or depict a centaur or a dragon when we are awake. The distinction is only that when we create fantastic figures while we are awake, the decisive thing is what impression we intend the new figment itself to make, whereas the composite formation in the dream is determined by a factor lying outside its figuration, the feature common to them in the dream-thoughts. Composite formations in dreams can be executed in many different ways. The simplest represents only the characteristics of the one thing, and this representation is accompanied by knowing that it also applies to another object. A more careful technique combines features from both objects into a new image, and as it does so it makes skilful use of similarities between the two objects drawn more or less from real life. The new formation can turn out to be an utter absurdity or even be a great success as a fantasy, depending on the wit and the subject-matter that go into composing it. If the objects that are to be condensed into a unity are too disparate, the dream-work is often content to create a composite formation with a more distinct centre, to which less distinct determinant factors attach themselves. It is as if in this case fusion into one image has not been successful; the two representations overlap and produce something like a competition between the visual images. If we wanted to demonstrate how a concept is formed out of many separate perceptions, we might do it by representing them like this in a drawing.

Of course, dreams are swarming with composite formations of this kind; I have already given some examples in the dreams I have analysed so far; I shall now add some more. In the dream on p. 240, in which the patient's life is 'told by the flowers', in flowery, that is, euphemistic style, the dream-self is carrying a branch of blossom in her hand. This, as we have learned, signifies both innocence and sexual sinfulness at the same time. In addition, the way the blossoms grow on the branch recalls *cherry* blossom; the blossoms themselves, taken singly, are *camellias*, so that the whole gives the impression of an *exotic* plant. The factor the elements in this composite formation have in common emerges from the dream-thoughts. The blossoming branch is put together from allusions to gifts, which moved her, or were supposed to move her, to yield to persuasion. In childhood the cherries, in later years the spray of camellias; the exoticism is an allusion to a much-travelled botanist who tried to win her favour with a drawing of flowers. Another patient created an intermediate thing in her dream out of seaside *bathing-huts*, *water closets*, and the *attic rooms* of our urban dwelling-houses. The first two elements share a reference to the naked body and exposure in a state of undress; by combining this with the third element, we may infer that (in her childhood) the attic too had been the scene of an exposure. Another dreamed that her elder brother promised to treat her to caviare, and that afterwards this brother's legs were covered in *black beads of caviare*. The element of *contagion* in the moral sense and the memory of a *rash* in her childhood, which made her legs appear covered with *red* spots rather than *black*, have combined with the beads of caviare into a new concept, that of '*what she got from her brother*'. Parts of the human body are treated in this dream like objects, as they are in other dreams.

I stated earlier that the dream has no means of expressing the relation of contradiction, or of the opposite to a statement, that is: 'No.' I shall now set about contradicting this statement for the first time. It is possible to represent one group of these cases we can sum up as 'opposites' simply by identification, as we have seen; that is, the opposite can be associated with an exchange, a replacement. I have given frequent examples of this. Another group of opposites, coming roughly under the category of '*vice versa*', '*on the contrary*', comes to be represented in the dream in the following remarkable, one might almost say witty, way. The 'vice versa' does not reach the content of the dream as itself, but makes its presence in the material known by representing a closely related piece of the already formed dream-content—retrospectively, as it were—*in reverse*. It is easier to illustrate the process than describe it. In the pleasant dream of 'up and down', the dream represents climbing in reverse, just as it represents the original model in the dream-thoughts, Daudet's introductory scene where Sappho is presented, by its opposite; movement in the dream is difficult at first and then easier, whereas in the scene in the novel the climb is easy at first and later becomes increasingly difficult. 'Above' and 'below' as they relate to the brother are also represented in the dream the other way round. This indicates that there is a relation of reversal or opposition existing in the dream-thoughts between two parts of the subject-matter, which we discovered when we found that in the dreamer's childhood fantasy he was carried by his nurse, the reverse of the way the hero carried his beloved in the novel. My dream of Goethe's attack on Herr M. (p. 280) also contains a 'vice versa' of this kind which has to be corrected before it becomes possible to interpret the dream. In my dream Goethe attacked a young man, Herr M.; in real life, as the dream-thoughts retained it, my friend, a man of some importance, was attacked by an unknown young writer. In my dream I calculate from the year of Goethe's death* onwards; in real life the calculation started from the year the paralysis-sufferer was born. The thought that was decisive for the dream-material turns out to be a contradiction to the idea that Goethe should be treated as if he were a madman. 'Vice versa,' says my dream, 'if you don't understand that book, it's you who are feeble-minded, not the author.' All these dreams of reversal, it seems to me, also imply the derogatory phrase 'seeing the *wrong side* of someone' (the reversal relating to the brother in the Sappho dream).

If we want to pursue the relationships between dream-content and dream-thoughts further, it is best at this stage if we set out from the dream itself and ask: what is the significance of certain formal characteristics in the representation of dreams as they relate to the dream-thoughts? Foremost among these formal characteristics which cannot but strike us in dreams are the differences in sensory intensity among the individual dream-constructions, and the variations in the degree of distinctness among particular parts of the dream or among entire dreams when compared with one another. The differences in sensory intensity run the gamut from a clarity of contour which one is inclined—though with no warrant for it—to judge greater than that of reality, down to an infuriating haziness which we declare is characteristic of dreams because it does not fully compare with any of the degrees of imprecision we occasionally perceive in objects in real life. Moreover, we usually describe an impression received from an indistinct object in our dream as 'fleeting', while the clearer dream-images, we think, have stood up to our perception of them for some little time. Now the question is: what conditions in the dream-material give rise to these variations in vividness among different parts of the dream-content?

At this point we must first take some steps to counter certain almost inevitable expectations. Since real sensations experienced during sleep can also belong to the material of the dream, one is likely to assume that these elements in the dream, or elements deriving from them, will stand out in the dream-content with particular intensity, or conversely that what strikes us as particularly vivid in the dream can be put down to real sensations of this kind made in our sleep. But my experience has never confirmed this. It is not correct that the elements in the dream that are the offspring of real impressions during sleep (nervous stimuli) will be more remarkable for their vividness than others that have their origin in memories. Reality does not count as a factor in determining the intensity of dream-images.

Moreover, one might still expect that the sensory intensity (the vividness) of the individual dream-images has some relation to the psychical intensity of the elements in the dream-thoughts corresponding to them. In the latter, degree of intensity coincides with degree of psychical value; the most intense and vivid elements are simply the most significant, and these form the centre of the dream-thoughts. Now we know, it is true, that these are the very elements which the censorship most prevents from entering the dream-content. All the same it could be that their nearest offspring, acting as their proxy, carry a higher degree of intensity, though, being only derivative, without necessarily forming the centre of the dream-representation. However, comparative observation of dream and dream-material will destroy this expectation too. The intensity of the elements in the dream-material has nothing to do with the intensity of the elements in the dream; between the two a total '*transvaluation of all psychical values*'* does in fact take place. It is often solely in the fleeting breath of a dream-element hidden by more powerful images that we are able to discover a direct descendant of what held such powerful sway in the dream-thoughts.

The intensity of the elements in the dream proves to be determined in a different way, that is, by two factors independent of each other. At first it is easy to see that those elements acting as the means of expression for the wish-fulfilment are represented with particular intensity. But then we learn from analysis that it is the most vivid elements of the dream that also generate the most trains of thought, that the most vivid are at the same time the best-determined. It does not alter the sense if we reformulate that last empirical statement as follows: the greatest intensity is shown by those elements in the dream which required the fullest and most complex *work of condensation* for their formation. We may anticipate that it will be possible to express this condition and the other condition of wish-fulfilment in one single formula.

I would like to prevent the problem I have just been dealing with—the causes of the greater or lesser intensity or distinctness of particular elements in a dream—from being confused with a different one concerning the variations in clarity to be found among entire dreams or sections of dreams. In the first, the opposites are clarity and haziness; in the second, clarity and confusion. It is evident, of course, that the rise and fall of the qualities on both scales occur in tandem. A part of the dream that appears clear to us usually contains intense elements; an unclear dream, on the contrary, is put together from less intense elements. Nevertheless, the scale from apparently clear to indistinct presents a far more complicated problem than the one presented by fluctuations in the vividness of the dream-elements; indeed, at this stage it is not possible to discuss it, for reasons I shall develop later. In a few individual cases one notes with some surprise that the impression of clarity or indistinctness made by a dream is not in the least significant for its structure, but has its origin in the dream-material as one of its components. In this connection I recall a dream of mine which on waking appeared to me to be so particularly well-structured, complete, and clear that, still drowsy as I was, I proposed to admit a new category of dreams which were not subject to the mechanism of condensation and displacement, but might be described as 'fantasies during sleep'. Closer scrutiny revealed that this rare dream displayed the same gaps and fissures in its structure as any other; so I gave up the category of dream-fantasies. However, the content of the dream was, in essence, that I was propounding to my friend* a difficult and long-sought

theory of bisexuality, and it was due to the wish-fulfilling power of
the dream that this theory—which the dream did not give, by the
way—appeared so clear and complete to us. What I had taken to be a
judgement on the finished dream was a part—and indeed the essential part—of the dream-content. You might say that the dream-work
was encroaching on my first waking thoughts, conveying to me in the
guise of a *judgement on* the dream that part of the dream-material it
had failed to represent exactly *in it*. I once came upon the exact
counterpart to this dream in a patient who did not want to tell her
dream at all at first, although it belonged in the analysis, 'because it is
so indistinct and confused'. Finally, protesting repeatedly that she
could not vouch with certainty for her account, she gave it: several
figures occurred in the dream, herself, her husband, and her father,
and it was as if she did not know whether her husband was her father
or who her father really was, or something like that. From combining
this dream with the ideas occurring to her during the consultation, it
emerged that her dream is about the pretty ordinary story of a maidservant who had to confess that she is expecting a child and has to
hear doubts as to 'who the father (of the child) really is'.[9] Here the
lack of clarity shown by the dream was also a part of the material that
initiated the dream. A part of this content had been represented in
the dream's *form.* In my experience, one very rarely arrives at a
situation like this one, where it is possible to interpret the clarity or
confusion of the dream in terms of certainty or doubt present in its
subject-matter. This qualitative scale from clarity to confusion is
essentially dependent on the operation of the factor in dream-
formation which I have so far left undiscussed, but which I shall be
obliged to reveal later on.

In many of the dreams which stay for a stretch firmly within a
certain situation and scene, interruptions occur which are described
by the following words: 'But then it is as if at the same time it were a
different place, and such and such happened there.' This kind of
interruption to the main action of the dream—which can be
resumed after a while—turns out to be a subordinate clause, an
interpolated thought. The conditional in the dream-thoughts is represented in the dream by simultaneity ('if' = 'when').

---

[9] Accompanying hysterical symptoms: absence of her periods and great ill humour,
this patient's main affliction.

What is the meaning of the sensation of inhibited movement, so close to anxiety, which appears so often in dreams? We want to move forward and cannot budge, we want to get something done and constantly come upon obstacles. The railway train is about to leave and we are unable to catch it; we raise our hand to avenge some insult and it fails us, and so on. We have already met this sensation in our discussion of exhibition-dreams, but we have not yet made a serious attempt to interpret it. It is convenient but inadequate to answer that motor paralysis occurs in sleep, making its presence felt in the said sensation. We are justified in asking: 'Then why do we not dream of inhibited movement all the time?', and in expecting that this sensation, which can always be summoned up in sleep, will be used for some representational purpose and will only be roused by a need for representation present in the dream-material.

This not-being-able-to-get-something-done does not always appear in dreams as a sensation, but also simply as a part of the dream-content. One such case is particularly suitable for explaining the significance of this item in our dreams. I will give a shortened version of a dream in which I appear accused of dishonesty. *The location is a jumble of a private clinic and several other places. A servant appears, summoning me to an examination.* In the dream I know that something has been missed, and that the examination is taking place because I am suspected of having appropriated what was lost. The analysis shows that 'examination' is to be taken as ambiguous, and includes 'medical examination'. Conscious of my innocence and of my function as consultant in this place, I accompany the servant unperturbed. At a doorway we are received by another servant, who says, pointing to me: 'You've brought him? But he's a decent man.' Then I enter a large hall, without the servant, where there are machines standing, and which reminds me of an Inferno with its diabolical punishments. Strung up on one apparatus I see a colleague who might have had every reason to be concerned about me; but he ignores me. Then I am told I can go now. I can't find my hat, and so I still can't go.*

The wish-fulfilment in the dream is obviously that I am acknowledged to be an honest man and allowed to go; so there must be all sorts of material in the dream-thoughts containing the contrary. Being allowed to go is the sign of my absolution; so if the ending of the dream introduces an occurrence that prevents me from going, the implication is that the suppressed contradictory material is using this feature to assert itself. So not finding my hat means: 'You're not an honest man after all.' Not-being-able-to-carry-something-out in this dream is an *expression of the contrary*, a '*No*'; hence, this qualifies my earlier claim that dreams are unable to express a negation.[10]

In other dreams, where not-being-able-to-move occurs as a sensation, not merely as a situation, the same contradiction is more powerfully expressed by this sensation of motor inhibition, as an impulse of willing opposed by a counter-willing. That is, the sensation of motor inhibition represents a *conflict of wills*. We shall hear later that this selfsame motor paralysis in sleep is one of the fundamental conditions of psychical activity while dreaming. Now the impulse that is transferred along the paths of motor activity is of course the will, and the fact that we are certain to feel this impulse inhibited while we are asleep is what makes the whole process so very appropriate for representing the *willing* and the '*No*' that opposes it. My explanation of anxiety makes it easy to grasp why the sensation of inhibited will is so close to anxiety and why it is combined with it so often in our dreams. Anxiety is an impulse of the libido, proceeding from the unconscious and inhibited by the preconscious. So in those dreams where the sensation of inhibition is combined with anxiety, it must be a matter of an impulse of willing which was once capable of developing libido, a matter of sexual stirrings.

(d) *Regard for Representability*

So far we have been occupied with examining how the dream represents relations between the dream-thoughts, but in doing so we frequently returned to the broader topic of the general nature of the changes undergone by the dream-material for the purposes of dream-formation. Now we know that the dream-material, largely divested

---

[10] In the complete analysis, an association with a childhood experience emerges by way of the following chain: 'The Moor has done his duty. The Moor *can go*.'* And then the joking question: 'How old is the Moor, when he has done his duty? One year old, for then he can walk/go.' (They tell me I had such a mop of black hair when I was born that my young mother declared I was a little Moor.)—Not being able to find my hat is an experience from the dream-day carrying many meanings. Our housemaid, a genius at putting things away, had hidden it.—This ending to my dream also conceals a rejection of sad thoughts of death: 'it will be a long time still before I have done my duty; I must not go yet.'—Birth and death, as in the dream of Goethe and the paralytic patient, which took place shortly before (p. 280).

of its logical relations, undergoes a concentration, while at the same time displacements of intensity among its elements necessarily bring about a psychical transvaluation of this material. The displacements we were considering turned out to be substitutions of one particular idea by another somehow closely associated with it; and they were useful in condensation, for in this way, instead of two elements, an intermediate factor common to them both gained entry to the dream. We have not yet mentioned another kind of displacement. But we learn from our analyses that there is such a thing, and that it makes its presence known in a *transposition in the words used to express* the thought concerned. In both cases it is a matter of displacement along a chain of associations, but the same procedure takes place in different psychical spheres, and the result of this displacement is that in one case one element is replaced by another, while in the other one element exchanges its verbal formulation for another.

This second kind of displacement occurring in the formation of dreams is not only of great theoretical interest; it is also particularly well suited to explain the appearance of fantastic absurdity in which dreams disguise themselves. As a rule, the displacement follows the direction taken when a colourless and abstract expression of the dream-thought is exchanged for a pictorial and concrete one. The advantage, and thus the intention of the substitution, is obvious. For the dream, what is pictorial is *capable of representation*, can be integrated into a situation where an abstract expression would cause similar difficulties for the dream-representation to those a political leading article, say, would make for an illustrated news-magazine. But not only representability has to gain from this exchange; the several interests of condensation and the censorship are able to do so too. Once the abstract, unusable thought is transformed into a pictorial language, the contacts and identities which the dream-work requires—and will create where they are not present—come about between this new expression and the rest of the dream-material more easily than before, for language has developed in such a way that the concrete words of every language are far richer in associations than its conceptual terms. One can imagine that a good bit of the intermediary work in the process of dream-formation takes place in this way—by appropriate linguistic transformation of the individual thoughts—for it aims at reducing the separate dream-thoughts to the most economical and unified expression possible in the dream. In the process one thought, whose expression perhaps for other reasons is fixed, will, in the way it distributes and selects, affect the expressive possibilities of another thought, and it may be that it does this from the outset, working as a poet does. If a poem is to rhyme, the second rhyming line is bound by two conditions; it has to express its due meaning, and it must find the same sound as the first rhyming line. The best poems, I suppose, are those where we do not notice the intention to find the rhyme, but where from the outset each thought has induced the other to choose the verbal expression that with a little adaptation will allow the rhyme to emerge.

In some cases this exchange of expression serves condensation by an even shorter route, by finding a form of words which, being ambiguous, will permit more than one dream-thought to be expressed. In this way the entire field of verbal punning is available for the dream-work to use. We should not be astonished at the role allotted to the word in dream-formation. You might say that the word, being the point of convergence for many kinds of ideas, is predestined for ambiguity; and the neuroses (obsessive ideas, phobias) take advantage of the word in their condensations and disguises no less brazenly than dreams. It is easy to show that dream-distortion too benefits from this displacement of expression. We are indeed misled if one ambiguous word is used instead of two unambiguous ones; and replacing our everyday, sober mode of expression by a pictorial one bars our understanding, particularly as the dream never states whether the elements it presents are to be interpreted literally or in a transferred sense, or whether they should be referred to the dream-material directly or via the mediation of interpolated phrases. I have already given several examples from dreams of representations which are only held together by the ambiguity of their expression ('Her mouth is wide open', in the injection-dream; 'I still can't go', in the last dream quoted, p. 253) and so on. I shall now relate a dream where the pictorial representation of abstract thoughts play a considerable part in its analysis. The distinction between this kind of interpretation and interpretation by means of symbolism can still be sharply defined; in symbolic dream-interpretation the key to the symbolization is arbitrarily chosen by the dream-interpreter; in our instances of verbal disguise these keys are generally known and given by established linguistic usage. If one has the right idea on the right occasion it is possible to resolve dreams of this kind wholly or piecemeal, even without recourse to what the dreamer has to say.

A lady with whom I am on friendly terms dreams: *She is at the opera. It is a performance of Wagner, which has gone on until 7.45 in the morning. In the stalls and the pit there are tables where people are eating and drinking. Her cousin, just back home from his honeymoon, is sitting at one of these tables with his young wife; nearby, an aristocrat. It is said about the latter that the young woman brought him something back from her honeymoon, quite openly, rather as one might bring a hat back from a honeymoon. There is a tall tower in the middle of the stalls, with a platform at the top surrounded by iron bars. The conductor is up there on high, wearing the features of Hans Richter;* he is constantly running round behind the bars, sweating frightfully, and from this position he is conducting the orchestra, which is ranged below around the base of the tower. She herself is sitting with a friend* (a lady of my acquaintance) in a box. Her younger sister makes to pass her a large lump of coal from the stalls, giving as her reason that she really didn't know that it would take so long and by now she must be bitterly cold. (Rather as if the boxes had to be heated during the long performance.)*

The dream is nonsensical enough, to be sure, though on the other hand it is skilfully made to suggest a situation. The tower in the middle of the stalls from which the conductor directs the orchestra; above all, the coal her sister passes up to her! I deliberately did not ask for an analysis of this dream; having some knowledge of the personal relations of the dreamer, I succeeded in interpreting parts of it without her aid. I knew that she had had much sympathy for a musician whose career had been interrupted by mental illness. So I decided to take the tower in the stalls literally. Then it emerged that the man she had wished to see in Hans Richter's place in her dream *towered high above* the other members of the orchestra. This tower can be described as a *composite formation made by apposition*; with its lower part it represents the man's greatness; with the bars at the top, behind which he is running round like a prisoner or an animal in a cage (allusion to the unhappy man's name*), it represents what later befell him. Something like '*Narrenturm*' ['Tower of Fools']* might be the word in which both thoughts could coincide.

After this revealed the dream's mode of representation, it was possible to attempt to resolve the second apparent absurdity, the one involving the coals her sister passes up to her, by using the same key. 'Coals' was bound to signify 'secret love'.

> *Kein Feuer,* keine *Kohle*
> kann brennen so heiß
> als wie *heimliche Liebe,*
> von der niemand was weiß.*
>
> [*No fire,* no *coal*
> Can burn as hot
> As a *secret love*
> Which the world knows not.]

She herself and her friend were *left sitting* [i.e. unmarried]; her younger sister, who still had prospects of marrying, passes the coals up to her 'because she really didn't know *that it would take so long*'. What would not take so long is not stated in the dream. If we were telling a story we would fill the gap with: 'the performance'. In the dream we may consider the sentence as it stands, declare it is ambiguous, and add: 'before she got married'. The interpretation 'secret love' is then supported by the reference to the cousin sitting in the stalls with his wife, and by the *open love affair* fabricated about the wife. The dream is dominated by the oppositions set up between secret and open love, the fire of her own love and the young wife's coldness. In both parts of the dream, by the way, we have *'someone high up'* as a composite formulation referring to both the aristocrat and the musician who raised such high hopes.

In the course of the foregoing discussions we have at last disclosed a third factor whose part in the transformation of dream-thoughts into dream-content is not to be underestimated: *regard for the representability of the peculiar psychical material used by the dream.* That is, usually, representability in visual images. Of the various subsidiary connections to the essential dream-thoughts, preference is given to the one allowing visual representation, and the dream-work does not flinch from the effort of first recasting the recalcitrant material, for instance, into a different verbal form, even if the formulation is more unusual, just as long as it makes representation possible and puts an end to the psychological distress of the pent-up activity of the thoughts. This process of pouring the thought-content into a different mould, however, can at the same time be employed for the work of condensation and create associations with another thought which would otherwise not be available. This other thought itself may—perhaps in order to meet the first halfway—have previously altered its original expression.

In view of the part played by verbal jokes, quotations, songs, and proverbs in the mental life of the educated, it would be entirely in accordance with expectation if disguises of this kind were used very frequently indeed in representing dream-thoughts. For example, what do carts signify in a dream, when each one is filled with a different vegetable? It is the wishful opposite of 'Kraut und Rüben' [cabbages and turnips], that is, 'all of a muddle', and accordingly stands for 'disorder'. I was surprised that this dream has only once been related to me. There is only a small range of subject-matter for which a universally applicable dream-symbolism has developed, on the basis of generally known allusions and verbal substitutions. Dreams, by the way, share a good deal of this symbolism with psychoneuroses, legends, and popular customs.

Indeed, looking at it more closely, one has to acknowledge that with this kind of substitution the dream-work is not doing anything original at all. To achieve its aims—in this case, representability free of censorship—it is simply walking the ways already laid down before it in unconscious thinking; it gives preference to those transformations of repressed material which are also allowed to reach consciousness in the guise of witticisms and allusions, and which fill all the fantasies of neurotics. At this point we suddenly gain an understanding of Scherner's dream-interpretations, with their nucleus of truth which I have defended elsewhere. Our preoccupation in our imaginations with our own bodies is by no means peculiar only to dreams, nor characteristic of these alone. My analyses have shown me that it is a regular occurrence in the unconscious thinking of neurotics, and can be traced back to the sexual curiosity which youths or maidens growing up develop about the genitals of the other sex, but also about their own. But, as Scherner and Volkelt emphasize quite correctly, the house is not the only sphere of representations used to symbolize the body, whether in dreams or in the unconscious fantasizing of neurosis. I am acquainted with patients who have, it is true, preserved the architectonic symbolism of the body and the genitals (though of course sexual interest extends far beyond the external genitals); to them, pillars and columns signify legs (as in the *Song of Songs**); every gateway reminds them of one of the body's orifices ('hole'); every water-supply pipe of the urinary apparatus; and so on. But the spheres of ideas belonging to plant life or to the kitchen are just as readily chosen as a hiding-place for sexual images. In the first case the ground has been abundantly prepared by linguistic usage, the deposit of fantasy-comparisons from the oldest of ancient times (the Lord's 'vineyard', the 'seed', the maiden's 'garden'* in the *Song of Songs*). Apparently innocuous allusions to the daily tasks of the kitchen let us think and dream the nastiest as well as the most intimate details of sexual life, and the symptoms of hysteria become simply uninterpretable if we forget that sexual symbolism can conceal itself behind the unremarkable things of everyday life as its best hiding-place. There is sound sexual meaning to it when neurotic children cannot bear the sight of blood or raw meat, or throw up on eating eggs and pasta, or when the natural human fear of snakes is monstrously intensified in the neurotic; and wherever neurosis makes use of this kind of disguise, it is walking the way that all mankind once travelled in ancient cultural eras, whose existence, beneath only a little debris, is still attested today by linguistic usage, superstition, and custom.

At this point I shall include the promised flower-dream of a patient, where I will draw attention to everything with a sexual interpretation. After this beautiful dream was interpreted, the dreamer liked it no longer.

(a) Introductory dream: *She goes into the kitchen to the two maid-servants and scolds them for not having finished preparing 'the bite to eat', and as she does so she sees so much crockery turned up on end to dry, crude crockery in piles.* Later addition: *the two maids go to fetch water, and as they do it is as if they are wading into a river which is rising right up to the house or into the yard.*[11]

(b) Main dream:[12] *She is climbing down from high up*[13] *over curious railings or fences, which are combined into large diamond shapes made up of interwoven fencing in small squares.*[14] *It is really not made for climbing; she has constant trouble in finding a foothold, and is glad that her dress*

---

[11] For the interpretation of this introductory dream as 'causal', see p. 240.

[12] The course of her life.

[13] High birth. Wishful opposite to the introductory dream.

[14] Composite formation combining two localities: the attic, as it was called, of her father's house, where she played with her brother, who was the object of her later fantasies, and the farm belonging to the wicked uncle who used to tease her.

doesn't catch on anything, so that as she is walking she remains decent.[15] *As she goes she is carrying a large branch in her hand,*[16] *actually like a tree, thickly covered with red blossoms, branched and spreading.*[17] *The idea of cherry-blossoms is present, but they look like camellias in full bloom, which, however, do not grow on trees. As she goes down, she has at first one, the suddenly two, and then again one.*[18] *As she gets to the bottom, the lower blossoms are already rather fallen. Now that she has reached the bottom, she sees a manservant who is, she might almost say, combing a tree just like hers, that is, he is ruffling thick tufts of hair hanging down from it like moss. Other workmen have cut down branches of this kind from a garden and thrown them onto the street where they are lying around, so that many people take them. But she asks whether it's all right, whether she too can take one for herself.*[19] *In the garden a young man is standing* (someone she knows, a foreigner), *and she approaches him to ask whether she can transplant such branches to her own garden.*[20] *He embraces her, but she struggles, and asks him what he is thinking of, and whether he thinks it is permitted to embrace her like that. He says there is nothing wrong, it is allowed.*[21] *He then declares he is ready to go with her into the other garden to show her how to plant it, and says something to her that she doesn't quite understand: 'anyway, I need three metres*—(later she says 'square metres') *or three fathom cords of ground.' It was as if in return for being helpful he would demand something of her, as if he intended to be compensated in her garden, or as if he wanted to cheat on some law, so that he would have an advantage and she come to no harm. She doesn't know whether he really showed her something then.*

I must mention yet another sphere of ideas which frequently serves to mask a sexual content in dreams, as it does in neurosis. I mean that involved in a *change of dwelling*. Moving out of an apartment can easily be replaced by *taking off* [*one's clothes*],* that is, by an

---

[15] Wishful opposite of a real recollection from her uncle's farm that she used to expose herself while asleep.

[16] Like the one carried by the angel in the Annunciation, a tall lily.

[17] For the explanation of this composite formation, see p. 240: innocence, period, *la dame aux camélias*.

[18] Indicating the number of figures serving her fantasies.

[19] Whether she could also pull one down,* that is, masturbate.

[20] The branch had by now taken over the function of proxy for the male genitals; it also, by the way, contains a very clear allusion to her family name.

[21] Refers, like the following, to precautions in marriage.

ambiguous word belonging to the sphere of ideas of dress. If the dream also contains a *lift*, then we recall that as a verb in English it also implies *to lift someone's clothes.*

Of course I have an excess of material of just this sort, but reporting it would take us too deep into a discussion of neurotic conditions. It all leads to the same conclusion, that we do not need to assume a specific symbolizing activity on the part of the psyche in the course of the dream-work. On the other hand, we may assume that the dream makes use of any symbolizations already present and waiting in unconscious thinking, because these satisfy the requirements of dream-formation better, both on account of their representability and also in most cases on account of their freedom from censorship.

(e) *Examples: Calculating and Speaking in Dreams*

Before I put the fourth factor controlling the formation of dreams in its due place, I will give some examples from my dream collection; some are able to illustrate the interaction of the three factors we are already familiar with; some to present belated evidence for certain unsupported assertions, or draw irrefutable conclusions from them. Indeed, in the foregoing account of the dream-work I have found it very difficult to prove my results by using examples. The instances I used to illustrate particular propositions only have any value as evidence in the context of a dream-interpretation; torn out of this frame of reference they lose their beauty, and a dream-interpretation that only skims the surface soon becomes so broad that it makes it easy to lose the thread of the argument it is supposed to be illustrating. I hope this reason of art will serve as my excuse for stringing together all sorts of examples whose only connection is that they relate to the text of the preceding section.

First, a few examples of particularly curious or unusual modes of representation in dreams. A lady's dream goes like this: *a maid-servant is standing on the ladder as if to clean the windows, and she has a chimpanzee and a gorilla–cat* (later corrected to: *angora cat*) *with her. She throws the animals onto the dreamer; the chimpanzee cuddles up to the dreamer, and that is most disgusting.* This dream has realized its intention by very simple means, by taking a turn of phrase literally and representing it as its wording says. 'Monkey' and the names of animals in general are pejoratives, insults, and the situation in the dream says just that: '*throwing insults around*'. This collection will shortly give further examples of the use of this simple trick in the dream-work.

Another dream proceeds in a similar way: *a woman with a child who has a strikingly malformed skull; she has heard it said of this child that he became like this on account of the way he was lying in his mother's womb. The doctor says it might be possible to give the skull a better shape by compressing it, but that would damage the brain. She thinks: as it's a boy, it will do him less damage.* This dream contains the concrete representation of the abstract concept: '*impressions of childhood*', which the dreamer has heard in the explanations of her therapy.

The dream-work strikes out on a rather different path in the following example. The dream includes the memory of an excursion to the Hilmteich* near Graz: *it is dreadful weather outside; a miserable hotel, with water dripping down the walls, the beds are damp.* (This last bit of the content is less direct in the dream than I have put it.) The dream signifies '*superfluous*'. The abstraction present in the dream-thoughts has first, quite forcibly, been made ambiguous, perhaps replaced by 'overflowing' or by 'fluid' and 'superfluous', and then successfully represented by a number of similar impressions. Water outside, water inside on the walls, water in the form of damp in the beds, all fluid and *super*fluous.*

It would be a separate task to collect modes of representation of this kind and arrange them according to the principles they are based upon.

The dream-work often succeeds in representing very recalcitrant material, such as proper names, by a forced use of very remote associations. In one of my dreams, *I was given a task to do by my old professor, Brücke. I am preparing a slide, and I pick something out of it that looks like crumpled silver paper.* (More of this dream later.) The idea attaching to it, which occurs to me with some difficulty, is 'Stanniol' [silver foil], and then I realize that what I am alluding to is the name *Stannius*, which is the name of the author of a treatise on the nervous system of fishes which I once regarded with awe. The first scientific task my teacher gave me did actually involve the nervous system of a fish, the Ammocoetes.* Clearly, the picture-puzzle could do nothing with this name.

We can learn a great deal from the numerals and calculations occurring in dreams about what the dream-work consists of and how it plays around with its material, the dream-thoughts. Superstitions regard dreaming of numbers as particularly auspicious, so I will produce a few examples from my collection.

I

From the dream of a lady, shortly before bringing her therapy to an end:

She wants to pay for something; her daughter takes 3 fl. 65 kr.* *from her purse; but she says: what are you doing? It only costs 21 kr.* This bit of the dream was clear to me on account of the dreamer's circumstances, without any further enlightenment from her. The lady was a foreigner who had found a place for her daughter in a Viennese educational establishment and was able to continue under my treatment for as long as her daughter remained in Vienna. In three weeks' time the school year would come to an end, and with that her therapy would end too. On the day before her dream, the principal of the seminary had put it to her that she might like to decide to keep the child there for a further year. She had clearly continued this suggestion in her own mind to the point of thinking that in that case she would also be able to extend her treatment for another year. Now this is what the dream is referring to, for a year equals *365* days and the three weeks to the end of the school year and of her treatment can be replaced by *21* days (though not by that number of consultations). The numerals that were present early in the dream-thoughts were allotted a cash value in the dream, though the meaning this expressed was nothing more profound than 'time is money'.* It is true, *365* Kreuzer make *3 Gulden 65 Kreuzer*. The very small sums appearing in the dream are obviously a wish-fulfilment; her wish reduced the costs of both her treatment and the year's education at the seminary.

II

The numerals in another dream lead to more complicated associations. A young lady, married for a number of years, learns that an acquaintance of hers, Elise L., who is almost the same age as she is, has just got engaged. Soon afterwards she dreams: *she is sitting with her husband in the theatre; one side of the stalls is entirely empty. Her husband tells her that Elise L. and her fiancé had also wanted to go, but had only got very bad seats, 3 for 1 fl. 50 kr., and of course they couldn't take those. In her opinion, that was no hard luck.*

Where do the *1 fl. 50 kr.* come from? From an intrinsically trivial occasion from the day before. Her sister-in-law had been given *150 fl.* as a present by her husband, and was in a hurry to spend it, using it to buy some jewellery. Let us note that 150 fl. is *100* times 1 fl. 50 kr. Where does the *3* for the theatre seats come from? Only one association emerges for that: the engaged girl is younger than she is by that number of months—three. When we pursued the question of what the dream meant by presenting one side of the stalls as empty, we found its solution. It is an allusion, unchanged, to a little occurrence that gave her husband good reason to tease her. She had wanted to go to one of the performances advertised at the theatre for that week, and to be on the safe side she bought tickets several days beforehand, which meant she had to pay an advance-booking fee. When they arrived in the theatre they discovered that one side of the auditorium was almost empty; she had no need *to be in such a hurry.*

I shall now replace the dream with the dream-thoughts. 'It was *nonsense* to marry so early; *I had no need to be in such a hurry*; I can see from Elise L.'s example that I would still have got a husband, indeed one *a hundred times* better (husband, dear one),* if I had only *waited* (opposite to her sister-in-law's *hurry*). I could have bought *three* such husbands for the money (her dowry)!' We note that the numbers in this dream have altered in meaning and context far more than in the one just discussed. The dream's work of transformation and distortion has been more elaborate here, which we interpret as indicating that these dream-thoughts had a particularly high degree of resistance to overcome from within the psyche. We should also not overlook an absurd element in the dream-content, that is, that *two* people are supposed to occupy *three* seats. We will be encroaching on the interpretation of absurdity in dreams when we note that in content this absurd detail is meant to represent the most emphatic of the dream-thoughts: it was *nonsense* to marry so early. The number 3, referring to a quite unimportant comparison between the two persons (the difference of 3 months in their ages), is then skilfully employed to produce the nonsense required for the dream. The reduction of the real-life 150 fl. to 1 fl. 50 kr. is the equivalent of the *low value* ascribed to the husband (or dear one) in the dreamer's suppressed thoughts.

III

Another example shows us the arithmetic of dreams which has brought them into such disrepute. A man dreams: *he is sitting in the home of the B's* (a family he used to know) *and says, 'It was nonsense that you didn't give me Mali.' Then he asks the girl, 'How old are you, then?' Her reply: 'I was born in 1882.'—'Ah, then you are 28 years old.'*

As the dream took place in 1898, it is clear that the reckoning is wrong, and the dreamer's weakness in arithmetic might admit comparison with the paralytic patient's inadequacies, if it did not allow of a different possible explanation. My patient is one of the sort whose thoughts can never let go of any woman they happen to see. For some months the patient who regularly followed him into my consulting-room was a young lady whom he would encounter and ask after frequently, meaning to be entirely courteous in his behaviour towards her. She it was whose age he reckoned to be 28. So much to explain the result of the ostensible calculation. However, 1882 was the year when he had married. He could not resist also getting into conversation with the two other female persons he met in my apartment, the two maidservants, by no means young, who used to open the door to him in turn, and when he did not find them very forthcoming, he explained to himself that they probably found him a '*settled*' elderly gentleman.

If we put these examples together with similar ones (to follow later), we may say: the dream-work is not doing arithmetic at all, it is not getting it either right or wrong; it is only putting together in the form of a calculation numerals occurring in the dream-thoughts which can be used as allusions to material resistant to representation. In doing so, it treats the numerals in exactly the same way as it does all other ideas, as it does names and speech which can be recognized as verbal presentations—that is, as material for expressing its intentions.

For the dream-work is also incapable of creating speech. However meaningful or irrational speech and reply in dreams may appear, the analysis tells us every time that in presenting them the dream has taken only fragments of speech spoken or heard in real life and dealt with them quite arbitrarily. It has not only torn them out of context and broken them up, accepting one bit and rejecting another, but often makes new combinations out of them, so that an apparently coherent speech in the dream will break down into three or four fragments in the analysis. In giving the words this new use, the dream has often departed from the meaning they had in the dream-thoughts, and discovered an entirely different meaning in the wording. On closer scrutiny it is possible to distinguish more distinct, compact elements in the dream-speech from others which function as connectives and have probably been filled in in the same way as we fill in missing letters and syllables when we are reading. Speech in dreams has something of the structure of breccia, in which larger fragments of various materials are bound together by a solidified matrix.

Strictly, it is true, this description applies only to those utterances in dreams which have something of the sensory quality of real speech, and can be described as 'speaking'. The others, which are not, as it were, felt, that is, heard as speech or uttered as speech (which are not accompanied by any acoustic or motor reinforcement in the dream, that is), are simply thoughts, appearing just as they do in our thought-activity when awake and passing unaltered into many of our dreams. Our reading-matter also seems to offer a full-flowing source, though hard to pursue, for the unimportant speech-material in our dreams. But everything that stands out conspicuously, in whatever way, submits to being traced back to speech pronounced in words we have ourselves uttered or heard in real life.

We have already found examples of the derivation of dream-utterances of this kind, which were made with other ends in mind. For example, in the 'innocuous market-dream' of p. 140, in which the words '*that's no longer available*' are used to identify me with the butcher, while a part of another speech, '*I don't recognize that, I won't have it*', really fulfils the task of making the dream innocuous. On the day before her dream, in fact, our dreamer had rebuked her cook for some impertinence with the words: '*I don't recognize that, behave yourself properly*,' and then she took the unimportant first part of this speech into her dream, in order to use it as an allusion to the later part, which would have fitted very well into the fantasy lying at the basis of the dream, but would also have revealed it.

A similar example, standing for many, which, indeed, all produce the same result:

A large yard, in which dead bodies are being burnt. He says: I'm going on. I can't bear the sight of it. (Not distinct as speech.) *Then he meets two butcher's boys, and asks: 'Well, did it taste good?' One of them answers: 'No, it didn't.' As if it were human flesh.*

The innocuous occasion for this dream is as follows: after their evening meal he paid a visit with his wife to their neighbours, good folk, but by no means *appetizing*. The hospitable old lady was just eating her supper, and *pressed* him (men have a joking compound word for it, with a sexual meaning) to taste some. He declined, he wasn't hungry any more. 'Oh, *go on*, you can manage it,' or words to that effect. So he has to taste it, and praises what she offered. '*That tastes good*.' Later, alone with his wife, he grumbles at the way his neighbour pushed herself on him, as well as at the quality of the food he had to taste. 'I can't bear the sight of it,' which was not definitely spoken even in his dream, is a thought referring to the physical charms of the lady who invited him to share her meal, and might be translated to mean that he has no desire to gaze on them.

The analysis of another dream will turn out to be more instructive. I shall relate it at this point on account of the very distinct speech forming its centre, but I shall not explain it until I deal with affects in dreams. My dream is very clear: *I have gone at night into Brücke's laboratory, and hearing a gentle knocking at the door I open it to* (the late) *Professor Fleischl, who comes in with several strangers and after a few words sits down at a table.* This is followed by a second dream: *My friend Fl. has come to Vienna inconspicuously; I encounter him in the street in conversation with my* (late) *friend P.,* and I walk with them to some place where they are sitting opposite each other as though at a small table, with myself to the fore at the narrow end at the little table. Fl. is telling us about his sister, and says: 'In three-quarters of an hour she was dead', and then something like: 'that is the threshold* [Schwele].'* *As P. does not understand him, Fl. turns to me and asks me how much of his concerns I have told P. Then, overcome by quite remarkable affect, I try to tell Fl. that P. (can't know anything at all, of course, because he) is no longer among the living. But what I say, noticing the error myself, is:* **Non vixit.** *Then I give P. a penetrating look; beneath my gaze he becomes pale, hazy; his eyes become sick and blue—and finally he dissolves away. This makes me unusually glad, and I understand then that Ernst Fleischl too was an apparition, a* revenant, *and I find it perfectly possible for a figure of that kind to persist for only as long as it pleases us, and that it can be removed by someone else's wish.*

This beautiful dream includes so many of the puzzling characteristics of dream-content: criticism operating within the dream itself, so that I notice my mistake of saying '*Non vixit*' instead of '*non vivit*';* sitting at ease in the company of the dead, who are declared to be dead by the dream itself; the absurdity of the conclusion I draw from this and the great satisfaction it gives me—so that I would 'gladly give my life' to offer a full solution to these riddles. But, in reality I am incapable of doing what in fact I do in my dream: sacrificing my regard for persons dear to me to my ambition. However, any disguise would ruin the dream's meaning—which I know very well. So I shall content myself with selecting some elements from the dream to interpret, first here and then at a later point.

The scene in which I annihilate P. with a glance forms the centre of the dream. As I do so, his eyes become strangely and uncannily blue, and then he dissolves away. This scene is a remarkable imitation of one I really experienced. I was a demonstrator at the Physiological Institute and had the early shift. Brücke had learned that on a few occasions I had arrived late at the students' laboratory. One day he came on the dot of opening-time and waited for me. What he said to me was brief and to the point; but the words did not matter. What was overwhelming were his terrible blue eyes and the glance he gave me; I dissolved away before it, like P. in my dream, but to my relief P. had exchanged roles with me. Anyone who can recall those wonderful eyes of the master's, still beautiful in extreme old age, and anyone who ever saw his wrath, will have no difficulty in sharing the affects of the young sinner of long ago.

For a long time, however, I just could not find a source for the '*Non vixit*' with which I pass that sentence in my dream, until I recalled that the two words were so strongly distinct in my dream not because they were heard or called, but because they were seen. Then I knew straight away where they came from. On the pedestal of the Monument* to Emperor Joseph II in the Hofburg in Vienna the beautiful words can be read:

Saluti patriae *vixit*
non diu sed totus.

From this inscription I had picked out what was suited to the one, hostile, set of thoughts in my dream-thoughts, and was meant to say: 'The fellow hasn't any right at all to interrupt. After all, he's dead.' And then I could not help remembering that I had had the dream a few days after the memorial to Fleischl had been unveiled in the university arcades, and that while I was there I had seen Brücke's memorial once again, and (in my unconscious) must have reflected with regret that my friend P., with his great talents and undivided devotion to science, had been robbed by his all too early death of his well-founded claim to a memorial in these halls. So I raised this monument to my friend in my dream; his first name was *Josef*.[22]

According to the rules of dream-interpretation, I would still have no justification for replacing the *non vivit*, which I need, by the *non vixit* that my memory of the Joseph memorial puts at my disposal. This must have been made possible by the contribution of another element in the dream-thoughts. It tells me to pay some attention to the fact that the scene in my dream is the meeting-place for two currents of thought towards my friend P., a hostile one and an affectionate one, the first one on the surface, the second hidden, which both contrive to be represented in the same words '*Non vixit*'. Because he has rendered great services to science, I raise a monument to him; but because he has been guilty of a malevolent wish (expressed at the end of the dream), I annihilate him. I have just formed a sentence there with a very distinctive pattern, and in doing so I must have been influenced by some model. But where is a similar antithesis to be found, placing two opposing reactions to the same person in parallel, each of which has a claim to be fully justified and yet has no wish to disturb the other? In one place only, but a deeply impressive one for the reader: in Brutus' justificatory speech* in Shakespeare's *Julius Caesar*. 'As Caesar loved me, I weep for him; as he was fortunate, I rejoice at it; as he was valiant, I honour him; but, as he was ambitious, I slew him.' Does this not show the same sentence-construction and antithetical thinking as the dream-thoughts I have uncovered? So I am playing the part of Brutus in my dream. If only I could find another, confirmatory trace of this surprising parallel connection in the dream-content! I think it could be the following: my friend Fl. comes to Vienna in *July*. This detail has no support at all in real life. To my knowledge my friend has never been in Vienna in the month of *July*. But the month of *July* was named after *Julius Caesar*, and so might very well represent the

---

[22] As a contribution to over-determination: my excuse for arriving late was that after working long into the night it was a long way from the *Kaiser-Josefstraße* to the Währingerstraße.

allusion I am looking for to the mediating thought that I am playing the role of Brutus.

Remarkably, I did once actually play Brutus. I performed the scene between Brutus and Caesar from Schiller's *Poems** before an audience of children. This was as a fourteen-year-old boy, together with my nephew, one year older than I, who had come to visit us from England—another *revenant*—for it was the playmate of my earliest childhood years who surfaced again with his return. Until I was almost four we had been inseparable, had loved each other and fought each other; and this childhood relationship has been decisive, as I have already suggested, for all my later feelings for companions of my own age. Since then my nephew John has had very many incarnations, bringing him back to life with now one side of his nature and now the other, as it is ineradicably fixed in my unconscious memory. He must have treated me very badly on occasion, and I must have shown courage towards my tyrant, for a little speech in my own justification has often been recounted to me, in which I defended myself when my father—his grandfather—called me to account: 'Why are you hitting John?' In the language of a child not yet two, it went: '*I hit him cos he hit me.*' It must be this childhood scene that turned the *non vivit* into *non vixit*, for in the language of later childhood 'hitting' is known by a word sounding just like *vixit*: *wichsen*; the dream-work is not above making use of connections of this sort. As for the hostility towards my friend P., which had so little cause in real life, he was my superior in many respects and therefore a suitable candidate to be a new edition of my playmate, so it certainly goes back to my complicated infantile relationship to John.

So I shall return to this dream again.

(f) *Absurd Dreams. Intellectual Performance in Dreams*

In our dream-interpretations so far we have come upon the element of *absurdity* so often that we are reluctant to put off any longer our investigation into where it comes from and what it means. Indeed, we recall that it was the absurdity of dreams which gave the opponents of their serious study one of their main arguments for regarding them as nothing but the meaningless products of a reduced and fragmented mental activity.

I shall begin with some examples in which the absurdity of the dream-content is only ostensible, disappearing as we go deeper into the meaning of the dream. They are dreams concerning—by chance, one might think at first—a dead father.

I

The dream of a patient who lost his father six years ago:

A great misfortune has befallen his father. He was travelling on the night train. There was a derailment. The seats collapsed, his head was jammed cross-wise between them. Then he sees him lying in bed, with a vertical wound just above his left eyebrow. He wonders that his father should have come to grief like this, for after all he is dead (he adds as he tells his story). *His eyes are so bright.*

According to the prevailing view of dreams, the content of this dream should be explained as follows: while he was imagining the accident to his father, the dreamer at first forgot that his father had been in the grave for years; as the dream proceeds, this memory is roused and causes him to be astonished at his own dream even as he is dreaming. However, analysis teaches us that it is quite unnecessary to look for explanations of this kind. The dreamer had ordered a bust of his father from a sculptor, and had first cast eyes on it two days before the dream. This is what seems to him to have *come to grief*. The sculptor has never seen his father, and is working from photographs in front of him. On the day before the dream, the devoted son sent an old family servant to the studio to see whether he too would pass the same judgement on the marble head, that is, that it turned out too narrow *in the cross-section* between the temples. Now follows the material from his memory that has contributed to the construction of this dream. When his father was troubled by business worries or family difficulties, he was in the habit of pressing both hands to his temples, as if his head had expanded and he wanted to press it together.—As a four-year-old child our dreamer was present when a pistol, which happened to be loaded, went off and blackened his father's eyes (*his eyes are so bright*).—When his father was alive, in his thoughtful or sad moods there was a deep vertical furrow to be seen in the place where the dream shows a wound. The substitution of a wound for this furrow points to the second occasion for the dream. The dreamer had taken a photograph of his little daughter; he had dropped the plate, and when he picked it up it showed a crack that ran like a vertical furrow across the little girl's forehead, reaching down to her eyebrow. At this, he could not hold off his superstitious forebodings, for the day before his mother died the photographic plate with her picture on it had cracked.

The absurdity of this dream is thus simply the consequence of a slipshod way we have of using words, making no distinction between a bust or photograph of a person and the person himself. We are all used to saying: 'Don't you think it's hit your father off?' Of course, the appearance of absurdity in this dream would have been easy to avoid. If it is admissible to judge so soon after learning of only one dream, one might say that this appearance of absurdity is permitted or intentional.

II

A second, very similar example from my own dreams (I lost my father in 1896):

After his death my father played a part in Magyar politics, united them politically (I see a small, indistinct picture showing this)*: a crowd of people, as though in the Reichstag; one person standing on one or on two chairs* [Stühlen]*, others around him. I recall how like Garibaldi** *he looked on his deathbed, and I am glad that this promise did come true after all.*

That is surely absurd enough. I dreamed it at a time when *obstruction* from Parliament had thrown Hungary into a state of disorder,* and the country was in the throes of the crisis from which it was rescued by Kálmán Széll. The trifling circumstance that the scene in the dream is made up of such small pictures is not without significance for elucidating this element. Usually the way dreams represent our thoughts visually is in images that give the impression of being more or less life-size; but the image in my dream is the reproduction of a woodcut bound into the text of an illustrated history of Austria, representing Maria Theresa* at the Reichstag in Pressburg; the famous scene of 'Moriamur pro rege nostro'.[23] Like Maria Theresa in the picture, in my dream my father is standing surrounded by the crowd. But he is standing on one or two chairs—so he is the *chairman*, or

---

[23] I do not recall the author or the work where I found a dream mentioned which was swarming with unusually tiny figures, and whose source turned out to be an etching by Jacques Callot* which the dreamer had been looking at during the day. Certainly Callot's etchings contain a tremendous number of very small figures; one set of them deals with the horrors of the Thirty Years War.

presiding judge [*Stuhlrichter*]. (He has *united* them. The intermediary here is the saying: 'We will not need a *judge*.') His resemblance on his deathbed to Garibaldi is something all those of us present did in fact remark. He had a *post-mortem* rise in temperature, his cheeks grew more and more flushed . . . involuntarily, we continue: 'Und hinter ihm, in wesenlosem Scheine lag, was uns alle bändigt, das Gemeine'* [And behind him, mere empty appearance, lay what confines us all, the common and mean].

These exalted thoughts act as a warning that the very thing we shall encounter is 'vulgarity'. The '*post-mortem*' describing the rise in temperature corresponds to the words '*after his death*' in the dream-content. The most painful part of my father's suffering was the complete paralysis of the intestine (*obstruction*) during his last weeks. All sorts of disrespectful thoughts attach themselves to this. I recall one of my contemporaries, who lost his father when he was still a schoolboy—which moved me, deeply stirred by his loss, to offer him my friendship. He once told me mockingly about the grief of a relative whose father had died in the street and was brought home, only for the family to find when they undressed the corpse that in the moment of death or *post mortem* his bowels had emptied of stools. It distressed the daughter so deeply that this nasty detail could not but spoil her remembrance of her father. With this we have got through to the wish embodying itself in this dream. '*To be a pure and great presence to one's children after one's death*'—who would not wish for that? What has become of the absurdity of this dream? It appeared absurd only because the dream gave a faithful representation of a perfectly admissible turn of phrase, whose components combine to produce between them the sort of absurdity which usually goes unremarked by us. Here too we cannot dismiss the impression that the appearance of absurdity is intentional, created on purpose.

III

In the example I am about to offer, I am able to catch the dream-work in the act of intentionally fabricating an absurdity which the material itself offers no occasion for. It comes from the dream suggested to me by my meeting with Count Thun before my holiday journey. *I am riding [fahre] in a hansom-cab and I tell the driver to drive me [fahren] to a railway station. 'Of course, I can't drive [fahren]* *with you on the railway line itself', I say, after he raised an objection, as if I had tired him out, although it is as if I had already driven [gefahren] with him on a stretch which one usually travels [fährt] by train.* Analysis provides this confused and nonsensical story with the following explanation: that day I had taken a hansom-cab which was meant to take me to a remote street in Dornbach. However, the cab-driver did not know the way, and, as these good folk do, he drove on and on until I noticed it and showed him the way, not sparing him a few scornful remarks. There is a train of thought spinning from this coachman to the aristocrat I shall meet later. For the moment just the pointer that one thing about the aristocracy we middle-class plebeians notice is how they prefer to take the driver's seat themselves. Count Thun himself certainly drives the Austrian state coach. However, the next sentence in the dream refers to my brother, whom I also identify with the cab-driver. This year I had called off our journey to Italy together ('*I can't drive with you on the railway line itself*'), and this refusal was a way of punishing him for his usual complaint that I normally *tire him out* on these journeys (which reaches the dream unchanged) in expecting him to make too many changes of place and take in too much in one day. That evening my brother had accompanied me to the station, but he jumped out at the Westbahnhof local railway station to take the local train to Purkersdorf.* I had remarked to him that he could go on with me a while longer if he did not take the local train, but took the main-line train from the Westbahnhof as far as Purkersdorf. Some of this entered the dream, where I am riding in the *cab* along a stretch which *one usually travels by train*. In reality it was the other way round (and '*Umgekehrt ist auch gefahren*' ['Travelling in the other direction is still travelling']); I had said to my brother: 'You can travel in my company in the main-line train along the same stretch as you're going to take the local.' I set up the entire confusion in the dream by saying 'cab' in it instead of 'local', which then of course serves very nicely to condense the figures of the cabby and my brother. Then I tease out some nonsense in the dream which this explanation seems scarcely fit to disentangle, and which virtually contradicts something I had said earlier ('I can't drive with you on the railway line itself'). As I have no need at all to mix the local train up with the cab, I must have shaped the entire puzzling tale in my dream intentionally.

But what was my intention? We shall now learn what absurdity in

dreams signifies, and the motives that allow it entry or create it. The
solution to the mystery in the present case is as follows: I need an
absurdity and something incomprehensible in my dream in connection with the element *fahren*,* because in my dream-thoughts there is
a certain judgement demanding to be represented. One evening, at
the house of that hospitable and witty lady who appears in another
scene of the same dream as a 'housekeeper', I had heard two riddles
which I could not solve. As my fellow-guests were already familiar
with them, I cut a rather ridiculous figure in my unsuccessful efforts
to solve them. They involved two puns on *Nachkommen* [those who
come after, descendants, following after] and *Vorfahren* [those who
go before, forebears, travelling or driving ahead of]:

> Der Herr befiehlt's,
> Der Kutscher thut's.
> Ein jeder hat's,
> Im Grabe ruht's. (*Vorfahren.*)

[The master commands it,
The driver does it,
Everyone has it,
It lies in the grave. (*To go/drive
ahead, those who go before, i.e. forebears*)]

It was confusing, too, that half of the second riddle was identical
with the first:

> Der Herr befiehlt's,
> Der Kutscher thut's.
> Nicht Jeder hat's,
> In der Wiege ruht's. (*Nachkommen.*)

[The master commands it,
The driver does it.
Not everyone has it,
It lies in the cradle. (*To drive after, those
who come after, i.e. children, descendants.*)]

Now when I saw Count Thun *driving ahead* so imperiously, and I
got into my Figaro-mood, judging it to be the only merit of these
grandees that they had taken the trouble to be born* (that they were
Nachkommen/descendants), these two riddles became intermediary
thoughts for the dream-work. As it is easy to mix up aristocrats with

coachmen, and as it used to be the custom in our part of the world to address the coachman as 'brother-in-law',* the work of condensation was able to draw my brother into the same representative figure. But the dream-thought at work behind it runs: *It's nonsense to be proud of one's forebears. I prefer to be a forebear myself, an ancestor.* On account of this judgement: 'It's nonsense', hence the nonsense in my dream. This now probably solves the last riddle left in this obscure part of the dream, where I dreamed that I had already *driven before* [*vorher gefahren*] with the cabby, that is, already *driven ahead* [*vorgefahren*] with him.

Dreams are made absurd, then, when one of the elements in the dream-thoughts contains the judgement 'that is nonsense'; when one of the dreamer's unconscious trains of thought is motivated by criticism and mockery. In this way the absurd becomes one of the means used by the dream-work to express contradiction, like its reversal of the relation between dream-thought and dream-content, like its exploitation of feelings of motor inhibition. But the absurd in dreams is not just to be translated by a simple 'No'; rather, it is meant to reproduce the dream-thoughts' disposition to laugh or mock at the same time as contradicting. The dream-work only provides something ridiculous if it is motivated by this intention. Once again it is transforming *part of the latent content into a manifest form.*[24]

Actually we have already met a convincing example of this kind of meaning in an absurd dream: the dream I interpreted without analysis of the Wagner performance that lasted till a quarter to eight in the morning, when the orchestra was conducted from a tower, etc. (p. 297). Clearly it means: this is a demented world and a deranged society. The deserving don't get their due, and the ones who don't care get it all—by which she means her own fate in comparison with

---

[24] That is, the dream is parodying the thought it labels as ridiculous by creating something ridiculous associated with it. This is how Heine* sets about it when he wants to mock the King of Bavaria's bad verse. He does so in even worse:

> Herr Ludwig ist ein großer Poet,
> Und singt er, so stürzet Apollo
> Vor ihm auf die Knie und bittet und fleht,
> Halt ein, ich werde sonst toll, oh!
> This Ludwig's a poet of renown;
> When he sings out one of of his lays, he
> Has Apollo begging on bended knees:
> 'Stop, stop! you're driving me crazy!'

her cousin's.—It is also far from accidental that our first examples of the absurdity of dreams should concern a dead father. The conditions for creating absurdity in dreams are to be found typically together here. The authority that characterizes the father provoked the child's criticism early on; the strict demands he made caused the child to keep a keen eye open for his father's every weakness; but the filial devotion which surrounds the father's person in our thoughts, especially after his death, only intensifies the censorship which prevents any expression of this criticism from becoming conscious.

IV

Another absurd dream about my dead father.

I receive a communication from the district council of the town where I was born relating to payment of costs for hospital accommodation in 1851, necessary on account of a seizure suffered in my house. I make fun of it, for in the first place, in 1851 I wasn't born, and in the second, my father, to whom it possibly refers, is already dead. I go in to him in the next room and tell him about it. To my surprise he remembers that once in 1851 he was drunk and had to be locked up or detained. It was when he was working for the firm of T... 'So you used to drink, too?' I ask. 'Did you get married soon afterwards?' I calculate that I was actually born in 1856, which seems to me to follow right after it.

In the light of the foregoing discussion, we can only translate this dream's blatant display of its absurdities as the sign of a particularly bitter and passionate polemic in the dream-thoughts. However, we are all the more astonished when we confirm that in this dream the polemic is quite open, and the father is identified as the figure who is made the butt of the mockery. Openness of this kind seems to contradict our assumptions about the part played by censorship in the dream-work. But it is a help to our understanding that the figure of my father is only a stand-in here, and that the dispute is actually carried on with someone else who only makes an appearance in the dream in a single allusion. While dreams usually deal with rebellion against other figures behind whom the father is hiding, here the pattern is reversed; the father is turned into a straw man to cover others, and that is why the dream is free to divert itself so undisguisedly with his otherwise sacrosanct figure, because the certain knowledge is also involved that it is not he who is meant. This is to be learned from what occasioned the dream. It happened, in fact, after I had heard that an older colleague, whose judgement was regarded as irreproachable, had expressed his disapproval and astonishment that one of my patients was continuing his psychoanalytic work with me into its *fifth year*. The introductory sentences of the dream indicate in transparent guise that for a time this colleague took over the duties that my father was no longer able to fulfil (*payment of costs, hospital accommodation*); and when the ties of our friendship began to loosen, I fell into the same conflict of feelings as the role and earlier achievements of the father provoke in the case of dissension between father and son. My dream-thoughts are defending themselves bitterly against the charge that *I am not getting on faster*, which then extends from the treatment of this patient to other things too. Does he know anyone who can do it any faster? Doesn't he know that conditions of this kind are otherwise absolutely incurable and last a lifetime? What are *four to five years* compared with the length of a whole life, especially when the burden of the patient's existence has been made so much lighter during treatment?

The mark of absurdity is produced in this dream largely by stringing sentences from different parts of the dream-thoughts next to one another without any intermediary transition. In this way the sentence: *I go in to him in the next room* abandons the theme which gave rise to the previous sentences and faithfully reproduces the circumstances when I informed my father of my own, independent, engagement. The sentence wants to remind me of the noble selflessness the old man showed then, and to contrast it with the behaviour of someone else, a new figure. I note at this point that this is why the dream is free to mock my father, because in the dream-thoughts he is fully acknowledged and held up as a model to others. It is in the nature of all censorship that in speaking of forbidden things one is permitted to say things that are not true sooner than the truth. The next sentence my father remembers, *that once he was drunk and so had to be locked up*, no longer contains anything referring to him in real life. The figure he is covering here is the great Meynert,* no less, whose footsteps I followed with such great reverence and whose behaviour towards me after a short period of favour suddenly changed to undisguised hostility. The dream reminds me of something he told me himself: that as a young man he had once been addicted to *using chloroform as an intoxicant* and so had had to *spend time in an institution*; the dream also reminds me of a second experience with him shortly before his end. I had conducted a bitter literary dispute with him on the subject of male hysteria, which he denied existed, and when I visited him in his last illness and asked how he was, he lingered over the description of his condition, and closed with the words: 'You know, I was always one of the finest cases of male hysteria.' This is how he admitted to my satisfaction *and to my astonishment* what he had obstinately struggled against for so long. However, my basis for being able to conceal Meynert behind my father in this scene in my dream is not the analogy I discovered between the two figures, but the brief, though entirely adequate, representation of a conditional clause in the dream-thoughts. In full, it goes like this: All right, if I were second generation, the son of a professor or Hofrat, then I would certainly *have got on faster*. In my dream I actually make my father a Hofrat and professor. The grossest and most disturbing absurdity in the dream is to be found in its treatment of the year *1851*, which does not seem to be at all different to me from *1856*, *as if the difference of five years meant nothing at all*. But that was the very thing that was meant to emerge from the dream-thoughts and find expression. *Four to five years*—that is the length of time I enjoyed the support of the colleague I mentioned at the outset; but it is also the length of time I made my fiancée wait to get married; and also the length of time, by a chance coincidence promptly exploited by the dream-thoughts, that I am now making the patient I am closest to wait to be completely cured. '*What are five years?*' my dream-thoughts ask. '*That's no time at all to me. It's just not an issue.* I have time enough ahead of me, and just as that finally came good, despite your lack of faith, so will this too.' Besides, the number *51*, detached from the century, is determined in yet another way, actually with the opposite meaning; it also occurs in this sense several times in the dream. 51 is the age when a man appears to be particularly vulnerable,* when I have seen colleagues die suddenly, among them one who had waited a long time but died a few days after being appointed professor.

V

Another absurd dream, which plays games with numerals.

One of my acquaintances, Herr M., has been attacked in an essay by no less a person than Goethe, with quite unjustifiable passion, we all think. Naturally, Herr M. is annihilated by this attack. He complains

*bitterly about it in company at table; but his reverence for Goethe has not
suffered, despite this personal experience. I try to throw some light on the
chronological pattern, which strikes me as improbable. Goethe died in
1832; as his attack must naturally have taken place earlier, Herr M. was
a very young man then. It seems plausible to me that he was eighteen
years old. But I am not sure what year we are in at present, and in this
way the entire calculation is plunged into darkness. The attack, by the
way, is included in Goethe's well-known essay 'On Nature'.*

We shall soon find a means of justifying the nonsense in this
dream. Herr M., whom I know from his *company at table*, recently
asked me to examine his brother, who was showing signs of *paralytic
insanity*. He was right in his surmise. During this visit a distressing
thing happened: without any cause the sick man *exposed* his brother
by alluding in conversation to the *exploits of the brother's youth*. I had
asked the patient the date of his birth, and repeatedly got him to do
small calculations to test his failure of memory—tests, by the way,
which he still passed quite well. I already note that in my dream I am
behaving like a sufferer from paralysis. (*I am not sure what year we are
in.*) Other material in the dream comes from another recent source.
The editor of a medical journal, a friend of mine, had published an
extremely unkind, '*annihilating*' criticism in his paper of the latest
book by my Berlin friend Fl., written by a very *youthful* reviewer not
fit to pass judgement. I believed I had a right to intervene and took
the editor to task. He deeply regretted having accepted the review,
but would not promise to print a correction. At this I broke off my
connection with the journal, and in my letter of resignation stressed
my expectation *that our personal relations would not suffer from this
occurrence.* The third source of the dream is the story, then still fresh
in my mind, told me by a patient of how her brother succumbed to
psychological illness, breaking into a frenzy with the cry '*Nature,
Nature*'.* His doctors were of the opinion that the cry derived from
reading that beautiful *essay of Goethe's* and was an indication that he
had been overworking at his studies in natural philosophy. I preferred to think of the sexual sense which even the less educated
among us imply when they speak of 'Nature', and the fact that the
unhappy young man mutilated himself in the genitals at least did not
suggest I was wrong. He was *eighteen years old* when his attack broke
out.

If I also add that my friend's book, so harshly criticized ('One wonders whether it is the author who is crazy, or oneself', another critic had said), deals with the *chronological patterns of life*, and even traces Goethe's long life back to the multiple of a biologically significant numeral, then it is easy to see that in my dream I am putting myself in the place of my friend. (*I try to throw some light on the chronological pattern.*) But I am behaving like a sufferer from paralysis, and the dream is revelling in its absurdity. That means, then, that the dream-thoughts are saying with irony: '*Naturally*, he is the fool, the madman, and you are the people of genius, who understand things better. But what if it were the other way round?' And this *reversal* is represented in the dream-content in quantity, for example, when *Goethe* attacks the young man, which is absurd, while even today a very young man could easily attack the immortal *Goethe*; and when I count forward from *the year of Goethe's death*, while I have my paralytic patient count forward from the *year of his birth*.

However, I have also promised to demonstrate that there is no dream that is not prompted by egoistic motives. Consequently, I must justify making my friend's cause my own in this dream, and putting myself in his place. It is not enough to call on the critical convictions of my waking mind for this. Now the story of the eighteen-year-old sufferer, and the different interpretations of his cry of 'Nature', allude to the position I have taken contrary to the majority of physicians in maintaining that the psychoneuroses have a sexual aetiology. I can say to myself: 'Just like your friend, that is how you will fare at the hands of the critics, indeed, you have already done so to some extent.' And now I am free to replace the 'he' of the dream-thoughts by a 'we'. 'Yes, you are right, we two are the fools.' I am reminded vigorously that 'mea res agitur'* by the reference to Goethe's incomparably beautiful little essay, for it was hearing this essay read at a popular lecture that decided me, when I was still an unsettled school-leaver, to study the natural sciences.

VI

I have not yet fulfilled my promise to analyse another dream in which my self does not occur to show that it, too, is egoistic. I mentioned a short dream on p. 207, in which Professor L. says: 'My son, the myope* . . .', and noted that it was only the preliminary dream to another, in which I have a part to play. Here is the missing main dream, which offers us an absurd and incomprehensible word-formation which needs explaining:

On account of some events in the city of Rome, it is necessary for the children to flee the city, which does in fact happen. The setting is then outside a gate, a double gate in the ancient style (the Porta Romana in Siena, as I know as I am dreaming). I am sitting on the edge of a fountain, very sorrowful, almost weeping. A female figure—an attendant, a nun—brings the two boys out and hands them over to their father—but I am not he. The older of the two is quite clearly my eldest son; I can't see the other's face. The woman who is bringing the boy wants him to kiss her goodbye. Her distinguishing feature is her red nose. The boy refuses her the kiss, but, giving her his hand in farewell, says: Auf Geseres, and to the two of us (or to one of us) he says: Auf Ungeseres. I have an idea that the latter indicates a preference.

This dream is built on a tangle of thoughts prompted by a play I had seen in the theatre, *Das neue Ghetto* [*The New Ghetto*].* The Jewish question, concern for my children's future, who cannot be given a fatherland of their own, concern about bringing them up in such a way that they can grow up able to move freely from place to place, these are easy to recognize in the relevant dream-thoughts.

'*By the waters of Babylon we sat down and wept.*'*—Like Rome, Siena is famous for its beautiful fountains; for Rome I have to find some substitute in my dream (see p. 148) among the places familiar to me. Not far from the Porta Romana in Siena we saw a large, brightly lit house. We learned that it was the *manicomio*, the lunatic asylum. Shortly before I had the dream I heard that someone who shared my religion had had to give up his hard-won position at a state asylum.

Our interest is roused by the spoken words: *Auf Geseres*, at a point in the situation retained in the dream where one should expect: *Auf Wiedersehen*; and by its quite nonsensical opposite: *Auf Ungeseres*.

Geseres, according to the information I have gathered from the scribes, is a genuine Hebrew word, deriving from the verb *goiser* and best rendered by 'suffering imposed upon one, destiny'. From its use in Jewish slang, one might suppose the word meant 'weeping and wailing'. *Ungeseres* is my very own word-formation, and first catches my attention, though to begin with I also have no idea what to do with it. The little remark at the end of the dream, that *Ungeseres* indicates some preference over *Geseres*, opens the gates to my ideas,

and so to my understanding. After all, we find a similar preference
between kinds of caviare: *unsalted* caviare is more highly regarded
than *salted*. Caviare to the general,* 'great expectations': this conceals a joking allusion to one of the members of my household,
younger than I, who will one day, I hope, take the future of my
children into her care. It fits well with this that another member of
my household, our good nanny, should be recognizable as the attendant (or nun) in the dream. However, there is an intermediary transition missing between the pair *salted–unsalted* and *Geseres–Ungeseres*.
It is to be found in the pair *'leavened–unleavened'*; in their *flight* from
Egypt, the children of Israel had no time to allow their dough to rise,
and in memory of this they still eat unleavened bread* at Easter to
this day. This is where I can accommodate the sudden idea that came
to me during this part of the analysis. I remembered how we took a
walk last *Easter* in the streets of Breslau, a town we did not know, my
Berlin friend and I. A little girl asked me the way to a certain street; I
had to make my excuses that I didn't know, and I then remarked to
my friend: 'I hope in later life the little girl has a keener eye in her
choice of persons to guide her.' Shortly afterwards I caught sight of a
physician's plate: 'Dr *Herodes*, consulting hours . . .' I remarked: 'I
hope our colleague is not actually a children's specialist.' My friend
had meantime been expounding his ideas on the biological significance of *bilateral symmetry* to me, and had introduced a sentence
with: 'If we just had one eye in the middle of our forehead like the
Cyclops . . .' That leads now to the words spoken by the professor in
the preliminary dream: *My son, the myope.* And this has led me to the
main source for *Geseres*. Many years ago, when this son of Professor
L.'s, who is today an independent thinker, was still *sitting on the
school benches*, he suffered from an eye complaint which the doctor
declared was a matter of some concern. In his opinion, as long as it
remained *on the one side* it was of no significance, but if it were to pass
over to the *other eye*, it would be serious. The trouble in the one eye
cleared up without leaving any damage; shortly afterwards, however,
signs of the infection really did appear in the other. The terrified
mother sent for the doctor at once to come out to the solitude of her
country lodgings. *'What sort of a "Geseres" are you kicking up?'* he
hectored. 'If it has got better *on the one side*, it'll get better *on the
other.'* And so it did.

And now its connection with me and mine. The *school bench* on which the son of Professor L. acquired his earliest wisdom passed as a gift from the boy's mother into the possession of my eldest son, the son, that is, I had speak the words of farewell in my dream. One of the wishes attached to this transference is now easy to guess. This school bench is also by its construction intended to protect the child from becoming *short-sighted* and *one-sided*. Hence the *myope* in my dream (and behind it *Cyclops*) and the discussion of *bilaterality*. My concern about one-sidedness has more than one meaning; as well as meaning physical one-sidedness, it can refer to intellectual development. Indeed, does it not seem that the craziness of the scene in the dream is a contradiction of these very concerns? After the child has spoken his words of farewell *to the one side*, he calls its very opposite *to the other side*, as if to set up a balance. *He is acting, as it might be, in observance of bilateral symmetry!*

Thus, dreams are often at their most profound when they appear at their craziest. Through the ages, those who had something to say and could not say it without risk would gladly don the fool's cap. The listener who was the target of the forbidden speech was prepared to tolerate it, as long as he could laugh and flatter himself with the view that the uncomfortable truths were obviously uttered by a fool. The Prince in the play who has to pretend to be a fool is behaving just as the dream does in reality, and so we can declare of the dream what Hamlet says of himself, as he replaces his true circumstances with his witty and unintelligible word-games: 'I am but mad north-north-west: when the wind is southerly, I know a hawk from a hand-saw.'[25]*

I have solved the problem of absurdity in dreams, then, to the point where we can say: the dream-thoughts are never absurd—at least not the dream-thoughts behind the dreams of sane and sensible people; and the dream-work produces absurd dreams or dreams with single absurd elements when criticism, mockery, and scorn are present in the dream-thoughts and waiting to be represented in its forms of expression. The important thing now is for me to show that the dream-work consists simply and solely of the interaction of the three

[25] This dream is also a good example of the generally valid proposition that the dreams of the same night, even if they are remembered separately, have grown from the ground of the same dream-thoughts. Incidentally, the dream-situation in which I have my children flee the city of Rome is distorted by a retrospective association with an analogous event that occurred in my childhood. Its meaning is that I am envious of relatives who took the opportunity many years ago to move their children to the soil of another country.

factors I have mentioned—and of a fourth I have yet to discuss; and to show that all it does is produce a translation of the dream-thoughts, while observing the four prescribed conditions; and to show that to ask whether the psyche is operating in the dream with all its mental capacities in action or only some of them is to put the wrong question and miss the real state of affairs. However, there are plenty of dreams containing judgements: they criticize, they acknowledge, they show astonishment at a single element in their content, they attempt explanations and set up arguments, so I must use selected examples to dispose of the objections arising from occurrences such as these.

My rejoinder is this: *everything in our dreams that ostensibly looks like the activity of the function of judgement is not to be understood as, say, an act of thinking on the part of the dream-work; rather, it belongs to the material of the dream-thoughts and has passed from there as a ready-made structure into the manifest dream-content.* For the moment, I can go one further. Even a good part of the judgements we make about our dreams as we remember them *after waking*, and the feelings summoned up in us as we reproduce them, belong to the latent dream-content and should be included in the interpretation of the dream.

I

I have already given a striking example illustrating this. A patient is reluctant to tell her dream, because it is *too unclear*. She has seen a figure in her dream and does not know *whether it was her husband or her father*. Then there follows a second part of the dream with a rubbish bin [Misttrügerl] in it, to which the following recollection is attached. As a young housewife she once mentioned jokingly to a young relative who was visiting that the next thing she had to do was get a new bin for the rubbish. The next morning one was sent to her, full of lilies of the valley. This part of the dream is a representation of the saying: 'It didn't grow on my own rubbish-heap.'* If we complete the analysis, we will find that a story she heard in her youth continued to leave its trace in the dream-thoughts: a girl had a baby, but *was quite unclear who the father was*. So the dream-representation is encroaching on her waking thoughts here, and causing the place of one element in the dream-thoughts to be taken by a waking judgement passed on the dream as a whole.

II

A similar case: one of my patients has a dream that strikes him as interesting, for immediately on waking he says to himself: *I must tell that to the doctor.* The dream is analysed and yields the clearest allusions to an affair he began in the course of his treatment, which he had decided *to tell me nothing about.*

III

A third example from my own dreams:

I am walking to the hospital with P. through a neighbourhood with houses and gardens. As we do so, the thought occurs that I have seen this neighbourhood in dreams several times before. I don't know my way around it very well; he shows me a path going across a corner to a restaurant (saloon, not garden); I ask there after Frau Doni and I learn that she is living in the back in a little room with three children. I go in that direction and before I get there I meet an indistinct figure with my two small daughters; then I take them with me after I have been standing with them a while. A kind of criticism of my wife for having left them there.

Then, when I wake, I feel a great *satisfaction*, which I explain as my expectation that I shall now learn from the analysis what is the meaning of: *I have already dreamed of this before.*[26] However, the analysis tells me nothing of the sort; it only shows me that my satisfaction belongs to the latent dream-content and not to my judgement about the dream. *It is the satisfaction that in my marriage I have had children.* P. is someone whom I accompanied for a while on the same path in life and who has gone much further than I have, socially and materially, but whose marriage has remained childless. The two occasions for the dream will serve instead of demonstration by a complete analysis. The previous day I read the obituary notice in the newspaper of *Frau Dona A . . . y* (which I turned into *Doni*), who had died in *childbed*. My wife told me that the departed had been looked after by the same midwife who had attended her when she had our two youngest. The name *Dona* occurred to me, for I had met it shortly before for the first time in an English novel. The other occasion for the dream is its date; it was the night before the birthday of my eldest boy, who has, it seems, a talent for poetry.

[26] A topic on which a long-drawn-out discussion has developed in the most recent issues of the *Revue Philosophique* (paramnesia in dreams).

IV

I am left with the same satisfaction after I wake from the absurd dream about my father playing a part in Magyar politics after his death; it is motivated by the continued feeling that accompanied the last sentence of the dream: *I recall how like Garibaldi he looked on his deathbed, and I am glad that this promise did come true after all. (Added on to this a continuation I have forgotten.)* From the analysis I am now able to fill in what belongs in this gap in my dream. It is a reference to my second son, whose first name I chose after a great figure in history* who had attracted me powerfully when I was a boy, particularly following my stay in England. All through the year when we were expecting him I had it in mind to use just this name, if it should be a son, and, *with great satisfaction*, I welcomed him with it the moment he was born. It is not difficult to see how the vaulting ambition which the father has suppressed is transferred in his thoughts onto his children. Indeed, it is not inconceivable that this is one of the ways by which such suppression, with which our life constrains us, comes about. The little boy earned his right of entry into the interconnections of this dream because he had the same accident—easily forgivable in a child or someone dying—of soiling his clothes. Compare the allusion to 'stools' and the dream-wish: 'To be a *pure and great* presence to one's children.'

V

If I am now to select expressions of judgement which are confined to the dream itself, and do not continue into our waking thoughts nor transfer themselves to them, it will be much easier for me to make use of dreams which I have already related with another aim in mind. The dream of Goethe and his attack on Herr M. seems to contain a large number of acts of judgement. '*I am trying to throw a little light on the the chronology, which strikes me as improbable.*' Does that not look like criticism of the nonsense that Goethe is supposed to have made a literary attack on a young man of my acquaintance? '*It seems plausible to me* that he was eighteen years old.' But that sounds like the result of an admittedly feeble-minded calculation; and '*I am not sure what year we are in*' would be an example of uncertainty or doubt in dreams.

However, I know from my analysis of this dream that the wording of these acts of judgement, ostensibly made only in the course of the dream, admits of another meaning which makes them indispensable for the dream-interpretation, and at the same time avoids any absurdity. With the sentence: '*I am trying to throw some light on the chronological pattern*' I am putting myself in the place of my friend, who really is trying to throw light on the chronological ordering of life. The sentence here loses its significance as a judgement passed on the nonsense of the preceding sentences. The interpolation '*it strikes me as improbable*' belongs with the later '*it seems plausible to me*'. I used more or less the same words in replying to the lady who told me of her brother's medical history: '*It seems to me unlikely* that his cry of "Nature, Nature" had anything to do with Goethe; *it is much more plausible to me* that it had the sexual significance familiar to you.' Now a judgement is certainly being passed here, though not in the dream but in reality, prompted by something the dream-thoughts had remembered and employed. The dream-content makes this judgement its own, just as it does any other fragment of the dream-thoughts.

The number *18*, with which the judgement in the dream is absurdly associated, still retains a trace of the context from which the real judgement was torn. Finally, my doubt that '*I am not sure what year we are in*' is meant simply to bring about my identification with the paralytic patient, for it was my examination of him that offered this one foothold for it.

In breaking down these apparent acts of judgement in the dream, we should remind ourselves of the rule for dream-interpretation given at the outset: we should regard the interconnectedness of the dream-components composed by the dream as inessential and illusory, and set it aside, for each individual dream-element should be traced back to its own source. The dream is a conglomerate which, for purposes of investigation, has to be broken up into fragments once more. However, on the other hand we should bear in mind that a psychical force is expressed in dreams which creates this apparent coherence, that is, it subjects the material produced by the dream-work to *a secondary revision*. We have expressions of that power here before us, which we will assess later as the fourth of the factors involved in the formation of dreams.

VI

I shall look for other examples of judgements made in dreams I have already related. In the absurd dream of the communication from the district council, I ask: '*Did you get married soon afterwards?*' *I calculate that I was of course born in 1856, which seems to me to follow straight after.* That is dressed up in the form of a line of reasoning towards a conclusion. My father married in 1851, soon after his attack; I am the eldest, born in 1856; so it all fits. We know that this is a false conclusion, effected in the interests of wish-fulfilment, and that the dominant sentence in the dream-thoughts is: '*four or five years, that is no time at all, it doesn't count.*' But the dream-thoughts give a different determination to every step in this line of reasoning towards a conclusion, in content and in form: it is my client, whose patience over five years my colleague is complaining about, who intends to get married as soon as his treatment is over. The way I treat my father in the dream recalls an *interrogation* or an *examination*, which reminds me of a university professor at Admissions who was in the habit of taking a complete military list of particulars: 'Date of birth?' '1856.'—'Patre?' The student would reply giving the father's first name with a Latin ending, and we students assumed that the high official *drew conclusions** from the first name of the father which he might not have been able to draw from the first name of the student being admitted. Accordingly, *drawing a conclusion* in the dream would be only a repetition of the *drawing a conclusion* that appears as a piece of material in the dream-thoughts. This tells us something new. If a conclusion occurs in the dream-content, it is certain to have come from the dream-thoughts; but it may be contained in these as a piece of remembered material or it can act as a logical connective to link a sequence of dream-thoughts. In each case a conclusion drawn in the dream represents a conclusion drawn in the dream-thoughts.[27]

This is a suitable point to continue the analysis of the dream. A memory of the Register of University Students (drawn up in Latin in my time) attaches itself to the professor's interrogation. And also to the course of my studies. The *five years* prescribed for the study of

---

[27] These results qualify my earlier account of the representation of logical relations (p. 237) on some points. That describes how the dream-work behaves generally, but does not take account of its subtlest and most scrupulous feats.

medicine were once again too few for me. I worked on unconcerned for some years more, and the circle of my acquaintances thought I was wasting my time, and doubted that I would be *finished*. Then I made a *quick* decision to take my examinations, and I was finished after all; *in spite of the postponement*. A fresh reinforcement for my dream-thoughts, which make up my defiant reply to my critics. 'And even though you wouldn't believe it, because I've taken my time over it: I shall finish, you'll see; I shall come to a conclusion after all. That is often the way it goes.'

The section at the beginning of the same dream contains some sentences which undeniably have the characteristics of argumentation. And this argumentation is not even absurd. It could just as easily belong to our thinking when we are awake. *In my dream I make fun of the communication from the district council, for in the first place, in 1851 I was not yet born, and in the second place, my father, to whom it possibly refers, is already dead.* Both propositions are not only intrinsically correct, but they also correspond completely to the arguments I would use in real life if I were to receive a communication of that kind. We know from our earlier analysis (p. 278) that this dream grew on the ground of dream-thoughts that were deeply embittered and full of scorn; if we assume that, in addition, the motives for censorship were also very strong, we will understand that the dream-work had every cause to create *an indisputable refutation of an absurd demand* after the model contained in the dream-thoughts. However, the analysis shows us that it is not for the dream-work to create this simulacrum freely; rather, it is obliged to use material from the dream-thoughts for it. It is as though an algebraic equation, in addition to the numbers, contained a plus and a minus sign for indicating a higher power or a root, and as though someone were to copy down this equation blindly, transferring the operative signs as well as the numerals into his copy and jumbling both sorts up together. The two arguments can be traced back to the following material. I find it distressing to think that many of the premises at the basis of my psychological solution to the psychoneuroses will produce incredulity and laughter once I have published them. That being the case, I have to maintain that impressions from their second year of life, sometimes even from their first, leave lasting traces in the emotional life of those who go on to fall ill; and these impressions, though much distorted and exaggerated in memory, can present us with the first and most fundamental reason for a hysterical symptom. When I find a suitable point to explain this to my patients, they are in the habit of parodying this newly acquired insight, declaring they are ready to look for memories from the time when they were *not yet in the land of the living.* I would also expect a similar reception if I revealed the unsuspected role played by the *father* in the earliest stirrings of sexuality in neurotic women (see the discussion on p. 198). And yet it is my well-founded conviction that both are true. In support of this, I have in mind particular examples where the father died when the child was very young, and where later, otherwise inexplicable occurrences prove that the child had indeed preserved memories of the figure who vanished from her life so soon. I know that both assertions are based upon *conclusions* whose validity will be disputed. It is thus a great achievement of wish-fulfilment when the very material of *these conclusions*, which I fear will be attacked, is used by the dream-work to establish *conclusions* that are indisputable.

VII

At the beginning of a dream that I have so far only touched upon, there is an explicit utterance of astonishment at its theme as it emerges.

*My old professor Brücke must have given me some task to do, **strangely enough it has to do with dissecting my own lower torso, pelvis, and legs,** which I can see in front of me as though I were in the dissecting room, but without feeling the lack of these limbs from my body, nor finding it at all gruesome. Louise N. is standing by and is helping me with the work. The pelvis has been eviscerated; one moment one has a view of it from above, the next a view from below, merging into each other. Thick, flesh-coloured tubercles are to be seen (which while I am still dreaming make me think of haemorrhoids). Also, something lying over it, looking like crumpled silver paper,[28] had to be carefully picked out. Then I was once again in possession of my legs and made my way through the city, but (out of tiredness) I took a cab. To my astonishment the cab drove in through the gateway of a house which opened up to it and let it pass along a passage which twisted at the end and finally led out into the open again.[29]*

---

[28] Silver foil [*Stanniol*]. Allusion to *Stannius, Nervensystem der Fische,* see p. 263.

[29] The location is the entrance hall of my apartment-building, where the children's prams belonging to the tenants are kept; but it is over-determined in several other respects.

Finally, I wandered through changing landscapes with an Alpine guide who was carrying my things. He carried me for a stretch out of consideration for my weary legs. The ground was swampy; we walked along the edge; people were sitting on the ground, like Red Indians or Gypsies, among them a girl. Just beforehand I had been moving on the slippery ground unaided, constantly surprised that I could manage so well after the dissection. At last we came to a little wooden house with an open window at the end. The guide set me down there and laid two wooden planks, which were standing ready, on the windowsill so as to bridge the chasm that had to be crossed from the window. This really filled me with fear for my legs. However, instead of the crossing I was expecting, I saw two grown men lying on wooden benches along the walls of the hut, and something like two children asleep next to them. As if not the planks, but the children, were to make the crossing possible. I wake with thoughts full of terror.

Anyone who has once acquired a proper impression of the sheer scope of condensation in dreams can easily imagine how many pages a detailed analysis of this dream must fill. Fortunately for the interconnections I shall borrow only the one example of surprise in dreams, which makes its presence known in that interpolated 'strangely enough'. I shall explain the occasion for the dream. It is a visit by that lady, Louise N., who is also helping me in my work in the dream. 'Lend me something to read.' I offer her *She** by Rider Haggard. 'A *strange* book, but full of hidden meaning,' I explain to her; 'the eternal-feminine,* the immortality of our emotions—' Then she interrupts me: 'I've read it. Haven't you anything of your own?'—'No, my own immortal works haven't been written yet.' 'Well, when can we expect what you call your latest insights,' she asked rather sarcastically, 'the ones you promise we too will find readable?' Now, when I come to think about it, I note that someone else is speaking through her to warn me, and I am silent. I think of the effort of self-conquest it is costing me to publish just my work on dreams, in which I am obliged to surrender so much of my innermost self. 'Das Beste, was Du wissen kannst, darfst Du den Buben doch nicht sagen'* [The best that you can know you cannot tell the children]. The task set me in the dream of *dissecting my own body, then, is the self-analysis* involved in relating my dreams. Old *Brücke* deserves to appear in this context; as early as my first years of scientific work it happened that I put a finding aside until his energetic urging made me publish it. But the further thoughts developing out of my conversation with Louise N. go too deep to become conscious; they are diverted by way of the material that was awakened incidentally in my mind by the mention of Rider Haggard's *She*. It is to this book, and to a second by the same author, *Heart of the World*,* that the judgement *strangely enough* refers, and many elements in the dream are taken from these two novels of fantasy. The swampy ground over which I am carried and the chasm to be crossed over planks we had brought with us come from *She*; the Red Indians, the girl, and the wooden house from *Heart of the World*. In both novels a woman is the guide; both of them are about a perilous journey, in *She* it is an adventurous way into the unexplored and scarcely trodden.* My weary legs, as I see from a note I made at the time of the dream, are a real sensation from those days. Their equivalent was probably a mood of weariness and the doubtful question: 'How far will my legs still carry me?' In *She*, the adventure ends when the guide, instead of leading herself and the others into immortality, goes to her death in the mysterious central fire. Fear of something like this had unmistakably stirred in my dream-thoughts. The *wooden house* is undoubtedly also the *coffin*, that is, the grave. But in its representation of this most undesirable of all thoughts by a wish-fulfilment the dream has achieved its masterpiece. In fact, I was once in a grave, but that was in an excavated Etruscan grave near Orvieto, a narrow chamber with two stone benches along the walls, on which the skeletons of two grown men were lying. The interior of the wooden house in my dream looks exactly like that, only with the stone replaced by wood. The dream seems to be saying: 'If you are to tarry in the grave, then let it be the Etruscan one'—and by making this underhand substitution, it transforms the most melancholy of expectations into a very desirable one. Unfortunately, as we shall hear, it can only change the imaginary idea accompanying the affect into its opposite, not always the affect itself as well. This is why I wake up with thoughts full of *terror*, after another idea has compelled my dream to represent it: that perhaps the children will achieve what was denied their father. This is yet another allusion to that strange novel in which one person's identity is preserved throughout a sequence of generations across 2000 years.

VIII

In the interconnections set up in another dream there is a similar expression of surprise at what is experienced in it, but this time it is linked to such a striking, far-fetched, and almost witty attempt at an explanation that I could not resist subjecting the entire dream to analysis just for its sake. *I am travelling overnight from the 18th to the 19th of July on the line south of Vienna, and in my sleep I hear the shout: 'Hollthurn in ten minutes!' At once I think of holothurians*— a museum of natural history—and that this is a place where brave men defended themselves unsuccessfully against the power of their reigning princes.—Of course, the Counter-Reformation in Austria!—as though it were a place in Styria or the Tyrol. Now I can see a little museum indistinctly, where the remains or the acquisitions of these men are pre-served. I would like to get down from the train, but I hesitate. There are women with fruit standing on the platform; they are crouched on the ground, holding their baskets out so invitingly.—I delayed, uncertain whether we still had time, and now we are still at a standstill.—All of a sudden I am in a different compartment, where the leather upholstery and the seats are so narrow that one's back bumps directly against the back of the seat.*[30] *I am surprised at this, but of course it is possible that I could have changed trains while I was still asleep. Several people, includ-ing an English brother and sister; a distinct row of books in a bookcase against the wall. I can see 'Wealth of Nations',* 'Matter and Motion'* (by Maxwell), thick books bound in brown linen. The man asks his sister about a book by Schiller,* whether she has forgotten it. One moment it looks as if the books are mine, the next as if they are theirs. I would like to intervene in the conversation to confirm or support— —I wake up,* my whole body sweating, because all the windows are closed. The train is stopping at *Marburg*.

As I am writing this down, a bit of the dream comes to mind which my memory wanted to pass over. *I say* [in English] *to the brother and sister of a certain work: 'It is from . . . ', but I correct myself: 'It is by . . .* The man remarks to his sister: 'Did you hear? He said it correctly.'*

The dream begins with the name of the station, which must have

---

[30] This description is incomprehensible to myself too, but I am following the principle of reproducing the dream in the words that occurred to me as I wrote them down. The wording itself is part of the representation by the dream.

woken me up, though only partially. I replace this name, which is
Marburg, by *Hollthurn*. That it was *Marburg* I heard the first, or
perhaps the second time it was called is proved by the reference to
Schiller in the dream, who of course was born in *Marburg*, though
not the one in Styria. Now I was travelling on this occasion in very
unpleasant circumstances, despite going first class. The train was
overfull; in the compartment I had encountered a gentleman and a
lady who seemed very superior persons and did not have the cour-
tesy, or did not think it worth taking the trouble, to conceal in any
way their displeasure at the interloper. My polite greeting was not
returned; although husband and wife were sitting side by side (their
backs to the engine), before my eyes the wife hurried to secure the
window-seat opposite her with an umbrella; the doors were shut at
once; demonstrative remarks exchanged about opening the windows.
They could, no doubt, tell my need for fresh air straight away. It was
a hot night, and the air in the totally closed compartment soon grew
stifling. In my experience, such inconsiderate and intrusive behaviour
is the mark of people who have not paid for their tickets, or who are
only travelling half-fare. When the guard arrived and I produced my
dearly bought ticket, there sounded from the lady's mouth,
unapproachable and like a threat: 'My husband has an authoriza-
tion.' She was a formidable figure, with ill-tempered features, in age
not far from the decline of feminine beauty; her husband never
uttered a word, he sat there without moving. I attempted to sleep. In
my dream I take a terrible revenge on my disagreeable travelling
companions; one would not guess what insults and humiliations are
hidden behind the torn fragments of the first half of my dream.
After this need was satisfied, the second wish asserted itself: to
change compartments. Dreams change their scene so often without
any protest being made at the transformation, so it would not have
been in the least remarkable if I had promptly replaced my travelling
companions with more pleasant ones from my memory. But here we
have a case where something objected to the change of scene and
thought it necessary to explain it. How did I suddenly get into a
different compartment? I certainly couldn't remember having
changed it. There was only one explanation: *I must have left the
carriage while I was still asleep*, a rare occurrence, but instances of it
are certainly known to neuropathologists. We know of persons who
have embarked upon railway journeys in a hazy state without reveal-

ing any sign of their abnormal condition until they come to completely at some station on their way and are then astonished at the
gap in their memory. So while I am still dreaming, I declare my case
to be one of *automatisme ambulatoire*.

The analysis allows us to find a different solution. That attempt at
an explanation, which amazes me when I had to ascribe it to the
dream-work, is not original, but copied from the neurosis of one of
my patients. I have already told the story elsewhere of a highly
cultivated and, in real life, tender-hearted man, who, shortly before
the death of his parents, began to accuse himself of murderous
desires, and now suffered from the precautionary measures he was
obliged to take as a safeguard against them. It was a case of severe
obsessive ideas, while maintaining total insight. At first he took a
dislike to walking down the street because of his compulsion to
account to himself for the disappearance of all the people he met; if
someone suddenly took evasive action to get away from his persecut-
ing glance, he was left with the distressing feeling, and the thought
that he might possibly have done away with him. There was a 'Cain-
fantasy' behind it, among other things, for 'all men are brothers'. As
this task was impossible to fulfil, he gave up going out for a walk and
spent his life incarcerated within his four walls. But the newspapers
constantly brought to his room news of murders that had taken place
outside, and his conscience would plant doubts in his mind that he
might be the murderer they were looking for. The certainty that he
had definitely not left his apartment for weeks protected him for a
while against these accusations, until one day the possibility
occurred to him that *he could have left the building in a state of
unconsciousness* and could have committed the murder in that way
without knowing anything about it. From then on he locked the
house door, gave the key to his old housekeeper, and forbade her
insistently to let it come into his hands, even if he demanded it.

That is the source of my attempt at explaining that I changed
carriages in a state of unconsciousness—it was transferred ready-
made into my dream from material in the dream-thoughts and is
obviously intended to be used by the dream as a means of identifying
me with the figure of that patient. My memory of him was prompted
in me by obvious association. A few weeks before I had made my last
overnight journey with this man. He was cured, and was accompanying me to the provinces to attend his relatives, who had called on my

services; we had a compartment to ourselves; we had all the windows open right through the night, and for as long as I was awake we enjoyed an excellent conversation. I knew that hostile impulses towards his father, dating from his childhood, in connection with sexuality, had been the root of his illness. So by identifying myself with him, I wanted to admit something analogous in myself. Indeed, the second scene in my dream actually dissolves into a riotous fantasy that the reason for the stand-offish behaviour of my two elderly travelling companions towards me is that my arrival disturbed the amorous exchanges they intended for the night. But this fantasy goes back to an early scene in my childhood when the child, driven no doubt by sexual curiosity, goes into his parents' bedroom and is driven from it by the father's mighty command.

It is superfluous to heap up further examples. They all would simply confirm what we have learnt from those already given: that an act of judgement in a dream is only a repetition of a model from the dream-thoughts. A repetition that is mostly out of place and introduced in an inappropriate context, but occasionally, as our last examples show, so cleverly employed that at first it is possible to have the impression of independent thinking. From this point we can turn our attention to that psychical activity which does not, it is true, seem to have a regular share in the formation of dreams, but where it does, endeavours to blend dream-elements of disparate origins into a dream that is meaningful and free of contradictions. However, before we do so we feel it is still imperative that we should first consider the expressions of affect that make their appearance in dreams, and compare these with the affects revealed by analysis in the dream-thoughts.

(g) *Affects in Dreams*

A shrewd remark of Stricker's has made us aware that the dream's expressions of affect will not allow us to dismiss them as contemptuously as we shake off its content once we are awake. 'If I dream I am frightened of robbers, the robbers are certainly imaginary, but the fear is real', and it is just the same when I dream I am happy. Our feeling testifies that the affects we live through in dreams are by no means inferior to the affects of similar intensity we feel when we are awake; and it is with the affects it contains, far more strongly than with the imagined ideas it contains, that the dream stakes its claim to be accepted as one of the real, formative, experiences of our soul. Now when we are awake we are unable to give these dream-affects their proper place, because the only way we know of assessing the psychical importance of an affect is from its connection with certain imagined ideas contained in the dream. If the affect and the content of ideas do not match in kind or intensity, then our waking judgement does not know what to make of it all.

We have always found it surprising that in our dreams the imagined ideas of the content are not attended by the effect upon our emotions that we would expect they would inevitably have in our waking thought. Strümpell said that ideas are stripped of their psychical values in dreams. However, there are plenty of dreams in which the opposite occurs: an intense expression of affect will make its appearance accompanying a content that does not seem to offer any occasion for the release of affect. I dream I am in a frightful, dangerous, repulsive situation, but I feel no fear or revulsion at all; at other times, on the contrary, I am filled with horror at something harmless, and with delight at something childish.

This puzzle will vanish, perhaps more suddenly and completely than any other presented by our dreams, once we pass from the manifest to the latent dream-content. We will not have to bother about explaining it, because it no longer exists. Analysis teaches us *that the imagined ideas in the dream-content have undergone displacements and substitutions, while the affects have remained in place unaltered.* No wonder that the ideas of the content, transformed as they are by dream-distortion, no longer match the unchanged affect; but no further astonishment either, once the analysis has put the right content in its former place.

Let us consider a psychical complex which has been subject to the influence of the censorship set up by resistance; the affects are that part of the complex which are most proof against the censorship, indeed, they are the only part that can give us a pointer towards filling the gaps. This is revealed in the psychoneuroses even more clearly than in dreams. In psychoneuroses the affect is always right, at least in its nature; although, of course, its intensity is increased by displacements of neurotic attention. If the sufferer from hysteria wonders that he is driven to fear a little thing so much, or the man with obsessive delusions wonders that such a distressing accusation should grow out of a trifle, both are misled, because they are taking the imagined idea—the little thing, the trifle—to be the essential thing, and they will be defending themselves in vain if they take these imagined ideas as a starting-point for their thinking. Psychoanalysis then puts them on the right track by acknowledging that, on the contrary, their affect is justified, and by looking for the idea relevant to it, which has been repressed and replaced by another. The assumption is that release of affect and content of imagined ideas do not form that indissoluble organic unity we usually treat them as being; rather, that both parts have been soldered onto each other in such a way that they can be separated by analysis. Dream-interpretation shows that this is in fact the case.

First of all I shall give an example where the analysis explains the apparent absence of affect accompanying the kind of imagined ideas in the dream-content which should have compelled its release.

I

She sees three lions in a desert. One of them is laughing, but she is not afraid of them. She must have run away from them, though, for she makes to climb a tree, but she discovers her cousin, a woman who is a teacher of French, already up there, etc.

The analysis brings the following material to bear: the unimportant occasion for the dream is a sentence from her English exercise, 'the mane is the lion's ornament'. Her father had a beard that framed his face like a *mane*. Her teacher of English is called *Miss Lyons*. An acquaintance sent her *Loewe's* ballads* [*Loewe*=lion]. These are her three lions, then; why should she be afraid of them?—She has read a story in which a Negro who has roused the others to revolt is hunted with hounds, and clambers up a tree to save himself. There follow, in a most playful spirit, remembered fragments, such as, 'Instructions on how to catch lions' from *Fliegende Blätter*: 'Take one desert and pass it through a sieve; the lions will be left in the sieve.' Then the very amusing, but rather improper, story of the official who is asked why he doesn't try harder to get into his boss's favour, and who replied that he has already tried crawling into it, but his immediate superior was already *up there*. The material all becomes intelligible when we learn that on the day of the dream the lady had been paid a formal visit by her husband's superior. He was very polite to her, kissed her hand, and *she was not at all afraid of him*, although he was such a big shot [in German idiom, 'ein großes Tier'=a big animal], and was much *lionized* in her country. So this lion can be compared to the lion in *A Midsummer Night's Dream*, who reveals himself to be Snug, the Joiner;* and all the lions we are not afraid of in our dreams are just like that.

II

For my second example I shall take the dream of the girl who saw her sister's little son lying dead in his coffin but, I add now, did not feel any grief or sadness at the sight. We know from the analysis why not. The dream only disguised her wish to see the man she loved again; the affect must have taken its tone from the wish, and not from its disguise. Hence, there was no reason at all for sadness.

In a number of dreams, the affect at least still keeps some contact with those ideas in the content which have taken the place of the right one. What happens then resembles what we learned of acts of judgement in dreams. If an important conclusion is drawn in the dream-thoughts, then the dream will also contain one; but it is possible that the conclusion in the dream has been displaced onto quite different material. Not infrequently this displacement takes place according to the principle of contraries.

I shall explain this last possibility in the following example of a dream which I have subjected to the most exhaustive analysis.

III

A palace on the sea. Later it does not lie directly on the edge of the sea, but on a narrow canal leading into the sea. A certain Herr P. is the governor. I am standing with him in a great reception room with three windows, and in front of them projecting walls rise like castle battlements. I have been assigned to the occupying force, perhaps as a volunteer naval officer. We are afraid of the imminent arrival of enemy warships, as we are in a state of war. Herr P. intends to leave; he gives me instructions about what is to be done if what we fear does happen. His ailing wife is with the children in the vulnerable palace. When the bombardment begins, the great hall is to be cleared. He is breathing heavily and makes to go away; I detain him, and ask how I can get news to him if necessary. He says something in reply, but then immediately falls down dead. I have probably overstrained him needlessly with my questions.

After his death, which doesn't make any further impression on me, thoughts about whether the widow will stay in the palace, whether I should report his death to headquarters and, as next in command, take over the direction of the palace. Then I am standing at the window, scrutinizing the ships as they pass; they are merchant ships, roaring past rapidly on the dark water, some of them with several funnels, others with bulging decks (which are very like the railway station buildings in the preliminary dream, not given here). *Then my brother is standing next to me and we are both looking out of the window on to the canal. One ship makes us start in alarm and call: The warship is coming. But it turns out that only the same ships already familiar to me are returning. Now there is a small ship passing by, oddly truncated, so that it ends at its broadest point; on deck there are some curious things to be seen, rather like cups or cans. We call as with one voice: 'That is the breakfast-ship.'*

The rapid movement of the ships, the deep, dark blue of the water, the brown smoke from the funnels—all this together creates a very tense and gloomy impression.

The localities in this dream are put together from several journeys to the Adriatic (Miramare,* Duino, Venice, Aquileia). A short, but enjoyable, Easter trip to Aquileia with my brother a few weeks before the dream was still fresh in my memory. *The naval war* between America and Spain,* too, and the worry attached to it for the fate of my relatives living in America, have a part in it. The operation of affect makes its presence felt in two places in this dream. In one place, an affect that might have been expected is absent; it is expressly emphasized that the governor's death makes no impression on me; in another place, where I think I see the warship, *I am filled with alarm*, and while I am asleep I feel all the sensations of terror. This well-constructed dream has accommodated affects in such a way that any noticeable contradiction is avoided. After all, there is no reason why I should be filled with alarm at the governor's death, and it is probably quite right that as commander of the palace I should be alarmed at the sight of the warship. However, the analysis points out that Herr P. is only a substitute for my own self (in my dream I am his substitute). I am the governor who suddenly dies. My dream-thoughts are concerned with the future of my relatives after my untimely death. This is the only distressing thought among them. The fear, which in my dream is soldered onto the sight of the warship, must have been detached from there and relocated here. On the contrary, analysis shows quite the reverse: that the region in the dream-thoughts from which the warship is taken is filled with the most cheerful reminiscences. It was the previous year in Venice; it was an enchantingly beautiful day and we were standing at the windows of our room on the Riva Schiavoni, looking at the blue lagoon where there was more movement than usual to be seen on that day. English ships were expected and were to be given a ceremonial welcome, when suddenly my wife cried out, as joyfully as a child: '*The English warship is coming!*' In my dream I am filled with alarm at the same words; once again we see that speech in dreams derives from speech in real life. I shall shortly show that even the element 'English' in these words was not lost to the dream-work. Between my dream-thoughts and the dream-content, then, I am turning joyfulness into alarm, and I need only suggest that with this transformation itself I am giving expression to a part of the *latent* dream-content. However, this example demonstrates that the dream-work is free to detach the occasion for an affect from its connections in the dream-thoughts and place it anywhere else in the dream-content.

I shall take the incidental opportunity to make a closer analysis of the *breakfast-ship*, whose appearance brings the rationally sustained situation of the dream to such a nonsensical conclusion. If I look more keenly at the object in my dream, it occurs to me in retrospect that it was black, and being truncated where it was widest, it bore a great similarity at this end to an object that had interested us in the museums in Etruscan cities. This was a rectangular tray of black pottery, with two handles, on which objects like coffee-cups or tea-cups were standing, not unlike a modern *breakfast table service*. When we enquired, we were told that it was for the toilette of an Etruscan lady, with bowls for holding make-up and face-powder on it; and we joked with each other that it wouldn't be a bad idea to take something like that back as a present for our wives. So the object in the dream means *en toilette wearing black* [schwarze Toilette], being in mourning, and it is a direct allusion to someone's death. With the other end, the object in my dream is a reminder of the barque [Nachen], from the root νέκυς, as my linguist friend informed me, on which the body was laid in ancient times and given up to the sea for burial. This provides a connecting-thread for the reason why in my dream the ships return.

Quiet, in the rescued boat, to the harbour the old man returns.*

It is the return after shipwreck; indeed, the breakfast-ship looks as if it is broken off at its broadest point. But where does the name 'breakfast'-ship come from? This is where the 'English' element, which we kept in reserve from the warships, is put to use. *Breakfast* in English means *breaking one's fast*. *Breaking* belongs to shipwreck [Schiff*bruch*] again, and *fasting* is connected to the black toilette.

However, only the name of this breakfast-ship was newly coined by my dream. The thing itself existed, and reminds me of one of the most enjoyable hours of our recent journey. Mistrusting the cooking in Aquileia, we had brought food with us from Görz* and bought a bottle of excellent Istrian wine in Aquileia; and while the little post steamer made its way slowly along the Canale delle Mee into the empty stretch of lagoons towards Grado,* as the only passengers we took our breakfast on deck in the most cheerful mood, enjoying it as we had rarely enjoyed a breakfast before. So that was the *breakfast-ship*, and it is precisely the memory of this good cheer and enjoyment of life behind which the dream is concealing the most grievous thoughts of an unknown and uneasy future.

This detachment of the affects from the masses of imagined ideas which have given rise to them is the most striking thing that happens to them in the formation of a dream, but it is neither the only change, nor the most essential, that they undergo on their way from the dream-thoughts to the manifest dream. If one compares the affects in the dream-thoughts with those in the dream, one thing becomes clear at once: where there is an affect present in the dream, it is also present in the dream-thoughts, but not the other way round. In general, the dream has fewer and weaker affects than the psychical material from which, as adapted, it has emerged. When I have reconstructed the dream-thoughts, I can see how the most intense emotions of the psyche are invariably fighting to assert themselves, mainly in a struggle with others sharply opposed to them. If I then look back at the dream, I often find it colourless, lacking in any intense tonality of feeling. The dream-work does not only reduce the content of my thinking to the level of trivality, but often mutes the tonality of its feeling as well. I could say that the dream-work brings about a *suppression of the affects*. Let us take the dream of the botanical monograph, for example. What corresponds to it in my thinking is a passionate and emotional plea for my freedom to act as I do and arrange my life in the way that seems right to me and me alone. The dream that emerged from that sounds trivial: I have written a monograph; it is lying in front of me; it has coloured plates; there are dried plants attached to each specimen. It is like the still-ness of a field strewn with corpses, with no trace remaining of the battle that once raged.

It is possible for it to work out differently, and for vivid expres-sions of affect to enter the dream itself; but let us first remain with the indisputable fact that so many dreams appear superficial, even trivial, whereas we cannot enter into the dream-thoughts without being deeply moved.

This is not the place to give a full theoretical explanation of this suppression of affect in the course of the dream-work; it would require us to go into the theory of affects and the mechanism of repression very thoroughly as the premiss of our argument. I will mention only two ideas at this point. I am compelled—on other grounds—to imagine the release of affect as a centrifugal process, directed towards the body's interior, analogous to the working of innervation in our motor and secretory processes. Just as in a state of sleep the transmission of motor impulses to the outside world appears suspended, so it is also possible that the centrifugal arousal of affects brought about by unconscious thinking could be hindered during sleep. If so, the stirrings of affect that come about as the dream-thoughts run their course would essentially be weak; and so those reaching the dream would be no stronger either. According to this line of thinking, the 'suppression of affects' would not be an achievement of the dream-work at all, but a consequence of the state of sleep. This may be so, but it cannot be the whole story. We must also remind ourselves that every dream of any greater complexity has also turned out to be the result of a compromise between two con-testing powers in the psyche. On the one hand, the thoughts forming the wish have to struggle against the opposition of a censoring agency; on the other, we have often seen that in the process of unconscious thinking itself, each and every train of thought was yoked together with its contradictory opposite. As all these trains of thought have the potential for affect, by and large we will hardly go wrong if we conceive the suppression of affect as a consequence of the inhibition exercised by the opposites on each other and by the censorship on both as it suppresses their efforts. *Inhibition of affect would then be the second achievement of the dream-censorship, as dream-distortion was its first.*

I shall include an example of a dream where the muted tone of feeling in the dream-content can be explained by the oppositions present in the dream-thoughts. I am obliged to relate the following short dream, which every reader will read with some revulsion.

IV

A hill, and on this something like an outdoor privy; a very long bench, at its end a large hole for the privy. The back edge is all covered with piles of faeces of all sizes and degrees of freshness. Behind the bench some bushes. I urinate onto the bench; a long stream of urine washes it all clear, the pats of excrement detach themselves easily and drop into the opening. As if at the end there were still some left.

Why did I feel no disgust at this dream?

Because, as the analysis will show, the most agreeable and satisfying thoughts had a share in bringing it about. In the analysis the *Augean stables,** cleared by Hercules, came to my mind at once. I am this Hercules. The hill and the bushes belong in Aussee, where my children are staying at present. I have discovered the aetiology of neuroses in childhood, and thus I have protected my own children from becoming ill. The bench (except for the hole, of course) is a faithful imitation of a piece of furniture given to me as a present by a devoted lady patient. It reminds me of how much my patients honour me. Indeed, even the museum of human excrement is capable of a heart-warming interpretation. However much it disgusts me, in my dream it is a recollection of the beautiful land of Italy, where in the little towns, as well we know, the WCs are not appointed differently. The stream of urine which washes everything clean is an unmistakable allusion to greatness. That is how Gulliver* puts out the great conflagration in Lilliput; though by doing so, it is true, he attracts the displeasure of the smallest of queens. But Gargantua* too, Master Rabelais's superman, takes this revenge on the people of Paris by aiming his stream of urine at the town as he rides towards Notre Dame. Only yesterday I was turning the pages of Garnier's illustrations to Rabelais before going to sleep. And, curiously, another proof that I am the superman! The platform of Notre Dame was my favourite spot in Paris; I used to climb the church towers among the monsters and gargoyles. The speedy disappearance of all the excrement alludes to the motto: *Flavit et dissipati sunt*,* which one day I shall use as a heading for the chapter on the therapy of hysteria.

And now for the operative occasion of the dream. It had been a hot summer afternoon; that evening I had given my lecture on the connection between hysteria and the perversions, and everything I could say displeased me utterly and seemed to me to be empty of all value. I was tired, had not a trace of pleasure in my arduous work, yearned to be away from this grubbing about in human dirt, longed for my children, and then for the beauties of Italy. In this mood I went from the lecture hall to a café to have a modest snack in the fresh air, having lost any pleasure in eating. But one of my audience came along with me; he asked if he might sit with me while I drank my coffee and choked down my roll, and began his flatteries. How much he had learned from me, how he now looked at everything with different eyes, how I had cleared the *Augean stable* of errors and prejudices in the theory of neuroses; in short, that I was a very great man. My mood was out of tune with his eulogy; I struggled with my disgust; went home earlier to get rid of him; read a few pages of Rabelais before going to bed, and read a novella by C. F. Meyer, *Die Leiden eines Knaben** [*A Boy's Sufferings*].

It was from this material that the dream emerged. Meyer's novella added the memory of scenes from childhood (compare the final image in the dream of Count Thun). The day's mood of disgust and dissatisfaction persisted in the dream to the extent that it was able to provide almost all the material for the dream-content. But in the night, the opposite mood of powerful and even excessive self-aggrandisement came to life and subsumed the first. The dream-content was obliged to find a form for itself that enabled it to use the same material to express both my delusion of inferiority and my overestimation of myself. This compromise-formation resulted in an ambiguous dream, but also in a muted tonality of feeling, as the opposites were inhibiting each other.

According to the theory of wish-fulfilment, this dream could not have come about if the opposite, megalomaniac train of thought, which—though suppressed—had a tonality of pleasure, had not come to join the thoughts of disgust. For distressing things are not to be represented in dreams; what we find distressing in our daytime thoughts can earn its entry into our dreams only if it will at the same time offer itself as a disguise for a wish-fulfilment.

The dream-work can also do something else with the affects of the dream-thoughts besides admitting them or reducing them to zero. It can *turn them into their opposite*. We have already learned the rule for interpretation that every element in a dream can also represent its opposite as well as itself. One never knows in advance whether to assume the one or the other; only the context will decide. An inkling of this state of affairs has clearly entered popular consciousness; dream-books often proceed on the principle of contrast when interpreting dreams. The intimate associative connection which in our thinking tethers the idea of a thing to that of its opposite makes this kind of transformation into the contrary possible. Like every other displacement it serves the purposes of the censorship, but it is also frequently the work of wish-fulfilment, for after all, wish-fulfilment is nothing but the replacement of a disagreeable thing by its opposite. Thus, just like our ideas of things, the affects of the dream-thoughts can also appear in the dream turned into their opposites, and it is probable that this transformation of an affect into its opposite is the work of the dream-censorship. The *suppression of affect* and the *transformation of affect into its opposite*, of course, also have their functions in our social life, which gave us the ready analogy to dream-censorship; above all, they serve *dissimulation*. If I am in conversation with someone I should treat with solicitude, when all the while I would like to say something hostile to him, it is almost more important for me to hide any expressive display of my affect than to moderate the wording of my thoughts. If I speak to him in words that are not impolite, but accompany what I say with a glance or gesture of hate, the effect I produce on that person is not much different from the one I would make if I had callously flung my contempt in his face. That is why the censorship bids me above all to suppress my affects, and, if I am a master of pretence, I will simulate the contrary affect, smile where I would rage, seem tender where I would destroy.

We are already familiar with an excellent example of the transformation of an affect into its opposite in the service of the censorship. In the dream of 'Uncle's beard' I feel great affection for my friend R., whereas and because the dream-thoughts are calling him a numbskull. This example of the transformation of affects into their opposite gave us our first clue to the existence of a dream-censorship. We also do not need to assume here that the dream-work creates a contrary affect of this sort wholly from scratch; it usually finds it ready and waiting in the material of the dream-thoughts and merely intensifies it with the psychical force of motives of defence until it becomes the predominant factor in forming the dream. In the dream of my uncle I have just mentioned, the contrary affect of affection probably has its source in my infancy (as the continuation of the dream suggests), for, from the special nature of my earliest childhood experiences (see the analysis on p. 271), the relationship between uncle and nephew has for me become the source of all my friendships and all my hatreds.

Certain suitable syntheses of fully analysed dreams will give us a good overview of these complicated processes of subsuming, diminishing, and turning into opposites which are the means by which the affects of the dream-thoughts finally turn into the affects in the dream. I will deal here with a few examples in which some of the instances I have discussed actually occur.

V

In the dream of the strange task my old professor Brücke gave me of dissecting my own pelvis, *I notice in the dream itself the absence of any appropriate feeling of horror.* Now this is wish-fulfilment in more than one sense. The dissection signifies the self-analysis that I am accomplishing, as it were, by publishing my dream-book, though in real life I have found it so embarrassing and painful that I have postponed printing the finished manuscript for more than a year. Now the wish is stirring that I should get over this sense of delay, which is why I do not feel any horror [Ger. *Grauen*, earlier rendered by the adjective 'gruesome'; homophone of *grauen*=to grow grey] in my dream. I would gladly notice the absence of *grauen* in the other sense; I am getting really grey; and this grey/*Grau* in my hair also reminds me not to delay any longer. Indeed, we know that at the end of the dream the thought reaches representation that I would have to leave it to the children to reach the goal of this difficult journey.

In the two dreams that transfer the expression of satisfaction to the moments immediately upon waking, this satisfaction is motivated in the one instance by the expectation that I shall now find out the meaning of 'I have dreamed of that before', and actually refers to the birth of my first children; in the other instance it is motivated by the conviction that 'what has been proclaimed by a sign' will now come to pass, and this is the same satisfaction that I felt when I welcomed my second son in his due time. In these cases the same affects persist in the dream as prevail in the dream-thoughts, but no dream works quite as simply as that. If we go a little deeper into the two analyses, we will learn that this satisfaction, which is not subject to censorship, draws added power from another source which does have the censorship to fear, and is charged with an affect that would certainly arouse opposition if it did not cover itself with the comparable affect of satisfaction, admissible and from an acceptable source, creeping in behind its back, as it were. Unfortunately I cannot demonstrate this from the example of this dream itself, but an instance from another field will make my meaning clear. I propose the following case: suppose there were someone near me whom I hate, so that I am moved by a strong feeling of joy when something happens to him. But my sense of morality does not give way to this emotion; I do not dare to utter my malediction, and when something he is not to blame for befalls him, I suppress my satisfaction and force myself to utter words and thoughts of commiseration. We have all found ourselves in such a position. But suppose the hated person does something wrong and gets into well-deserved trouble. Then I may give free rein to my satisfaction that he has been justly punished, and I express my agreement with many others who have no such axe to grind. However, I can observe that my satisfaction turns out to be more intense than the others'; it has been reinforced from the source of my hatred, which until now has been prevented by my inner censorship from releasing its affect; but under the changed circumstances it is no longer hindered from doing so. This case applies to society in general, when persons who are disliked, or members of an unwelcome minority, make themselves culpable in some way. Their punishment then is not usually commensurate with the wrong they have done, but with the wrong plus the ill will directed against them, which until now has been ineffective. Those carrying out the punishment are committing an injustice, there is no doubt about that; but their awareness of it is hindered by the satisfaction they get from the suspension of a long-held suppression within them. In cases like this, it is true the affect is justified in its nature, but not in its degree; and the self-criticism which can rest easy on the one issue only too readily avoids scrutinizing the second. Once the doors are opened, more people will force their way through than it was originally intended to admit.

It is a striking feature of the neurotic character that causes with affective potential give rise to an affect in the neurotic which is justified in its quality, but in quantity exceeds all measure. It can be explained in the following way—insofar as it admits of a psychological explanation at all. The excess derives from sources of affect that have remained unconscious and have so far been suppressed, and which are able to set up an associative connection with the real cause, while the desired route for their release is opened up by the irreproachable and admissible source of affect. This makes us aware that we should not focus exclusively on the relation of reciprocal inhibition between the suppressed and the suppressing agencies in the psyche. Just as much attention should be paid to those cases where both agencies work together and reinforce each other to bring about a pathological effect. Let us now apply these suggestions on the mechanics of the psyche to understanding how affects manifest themselves in dreams. A satisfaction that makes its presence known in the dream, and of course is promptly to be found in its place in the dream-thoughts, is not always fully explained by this evidence alone. As a rule, one would have to look in the dream-thoughts for a second source for it, one which is under pressure from the censorship. Under this pressure the source would have given rise, not to the affect of satisfaction, but rather to its opposite; however, the presence of the first source enables this second source to free its affect of satisfaction from repression and allow it to join with the satisfaction from the first source and reinforce it. In this way the affects in the dream appear to be made up of many tributaries flowing into them, and to be over-determined in respect of the material in the dream-thoughts. *Sources of affect which can give rise to the same affect come together in the process of dream-work to produce it.*

We get a little insight into these complicated circumstances from the analysis of the beautiful dream that has '*Non vixit*' as its centre (see p. 268). In this dream there are two places in the manifest content where expressions of affect of a different nature are condensed. Hostile and distressing emotions (in the dream itself it says 'overcome by quite remarkable affect') overlap at the point where I annihilate my friend and rival with the two words. At the end of the dream I am unusually glad and I make a positive judgement about a possibility I would recognize as absurd when awake, that there are in fact such things as *revenants*, which can be banished merely by wishing them away.

I have not yet related the occasion for this dream. It is of the essence, and leads us deep into understanding it. I received news from my friend in Berlin (whom I have identified by the initial Fl.) that he was to undergo an operation, and that relatives of his living in Vienna would let me know further how he fared. The first news after the operation was not satisfactory, and left me worried. Most of all I would have liked to travel to Berlin and see him myself, but just at that time I was suffering from a painful complaint which made every movement a torment. Now I learn from the dream-thoughts that I feared for the life of my dear friend. His only sister, whom I had not met, had died young after the briefest of illnesses, as I knew. (In my dream: *Fl. is telling us about his sister and says: in three-quarters of an hour she was dead.*) I must have imagined that his own nature was not much more resilient, and got the idea that in the end I would be making the journey in response to far worse news—and would arrive too *late*, which would cause me to reproach myself for ever.[31] This rebuke for coming too late has become the centre of the dream, but it has represented itself by a scene in which it is Brücke, the revered master of my student years, who rebukes me with a terrible glance from his blue eyes. It will soon emerge what brought about this shift of scene; the dream is unable to reproduce the scene in the way I experienced it. It is true, it gives the blue eyes to the other figure, but it gives the annihilating role to me, a reversal which is obviously the work of wish-fulfilment. My concern for my friend's life, my self-reproach that I am not making the journey to see him, my shame (he came to Vienna—to me—*inconspicuously*), my need to regard my illness as my excuse, all this goes into composing the storm of feeling that I felt distinctly in my sleep, and which rages in that region of the dream-thoughts.

However, there was something else about the occasion for the dream that had the completely opposite effect upon me. When I was given the adverse news of the first days after the operation, I was also

[31] It is this fantasy from the unconscious dream-thoughts that imperiously demands *non vivit* instead of *non vixit*. 'You have come too late. He is no longer alive.' It is noted on p. 269 that the manifest situation of the dream also aims for *non vivit*.

warned not to speak to anyone about the entire matter, which I found insulting, because it was premised on an unnecessary mistrust of my discretion. Of course I knew that this did not come from my friend, but I was hurt and embarrassed by the hidden rebuke, because it was—not entirely unjustified. Only a rebuke that 'has something in it' will sting, will have the power to stir our feelings, not the other sort, as we know. Not with regard to my friend, it is true, but once before, when I was much younger, in the case of two friends who both—to my honour—wanted to call me by that name, I quite unnecessarily babbled out something the one had said about the other. Nor have I forgotten the reproaches I got to hear then. One of the two friends between whom I played disturber of the peace was Professor *Fleischl*; the other can be replaced by his first name, *Josef*, which was also the name of my friend and rival P.* who appeared in the dream.

As evidence in the dream for the charge that I cannot keep anything to myself there are the elements *inconspicuous* and Fl.'s question, *how much of his concerns have I told P.?* However, it is the intervention of this memory that transposes the rebuke of coming too late from the present to my time in Brücke's laboratory. And in replacing the second figure in the annihilation-scene of the dream by someone called *Josef*, I make this scene represent not only the rebuke that I have come too late, but also the charge more strongly affected by repression: that I cannot keep a secret. The dream's work of condensation and displacement, as well as the motives for it, are evident here.

However, my petty present-day annoyance at the warning not to reveal anything is reinforced from sources flowing in the depths, and thus augmented, it swells to a torrent of hostile feelings towards persons who in real life are dear to me. The source providing the reinforcement flows at the infantile level. I have already related how my warm friendships and my enmities with my contemporaries go back to the company I kept as a child with my nephew, one year older than I. In our relations he had the upper hand; I learned to defend myself early; we were inseparable from each other; we loved each other; in between, so our elders tell me, we fought and—*told tales on each other*. All my friends are in some sense incarnations of this first figure, 'who came before my clouded gaze so long ago',* *revenants*. My nephew himself came back to visit as an adolescent, and then we performed Caesar and Brutus together. An intimate friend and a hated foe have always been necessary to my emotional life; I have always been able to create for myself fresh embodiments of both, and not infrequently my childhood ideal went so far that friend and foe coincided in the same person—no longer at the same time, of course, or switching repeatedly from one to the other, which was probably the case in my earliest childhood years.

At this point I do not intend to pursue the way in which, given such circumstances, a recent occasion for affect is able to hark back to one from infancy, in order to use it as a substitute for itself to produce the affect. It belongs to the psychology of unconscious thinking, and would have its proper place in a psychological explanation of the neuroses. Let us assume for purposes of interpreting the dream that a memory from childhood or one created in fantasy presents itself, with something like the following content: the two children start quarrelling over some object—exactly what, we can leave open, although the recollection, or the illusory recollection, has something quite definite in mind;—each one of them maintains that he *came sooner*, that is, he has first claim on it; a fight develops; might is right; the dream suggests that I could have known I was in the wrong (*I notice my mistake*); but this time I am the stronger; I hold the field; the defeated combatant hurries to my father, his grandfather; tells on me, and I defend myself with the words familiar from my father's account: *I hit him because he hit me.* Thus, this memory, or more probably fantasy, which forces its way into my mind in the course of the analysis—without further evidence, I myself don't know how—is a central part of the dream-thoughts, gathering the affects prevailing there in the same way as a fountain-bowl collects the waters streaming into it. From here the dream-thoughts flow along the following channels: it serves you right that you have to get out of the way for me; why did you want to get me out of the way? I don't need you, I'll find someone else to play with, etc. Then the channels open up along which these thoughts return and flow into the dream-representation again. I must have charged my dead friend Josef with some such 'Ôte-toi que je m'y mette'* at the time. He had followed in my footsteps in Brücke's laboratory, but promotion there was slow and difficult. Neither of the two assistants showed signs of moving. The young scientists were growing impatient. My friend, who knew he did not have many years to live, and who had no obligations to the man ahead of him from any bonds of intimacy, was on occasion loud in expressing his impatience. As the member of staff ahead of him was a very sick man, the wish to get him out of the way, besides implying 'by promotion', also admitted an odious secondary meaning. Some years earlier I had naturally felt the same wish even more strongly to take up a position that had been vacated. Wherever there are hierarchies and promotions to be found in the world, the way is clear for wishes requiring suppression. Not even at the bed of his sick father can Shakespeare's Prince Hal* avoid the temptation of trying on the crown to see how it suits him. But, as one might expect, my dream punishes Josef, not me, for this ruthless wish.[32]

'As he was ambitious, I slew him.'* As he could not wait for the other to get out of the way for him, the dream got him out of the way. I nurse these thoughts right after attending the unveiling of the memorial to the other at the university. So one part of the satisfaction I felt in my dream can be interpreted as: a just punishment; it serves you right.

At my friend's funeral, a young man made the apparently unsuitable remark that the speaker addressed us as though the world could not go on without this one human being. He was protesting as a truthful person whose grief was offended by exaggeration. But my dream-thoughts connect with what he said: no one is really irreplaceable; how many I have already accompanied to the grave; but I am still alive, I have outlived them all, I hold the field. Such a thought, in the moment when I fear I shall not meet my friend again among the living when I make the journey to see him, allows the interpretation to unfold in only one way: once again I am glad to outlive someone; glad that it is not *I* who am dead, but *he*; that I hold the field as I did then in the fantasy of that childhood scene. This satisfaction, deriving from an infantile level, that I hold the field accounts for the greater share of the affect taken up into the dream. I am delighted that I am the survivor, I express it with the naive egoism of the married couple in the anecdote: 'If one of us dies, I'll go and live in Paris.' In my expectations, it goes without saying that I am not the one.

[32] It will have been noticed that the name of *Josef* plays such a large part in my dreams (see the dream of my uncle). In my dreams it is particularly easy for me to conceal my self behind figures with this name, for *Joseph* was also the name of the well-known *dream-interpreter* in the Bible.

One cannot deny that it requires arduous self-conquest to interpret and report one's own dreams. The interpreter has to expose himself as the only villain among all the noble figures who share his life. So I find it quite understandable that the *revenants* should only exist for as long as one wants them to, and that they can be removed at a wish. That is, of course, what my friend Josef was punished for. However, the *revenants* form the sequence of incarnations of my childhood friend; so I am also satisfied that I have replaced this figure over and over again, and a replacement will soon turn up for the one I am now about to lose. No one is irreplaceable.

But what has become of the dream-censorship in this? Why doesn't it raise the strongest objections to this grossly selfish train of thought, and transform the satisfaction clinging to it into grave unpleasure? I think it is because other, unobjectionable trains of thought about the same figures also end in satisfaction, and cover with their affect the one from the forbidden infantile source. In another stratum of my thoughts, I said to myself at that solemn unveiling of the memorial: I have lost so many dear friends, one through death, another when our friendship broke up; it is good, all the same, that I have found a replacement for them and gained this one friend who means more to me than the others could; and now, at the age when it is no longer easy to make new friendships, I shall hold him close for ever. I can transfer my satisfaction at having found this substitute for my lost friends into my dream undisturbed, but the hostile satisfaction from the infantile source slips in behind it too. Certainly, infantile tenderness helps to reinforce my present-day, justified affection; but infantile hatred, too, has made its way into the dream-representation.

In addition, however, the dream contains a distinct allusion to another train of thought which is allowed to end in satisfaction. After long waiting, my friend had shortly before had a baby daughter. I know how much he had mourned the early loss of his sister, and I wrote to him that he would transfer to this child the love he felt for his sister. At last this little girl would make him forget his irreplaceable loss.

So this sequence, too, again links on to the intermediary thoughts of the latent dream-content, from which the paths diverge in opposite directions: no one is irreplaceable. Look, only *revenants*; everyone we have lost returns to us. And now the associative bonds between the contradictory components of the dream-thoughts are drawn closer by the chance circumstance that my friend's little daughter has the same name as my own little playfellow, who was the same age as I was, the sister of my oldest friend and rival. I heard the name 'Pauline' with *satisfaction*, and as an allusion to this coincidence, I substituted one Josef for another Josef in my dream, and found it impossible to suppress the same initial sound in the names Fleischl and Fl. This becomes the starting-point then for a line of thought to the naming of my own children. I insisted that their names should not be chosen according to fashion, but should be in remembrance of persons dear to us. Their names turn the children into *revenants*. And finally, is having children not the only access any of us has to *immortality*?

I shall only add a few more remarks from another angle on affects in dreams. It is possible for a tendency to an affect—what we call a mood—to be present in the sleeper's psyche as the dominant element and then for it to share in determining the dream. This mood can proceed from the experiences and thoughts of the day; it can have somatic origins; in both cases they will be accompanied by the trains of thought appropriate to them. As far as the formation of dreams is concerned, it does not matter whether the content of imagined ideas in the dream-thoughts is the primary determinant of the tendency to affect, or whether it is itself aroused secondarily by the sleeper's emotional disposition, which can be explained by its somatic basis. In all cases, dream-formation operates under restriction: it can only represent a wish-fulfilment, and it is only from the wish that it can draw its psychic energy. The currently active mood will be treated in the same way as active sensation during sleep (see p. 181), which is either ignored, or reinterpreted as a wish-fulfilment. Moods of distress in sleep become the driving forces of the dream as they arouse energetic wishes which the dream is intended to fulfil. The material they cling to is worked over until it becomes usable as an expression for fulfilling them. The more intense and dominant the mood of distress is as an element in the dream-thoughts, the more certain it is that the most strongly suppressed wishes will use this opportunity to get themselves represented. For unpleasure, which they usually have to generate for themselves, is already present and active, so they discover that the most difficult part of their efforts to become

represented has already been done. And this discussion touches once
again on the problem of anxiety-dreams, which will turn out to be
the borderline case for dreams and their functioning.

(h)* *Secondary Revision*

Let us at last raise the subject of the fourth factor in the formation of
dreams.

If we continue our examination of the dream-content in the way
we have been doing, by referring occurrences that strike us as noticeable in the dream-content back to their origins, we will come upon
elements which will need an entirely fresh assumption to explain
them. I have in mind those instances where the dreamer is astonished or annoyed as he dreamed, or where he recoiled—in fact from
part of the dream-content itself. Most of these stirrings of criticism
in our dreams are not aimed at the dream-content but, as I have
shown from suitable examples, they turn out to be parts of the
dream-material taken over into the dream and put to appropriate use
there. However, some criticism in a dream refuses to be accommodated by a derivation of this kind; it is not possible to find its
correlate in the dream-material. What is the meaning, for instance,
of the criticism we meet quite frequently in a dream: 'After all, it's
only a dream'? This is a real criticism of the dream, of the sort I
could make when awake. Quite often, too, it is just the forerunner of
our waking; more frequently it is itself preceded by a feeling of
distress which is put to rest by telling ourselves that we are dreaming. However, the thought: 'After all, it's only a dream' while we are
still dreaming has the same intention as the one Helen of Troy* gives
it on the open stage in Offenbach's comic opera; it wants to reduce
the significance of what has just been experienced and help to make
what follows bearable. It serves to lull to sleep a certain agency,
which might have every cause to stir at the given moment and forbid
the continuation of the dream—or scene. But it is more convenient
to go on sleeping and endure the dream 'because it's only a dream
after all'. As I see it, the scornful criticism, 'after all, it's only a
dream', occurs in the dream when the censorship, which never falls
entirely asleep, feels caught unawares by the dream that has already
been admitted. It is too late to suppress it; accordingly, the censorship responds with this comment to the anxiety or feeling of distress

aroused by the dream. It is an expression of the *esprit d'escalier* on the part of the psychical censorship.

However, this example offers indisputable proof that not everything contained in the dream comes from the dream-thoughts, but rather that a function of the psyche indistinguishable from our waking thoughts can make some contribution to the dream-content. Now the question is whether this is wholly exceptional, or whether the psychical agency which usually only functions as censorship may claim to have a regular share in the formation of dreams.

We are bound to decide unhesitatingly for the latter. There is no doubt that the censoring agency, whose influence we have so far observed only in restrictions and omissions in the dream-content, is also responsible for interpolations and additions. These interpolations are often easy to recognize; they are announced timidly, introduced with an 'as if', are not in themselves particularly vivid, and they are always to be found in places where they can function to link two bits of the dream-content or set up a connection between two parts of the dream. The memory retains them less easily than the true offspring of the dream-material; if the dream is forgotten, they are the first to vanish, and I have the strong suspicion that our frequent complaint that we have dreamed so much but forgotten most of it and retained only fragments is due to the prompt disappearance of just these cementing thoughts. In a complete analysis these interpolations sometimes betray themselves because no material relating to them is to be found in the dream-thoughts. However, on closer scrutiny I have to say that this case occurs less frequently; still, these connecting thoughts do on the whole allow us to trace them back to material in the dream-thoughts, but material which was not able, either on its own account or by virtue of its over-determination, to claim admittance into the dream. It would seem that the psychical function in dream-formation we are now considering will make the effort to produce new creations only in extreme cases; as long as possible, it will turn to account whatever it is able to select as being suitable from the dream-material.

What marks this part of the dream-work out and exposes it to view is its purpose. This function proceeds rather as the poet* maliciously declares philosophers do: with its snippets and scraps it patches the gaps in the dream's structure. The result of its labours is that the dream loses its appearance of absurdity and incoherence, and approaches the pattern of an intelligible experience. But its labours are not always crowned with total success. In this way, dreams come about which might appear perfectly logical and rational; they start out from a plausible situation, continue it through changes free of contradictions, and bring it—though this happens less often—to an unsurprising conclusion. These dreams have gone through a very deep and thorough working-over from this function of the psyche which resembles waking thought; they seem to make sense, but this sense is also furthest from the real meaning of the dream. If we analyse them, we are convinced that here the secondary revision of the dream has played around with the material most freely, and retained the relations in it least. These are dreams that have already been interpreted, you might say, before we submit them to interpretation when we are awake. There are other dreams where this purposeful revision has only partially succeeded; coherence seems to be in control up to a point, then the dream becomes non-sensical or confused, and then perhaps for the second time in its course it goes on to make ostensible sense. In other dreams the revision has given up entirely; we are helpless in the face of a mean-ingless heap of fragmentary material.

I would not like to declare out of hand that this fourth shaping power has no capacity to contribute something new to the dream, for after all, it will soon appear that we are acquainted with it, indeed, it is the only one among our four dream-composers we are already familiar with. However, it is certainly the case that its influence, like that of the others, is manifested mainly in the preference and choice it makes from already-formed psychical material in the dream-thoughts. There is only one case where it is largely spared its work of building a façade onto the dream, as it were, and that is if such a structure is already present in the material of the dream-thoughts, ready and waiting to be used. The element in the dream-thoughts I have in mind I usually call a *fantasy*; it will avoid misunderstandings, perhaps, if I identify the *daydream*[33] as its equivalent in waking life. The part played by this element in the life of the psyche has not yet been fully recognized or revealed; M. Benedikt has made a start, and a very promising one, it seems to me, with his assessment. The significance of the daydream has not escaped the unerring insight of

---

[33] *Rêve, petit roman*—daydream, story.*

the poets; Alphonse Daudet's description of the daydreams of one of the minor figures in his *Nabab** is widely known. The study of the psychoneuroses leads to the surprising insight that these fantasies or daydreams are the immediate predecessors of hysterical symptoms—at least of a large number of them; hysterical symptoms cling not to the memories themselves but only to the fantasies constructed on the basis of the memories. The frequent occurrence of conscious fantasies during the day draws our attention to these formations; but just as conscious fantasies of this kind exist, there are also plenty of unconscious ones which cannot but remain unconscious because of their content and their origin in repressed material. If we immerse ourselves more deeply in the nature of these daytime fantasies, we find that they are quite justifiably called by the same name that we give to the productions of our thinking at night: *dreams*. They share certain essential characteristics with our night-time dreams; investigating them could actually have opened up for us the best and nearest access to understanding dreams.

Like dreams, they are wish-fulfilments; like dreams, they are based in large part on our infantile experiences; like dreams they enjoy a certain relaxation of the censorship for their creations. If we go in pursuit of their structure, we become aware of how the wishful motive at work in their production and the material from which they are constructed are thrown into confusion, rearranged, and composed into a new whole. Their relation to the childhood memories they go back to is rather like the relation of many of the baroque palaces in Rome to the ancient ruins whose stones and pillars have provided the material for building in more modern forms.

In the 'secondary revision' exercised on the dream-content which we have ascribed to our fourth shaping factor, we find the same activity as the one that expresses itself freely and unconfined by other influences in the creation of daydreams. We might say without further ado that our fourth factor attempts to shape *something like a daydream* out of the material available to it. But in cases where a daydream of this sort is already formed in the web of the dream-thoughts, this factor in the dream-work will for preference take over the daydream and aim for it to enter the dream-content. There are such dreams consisting only of the repetition of a daytime fantasy, for example, the dream of the boy that he was riding in the war-chariot with the heroes of the Trojan War. In my *Autodidasker* dream, the second part of the dream at least is a faithful repetition of a daytime fantasy, innocuous in itself, about my relations with Professor N. The fantasy already present more frequently forms only a part of the dream, or only a part of it gets through to the dream-content; this is due to the complicated conditions the dream has to satisfy as it emerges. Then the fantasy is usually treated like any other component of the latent material; but once in the dream it is often still recognizable as a whole. In my own dreams there are often parts that stand out, making a different impression from the rest. They appear fluent, more coherent, but also more evanescent than other parts of the same dream; I know these are unconscious fantasies entering my dream as a coherent part of it, but I have never succeeded in pinning any of them down. For the rest, these fantasies, like all the other components of the dream-thoughts, are jostled up against one another, they are condensed, they overlay one another and the like; but there are transitional instances between those cases where they are free to form the dream-content, or at least the dream-façade, almost without alteration, and those at the opposite end of the range where they are represented in the dream-content only by one of their elements, or by some remote allusion to one of them. Obviously what befalls the fantasies in the dream-thoughts will depend crucially on any advantages they may have to offer against the demands of the censorship and the pressures towards condensation.

In choosing my examples for interpretation, I have as far as possible steered clear of dreams in which unconscious fantasies have played a relatively important part, because the introduction of this element of the psyche would have required lengthy explanations of the psychology of unconscious thinking. Nevertheless, I cannot entirely avoid discussing 'fantasies' in the present context, as they frequently enter the dream fully fledged, and even more frequently shimmer clearly through it. I would perhaps mention just one more dream, which appears to be made up of two different fantasies, opposites, but overlapping each other in certain places; one of these is superficial, the other becomes, as it were, the interpretation of the first.

The dream—the only one I have no careful notes for—runs roughly as follows: the dreamer—a young bachelor—is sitting in his regular inn, which looks as it usually does; several people appear on the scene to take him away, among them one who makes to arrest him. He says to his companions at table: 'I'll pay later. I'll be back.' But they smile and sneer: 'We've heard that before. That's what they all say.' One guest calls after him: 'There's someone else on his way out!' He is then led into a small room where he finds a woman with a child in her arms. One of his escorts says: 'This is Herr Müller.' A commissioner, or some other kind of official, turns the pages of a pack of notes or papers, repeating as he does so: 'Müller, Müller, Müller.' Finally, he asks him a question, which he answers with 'Yes'. He then looks round for the woman, and notices that she has grown a large beard.

The two components here are easy to distinguish. The superficial one is a *fantasy of being arrested*, and seems to be freshly formed by the dream-work. But behind it, material that has been slightly adapted by the dream-work comes into view: the *fantasy of getting married*, and the features that both could have in common once again stand out with particular clarity, as in one of Galton's composite photographs. The promise made by the young man, still a bachelor so far, that he will come back to his regular place at table, the scepticism of his drinking fellows, who joke from long experience, 'There's someone else on his way out (to get married)', these items make good sense in the other reading as well. So does the answer 'Yes' that he gives the official. Leafing through a pile of papers and repeating the same name the while correspond to a minor, but recognizable feature of marriage celebrations, that is, reading out the telegrams of congratulation arriving in piles, which are, of course, all addressed to the same name. With the personal appearance of the bride in this dream, the marriage-fantasy has even triumphed over the fantasy of being arrested which covers it. I was able to clear up the bride's beard at the end of the dream by making an inquiry—we did not get as far as an analysis. The day before, the dreamer had crossed the road with a friend who was just as averse to marriage as he was, and the friend had drawn his attention to a pretty brunette coming towards them. However, the friend had remarked: 'Fine, if only these women didn't grow beards like their fathers as they get older.'

Naturally, there are plenty of elements in this dream where dream-distortion has been at work more deeply and thoroughly. It may be that the words 'I'll pay later' refer to the way he fears his father-in-law might behave with regard to the dowry. Obviously all sorts of doubts are holding the dreamer back from relaxing and enjoying his marriage-fantasy. One of these doubts—that with marriage he will lose his freedom—was embodied in the transformation of the scene into an arrest.

If we return to our proposition that the dream-work is happy to make use of a fantasy already present and available instead of putting a new one together out of the material in the dream-thoughts, this insight may perhaps solve one of the most interesting puzzles offered by dreams. On page 24, I related a dream of Maury's [48], who was struck on the back of his neck by a board and woke from a long dream, a complete novel, set in the time of the French Revolution. As the claim is made that the dream was coherent, and its explanation is ascribed wholly to the stimulus that woke the sleeper, one quite out of his ken, all we seem to be left with is the one assumption that the entire dream, in all its profusion, must have been composed and set in train in the brief space of time between the moment the board fell onto the vertebra of Maury's nape and his waking up on account of the blow. We would not dare to ascribe such speed to the activity of our waking thoughts, so this might lead us to grant that the dream-work has the advantage of remarkable acceleration as the dream unfolds.

This conclusion quickly became popular, but recent authorities (Le Lorrain [45], Egger [20], and others) have raised strong objections to it. Partly they are sceptical of the accuracy of Maury's account of his dream, partly they are trying to prove that our speed of thinking in waking life is no less than that of our dreams, whose feats need not be played down. The discussion raises questions of principle whose answers seem to me to be still very far away. But I must confess that I do not find the arguments—Egger's, for example—convincing, especially his objections to Maury's guillotine dream. I would suggest the following explanation for this dream: would it be so very unlikely that Maury's dream might represent a fantasy which was preserved ready-made for years in his memory and was roused—I would say *alluded to*—when he responded to the stimulus that woke him? To start with, this disposes of the whole difficulty of composing such a long story with all its details in the extremely short space of time available to the dreamer; it is already composed. If the board had struck the back of Maury's neck while he was awake, there would have been room for a thought such as: 'that is just as if I were being guillotined.' But since he was struck while he was asleep, the dream-work quickly made use of the stimulus reaching it to produce a wish-fulfilment, *as if* it were thinking (this is to be taken entirely in a figurative sense): 'This is a good opportunity to make the wishful fantasy from my reading of yore come true.' It seems beyond dispute to me that the romance he dreamed is just the sort an adolescent habitually makes up under the influence of powerful and exciting impressions. Who would not have felt gripped—especially if you were French, and a historian of culture—by descriptions from the Reign of Terror, when the nobility, men and women, the flower of the nation, showed how one could die with a serene spirit, and kept their sharp wit and delicate manners up to their fatal departure from this life? How attractive to fantasize that you are a young man in their midst, kissing your lady's hand as you bid her farewell, and climbing the scaffold unafraid! Or, if ambition was the main motive for the fantasy, to imagine yourself into the figure of one of those mighty individuals who, by the power of their thoughts and their blazing eloquence alone, rule the city at the time when the heart of humanity is throbbing there; who out of conviction send thousands of human beings to their deaths as they pave the way for the transformation of Europe; who, even as they do so, know that their own heads are not safe, and that one day they will lay them beneath the knife of the guillotine! To do so perhaps in the role of the Girondistes,* or the heroic Danton?* That Maury's fantasy was motivated by ambition seems to be suggested by the feature retained in his memory: 'accompanied by an enormous crowd'.

However, this fantasy, completed long ago, does not even need to be run through; it is enough if it is, as it were, 'touched on'. This is what I mean: if a few bars of music are quoted (as they are in *Don Giovanni**), and someone says 'That's from Mozart's *Marriage of Figaro*', then all of a sudden I am overwhelmed by a surge of memories and I cannot for the moment bring particular ones to consciousness. The stimulus-word acts as a breaching-place in my memory through which a whole mass of recollections are set in motion all at the same time. It need not be any different in our unconscious thinking. The stimulus to waking rouses the psychical breaching-place, which opens up access to the entire guillotine-fantasy. But this will not run its full course while the fantasist is still asleep, only when he remembers it on waking up. Once awake, he remembers all the details of the fantasy that was touched on as a whole in his dream. But he has no means of being certain that he is remembering something he has really dreamed. The same explanation—that it is a question of ready-made fantasies roused in their entirety by the stimulus to waking—can be applied to other dreams dependent on a stimulus to waking, for example, Napoleon's dream of a battle just before the infernal machine went off. I do not want to assert that all dreams upon waking admit of this explanation, or that the general problem of acceleration in the course of the dream can be disposed of in this way.

We are now at the stage where we cannot avoid dealing with the relationship of this secondary revision of the dream-content to the other factors governing the dream-work. Does the process go something like this: the dream-forming factors—the efforts of condensation, the compulsion to escape the censorship, and regard for representability by the psychical means available to dreams—first form a provisional content out of the material given, and then this is reshaped retrospectively until it answers the requirements of a second agency as best it can? This is hardly likely. We should rather assume that the requirements set by this factor make one of the conditions the dream has to satisfy, and that this condition will operate by selecting from the broad mass of material in the dream-thoughts, enabling them to enter the dream, that is, it will function just as the factors of condensation, the censorship set up by resistance, and representability do. However, of the four conditions we have identified for the formation of dreams, this most recent one is in any case the one whose requirements appear to be the least compelling for the dream. It is highly likely that our identification of this psychical function, which performs what we have called the secondary revision of the dream-content, with the operation of our waking thought, arises from the following consideration: our waking (preconscious) thought behaves towards whatever random material presents itself to our perception in the same way as the function in question behaves towards the dream-content. It comes naturally to it to create order out of such material, to set up relations and locate it where we can expect an intelligible context. But this is probably going too far. The reason we are fooled by conjurers' tricks is because they rely on this intellectual habit of ours. In our efforts to make a coherent and intelligible whole of the sensory impressions presenting themselves to us, we often make the oddest mistakes or even falsify the truth of the material before us. The proofs of this are too widely known to need further demonstration. We read over misprints that spoil the sense, and create an illusion of the correct word. One editor of a widely read French journal is said to have dared to bet that in the course of printing he would have 'from the front' or 'from behind' slipped into every sentence of a long article without one of his readers noticing. He won the bet. Reading a newspaper some years ago, I was struck by an amusing example of making the wrong connection. After that sitting of the French Chamber of Deputies when Dupuy's* brave words 'La séance continue' put an end to the alarm caused by the explosion when an anarchist's bomb was thrown into the Chamber, visitors to the gallery were questioned as witnesses about their impressions of the assassination attempt. Among them were two visitors up from the provinces; one of them said he had certainly heard an explosion right after the end of a speech, but had thought it was the custom in Parliament to fire a shot whenever a speaker had finished. The other, who had probably heard several speakers already, made the same judgement, but with the variation that shots of this kind were made as a commendation, and only happened after particularly successful speeches.

It is probable, then, that the agency requiring the dream-content to be intelligible is none other than our normal thinking; it subjects it to a first interpretation, and by doing so brings about its complete misunderstanding. For our interpretation, it remains mandatory in all cases to pay no attention to the ostensible coherence of a dream, as having a suspect source, and to take the same route back to the dream-material, whether the dream is lucid or confused.

As we do so, however, we recall from our earlier discussion (p. 251) what it is that the qualitative scale from confusion to clarity essentially depends upon. The parts of the dream that appear clear to us are the ones where the secondary revision was able to accomplish something; in the other parts, which seem confused, the powers of this ability failed. As the confused parts of the dream are also very often less vivid and distinctive, we may draw the conclusion that the secondary dream-work is also to be held responsible for some contribution to the intensity of sensuous realization in particular elements of the dream.

If I am to look anywhere for something comparable to the definitive formation of a dream when normal thinking has a share in shaping it, the only things that come to mind are those puzzling inscriptions with which the *Fliegende Blätter* used to entertain its readers for so long. They set up the expectation that a certain sentence—in dialect for the contrast and with as comical a meaning as possible—contained a Latin inscription. To do this, the letters of the words are torn out of their proper order as syllables and rearranged. Now and again a genuine Latin word will come about, in other parts we think we can see abbreviations of such words, and in other parts of the inscription again we are willing to be taken in by the meaninglessness of solitary letters, assuming that the passages are apparently weathered, or that there are gaps in the inscription. If we don't want to be taken in by the joke, we have to ignore all the requirements for an inscription, keep our eye on the letters, and, without troubling about the required arrangement, put them together to make words in our mother-tongue.

I shall now set about summing up this lengthy discussion of the dream-work. We were confronted with the question of whether the psyche applies all its powers without any restrictions to the formation of dreams, or whether it employs only a fragment of them, inhibited in capability. Our investigations lead us to reject the terms of this question entirely, as inappropriate to the situation. Indeed, if we were to reply on the same terrain as the question, we should have to answer both views in the affirmative, even though as opposites they appear to be mutually exclusive. The work of the psyche in the formation of dreams can be broken down into two tasks: it generates the dream-thoughts, and it transforms them into the dream-content. The dream-thoughts are entirely reasonable, and are formed with all the expense of psychical energy we are capable of; they belong to that dimension of our thinking which has not become conscious, and from which, by some transposition, our conscious thoughts also arise. However many unanswered questions and puzzles the dream-thoughts raise, all the same these puzzles do not have any particular relation to dreams, and do not merit treatment among the problems of dreams. On the other hand, the other task of transforming the unconscious thoughts into the dream-content is peculiar to the life of dreams and characteristic of it. This is the true dream-work, and it is far more remote from the model of waking thought than even the most determined belittlers of the psyche's feats of dream-formation have thought. It is not that it is more negligent, more unreasonable, more forgetful, more incomplete, say, than waking thought; it is qualitatively something completely different from it, and so at first not comparable to it. It does not think, calculate, judge in any way at all; it confines itself to reshaping. It can be described exhaustively if we keep our eye on the conditions which its product has to satisfy. Above all, this product—the dream—has to be removed from the influence of the *censorship*, and for this purpose the dream-work makes use of the *displacement of psychical intensities* to the point of a transvaluation of all psychical values; thoughts are to be reproduced exclusively or predominantly in terms of the material provided by visual and aural memory-traces, and this requires the dream-work to *take account of representability*, which it does by setting up new displacements. Greater intensities than the dream-thoughts have at their disposal at night are (probably) to be created, and this purpose is served by the ample *condensation* undertaken with the elements of the dream-thoughts. Little account is taken of the logical relations in the thought-material; they are ultimately given a hidden representation in particular *formal* features of the dreams. The affects of the dream-thoughts are subject to lesser modifications than the imagined ideas of their content are. As a rule they are suppressed; where they are retained, they are separated from their ideas and combined with affects of a similar tonality. Only one part of the dream-work, the revisions, variable in extent, made by our partially roused waking thought, conforms to the conception our authorities would apply to the entire activity of dream-formation.

VII

THE PSYCHOLOGY OF THE DREAM-PROCESSES

Among the dreams I have learned of through others, there is one that now has very special claims on our attention. It was told me by a patient who had heard it herself in a lecture on dreams; its actual source remains unknown to me. However, its content made an impression on the lady, for she very soon 'copy-dreamed' it, that is, repeated elements of the dream in a dream of her own, using this transference to express a point of resemblance to it.

The prior conditions for this model dream are as follows: for days and nights a father has been watching at his child's sickbed. After the child's death, he lies down to rest in a room nearby, but leaves the doors open so that he can look from his bedroom into the room where the child's body is laid out, surrounded by tall candles. An old man has been set to keep watch, sitting near the body and murmuring prayers. After a few hours' sleep, the father dreams *that the child is standing at his bedside, grasps him by the arm and whispers to him reproachfully, 'Father, can't you see that I am burning?'* He wakes up, notices a bright light coming from the room where the body is lying, hurries over, and finds the old attendant fallen asleep, the shroud and an arm of the beloved body burnt by a lighted candle that had fallen across it.

The explanation of this touching dream is simple enough, and was also given correctly by the lecturer, so my patient informed me. The bright light came through the open doors and fell on the father's eyes, leading him to draw the same conclusion as he would have made if he had been awake: that a fire had started when a candle fell over near the body. Perhaps the father had carried into his sleep the worry that the aged attendant might not be up to his job.

We too would find nothing to alter in this interpretation, unless it were to add the condition that the content of the dream must be over-determined, and that what the child said must have been put together from words he had really used in life in a context of events that were important to the father. Such as the complaint 'I'm burning'—of his feverishness when he died, and the words: 'Father, can't you see?' on some other occasion unknown to us, but charged with deep affect.

However, after we have acknowledged this dream to be a meaningful occurrence with a proper place in the context of what was going on in the father's psyche, we might well wonder that under such circumstances a dream came about at all, when it was advisable to wake up as quickly as possible. We will notice then that this dream too is not without its wish-fulfilment. In the dream the dead child behaves as if he were alive, he warns his father himself, he comes up to his bed and tugs him by the arm, just as he probably did in that memory from which the dream took the first bit of what the child said. Now, it was for the sake of this wish-fulfilment that the father prolonged his sleep for a moment. He gave the dream a prior claim over his waking reflection because it was able to show him the child alive again. If he had woken first and then drawn the conclusion that took him into the room where the child's body was lying, he would have shortened the child's life by this one moment, as it were.

There can be no doubt which distinctive feature of this little dream has captured our interest. So far we have mainly been concerned with probing after the hidden meaning of dreams, the route we should take to discover it, and the means the dream-work has employed to hide it. And now we come upon this dream, which offers no problems of interpretation, whose meaning is given undisguised, and we note that it still retains the essential characteristics that distinguish a dream sharply from our waking thought and rouse our need for explanation. Only when we have got rid of everything that has to do with the work of interpretation can we see how incomplete our psychology of dreams still is.

But before we take our thoughts along this new path, let us pause and look back, to see whether on our journey so far we have not left anything important unremarked. For we must be clear in our minds: the stretch of our way that makes for easy going lies behind us. Until now, if I am not much mistaken, all the paths we have trodden have led us into the light, to enlightenment and to full understanding; from the moment we propose to go more deeply into the psyche's inner processes of dreaming, all our ways lead into the dark. It is impossible for us to get as far as *explaining* the dream as a psychical process, for explaining means tracing back to what is already known, and at present the psychological knowledge does not exist that we could use as an explanatory framework for what we have been able to deduce from our psychological scrutiny of dreams. On the contrary, we shall be obliged to put forward a set of new assumptions touching speculatively on the structure of the psychical apparatus and the play of forces active in it, though we must take care not to spin them out too far beyond their first logical links, for if we do, their worth will vanish into uncertainty. Even if we make no errors of deduction, and take account of all the logical possibilities, there is still the threat that our calculations will go utterly wrong because the elements we start from are probably incomplete. There is no possibility of acquiring any information about—or at least of accounting for—how the instrument of our psyche is constructed or how it operates, from even the most careful examination of the dream or of any other psychical attainment *by itself*; for this, we will have to compare a number of the psyche's functions and from this study compile the requirements that turn out to be constants among them all. As we do so, the psychological assumptions that we draw from our analysis of dream-processes will have to wait at the station, as it were, until they have caught the connection to the results of other investigations attempting to reach the heart of the same problem from another point of attack.

(a) *Forgetting in Dreams*

I suggest, then, that we should first turn to a topic that raises an objection we have so far disregarded, but which is apt to cut the ground from under our efforts at dream-interpretation. We have heard the charge from more than one side that we do not have any actual knowledge of the dream we are proposing to interpret, or, more correctly, we have no guarantee that we know it in the way it really happened (compare p. 40). What we remember of the dream, and what we practise our arts of interpretation upon, is first of all damaged by the inaccuracy of our memory, which seems to be particularly incapable of retaining the dream, and in fact has probably lost the most important part of its content. Indeed, when we want to pay attention to our dreams, we so often find that we have cause to complain that we dreamed much more, but unfortunately we cannot remember any more than this one fragment, and even that seems to us curiously uncertain. Secondly, everything suggests that our memory not only reproduces the dream incompletely and inaccurately, but also falsifies it. Just as on the one hand one may doubt whether the dream really was as incoherent and confused as we relate it, so on the other hand it is possible to query whether it was as coherent as we relate it, whether in attempting to reproduce it we are not filling gaps—which may indeed be there or have been created by our forgetting—with arbitrarily chosen new material, decorating, tidying up, rounding off our dream, so that any judgement as to what its real content was is rendered impossible. Indeed, we found one authority (Spitta [64]) surmising that any kind of order or coherence in the dream at all is imposed upon it only when we attempt to recall it. In this way, we are in danger of having the very object whose value we have undertaken to assess wrested from our hands.

In our interpretations so far we have not listened to these warnings. Indeed, we have found the smallest, the most inconspicuous, the most uncertain components of the dream's content demanding interpretation no less audibly than its distinct and securely retained elements. In the dream of Irma's injection, there are the words: 'I *quickly* summon Dr. M.', and we assumed that even this extra little item would not have got into the dream if it did not admit of a particular derivation. In this way we arrived at the story of that unfortunate patient to whose bedside I 'quickly' summoned my older colleague. In the ostensibly absurd dream that treats the difference between 51 and 56 as a *quantité négligeable*, the number 51 was mentioned several times. Instead of taking this for granted or finding it unimportant, we inferred from it a second train of thought in the latent dream-content which led us to the number 51, and the trace we then pursued further led us to our fear that the age of 51 sets a limit to our life, all in sharpest contrast to a dominant trait of thought which was lavish in its grandiose expenditure of the days of our years. In the *Non vixit* dream there was the inconspicuous little insertion, which at first I did not notice: '*As P. doesn't understand him, Fl. asks me etc.*'. When the interpretation then came to a halt, I went back to these words and discovered the route from them to the childhood fantasy that makes its entrance into the dream-thoughts as an intermediary junction-point. It happened via the poet's lines:

Selten habt Ihr mich *verstanden*,
Selten auch verstand ich Euch,
Nur wenn wir im *Koth* uns fanden
So verstanden wir uns gleich!*

Seldom did you understand me,
Nor I you, in all the past;
Only when in filth we land, we
Understand each other fast.   (tr. Hal Draper)

Examples from every analysis could confirm how it is precisely the slightest features of a dream that are indispensable for its interpretation, and how long the delay in completing the task drags out if we notice these things only late in the day. In interpreting dreams, we paid equal attention to every nuance of the verbal form in which the dream before us was expressed; indeed, if we were presented with nonsensical or inadequate wording, as if the effort to translate the dream into the right version had not succeeded, we heeded these faults of expression as well. In short, what in the opinion of our authorities is supposed to be an arbitrary improvisation, concocted when at a loss, we have been treating like a sacred text. This contradiction needs explaining.

The explanation is in our favour, though without putting the other writers in the wrong. From the point of view of our newly gained insights into the origins of dreams, the contradictions are reconciled in their entirety. It is correct that we garble the dream in our attempt to reproduce it; in this distortion we meet again what we have called the secondary—and often misleading—revision of the dream by the agency of normal thinking. But this distortion is itself nothing but a part of the revision which the dream-thoughts regularly* undergo as a consequence of the censorship. In this regard, the authorities have senses or seen that part of the dream-distortion is at work in the manifest dream; this is of little use to us, for we know that a much more far-reaching work of distortion, less easy to grasp, has already chosen the dream, motivated by the hidden dream-thoughts. The authorities are wrong only in regarding the modifications the dream undergoes when remembered and put into words as being arbitrary, impossible to interpret further, and so very likely to put us on the wrong track in understanding the dreams. They underestimate the factor of determination in matters of the psyche. Nothing is arbitrary there. It can be shown quite generally that a second train of thought will promptly take over the determination of an element left undetermined by the first. For example, I try to think of a number quite at random; it is not possible; the number that occurs to me is unambiguously and necessarily determined by thoughts within me that may well be quite remote from my present intention. The changes the dream goes through as we edit it when awake are just as far from being arbitrary. They are still linked by association to the content they replace, and they serve to point us the way to this content, which may itself in turn be the proxy for another.

When I am analysing their dreams with my patients I am in the habit of putting this assertion to the test, never without success, in the following way. If the account of a dream appears difficult for me to understand at first, I ask its narrator to repeat it. He rarely does so in the same words. But the passages where he has altered his narrative are the ones revealed to me as the weak spots in the dream's disguise; they serve me as the embroidered sign on Siegfried's cloak* served Hagen. That is where the dream-interpretation can make a start. The narrator has been warned that I intend to take particular care in solving the dream; so under the pressure of resistance, he quickly protects the weak spots in the dream's disguise by replacing a revealing expression by one more remote. In this way he draws my attention to the expression he has dropped. From the trouble taken to defend the dream against being solved, I am able to infer how much care has gone into weaving the dream its cloak.

The authorities are less justified in devoting so much space to our doubts as we judge our accounts of dreams. For these doubts have no intellectual warrant; our memory has no guarantees at all, and yet we bow more often than is objectively justified to the compulsion to believe what it says. Our doubts about the correct reproduction of a dream, or particular items in a dream, are again only the offspring of the dream-censorship, our resistance to the possibility that the dream-thoughts might penetrate into consciousness. This resistance does not always come to an end with the displacements and substitutions it has carried out, it still clings to what has been allowed through in the form of doubts. We fail to recognize this doubt the more readily because it takes care never to attack intense elements in the dream, merely weak or indistinct ones. But by now we already know that between dream-thoughts and dream a total transvaluation of all psychical values has taken place; distortion was only made possible by the withdrawal of value, it invariably expresses itself in this way, and is sometimes content to leave it at that. If in addition some doubt comes and attaches to an indistinct element in the dream-content, we are able to follow this pointer and recognize the doubt as being a more direct descendant of one of the outlawed dream-thoughts. It is like the situation after a great upheaval in one of the republics of the Ancient World or the Renaissance. The powerful dynasties who once ruled are now banished, all the high positions are occupied by upstarts; in the city only utterly impoverished and powerless relatives or supporters of the overthrown powers are tolerated. But even these do not enjoy full civil rights and are mistrustfully kept under surveillance. In our case, the place of mistrust in the example is taken by doubt. That is why, when analysing a dream, I insist that any scale indicating degrees of certainty should be abandoned entirely, and the slightest possibility that something of one sort or another might have occurred in the dream should be treated as being absolutely definite. As long as anyone has not decided to let go of the question of certainty when tracing an element from the dream, the analysis will come to a standstill until he has. If the analysand dismisses the element in question as unimportant, the psychical effect will be that the involuntary ideas behind the element will not attempt to enter his head. An effect of this kind is not really a matter of course; it would not be absurd for someone to say: I am not certain whether this or that was contained in my dream, but the following comes to mind in relation to it. No one ever does say this, and it is this very effect of doubt which disturbs the analysis and unmasks it as the offspring and instrument of psychical resistance. Psychoanalysis is right to be mistrustful. One of its rules runs: *whatever disturbs the continuation of the work of analysis is a resistance*.

Forgetting dreams, too, will remain inexplicable unless we also include the power of the psychical censorship in our explanation of it. The feeling that we have dreamed a great deal in the night and only retained a little of it may have a different meaning in a number of cases, perhaps that the dream-work has palpably gone on right through the night and only left the one brief dream behind. In other cases, it is impossible to doubt the fact that after we wake we increasingly forget our dreams. We often forget them despite strenuous efforts to remember them. However, it is my view that just as we invariably overestimate the scope of this forgetting, we also over-estimate how much our knowledge of our dreams loses from their fragmentary and piecemeal nature. Everything we have lost in for-getting the dream-content can often be retrieved by the analysis; in a fair number of cases at least, it is possible to start from a single remaining shard and recover, if not the dream—but after all, that is not the important thing—then the dream-thoughts, all of them. It requires some effort of attention and self-overcoming on our part in the course of the analysis; that is all, but it does indicate that the act of forgetting the dream was not without a hostile purpose.

We are provided with convincing proof that forgetting our dreams is purposeful, serving the ends of psychical resistance,[1] when we observe a preliminary stage of forgetting in the course of certain analyses. It quite often happens that suddenly, in the middle of the work of interpretation, there comes to the surface a part of the dream that has been left out, but is described as forgotten until that moment. This part of the dream, rescued from oblivion, is always the most important part; it lies along the shortest route towards solving the dream and for that reason was most liable to be resisted. Among the examples of dreams I have included in the course of this treatise, there happens to be one where I have to interpolate a bit of dream-content retrospectively. It is my travelling-dream, the one that takes revenge on the lady who was my disagreeable travelling-companion,* which I have left almost uninterpreted, partly on account of its grossly indecent content. The omitted part runs: *I say [in English] about a book by Schiller: 'It is from . . .' but correct myself, noticing the error myself: 'It is by . . .' At that the man observes to his sister: 'He did say it correctly.'*

Self-correction in dreams, which seemed so marvellous to many of our authorities, probably does not require our attention. As the model for the linguistic error in this dream I shall rather point to one in my memory. I was seventeen years old,* making my first visit to England, and I spent a whole day on the shore of the Irish Sea. I was naturally lost in pleasure gathering the sea-creatures left behind by the tide, and I was just occupied with a starfish (the dream begins with *Hollthurn—holothurians* [sea-slugs]) when a charming little girl

---

[1] On the subject of intention in forgetting, compare my essay 'Über den psychischen Mechanismus der Vergeßlichkeit' ['The Physical Mechanism of Forgetfulness'], in the *Monatschrift für Psychiatrie und Neurologie*, 1898 [SE iii. 289].

came up to me and asked, 'Is it a starfish? Is it alive?' I replied, 'Yes, *he* is alive', but was then embarrassed at the inaccuracy, and repeated the sentence correctly. Instead of the linguistic error I made then, the dream replaces it by another, which is just as easy for a speaker of German to make. '*Das Buch ist von Schiller*' should not be translated as 'the book is from Schiller', but as 'by . . .' The dream-work makes this substitution because the matching sound of '*from*' creates a splendid condensation with the German adjective '*fromm*' ['pious']—and from all we have heard of the dream-work's intentions and of its ruthlessness in choosing its means, we should no longer be amazed that it should do so. But what does this innocuous memory of the seashore have to say in the context of my dream? It uses the most innocent example possible to elucidate my misuse of an article designating *gender*, introducing *gender and sex (he)* where it does not belong. This is of course one of the keys to solving the dream. Anyone who has heard where the title of the book *Matter and Motion* comes from (*Molière* in *Le Malade Imaginaire*: La *matière* est-elle laudable?*—a *motion* of the bowels) will be able to complete the interpretation himself.

I can, by the way, settle the question of adducing proof that forgetting dreams is to a large extent the work of resistance with a demonstration *ad oculos*. A patient tells me he has had a dream, but has forgotten it without a trace; at that stage it is simply counted as not having happened. We continue our work, I come upon a resistance, make something clear to the patient, by persuasion and pressure help him to reconcile himself to some unpleasant thought, and no sooner has this succeeded than he cries: 'Now I remember what it was I dreamed.' The same resistance that disturbed him in the day's work of analysis also made him forget his dream. By overcoming this resistance, I have coaxed the dream back into memory.

Similarly, a patient who has reached a certain point in the work of analysis is able to remember a dream that occurred three, four, or more days before, but which meantime has been reposing in oblivion.

An experience I had in the course of writing this manuscript is an indication that dreams are just as unforgotten as other acts of the psyche, and that in this respect too, in their persistence in the memory, they are the full equal of the psyche's other feats. I had kept notes of plenty of my own dreams which for some reason at the time I could only subject to a very incomplete interpretation, or to none at all. Now, one to two years later, I have made the attempt to interpret some of them, intending to use them as material to illustrate my assertions. The attempts were successful in every case; indeed, I would even say the interpretation went along more easily such a long time later than it did at the time when the dreams were still fresh in my experience. I would suggest that a possible explanation for this lies in the fact that meantime I have gone beyond a number of resistances within myself which were disturbing me then. In making these retrospective interpretations, I compared the results I had at the time in tracing the dream-thoughts with my current, mostly far richer, results, and discovered the earlier ones present unchanged among the new ones. I cut short any astonishment at this when I reflected that, after all, it has long been my practice to have my patients interpret dreams they sometimes tell me dating from earlier years, as though they were dreams from the previous night, according to the same method and with the same success. When I come to discuss anxiety-dreams, I shall report two examples of belated dream-interpretation of this kind. When I made this experiment for the first time, I was led by the justified expectation that in this respect too the dream would behave just like a neurotic symptom. For when treating a psychoneurotic, a hysteric, say, psychoanalytically, I have to find an explanation for the earliest symptoms of his complaint, long ago mastered and done with, as well as for the current symptoms that brought him to me; and I find it far easier to solve the former problem than the present, urgent, task. As early as my *Studies on Hysteria*,* published in 1895, I was able to give the explanation for the first hysterical attack which a woman of over forty suffered at the age of fourteen.

In a looser sequence, I should like to add some further observations on the interpretation of dreams, which will perhaps provide some orientation for the reader who wants to check my account by working on his own dreams.

No one would expect the interpretation of his dreams to fall into his lap without any effort. It needs practice just to become aware of endoptic phenomena and other sensations normally out of range of our attention, although there is no psychical motive to baulk at these perceptions. It is considerably more difficult to get hold of 'involuntary ideas'. Anyone wanting to do this will have to fulfil the conditions this treatise has raised, and in following the rules it has given, he must take pains to restrain any criticism, any prejudice, any bias of affect or intellect during the work of analysis. He will bear in mind the precept Claude Bernard* proposed for the experimenter in the physiological laboratory: 'Travailler comme une bête', that is, to work as doggedly as a beast, but also with as little concern about the results. Anyone following this advice will no longer find the task difficult. However, interpreting a dream is not always accomplished at one fell swoop; quite often one's interpretive powers feel at the end of their tether after pursuing a chain of ideas, when the dream ceases to say anything more that day; then it is as well to break off and return to the work of analysis another day. Then a different bit of the dream-content will draw attention to itself, and one gains access to a fresh stratum of the dream-thoughts. This procedure might be called 'fractional' dream-interpretation.

The most difficult thing is to persuade the beginner in dream-interpretation to recognize the fact that his task is not over when he has a complete interpretation of a dream in his hands, one that is meaningful and coherent, and enlightens him about all the elements in the dream-content. Besides this, it is possible that there is an overarching interpretation of the dream which has escaped him. It is really not easy to get an idea of the wealth of unconscious trains of thought in our thinking, all struggling for expression, nor to believe how clever the dream-work is in its polysemous mode of expression, killing seven flies at one blow, like the Little Tailor* in the fairy-tale, as it were. The reader will always be inclined to accuse the author of overloading every rift with ore; but anyone who has gained experience of interpretation himself will have learned better.

The question whether every dream is amenable to interpretation is to be answered by 'No'. It should not be forgotten that the interpreter has against him those same psychical powers that are responsible for the distortion in the dream. In this way it becomes a contest of relative strength whether one's intellectual interest, capacity for self-overcoming, psychological insight, and practice in the interpretation of dreams can master the inner resistances. For a stretch it is always possible, enough at least to be convinced that the dream is a meaningful formation, and mostly, also, to acquire an inkling of that meaning. Very often a dream following hard on the heels of the one we are interpreting will enable us to establish a reading we have assumed for the first, and to carry it further. A whole set of dreams, carrying on for weeks or months, often rests on common ground, and is to be interpreted in its interrelations. In cases where we have a sequence of dreams, it can often be noticed how one dream will take for its centre what the next only alludes to on the periphery, and the other way round, so that the two complement each other for purposes of interpretation as well. I have already used examples to show how the various dreams of the same night are quite regularly to be treated as a whole.

The best-interpreted dreams often have a passage that has to be left in the dark, because we notice in the course of interpretation that a knot of dream-thoughts shows itself just there, refusing to be unravelled, but also making no further contribution to the dream-content. This is the dream's navel, and the place beneath which lies the Unknown. Indeed, the dream-thoughts we come upon as we interpret cannot in general but remain without closure, spinning out on all sides into the web-like fabric of our thoughts. Out of a denser patch in this tissue the dream-wish then arises like a mushroom from its mycelium.

Let us return to the facts about forgetting dreams. For we have omitted to draw one important conclusion from them. If our waking life shows the unmistakable intention of forgetting the dream that was formed at night, either as a whole immediately after we wake, or bit by bit in the course of the day, and if we identify the main party to this forgetting as our psychical resistance to the dream—which has already done its utmost to the dream in the night—then the question arises, what has actually enabled the dream to be formed at all in face of this resistance? Let us take the most glaring case, when our waking life does away with the dream as though it had never happened. In this case, if we take the play of psychical forces into account, we would have to say that the dream would not have come into existence at all if the resistance had held sway at night as it does by day. Our conclusion is that during the night it has lost a part of its power; we know it has not been entirely suspended, for we have demonstrated the distorting part it plays in forming the dream. But we are aware of the possibility that it has been reduced at night, that this lowering of resistance makes the formation of dreams possible; and thus it is easy to understand how, once restored to full force on waking, it promptly gets rid of what it had to admit while it was weak. Indeed, descriptive psychology instructs us that the main condition for the formation of dreams is the sleeping state of the psyche; so we can now add the explanation: *the state of sleep makes the formation of dreams possible by reducing the endopsychic censorship*.

It is certainly tempting to regard this conclusion as the only one it is possible to draw from the facts about forgetting dreams, and to develop further inferences from it about the ratio of energy between sleeping and waking. However, let us pause here for the moment. Once we have immersed ourselves rather more deeply in the psychology of dreams, we will learn that there are still other ways of imagining how the formation of dreams is made possible. It might also be possible to evade the resistance to bringing the dream-thoughts into consciousness without the resistance being abated. It is also plausible that the state of sleep helps to bring about both the factors favourable to the formation of dreams at the same time, that is, the reduction of resistance as well as its evasion. Let us break off here, and pick up the thread a little later.

There is another set of objections to our procedure in interpreting dreams which we must now deal with. Of course we proceed by abandoning all the purposive ideas that normally dominate our reflections, concentrating on one particular element in the dream, and then noting what involuntary thoughts it calls up in us. Then we take up the next component in the dream-content, go through the same work with this one, and allow ourselves to be carried along by our thoughts with no care for the direction in which they are moving, even though they take us, as they say, all over the shop. We do so in the confident expectation that in the end, without any intrusion on our part, we shall come upon the dream-thought that gave rise to the dream. The objection made in criticism of this procedure runs more or less as follows: there is nothing wonderful about getting from one particular element in a dream to anywhere at all. *Something or other* can be linked by association to every idea; the only remarkable thing is that by this aimless and arbitrary drift of thoughts you are supposed to arrive straight at the dream-thoughts. That is probably a self-deception; you trace the train of associations from the one element until you note that for some reason it breaks off; if you take up a second element, it is only natural that the original openness of association should now undergo a certain limitation. You still have the earlier chain of thoughts in mind and so, when analysing the second imagined idea from the dream, thoughts come to mind which also have something in common with the earlier chain. Then you imagine you have found a thought which represents a junction-point between two dream-elements. As you allow yourself every liberty in combining thoughts, really excluding only the transitions from one idea to another that are operative in normal thinking, ultimately it is not difficult to take a sequence of 'intermediary thoughts' and concoct something you call the dream-thoughts, claiming with no warrant, as they are completely unknown, that these are the psychical replacement of the dream. But it is all arbitrary, a clever-seeming exploitation of sheer chance. And the person who subjects himself to this useless labour can take any old dream and along these lines conjure up any old interpretation.

If we are really presented with such objections, we can defend ourselves by referring to the impression our dream-interpretations make, to the surprising combinations with other dream-elements that emerge in the course of tracing particular imagined ideas, and to the unlikelihood that something that covers the dream as exhaustively and illuminatingly as one of our interpretations could be reached in any other way than by following the traces of psychical connections set up earlier. We could also justify ourselves by pointing out that our procedure when interpreting dreams is identical with our method in treating hysterical symptoms, where we do have a guarantee that the method is correct in the appearance and disappearance of symptoms in their place, that is, where our reading of the text is supported by the interpolated illustrations. However, there is no reason for us to avoid the problem of how it should be possible that, by tracing a chain of thoughts spinning out arbitrarily and aimlessly, we can reach a pre-existent destination, for though we cannot solve this problem, we are in a position to dispose of it completely.

For it is demonstrably wrong to say that we are being borne along an aimless flow of ideas when we relax our reflectiveness and let the involuntary ideas come to the surface, as we do when we are interpreting dreams. It can be shown that the only purposive ideas we are able to relinquish are the ones known to us, and the moment these cease, unknown—or, as we would loosely say, unconscious—purposive ideas take over and then determine the course taken by the involuntary ideas. There is no way that our own influence on the life of our psyche can bring about a kind of thinking without purposive ideas; nor am I acquainted with any state of psychical disorder that might do so. In this respect the psychiatrists have dispensed with the stability of the psyche's interconnected structure much too soon. I know that an uncontrolled flow of thoughts with no purposeful ideas is not present in hysteria or paranoia, just as it is not to be found in the formation or the solution of dreams. It may be that it does not occur at all in the endogenous psychical illness; even the delirious fantasies of the mad, according to Leuret's brilliant surmise, are meaningful, and are only unintelligible to us because of what they have left out. I have received the same conviction on the occasions I have had for observation myself. The delirious fantasies are the work of a censorship that no longer bothers to hide its supremacy, and instead of sharing in the creation of an inoffensive version, it ruthlessly deletes what it objects to—leaving the remainder incoherent. This censorship proceeds just like the Russian newspaper censorship at the borders; it allows foreign journals to come into the hands of the readers under its protection only when passages are heavily blacked out.

It may be that the free play of ideas along a random chain of associations is present in destructive organic processes of the brain; what is regarded as such in the psychoneuroses can be explained in every case by the effect of censorship on a sequence of thoughts thrust into the foreground by still hidden purposive ideas. It has been regarded as an unmistakable sign of associations without any purposive ideas if the imagined ideas (or images) coming to the surface appear to be connected to one another by the links of what we call superficial associations, that is, by assonance, verbal ambiguity, coincidence in time without any relation in meaning, all the associations we permit ourselves in jokes and word-play. This characteristic applies to the thought-connections that lead us from the elements in the dream-content to the collaterals and from these to the actual dream-thoughts; we have found examples of this in a number of dream-analyses, which were bound to arouse our surprise. No connection was too loose, no joke too bad to form the bridge from one thought to another. But we are not far from a true understanding of such indulgence. *Whenever one psychical element is connected with another by an offensive or superficial association, there also exists a proper and deeper link between the two, which is subject to the resistance of the censorship.*

The pressure of censorship, not the suspension of purposive ideas, is the real reason for the predominance of superficial associations. In the representation, the superficial associations replace the deep associations when the censorship has made the latter's normal connecting routes impassable. It is as if something causing a general traffic hold-up, a flood, for example, has made the broad highways in the mountains impassable; the traffic is kept going along steep and difficult footpaths, normally trodden only by the huntsman.

We can distinguish two cases here, though they are essentially one. In the first instance the censorship is aimed only at the connection between two thoughts which, when taken separately, are not subject to its disapproval. In this case, the two thoughts enter consciousness severally, one after the other; their connection remains hidden; instead, however, some superficial link between them occurs to us, which we would not otherwise have thought of, and which as a rule begins at a different corner of the complex of ideas from the place where the suppressed, but essential connection starts out. Alternatively, in the second case both thoughts are subject to the censorship in their own right, on account of their content; then neither appears in its proper form, but in some modified, substitute guise, and the two substitute thoughts are chosen in such a way that the superficial association between them reproduces the essential connection between the thoughts they have replaced. *In both these cases, under pressure from the censorship, a displacement has taken place from a normal association, to be taken seriously, to one that is superficial and seemingly absurd.*

Knowing of these displacements, we are quite confident in also relying on superficial associations in the course of interpreting dreams.[2]

The two propositions—that when conscious purposive ideas are relinquished, command over the flow of ideas passes to hidden purposive ideas; and that superficial associations are only displaced substitutes for deeper suppressed associations—are most fully used

---

[2] Of course the same considerations also apply to cases when the superficial associations are exposed in the dream-content, as they are, for example, in the two dreams related by Maury (p. 51: *pélerinage—Pelletier—pelle*; *Kilometre—Kilogramme—Gilolo—Lobelia—Lopez—Lotto*). I know from my work with neurotics which reminiscence it is that prefers this kind of representation. It is from looking up the encyclopaedia (all reference works) at the time of puberty, when their curiosity is roused, that most young people have satisfied their need for an explanation of the riddle of sexuality.

by psychoanalysis in the treatment of neuroses; indeed, the two propositions become the fundamental pillars of its technique. When I bid a patient relax all his reflectiveness, and tell me whatever comes into his mind then, I am relying on the premiss that he cannot let go of the purposive ideas behind the treatment, and I consider I am justified in concluding that the seemingly most harmless and wayward things he tells me are related to his illness. Another purposive idea, which the patient has no inkling of, is the idea of my own person. Accordingly, a complete account of this procedure, as well as a thorough proof of both explanations, properly belongs in a presentation of psychoanalytic technique as a method of therapy. At this stage we have come to one of those points of contact where we have in principle left the subject of dream-interpretation.

Only one conclusion left from these objections is correct, and that is that we do not need to ascribe all the ideas that come to mind in the course of interpretation to the dream-work of the night as well. Of course, as we interpret when we are awake, we are taking a path leading back from the dream-elements to the dream-thoughts. The dream-work took the opposite way, and it is highly unlikely that these paths are passable in both directions. What emerges is rather that by day we create passageways via fresh thought-associations which reach the intermediary thoughts and the dream-thoughts now in one place, now in another. We can see how the fresh thought-material of the day pushes into the interpretive trains of associations, probably also forcing the intensified resistance which has set in since the night to find new and more remote detours. The number and kind of the collaterals that we spin out by day, however, is psychologically quite insignificant, as long as it leads us along the path to the dream-thoughts we are looking for.

(b) *Regression*

But now that we have guarded ourselves against these objections, or at least indicated where our weapons of defence are resting, we can no longer put off broaching the psychological investigations for which we have long been arming ourselves. Let us sum up the main results of our inquiry so far. Dreams are fully paid-up psychical acts; their driving-force is a wish in need of fulfilment; their unrecognizability as wishes, and their many oddities and absurdities, derive from the influence of the psychical censorship which they have gone through in the course of their formation; as well as the compulsion to escape this censorship, the following factors have shared in forming them: the compulsion to condense the psychical material, regard for representability in visual or other sensory images, and—though not invariably—regard for a rational and intelligible appearance for the dream's structure. From each of these propositions, the way leads on to psychological postulates and conjectures. The reciprocal relationship between the wish as motive and the four conditions, as well as their relations among themselves, is still to be investigated, and the place of dreams in the interconnected life of the psyche is still to be located.

We placed a dream at the head of this chapter to remind us of the puzzles that still remain to be solved. We had no difficulty in interpreting this dream of the burning child, even though it was not told as completely as we would have it. We asked ourselves why the father should have dreamed at all, instead of waking up, and we recognized that one motive for the dream was the wish to imagine the child alive. Another wish also had a part in this, as we shall see from a later discussion. At first, then, it was for the sake of the wish-fulfilment that the processes of thought were transformed into a dream during sleep.

If we reverse this process, there is only one characteristic left that distinguishes the two kinds of psychical occurrence from each other. The dream-thought would have gone like this: 'I can see a light coming from the room where the body is lying. Perhaps a candle has fallen over, and the child is burning!' The dream reproduces the result of this reflection unaltered, but represented in a situation that is immediate and to be apprehended with the senses as if it were a waking experience. But that is the most distinctive and striking characteristic of dreaming in general; a thought—as a rule the wishful thought—is objectified in the dream, represented or, as we imagine, experienced as a scene.

Now how are we to explain this characteristic peculiarity of the dream-work, or, to put it less ambitiously, to find a place for it in the interconnections of the psychical processes?

If we look more closely, we are likely to notice that two distinctive characteristics, almost independent of each other, are perceptible in the dream in the form in which it appears. One is representation in terms of an immediate situation, with no 'perhaps' about it; the other is the transposition of the thought into visual images and into speech.

The transformation undergone by the dream-thoughts when the expectation they express is put in the present tense may not appear very striking in this particular dream. This is related to the curious, actually secondary role of wish-fulfilment in this dream. Let us take another dream, where the wish in the dream is not separated from the waking thoughts continued into it, for example, the dream of Irma's injection. The dream-thought that reaches representation here is an optative: if only Otto were to blame for Irma's illness! The dream represses the optative and replaces it by a simple present: Yes, Otto is to blame for Irma's illness. This, then, is the first of the transformations that even a dream with no distortions performs with the dream-thoughts. However, we shall not linger long over this first peculiarity shown by dreams. We can settle it by referring to conscious fantasies, to daydreams, which treat their content of imagined ideas in the same way. When Daudet's M. Joyeuse* wanders idle and unemployed through the streets of Paris while his daughters are obliged to believe he is sitting in his office holding down a job, he daydreams of the chance events that are to help him towards a patron and a position, likewise in the present tense. The dream, then, uses the present in the same way, and with the same justification, as the daydream does. The present is the tense in which the dream is represented as fulfilled.

However, only the second characteristic is peculiar to the dream as distinct from the daydream: its content of imagined ideas is not framed as thoughts, but transformed into sensory images which we believe in, and which we think we are actually experiencing. Let us add at once that not all dreams display this transformation of imagined idea into sensory image; there are dreams consisting only of thoughts, which we would not dispute were still essentially dreams. My dream '*Autodidasker*—the daytime fantasy with Professor N.' is one of this kind, which had elements intruding into it which were hardly more sensory than if I had thought up its content by day. Also, in every dream of any length there are elements that have not shared the sensory transformation, but are simply thought or known in the way we are used to thinking or knowing them when awake. At this point let us further bear in mind that this kind of transformation of ideas into sensory images does not only characterize dreams, but also hallucinations, the visions that appear independently in states of health, say, or as the symptoms of psychoneuroses. In short, no aspect of the relation we are investigating here is an exclusive one; nevertheless, it remains the case that this characteristic of dreams, where it occurs, seems to us the one that is the most remarkable, so that the life of dreams seems unthinkable without it. However, to understand it will require far-reaching discussion.

Among all the observations on the theory of dreams to be found among the authorities, I would like to draw attention to one as offering a valuable starting-point. In his *Psychophysik* (Vol. II, p. 520) the great G. T. Fechner [25]* speculates, in a discussion devoted to dreams, that *the theatre where our dreams are enacted is a different one from the scene of action where our ideas are generated in waking life*. This is the only assumption that will enable us to understand the peculiar characteristics of the dream-life.

The idea it puts at our disposal is that of *location in the psyche*. Let us put aside entirely the fact that the psychical apparatus we are dealing with here is also familiar to us as an anatomical specimen; and let us take care to avoid being tempted to define the psychical location in broadly anatomical terms. We shall remain on psychological terrain, bearing in mind only to follow the requirement that we should think of the instrument serving the functions of the psyche as acting like a composite microscope, say, or a photographic apparatus. The psychical location then corresponds to a place within this apparatus where one of the preliminary stages of the image comes about. In the microscope and telescope, as we know, these are partly hypothetical locations, places where no tangible component of the apparatus is sited. There is no need, I think, to apologize for the inadequacy of this figure, nor of all the others like it. These metaphors are only meant to support us in the attempt to make the complexity of the psyche's achievements intelligible by analysing the apparatus into its components and ascribing particular functions to particular parts of it. To my knowledge, this is the first time anyone has ventured to conjecture from this kind of analysis how the instrument of the psyche is composed. It seems harmless enough to me. In my view, we may give free rein to our speculations as long as we keep our judgement cool as we do so, and do not mistake the scaffolding for the building. Since all we need on first approaching something unknown is the support of some provisional ideas, let us begin by turning to the crudest and most tangible hypotheses.

Let us, then, imagine the psychical apparatus as a composite instrument, whose parts we shall call *agencies* or, to put it more concretely, *systems*. In doing so, we raise the expectation that these systems may be in a constant spatial orientation towards one another, rather as the various systems of lenses in a telescope are located one behind the other. Strictly speaking, we do not need to assume a real spatial arrangement for the psychical systems. It is sufficient if a firm sequence can be set up by establishing that in certain psychical processes the systems go through a definite temporal sequence in their arousal. This sequence may undergo alteration in other processes; let us, for preference, leave this possibility open. From now on, for the sake of brevity, we shall refer to the component parts of the apparatus as 'ψ-systems'.

Now the first thing that strikes us about this apparatus composed of ψ-systems is that it has a direction. All our psychical activity starts from (internal or external) stimuli and ends in innervations. Accordingly, we shall ascribe to the apparatus one sensory and one motor end; at the sensory end a system is located for receiving our sense-perceptions; at the motor end there is another which opens the floodgates to motor activity. The psychical process generally runs its course from the perceptual end to the motor end. The most general diagram for the psychical apparatus, then, would look as in Figure 1.

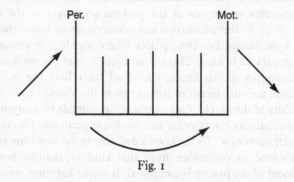

Fig. 1

But that does no more than fulfil a requirement long familiar to us, that the psychical apparatus must be constructed like a reflex apparatus. The reflexive process is still the model of all psychical performance too.

We now have a reason to hypothesize the first appearance of a differentiation at the sensory end. A trace of the perceptions impinging upon us remains in our psychical apparatus, and this we can call a '*memory-trace*'. Indeed, we call the function relating to this memory-trace our 'memory'. If we are serious about intending to link psychical processes to systems, then the memory-trace can only consist in permanent alterations to the elements of the systems. Now there are difficulties about this, as pointed out elsewhere,* if one and the same system on the one hand wants to preserve faithfully any alterations to its elements, and on the other is still supposed to encounter new occasions for change with fresh receptivity. According to the principle guiding our experiment, we shall distribute these two activities between different systems. We assume that an outermost system of the apparatus is the receptor for the perceptual stimuli, but that it does not retain anything of them, that is, it has no memory; we assume too that behind this system there is a second one that trans-forms the momentary excitation of the first into permanent traces. If so, this would be the diagram of our psychical apparatus (Fig. 2).

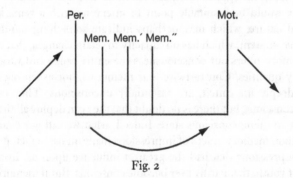

Fig. 2

We know that there is something else we retain permanently from the perceptions impinging upon the *Per* system. besides their content. Our perceptions also turn out to be linked to one another in our memory, above all if they occurred at the same time. We call this fact *association*. Now it is clear that if the *Per*.-system has no memory at all, it cannot retain the traces for association either; the particular

Per.-elements would be intolerably obstructed in their function if some remnant of an earlier link were to assert itself against a fresh perception. So we must assume, rather, that the basis for association is the memory-system. If so, the fact of association then consists of a process where, as a consequence of reductions in resistance and of pathways set up from one of the *Mem.*-elements, the excitation is passed on to one *Mem.*-element rather than another.

If we go into it further, it becomes necessary to assume not one but several *Mem.*-systems of this kind, in which the same excitation, passed on by the *Per.*-elements, is fixed permanently in several different ways. In any case, the first of these *Mem.*-systems will contain the permanent association brought about by coincidence in time; in the more remote *Mem.*-systems the same stimulus-material will be arranged according to other kinds of coincidence, so that relations of similarity, say, and other kinds, would be represented by these later systems. Of course, there would be little point in trying to put the psychical significance of a system of this kind into words. Its character would lie in its intimate relation to elements in the raw material of memory, that is—if we wanted to point towards a more far-reaching theory—it would lie in the gradations of conductive resistance in the transmission of excitations to these elements.

This would be a suitable point to intervene with a remark of a general nature, which may perhaps indicate something significant. The *Per.*-system, which has no capacity to retain changes, that is, has no memory, offers our consciousness the entire range and variety of sensory qualities. Contrariwise, our memories, not excepting those most deeply imprinted, are essentially unconscious. They can be made conscious; but there is no doubt that they can deploy all their influence in the unconscious state. Indeed, what we call our character rests upon memory-traces of impressions made on us; in fact, it is the very impressions that had the greatest influence upon us, from our earliest youth, that hardly ever become conscious. But if memories do become conscious, they do not display any sensory quality, or only a very slight one in comparison with our perceptions. If it could be confirmed *that in the ψ-systems, memory and quality in our consciousness are mutually exclusive*, then a most promising insight into the conditions governing the excitation of neurones is opened up for us.

What we have been assuming so far about the composition of the psychical apparatus at its sensory end has been done without considering dreams or any psychological explanations that might derive from them. However, dreams provide the proof for our knowledge of another part of the apparatus. We have seen that it was impossible for us to explain the formation of dreams if we did not venture the hypothesis that there were two psychical agencies, and that one of these subjected the other to criticism, with the consequence that the second was excluded from becoming conscious.

The criticizing agency, we decided, entertained closer relations to consciousness than the criticized. It stands between the latter and consciousness like a protective screen. We also found some grounds for identifying the criticizing agency with the one that guides our waking life and decides our voluntary and conscious doings. If we follow our hypothetical pattern, then, and replace these agencies by systems, then the insight just mentioned shifts the criticizing system to the motor end. We will now introduce the two systems into our diagram (Fig. 3), expressing their relation to consciousness in the names we give them.

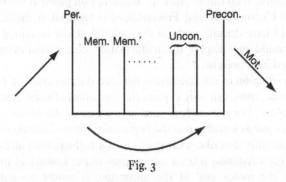

Fig. 3

The last of the systems at the motor end we shall call the *Preconscious*, to indicate that the processes of excitation going on in it are able to reach consciousness without further hindrance, as long as certain further conditions are satisfied, for example, that they should have reached a certain intensity, attracted a certain share of the function we have to call attention, and the like. At the same time, it holds the key to our voluntary motor actions. The system behind it we call the *Unconscious*, because it has no access to consciousness *except by way of the Preconscious*, while its processes of arousal have to put up with alterations to them as they make their passage through.

In which of these systems, then, shall we place the impulsion to form dreams? For the sake of simplification, in the *Uncon.*-system. True, we shall hear in later discussions that this is not entirely correct, and that the formation of dreams is bound to start out from dream-thoughts belonging to the preconscious system. However, we shall also learn, when we come to discuss the dream-wish, that the motive force of the dream is contributed by the *Uncon.* On account of this factor, let us assume that the unconscious system is the starting-point for the formation of dreams. Like all other thoughts in process of formation, the dream aroused here will express the urge to move on into the *Precon.*, and from there to gain access to consciousness.

Experience tells us that, for the dream-thoughts in daytime, this route leading through the Preconscious to consciousness is blocked by the censorship of resistance. At night they are able to make their own way to consciousness; but the questions arise, what path do they take, and what changes enable them to take it? If the dream-thoughts were enabled to do this because the resistance on guard at the border between Unconscious and Preconscious is reduced at night, then we would have dreams made of the material of our imagined ideas which would not display the hallucinatory characteristics we are interested in at present.

The reduction of the censorship between the two systems *Uncon.* and *Precon.*, then, can only explain the formation of such dreams as *Autodidasker*, but not such dreams as the one of the *burning child*, which we put as a problem at the beginning of these investigations.

We can only describe what goes on in a hallucinatory dream by saying: the excitation takes a *retrogressive* route. Instead of moving towards the motor end of the apparatus, it moves towards the sensory end, and finally reaches the system of perceptions. If we call the direction in which psychical processes move from the unconscious when we are awake the *progressive* direction, then we may say of dreams that they have a *regressive* character.

In that case, this regression is certainly one of the most important psychological features characterizing the process of dreaming; but we must not forget that it does not only characterize dreams. Intentional remembering, too, and other processes that are part of our normal thinking correspond to a backward direction taken in the psychical apparatus, starting from a complex act generating imagined ideas and moving back to the raw material of the memory-traces at its basis. When we are awake, however, this backward reach never stretches further than the remembered images; it is unable to produce the hallucinatory vividness of perceptual images. Why is this different in dreams? When we discussed the work of condensation in dreams, we could not avoid the assumption that the intensities attaching to imagined ideas are transferred in their entirety from one idea to another by the dream-work. It is probably this modification in the normal psychical processes that makes it possible to charge the *Per.*-system with energy in the contrary direction, starting out from the thoughts and going all the way to the height of sensory vividness.

I hope we are far from deceiving ourselves about the importance—or otherwise—of these reflections. All we have done is give a name to an inexplicable phenomenon. We call it regression when an idea transforms itself in dreams back into the sensory image from which it once, at some time, emerged. But this step too needs to be justified. Why find a name, if it does not teach us anything new? Now it is my view that the name 'regression' is useful insofar as it connects a fact familiar to us to the scheme of a psychical apparatus characterized by its tending in a certain direction. This is the point where for the first time it has been worthwhile to have set up such a scheme. For it is only with the help of this scheme that we will be able to understand another characteristic of dream-formation without considering the problem anew. If we regard the process of dreaming as a regression within our hypothetical psychical apparatus, this explains without further ado the empirically established fact that all the logical relations between the dream-thoughts are lost in the course of the dream-work, or only expressed with difficulty. According to our diagram, these intellectual relations are not located in the first *Mem.*-systems, but are contained in those lying further to the right, and except for the perceptual images, they are bound to lose their specific form of expression in the course of regression. *In the course of regression, the close-knit web of dream-thoughts is unravelled into its raw material.*

What changes make this regression, impossible by day, possible in our dreams? We will leave it to conjectures on this point. It must, I suppose, be a matter of changes in the degree of energy charging the particular systems, making them more suitable, or less, as paths for the excitation to travel; but in every apparatus of that kind the same effect on the path of the excitation could be brought about by more than one kind of modification. One thinks at once, of course, of the state of sleep, and of the changes in energy-charge that it produces at the sensory end of the apparatus. By day there is a continuous current from the ψ-system of the *Per.* to acts of motion; at night it comes to an end, and would no longer be able to prevent the current of excitation from flowing back in the reverse direction. This would be the 'withdrawal from the external world' which is supposed, in the theory of some authorities (see p. 44), to explain the psychological nature of dreams. Meantime, in explaining regression in dreams we shall have to take into consideration those other regressions that come about in waking states and that are pathological. In these forms, of course, what I have just said is of no help at all. Regression occurs in spite of the uninterrupted sensory current flowing in a progressive direction.

For the hallucinations of hysteria and paranoia, and the visions of people of sound mind, I can offer the explanation that they do in fact correspond to regressions, that is, that they are thoughts transformed into images, and that the only thoughts to undergo this transformation are those that have intimate connections with suppressed or still unconscious memories. For example, one of my youngest patients suffering from hysteria, a boy of twelve years old, is prevented from sleeping by '*green faces with red eyes*', which fill him with horror. The source of this apparition is the memory, suppressed but once conscious, of a boy he saw very often four years ago, and who offered him a repellent embodiment of a number of children's bad habits, among them masturbation, which my patient accused himself in retrospect of having committed. His mama had remarked at the time that the badly behaved boy had a *greenish* colour to his face and *red* (that is, *red-rimmed*) eyes. Hence the terrifying ghoul, which, by the way, is only intended to remind him of another prediction of his mother's, that boys like that become weak-minded, cannot learn anything at school, and die young. Our little patient makes part of the prophecy come true; he makes no progress at school, and, as he shows on being questioned about the ideas involuntarily entering his mind, he is terribly frightened of the second part. However, after a short time his treatment has brought the successful result that he is able to sleep, is losing his fears, and is finishing his school year with an excellent report.

At this point I can add the resolution of a vision which a forty-year-old patient with hysteria told me from her days of good health. One morning she opens her eyes and sees her brother in the room, but, as she knows, he is in a lunatic asylum. Her little son is asleep in the bed next to her. So that the child should not be *frightened* and *suffer convulsions* when he sees his *uncle*, she draws the *sheet* over him, and then the apparition vanishes. The vision is a reworking of a childhood memory of the lady's, which was conscious, it is true, but was most intimately related to all the unconscious materials in her psyche. Her nurse had told her that her mother, who died early (my patient was only eighteen months old when her mother died), had suffered from epileptic or hysterical *convulsions*, in fact, ever since a fright she had when her brother (my patient's *uncle*) appeared to her as a ghost with a *sheet* over his head. The vision contains the same elements as the memory: the brother's apparition, the sheet, the fright, and its effect. However, these elements are arranged in a different context and transferred to other figures. The obvious motive for the vision, the thought it replaces, is the worry that her little son, who has such a close physical resemblance to his uncle, could share the same fate.

The two examples I have quoted are not entirely free from all connection with the state of sleep, and so they are perhaps not wholly suitable for making the proof I need them for. I refer, then, to my analysis of a patient suffering from hallucinatory paranoia,[3] and to the results of my still unpublished studies of the psychology of the psychoneuroses, to reinforce my argument that in these cases of thoughts regressively back-transformed, one should not overlook the influence of a suppressed or unconscious memory, most often one from infancy. This memory draws the idea connected to it and denied expression by the censorship into the regression, as it were, which is the form of representation in which it has its own psychical presence. I may quote one result from my *Studies on Hysteria*, that when we are successful in bringing the scenes from childhood (whether they are recollections or fantasies) into consciousness, they are seen as hallucinations, and only cast off this character when they are communicated. It is also widely known that even in people who do not normally have a visual memory, their earliest childhood

---

[3] 'Weitere Bemerkungen über die Abwehr-Neurosenpsychosen' ['Further Remarks on the Neuropsychoses of Defence']. *Neurologisches Centralblatt*, 1896, Nr. 10 [SE iii. 159].

recollections are characterized by a sensory vividness that is retained and persists into later years.

If we recall the part played in the dream-thoughts by infantile experiences or by fantasies based upon them, and bear in mind how often bits of them resurface in the dream-content, and how the dream-wishes themselves are often derived from them, then we will not reject the probability that in the dream, too, the transformation of thoughts into images may also be the consequence of the *attraction* that their memory, represented now in visual terms and aiming for revival, exercises on the thoughts cut off from consciousness and struggling for expression. According to this view, the dream could also be described as *the substitute for the scene from infancy, altered by transferring the scene onto recent experiences*. The scene from infancy cannot be renewed; it has to be satisfied with its return as a dream.

One of the hypotheses put forward by Scherner and his disciples is made superfluous when we point out the significance of infantile scenes (or of their repetition in fantasies) as, to some extent, a model for the dream-content. Scherner assumes a condition of 'visual stimulus', or excitation within the organ of sight, when the visual elements of dreams are particularly vivid or profuse. There is no need for us to object to this assumption if all we are doing is confirming that a condition of excitation of this kind applies simply to the perceptual system of the organ of sight; but we shall argue that this condition of excitation is a renewal of a visual stimulus that once actually happened, brought alert by the memory of it. I have at hand a good example from my own experience of this kind of influence from an infantile recollection; my own dreams have in general fewer sensory elements than I have to reckon with in the dreams of others; but in the most beautiful and vivid dream I have had in recent years, it is easy for me to trace the hallucinatory clarity of the dream-content back to the sensory qualities of recent impressions. I mentioned a dream on p. 301, in which the deep blue colour of the water, the brown colour of the smoke from the ships' funnels, and the dark brown and red of the buildings I saw left a profound impression on me. If any dream was to be interpreted in terms of visual stimulus, then it was this one. And what had put the organ of my sight into this stimulated state? A recent impression, which joined with a number of earlier ones. The colours I saw were first of all the colours of the building-blocks which the children had been playing with on the day before my dream, putting up a wonderful edifice for me to admire. They had the same dark red for the big bricks, and the blue and the brown for the small ones. This was joined by impressions of colour from my last Italian journey, the lovely blue of the Isonzo and the lagoons, and the brown of the Carso.* The beautiful colours in my dream were only a repetition of what I saw in recollection.

Let us sum up what we have learned about the peculiar ability of the dream to recast the content of its imaginary ideas into sensory images. We have not explained this characteristic of the dream-work by tracing it back to known laws of psychology, say; rather, we have picked it out because it is a pointer towards unknown conditions, and we have distinguished it by calling it a 'regressive' characteristic. It was our view that wherever it occurs, this regression is probably an effect of resistance, as it pits itself against the entry of the dream-thought into consciousness along the normal way, as well as being an effect of the attraction exercised on it at the same time by the presence of strong sensory memories. It may be that in dreams regression is made easier as, in addition, the progressive current flowing from the sensory organs during the day also ceases; in other forms of regression, the absence of this auxiliary factor has to be made up for by a reinforcement of other motives for regression. Let us not forget to note also that in these cases of pathological regression, as in dreams, the process of transmitting energy may well be different from that of regression in normal psychical life, as it enables the perceptual system to carry a full hallucinatory charge. What we described when we analysed the dream-work as 'having regard to representability', we might perhaps relate to the *selective attraction* exercised by the scenes in our visual memory which the dream-thoughts have touched upon.

It may be that we ourselves have not found this first part of our psychological study of dreams particularly satisfactory. Let us console ourselves that of necessity, we are building out into the dark. If we have not gone entirely astray, we are bound to come upon another point of attack in approximately the same region, where we shall then, it may be, find our way more surely.

(c) *On Wish-Fulfilment*

The dream of the burning child at the head of this chapter offers a welcome occasion to assess the difficulties encountered by the theory of wish-fulfilment. We have all certainly heard with some surprise that the dream is supposed to be nothing but a wish-fulfilment, and not only because this seems to be contradicted by anxiety-dreams. For after hearing the first explanation claim that behind dreams there are concealed meaning and psychical value, we would hardly have expected such a straightforward definition of what this meaning might be. According to Aristotle's correct, but meagre definition, the dream is a process of thinking continued into sleep—insofar as one is sleeping. Now if by day our thinking can create such a variety of psychical acts—judgements, inferences, refutations, intentions, and the like—why should it have to limit itself solely to producing wishes? Are there not plenty of dreams that render a different kind of psychical act in an altered form—a care or concern, for example—and is not the father's particularly transparent dream at the head of this chapter one just of this kind? In his concern, he concludes from the light striking his eye, even though he is asleep, that a candle has fallen over and might have set fire to the body; he transforms this inference into a dream by clothing it in a meaningful situation and putting it into the present. What part does wish-fulfilment play in this, and are we not misjudging the predominance of the thought in it, continuing from waking life or aroused by the fresh sense-impression?

That is all perfectly correct, and it compels us to go more closely into both the part played by wish-fulfilment in dreams, and the significance of waking thoughts as they continue into sleep.

Wish-fulfilment itself has already made us distinguish two groups of dreams. We have found dreams that openly professed that they were wish-fulfilments; others where the wish-fulfilment was unrecognizable, and often hidden by all the devices of the dream-work. These latter, we saw, were performed by the dream-censorship. The wishful dreams that were undistorted we found were mainly children's dreams; short, frank wishful dreams *appeared*—I emphasize this proviso—to occur in adults too.

We may now ask where the wish realized in the dream comes from. But when we ask 'where from?', what are our points of reference, contrast and differentiation? In my view, the contrast is between the life of the day as it has entered consciousness, and a psychical activity which has remained unconscious and can only make itself felt at night. In this light, I can identify three possible sources for a wish. (1) It can have been aroused in the course of the day, but on account of external circumstances left unappeased; if so, there emerges at night a frank and unappeased wish. (2) It can have surfaced during the day, but have been rejected; if so, there emerges an unappeased but suppressed wish. Or (3), it can have no connection to the life of the day, and belong to those wishes that only stir within us at night, arising from what has been suppressed. If we apply our scheme of the psychical apparatus, we will locate a wish of the first kind in the *Precon.*-system; we assume of the second kind of wish that it has been driven from the *Precon.*-system back into the *Uncon.*, and persists only there, if at all; and we believe that the wishful impulse of the third kind is not capable of going beyond the borders of the *Uncon.*-system at all. Now, do wishes from these different sources have the same value for dreams—do they have the same power to initiate a dream?

A survey of the dreams available to us to answer this question reminds us first of all to add a fourth source for the wishes in dreams: the wishful impulses that become activated at night (e.g. responses to the stimulus of thirst, or sexual need). Once we do so, it seems probable that the origin of the dream-wish makes no difference to its capacity to initiate a dream. I recall the little girl's dream, which continued the trip across the lake interrupted in the daytime, as well as the other children's dreams quoted in the same context. They are explained by an unfulfilled, but unsuppressed daytime wish. Examples of a wish suppressed by day and breaking out at night can be pointed out in vast numbers; I could add a very simple instance here. A lady with some taste for mockery had a younger friend who had become engaged; throughout the day she would answer the questions of acquaintances—whether she knew her friend's fiancé and what she thought of him—with unqualified praise; in doing so she silenced her judgement, for she would have liked to tell the truth: *you could buy him for ten a penny.** At night she dreams that the same questions are put to her, and she replies with the tradesman's phrase: *for repeat orders, just give the number*. Finally, we have learned from a great many analyses that in all dreams subject to distortion, the wish comes from the unconscious and is imperceptible by day. It seems at first, then, that in the formation of dreams all wishes have the same value and the same power.

I am not able to prove here that the situation is actually quite different from this, but I am very much inclined to assume a stricter determination for dream-wishes. Of course, the children's dreams leave no room for doubt that a wish left unsatisfied by day can initiate a dream. But we should not forget that this is a child's wish, with the peculiar strength of infantile experience. I am very doubtful whether the unfulfilled daytime wish of an adult is sufficient to create a dream. It seems to me rather that, as our thinking takes progressive control over the life of our impulses in creating or retaining intense wishes, such as children experience, we renounce them more and more, giving them up as good for nothing. It may be that individual differences hold good here, one type of person preserving infantile psychical processes longer than another—just as, indeed, differences of this kind also apply to the weakening of a mode of imagination that originally was strongly visual. But in general, I believe, the wish left unfulfilled from the day is not strong enough in adults to create a dream. I readily grant that a wishful impulse coming from the conscious will contribute towards arousing the dream, but probably no more than that. The dream would not arise if the preconscious wish had no other source where it could get reinforcement.

That source is the Unconscious. *I imagine that the conscious wish becomes the initiator of a dream only if it succeeds in wakening an unconscious wish consonant with it, and drawing reinforcement from this.* Following indications from the psychoanalysis of neuroses, I consider that these unconscious wishes are always alive, ready at all times to seek out expression if the opportunity offers, always ready to ally themselves with some impulse from the conscious, and to transfer their own great intensity to the less intense charge of the conscious impulse.[4] It is then bound to appear as if the conscious wish alone were realized in the dream; however, one striking little thing about the form taken by the dream will act as a pointer to the track of the powerful accomplice from the Unconscious. These wishes of our Unconscious, ever stirring, never dying—immortal,

---

[4] They share this characteristic of indestructibility with other really unconscious psychical acts, i.e. acts that belong to the *Uncon.*-system only. These are paths laid down once and for all, which are never out of use, and which, whenever an unconscious excitation recharges them, always act as a conduction-route to discharge the process of arousal. To use a comparison: their only kind of annihilation is that of the shades in the underworld of the *Odyssey**—who waken to new life once they have drunk blood. The processes dependent on the preconscious system are destructible in a quite different sense. The psychotherapy of neuroses is based on this distinction.

one might say—remind us of the legendary Titans whose shoulders from time immemorial bore the great mountain-masses laden upon them by the victorious gods, which even now still quake from time to time from the convulsions of their limbs—these repressed wishes, I say, themselves have infantile origins, as we learned from our investigations into the psychology of neuroses. I would therefore like to dismiss the statement I made earlier that it does not matter what the origin of the wish behind the dream might be, and replace it by another one as follows: *the wish represented in the dream has to be an infantile one*. In adults, then, it comes from the *Uncon.*; in children, where there is as yet no division or censorship between *Precon.* and *Uncon.*, or where this is only gradually being established, it is an unfulfilled, unrepressed wish from waking life. I know this intuition cannot be demonstrated universally; but I maintain that it can be demonstrated frequently, even in cases where one might not have suspected it, and that it is not to be generally refuted.

As far as the formation of dreams is concerned, then, I shall let the wishful impulses arising from conscious waking life take a back-seat. The only function I will grant them is possibly to provide material for active sensations during sleep (cf. p. 176). I shall stay on the course laid down by this line of thought when I now consider the other psychical stimuli remaining from the life of the day which are not wishes. It is possible for us to put a provisional end to the energy charges of our waking life when we decide to go to sleep. Anyone who can do that well is a good sleeper; Napoleon I is supposed to have been a model of this kind. It is not always successful and not always complete. Problems needing to be settled, cares tormenting us, impressions overwhelming us continue the activity of our thoughts into our sleep too, and keep psychical processes going in the system we have called the Preconscious. If we want to classify these stirrings of thought that continue into sleep, we can set up the following groups: (1) what has been left unfinished by some chance delay during the day; (2) what has been left unsettled, unsolved by some failure of our powers of thought; (3) what has been rejected and suppressed by day. These are joined by the powerful fourth group, which has been stirred in our *Uncon.* by the work of the Preconscious in the course of the day; and finally we can add the fifth group: the unimportant—and hence unresolved—impressions of the day.

There is no need to underestimate the psychical intensities that these remains of the day introduce into the condition of sleep, especially from the group of unresolved problems. It is certain that these impulses are still struggling for expression at night too, and we may assume just as surely that the state of sleep makes it impossible for the usual process of excitation to continue in the Preconscious, ceasing as it becomes conscious. Insofar as we are able in the normal way to be conscious of our thinking processes at night too, we are simply not asleep. What kind of change in the *Precon.* system is brought about by the state of sleep, I cannot say; but there is no doubt that the psychological characteristic of sleep is to be looked for essentially in the changes of energy charge in this system, which also controls access to our power of movement, which is paralysed in sleep. Against this, there is nothing I know of in the psychology of dreams that bids us assume that sleep is anything but a secondary factor in bringing about changes in the *Uncon.* system. No other way is left, then, for the night-time excitation in the *Precon.* than the one the wishful impulses from the *Uncon.* take; it has to look to the *Uncon.* for reinforcement and join in following the detours of the unconscious excitations. However, what is the attitude of the preconscious remains of the day towards the dream? There is no doubt that they enter the dream in quantity, and make use of the dream-content to make their presence felt by the consciousness, even at night; indeed, on occasion they dominate the dream-content, compelling it to continue the work of the day; it is also certain that the remains of the day can just as easily be characterized by other things besides wishes; but even so, it is very instructive, and for the theory of wish-fulfilment quite decisive, to see what condition they have to accept to gain entry into the dream.

Let us take one of our earlier examples, for example, the dream that had my friend Otto appear with the symptoms of Basedow's disease (p. 207). During the day my thoughts were troubled on account of Otto's appearance, and the disquiet worried me deeply, like everything touching this person. It also pursued me, I assume, into my sleep. Probably I wanted to find out what was the matter with him. At night, this concern found expression in the dream I have related; in the first place, its content was nonsensical, and in the second, it did not correspond to any wish-fulfilment. However, I began to investigate where this inappropriate expression of the concern I had felt in the day came from, and in the course of analysis I discovered a connection by which I identified him with a certain Baron L., and myself on the other hand with Professor R. There was only one explanation for why I was obliged to choose this particular substitute for my daytime thought. In my *Uncon.*, I must always have been prepared to identify with Professor R., for this was the fulfilment of one of my immortal childhood wishes, my rage for greatness. Ugly thoughts towards my friend, which I would certainly repudiate by day, had exploited the opportunity to slip into the representation and become part of it, but my daytime worry, too, had also found some sort of expression by means of a substitute in the dream-content. The daytime thought, which was not in itself a wish, but on the contrary a worry, was obliged to find some route to a connection to an infantile wish, one now unconscious and suppressed. The wish then enabled the worry to 'originate', though duly dressed up, in consciousness. The more dominating this worry was, the more violent the yoking required could be; there was no need for any connection at all to exist between the content of the wish and the content of the worry, nor was there any in our example.

I am now able to give a precise account of the significance of the unconscious wish for dreams. I grant that there is an entire group of dreams which are *initiated* mainly, or even exclusively, by the remains of the day, and I think that even my wish to become a professor extraordinarius at long last could have allowed me to sleep in peace that night, if my disquiet about my friend's health had not still been stirring from the day. But even so, this worry would still not have produced a dream; the *driving-force* that the dream needed had to be contributed by a wish; it was up to the worry to find a wish for itself that would act as the driving-force of the dream. To put it in the form of a comparison: the daytime thought might possibly play the part of *entrepreneur* for the dream; but the entrepreneur who has the idea, as we say, and the will to translate it into action, still cannot do anything without capital; he needs a *capitalist* to take on the expenses, and the capitalist in this case, who contributes the psychical expenditure for the dream, is always and unfailingly, whatever the daytime thought may be, *a wish from the Unconscious*.

On other occasions the capitalist is himself the entrepreneur; in dreams, indeed, that is the more usual case. An unconscious wish has been aroused by the day's work, and it now creates the dream. All the other situations possible in the economic circumstances I have just suggested as an example also have their parallels in the procedures of the dream; the entrepreneur is in a position to contribute a small amount of capital himself; several entrepreneurs might turn to the same capitalist; several capitalists might club together and provide what the entrepreneurs require. Likewise, there are also dreams that are supported by more than one wish, and there are further variations of a similar kind, which can easily be reviewed, and are of no more interest to us. We shall only later be in a position to fill any gaps there may be in this account of the dream-wish.

The *tertium comparationis** of the analogies I have been drawing— the appropriate amount made available—can be used with finer differentiation to elucidate the structure of the dream. In most dreams it is possible to recognize a centre endowed with particularly strong sensory intensity, as I described on p. 232. As a rule this is the direct representation of the wish-fulfilment, for if we put the displacements of the dream-work into reverse, we find the psychical intensity of the elements in the dream-thoughts replaced by the sensory intensity of the elements in the dream-content. The elements in the neighbourhood of the wish-fulfilment often have nothing to do with its meaning; rather, they turn out to be the offspring of distressing thoughts going against the grain of the wish. However, from their often-contrived connection with the element at the centre, enough intensity has rubbed off on them to give them the potential for representation. In this way the wish-fulfilment's power of representation is diffused across a certain contextual sphere, and within this all the elements, even the weakest, are enabled to arrive at representation. In dreams driven by several wishes, it is easy to distinguish the spheres of the particular wish-fulfilments from one another, and often to read the gaps in the dreams as border-zones as well.

Although these observations have limited the significance of the remains of the day for the dream, it is still worth our while to pay some further attention to them. After all, they must be a necessary ingredient in forming the dream, if we are surprised at the fact that every dream shows some link to a recent impression of the day, often of the most trifling sort, as part of its content. We have not yet been able (p. 139) to understand the necessity for this added ingredient to the dream-mélange. And we will only do so if we hold fast to the part played by the unconscious wish and then turn to the psychology of neuroses for information. There we learn that an unconscious idea as such is incapable of entering the Preconscious, and that it is only able to effect any expression by attaching itself to an innocuous idea already present in the Preconscious; it transfers its intensity onto this, concealing itself behind it. This is the fact of *transference*, which contains the explanation for so many striking occurrences in the inner life of neurotics. The transference can leave the idea from the Preconscious unchanged, giving it an undeservedly great intensity; alternatively, it can forcibly modify the idea from the Preconscious by the content of the idea transferring from the Unconscious. Forgive my liking for analogies from everyday life, but I am tempted to say that the situation of the repressed idea resembles that of an American dentist in our own dear country, who may not practise his profession unless he makes use of a formally qualified doctor as his ostensible brass plate or cover before the law. And just as it is not exactly the doctors with most work of their own who enter these alliances with the dental technicians, in the operations of the psyche it is not those preconscious or conscious ideas which have attracted ample attention to themselves in the Preconscious that are elected to cover a repressed idea. For choice, to spin its web of connections around them, the Unconscious actually prefers pre-conscious impressions and ideas that have either been ignored as unimportant, or, if considered, have promptly been rejected. It is a well-known proposition of association theory, empirically confirmed, that ideas which have set up an intimate connection with one aspect, will keep aloof, as it were, from entire groups of new connections; I once attempted to base a theory of hysterical paralysis on this proposition.

If we assume that the same need for transference by repressed ideas as we recognized in analysing neuroses also holds good in dreams, this will explain at one blow two of the puzzles we have encountered in dreams: that every analysis of a dream is able to draw attention to the interweaving of a recent impression; and that this recent element is often of the most trifling sort. We can add to this what we have already learned elsewhere: that these recent and trifling elements reach the dream-content so frequently as substitutes for the earliest and oldest of our dream-thoughts, because they also have the least to fear from the censorship set up by resistance. However, while freedom from censorship only explains the preference for the trivial elements, the constant occurrence of recent elements reveals the need for transference. The demand of the repressed for material that is as yet free of associations is satisfied by both groups of impressions, the trivial because they have not given any occasion for a wide range of connections, and the recent because there has not been time for it.

Thus we can see that the remains of the day, to which we may now give credit for the trivial impressions, not only borrow something from the *Uncon.* when they get a share in forming a dream—that is, the driving-force at the disposal of the repressed wish—but they also have something indispensable to offer the Unconscious, the point of attachment it needs for transference. If we wanted to go more deeply into the inner processes at this point, we would have to cast a brighter light on the play of excitations between Preconscious and Unconscious—indeed, the study of the psychoneuroses presses us to do so, but dreams simply do not offer any support for it.

Just one further remark on the remains of the day. There is no doubt that they are the real disturbers of sleep, not dreams, which endeavour rather to guard our sleep. We shall come back to this later.

We have up until now been pursuing the wish behind the dream, we have derived it from the field of the *Uncon.*, and analysed its relationship to the remains of the day, which for their part may be wishes or psychical impulses of any other kind, or simply recent impressions. In this way we made room for the claims that can be made for the importance of our multifarious waking thought in forming dreams. It would not even be impossible to use this train of reasoning as the basis for explaining those extreme cases in which the dream continues the work of the day and brings an unsolved problem of our waking life to a happy conclusion. We only lack an example of the kind where analysis would reveal the infantile or repressed source of the wish that, when called upon, so successfully reinforced the efforts of preconscious activity. However, we have not come a single step closer to solving the puzzle of why all the Unconscious is able to offer in sleep is the driving-force to produce a wish-fulfilment. The answer to this question is bound to shed light on the psychical nature of wishing; it will be given with the aid of our schematic picture of the psychical apparatus.

We have no doubt that this apparatus too only reached its present perfection by way of a long development. Let us attempt to transpose it back to an earlier stage of its functioning. Hypotheses requiring a different kind of substantiation tell us that at first the apparatus aimed to maintain itself as far as possible without stimulus, and so in its earliest structure it assumed the scheme of the reflexive apparatus, which enabled it to discharge at once in motor activity any sensory excitation reaching it from outside. But this simple function is disturbed by the exigencies of life; it is to these that the apparatus also owes the impulsion to further development. The exigencies of life first approach it in the form of the great bodily needs. The excitation caused by internal need will seek some discharge into a motor activity we might describe as an 'internal change' or an 'expression of emotion'. A hungry child will cry or flail about helplessly. However, the situation remains unaltered, for the excitation coming from an internal need is not consistent with an intermittent force but with one that is continuously in operation. A change can only take place if in some way—for the child, if someone else comes to its aid—the *experience of satisfaction* is felt, annulling the internal stimulus. An essential component of this experience is the appearance of a certain perception (of food, in our example); from now on its remembered image will remain associated with the trace left in the memory by the excitation aroused by the need. The next time this need appears, an impulse in the psyche will arise, thanks to the association created, which will invest the remembered image with that perception and evoke the perception itself; what it really wants, then, is to restore the situation of its original satisfaction. An impulse of this kind is what we call a wish; the reappearance of the perception is the fulfilment of the wish; and when the perception is fully charged with the excitation roused by the need, that is the shortest path to the wish-fulfilment. There is nothing to hinder us from assuming a primitive state of the psychical apparatus when this path really was taken in this way, and when wishing ended in hallucinating. This earliest activity of the psyche, then, aims at a *perceptual identity*, that is, at a repetition of the perception linked to the satisfaction of the need.

Bitter experience of life must have modified this primitive thought-activity into a more adaptable, secondary one. Elsewhere, the creation of a perceptual identity on the short, regressive path within the apparatus does not have the same result as when the same perception is charged from outside. The satisfaction does not set in;

the need goes on. To make the internal charge equivalent to the external, it must be constantly kept going—which does actually happen in hallucinatory psychoses and hunger-fantasies, whose only psychical feat is *that they hold on to* the desired object. To put the psychical force to more purposefully adapted use, it is necessary to halt the process of complete regression so that it does not go beyond the remembered image; then it can set off from the remembered image to seek out other paths, which will finally lead to creating the desired perceptual identity from the direction of the external world. This inhibition, as well as the consequent diversion of the excitation, is a function of a second system governing voluntary movement, that is, coming into operation only once movement is used to carry out purposes that have already been remembered beforehand. Still, all the complicated activity of thought spinning out from the remembered image to the creation of perceptual identity by the external world only represents the *long way round to wish-fulfilment*[5] which experience has made necessary. Thought, after all, is nothing but a substitute for an hallucinatory wish, and to say that the dream is a wish-fulfilment is self-evident, for nothing but a wish is capable of putting our psychical apparatus to work. The dream, which fulfils its wishes along short, regressive paths, has preserved for us a mere sample of the psychical apparatus's *primary*—discarded—way of functioning, discarded, that is, as inexpedient. It seems banished to the night, though it once governed our waking, when the life of the psyche was still young and helpless, rather as we find the primitive adult weapons, the bow and arrow, which the human race has laid aside, in the nursery still. *Dreaming is a part of the—surmounted—childhood life of the psyche.* In the psychoses, these primary ways of functioning in the psychical apparatus, which are normally suppressed in waking life, will come forcibly into their own again, and then reveal how incapable they are of satisfying our needs with regard to the external world.

Clearly, the unconscious wishful impulses also seek to assert themselves by day as well, and we learn from the fact of transference as well as from the psychoses that they are striving by way of the

[5] Le Lorrain [45] rightly praises the wish-fulfilling function of the dream: 'Sans fatigue sérieuse, sans être obligé de recourir à cette lutte opiniâtre et longue qui use et corrode les jouissances poursuivies' ['Without major fatigue, without the obligation to resume that stubborn struggle which wears out and spoils the pursued delights'].

preconscious system to get through to consciousness and take control of movement. It is the censorship between *Uncon.* and *Precon.*, then, which dreams really compel us to assume, that we must acknowledge and honour as the guardian of our mental health. Now, is it not imprudent of this guardian to reduce his activity at night, allowing the suppressed impulses of the *Uncon.* to find expression, and making hallucinatory regression possible again? I do not think so, for when the critical guardian takes his rest—and we have evidence in any case that his slumber is not deep—he also closes the gateway to movement. Whatever impulses from the normally inhibited *Uncon.* may go rampaging upon the scene, they can be left to their own devices, they remain harmless, because they are unable to set the motor apparatus going, which is the only thing whose impact can change the external world. The state of sleep ensures the safety of the stronghold to be guarded. The situation is less harmless if the displacement of forces is brought about not by the relaxation at night of the critical censorship's expenditure of energy, but by its pathological reduction, or by a pathological reinforcement of the unconscious excitations, while the Preconscious is still charged with energy and the gates to movement are open. Then the guardian is overwhelmed, the unconscious excitations overcome the *Precon.*, and from there they take control of what we say and do, or forcibly bring about hallucinatory regression, and direct the course of the apparatus, which was not intended for them, by virtue of the attraction exercised by perceptions on the distribution of our psychical energy. We call this condition psychosis.

This puts us well on the way to building further on our psychological scaffolding, which we left at the point where we had included the two systems *Uncon.* and *Precon.* But we still have reasons enough to linger with our assessment of the wish as the sole psychical driving-force of the dream. We have accepted the explanation that the dream is always a wish-fulfilment because it is a creation of the *Uncon.*-system, whose only aim is wish-fulfilment, and which has at its disposal only the forces of the wishful impulses. Now if we want, even for a moment longer, to maintain our right to start out from the interpretation of dreams on very wide-ranging psychological speculations, we are under an obligation to show that we can use them to locate the dream in a context of interconnecting which can also include other psychological formations. If a system of the

Uncon.—or for the sake of discussion, something analogous to it— does exist, then the dream cannot be its only expression; every dream may well be a wish-fulfilment, but there must be other forms of abnormal wish-fulfilments besides dreams. And really, the theory of all psychoneurotic symptoms culminates in the proposition *that they too have to be conceived as wish-fulfilments of the Unconscious.* Our explanation makes the dream only the first item in a series which is of great significance to the psychiatrist, for understanding it would mean being able to solve the psychological part of the psychiatrist's work. However, the other items in this series of wish-fulfilments, for instance, hysterical symptoms, have one essential characteristic that I have not yet encountered in dreams. For I know from investigations I have alluded to frequently in the course of this treatise that for a hysterical symptom to be formed, both currents of our psychical life must come together. The symptom is not merely the expression of an unconscious wish realized; another wish from the Preconscious has to join it, realized by the same symptom, so that the symptom is determined *at least* doubly, once from each of the conflicting systems. As in the dream, there is no limit set to any further over-determination. The determinant that does not come from the *Uncon.* is, as far as I can see, invariably a train of thought reacting to the unconscious wish, for example, self-punishment. In general, then, I can say that *a hysterical symptom only comes into being when two opposing wish-fulfilments, each with its source in a different psychical system, are in a position to coincide in one expression.* Examples would be of little use here, for only a complete exposé of the complications present would be convincing. So I shall leave it at the assertion, and only offer an example as an illustration, not for any value it may have as evidence. A patient's hysterical vomiting, then, turned out on the one hand to be the fulfilment of an unconscious fantasy from her years of puberty—the wish, in fact, to be constantly pregnant and have countless children; later this was expanded to: by as many men as possible. A powerful defensive reaction had set in against this unbridled wish. However, as the patient was in danger of losing her fine figure and her good looks through this vomiting, so that no man would take a fancy to her, her symptom was also perfectly acceptable to her self-punishing train of thought, and so, being admissible to both sides, it could be realized. It is the same manner of dealing with a wish-fulfilment as it pleased the Parthian queen to use against the triumvir Crassus.* She thought he went on the campaign for love of gold; so she had molten gold poured down the throat of his dead body. 'Now you've got what you wished for.' Until now, all we know of the dream is that it expresses a wish-fulfilment of the Unconscious; it seems that the dominant preconscious system tolerates this, once it has imposed certain distortions upon the dream. In general, one cannot actually demonstrate a train of thought opposed to the dream-wish that is also, like its adversary, realized in the dream. We come across some signs of reaction-formations in our analyses of dreams, but only now and again, for example, my affection for my friend R. in the dream of my uncle (p. 109). However, the missing ingredient from the Preconscious can be discovered elsewhere. After undergoing all sorts of distortions, the dream is free to express a wish from the *Uncon.*, while the dominant system has withdrawn into the *wish to sleep*, realizing it by the changes it is able to bring about in the charges of energy within the apparatus of the psyche, and finally holding on to it for as long as sleep lasts.[6]

This firmly held wish of the Preconscious to sleep generally has the effect of making it easier for dreams to be formed. Let us consider the dream of the father who was led by the light coming from the dead child's room to conclude that the body might have caught fire. We have indicated that one of the psychical forces deciding that the father should draw this conclusion rather than be woken up by the light was the wish to prolong the life of the child imagined in the dream by just that moment. Other wishes arising from what has been repressed are likely to escape us, because we are not in a position to analyse this dream. But we may in addition take the father's need of sleep to be its second driving-force; just as the dream prolongs the child's life, the father's sleep too is lengthened by a moment. Let the dream go on, was his motivation, otherwise I shall have to wake up. As it does in this dream, the wish to sleep lends its support to the unconscious wish in all other dreams. On p. 99 we gave an account of dreams that presented themselves frankly as dreams of convenience. Actually, all dreams can lay claim to this description. The effectiveness of the wish to go on sleeping can be seen most easily in the dreams we have when we are woken up, as they adapt the external sensory stimulus in such a way that it is compatible with

---

[6] I have taken this idea from Liébault's theory of sleep; it is to him we are indebted for the revival of research into hypnosis in our time.

continuing sleep, and weave it into a dream to remove the demands it might make as a reminder of the outside world. However, this wish must also have a share in making possible all those other dreams that can only attempt to wake us up by disturbing our state of sleep from within. What the *Precon.* often says to our consciousness when the dream goes too far, is: 'Don't worry! Go on sleeping. After all, it's only a dream.' Even though this is never uttered aloud, it is a good general description of the attitude of the dominant activity of our psyche towards dreams. I am bound to draw the conclusion *that, throughout the entire state of sleep, we know just as certainly that we are dreaming as we know that we are asleep.* We do not have to pay any attention to the objection that our consciousness is never directed to the one item—the knowledge that we are asleep—and that it attends to the other—the knowledge that we are dreaming—only on particular occasions, when the censorship feels as if it has been caught unawares.

(d) *Arousal by Dreams. The Function of Dreams. Anxiety-Dreams*

Knowing as we do now that throughout the night the Preconscious is set on the wish to sleep, we can pursue the process of dreaming with greater understanding. But let us first summarize what we know about it so far. We would say, then, that a residue from the day is left from our waking activity, and that its charge of energy does not completely withdraw at night; alternatively, our waking activity has stirred one of our unconscious wishes during the day; or again, both may happen together—we have already discussed several possibilities in this respect. Either the unconscious wish has already been making its way towards the day's remnants in the course of the day, or this may not happen until the state of sleep sets in, when the wish brings about a transference onto them. A wish then emerges which has been transferred onto the recent material; alternatively, the suppressed recent wish has been revivified by reinforcement from the Unconscious. Its intention is to make its way into consciousness along the normal route taken by thought-processes via the *Precon.* But it comes up against the censorship—which still persists—and is now subject to its influence. At this stage it takes the distorted form for which the way was already prepared by its transference onto recent events. Up to this point it is on the way to becoming something similar to an obsessive idea or illusion or the like, that is, a thought reinforced by the transference and distorted in its expression by the censorship. However, the state of sleep does not allow the Preconscious to penetrate any further; probably the system has protected itself against penetration by reducing its excitations. The process of dreaming, then, takes the route of regression opened up by this characteristic of the state of sleep, and as it does so it follows the attraction exercised on it by groups of memories, some of which are only charged with visual intensity, not translated into the terms of the later systems. On the way to regression, it acquires representability. We shall deal with the question of compression later. The process of dreaming has now travelled the second stretch of its zigzag course. The first part extended progressively from the unconscious scenes or fantasies to the Preconscious; the second part moves from the borders of censorship on towards the perceptions again. However, once a dream-process has become the content of a perception, it has, you might say, evaded the obstacles placed on it in the *Precon.* by the censorship and the state of sleep. It is now able to draw attention to itself and be noticed by consciousness. For consciousness, which we regard as a sensory organ for the apprehension of psychical qualities, can be aroused from two locations when we are awake. First and foremost from the periphery of the whole apparatus, the perceptual system; besides this, from the excitations of pleasure and unpleasure which are the only psychical quality to emerge from the transfers of energy within the apparatus. All the other processes in the ψ-system, even those in the *Precon.*, lack any psychical quality, and so they are not an object of consciousness, in so far as they do not provide pleasure or unpleasure for our perception. We shall have to assume that *these releases of pleasure and of unpleasure automatically regulate the processes of energy-charging.* However, in order to make more fine-tuned performance possible, it later turned out to be necessary to shape the course of ideas so that it was more independent of signs of unpleasure. To this end, the *Precon.* system needed qualities of its own, able to attract consciousness, and it most probably acquired them by setting up the connection between preconscious processes and the memory-system of linguistic signs—which was itself not without qualities. Through this system's qualities, consciousness, which previously was only a sensory organ for perceptions, now also becomes the sensory organ for part of our thinking processes. There are now, as it were, two sensory surfaces, one turned towards processes of perceiving, the other towards processes of thinking.

I have to assume that the state of sleep makes the sensory surface of consciousness that is turned towards the *Precon.* far less susceptible to excitation than the surface turned towards the *Per.*-systems. Of course, there is also a purpose to giving up interest in thought-processes at night. Nothing is supposed to happen in our thinking; the *Precon.* wants to sleep. However, once the dream has become a perception, it is able to use the qualities it has now acquired to arouse consciousness. This excitation of the senses achieves what it is its function to achieve; it makes a part of the energy-charge available in the *Precon.* pay attention to what is arousing it. So it has to be admitted, then, that the dream always *arouses* us, it sets in action part of the force at rest in the *Precon.* The dream then undergoes what we have described as secondary revision, which takes account of coherence and intelligibility. That is to say, it treats the dream like any other perceptual content: its ideas are subjected to the same expectations, that is, insofar as its subject-matter allows. As for the direction taken by the course of this third part of the dream-process, it is again a progressive one.

To avoid misunderstandings, a word about the temporal characteristics of these dream-processes is probably called for. A very attractive line of thought was put forward by Goblot [29], which was obviously set off by the puzzle presented in Maury's guillotine dream: he attempts to show that dreams take up only the time of the transitional period between sleeping and waking. Waking up takes time; the dream occurs in this time. In this view, the last image of the dream was so strong that it forced the sleeper to wake up. In reality, the image was so strong only because with it we were already so close to waking. 'Un rêve c'est un réveil qui commence.'*

Dugas [18] has already emphasized that Goblot has to throw out a great deal of factual material to make his thesis generally valid. There are also dreams from which we do not wake, for example, many where we dream that we are dreaming. From our knowledge of the dream-work, we cannot possibly agree that it only lasts for the period of waking. On the contrary, it must be more likely that the first part of the dream-work is already beginning during the day, when it is still governed by the Preconscious. The second part of the dream-work—the changes imposed by the censorship, the attraction exercised by the unconscious scenes, the breakthrough to perception—probably goes on throughout the night, and to that extent we may always be right when we claim we have been dreaming all night long, even though we are unable to say what. However, I do not believe that the processes of the dream really follow the temporal sequence we have been describing: first the presence of the transferred dream-wish, then the distortion by the censorship, and after that the shift in the direction of regression, etc. We have had to construct this kind of sequence in describing it; in reality it is much more likely to be a matter of simultaneously trying out this or that path, a toing and froing of excitations until finally they accumulate in the way most suitable for the one lasting constellation to emerge. Some experiences of my own lead me to think that the dream-work often needs more than a day and a night to deliver its results, though if that is so, the extraordinary art shown in constructing the dream loses its wonder. Even the consideration it gives to intelligibility as a perceptual event can, in my opinion, come into effect before the dream has attracted consciousness to itself. On the other hand, from then on the process is accelerated, for after all, the dream now goes through the same treatment as anything else perceived. It is like a firework that has been hours in the preparation, and then blazes up in a moment.

Either the dream-process is enabled by the dream-work, quite independently of the time or the depth of sleep, to gain enough intensity to attract consciousness to itself and rouse the Preconscious; or its intensity is not sufficient for this, and it has to remain at the ready until it attracts attention—which becomes more mobile then—immediately before waking. Most dreams appear to operate with relatively low psychical intensities, for they are waiting until it is time to wake. But this also explains how we are, as a rule, aware of something we have dreamed if we are suddenly jolted out of deep sleep. Just as when we wake up naturally, the first thing we see is the perceptual content created by the dream-work, and next after that what is given by the outside world.

However, greater theoretical interest applies to the dreams that are able to wake us up in the midst of our sleep. If we bear in mind its efficacy demonstrable everywhere else, we may well ask why the dream, that is, the fulfilment of the unconscious wish, is still left with the power to disturb sleep, that is, the fulfilment of the pre-conscious wish. The cause must lie in their energy relations, of which we have no knowledge. If we did, we would probably find that letting the dream run on, and expending a certain detached attention on it, represents a saving of energy in contrast to keeping the Unconscious within the same bounds at night as during the day. Our experience shows that dreaming, even if it interrupts our sleep several times in one night, is compatible with sleep. We wake up for a moment, and go back to sleep again at once. It is as if we were brushing away a fly in our sleep; we wake up *ad hoc*. When we go back to sleep, we have removed the disturbance. Fulfilling the wish to sleep, as familiar examples of nurses' sleep and the like show us, can be combined with a certain expenditure of attention in a specific direction.

However, at this point an objection which is based on better knowledge of unconscious processes demands a hearing. We have described even unconscious wishes as being constantly alive and active. Nevertheless, during the day they are not strong enough to make themselves audible. But in the state of sleep, if the unconscious wish has had the power to form a dream and arouse the Preconscious with it, why does this power seep away once we are aware of the dream? Rather, should not the dream renew itself constantly, just as the disturbing fly is fond of coming back again and again to the spot it was driven away from? What right had we to assert that dreams get rid of any disturbance to our sleep?

It is quite correct that the unconscious wishes always remain alive and active. They represent paths that are always passable, whenever a quantity of excitation makes use of them. It is even the salient feature of unconscious processes that they are indestructible. In the Unconscious, nothing is brought to an end, nothing is past or forgotten. We get the strongest impression of this from the study of neuroses, especially of hysteria. The unconscious path of thoughts, leading to discharge in an attack, can be travelled again at once, if sufficient excitation has accumulated. An injury experienced thirty years ago, once it has gained access to the unconscious sources of affect, will continue throughout all those thirty years to act just like a recent one. Whenever the memory of it is touched, it comes to life again charged with excitation, which is then discharged in a motor attack. It is just here that psychotherapy can intervene. Its job is to deal with the unconscious processes, settling them and making it possible to forget them. In fact, what we are inclined to regard as self-evident, and to explain by the primary influence of time on the remnants of memory in the psyche, by waning memories and the low intensity of fading impressions, are in reality secondary changes which have come about by hard labour. It is the Preconscious that does this work, and the only route that psychotherapy can take is to subdue the *Uncon.* to the authority of the *Precon.*

For a particular unconscious process of excitation, then, there are two outcomes. On the one hand, it is left to itself; if so, it will finally break out somewhere and for this once it will discharge its excitation in movement. Alternatively, it succumbs to the influence of the Pre-conscious, which *binds* the excitation, instead of *venting* it. *But it is the latter that takes place in the process of dreaming.* The charge of energy coming from the Preconscious towards the dream (which has now become perceptual) because it has been diverted there by the excitation of consciousness, binds the unconscious excitation of the dream and neutralizes its capacity to disturb. If the dreamer wakes for a moment, he really has brushed away the fly that threatened to disturb his sleep. We can now have some idea that it really was more convenient and more economical to let the unconscious wish run its course, opening up its path to regression so that it can form a dream, and then to deal with the dream, binding it by a small expenditure of preconscious work, than to keep a tight rein on the Unconscious throughout the entire time spent asleep as well as waking. It was, of course, to be expected that even if dreaming was not originally a process with a purpose, it would have found itself a function within the play of forces in the psyche. We can now see what that function is. Dreaming has taken on the task of bringing the excitation of the *Uncon.*, which was left free, back under the control of the Pre-conscious. In doing so, it discharges the excitation of the *Uncon.*, acts as a safety-valve for it, and at the same time ensures the sleep of the Preconscious in exchange for a small expenditure of waking activity. In this way it presents itself as a compromise, just like all the other psychical formations in the series it belongs to, serving both systems at the same time as it fulfils the wishes of both, in so far as they are compatible with each other. A glance at Robert's 'excretion theory' explained on p. 66 indicates that we have to admit this authority was right on the main question of the function of dreams, though we part company from him in our assumptions and in our assessment of the dream-process.

The qualification, *insofar as the wishes are compatible with each other*, suggests possible cases where the function of a dream may miscarry. The process of dreaming is first admitted as a wish-fulfilment of the Unconscious; if this attempted wish-fulfilment gives such a violent jolt to the Preconscious that it can no longer preserve its repose, the dream has broken the compromise, and no longer fulfils the other part of its task. If this happens, it is inter-rupted at once and replaced by a fully wakened state. In this case too, it is not actually the fault of the dream if, though normally the guardian of sleep, it has to appear as its disturber, and this need not make us doubt its fitness for its purpose. This is not the only instance in the organism where a useful arrangement becomes use-less and disturbing as soon as there is some change in the conditions under which it comes into being; in these cases the disturbance at least serves the new purpose of signalling the change and summon-ing up the organization's regulatory means against it. I have in mind, of course, the case of anxiety-dreams, and—so as not to appear to be avoiding this evidence against the theory of wish-fulfilment, wherever I come upon it—I propose to approach an explanation of anxiety-dreams, at least with some suggestions.

By now we no longer regard it as a contradiction that a psychical process producing anxiety can still, for that reason, be a wish-fulfilment. We are able to explain it to ourselves as follows: the wish belongs to one system, the *Uncon.*, while the system of the *Precon.* has rejected and suppressed this wish. Even in cases of complete psychical well-being, the *Uncon.* is not totally subject to the *Precon.*; the measure of this suppression indicates the degree of our psychical normality. The symptoms of neurosis show us that the two systems are in conflict with each other; they are the compromise results of the conflict, putting a provisional end to it. On the one hand they enable the *Uncon.* to find an outlet for the discharge of its excitation, act as a sally-port for it, and on the other, they still offer the *Precon.* the possibility of having some control over the *Uncon.* It is instruct-ive, for example, to consider the significance of a hysterical phobia or of agoraphobia. Say that a neurotic is incapable of crossing the road alone, which we rightly describe as a 'symptom'. Suppose we then nullify this symptom by forcing him to perform the action he believes he cannot take. If we do, it results in an attack of anxiety, as, indeed, an attack of anxiety in the street has often become the occasion for agoraphobia to set in. In this way we learn that the symptom has been created in order to prevent the outbreak of anxiety; the phobia is situated like a frontier stronghold against the anxiety.

We will not be able to take our account further without looking at the part played by the affects in these processes, which can only be done incompletely at this point. So let us propose that the suppression of the *Uncon.* is necessary above all because, if left to itself, the course of ideas in the *Uncon.* would develop an affect which was originally characterized by pleasure but, since undergoing the process of *repression*, is characterized by unpleasure. The aim of the suppression—but also its consequence—is to prevent this development of unpleasure. The suppression extends as far as the content of the ideas in the *Uncon.*, because the release of unpleasure could take off from there. This proposition is based on a quite specific assumption about the nature of the development of affect, which it regards as being accomplished by the motor or secretory systems, seeing the key to its innervation as located in the imagined ideas of the *Uncon.* These ideas are strangled, as it were, by the *Precon.*'s control of them, and inhibited from transmitting the impulses developing the affect. If this charge of energy from the *Precon.* stops, then the danger is that the unconscious excitations will release an affect, which—as a consequence of its earlier suppression—can only be felt as unpleasure, as anxiety.

This danger is let loose if the dream-process is allowed to run its course. The conditions for its realization are if repressions have taken place and if the suppressed wishful impulses are able to become sufficiently strong—conditions, in fact, which are entirely outside the psychological framework of dream-formation. If it were not that our topic is connected to that of the development of anxiety by this one factor—the freeing of the *Uncon.* during sleep—I could dispense with discussing anxiety-dreams and spare myself all the obscurities attaching to them.

The theory of anxiety-dreams, as I have already said many times, belongs to the psychology of neuroses. We have nothing further to do with it now that we have indicated the place where it touches our topic, which is the process of dreaming. There is just one more thing I can do. As I have maintained that neurotic anxiety arises from sexual sources, I can submit anxiety-dreams to analysis to point out the sexual material in their dream-thoughts.

I have good reasons to refrain from using any of the examples which my neurotic patients offer me in plenty, and I shall give preference to anxiety-dreams from young persons.

I have no longer had a real anxiety-dream myself for decades. I remember one from my seventh or eighth year, which I submitted to interpretation some thirty years later. It was very vivid, and it showed me *my beloved mother with a distinctively tranquil, sleeping expression on her face, who was being carried into the room by two (or three) people with birds' beaks, and laid on the bed.* I woke up crying and screaming, and disturbed my parents' sleep. The—curiously draped—elongated figures with the birds' beaks I had taken from the illustrations to *Philippson's* edition of the Bible;* I believe they were gods with falcons' heads from an Egyptian tomb relief. Besides this, the analysis provided me with the memory of a badly behaved boy, our caretaker's son, who used to play with us children in the field in front of the house, and I rather think he was called *Philipp*. I have the feeling as though it was from this boy that I first heard the vulgar word for sexual intercourse for which the educated substitute a Latinate word, 'coition', but which is characterized clearly enough by the choice of falcons' heads.* I must have guessed the sexual meaning of the word from the face of my experienced mentor. The expression on my mother's face in the dream was copied from the sight of my grandfather, whom I had seen snoring in a coma a few days before his death. So the interpretation in the secondary revision of the dream must have been that my mother *is dying*—the *tomb* relief also chimes with this. I woke up in this state of anxiety, and did not stop until I had wakened my parents. I remember I calmed down all of a sudden when I saw my mother, as though I needed the reassurance: so she is not dead, after all. But this secondary interpretation of the dream already happened under the influence of the anxiety released. Not that I was anxious because I had dreamed that my mother was dying; but I interpreted the dream in its preconscious version in this way because I was already under the power of anxiety. But the anxiety could be traced back by way of repression to a dark, obviously sexual desire which had found an appropriate expression in the visual content of the dream.

A twenty-seven-year-old man, who has been very ill for a year, dreamed several times between the ages of eleven and thirteen with feelings of great anxiety, *that a man with a hatchet was coming after him; he wants to run, but feels as if he is paralysed and cannot move from the spot.* That is probably a good model of a very common anxiety-dream, beyond any sexual suspicion. In the course of analysis, the dreamer at first comes upon a—chronologically later—story of his uncle, who was attacked in the street at night by a suspicious individual, and he makes his own inference from this that he might have heard of a similar experience at the time of the dream. The hatchet rouses the recollection that at the time he once hurt himself with a hatchet when he was chopping kindling. Then he comes directly upon his relationship with his younger brother, whom he used to maltreat and knock about, and he remembers one occasion particularly when he kicked him in the head with his boot, so that the boy bled and his mother exclaimed: 'I'm afraid he'll kill him one day.' While he seems fixed on the topic of violence, another memory from his ninth year suddenly surfaces. His parents had come home late and went to bed, while he pretended to be asleep, and he heard a panting and other sounds that seemed uncanny to him, and he could also guess at the position of the two in bed. His further thoughts show that he had set up an analogy between this relationship of his parents' and his own to his younger brother. He subsumed what happened between his parents under the concept: *violence and fighting.* As proof of this conception he noticed that there was often *blood in his mother's bed.*

It is, I would say, a matter of everyday experience that the sexual intercourse of adults seems uncanny to the children who observe it, and arouses anxiety in them. I have explained this anxiety as a matter of sexual excitation which their understanding cannot cope with; probably it also gets repudiated because the parents are involved in it, and so it is transformed into anxiety. At an earlier period of life the stirrings of sexuality felt towards the parent of the opposite sex do not yet meet with repression, and express themselves freely, as we have heard (p. 197).

I would have no doubts about applying the same explanation to the night-time attacks of anxiety accompanied by hallucinations (the *pavor nocturnus*) suffered so often by children. There too it can only be a matter of stirrings of sexuality which are not understood, and rejected. A record of them would probably also indicate a temporal periodicity, for sexual libido can be intensified as much by arousal from chance impressions as by the spontaneous, intermittent processes of development.

I lack the empirical material needed to carry this explanation through to the end. On the other hand, the paediatricians seem to lack the one point of view that would allow them to understand the entire series of phenomena from the somatic as well as the psychical aspect. As a comic example of how close one can get to an understanding of such cases, and then, blinded by the blinkers of medical mythology, walk right past it, I would like to quote a case I found in Debacker's [17] thesis of 1881 on *pavor nocturnus* (p. 66).

A thirteen-year-old boy in poor health began to become timid and dreamy; his sleep became restless, and was broken almost once every week by a bad attack of anxiety with hallucinations. His memory of these dreams was always very distinct. He was able to relate that the devil had shouted at him: 'Now we've got you, now we've got you,' and then there was a smell of sulphur and brimstone, and the fire burned his skin. He would wake from this dream in terror, but at first was not able to cry out until he had found his voice, and he was heard to say distinctly: 'No, no, not me, I haven't done anything,' or: 'Please, don't. I'll never do it again.' Sometimes he would also say: 'Albert didn't do that.' Later he avoided getting undressed 'because the fire would only get him if he was undressed'. In the middle of these dreams of the devil, which put his health in danger, he was sent to the country, where he recovered in the course of eighteen months, and then, when he was fifteen years old, he once confessed: 'Je n'osais pas l'avouer, mais j'éprouvais continuellement des picotements et des surexcitations aux *parties*;[7] à la fin, cela m'énervait tant que plusieurs fois, j'ai pensé me jeter par la fenêtre du dortoir.'*

It is probably not difficult to guess: (1) that in earlier years the boy masturbated, probably denied it, and was threatened with heavy punishments for his bad habit. (His admission: 'Je ne le ferai plus'; his denial: 'Albert n'a jamais fait cela'); (2) that in the turmoil of puberty, the temptation to masturbate was aroused again with the tickling in his genitals; but that now (3) a repressive struggle broke out within him, suppressing the libido and transforming it into an

---

[7] My italics; but in any case not to be misunderstood.

anxiety which resumed retroactively the punishments he had once been threatened with.

By contrast, let us hear the conclusions drawn by our authority (p. 69). 'We may conclude from these observations that (1) the influence of puberty on a boy of weakened heath can produce a condition of great weakness, and that it can go as far as *a very considerable cerebral anaemia*.[8]

'(2) This cerebral anaemia produces a change in the character, demonomanic hallucinations and states of intense anxiety at night, and perhaps also by day.

'(3) The demonomania and the boy's self-accusations derive from the effects of his religious education, which influenced him as a child.

'(4) As the consequence of a fairly long stay in the country, physical exercise, and the return of his strength at the end of puberty, all the phenomena disappeared.

'(5) Perhaps one may ascribe the child's predisposition to this cerebral condition to heredity and to his father's earlier syphilis.'

The final word: 'Nous avons fait entrer cette observation dans le cadre des délires apyrétiques d'inanition, car c'est à l'ischémie cérebrale que nous rattachons cet état particulier.'*

(e) *Primary and Secondary Process. Repression*

In venturing further into the psychology of dream-processes, I have taken on a difficult task to which my expository skills, also, are scarcely equal. To express the simultaneity of such complicated interrelationships in terms of linear sequence in my description of them, while ensuring that each proposition I put forward does not appear to be based on prior assumptions, is likely to be too much for my powers. It is brought home to me now that in giving an account of the psychology of dreams I am not able to follow the historical development of my insights. My perspective on dreams was given me by my previous work on the psychology of neuroses, which I ought not to use as a point of reference here, although I shall have to do so again and again as I proceed in the opposite direction, starting out from dreams with the intention of making the connection to the

[8] My italics.

psychology of neuroses. I am aware of all the difficulties this will cause the reader, but I do not know how to avoid them.

Dissatisfied as I am by this state of affairs, I am happy to linger on a different aspect which seems to me to increase the value of my labours. As the introduction to my first chapter has indicated, I found a topic dominated by the sharpest contradictions among the opinions of the authorities. Our own treatment of the problems raised by dreams has found room for most of these contradictions. We ourselves had to argue decisively against only two of the views raised: that the dream has no meaning, and that it is a somatic process; but otherwise we were able to acknowledge that all these mutually contradictory opinions were right on some point in these complicated interrelationships, and to demonstrate that they had discovered something that was correct. By exposing the hidden dream-thoughts, we have confirmed in general that the dream does continue the motivation and interests of waking life, for dream-thoughts are engaged only with what seems to be important and of great interest to us. Dreams are never concerned with trivia. But we have also admitted the opposite, that dreams will also pick up the rejected trifles of the day, and will not make a major interest of the day their own until this has to some extent withdrawn from the work of our waking hours. We found this held good for the dream-content, which expresses the dream-thoughts in a form altered by distortion. For reasons to do with the mechanics of association, we said, the process of dreaming more readily takes possession of fresh or unimportant representations for its material, which have not yet been requisitioned by our waking thought; and for reasons of censorship, the process of dreaming transfers psychical intensity from what is important, but also objectionable, onto what is insignificant. The hypermnesia of dreams and their command of childhood material have become the two pillars on which our theory rests; our theory of dreams has ascribed to wishes deriving from childhood the part of indispensable moving-force in the formation of dreams. Of course it would not occur to us to doubt the importance, experimentally demonstrated, of external sensory stimuli during sleep, but we have given this material the same place relative to the dream-wish as we have the remnants of thought left over from the work of the day. We do not need to dispute that the dream interprets the objective sensory stimulus as if it were an illusion; but where the authorities left the motive for this interpretation uncertain, we have put it in. The interpretation occurs in such a way that the object perceived is deprived of its power to disturb our sleep and becomes available for purposes of wish-fulfilment. It is true, we do not accept that subject-ive states of excitation in the sensory organs occurring during sleep are a particular source of dreams, though this appears to have been demonstrated by Trumbull Ladd [40]. However, we are able to explain them as a regressive revival of memories operating behind the dream. Internal organic sensations, too, which are seized on as the key point in explaining dreams, also retain their function in our conception, but with a more modest scope. In our view, these sensations—of falling, floating, being inhibited—represent material available at all times for the dream-work to use to express the dream-thoughts whenever it needs to.

That the process of dreaming is rapid and momentary appears to us to be true of the perception by consciousness of the ready-made dream-content; but we have found it more likely that the preliminary parts of the dream-process take a slow, drifting course. With regard to the puzzle of a dream-content abounding in ideas but concen-trated into the briefest moment, we were able to add that these are cases where the dream admits structures ready-made and already present in the life of the psyche. We agreed that dreams are distorted and deformed by memory, but we found this no obstacle, for this is only the last, manifest part of a work of distortion operative from the start of the process of dream-formation. In the embittered, seem-ingly irreconcilable dispute over whether our inner life sleeps at night or still has all its capacities at its disposal as it does by day, we were able to say that both sides were right, but that neither of them was entirely right. We were able to discover in the dream-thoughts proof of highly complicated intellectual performance, operating with almost all the instrumentation of the psychical apparatus; but it still cannot be denied that these dream-thoughts originated in the day-time, and it is essential to assume that there is such a thing as a state of sleep for the inner life. This is how even the theory of partial sleep came into its own; but the state of sleep, we found, is not character-ized by the disintegration of psychical interconnections, but by the focus on the wish to sleep by the psychical system in control of the day. Withdrawal of attention from the external world, too, retained its importance in our conception of the dream; although it is not the only factor, it helps to make the regressive nature of representation in dreams possible. There is no disputing that voluntary direction of the course of ideas is abandoned; but this does not mean that the life of the psyche becomes purposeless, for we have heard that once the voluntary purposes are relinquished, involuntary purposes take control. We have not only acknowledged the existence of loose associative connections in dreams, but we have given them a much wider scope than could have been suspected; however, we discovered that they were only imposed substitutes for other—proper and meaningful—associations. Certainly, we too called the dream absurd; but we learned from examples how clever the dream is when it is pretending to be absurd. We do not disagree on the functions that have been ascribed to the dream. That the dream, like a safety-valve, allows the psyche to let off steam; and that, as Robert puts it, by imagining it in the dream, all sorts of harmful stuff is rendered harmless—this not only coincides exactly with our theory of the dream's double wish-fulfilment, but it becomes more intelligible in our theory than in Robert's, even in its formulation. The psyche's revelling in the free play of its capacities can also be found in our theory, in the way preconscious activity allows the dream to run on. The 'return of our inner life to the embryonic point of view in dreams', and the words of Havelock Ellis [23], 'an archaic world of vast emotions and imperfect thought', appear to be happy anticipations of our own argument, which has *primitive* ways of working, suppressed by day, taking part in the formation of dreams; and like Delage [15], we regard 'the *suppressed*' as the motive force of dreaming.

We have fully recognized the part Scherner ascribes to the dream-imagination, as well as Scherner's own interpretations, but we have had to allocate them, as it were, a different place in the problem. It is not that the dream forms the imagination, but that the unconscious activity of the imagination has the greatest share in the formation of the dream-thoughts. We are still indebted to Scherner for drawing our attention to the source of dream-thoughts; but almost everything that he ascribes to the dream-work is to be put down to the activity of the Unconscious during the day, which provides the spur for dreams no less than for neurotic symptoms. We had to distinguish the dream-work from this activity as something quite different and far more specific. Finally, we have certainly not given up the relation between dreams and disorders of the psyche; rather, we have set it more firmly on a fresh basis.

What is new in our theory of dreams acts as a kind of greater whole, holding the most various and contradictory conclusions of our authors together and including them in our structure, with many of them altered and only a few entirely rejected. But our building too is still incomplete. Quite apart from the many uncertainties we have brought upon ourselves by advancing into the darkness of psychology, there is also a fresh contradiction that seems to weigh upon us. On the one hand, we had the dream-thoughts come about by means of completely normal mental activity, but on the other, we discovered a number of quite abnormal thought-processes among the dream-thoughts, and we made our way from them to the dream-content; we then go over them again in our interpretation of the dream. Everything we have called the 'dream-work' appears to depart so far from psychical processes we know to be rational, that the harshest judgement passed by our authors on the low psychical performance of dreaming cannot fail to seem perfectly right and proper.

At this point it may be that we will gain aid and enlightenment only by advancing still further. I will single out one of the constellations leading to the formation of dreams:

We have learned that the dream takes the place of a number of thoughts that come from the life of the day and are connected in a perfectly logical way. This removes any doubts that these thoughts have their origin in our normal mental life. All the characteristics we admire in our thought-processes, and which mark them out as complicated feats of a high order, can also be found in the dream-thoughts. But there is no need to assume that this intellectual work is accomplished during sleep—that would throw our idea of the psychical state of sleep, firmly held so far, into dire confusion. Rather, these thoughts could very well come from the day, and from their first prompting could have gone on unnoticed by our consciousness, and could already have been completed when we fell asleep. If we are to gather anything from this situation, it is at most *that the most complicated feats of thinking are possible without the participation of consciousness*—which in any case we were bound to learn from every psychoanalysis of a hysteric or person with obsessional ideas. These dream-thoughts are in themselves certainly not incapable of becoming conscious; if they have not become conscious to us in the course of the day, there may be several reasons for it. Becoming conscious is connected with the application of a particular psychical function, attention, which it seems is used only in a particular quantity, and this latter may be diverted from the train of thought in question by other aims. Another way in which such trains of thought can be withheld from consciousness is the following: we know from our conscious reflection that when we are paying attention, we are pursuing a definite path. If, as we go along this path, we come upon an idea that does not stand up to criticism, we break off; we let the charge of our attention drop. Now it seems that the train of thought we embarked on and abandoned can carry on spinning itself out, even though our attention is no longer turned to it, provided that the process does not reach a particularly high intensity at any point, forcing attention onto it. A train of thought may be rejected at the beginning, probably consciously, by a judgement that it is wrong, or useless for the present purpose of the act of thinking, so it is possible that this is the reason why it will continue, unnoticed by consciousness, until we fall asleep.

Let us sum up: we call a train of thought of this kind *preconscious*; we regard it as completely rational, and it can just as readily be one that has been merely neglected as one that has been interrupted or suppressed. Let us also state outright how we visualize the course that a train of ideas follows. We believe that, starting from a purposive idea, a certain amount of excitation that we call 'charging energy' is displaced along paths of association selected by this purposive idea. A 'neglected' train of thought has not received such a charge of energy; a 'suppressed' or 'rejected' train of thought has had it withdrawn; both are left to their own excitations. A train of thought that has been purposively charged will, under certain circumstances, be capable of attracting the attention of consciousness to itself, and via this mediating agency it will then receive a '*supercharge*'. We shall have to explain our assumptions about the nature and function of consciousness a little later.

A train of thought set going in the Preconscious in this way can die down of its own accord or it can hold its own. We envisage the first outcome as occurring if the energy of the train of thought has been diffused in all the associative directions leading out from it, putting the entire chain into a state of excitation that lasts for a while, but then fades away as the excitation needing discharge is transformed into a quiescent charge. If this first outcome does occur, the process has no further significance for the formation of dreams. However, there are other purposive ideas lurking in our Preconscious which come from the sources of our unconscious and ever-active wishes. These can take over the excitation in the sphere of thoughts left to themselves, set up a connection between these and the unconscious wish, *transfer* to them the energy belonging to the unconscious wish, and from now on the neglected or suppressed train of thought is in a position to hold its own, though this reinforcement does not give it any right to be admitted to consciousness. We may say that the train of thought, preconscious until now, has been *drawn into the Unconscious*.

Other constellations leading to the formation of a dream might be, if from the start the preconscious train of thought were linked with the unconscious wish and for that reason came up against rejection from the dominant purposive charge; or if an unconscious wish became active from other (perhaps somatic) causes, and were to look for a transference onto the psychical residues that are not charged by the *Precon.* and do not come halfway to meet it. All three cases have the same result in the end: a train of thought comes about in the Preconscious, deserted by the preconscious energy-charge, but receiving one from the unconscious wish.

From then on the train of thought undergoes a series of transformations which we no longer recognize as normal psychical processes, and which produces a disconcerting result, a psychopathological formation. Let us single them out and put them together.

(1) The intensities of the individual ideas in their total amount become capable of discharge and pass over from one idea to another, so that individual ideas are formed which are invested with great intensity. With the frequent repetition of this process, the intensity of an entire train of thought can finally be concentrated in a single one of its elements. This is the fact of *compression* or *condensation* which we got to know in the course of the dream-work. It is condensation that is mainly to blame for the disconcerting impression made by dreams, for we are quite unfamiliar with anything analogous to it in our normal inner life accessible to consciousness. Here too we have ideas possessing great psychical significance as points of intersection or as the final result of entire chains of thought, but

their importance is not expressed by any characteristic obviously discernible to internal perception; the importance of the idea in this respect does not make what is presented in it any more intense. However, in the process of condensation all the psychical inter-connections are converted into the *intensity* of the ideational content. It is the same as if I were having a book printed, and had a word I regarded as overwhelmingly important for understanding the text printed in italics or bold. In speaking, I would pronounce the word loudly and slowly and with emphasis. The first comparison takes us directly to one of the examples borrowed from the dream-work (*Trimethylamine* in the dream of Irma's injection). Art historians remind us that the oldest historical sculptures follow a similar prin-ciple to express the rank of the personages represented by their size in the sculpture. The king is represented as two or three times bigger than his entourage or his vanquished enemy. A sculpture from the Roman period will make use of more subtle means for the same purpose. It will place the figure of the Emperor in the middle, show him raised high, devote particular care to the modelling of his figure, lay his enemies at his feet, but no longer have him appear as a giant among dwarfs. Meanwhile, the bow the inferior makes to his superior among ourselves today is still a late echo of that ancient principle of representation.

The direction taken by the condensations in the dream is pre-scribed on the one hand by the rational preconscious relations of the dream-thoughts, on the other by the attraction of the visual memories in the Unconscious. The work of condensation aims to produce those intensities required to break through to the perceptual systems.

(2) Again, intermediary ideas, rather like compromises (see the numerous examples), are created by the mobility with which these intensities can be freely transferred, also in the service of condensa-tion. This is something equally unheard of in the normal processing of ideas, where what matters most is the selection and retention of the 'right' element among them. By contrast, composite and com-promise formations occur with extraordinary frequency when we are searching for the words to express preconscious thoughts; these are described as varieties of 'slips of the tongue'.

(3) The ideas that transpose their intensities from one to the other have the *loosest relations* to one another, and are linked by associations of a kind scorned by our normal thinking and left to be exploited for

comic effect. In particular, verbal associations based on punning and similarities of sound are regarded as being equal in value to the others.

(4) Thoughts contradicting each other do not aim to cancel each other out, but persist side by side, often combining *as if there were no contradiction* into products of condensation, or they form compromises which we would never forgive our logical thinking for committing, but often approve of in our actions.

These are some of the most striking of the abnormal processes which the dream-thoughts, having previously had a rational form, undergo in the course of the dream-work. As we see, what chiefly characterizes them is the importance attached to making the charge of energy mobile and *capable of discharge*; the content and the proper meaning of the psychical elements carrying the charge become unimportant. One might still suppose that condensation and the formation of compromises take place only to help to bring about regression, if it is a matter of transforming thoughts into images. However, the analysis—and still more clearly the synthesis—of dreams that dispense with any regression to images, for example, the dream '*Autodidasker*—conversation with Professor N.', reveal the same processes of displacement and condensation as the rest.

Thus, we cannot deny the insight that two essentially different psychical processes play a part in forming dreams; the one creates perfectly rational dream-thoughts, just as valid as normal thinking; the other treats these in a most disconcerting, irrational manner. We have already isolated the second in Chapter VI as the true dreamwork. What have we to say now about the origins of this second psychical process?

We could not give an answer at this point if we had not already gone some way into the psychology of neuroses, particularly of hysteria. From this we learn that the same irrational psychical processes—and others I have not enumerated—control the production of hysterical symptoms. In hysteria too we first discover a set of completely rational thoughts, entirely equal in validity to our conscious thoughts; but we are unable to find out anything about their existence in this form and can only reconstruct them in retrospect. If they make their way through to our perceptions at some place, we see from our analysis of the symptoms formed that these normal thoughts have undergone abnormal treatment, and *by means of condensation and compromise-formation, by way of superficial associations under cover of contradictions, and possibly along the path of regression, they have been transposed into the symptoms.* Given this total identity between the characteristics of the dream-work and the psychical activity whose outcome is psychoneurotic symptoms, we consider we are justified in carrying over to dreams the conclusions that hysteria forces us to draw.

From the theory of hysteria we take the following proposition: *a normal train of thought is subject to this kind of abnormal treatment only if an unconscious wish originating in infancy and in a state of repression has been transferred to it.* It is for the sake of this proposition that we have built our theory of the dream on the assumption that the wish motivating the dream always originates from the Unconscious— which, as we have admitted, cannot be proved to be universally applicable, though it cannot be disproved either. But to be able to say what '*repression*' is, a name we have played with so often, we will have to go on building our psychological scaffolding for a while longer.

We gave our attention to the fiction of a primitive psychical apparatus whose activity was regulated by the attempt to avoid the build-up of excitation and maintain itself as free of excitation as possible. That is why it was constructed along the lines of a reflex apparatus; the power of movement, which first of all provides a route to changes within the body, was the path of discharge at its disposal. We then discussed the psychical consequences of the experience of satisfaction, and in doing so, we could already have included our second assumption, that a build-up of excitation—following various modalities which need not concern us here—is felt as unpleasure, and puts the apparatus into action in order to restore the experience of satisfaction in which the reduction of excitation is felt as pleasure. A current of this kind in the apparatus, starting out from unpleasure and aiming for pleasure, we call a wish; we said that only a wish can set the apparatus in motion, and that the course of excitation in it is automatically regulated by the perceptions of pleasure and unpleasure. The first wishing was perhaps a hallucinatory charging of the memory of satisfaction. However, this hallucination, if it was not to be retained to the point of exhaustion, turned out to be no good at bringing about the cessation of the need, and hence the pleasure, bound up with the satisfaction.

This made a second activity—in our terms, the activity of a second system—necessary, which did not allow the memory-charge to get as far as perception and from there to bind the forces of the psyche, but diverts the excitation caused by the need along a detour; by way of voluntary movement, this indirect route ultimately alters the external world in such a way that a real perception of the object of satisfaction can come about. Up to this point we have been following our schematic plan of the psychical apparatus; the two systems are the germ of what we have put in place as the *Uncon.* and *Precon.* in the fully developed apparatus.

To be able to alter the external world effectively by movement, it is necessary to build up a large number of experiences in the memory-systems and to have a variety of firmly fixed associations that are summoned up in this memory-material by different purposive ideas. Let us now take our assumptions further. The activity of the second system, multifariously feeling its way, emitting charges of energy, withdrawing again, on the one hand needs to have all the memory-material freely at its disposal; on the other, it would be an unnecessary expense of effort if it were to send vast quantities of energy-charge along particular paths of thought, which would then discharge uselessly and reduce the quantity needed for altering the external world. I postulate, then, that it is for the sake of efficiency that the second system manages to keep the greater part of the energy-charges quiescent, and uses only a smaller part for displacement. The mechanics of these processes is quite unknown to me; anyone wanting to take these ideas seriously would have to look for analogies to them in physics and find a way of visualizing the process of movement as it occurs in the excitation of neurones. But I do maintain that the activity of the first ψ-system is directed towards *the free discharge of quantities of excitation*; and that the second system *inhibits* this discharge by emitting its own energy-charges, transforming the charge into a quiescent one and probably raising its level. I am assuming, then, that the discharge of excitation as governed by the second system is linked to quite different mechanical conditions from those present when governed by the first. Once the second system has ended its exploratory thought-activity, it also suspends its activity of inhibiting and damming the excitations, allowing them to be discharged in movement.

Some interesting thoughts arise if we look at the relation of this inhibition of discharge by the second system to regulation by the unpleasure principle. Let us consider the counterpart to the primary experience of satisfaction, the *experience of an external shock*. Suppose a perceptual stimulus, the source of an excitation of pain, impinges on the primitive apparatus. If so, this will be expressed in spasmodic movements until one of them removes the apparatus from the perception and at the same time from the pain; if the perception reappears, this process will promptly be repeated (as a movement of flight, say), until the perception has disappeared once more. But in this situation no inclination will remain to recharge the perception of the source of pain with hallucinatory, or any other kind of intensity. Rather, if this painful memory-image is aroused in some way, there will be an inclination in the primary apparatus to abandon it at once, for after all, any overflow of its excitation would call up unpleasure (or, more precisely, would begin to call it up). Turning away from the memory, which is only a repetition of the earlier flight from the perception, is made easier because, unlike the perception, the memory does not possess enough quality to excite consciousness and in this way attract a fresh charge of energy. This effortless and regular way the psychical process has of turning away from the memory of what was once painful offers us the model and the first example of *psychical repression*. It is widely recognized how much of this avoidance of what is painful—ostrich tactics—is still demonstrably to be found in the inner life of normal adults.

As a consequence of the unpleasure principle, then, the first ψ-system is utterly incapable of taking anything unpleasant into the context of its thoughts. All the system can do is wish. If this were to remain so, it would hamper the thinking-activity of the second system, which needs to have at its disposal all the memories laid down in experience. Two paths are now possible. Either the work of the second system frees itself completely from the unpleasure principle, and continues on its own way without bothering about the unpleasure roused by a memory; or it can charge the unpleasurable memory in such a way that the release of unpleasure is avoided. We can reject the first possibility, for the unpleasure principle is patently the regulator for the course of excitation in the second system. This leaves us with the second possibility: that this system is able to charge memories in such a way that they inhibit discharge, and thus also inhibit any discharge—comparable to the inhibition of a motor innervation—in the direction of the development of unpleasure. We have, then, two points of departure—the account taken of both the unpleasure principle and the principle of the least expenditure of innervation—leading us to the hypothesis that charging by the second system also represents an inhibition on the discharge of excitation. But let us hold on to the thought—it is the key to the theory of repression—*that the second system can only charge an idea if it is in a position to inhibit the development of unpleasure issuing from it.* Anything that might perhaps escape this inhibition would also be inaccessible to the second system, and as a consequence of the unpleasure principle would promptly be dropped. However, the inhibition of the unpleasure need not be total; the beginnings of unpleasure must be allowed, for they give the second system some indication of the nature of the memory and perhaps of its unsuitability for the purpose intended by the thinking-process.

I shall now give the name of *primary process* to the psychical process which the first system alone allows; and the one resulting from the inhibition imposed by the second system I shall call the *secondary process.* There is another point where I can show why the second system is bound to act as a corrective to the primary process. The primary process aims to discharge excitation in order to set up a *perceptual identity*, using the amount of excitation accumulated in this way to do so; the secondary process has abandoned this intention and taken up another in its place—to set up a *thought-identity*. All thinking is only a roundabout way from the memory of a satisfaction, adopted as its purposive idea, to an identical charge of the same memory, which, it is intended, will be regained by way of motor experiences. Thinking must interest itself in the connecting paths between ideas without allowing itself to be led astray by their intensities. But it is clear that condensations of ideas, intermediary and compromise-formations, are an obstacle to attaining this goal of identity; by replacing one idea with another, they diverge from the path that led on from the first. So in secondary thinking, processes of this kind are carefully avoided. It is also easy to see that the unpleasure principle also puts difficulties in the way of the thinking process in its pursuit of thought-identity, though otherwise the principle offers it very important clues. Thinking, then, must move towards freeing itself more and more from the exclusive regulation of the unpleasure principle, and towards limiting the development of affect by thought-activity to the minimum that can still function as a signal. This finer differentiation of functioning is meant to be achieved by a fresh supercharge, mediated by consciousness. But we are well aware that this is rarely a complete success, even in the most normal inner life, and that our thinking always remains vulnerable to falsification by interference from the unpleasure principle.

But this is not the flaw in the efficient functioning of our psychical apparatus that makes it possible for thoughts, which present themselves as the products of secondary thought-activity, to fall victim to the primary psychical process ('primary psychical process' is now the formula we can use to describe the activity that leads to dreams and to hysterical symptoms). Inefficiency arises from the encounter of two factors from our evolutionary history: the one devolves entirely onto the psychical apparatus, and has exercised a crucial influence on the relations between the two systems. But the other comes into its own fitfully, introducing driving-forces of organic origin into the inner life. Both have their origins in infancy, and are the deposit of the changes that our psychical and somatic organism has gone through since the time of childhood.

When I called a process in the psychical apparatus a *primary* one, it was not only with an eye to its place in a hierarchy or to its efficiency, but rather because in choosing this name I also wanted to include some reference to time. It is true, a psychical apparatus that would only possess the primary process does not to our knowledge exist, and to that extent it is a theoretical fiction; but we do know as a fact that the primary processes are present as a given from the start, while the secondary processes only develop gradually in the course of our life; they inhibit and overlay the primary processes, perhaps not attaining complete control over them until the prime of life. As a consequence of this belated entry of the secondary processes, the heart of our being, made of the unconscious wishful impulses, cannot be comprehended or inhibited by the Preconscious, whose function is restricted once and for all to indicating the most convenient paths to the wishful impulses from the Unconscious. These unconscious wishes exert a compulsion on all the psyche's later aims and efforts, which have to adapt themselves to this pressure, or labour to divert it, redirecting it to higher aims. As a further consequence of this belated appearance, a wide field of memory-material also remains inaccessible to preconscious charging.

Now among these wishful impulses originating in our infancy, which cannot be destroyed or inhibited, there are also some whose fulfilment is a contradiction to the purposive ideas pursued by secondary thinking. The fulfilment of these wishes would no longer produce an affect of pleasure, but of unpleasure, *and it is this very transformation of affect that makes up the nature of what we call 'repression'.* How a transformation of this kind occurs, what paths it takes, what motive forces drive it—these questions make up the problem of repression, which we need only touch upon here. It is enough for us to hold on to the idea that a transformation of affect of this sort occurs in the course of our development (we only have to think of the emergence in a child's life of disgust, which was absent at the start), and that it is linked to the activity of the second system. The memories that are the starting-point for the unconscious wish to summon the release of affect, were never accessible to the *Precon.*; that is why the release of the affect belonging to them cannot be inhibited either. Precisely because of this emergence of affect, these ideas are now inaccessible even from the preconscious thoughts onto which they have transferred their wishful force. On the contrary, the unpleasure principle takes over, and causes the *Precon.* to turn away from these transference-thoughts. These are left to themselves, 'repressed', and so it is that the presence of a store of infantile memories, unavailable to the *Precon.* from the start, becomes the prerequisite for repression.

In the most favourable cases, the production of unpleasure comes to an end as soon as the energy-charge is withdrawn from the transferred thoughts in the *Precon.* This successful result indicates that the intervention of the unpleasure principle has been effective. However, it is a different matter if the repressed unconscious wish experiences an organic reinforcement, which it lends to its transference-thoughts; doing so puts them in a position to attempt to force their way through with their excitation, even if they have lost their energy-charge from the *Precon.* A defensive struggle ensues, in which the *Precon.* reinforces the opposition to the repressed thoughts; there follows a breakthrough of the transference-thoughts, which are the vehicle of the unconscious wish, into some form of compromise by forming a symptom. But from the moment the repressed thoughts are powerfully charged with the unconscious wishful excitation, and on the other hand have been deserted by their preconscious charge, they are subject to the primary process, and their only aim is motor discharge or, if the way is open, hallucinatory revival of the desired perceptual identity. Earlier, we found empirically that the irrational processes we described only unfold with thoughts that are in a state of repression. Now we are able to understand yet another part of these relationships. These irrational processes are the *primary* ones in the psychical apparatus; they always make an appearance wherever imagined ideas are deserted by their preconscious charge and left to themselves, when they can be invested with the uninhibited energy of the Unconscious as it strives for discharge. There are, in addition, some other observations to support the view that these processes which I have called irrational are not falsifications of normal processes, not intellectual errors, but modes of activity of the psychical apparatus that are free of inhibition. Thus we can see that the shift from preconscious excitation to motor action follows the same processes, and that the attachment of preconscious imagined ideas to words can easily show the very same displacements and confusions which we normally ascribe to inattention. Finally, evidence of the increase in work that becomes necessary with the inhibition of these primary modes of functioning comes from the fact that we produce a comic effect, a surplus to be discharged in laughter, if we let these modes of functioning in our thinking force their way into consciousness.

The theory of the psychoneuroses maintains with absolute certainty that only wishful impulses from infancy that are sexual in nature and have been subject to repression (transformation of affect) are capable of revival in later periods of development, whether as a consequence of the individual's sexual constitution—which, of course, developed out of an original bisexuality—or as a consequence of unfavourable influences on his sex-life; if this is the case, they will provide the driving-force for the formation of all psychoneurotic symptoms. It is only by introducing these sexual forces that the demonstrable gaps in the theory of repression can be filled. I will leave it an open question whether sexual and infantile factors should also be required for the theory of dreams; I leave this theory unfinished at this point, for I have already taken a step beyond what can be demonstrated by assuming that dream-wishes always originate in the Unconscious.[9] Nor will I go any further in my investiga-

---

[9] Here as elsewhere, there are gaps in my treatment of the topic which I have left intentionally, because to fill them would require on the one hand too much effort, and on the other reliance on material alien to dreams. Thus, for example, I have avoided indicat-

tion into what makes the difference between the interplay of psychical forces in the formation of dreams and in the formation of hysterical symptoms; after all, we do not have accurate enough knowledge of one of the two objects of comparison. But there is another point which I regard as very important, and I will preface it by confessing that it is only for the sake of this point that I have included my entire discussion of the two psychical systems, with their modes of activity and repression. For it is not now a matter of whether my conception of these is halfway correct, or—easily possible in such difficult matters—whether it is skewed and incomplete. However much the interpretation of the psychical censorship and of the rational and the abnormal revisions of the dream-content may change, it will still hold good that processes of this kind are active in the formation of dreams, and are in essentials most closely analogous to the processes identified in the formation of hysterical symptoms. Now the dream is not a pathological phenomenon; it does not presuppose a disturbance of the psychical equilibrium; it does not leave any reduction in efficiency behind it. The objection that my own dreams and the dreams of my neurotic patients do not allow any conclusions to be drawn about the dreams of normal persons may well be dismissed without consideration. So when we argue from the phenomena to the forces driving them, we are recognizing that the psychical mechanism which the neurosis makes use of is not first created by a pathological disorder attacking the inner life, but is already present

---

ing whether I attach different meanings to the word 'suppressed' [*unterdrückt*] and the word 'repressed' [*verdrängt*]. I only need to make it clear that the latter emphasizes its affiliation to the Unconscious more strongly than the former. I have not gone into the closely related* problem of why the dream-thoughts undergo distortion by the censorship, even in cases where they give up their progressive movement towards consciousness and opt for the path of regression—and further such omissions. What I was chiefly concerned to do was to give some impression of those problems we are led towards by further analysis of the dream-work, and to indicate the other topics such analysis encounters on its way. I have not always found it easy to decide where to break off from pursuing them.—The fact that I have not dealt exhaustively with the part played by sexual ideas in dreams, and have avoided interpreting dreams with an obviously sexual content, has a particular reason, which may not coincide with the reader's expectations. It is utterly foreign to my opinions and the theoretical views I put forward in neuropathology to regard the sexual life as a shameful thing which neither physician nor scientist should be concerned with. And, in my opinion, the moral indignation that moved the translator of Artemidorus of Daldis [2] to withhold the chapter on sexual dreams from the reader is ridiculous. What decided me was solely the realization that in explaining sexual dreams I would have to become deeply involved in the still unsolved problems of perversion and bisexuality, and so I kept this material for another occasion.

in the normal structure of the psychical apparatus. The two psychical systems, the censorship on the transit between them, the inhibition and overlaying of one activity by the other, the relations of both to consciousness—or whatever a more correct interpretation of the actual circumstances may have to offer instead of these—all these belong to the normal structure of our psychical instrument, and dreams show us one of the ways leading to an understanding of that structure. If we are content with a minimum of completely guaranteed new knowledge, we will be able to say that dreams prove to us *that what is suppressed continues to exist in normal persons too, and remains capable of psychical functioning*. The dream itself is one of the expressions of what is suppressed; in theory, this is so in all cases; palpably and empirically it is so at least in a great number of instances, and these, in fact, display the striking characteristics of the dream-life at their clearest. In waking life, what is suppressed in the psyche is thwarted in its attempts at expression by the *removal of contradictions by their opposite** and cut off from internal perception; at night, and in the power of compromise-formations, it finds ways and means of forcing its way into consciousness.

*Flectere si nequeo superos, Acheronta movebo.**

By pursuing the analysis of dreams, we can get a little further in our understanding of how this most marvellous and mysterious instrument is composed; true, it is only a little further, but it is a beginning, enabling us to push on further in their analysis, starting from other formations which have to be described as pathological. For illnesses— at least those that are rightly called functional—do not have the destruction of this apparatus or the creation of new splittings within it for their precondition; they are to be explained *dynamically* by the strengthening and weakening of the components in the interplay of forces, so many of whose effects are hidden while they are functioning normally. I hope to show elsewhere how the composition of the apparatus out of the two agencies also allows a finer differentiation in normal functioning too, which would not be possible for one only.[10]

---

[10] Dreams are not the only phenomenon allowing us to base psychopathology on psychology. In a short series of articles, not yet completed, in the *Monatschrift für Psychiatrie und Neurologie* ('The Psychical Mechanism of Forgetfulness', 1898 [SE iii, 289]; 'Screen Memories' [SE iii, 301]) I attempt to interpret a number of everyday psychical phenomena in support of the same insight.

(f) *The Unconscious and Consciousness. Reality*

If we look more closely, it is not the existence of two systems near the motor end of the apparatus, but the existence of two different processes of excitation and two modes of its discharge that were suggested by our psychological discussions in the previous section. For us it would scarcely matter, for we must always be prepared to drop our provisional assumptions if we think we are in a position to replace them with something else closer to the unknown reality. Let us now try to correct some notions which could become misleading if we view the two systems in the crudest and most immediate sense as two locations within the psychical apparatus, notions that have left their mark in the terms 'repressing', or 'pushing back', and 'pushing through'. So when we say that an unconscious thought is aiming to be carried over into the Preconscious so that it can then push through to consciousness, we do not mean that a second thought is supposed to be formed in a new place, like a copy with the original existing concurrently with it. And as for pushing through to consciousness, let us also take care to detach it from any idea of a change of place. When we say a preconscious thought is pushed back and repressed, and then taken over by the Unconscious, we might be tempted by these images drawn from the sphere of ideas about battles for territory to assume that a constellation in one locality of the psyche is really being dissolved and replaced by a new one in the other locality. Instead of these metaphors, let us say what seems to correspond more closely to the real state of affairs: that a charge of energy is invested in a particular constellation, or is withdrawn from it, so that the psychical structure comes under the control of an agency, or is removed from it. Again, we are replacing a topographical mode of representation here by a dynamic one. What is mobile, it seems to us, is not the psychical formation, but rather its innervation.

All the same, I think it is useful and justifiable to keep this graphic way of representing the two systems. We will avoid any misuse of this mode of representation if we remind ourselves that ideas, thoughts, psychical formations generally are not to be located in organic elements of the nervous system at all, but, as it were, *between them*, where resistances and accesses form their corresponding correlatives. Everything that can become the object of our inner perception is *virtual*, like the image in the telescope made by the passage of light-rays. However, we are justified in assuming that the systems—which are not of a psychical nature themselves and will never be accessible to our psychical perception—are like the telescope lenses that create the image. If we continue this comparison, the censorship between the two systems would correspond to the refraction of a ray of light as it passes over into a new medium.

Up to now we have been psychologizing off our own bat. It is time to take a look at the theoretical opinions dominating contemporary psychology and examine how they relate to our propositions. The question of the Unconscious in psychology is, in Lipps's[11] forceful words, not so much a psychological question as *the* question of psychology. As long as psychology settled this question with the merely verbal explanation that 'the Psychical' was simply 'the Conscious', and 'unconscious psychical processes' were palpable nonsense, the door was closed to any psychological evaluation of the observations a physician was able to gain from abnormal psychical states. The physician and the philosopher will only meet when both recognize that 'unconscious psychical processes' is 'the most appropriate and considered expression for a well-established fact'. All the physician can do is to dismiss with a shrug of the shoulders the assertion that 'consciousness is the definitive characteristic of what is psychical', perhaps assuming, if his respect for the philosopher's remarks is still strong enough, that they have not been dealing with the same object nor pursuing the same science. For even one single perceptive observation of the inner life of a neurotic, one single analysis of a dream, is bound to urge upon him the unshakable conviction that it is possible for the most complicated and logical thought-processes, which cannot after all be denied the name of psychical processes, to occur without arousing the person's consciousness. Certainly, the physician does not learn of these unconscious processes until they have exercised some effect upon consciousness that can be communicated or observed. But this effect upon consciousness can display a psychical character that is wholly at variance with the unconscious process, so that it is impossible for our internal perception to recognize the one as a substitute for the

---

[11] 'The Concept of the Unconscious in Psychology', Lecture held at the Third International Congress for Psychology in Munich, 1897.

other. The physician must maintain his right to use an *inferential method* to make his way from the effect on consciousness to the unconscious psychical process; on his way he learns that the effect on consciousness is only a remote psychical effect of the unconscious process, and that the latter has not become conscious as such; also that it was present and in operation without revealing itself to consciousness in any way.

The essential preliminary to true insight into the psyche's way of working is to get away from overestimating the attribute of consciousness. The Unconscious must, as Lipps puts it, be assumed to be the general basis of the life of the psyche. The Unconscious is the greater sphere that includes the smaller sphere of the Conscious; everything conscious has a prior stage that is unconscious, whereas the Unconscious can remain at this stage and still claim to have the full value of a psychical function. The Unconscious is the true reality of the psyche, *its inner nature just as unknown to us as the reality of the external world, and just as imperfectly revealed by the data of consciousness as the external world is by the information received from our sensory organs.*

Now that the old antithesis between conscious life and the life of dreams as the psychical Unconscious has been put in place, a number of the problems of dreams, which were still profoundly engaging the earlier authors, have been removed. So many feats performed in dreams which made them marvel are now no longer to be credited to dreams, but to unconscious thinking, which is also active by day. If, as Scherner says, dreams seem to play with a symbolizing representation of the body, this is the feat of certain unconscious fantasies, which probably arise in response to sexual impulses, and are expressed not only in dreams but also in hysterical phobias and other symptoms. If a dream continues the work of the day and completes it, and even has valuable ideas and brings them to light, all we have to do is simply divest it of its dream-disguise as being the achievement of the dream-work and a sign of assistance from the dark powers in the depths of our soul (cf. the Devil in Tartini's* sonata dream). The intellectual feat itself is due to the same psychical powers that achieve all such feats during the day. We are probably far too much inclined to overestimate the conscious character even of intellectual or artistic production. However, from what some highly productive people, such as Goethe and

Helmholtz* tell us, we learn rather that the new and essential elements of their creations came into their mind suddenly and entered their perception almost complete. There is nothing odd about the contribution of consciousness in other instances where the efforts of all the mental powers were required. But it is the much-abused privilege of consciousness that, wherever it has a share, it conceals from us all the other activities of the psyche.

It is scarcely worth proposing the historical significance of dreams as a particular topic. Cases where a dream caused some commander to undertake a great enterprise whose success changed the course of history only present a new problem if we treat the dream as an alien force in contrast to other, more familiar psychical powers; but no longer if we regard the dream as a form of expression for impulses which are hampered by resistance by day, but are able to draw reinforcements from deep sources of excitation by night. But the respect ancient peoples paid to dreams is a tribute, based on a true psychological intimation, to the untamed, indestructible elements in the human soul, the *daemonic* powers* that produce the dream-wish and that we rediscover in our Unconscious.

I say '*in our Unconscious*' deliberately, for what we have given this name to is not identical with the Unconscious of the philosophers, not even with the Unconscious as Lipps conceives it. To the philosophers, it is simply meant to denote the opposite of the conscious. Lipps goes further and tells us that everything psychical is present in an unconscious state, and some of that is also present in a state of consciousness. But it is not as evidence for *this* proposition that we have called on the phenomena of dreams and the formation of hysterical symptoms; observation of our everyday life alone is enough to establish it beyond any doubt. The new thing we have learned from our analysis of psychopathological formations, indeed, from the first of the series, the dream, is that the Unconscious—that is, the essential nature of the psyche—occurs as the function of two separate systems, and does so in normal psychical life. Thus there are *two kinds of Unconscious* which, we find, the psychologists have not yet distinguished. Both are unconscious as psychology understands the term; but in our conception, the one we have called *Uncon.* is also *incapable of reaching consciousness*, whereas we have called the other *Precon.* because, although it is true it has to keep to certain rules, and may have to submit to a fresh censorship, its excitations are able to reach consciousness—still without taking account of the

Uncon.-system. The fact that, in order to reach consciousness, the excitations have to make their way through an immutable sequence of agencies, which we discovered from the changes imposed by the censorship they exercised, enabled us to set up a spatial analogy. We described the relations of the two systems to each other and to consciousness by saying that the *Precon.*-system stood like a partition-screen between the *Uncon.*-system and consciousness. The *Precon.*-system did not only block access to consciousness, we said, it also governed access to voluntary movement and directed the transmission of a mobile energy-charge, a part of which is familiar to us in the form of attention.

We also have to distance ourselves from the distinction between *supraconsciousness* and *subconsciousness* which has become so popular in recent literature on the psychoneuroses, as this above all seems to emphasize that what is psychical and what is conscious enjoy equal status.

What role is left in our account for once-omnipotent consciousness, which hid everything else from sight? No more than *that of a sensory organ for perceiving psychical qualities*. In accordance with the ideas at the basis of our attempted scheme, we can only conceive conscious perception as a function peculiar to a particular system, to which we may appropriately give the abbreviation *Con.* We conceive this system to be similar in its mechanical characteristics to the perception-system *Per.*, that is, susceptible to excitation by qualities and incapable of retaining any trace of alteration, that is, without memory. The psychical apparatus, which is turned towards the external world with the sensory organ of the *Per.*-systems, is itself the external world for the sensory organ of the *Con.*, which has its teleological justification in this state of affairs. Here again we encounter the principle of a series of agencies that seems to govern the structure of the apparatus. The excitatory material flows to the sensory organ of the *Con.* from two directions: from the *Per.*-system, where its excitation, determined by the qualities, probably undergoes fresh revision until it becomes a conscious sensation; and from within the apparatus itself, where the quantitative processes are felt qualitatively as the series pleasure–unpleasure, once they have achieved certain alterations.

Those philosophers who became aware that rational and highly composed thought-formations are possible even without a contribution from consciousness then had difficulties in ascribing any function to consciousness; it seemed to them to be a needless mirror-image of the completed psychical process. We are rescued from this embarrassment by the analogy between our *Con.*-system and the perceptual systems, for we can see that perception by our sensory organs has the result of directing a charge of attention towards the paths where the approaching sensory excitation is spread; the qualitative excitation of the *Per.*-system serves to regulate the discharge of the mobile quantity in the psychical apparatus. We can claim the same function for the overlying sensory organ of the *Con.*-system. In perceiving new qualities, it makes a new contribution to directing the mobile quantities of energy-charge, and to distributing them suitably. By its perception of pleasure and unpleasure, it influences the course of the energy-charges within the psychical apparatus, which otherwise operates unconsciously and by means of displacement of quantities. It is probable that at first the displacement of energy-charge is regulated automatically by the unpleasure principle, but it is quite possible that consciousness of these qualities adds a second, and finer, regulation, which can even be at odds with the first, completing the efficiency of the apparatus by enabling it, quite contrary to its original disposition, to submit even what is connected with the release of unpleasure to the processes of energy-charge and revision. We learn from the psychology of neuroses that a major part in the functioning of the apparatus is assigned to this regulation by the qualitative excitations of the sensory organs. The automatic domination of the primary unpleasure principle and the restriction of efficiency this involves are broken by the processes of sensory regulation, which are themselves automatic actions. We learn that repression, which originally served a purpose but nevertheless ends in a harmful loss of inhibition and inner control, is more easily brought to bear on memories than on perceptions, because they cannot receive any additional energy-charge from the excitation of the psychical sensory organ. If a thought to be fended off does not enter consciousness on the one hand because it is subject to repression, it can at other times only be repressed because it has been withdrawn from conscious perception for other reasons. These are the hints we make use of in our therapy to reverse the course of repressions that have already taken place.

From a teleological standpoint, the value of a supercharge of energy, which is produced by the regulatory influence of the *Con.* sensory organ on the mobile quantities, cannot be better demonstrated than by its ability to create a new series of qualities and thereby a new regulatory process—which is what constitutes the superiority of human beings over animals. For thought-processes are in themselves without quality, apart from the pleasurable and unpleasurable excitations accompanying them, which, as possible disturbances to thought, are after all meant to be kept within bounds. In order to invest them with some quality, they are associated in human beings with verbal memories, whose residual quality is sufficient to attract the attention of consciousness to them, which will then invest the thinking with a fresh charge of mobile energy.

We can only gain an overall view of the problems of consciousness in all their variety when we analyse hysterical thought-processes. When we do, we have the impression that the charge passing from the Preconscious to consciousness is also associated with a censorship similar to the censorship between *Uncon.* and *Precon.* This censorship too only sets in when a certain quantitative limit is reached, so that less intense thought-formations escape it. All the possible cases in which thoughts refuse to enter consciousness, or force their way into it only under limitations, are to be found together within the framework of psychoneurotic phenomena; they all point to the intimate reciprocal relationship between censorship and consciousness. I will close these psychological reflections with a report of two examples that illustrate this.

A consultation last year took me to an intelligent and unembarrassed-looking girl. Her style of dressing is disconcerting; where women's clothes are normally attended to down to the last pleat, one of her stockings is hanging down and two buttons of her blouse are open. She complains about having pains in one leg, and exposes her calf without being asked. But her main complaint, in her own words, is: *she has a feeling in her body as if something were sticking in it that is moving to and fro and shaking her through and through. When that happens, her whole body seems to grow stiff.* My colleague, also present, catches my eye; he has no difficulty in understanding her complaint. It seems remarkable to both of us that the patient's mother seems to make nothing of it, though she must have found herself repeatedly in the situation that her daughter is describing. The girl herself has no idea of the meaning of what she is saying; if she had, she would not utter it. In her case, the censorship has been successfully obscured, so that a fantasy that would otherwise remain in the Preconscious is admitted into consciousness under the seemingly innocuous mask of a complaint.

Another example. I begin the psychoanalytic treatment of a fourteen-year-old boy suffering from *tic convulsif*, hysterical vomiting, headaches, and the like by assuring him that when he closes his eyes he will see images, or ideas will come into his mind which he should tell me. He answers in images. The last impression he had before he came to me is revived visually in his memory. He had been playing a board game with his uncle, and now sees the board in front of him. He considers various positions that are favourable or unfavourable, moves that one should not make. Then he sees a dagger lying on the board, an object which his father owns, but which his imagination has removed onto the board. Then there is a sickle on the board, then it is joined by a scythe, and now the image of an old farmer makes its appearance, mowing the grass in front of the boy's faraway home with a scythe. After a few days I came to understand this sequence of images. Unhappy family circumstances have upset the boy. A harsh, irascible father, constantly quarrelling with his mother, with a method of bringing up his son by threats; his father's divorce of his gentle, tender mother; the remarriage of his father, who brought a young woman home one day to be his new mama. It was in the first days after this happened that the fourteen-year-old's illness broke out. The suppressed rage against his father composed those images into intelligible allusions. A recollection from mythology provided the material. The sickle is the one Zeus used to castrate his father, the scythe and the image of the farmer represent Cronos, the violent old man who devours his children, and on whom Zeus takes such unfilial revenge. The father's marriage was an occasion to throw back at him the accusations and threats which the boy had previously heard from him because he had been *playing* with his genitals (the board game; the forbidden moves; the dagger one can use to kill). In this case, it is long-repressed memories and their unconscious offspring that have slipped into consciousness by the roundabout routes opened up to them in the form of *apparently meaningless images*.

I would, then, look for the theoretical value of an interest in dreams in the contributions it makes to our psychological knowledge and in the start it makes towards our understanding of the psycho-neuroses. Who can guess how important a thorough acquaintance with the structure and functions of a psychical apparatus may become, when even the present-day state of our knowledge enables our therapies to have a fortunate influence on the essentially curable forms of psychoneuroses? And what of the practical value of this interest, I hear it asked, for our knowledge of the psyche, and for the revelation of hidden character traits in the individual? Do not the unconscious impulses revealed in dreams possess the value of real forces in our inner life? Is the ethical significance of our suppressed wishes to be treated as an unconsidered trifle, for just as they create dreams, they may one day create other things?

I do not feel justified in answering these questions. My thoughts have not pursued the problem of dreams under this aspect. I only think that, in any case, the Roman Emperor was wrong to have his subject put to death because he dreamed he had murdered his Emperor. He should have been concerned first with what the dream meant; most likely it was not the same as it appeared to be. And even if a dream with a different tenor had this treasonable meaning, it would still be fitting for us to bear Plato's observation in mind, that the virtuous man is content to dream what the wicked man actually does. In my view, then, it is best to absolve dreams. Whether we should ascribe *reality* to unconscious wishes, I cannot say. Of course we cannot grant it to any of the transitional or intermediary thoughts. Looking at these unconscious wishes reduced to their ultimate, their truest expression, we must bear in mind that what has psychical reality too can have more than just one form of existence.* To answer our practical need to judge men's characters, their actions and consciously uttered opinions are mostly sufficient. Actions, above all, deserve to be put in the forefront, for many impulses which have forced their way through to consciousness are still often annulled by real forces in our inner life before they have issued in action; indeed, that is why they often do not encounter any psychical obstacle on their way, because the Unconscious is certain they will be prevented at another point. It is still instructive in any case to get to know the much-disturbed soil on which our virtues proudly grow. The complexity of a human character, moved dynamically this way and that, can very seldom be resolved by deciding between simple alternatives, as our superannuated morality would have it.

And what of the value of dreams for our knowledge of the future? Of course that is out of the question. Instead, one should rather ask: for our knowledge of the past. For in every sense, dreams come from the past. It is true, the ancient belief that dreams show us the future is not entirely without some truth. For by representing a wish as fulfilled, a dream does indeed take us into the future; but this future, taken by the dreamer to be in the present, is shaped by the indestructible wish into the image of that past.

FREUD'S BIBLIOGRAPHY*

1. **Aristotle.** *Ueber Träume und Traumdeutungen.* Trans. by Bender.
2. **Artemidorus.** *Symbolik der Träume.* Trans. by Friedrich S. Krauss. Vienna 1881.
3. **Benini, V.** 'La memoria e la durata dei sogni'. *Rivista italiana di filosofia.* XIIa. 1898.
4. **Binz, C.** *Ueber den Traum.* Bonn 1878.
5. **Börner, J.** *Das Alpdrücken, seine Begründung und Verhütung.* Würzburg 1855.
6. **Bradley, F. H.** 'On the failure of movement in dream'. *Mind.* III. 1894.
7. **Brander, R.** *Der Schlaf und das Traumleben.* Leipzig 1884.
8. **Burdach, K. F.** *Die Physiologie als Erfahrungswissenschaft*, vol. III. 3rd edn. 1826–32.
9. **Büchsenschütz, B.** *Traum und Traumdeutung im Alterthum.* Berlin 1868.
10. **Chaslin, P.** 'Du rôle du rêve dans l'évolution du délire'. Thesis, Paris 1887.
11. **Chabaneix, P.** *Physiologie cerebrale: Le subconscient chez les artistes, les savants et les écrivains.* Paris 1897.
12. **Calkins, Mary Whiton.** 'Statistics of dreams'. *Amer. J. of Psychology.* V. 1893.
13. **Clavière.** 'La rapidité de la pensée dans le rêve'. *Revue philosophique.* XLIII. 1897.
14. **Dandolo, G.** *La coscienza nel sonno.* Padua 1889.
15. **Delage, Yves.** 'Une théorie du rêve'. *Revue industrielle*, II. 1891.
16. **Delboeuf, J.** *Le sommeil et les rêves.* Paris 1885.
17. **Debacker, F.** 'Des hallucinations et terreurs nocturnes des enfants'. Thesis, Paris 1881.
18. **Dugas, L.** 'Le souvenir du rêve'. *Revue philosophique.* XLIV. 1897.
19. —— 'Le sommeil et la cérébration inconsciente durant le sommeil'. *Revue philosophique.* XLIII. 1897.
20. **Egger, V.** 'La durée apparente des rêves'. *Revue philosophique.* XL. 1895.
21. —— 'Le souvenir dans le rêve'. *Revue philosophique.* XLVI. 1898.
22. **Ellis, Havelock.** 'On dreaming of the dead'. *The Psychological Review.* II, No. 5. September 1895.
23. —— 'The stuff that dreams are made of'. *Appleton's Popular Science Monthly.* LIV. April 1899.

24. **Ellis, Havelock.** 'A note on hypnagogic paramnesia'. *Mind.* VI. 1897.

25. **Fechner, G. T.** *Elemente der Psychophysik.* 2nd edn. 2 vols. Leipzig 1889.

26. **Fichte, I. H.** *Psychologie. Die Lehre vom bewussten Geiste des Menschen.* 2 vols. Part I. Leipzig 1864.

27. **Giessler, M.** *Aus den Tiefen des Traumlebens.* Halle 1890.

28. —— *Die physiologischen Beziehungen der Traumvorgänge.* Halle 1896.

29. **Goblot, E.** 'Sur le souvenir des rêves'. *Revue philosophique.* XLII. 1896.

30. **Graffunder, P. C.** *Traum und Traumdeutung.* 1894.

31. **Griesinger, W.** *Pathologie und Therapie der psychischen Krankheiten.* 3rd edn. Stuttgart 1871.

32. **Haffner, P.** 'Schlafen und Träumen'. *Frankfurter zeitgemässe Brochüren.* Vol. 5, no. 10. 1884.

33. **Hallam, F.** and **S. Weed.** 'A study of the dream consciousness'. *Amer. J. of Psychology.* VII. 1896.

34. **Hervey de Saint-Denys, Marquis d'.** *Les rêves et les moyens de les diriger.* Paris 1867. (anonym.)

35. **Hildebrandt, F. W.** *Der Traum und seine Verwerthung für's Leben.* Leipzig 1875.

36. **Jessen, P.** *Versuch einer wissenschaftlichen Begründung der Psychologie.* Berlin 1855.

37. **Jodl, F.** *Lehrbuch der Psychologie.* Stuttgart 1896.

38. **Kant, J.** *Anthropologie in pragmatischer Hinsicht.* Kirchmann edn. Leipzig 1880.

39. **Krauss, A.** 'Der Sinn im Wahnsinn'. *Allgemeine Zeitschrift für Psychiatrie.* XV and XVI. 1858–9.

40. **Ladd, G. T.** 'Contribution to the psychology of visual dreams'. *Mind.* I. 1892.

41. **Leidesdorf, M.** *Das Traumleben.* Vienna 1880.—*Sammlung der 'Alma Mater'.*

42. **Lemoine, A.** *Du sommeil au point de vue physiologique et psychologique.* Paris 1855.

43. **Liébeault, A.** *Le sommeil provoqué et les états analogues.* Paris 1889.

44. **Lipps, T.** *Grundthatsachen des Seelenlebens.* Bonn 1883.

45. **Le Lorrain, J.** 'Le rêve'. *Revue philosophique.* XL. 1895.

46. **Maudsley, H.** *Physiology and the Pathology of Mind.* 2nd edn. London 1868.

47. **Maury, A.** 'Nouvelles observations sur les analogies des phénomènes du rêve et de l'aliénation mentale'. *Annales méd. psych.* 1855.

48. —— *Le sommeil et les rêves.* Paris 1878.

49. **Moreau, J.** 'De l'identité de l'état de rêve et de folie'. *Annales méd. psych.* I. 1855.

50. **Nelson, J.** 'A study of dreams'. *Amer. J. of Psychology.* I, 1888.

51. **Pilcz, A.** 'Ueber eine gewisse Gesetzmäßigkeit in den Träumen'. Author's abstract in *Monatsschrift für Psychologie und Neurologie.* V. 1899.

52. **Pfaff, E. R.** *Das Traumleben und seine Deutung nach den Principien der Araber, Perser, Griechen, Indier und Aegypter.* Leipzig 1868.

53. **Purkinje, J. E.** 'Wachen, Schlaf, Traum und verwandte Zustände', in Wagner's *Handwörterbuch der Physiologie.* vol. 3. Braunschweig 1846.

54. **Radestock, P.** *Schlaf und Traum.* Leipzig 1879.

55. **Robert, W.** *Der Traum als Naturnothwendigkeit erklärt.* Hamburg 1886.

56. **Sanctis, Sante de.** 'Les maladies mentales et les rêves'. Extrait des *Annales de la Societé de médecine de Gand.* LXXVI. 1897.

57. ——— 'Sui rapporti d'identità, di somiglianza, di analogia e di equivalenza fra sogno e pazzia'. *Rivista quindicinale di Psicologia, Psichiatria, Neuropatologia.* 15 Nov. 1897.

58. **Scherner, K. A.** *Das Leben des Traums.* Berlin 1861.

59. **Scholz, F.** *Schlaf und Traum.* Leipzig 1887.

60. **Schopenhauer, A.** 'Versuch über das Geistersehen und was damit zusammenhängt'. *Parerga und Paralipomena,* 2nd edn. Berlin, vol. I, 1862.

61. **Schleiermacher, F.** *Psychologie, Gesammelte Werke,* ed. L. George. vol. VI, pt. 3. Berlin 1862.

62. **Siebeck, H.** *Das Traumleben der Seele.* Berlin 1877.

63. **Simon, M.** *Le monde des rêves.* Paris 1888. Bibliothèque scientifique contemporaine.

64. **Spitta, H.** *Die Schlaf- und Traumzustände der menschlichen Seele.* 2nd edn., Tübingen 1892.

65. **Stumpf, E. J. G.** *Der Traum und seine Deutung.* Leipzig 1899.

66. **Strümpell, L.** *Die Natur und Entstehung der Träume.* Leipzig 1877.

67. **Tannery, M. P.** 'Sur la mémoire dans le rêve'. *Revue philosophique.* XLV. 1898.

68. **Tissié, P.** *Les rêves, physiologie et pathologie.* Paris 1898. Bibliothèque de philosophie contemporaine.

69. **Titchener, E. B.** 'Taste dreams'. *Amer. J. of Psychology.* VI. 1895.

70. **Thomayer, S.** 'Sur la signification de quelques rêves'. *Revue neurologique.* No. 5, 1897.

71. **Vignoli, T.** *Von den Träumen, Illusionen und Hallucinationen.* Internationale wissenschaftliche Bibliothek. Vol. 47.

72. **Volkelt, J.** *Die Traum-phantasie.* Stuttgart 1875.

73. **Vold, J. Mourly.** *Expériences sur les rêves et en particulier sur ceux d'origine musculaire et optique.* Christiania 1896. Report in *Revue philosophique.* XLII. 1896.

74. ——*Einige Experimente über Gesichtsbilder im Traum.* Report on Third international Congress for Psychology in Munich, *Zeitschrift für Psychol. Sinnesorgane.* XIII. 1897.

75. **Weygandt, W.** *Entstehung der Träume.* Leipzig 1893.

76. **Wundt, W.** *Grundzüge der physiologischen Psychologie.* 2 vols. 2nd edn. 1880.

77. **Stricker, S.** *Studien über das Bewusstsein.* Vienna 1879.

78. —— *Studien über die Association der Vorstellungen.* Vienna 1883.

POSTSCRIPT

Only as I was correcting the final proofs in September 1899, I learned of a short work, *Induktive Untersuchungen über die Fundementalgesetze der psychischen Phenomene* [*Inductive Investigations into the Fundamental Laws of Psychical Phenomena*] by Dr C. Ruths, 1898, announcing a larger work on the analysis of dreams. From what the author has indicated, I may expect that on many points his results will agree with mine.

EXPLANATORY NOTES

Any annotator of *The Interpretation of Dreams* owes a great debt to Alexander Grinstein, who in his book *On Sigmund Freud's Dreams* (Detroit, 1968) has tenaciously pursued many of the literary and other allusions and summarized some of the lesser-known books to which Freud refers. Much of the historical material is elucidated by William McGrath in *Freud's Discovery of Pycho-analysis* (Ithaca, NY, 1986).

1 [Epigraph] *'Flectere si . . . movebo'*: Virgil, *Aeneid* vii. 313: 'If Heaven I cannot bend, then Hell I will arouse.' Freud took this motto, not directly from Virgil, but from a political text by Ferdinand Lassalle (1825–64) on the Austro-Italian War of 1859.

7 *Aristotle*: Greek philosopher (384–322 BC). The number in square brackets following the title refers to the entry in Freud's original Bibliography (pp. 413–16).

8 *Schelling*: Friedrich Wilhelm Joseph Schelling (1775–1854), a leading post-Kantian philosopher, established himself with his early treatise *On the World-Soul* (1798) as an exponent of 'Naturphilosophie' which sought to understand the natural world as the harmonious expression of an indwelling spiritual force.

10 *. . . ou fait*: 'We dream about what we have seen, said, desired, or done.'

Xerxes: this story is told by Herodotus (*c*.490–425 BC) in Book VII of his *Histories*. The King of Persia, Xerxes, when preparing to invade Greece, was terrified by ominous dreams. His counsellor Artabanus told him: you say that you're being haunted by a dream figure, the emissary of some god, who refuses to let you cancel the expedition. In actual fact, though, dreams don't come from the gods, my son. I have lived many more years than you, so I can explain what these dreams are that drift into us. The visions that occur to us in dreams are, more often than not, the things we have been concerned about during the day. And, you see, we have been extremely occupied with this expedition for some days now.' (Trans. Robin Waterfield, Oxford World Classics edn. (Oxford, 1998), 413–14).

11 *Lucretius*: Titus Lucretius Carus (*c*.100–*c*.55 BC), author of the philo-sophical poem *On the Nature of the Universe*, devoted to explaining the universe in purely natural terms without need for gods. Quotation from iv. 962 ff.:

> And those pursuits which most we love to follow,
> The things in which just now we have been engaged,
> The mind being thus the more intent upon them,
> These are most oft the substance of our dreams.

Lawyers argue their cases and make laws,
Generals fight battles, leading troops to war . . .

(trans. Ronald Melville, Oxford World's Classics edn. (Oxford, 1999),
127).

11 *Cicero*: Marcus Tullius Cicero (106–43 BC), Roman orator and statesman. *De divinatione* ('On Divination', composed *c.*44 BC) is a dialogue
undermining belief in predicting the future by dreams, augury, or other
forms of divination. Quotation: 'It is chiefly the remains of those things
we have thought about or done during the day that are moved and agi-
tated in our souls.'

14 *Scaliger*: Julius Caesar Scaliger (1484–1558) and his son Joseph Justus
Scaliger (1540–1609), important classical scholars.

19 *. . . au jour*: 'That every impression, even the most insignificant, leaves
an unalterable trace, indefinitely capable of reappearing.'

23 *June days of 1848*: the suppression of a revolutionary uprising in Paris.

24 *infernal machine*: an explosive device used in warfare.

the Tagliamento: a river in Friuli in northern Italy; Napoleon had this
dream when, as commander-in-chief of French forces under the Direc-
tory, he fought a campaign against the Austrians in Lombardy, which was
then under Austrian rule.

Robespierre . . . Fouquier-Tinville: Maximilien de Robespierre (1753–94)
and Jean-Paul Marat (1763–93), leaders of the French Revolution;
Antoine-Quentin Fouquier-Tinville (1746–95), public prosecutor during
the Reign of Terror.

25 *. . . exclusive*: 'a certain affinity, but which is not unique or exclusive'.

27 *Gulliver's Travels*: in this satire (1726) by Jonathan Swift (1667–1745),
Gulliver's second voyage takes him to the giants of Brobdingnag, his
fourth to the intelligent and virtuous horses (Houyhnhnms) who keep
humans (Yahoos) as domestic animals.

32 *Schopenhauer*: Arthur Schopenhauer (1788–1860), the philosopher of
pessimism and author of *The World as Will and Idea* (1819) and *Parerga
and Paralipomena* (1851). The latter includes 'Versuch über das
Geistersehen und was damit zusammenhängt' ('Essay on Seeing Spirits
and Related Matters'), to which Freud is referring.

37 *. . . de dehors*: 'Dreams of purely psychic origin do not exist . . . the
thoughts of our dreams come to us from outside . . .'

41 *'. . . bonnes methodes'*: '. . . the observation of dreams involves special
difficulties, and the only way to avoid all errors in such a case is to set
down on paper without the least delay whatever one has just felt and
noticed; otherwise partial or complete forgetfulness takes over; total forgetfulness is not important; but partial forgetting is treacherous; for
if one sets out straight away to recount what is not forgotten, one is

tempted to use the imagination to complete the fragments provided by memory . . . one becomes an artist unwittingly, and the narrative, periodically repeated, imposes itself on its author's own belief, and in all good faith he presents it as authenticated fact, duly established in accordance with proper technique . . .'

42 *'a dream came to me'* . . . *'I dreamed'*: the impersonal formulation in German is 'mir hat geträumt', as distinct from the form with the active subject, 'ich habe geträumt' (J.C.).

48 *'. . . absurdité'*: 'there are no absolutely rational dreams, which do not contain some incoherence, anachronism, absurdity.'

'. . . spirituel': 'The dream is the anarchy of the psyche, the emotions, and the mind, it is the play of functions that are left to their own devices, acting without control and without purpose; in the dream the mind is a spiritual automaton.'

'. . . somniare': 'Nothing can be imagined that is so absurd, so incoherent, or so bizarre that we are not able to dream it.'

49 *Charles XII. . . Pultava*: at the battle of Poltava in 1709, Russian forces inflicted a massive though not final defeat on the ambitious Swedish king Charles XII (1682–1718).

'. . . et raisonnante': 'The production of these images, which in the waking man are usually the product of the will, is the intellectual equivalent of those movements, in the sphere of motility, which are to be seen in cases of chorea and paralytic illnesses . . . a whole series of degradations of the thinking and reasoning faculty.'

51 *'. . . idées'*: '(1) a spontaneous and, as it were, automatic mental action; (2) a perverse and irregular association of ideas.'

52 *'. . . irraison pur'*: 'The dream is neither wholly unreasonable nor wholly irrational.'

'. . . les anges': 'In sleep, apart from perception all the mental faculties—intelligence, imagination, memory, will, morality—remain essentially intact; only they apply themselves to imaginary and unstable objects. The dreamer is an actor who plays at will fools and wise men, executioners and victims, dwarfs and giants, devils and angels.'

53 *'. . . du fait présent'*: 'The Marquis d'Hervey allows the intelligence, during sleep, all of its liberty of action and attention, and seems to think that sleep consists only in the shutting-off of the senses, their separation from the external world; so that according to his view the sleeping man is hardly different from the man who lets his mind wander while closing off his senses; the only difference marking off ordinary thinking from that of the dreamer is that the latter's ideas take on a visible, objective form which could be mistaken for that which is caused by external objects; memory takes on the appearance of an actual event.'

53　'... *l'éveillé*': 'there is a further and most important distinction, in that the intellectual faculties of the sleeper do not have the same stability that they have in the man who is awake.'

54　*Schubert*: Gotthilf Heinrich Schubert (1780–1860), a physician who helped to popularize Schelling's 'Naturphilosophie' and strongly influenced later Romantic writers through his *Views of the Night-Side of the Natural Sciences* (1808) and *The Symbolism of Dreams* (1814).

　　the younger Fichte: Immanuel Hermann Fichte (1796–1879), son and editor of the philosopher Johann Gottlieb Fichte, and himself a noted philosopher and theologian. Freud quotes from his *Psychologie* (1864).

57　*Kant's categorical imperative*: formulated in Kant's *Groundwork of the Metaphysics of Morals* (1785) and developed in his *Critique of Practical Reason* (1788), this is the moral injunction to act only according to principles which one thinks universally binding.

59　... *is a murderer*: 1 John 3: 15.

　　... *evil thoughts*: Matthew 15: 19.

60　*Kant*: editors have been unable to find this passage in the *Anthropologie* (1804). In the section headed 'On involuntary poetry in a healthy state, i.e. on the dream', Kant follows the Enlightenment tendency to explain dreams by physiological stimuli. Elsewhere Kant describes dreams disparagingly as 'nothing but wild and distasteful chimeras' in which 'ideas of the imagination are tossed together with those of the external senses': *Dreams of a Spirit-Seer* (1766).

　　'... *vengono dinanzi*': 'Some of our desires which we believed had been suppressed and extinguished for a time are reawakened; old, dead passions come back to life; things and people we never think about appear before us.'

62　'... *à refouler*': 'It is our inclinations which speak and make us act, without conscience holding us back, although sometimes it gives us warning. I have my faults and wicked inclinations; while awake, I try to struggle against them and usually manage not to give way to them. But in my dreams I always give way, or to put it better, I act according to their commands, without fear or remorse ... Clearly the visions which appear before my mind and constitute the dream are suggested to me by the impulses whose effects I feel, and which my absent willpower does not try to suppress.'

　　'*En rêve ... dans le rêve*'. 'In dreaming man is revealed to himself in all his nakedness and native wretchedness. As soon as he suspends the exercise of his will he becomes the plaything of all the passions from which, when awake, he is defended by conscience, his sense of honour, and fear ... In dreaming, it is above all the instinctive man who is revealed ... Man returns, so to speak, to the state of nature when he dreams; but the less his mind has been influenced by acquired ideas, the more it is still under the influence of inclinations that clash with them in the dream.'

65 *Mephisto*: in the scene 'Faust's study (I)' in Goethe's *Faust, Part One* (1808), the devil Mephistopheles complains: 'The earth, | The air, the water, all give birth: | It germinates a thousandfold, | In dry or wet, in hot or cold!' (trans. David Luke, Oxford World's Classics edn. (Oxford, 1987); all subsequent quotations are from this version).

68 '. . . *odieuse*': 'If they were deeply in love they almost never dreamed about one another before marriage or during the honeymoon; and if they had erotic dreams they were of being unfaithful with some indifferent or unattractive person.'

   . . . *ressorts tendus*: 'so many wound-up springs'.

69 '. . . *le sommeil*': 'In short, the dream is the product of the mind wandering without purpose and direction, fastening in turn upon such thoughts as have retained enough strength to put themselves in its way and arrest its course, establishing connections between them, sometimes weak and unclear, sometimes strong and tighter, according to the degree to which the brain's activity is more or less impaired by sleep.'

   . . . *to the grave*': quotation from the novel *Heinrich von Ofterdingen* (1802) by Novalis (pseudonym of Friedrich von Hardenberg, 1772–1801), where the poet Heinrich defends dreams against his sceptical father. Heinrich's mild plea does not fit the extraordinary symbolic, prophetic, and erotic dream that he himself has just experienced.

74 . . . *de la folie*: 'the real determining cause of the madness'.

79 *Artemidorus*: Artemidorus of Daldis in Asia Minor (second century AD) wrote a treatise on dreams in five books entitled *Oneirocritica*, considering how to interpret them as predictions of the future.

84 '. . . *problème obscure*': 'Any psychologist is obliged to confess even his failings if he thinks he can thus cast light on some obscure problem.'

   Irma: Anna Hammerschlag, daughter of Freud's Hebrew teacher Samuel Hammerschlag, and a close friend of Freud's wife Martha; in 1885 she married Rudolf Lichtheim of Breslau, son of a neurologist who was a long-standing friend of Freud's associate Josef Breuer. Her brother Paul married Breuer's daughter Bertha in 1893. This illustrates the close web of professional and family ties within the acculturated Jewish community to which Freud belonged.

   Otto: Dr Oskar Rie (1863–1931), a lifelong friend of Freud's, paediatrician to his children.

85 *Dr M.*: Josef Breuer (1842–1925), Freud's close colleague for some ten years and collaborator on the *Studies on Hysteria* (1895). By the late 1890s their friendship had cooled and Freud had transferred his devotion to Fliess; hence Breuer figures here as a blunderer.

   Leopold: Ludwig Rosenberg, a paediatrician, colleague and friend of Freud's. He and his brother-in-law Oskar Rie belonged to the group which met in Freud's house to play the card-game Tarock every Saturday evening from the 1890s till the death of the fourth player, Professor Leopold Königstein, in 1924.

88 *1885*: a mistake for 1884, when Freud published his first study of cocaine. The friend who abused it was Ernst Fleischl von Marxow (1846–91); see Introduction, p. xxiv.

90 *Inspector Bräsig and his friend Karl*: characters from the Low German dialect novel *Ut mine Stromtid* ('From my Time as a Farm Manager', 1862–74) by Fritz Reuter (1810–74), who was popular for his Dickensian humour. There is an English version entitled *An Old Story of my Farming Days*, translated by M. W. MacDowall, 3 vols. (London, 1878). In *On Sigmund Freud's Dreams* Grinstein gives a plot summary (pp. 33–6) and relates it to Freud's associations (pp. 37–40).

91 *dysentery . . . diphtheria*: the German 'Dysenterie' and 'Diphtherie' are closer in sound than their English equivalents (J.C.).

93 *another friend*: Wilhelm Fliess (see Introduction, pp. xxiii–xxiv).

100 *A young colleague*: Rudi Kaufmann, Josef Breuer's nephew; see Freud's letter to Fliess, 4 March 1895.

101 *Alphonse Daudet . . . Prévost*: French novelists: Alphonse Daudet (1840–97), now best remembered for *Lettres de mon moulin* (1869); Paul Bourget (1852–1935), author of *Le Disciple* (1889); Marcel Prévost (1862–1941), whose many novels include *L'Automne d'une femme* (1893).

102 *Aussee . . . Hallstatt*: Aussee is a popular Alpine holiday resort, with salt-baths, in Styria. Hallstatt is a village on a lake in the Salzkammergut, some 12 miles from Ischl (mentioned below).

the Dachstein: a mountain massif south of Hallstatt, rising to 2,995 metres (9,827 feet).

vale of E[s]cher: correctly Echerntal, a wooded valley with waterfalls near Hallstatt. The atmosphere of this holiday is best conveyed by Baedeker: 'The Waldbach-Strub (2060 ft.), in the well-wooded Echern-Thal, 1 hr. to the S .W. of Hallstatt, is precipitated in three leaps from a height of 330 ft. through a cleft in the rocks. The Schleier Fall, of about equal height, descends into the same abyss. Both are insignificant in dry seasons. A picturesque path [*Malersteig*] leads along the Waldbach from Croallo's Inn (halfway through the Echern-Thal) to the Lahn and back to Hallstatt.'

lodge: 'Hütte', a word whose semantic range, from 'cottage' via 'cabin' to 'shack' or 'kennel', makes it difficult to translate: here it means a building which, having originally been a cabin providing refuge for climbers, has developed into a modest hotel.

103 *Dornbach*: a village in the Vienna Woods, immediately west of Vienna. Again, Baedeker supplies the atmosphere: 'The chief attraction here is the Park of Prince Schwarzenberg, through which a road ascends from the tramway terminus to the (3 M[iles]) Hameau, or Holländer Dörfel

(1515 ft.; Inn), a fine point of view ... From the Holländer Dörfel a pleasant path leads in ¾ hr. to the Sofien-Alpe (1595 ft.; Inn), which may also be reached direct in 1¼ hr. by a picturesque path from Neuwaldegg via the Rohrer-Hütte (Inn).'

106 ... *with which you have been pleased to draw attention to yourself of late*: later editions tone down the criticism of the 'unjustified generalizations' to '... die sich zum Glück leicht zurückweisen läßt': Strachey: '... though fortunately one which it is easy to disprove' (J.C.).

108 *professor extraordinarius*: a professor who is not among the established professors ('Ordinarien') and does not share their administrative and supervisory duties.

considerations of religion: a euphemistic reference to anti-Semitism.

109 *Uncle Josef ... sad one*: Josef Freud, Freud's paternal uncle, was imprisoned in 1866 for dealing in counterfeit roubles; Freud's father may have been implicated as well.

110 *Galton*: Sir Francis Galton (1822–1911), British scientist, anthropologist, and eugenicist, who believed that both physical and mental traits were inherited. His composite photographs were intended to bring out the basic anthropological type represented by various individuals.

111 *infected*: the first edition has 'Infection', seemingly a mistake for 'Injection'; Strachey translates as 'injected'.

112 '*Das Beste ... sagen*': words spoken by Mephistopheles in the scene 'Faust's Study (II)' of Goethe's *Faust, Part One*. In his many quotations from *Faust*, Freud shows especial fondness for the words of the devilish tempter Mephisto, the 'Spirit of Perpetual Negation' who cynically questions the high-flown aspirations of the hero—a model for Freud's analysis of unconscious motives? This qualifies the widespread view, put forward by Thomas Mann among others, that Freud identified with the overweening ambitions of Faust. Also quoted on p. 293.

115 *Goethe*: the poem 'Totality' (*c*.1814) runs in full:

> Ein Kavalier von Kopf und Herz
> Ist überall willkommen;
> Er hat mit feinem Witz und Scherz
> Manch Weibchen eingenommen;
> Doch wenn's ihm fehlt an Faust und Kraft,
> Wer mag ihn dann beschützen?
> Und wenn er keinen Hintern hat,
> Wie mag der Edle sitzen?

['A Cavalier in head and heart is welcome everywhere; with his refined wit and jests, he's turned many a woman's head; but if he lacks a powerful fist, then who wants to protect him? And if he hasn't a backside, how can the lord be seated?'] The title 'Totality' refers to the need for perfection in all bodily parts.

116 *Bernheim*: Hippolyte Bernheim (1840–1919), a leading medical hypnotist, whom Freud visited at Nancy in 1889 in order to study his methods.

123 *Lenau*: Nikolaus Lenau (pseudonym of Nikolaus Franz Niembsch, Edler von Strehlenau, 1802–50), Austrian poet of *Weltschmerz* (cosmic suffering). His poem 'Das tote Glück' ('Dead Happiness') seems to be about infanticide; it could imply abortion, but not contraception.

128 *Böcklin*: Arnold Böcklin (1827–1901), Swiss painter; Freud may be thinking of his *The Island of the Dead* (1880).

Dreyfus: in 1894 Captain Alfred Dreyfus, a Jewish officer with French Military Intelligence, was found guilty of spying for Germany and sent to the penal settlement of Devil's Island in the West Indies; in 1897 evidence suggesting his innocence was brought to light and led to the Dreyfus Affair which divided French society.

129 *Berlin friend*: Fliess.

134 *in Hamlet*: I. v. 129–30.

135 *Hänschen Schlau*: one of the epigrams written in the 1750s by Gotthold Ephraim Lessing (1729–81) runs:

> 'Es ist doch sonderbar bestellt',
> Sprach Hänschen Schlau zu Vetter Fritzen,
> 'Daß nur die Reichen in der Welt
> 'Das meiste Geld besitzen.'

['It's really very odd,' said Jacky Sly to Cousin Fred, 'that only the rich people in the world have most of the money.']

141 *a certain kind of carelessness*: i.e. appearing in public with one's fly unbuttoned.

'I won't take it' . . . *dream-content*: the translation unavoidably disguises the overlap between 'Das nehm ich nicht' ('I won't have it') and 'Benehmen Sie sich anständig' ('Behave properly').

143 *Apollo candles* . . . : the missing words are supposed to be 'and masturbates'.

146 *Nansen*: Fridtjof Nansen (1861–1930), Norwegian explorer, who in 1893–6 explored the Arctic Ocean in a ship, the *Fram*, that was specially designed to be lifted, not crushed, by ice-floes. Nansen was also a scientist, and on returning from his expedition was made professor of zoology at the University of Christiania (Oslo).

division of the Chinese Empire: especially between 1897 and 1900, Germany sought to acquire territory and influence in the vulnerable Chinese Empire.

148 *Prater*: a park north-east of the centre of Vienna, popular for its restaurants and puppet-theatres.

Bourgeois Ministry: 'Bürgerministerium'. In 1868 the Emperor Franz Joseph appointed a cabinet led by the liberally inclined aristocrat Prince

'Carlos' Auersperg and consisting mainly of middle-class ministers such as Eduard Herbst (Justice), Karl Giskra (Interior), and Johann Nepomuk Berger (without portfolio; succeeded in 1871 by Joseph Unger).

satchel: an allusion to Napoleon's alleged remark, 'Every French soldier carries in his cartridge-pouch the baton of a marshal of France', indicating that in his army any gifted soldier could reach the highest rank. In fact the saying was uttered by Napoleon's adversary Louis XVIII in an address to cadets in 1819.

Rome: on Freud's long-inhibited desire to visit Rome, see Ernest Jones, *Sigmund Freud: Life and Work* (London, 1953–7), ii. 17–21.

149 *Lübeck*: a North German port near Hamburg, where Freud's wife came from.

Gleichenberg: a popular holiday resort near Graz in Styria, overlooked by an old castle on a high crag.

Karlsbad: now Karlovy vary, a town in the narrow valley of the River Tepl, still a popular resort; in Freud's day, according to Baedeker, it attracted over 30,000 visitors a year, many of them seeking relief from liver complaints in the local mineral springs.

150 *not be a very comfortable place for Germans*: because of the growing strength of Czech nationalism. From the 1880s on, figures recording the growth of the Czech-speaking population and the decline of the German speakers were officially displayed outside the Prague city hall in order to hearten Czechs. Tensions exploded in the anti-German riots of December 1897.

in my seventeenth year: Freud revisited Freiberg (Příbor), his birthplace, in August and September 1872, when he was sixteen. On the accuracy or otherwise of his recollection, see Jones, *Freud*, i. 35–6.

one of our classic writers: in 1925 Freud identified this writer as the humorous Romantic author Jean Paul Friedrich Richter (1763–1825).

Winckelmann: Johann Joachim Winckelmann (1717–68), a Prussian schoolteacher, who went to Rome in 1755, became librarian to Cardinal Albani, and wrote an epoch-making history of classical art.

Hannibal: Carthaginian general (247–182 BC) who fought against the Romans in the Second Punic War, defeating them at Lake Trasimene (217 BC) and elsewhere, and conquering the South Italian province of Campania.

151 *Hasdrubal*: Freud here confuses Hannibal's brother Hasdrubal with his father Hamilcar Barca. He corrected this mistake in later editions and commented on it in *The Psychopathology of Everyday Life*, ch. 10.

Thiers: Adolphe Thiers (1797–1877), French historian and statesman, author of *Histoire du consulat et de l'empire* (1845–62).

Masséna: André Masséna (1758–1817), later duc de Rivoli, one of Napoleon's outstanding generals; widely though wrongly supposed to be a Jew called Menasse or Manasseh.

155 *Graben*: a major shopping street in the centre of Vienna.

157 *Pélagie*: Grinstein has identified this novel as *Hypatia* (1853) by Charles Kingsley (1819–75). Set in early Christian Alexandria, it has as hero the monk Philammon who admires the learned pagan Hypatia but is attracted to the courtesan Pelagia, who is really his sister.

158 *you owe Nature a death*: probably an inaccurate recollection of Shakespeare's *1 Henry IV*, v. i. 126: 'thou owest God a death.' Freud uses the same misquotation in his letter to Fliess of 6 February 1899.

159 *Brücke*: Freud's teacher Ernst Brücke (1819–92).

'. . . *gelüsten*': from the dialogue between Mephisto and the student in the scene 'Faust's Study (II)' of Goethe's *Faust, Part One*.

Fleischl: see note to p. 88 above.

Spalato: Spalato (stress on first syllable), now Split in Croatia, was then an important town of some 20,000 inhabitants in the Austrian crownland of Dalmatia.

Stettenheim: Julius Stettenheim (1831–1916), Jewish journalist and satirist, active in Hamburg and Berlin.

160 '*Der Du . . . Kothe*': quotation from Part II (1812) of Goethe's autobiography *Aus meinem Leben: Dichtung und Wahrheit* (*From my Life: Poetry and Truth*, 1811–33), Book 10: on receiving a letter in mockclassical verse from his friend Johann Gottfried Herder (1744–1803), requesting the loan of a book and punning on Goethe, *Goten* (Goths) and *Kot* (excrement), Goethe was understandably offended; he reflects: 'It was certainly indelicate to permit himself this joke on my name; for a person's own name is not like a cloak that merely hangs upon him and can be tugged and twitched, but a perfectly fitting garment, indeed like his own skin, that has grown around him, and cannot be scraped and flayed without doing him an injury.'

'*So seid . . . Staub*': from Goethe's play *Iphigenie auf Tauris* (1787), II. ii. Iphigenie says this on learning how many Greek heroes have perished in the siege of Troy. The line helps to introduce the ambiguity, crucial for the action, between 'divine image' as a statue of a god and as a description of a human being made in the gods' image.

Cattaro: Cattaro (stress on first syllable), now Kotor in Croatia, southeast of Dubrovnik; then an Austrian naval base and fortress town near the frontier with Montenegro.

Ischl: a fashionable spa and holiday resort in the Salzkammergut, southeast of Salzburg, where the Emperor generally resided from July to September.

Count Thun: Count Franz Anton Thun (1847–1916), a member of a great feudal family in Bohemia, who became Prime Minister of Austria in March 1898 and made concessions to the Czechs which only inflamed further the nationalism of the Germans; he resigned in October 1899.

161 *The Marriage of Figaro*: *Le Nozze di Figaro*, opera by Mozart with libretto by Lorenzo da Ponte, first produced in Vienna in 1786; based on the seemingly subversive comedy *La Folle Journee ou Le Mariage de Figaro* (*The Crazy Day or The Marriage of Figaro*, 1781) by Pierre-Augustin Caron de Beaumarchais (1732–99).

162 *Taaffe*: Count Eduard Taaffe (1833–95) became Prime Minister of Austria in 1879 and continued till 1893; the remaining Liberals soon left his government and entered opposition, leaving the 'Iron Ring' of conservative, clerical, and pro-Slav politicians. Taaffe's premiership thus marks the end of the Liberal era in Austria.

Krems or Znaim: *Krems*, an old town on the Danube above Vienna. *Znaim*, a town in Moravia, now Znojmo in the Czech Republic, just across the Austrian border.

Graz: one of the main cities in Austria, capital of Styria.

163 *the Wachau*: a picturesque stretch of the Danube above Vienna, where the river flows through a narrow rocky defile, extending from Melk to Krems.

Emmersdorf: a village in the Wachau, famous for its late-medieval church.

Fischhof: Adolf Fischhof (1816–93), a doctor, who was among the leaders of the 1848 Revolution in Vienna, later a respected leader of Austrian Liberalism.

'Fifty years ago': Grinstein (p. 104) suggests this refers to Tennyson's poem 'The Roses on the Terrace', beginning 'Rose, on this terrace fifty years ago', which links up with Freud's later reference to the Wars of the Roses.

a fellow-student: Heinrich Braun (1854–1927), a converted Jew, later a prominent Socialist politician in Germany. See Freud's letter to his widow Julie Braun-Vogelstein, October 1927 (in *Letters 1873–1939*, ed. Ernst L. Freud (London, 1961)). As she was Braun's fourth wife, Freud seems to be comparing him with Henry VIII in respect of sexual energy as well as resistance to authority.

aristocrat: identified by McGrath as Robert Edler von Siebenrock.

white and red roses: *3 Henry VI*, i. i.

164 *A colleague*: Victor Adler (1852–1918), founder of the Austrian Social Democratic Party, and brother-in-law of Heinrich Braun. Adler said that Freud, despite his radicalism, would imitate the Prodigal Son by returning to his father's house (see Luke 15). 'Adler' is the German word for 'eagle'.

Zola's Germinal: Émile Zola (1840–1902); *Germinal* (1885) recounts a miners' strike in northern France. The title refers to the seventh month in the French Revolutionary calendar. These associations may explain its substitution for *La Terre* (*Earth*, 1887).

165 *Flavit et dissipati sunt*: 'He blew and they were destroyed.'

165 *incontinentia alvi*: physical incontinence.

Grillparzer: Franz Grillparzer (1791–1872), Austrian dramatist; in his tragedy *Des Meeres und der Liebe Wellen* (1831) the repressive uncle of the priestess Hero ensures that the lamp, which is intended to guide her lover Leander as he swims across the Hellespont to her tower, is blown out, so that Leander perishes.

166 *Rabelais*: François Rabelais (*c*.1483–1553); in his *Gargantua* (1534), ch. 17, the giant Gargantua visits Paris: 'Then smiling, he untied his fair braguette, and drawing out his mentul into the open air, he so bitterly all-to-bepissed them, that he drowned two hundred and sixty thousand four hundred and eighteen, besides the women and little children' (Urquhart's translation).

167 *Odhin's Consolation*: *Odhins Trost*, a novel (1880) by Felix Dahn (1834–1912), the prolific author of once-popular historical and legendary novels about the early Germanic past.

La Terre: the old peasant Fouan is maltreated by his brutal son.

Panizza: the Munich satirist Oskar Panizza (1853–1921) wrote the scandalous play *Das Liebeskonzil* (*The Council of Love*, 1895), set during the Renaissance: a decrepit God decides to punish humanity for its vices by commissioning the Devil to invent syphilis and beget an irresistible woman to infect mankind, beginning with the Pope.

179 *Sunday rider*: in a letter to Fliess of 7 July 1898, Freud writes, referring to an enclosed essay: 'It completely follows the dictates of the unconscious, on the well-known principle of Itzig, the Sunday rider. "Itzig, where are you going?" "Do I know? Ask the horse."'

181 *Arcole*: Napoleon Bonaparte defeated Austrian troops at Arcola (the usual form of the name) in northern Italy on 16 November 1796. He became First Consul by his *coup d'état* of 18 Brumaire (= 9 November) 1799.

'the nightingale': 'Wilt thou be gone? It is not yet full day. | It was the nightingale and not the lark | That pierced the fear-full hollow of thine ear': Juliet in *Romeo and Juliet*, III. v. 1–3.

187 *Andersen*: Hans Christian Andersen (1805–75), Danish writer of fairy-tales.

Fulda: Ludwig Fulda (1862–1939), in his day a very popular German dramatist. *Der Talisman* (1893) dramatizes the story of the Emperor's new clothes. The 'talisman' of the title is explained as the courage of truth ('der Mut der Wahrheit').

188 *. . . sexual life and the work of culture begins*: how closely Freud conceived the two in the development of culture is indicated by his use of a singular verb for a plural subject here, perpetuated in later editions (J.C.).

190 *Keller's . . . man's eternal nature*: at the beginning of Book VI of Homer's *Odyssey*, the shipwrecked Odysseus is found washed up on the shore of Phaeacia by the king's daughter Nausicaa. The great Swiss novelist Gott-

fried Keller (1819–90) wrote as his masterpiece *Der grüne Heinrich* (2 versions, 1854–5 and 1879–80). Heinrich Lee, the hero, receives this advice from his art teacher Römer, and it is doubly confirmed, first when Römer dies in misery and insanity in Paris, and later when Heinrich, having studied art unsuccessfully in Munich, returns home destitute.

192 *the Odyssey*: in Book XI of the *Odyssey*, Odysseus summons up the souls of the dead by sacrificing sheep and giving their blood to the souls to drink.

195 *angel-maker*: this word (*Engelmacherin*) is also the vulgar term for an abortionist.

196 '*. . . no traveller returns*': *Hamlet*, III. i.81–2.

197 *Fourth Commandment*: the commandment 'Honour thy father and thy mother' is for Freud the fourth, as it is in both the Catholic and Lutheran Churches, adopting the division established by St Augustine, whereas the Reformed Churches and the Church of England count this as the fifth, following the order in Exodus 20 rather than that in Deuteronomy 5.

201 *Oedipus*: the protagonist of the plays *Oedipus the King* and *Oedipus at Colonus* by Sophocles (496–406 BC).

   . . . far-distant crime: trans. E. F. Watling (Harmondsworth, 1964), 28. Subsequent quotations are from this version.

202 *later tragedies of fate*: Freud is referring to a genre of early nineteenth-century German dramas where a curse is worked out; an example is *Die Ahnfrau* (*The Ancestress*, 1817), a popular but immature play by Grillparzer.

204 '*sicklied o'er . . . thought*': *Hamlet*, III. i. 87. Goethe's interpretation of *Hamlet* occurs in his novel *Wilhelm Meisters Lehrjahre* (*Wilhelm Meister's Apprenticeship*, 1795–6): Shakespeare intended to portray 'the effects of a great action laid upon a soul unfit for the performance of it'; Hamlet's is 'a lovely, pure and most moral nature, [which] without the strength of nerve which forms a hero, sinks beneath a burden which it cannot bear and must not cast away' (Book IV, ch. 13, in Thomas Carlyle's translation).

Brandes: the Danish critic Georg Brandes (1842–1927), internationally famous in his day, published *William Shakespeare* in German in 1896.

Hamnet: the Stratford parish register records the death of Shakespeare's son Hamnet, aged eleven, on 11 August 1596. The burial of John Shakespeare, the dramatist's father, is recorded on 8 September 1601. *Hamlet* is entered in the Stationer's Register on 26 July 1602 and said to have been 'lately acted by the Lord Chamberlain his servants'; the Oxford editors believe that Shakespeare wrote it in about 1600 and revised it later. Brandes's conjecture thus looks unlikely.

'*Macbeth . . . childlessness*': see the (unjustly ridiculed) discussion of this subject in A. C. Bradley, *Shakespearean Tragedy* (1904), note EE.

206 *Dr Lecher*: Dr Otto Lecher, Liberal member of the parliamentary opposition, delivered a speech lasting twelve hours on 28–9 October 1897
against the government's support for the use of Czech in schools and
offices in Bohemia and Moravia. Lecher himself represented Brünn, now
Brno, in Moravia.

207 *'My son, the myope'*: this dream is more fully analysed in the section on
'Absurd Dreams' in Chapter VI. The German words '*Myop*' and
'*Cyclop*' resemble each other more closely in sound than the corre-
sponding English 'myope' and 'cyclops' (p. 284) (J.C.).

Basedow's disease: a swelling of the thyroid gland in the throat, producing
a goitre or *struma* (mentioned below), along with the symptoms described
here.

208 *Basedow*: Johann Bernhard Basedow (1723–90), educational reformer
who founded the Philanthropinum at Dessau; a friend of Goethe, mentioned in the poem 'Diner zu Koblenz' ('Dinner at Koblenz', 1774).

210 *'dies irae, dies illa'*: from the medieval hymn by Thomas of Celano beginning 'That day of wrath, that day will dissolve the world into ashes',
anticipating the Day of Judgement when 'even the righteous will barely
be saved'. Three verses are familiar from being quoted in the 'Cathedral'
scene of *Faust I*.

216 *'Ein Tritt ... schlägt'*: another quotation from the dialogue between
Mephisto and the student in the scene 'Faust's Study (II)' of *Faust, Part
One*.

218 *dyspnoea*: difficulty in breathing.

Sappho: a novel (1884) by Daudet (see note to p. 101) about a young
man's relationship with a courtesan known as 'Sappho' after the Greek
woman poet, having once posed for a sculpture of her; for a plot summary see Grinstein, pp. 257–60.

Von Stufe zu Stufe: a play, first performed in 1869 or earlier, by the
German actor and director Hugo Müller; *Rund um Wien* has not yet been
traced. I owe this information to W. E. Yates.

219 *Uhland*: Ludwig Uhland (1787–1862), late-Romantic poet, author especially of ballads.

'Einst hatt' ich ... trägt': from the 'Walpurgis Night' scene of *Faust, Part
One*, where Faust almost succumbs to erotic temptation before having an
involuntary vision of Gretchen, the lover whom he has abandoned.

221 *may-beetles*: Maikäfer. The exact English rendering is 'cockchafer', but
the dream-interpretation requires a reference to 'May' ('She was born
in *May* and had been married in *May*, p. 222), so 'may-beetles' is
preferred (J.C.).

222 *Adam Bede*: a novel (1859) by George Eliot (pseudonym of Mary Ann
Evans, 1819–80), in which the pretty but foolish Hetty Sorrel is seduced
by Arthur Donnithorne, while the noble-hearted workman Adam Bede
marries the plain but admirable Methodist preacher Dinah Morris.

Maupassant: Guy de Maupassant (1850–93), some of whose fiction featuring prostitution (*La Maison Tellier*, 1881) or adultery (*Bel-Ami*, 1885) might well be thought immoral.

Le Nabab: Daudet's *Le Nabab* (1877), a novel sketching Paris life in the Second Empire, focusing on a politician and financier who has made a fortune in Egypt and who attaches himself to the duc de Mora.

The Magic Flute: opera by Mozart with libretto by Emmanuel Schikaneder, first produced in Vienna in 1791. The words quoted are spoken by the wise Sarastro to his adoptive daughter Pamina.

223 *Das Käthchen von Heilbronn*: a play (1810) by Heinrich von Kleist (1777–1811), in which the heroine, of humble birth, is devotedly and at last successfully in love with a nobleman. In Act IV, scene ii, Käthchen speaks to the Count in her sleep and reveals his previously unconscious awareness that he loves her: 'You are as much in love with me as a beetle.' In the first edition, Freud transposed the words to: 'Verliebt ja bist Du wir ein Käfer mir.' 'Beetle' (*Käfer*) was a regional term of endearment (I owe this information to Mrs Hilda Brown).

Tannhäuser: Wagner's opera, first performed in 1845. Freud misquotes the Pope's condemnation of Tannhäuser, which begins: 'Hast du so böse Lust geteilt' ('If you have shared such foul desire'): Tannhäuser, having succumbed to the pagan sensuality of Venus, seeks absolution from the Pope but is told he can no more be absolved than the Pope's staff can blossom; the self-sacrifice of the saintly Elisabeth brings about this miracle, destroys Venus, and redeems Tannhäuser.

Penthesilea: a tragedy by Kleist, written in 1807, published in 1808; the heroine, an Amazon queen prone to violent mood-swings, feels belittled by her lover Achilles, sets her dogs on him, and devours his flesh.

225 *Propylea*: a propylaeum in Greek architecture is a porch supported by columns at the entrance to a sacred enclosure, such as the entrance-hall of the Acropolis in Athens; the name 'Propyl(a)ea' is also given to neo-classical works like the monumental gateways in Munich, completed in 1862.

227 *Ibsen*: Nora is the heroine of *A Doll's House* (1879) and the Ekdal family feature in *The Wild Duck* (1884), both by Henrik Ibsen (1828–1906).

Olmütz: now Olomouc, then an important garrison town of some 20,000 inhabitants in Moravia.

Jubilee Exhibition: in 1898, marking the fiftieth anniversary of the accession of the Emperor Franz Joseph.

228 *The first reader*: Wilhelm Fliess. Freud inserted this footnote in response to an objection by Fliess (see letter of 11 September 1899); the analogy between dreams and witticisms was to be explored in *Jokes and their Relation to the Unconscious*.

B.: Berlin.

229 *Fliegende Blätter*: a much-read German comic paper.

Lasker: Eduard Lasker (1829–84), a leading German politician of Jewish origin who helped to found the National Liberal Party.

Lassalle: Ferdinand Lassalle (1825–64), German Socialist politician, son of a Jewish businessman; killed in a duel.

J. J. David: Jakob Julius David (1859–1906), born, like Freud, in Moravia, though at Weisskirchen; he was brought up nearby at Fulnek, close to the boundary with Austrian Silesia. David was well known at this time for realistic stories of village life.

230 *Breslau*: now Wrocław in Poland; then the capital of the German province of Silesia.

L'Œuvre: Zola's *L'Œuvre* ('The Work [of Art]', 1886), a novel about artists whose hero, Claude Lantier, is based on Zola's friend Paul Cézanne; Zola himself appears as the novelist Pierre Sandoz.

235 *Is fecit cui profuit*: a legal maxim: 'he who profited from it, did it.'

239 *School of Athens*: a fresco by Raphael (Raffaello Sanzio, 1483–1520) painted between 1509 and 1511 in the Vatican.

242 *the night before my father was buried*: in a letter to Fliess of 2 November 1896, Freud says this dream took place the night after the funeral.

243 *dame aux camélias*: the play *La Dame aux camélias* (*The Lady with the Camellias*, 1852) by Alexandre Dumas *fils* (1824–95), best known as the source of Verdi's opera *La Traviata* (1853).

Goethe's poem: 'Der Müllerin Verrat' ('The Treachery of the Miller's Daughter', 1798), a ballad in which a lover, himself a two-timer, complains of how his girlfriend has betrayed their love to her family.

249 *Goethe's death*: in 1832.

250 *transvaluation of all psychical values*: borrowed from a phrase often used by Friedrich Nietzsche (1844–1900), e.g. in *The Genealogy of Morals* (1887), where Nietzsche announces that he is preparing a work called *The Will to Power: An Attempt at a Transvaluation of all Values* (Part 3, sec. 27). A book under this title was compiled from his notebooks by his friend Peter Gast and his sister Elisabeth Förster-Nietzsche and published posthumously in 1901.

251 *my friend*: Fliess. For his theory of bisexuality, see the Introduction, pp. xxiii–xxiv.

253 *... summoning me to an examination*: the German 'Untersuchung' doubles the meanings of '(medical) examination' and '(legal) investigation' here (J.C.).

254 *'The Moor has done his duty ...'*: from Schiller's play *Fiesco* (1784), III. iv; the conspirator Fiesco dismisses his Moorish servant and accomplice, Muley Hassan, with what the latter considers ingratitude. (German *gehen* can mean both 'go' and 'walk' (J.C.).)

257 *Hans Richter*: conductor (1843–1916); an assistant to Wagner, he conducted the premiere of the *Ring* at Bayreuth in 1876; he often conducted in London, and was conductor of the Hallé Orchestra in Manchester from 1900 to 1911.

the unhappy man's name: given in a 1925 addition as Hugo Wolf (1860–1903), the composer whose works include the opera *Der Corregidor* (1896) and many songs to words by Goethe, Mörike, and Eichendorff. As music critic for the Vienna *Salonblatt*, 1884–7, he was a passionate Wagnerian and opponent of Brahms. In 1897 he suffered a mental breakdown; after a brief and illusory recovery, he was sent in December 1898 to an asylum where he stayed until his death.

Tower of Fools: 'Narrenturm', an old term for a lunatic asylum.

258 *'Kein Feuer, keine Kohle ... weiß'*: an anonymous folk-song, of which a version entitled 'Heimlicher Liebe Pein' ('The Pain of Secret Love') is in the famous German collection *Des Knaben Wunderhorn* (*The Boy's Magic Horn*, 1806–8), compiled by Achim von Arnim and Clemens Brentano.

259 *Song of Songs*: 5: 15, 'His legs are as pillars of marble, set upon sockets of fine gold.'

260 *garden*: Song of Songs 4: 12: 'A garden shut up is my sister, my bride.'

261 *pull one down*: in German, 'sich einen herunterreißen'.

... clothes: ausziehen, a pun, condensing the meanings of 'moving out (of a house)' and 'taking off (one's clothes)'. This paragraph was omitted in subsequent editions (J.C.).

263 *the Hilmteich*: a large pond, with boats for hire and a restaurant nearby, just outside Graz.

fluid and superfluous: Überflüssig = superfluous; *überfließend* = overflowing; *flüssig* = fluid; *über'flüssig* = super'fluous: the alliterative and punning connections are glaring in German, less apparent in English (J.C.).

Ammocoetes: Freud's short paper on the roots of the nerves in the spine of the *Ammocoetes* was published in the proceedings of the Vienna Academy of Sciences in 1877.

264 *3 fl. 65 kr.*: fl. = Florin or Gulden; kr. = Kreuzer. This is the old currency before Austria adopted the gold standard in 1892, whereupon the Gulden was replaced by the Krone at the rate of 2 Kronen to one old Gulden. Twelve Gulden would correspond roughly to one pound sterling.

'time is money': in English in the original.

265 *... dear one*: Schatz, a term of endearment, literally 'treasure', so establishing a link with buying jewellery and with the value of the husband in the dream (J.C.).

268 *Fl. ... P.*: Fliess, and Josef Paneth (1857–90), Freud's friend, colleague, and successor at the Vienna Institute of Physiology.

threshold: Freud uses a non-existent and unintelligible word, *Schwele*, which sounds like *schwelen* ('to smoulder') or *Schwelle* ('threshold').

269 *Non vixit*: 'he has not lived'; *non vivit*: 'he is not alive'.

Monument: the monument to the Emperor Joseph II (reigned with his mother Maria Theresa from 1765, and alone from 1780 to his death in 1790), Austria's Enlightened despot. An equestrian statue of him by Zauner stands on the Josefsplatz adjacent to the Hofburg (the Imperial residence in the centre of Vienna). The inscription means: 'He lived for his country's good, not long, but entirely.' Freud noted in 1925 that it actually read 'Saluti publicae . . .', 'for the public good'.

270 *Brutus' justificatory speech*: *Julius Caesar*, III. ii. 282–4.

271 *Schiller's Poems*: the poem comes from Schiller's play *Die Räuber* (*The Robbers*, 1781), IV. v, where the hero Karl Moor sings it accompanying himself on the lute.

273 *Garibaldi*: Giuseppe Garibaldi (1807–82), Italian patriot and republican, who contributed to his country's unification by conquering Naples and Sicily with his guerrilla Redshirts.

state of disorder: the Hungarian political crisis in 1898–9 was initiated by the fall of Count Badeni's government in Austria in November 1897: proponents of Hungarian independence sought to replace Hungary's customs union with the Austrian half of the Dual Monarchy by a separate tariff on exports, and refused to accept the compromise worked out by the Prime Minister Baron Bámffy; his successor Kálmán Széll formed a coalition which governed from 1899 to 1903.

Maria Theresa: Empress of Austria from 1740 to 1780. When Frederick the Great of Prussia invaded the Austrian province of Silesia in 1740, the young Empress appealed for Hungarian help at the Diet of Pressburg (now Bratislava) in 1741. The response was 'We will die for our ruler'.

274 *'Und hinter ihm . . . Gemeine'*: from Goethe's poem 'Epilog zu Schillers "Glocke"' (1815).

273 *Callot*: Jacques Callot (1592–1635) made many etchings of courtiers, beggars, and hunchbacks, and recorded the horrors of the Thirty Years War in his series *Les Grandes Misères de la guerre* (1633), partly inspired by the French invasion of Lorraine.

275 *Purkersdorf*: a small town some 8 miles west of Vienna, on the main railway line.

276 *. . . the element 'fahren'*: *fahren* (to go, travel) is a basic semantic unit used in a wide variety of compounds, seen in Freud's punning on 'Vorfahren'. He uses the word itself frequently in the account of his dreams (J.C.).

taken the trouble to be born: a quotation from Beaumarchais's *Le Mariage de Figaro* (see note to p. 161): 'Because you are a great lord, you believe yourself to be a great genius! . . . You took the trouble to be born, and that is all.'

277 *brother-in-law*: an example of this usage with which Freud would have been familiar is found in Goethe's early poem 'An Schwager Kronos' ('To the Coachman Kronos'), written during a journey by coach in 1774.

Heine: from 'Lobgesang auf König Ludwig' by Heinrich Heine (1797–1856), one of Freud's favourite writers (translation from Hal Draper, *The Complete Poems of Heinrich Heine: A Modern English Version* (OUP, 1982), 539). The poem, published in February 1844 in Karl Marx's *Deutsch-Französische Jahrbücher*, is aimed at the reactionary King Ludwig I of Bavaria. On Freud's use of Heine, see Sander L. Gilman, 'Freud reads Heine reads Freud', in Mark H. Gelber (ed.), *The Jewish Reception of Heinrich Heine* (Tübingen, 1992), 77–94.

279 *Meynert*: Theodor Meynert (1833–92), Professor of Psychiatry at the University of Vienna.

280 *'51 is the age ... vulnerable'*: this alludes to Wilhelm Fliess's efforts to find significant periodicities and a 'chronological pattern' in life' (p. 282) based on combinations of 28 and 23 (= 51). See Introduction, pp. xxiii–xxiv. On the harsh review mentioned on p. 281, see Frank Sulloway, *Freud: Biologist of the Mind*, 2nd edn. (Cambridge, Mass., and London, 1992), 144.

281 *'On Nature'*: this essay, long attributed to Goethe, was in fact written by his acquaintance, the Swiss clergyman G. C. Tobler, who visited Goethe in Weimar in 1781, conversed with him about natural science and natural theology, and published the product of these discussions in the *Tiefurt Journal* in the winter of 1782–3.

'Nature, Nature': this sounds very like the young Goethe: see his essay 'On Shakespeare's Birthday' (1773): 'And so I cry "Nature, nature! nothing so natural as Shakespeare's people."'

282 *mea res agitur*: 'this concerns me'.

my son the myope: see note to p. 207.

283 *The New Ghetto*: a play by the Zionist leader Theodor Herzl (1860–1904), in which an upright Jewish lawyer, ostensibly assimilated to Gentile society, finds himself rejected and confined to an invisible (hence 'new') ghetto. The importance of this play for Freud was first explored by Peter Loewenberg in 'A Hidden Zionist Theme in Freud's "My Son, the Myops" Dream', *Journal of the History of Ideas*, 31 (1970), 129–32, and is developed by McGrath, pp. 236–44.

'By the waters of Babylon ... wept': Psalm 137.

284 *'Caviare to the general'*: Hamlet, II. ii. 437.

unleavened bread: see Exodus 12: 17.

285 *'I am but mad ... hand-saw'*: Hamlet, II. ii. 379.

286 *'... rubbish-heap'*: 'rubbish' here is *Mist*, literally, 'dung'. To condense 'Misttrügerl' and 'Nicht auf meinem eigenen *Mist* gewachsen' plausibly, the English is more genteel than the German (J.C.).

288 *a great figure in history*: Freud named his second son Oliver after Oliver Cromwell (1599–1658), Lord Protector of England from 1653 to 1658.

290 *drew conclusions*: presumably about the student's Jewish origins.

293 *She*: the novel (1887) by H. Rider Haggard (1856–1925); its entrancing heroine, the queen of a lost Central African kingdom, has survived without ageing for 2000 years.

'the eternal feminine': the last words of Goethe's *Faust, Part Two* are: 'das Ewig-Weibliche | Zieht uns hinan'—'Eternal Womanhood | Draws us on high'.

'Das Beste . . . sagen': see note to p. 112.

294 *Heart of the World*: a novel (1896) by Rider Haggard centring on a hidden Mexican city where the Aztec priesthood survives, and on a heart-shaped stone whose two halves, when reunited, are expected to enable the Aztecs to reconquer Mexico; this prophecy is frustrated by a sexual conflict. For a plot summary, see Grinstein, pp. 404–11.

'into the unexplored and scarcely trodden': a hidden allusion also to Faust's descent to the Mothers in order to reanimate Helen of Troy: 'A path untrodden | Which none may tread; a way to the forbidden, | The unmoved, the inexorable' (*Faust, Part Two*, 'A Dark Gallery').

295 *holothurians*: sea-slugs.

Wealth of Nations: in full *An Enquiry into the Nature and Causes of the Wealth of Nations* (1776), a famous book on economics by Adam Smith (1723–90).

Matter and Motion: a book on physics (1877) by James Clerk Maxwell (1831–79).

Schiller: Friedrich Schiller (1759–1805), the dramatist and philosopher, was born not in Marburg (in Central Germany) but in Marbach am Neckar near Stuttgart. The Austrian town of Marburg is near Graz.

'It is from' . . . 'It is by': in English in the original. (The German word *von* can mean either 'from' or 'by', according to context (J.C.).)

300 *Loewe's ballads*: Carl Loewe (1796–1869) composed many ballads which long remained popular as family entertainment.

301 *Snug, the Joiner*: see *A Midsummer Night's Dream*, V. i. 221.

302 *Miramare*: near Trieste on the Adriatic, has a chateau which once belonged to the Emperor Maximilian of Mexico. Nearby are the castle of Duino, later famous as the place where Rilke began the *Duino Elegies* in 1914, and the remains of the Roman city of Aquileia.

'naval war between America and Spain': in 1898. McGrath, pp. 256–8, relates this dream to contemporary events and points out that the conflict between democratic America and Roman Catholic Spain formed a parallel in Freud's imagination to the conflict between Hannibal and Rome.

304 *'Quiet . . . returns'*: from one of Schiller's epigrams, 'Erwartung und Erfüllung' ('Expectation and Fulfilment'): 'In den Ozean schifft mit tausend Masten der Jüngling, | Still, auf gerettetem Boot, treibt in den Hafen der Greis' ('The youth launches into the ocean with a thousand masts, | Quiet, in the rescued boat, to the harbour the old man returns').

Görz: now Gorizia in north-eastern Italy.

Grado: a small fishing port and tourist resort on the Adriatic.

306 *the Augean stables*: the fifth of Hercules' ten labours was to clean out many years' accumulation of dung from the cattle-yard belonging to King Augeias, who owned many hundreds of cattle; he did this by diverting two rivers to run through the yard.

Gulliver: see Swift, *Gulliver's Travels*, 'A Voyage to Lilliput', ch. 5.

Gargantua: see note to p. 166.

307 *Flavit . . . sunt*: see note to p. 165.

Die Leiden eines Knaben: a story (1883) by Conrad Ferdinand Meyer (1825–98) about a boy at the court of Louis XIV suffering under the strict and uncongenial educational regime of the Jesuits.

313 *P.*: Josef Paneth; see note to p. 268.

'at whom . . . ago': 'Die früh sich einst dem trüben Blick gezeigt' from the prefatory poem to *Faust, Part One*, 'Zueignung' ('Dedication'), in which Goethe reflects on his lifelong preoccupation with this work.

314 *'Ôte-toi que je m'y mette'*: 'Come out so that I may have your place' (a sexual double entendre).

315 *Prince Hal*: see *2 Henry IV*, IV.v.

'As he was ambitious . . . him': from the speech in which Brutus justifies killing Caesar in *Julius Caesar*, III. ii. 27.

318 *(h)*: wrongly labelled '(g)' in the first edition, a small instance of the hasty proof-reading that characterizes the volume (J.C.).

Helen of Troy: *La Belle Hélène*, operetta by the German-French Jacques Offenbach (1819–80), first produced in 1864; from the love-duet between Helen and Paris in Act II.

319 *the poet*: Heine in no. 58 of the 'Homecoming' section of the *Book of Songs* (1827), translated as follows by Hal Draper:

> Life and the world's too fragmented for me!
> A German professor can give me the key.
> He puts life in order with skill magisterial,
> Builds a rational system for better or worse;
> With nightcap and dressing-gown scraps as material
> He chinks up the holes in the Universe.

320 *daydream, story*: in English in the original (J.C.).

321 *Nabab*: see note to p. 222.

325 *Girondistes*: properly Girondins, a radical faction in the French Revolution, named after the Gironde region from which three of their leaders came; tried and guillotined in October 1793.

Danton: Georges Danton (1759–94), revolutionary leader.

325 *Don Giovanni*: opera by Mozart, first performed in Prague in 1787. Freud is referring to the banquet scene in the final act.

327 *Dupuy*: Charles-Alexandre Dupuy (1851–1923), French politician, elected President of the Chamber of Deputies on 5 December 1893; during his first week in office an anarchist, Auguste Vaillant, threw a bomb at him, whereupon Dupuy said calmly: 'The session continues, gentlemen.' It was during his period as Prime Minister of France (May 1894 to January 1895) that Captain Dreyfus was exiled to Devil's Island.

334 *Selten . . . gleich*: *Heine*: no. 78 of 'The Homecoming' (cf. note to p. 319).

regularly: an under-translation. Freud does not in fact use '*regelmäßig*' here, but '*gesetzmäßig*', i.e. as governed by laws (which he has been working out in his dream-book). However, to spell out this passing claim in the text would be to over-translate, so the translator makes things easy for herself (J.C.).

335 *the embroidered sign on Siegfried's cloak served Hagen*: in the *Nibelungenlied* (written *c*.1200), the sign marks the single vulnerable spot on Siegfried's body and enables Hagen to murder him.

337 *. . . the lady who was my disagreeable travelling-companion*: in the 1st edition Freud reserves his animus for the lady alone; in later editions he applies it to her and her husband: 'two disagreeable fellow-travellers' (Strachey) (J.C.).

seventeen years old: changed in later editions to 'nineteen'. Freud first visited Britain in 1875, when he stayed with relatives in Manchester.

338 *'La matière est-elle laudable?'*: i.e. is the patient's stool normal?— Molière, *Le Malade imaginaire* (*The Hypochondriac*, 1673).

339 *Studies on Hysteria*: Freud is referring to 'Frau Cäcilie M.', whose story is told as part of the fifth case-history in the *Studies on Hysteria* and in an extended footnote to the second. Born Baroness Anna von Todesco in 1847, she married the Jewish banker Leopold, Baron von Lieben, in 1872; her mother belonged to the wealthy Gomperz family. These and other connections deterred Freud from recounting her case in full detail, although she was his patient for over five years, from 1888 (possibly 1887) to the autumn of 1893. She died in 1900.

340 *Claude Bernard*: French physiologist (1813–78).

Little Tailor: the hero of the tale 'The Brave Little Tailor' in the Grimms' *Tales* (1815); he shows his valour by killing seven flies at a stroke.

348 *M. Joyeuse*: from Daudet's *Le Nabab* (see note to p. 222 above).

349 *Fechner*: Gustav Theodor Fechner (1801–87) developed the Romantic philosophy of nature in a number of works including *Elements of Psychophysics* (1860).

351 *as pointed out elsewhere*: by Josef Breuer in the *Studies on Hysteria*, in a footnote to Section I of the theoretical essay he contributed.

359 *Carso*: described by Baedeker as 'an inhospitable and dreary plain, strewn with blocks of limestone, called the Karst (Ital. *Carso*, Slav. *Kras*), which extends from Fiume to Gorizia'.

361 *You could buy him for ten a penny*: more literally, the German 'Er ist ein Duzendmensch' would yield 'his sort are turned out by the dozen'. But for once, 'established linguistic usage' in English offers a serviceable equivalent for the commercial idiom (J.C.).

362 *Odyssey*: see note to p. 192.

366 *tertium comparationis*: the third item to which two others are compared.

373 *Crassus*: Marcus Licinius Crassus (d. 53 BC), a wealthy Roman politician, general, and property-owner. This anecdote is told by the historian Dio Cassius (AD 150–235). I owe this information to Nicholas Purcell.

376 *. . . qui commence*: 'A dream is the beginning of waking.'

382 *Philippson's edition of the Bible*: an edition of the Old Testament in Hebrew and German. The pictures described here, illustrating Deuteronomy 4, are reproduced in McGrath, pp. 41, 43.

. . . falcons' heads: *Vogel* = bird: in interpreting the dream, Freud relates it to *vögeln* (slang) = to fuck (J.C.).

384 *'Je n'osais . . . dortoir'*: 'I didn't dare admit it, but I kept having prickly feelings and overexcitations in my *parts*; finally it got on my nerves so much that I thought several times of throwing myself out of the dormitory window.'

385 *'Nous avons . . . particulier'*: 'We have classified this observation among the apyretic deliria proceeding from inanition, for we attribute this particular state to cerebral ischaemia.' 'Ischaemia' is a deficiency in the supply of blood to any organ.

401 *closely related*: the first edition has *nahe liegende*; SA, *naheliegende*; Strachey, 'obvious'. I have translated the words as they occur—meaningfully—in the first edition. The later text, as established, may be evidence of rethinking or the correction of a misprint (J.C.).

402 *removal . . . opposite*: see p. xliv, n. 8.

'Flectere . . . movebo': see note to p. 1, above.

405 *Tartini*: the composer Giuseppe Tartini (1692–1770) wrote a sonata known as the 'Trillo del Diavolo' ('The Devil's Trill') in 1714; it is said that he dreamed of selling his soul to the Devil, who then played him this sonata, and on waking he wrote down what he could remember.

Helmholtz: Hermann von Helmholtz (1821–94; ennobled in 1882), wide-ranging German scientist who made major advances in both physics and physiology; in the latter, his measurements of nervous stimuli enabled him to establish a strictly material and quantitative physiology. This approach, associated with the 'Helmholtz School', was transmitted to the young Freud via his teacher Brücke.

406 *daemonic powers*: this tenacious German concept was formulated by Goethe in a famous passage in Book 20 of his autobiography *Dichtung und Wahrheit* (*Poetry and Truth*): 'He [the young Goethe] believed that in Nature, both living and lifeless, animate and inanimate, he had discovered something which manifested itself only in contradictions and therefore could not be grasped by any concept, far less by a word. It was not divine, for it seemed devoid of reason; not human, for it had no intellect; not devilish, for it was beneficent; not angelic, for it often displayed malice [*Schadenfreude*]. It seemed like chance, for it showed no regularity; it resembled Providence, for it revealed interconnections. It seemed able to penetrate all the limits imposed on us; it seemed to deal as it pleased with the necessary elements of our existence; it contracted time and extended space. It seemed to enjoy only the impossible and to spurn the possible with contempt. To this being, which seemed to intervene among all others, separating and uniting them, I applied the term "daemonic", following the example of the ancients and of those who had perceived something similar.'

411 *... we must bear in mind that what has psychical reality too can have more than just one form of existence*: this is a concluding proposition which Freud revised and varied considerably for later editions. First edition: '... so muß man sich wohl erinnern, daß auch dem psychisch Realen mehr als nur eine Existenzform zukommt.' This was modified successively in the 1914 and 1919 editions to: '... so muß man wohl sagen, daß die *psychische* Realität eine besondere Existenzform ist, welche mit der *materiellen* Realität nicht verwechselt werden soll', and followed by a further paragraph developing the distinction. Strachey: '... we shall have to conclude, no doubt, that *psychical* reality is a particular form of existence not to be confused with *material* reality. ...' (J.C.).

413 *Freud's Bibliography*: These are the texts and references listed by Freud at the end of the first edition. As they originally included a number of errors, they have been minimally adjusted according to the corrections made by Angela Richards for the SE volume and, in her train, by the editors of *Die Traumdeutung*, vol. ii of Sigmund Freud, *Studienausgabe* [*der gesammelten Werke*], 10 vols. and supplementary vol. (Frankfurt am Main, S. Fischer Verlag, 1969–75) (J.C.).

INDEX OF DREAMS

Note. The name or description of the dreamer is to be found in brackets after the dream.

GENERAL INDEX

Note. Information to be found in footnotes is indicated by n. after the page number. Information from notes at the end of the book is entered under the page number.